MODERN PAINTERS

A self-portrait by John Ruskin, 1873
(By kind permission of the trustees of Brantwood, Coniston, Cumbria)

MODERN PAINTERS

by

John Ruskin

Edited and abridged by David Barrie

. . . . "Accuse me not
Of arrogance, ...
If, having walked with Nature,
And offered, far as frailty would allow,
My heart a daily sacrifice to Truth,
I now affirm of Nature and of Truth,
Whom I have served, that their Divinity
Revolts, offended at the ways of men,
Philosophers, who, though the human soul
Be of a thousand faculties composed,
And twice ten thousand interests, do yet prize
This soul, and the transcendent universe,
No more than as a mirror that reflects
To proud Self-love her own intelligence."
WORDSWORTH

Alfred A. Knopf
New York
1987

THIS IS A BORZOI BOOK
PUBLISHED BY ALFRED A. KNOPF, INC.

Introduction and compilation copyright © 1987 by David Barrie

Published in the United States by Alfred A. Knopf, Inc., New York.
Distributed by Random House, Inc., New York.
Originally published in Great Britain by
André Deutsch Limited, London.

Library of Congress Cataloging-in-Publication Data

Ruskin, John, 1819-1900.
  Modern painters.

  1. Painting. 2. Aesthetics. I. Barrie, David,
  1953– . II. Title.
  ND1135. R8 1988 750'.1 87-82285
  ISBN 0-394-56846-X

First published, Volume I 1843, Volume II 1846, Volumes III and IV 1856, Volume V 1860
First complete edition, 1873

Printed in the United Kingdom. Bound in the United States of America
First American edition of this abridgement

CONTENTS

VOLUME II

PART III Of Ideas of Beauty

Contents

VOLUME III

PART IV Of Many Things

LIST OF
ILLUSTRATIONS
Black and White

Colour

PREFACE

Considered merely as a writer, he is in the very highest rank of
English stylists. The vigour and splendour of his eloquence are not
more remarkable than its precision, and the delicate truthfulness
of his epithets.

George Eliot, reviewing
Volume III of *Modern Painters* in 1856

Ruskin was one of the most remarkable men, not only of England
and our time, but of all countries and all times. He was one of
those rare men who think with their hearts . . . and so he thought
and said not only what he himself had seen and felt, but what
everyone will think and say in the future.

Tolstoy, on Ruskin's death in 1900

. . .when I see how mightily this dead man lives. . .I know how
slight a thing death is.

Proust, 1900

John Ruskin was the most eloquent and influential interpreter of the
visual arts that Britain has ever produced. He was also a passionate
opponent of Victorian capitalism. In his own lifetime, he was revered not
just as a critic or social reformer, but as a master of English prose. His
magnum opus, *Modern Painters*, has been described by Sir Ernst Gombrich
as 'the most ambitious work of scientific art criticism ever attempted'.
Nevertheless, Ruskin's reputation quickly declined after his death. Even
now, despite the revival of academic interest in his works that has taken
place over the last twenty-five years or so, most of Ruskin's books
(including *Modern Painters*) remain out of print. Today he is probably
remembered more for his disastrous marriage and his ill-judged attack on
Whistler than for his enormous contributions to the culture of the
English-speaking world.

The sheer length of many of Ruskin's major works is undoubtedly one
of the main reasons for their continued neglect. *Modern Painters*, in its
original form, runs to over six hundred thousand words. Very few non-
specialists have the time, energy or inclination to plough through a work

of this size, even if they have access to a copy. As Ruskin himself rightly observed in the preface to the final volume: 'Had I wished for future fame I should have written one volume, not five.'

The purpose of the present abridgement is to make this masterpiece available again in a manageable form to the ordinary reader. It would be idle to pretend that in reducing its length by roughly half, much has not been sacrificed. But anyone who is familiar with Ruskin's writings will know how freely he indulges in digression and repetition. I believe that even in its present truncated form, most of the principal ideas and themes of the original survive. Of course, to the real Ruskin enthusiast (and I count myself one of them), every word is a joy and any omission a reason for regret. Nevertheless, I take comfort from the fact that Ruskin himself authorised the production of an abridged version of *Modern Painters*, though the project was never realised.* In any event, I genuinely hope that the present volume may help to widen the circle of his admirers and that some at least of those who read it may be tempted to seek out the original.

ACKNOWLEDGEMENTS

I have received help, advice and encouragement from many people, but I would particularly like to record my gratitude to Susie and Meirion Harries, Peter Day, Caroline Dawnay, Dr Roland Mayer, Robert Tear, Anthony Browne, Noël Annesley, W.J. Plomer, Gianfranco Varvesi, the staff of the London Library, the private collectors who kindly gave permission for works in their possession to be reproduced, and, above all, my wife Mary.

*The details of this ill-fated project emerge from *The Correspondence of John Ruskin and Charles Eliot Norton*, edited by John Bradley and Ian Ousby (Cambridge, 1987). See for example Letters 318, 327, 328 and 329.

INTRODUCTION

THE first volume of *Modern Painters* was published in 1843 when Ruskin was only twenty-four. It was the realisation of a project on which he had first embarked in 1836, when he read a vicious review in *Blackwood's Magazine* of some paintings by Turner in that year's Royal Academy exhibition. Ruskin immediately wrote a long letter to the editor defending the artist but, on the advice of Turner himself (whom Ruskin's father consulted), it was never sent. It was not until 1842 that another outburst of philistine critical abuse reawoke Ruskin's indignation; this time he was determined to 'blow the critics out of the water'.

Ruskin little realised that what he had initially envisaged as a polemical pamphlet defending the reputation of a single artist would grow in size and scope until it became not just a five volume treatise on art, but a prolonged meditation on the relationship between man, God and the natural world. The composition of this great work spanned a period of seventeen years and, in the very last chapter of the final volume, Ruskin acknowledged that he found it impossible to conclude a project which had, he rightly said, led him 'into fields of infinite enquiry'. He could only bring it to an end.

Ruskin followed his father's cautious advice not to attach his name to Volume I for fear that knowledge of his age would tell against it. Instead it was attributed to 'A Graduate of Oxford'. It was published in May 1843 and sold slowly at first. But despite hostile reviews in some august journals, it had, within a year or so, begun to attract a following among leading figures in the literary world. Wordsworth declared the author 'a brilliant writer' and Charlotte Brontë wrote to a friend: 'Hitherto I have only had instinct to guide me in judging art; I feel now as if I had been walking blindfold — this book seems to give me eyes.' The Brownings, though disagreeing strongly with some of Ruskin's harsh judgements on the old masters, were none the less much impressed by the style in which it was written. Elizabeth Barrett Browning commented that it was a great thing 'for a critic to be so much of a poet'. George Eliot wrote that she venerated Ruskin as 'one of the great teachers of the day'. In the United States, Walt Whitman was later to write approvingly of Ruskin's 'dashy, manly, clear-hearted style' and recommended Volume I to 'every lover of what we must call intellectual chivalry, enthusiasm, and a high-toned sincerity'. The praise came not only from literary figures but also from rising academics such as Benjamin Jowett, the future Master of Balliol, who 'read it all through with the greatest delight' and Henry Liddell, the future Dean of Christ Church, to whom it came as 'a revelation'. The later volumes confirmed and strengthened the favourable impression created by the first.

The reaction of the artistic establishment to Volume I was, however, distinctly cool. Turner himself seems to have been rather embarrassed by the extravagant praise heaped upon him and no doubt shook his head over Ruskin's rough treatment of Claude, whom he deeply respected. It was some time before he gave Ruskin — who was by then a personal friend — any hint that he had even read the book. Not surprisingly, some painters were offended by the prominence given to Turner. More than forty years later, Ruskin summed up the reaction of the leading artists mentioned in Volume I in his autobiographical work *Praeterita*: 'Taken as a body, the total group of Modern Painters were... more startled than flattered by my schismatic praise.'

The rising generation of young artists had less at stake and shared the delight of the general reader in discovering such an inspiring and intrepid critical voice. William Holman Hunt, one of the principal founders of the Pre-Raphaelite Brotherhood, which was to revolutionise painting in Britain in the 1850s, first read the second volume of *Modern Painters* in 1847 with the feeling that it had been written expressly for him. Many years later he wrote to Ruskin that it had been for him 'the voice of God'. Another Pre-Raphaelite, the sculptor Thomas Woolner, was convinced that it 'must do an incalculable amount of good' since it stated 'truths hitherto but dimly understood by many fine artists and totally disregarded by the bulk'. With the passing of time, further admirers were steadily recruited, including two Oxford undergraduates who were to become devoted followers of Ruskin's teachings: Edward Burne-Jones and William Morris. In 1856 Burne-Jones wrote an article, which also reflected Morris's views, in which he described Ruskin as a 'Luther of the arts' rising out of the slough of contemporary criticism.

Biographical Background

John Ruskin was born in 1819, the only son of a Scottish sherry merchant who had married his first cousin, the daughter of an inn keeper in Croydon. His social background was therefore modest but his father, John James Ruskin, was an able and industrious man whose recently established business soon began to prosper. It was the fortune made by his father which ensured Ruskin's financial security and enabled him to spend his life travelling, drawing, studying, teaching and writing books on whatever subjects interested him, untroubled by commercial considerations.

From an early age Ruskin's precocious literary talents were encouraged by his father, who was a great admirer of the Romantic poets. While still a child Ruskin was writing fluent, though not always very original verse modelled on the works of Wordsworth, Byron and Scott. His first poem was published when he was only thirteen and he reached the summit of his poetic career when, in 1839 (admittedly at the third attempt), he won the prestigious Newdigate prize at Oxford. It was his father's dream that he would one day make his name as a poet but Ruskin gave up writing poetry more or less completely after 1845. In that year he wrote to his father from Italy that the life he led was 'too comfortable and regular, too hardening' for him to be able to write first-rate verse: 'I don't see how it is possible for a person who gets up at four, goes to bed at ten, eats ices when he is hot, and beef when he is hungry, gets rid of all claims of charity by giving money which he hasn't earned, and those of compassion by treating all distresses more as picturesque than real: I don't see how it is at all possible for such a person to write good poetry . . .'

Margaret Ruskin, a devout evangelical Christian, was no less ambitious for her son than her husband, but her hope was that he would enter holy orders. From a very early age Ruskin read the Bible with his mother every morning and learned selected passages by heart. Like all fundamentalists, Margaret Ruskin believed that the Bible was the literal word of God, and she passed this belief on to her son. But Ruskin soon learnt from his mother — and from the Anglican evangelical preachers whose sermons he regularly heard — that the Bible sometimes needed to be interpreted symbolically. For example, many episodes in the Old Testament (e.g. the sacrifice of Isaac) could be read as prefigurations (or 'types') of events in the life of Christ. The young Ruskin quickly acquired skill in applying the technique of typological interpretation not just to the Bible but to the world around him. Since God was the creator of all things, and since nothing was created without purpose, he believed that it was in principle possible to uncover divine significance in anything. The daily Bible reading sessions therefore provided Ruskin with much more than just an encyclopaedic knowledge of the scriptures; they gave him exercise in the task of interpretation and established in him the habit of delving beneath the surface of all things — whether paintings or mountains — for their symbolic significance. Ruskin's remarkable exegetical skills and his advocacy of the use of symbols in art owed a great deal to this early discipline. At the same time, the Bible and the evangelical preachers left a deep mark on his prose style.

From his earliest years Ruskin frequently enjoyed experiences of almost mystical communion with nature similar to those described by poets like Wordsworth and Traherne. For him, as for Wordsworth, this kind of exaltation was associated particularly with the grandeur of mountain scenery. One of his very first memories was of seeing Derwent Water in 1824 (see page 414). This experience occurred when he and his parents were on one of the annual tours which played such a crucial part in the development of his aesthetic outlook. Almost every summer the family

fig.1   Samuel Prout, *Antwerp*

would set off by carriage to visit some picturesque corner of Britain and in 1833, inspired by some of Samuel Prout's engravings [fig.1] they undertook their first lengthy tour on the continent. Their journey took them down the Rhine; a famous passage in *Praeterita* records Ruskin's first sight of the great range of mountains that were to hold him in thrall for the rest of his days:

> It was drawing towards sunset, when we got up to some sort of garden promenade — west of the town, I believe; and high above the Rhine, so as to command the open country across it to the south and west. At which open country, far into the blue, gazing as at one of our distances from Malvern of Worcestershire, or Dorking of Kent, — suddenly — behold — beyond!
>   There was no thought in any of us for a moment of their being clouds. They were clear as crystal, sharp on the pure horizon sky, and already tinged with rose by the sinking sun. Infinitely beyond all that we had ever thought or dreamed, — the seen walls of lost Eden could not have been more beautiful to us; nor more awful, round heaven, the walls of sacred Death... Thus, in perfect health of life and fire of heart, not wanting to be anything but the boy I was, not wanting to have anything more than I had; knowing of sorrow only just so much as to make life serious to me, not enough to slacken in the least its sinews; and with so much of science mixed with feeling as to make the sight of the Alps not only the revelation of the beauty of the earth, but the opening of the first page of its volume, — I went down that evening from the garden terrace at Schaffhausen with my destiny fixed in all of it that was to be sacred and useful...

Ruskin's intense love of nature undoubtedly received nourishment from his reading of Wordsworth (the epigraph to each successive volume of *Modern Painters* was a quotation taken from *The Excursion*, reprinted on the title page of this edition), but he differed from Wordsworth in possessing the investigative curiosity of the true scientist. In Volume III, Ruskin himself draws out this contrast, claiming that 'the chief narrowness of Wordsworth's mind' lay in his inability to understand that 'to break a rock

fig.2 engraving after J.M.W. Turner, *Aosta*, from *Italy* by Samuel Rogers

with a hammer in search of crystal may sometimes be an act not disgraceful to human nature, and that to dissect a flower may sometimes

be as proper as to dream over it' (page 412). His scientific bent first emerged
when he began collecting rocks and minerals as a child. But it was his
reading of the classic *Voyages dans les Alpes* by de Saussure, which was given
to him for his fifteenth birthday, that prompted him to take up the study of
geology seriously. It was a science which was still in its infancy and there
was room for the amateur. Ruskin not only read the journals and attended
meetings of the Geological Society but managed to make a small contri-
bution of his own in the form of a short article on the reasons for the colour
of the waters of the Rhine, which appeared in 1834 and was his first published prose work. In 1839 he was made a Fellow of the Geological Society
and for the rest of his life he continued to take a close interest in geology,
though his own writings on the subject were often highly idiosyncratic.

Ruskin's devotion to the beauties of the natural world also found an
outlet in the practice of landscape art. Like most children of wealthy
parents in those days, he learnt to draw using pencil and watercolour and
showed great aptitude as well as remarkable powers of concentration. He
and his father also regularly attended exhibitions of the Society of Painters
in Water-colours (commonly known as the 'Old Water-colour Society') at
which they collected drawings and got to know some of the artists
personally. In fact Ruskin was to receive lessons from two prominent
members of the Old Water-colour Society, Anthony Vandyke Copley
Fielding and James Duffield Harding. Through his exposure to the work
and teaching of professional artists like these, Ruskin absorbed a taste for
the picturesque topographical art which was then at the height of fashion
and was soon producing accomplished landscape and architectural
drawings in the approved manner.

Ruskin's admiration for Turner, whom he was later to call 'his first
earthly master', began when he was given for his thirteenth birthday a
copy of Samuel Rogers' narrative poem *Italy* which included vignettes
based on his works [fig.2]. He was entranced by these delicate,
atmospheric studies and tried to imitate them. But his discovery of the full
range and power of Turner's art, by comparison with which even the best
work of his contemporaries seemed insipid and conventional, came four
years later, in 1836. At the Royal Academy exhibition that year he saw
three major oil paintings by Turner which bowled him over; it was the
intemperate attack on these works by the *Blackwood's* critic which, as we
have seen, first prompted him to spring to the artist's defence. In his
unpublished letter to the editor of *Blackwood's* Ruskin fearlessly described
Turner's imagination as 'Shakespearian in its mightiness' and likened him
to 'a meteor, dashing on in a path of glory which all may admire, but
which none can follow'. Turner's imitators, he added, 'must be, and
always have been, moths fluttering about the lights, into which if they
enter they are destroyed'.

When Ruskin went up to Oxford in 1837 he continued to cultivate his artistic skills, specialising at first in the production of meticulous architectural studies in the style of Samuel Prout [fig.3] and later falling under the influence of David Roberts, whose renderings of Near-Eastern subjects he saw exhibited in 1840. But over the next few years his whole aesthetic outlook underwent a radical transformation. According to the account given in *Praeterita*, the change was precipitated by two crucial experiences which occurred in 1842, shortly before he began work on *Modern Painters*:

fig.3   John Ruskin, *Peterborough Cathedral*, 1837

One day on the road to Norwood, I noticed a piece of ivy around a thorn stem, which seemed, even to my critical judgement, not ill 'composed'; and proceeded to make a light and shade pencil study of it in my grey paper pocket book... When it was done, I saw that I had virtually lost all my time since I was twelve years old, because no-one had ever told me to draw what was really there! All my time, I mean, given to drawing as an art; of course I had the records of places, but I had never seen the beauty of anything, not even of a stone — how much less of a leaf!

The second revelation followed shortly afterwards when Ruskin was drawing an aspen tree in the forest of Fontainebleau:

Languidly, but not idly, I began to draw it; and as I drew, the languor passed away: the beautiful lines insisted on being traced, — without weariness. More and more beautiful they became, as each rose out of the rest, and took its place in the air. With wonder increasing every instant, I saw that they 'composed' themselves, by finer laws than any known to men. At last the tree was there, and everything that I had thought before about trees, nowhere...

Whether or not the crucial change in outlook which these passages record was in fact a sudden one, there can be no doubt that around this time Ruskin began to abandon his previous adherence to fashionable stylistic conventions. His eyes had been opened and his own unique artistic and critical personality began to emerge.

During his time at Oxford, Ruskin published a series of essays on architecture (later collected in book form as *The Poetry of Architecture*). He also underwent a long drawn-out emotional ordeal which resulted from his hopeless infatuation with Adèle Domecq, the daughter of his father's business partner. He was first captivated by Adèle early in 1836, when she and her sisters came to stay with the Ruskins. As she was a Roman Catholic, his mother would have had grave reservations about their marriage, but in any case Adèle showed not the slightest interest in him. He would no doubt eventually have forgotten her had his parents not made the mistake of again inviting her and her sisters to stay for Christmas in 1838. As it was, his passion was rekindled and he continued to nourish hopes of winning her love until, in the summer of 1840, he was shattered by the unexpected news that she had married. Just three weeks later he was taken seriously ill with a pulmonary complaint, possibly tuberculosis, and was forced to break off the rigorous programme of work which he was pursuing for his final examinations.

Ruskin passed the rest of the summer in London and it was then that he first met Turner. The great artist was more than forty years older than him as well as being difficult and far from sociable. It therefore says much for Ruskin's charm and enthusiasm that, over the next few years, he was able to establish a close relationship with him. Much to his regret, however, Ruskin learned very little from Turner about his techniques or the reasons behind his choice of subject matter: the artist was very tight-lipped about such things. Although their relationship later deteriorated as the result of some insult that Ruskin felt he had suffered at Turner's hands, Ruskin was named as an executor of Turner's will and eventually undertook the preservation and cataloguing of the nineteen thousand drawings which Turner left to the nation.*

In the autumn of 1840 Ruskin's parents took him south to pass the winter in Italy, in the hope that the warmer climate would help to restore his health. The tour lasted until the following summer and took the family as far as Naples. It was a very difficult time. Ruskin was afraid that he might not have much longer to live and was in a delicate physical condition. He was also plagued by doubts about whether he should enter holy orders, as his mother had always wished. He disliked both Naples and Rome but during their stay in Rome he got to know the painters Joseph Severn and George Richmond. Severn had nursed the dying Keats and Richmond had been one of William Blake's young disciples. Both men showed Ruskin great sympathy and were to become life-long friends. Ruskin's strength began to return during the family's stay in Venice, a city with which he now began to fall in love. It was only, however, on the journey home, as they crossed the Alps, that the clouds finally lifted. By then he was sure that he would get well.

After taking his finals in May 1842, Ruskin again set off for the continent with his parents and passed much of the summer in Switzerland. It was there that he read the review which spurred him to write Volume I of *Modern Painters*. On the family's return, Ruskin started work, making frequent trips to the Dulwich Picture Gallery (which was close to his new home in Denmark Hill), the National Gallery and certain private collections to which he had access. He wrote quickly and in secret; only his family were aware of what he was doing and Ruskin sought advice from no one but them. His father found a publisher and the book appeared in May 1843, under the ponderous title (which was not Ruskin's own choice): *Modern Painters: their superiority in the art of Landscape Painting to all the Ancient Masters*. Not surprisingly, it soon came to be known simply as *Modern Painters*.

---

* These works, together with the oil paintings in the Turner bequest, have at last been gathered under one roof as Turner intended. They are housed in the Clore Gallery, an extension of the Tate Gallery in London, which opened in April 1987.

Ruskin's ambitious aim, as set out in the Preface, was to 'demonstrate' the superiority of the 'modern school' of landscape art deductively, on the pattern of a geometrical proof. It has sometimes been suggested that Ruskin was totally ill equipped for the task he had undertaken. But this is a gross exaggeration. He had read widely in the field of aesthetics and art criticism, disciplines which were then a great deal less cultivated than they are today. He was already familiar with much of the English writing on art of the eighteenth century, notably Reynolds's *Discourses*, the lectures of Fuseli and Barry, Burke's *Treatise on the Sublime and the Beautiful*, and Johnson's essays, and he was also well acquainted with the works of Plato and Aristotle. Nor should the enormous value of his own experience as a draughtsman and of his contacts with professional artists be underestimated.*

It is true that Ruskin's knowledge of European art was not extensive and that his tastes were as yet rather parochial; but it was sufficient for his immediate purposes to show that those critics who accused Turner of unfaithfulness to nature were wrong and that the old masters with whom they unfavourably contrasted him, were in fact less faithful to nature than he. And he had several great advantages. He was gifted with quite extraordinary powers of expression and was fired by a passionate sense of indignation. At the same time, his religious devotion to the study of the natural world, coupled with his capacity for minute observation and analysis, enabled him to speak with real authority when comparing the representational merits of paintings by the relatively small group of artists whom he singled out for detailed attention.

The greatest influence apparent in Volume I — apart from the works of Turner himself — is Wordsworth. In accordance with his espousal of the ancient theory that saw painting and poetry as 'sister arts', Ruskin draws on Wordsworth for examples of good landscape 'painting'; but his debt to Wordsworth extends also to the theoretical level. The basic argument of Volume I is closely analogous to that proposed by Wordsworth in the Preface to the *Lyrical Ballads*, the first publication of which in 1800 marked the birth of English Romantic poetics. Just as Wordsworth rejected the artifice of classical poetic diction in favour of 'the real language of men', so Ruskin, more than forty years later, attacked the attempts by classical landscape painters to 'improve' or idealise nature,

* In *The Image and the Eye*, Sir Ernst Gombrich has raised the intriguing possibility that Ruskin may have heard the lectures delivered by Constable in 1836 in which he set out his scientific theory of painting. Constable's approach is neatly summarised in an aphorism which could well have come from Ruskin: 'We see nothing truly till we understand it' (see Leslie's *Memoirs of the Life of John Constable*, ed. Andrew Shirley, 1937, p.398).

contrasting their distortions of reality with the 'truthfulness' of Turner.

While Volume I is highly successful on a polemical level, the opening analytical chapters are marred by the rather pretentious style in which they are written, and despite Ruskin's efforts to tone down the language in later editions, the entire volume bears the marks of the narrow and intolerant faith in which he had been brought up. Ruskin himself soon recognised the shortcomings of this his first major work. As early as October 1844 he was lamenting its overbearing tone in a letter to a close friend and complained that it was marked throughout by 'a nasty, snappish, impatient, half-familiar, half-claptrap web of young mannishness.'

In Volume II Ruskin addressed the fundamental question: what is the nature of beauty? He was faced with a daunting task. He therefore devoted much of the next two years to further study, and sought help and advice from some of his Oxford friends. A letter written to one of them in 1844 is very revealing about Ruskin's overall aims and shows that, having by now abandoned the idea of taking holy orders, he nonetheless believed that he could discharge an almost priestly function as a critic. 'I am not,' he said, 'engaged in selfish cultivation of critical acumen, but in ardent endeavour to spread the love and knowledge of art among all classes... the love and knowledge I would desire to communicate are not of technicalities and fancies of men, but of the universal system of nature – as interpreted and rendered stable by art.' Later in the same letter he questioned whether there could be any better use of his talents than 'in showing the functions, power, and value of an art little understood; in exhibiting the perfection, desirableness, and instructiveness of all features, small and great, of external nature, and directing the public to expect and the artist to intend – an earnest and elevating *moral* influence in all that they admire and achieve'.

As it turned out however, the illustrative material in Volume II was not to be drawn primarily from 'external nature'. Instead, the human figure became the focus of Ruskin's attention. One of the reasons for this unexpected change of direction was Ruskin's recognition that, prior to the seventeenth century, landscape had generally provided little more than a backcloth for the treatment of the figure. In order to provide a sound basis for a comprehensive theory of beauty he felt obliged to study acknowledged examples of the highest artistic perfection in the treatment of the human form. Already in 1844 he was at work in the British Museum, studying the Elgin Marbles. But the direction which Ruskin's interests now took was strongly influenced by his reading around this time of a work by the French art historian, Alexis François Rio, entitled *De la Poésie Chrétienne dans son principe, dans sa matière et dans ses formes* (Paris, 1836), which extolled the virtues of the Italian primitives. Rio's admiration for the early Italian masters was not particularly novel; they had, for example, been discovered and emulated as much as thirty years earlier by the Nazarene school of painters in Germany who in turn had influenced a number of English artists. But Ruskin was greatly impressed by Rio's book and decided that he had to visit Italy again before taking the next volume any further. The increasing fascination with the mediaeval world which marks Ruskin's career after 1845 probably owed much to Rio's inspiration.

Ruskin travelled to Italy in the summer of 1845, and for the first time he went without his parents. It was to be a turning point in his career. Following in Rio's footsteps, he headed for Tuscany where he spent several weeks in a frenzy of activity in Lucca, Pisa and Florence, drawing, making notes and reading a mixture of Dante and mediaeval Italian history [figs.4 & 5]. The provincialism and religious intolerance which, on his last visit to Italy, had made it difficult for him to respond to Italian sacred art, now began to evaporate. He was enormously excited by the works of Giotto, Masaccio and Ghirlandaio and by the frescoes in the Campo Santo at Pisa, but it was Fra Angelico who made the deepest impression on him — for the time being. Overwhelmed by what he had seen and appalled by the lack of respect which the Italians showed for their artistic heritage, Ruskin retreated to the mountains for rest. There he was joined by his old teacher Harding with whom he travelled on to Venice where another revelation awaited him. Tintoretto was not at that time held in high public esteem and it was almost by chance that the two men ventured into the Scuola di San Rocco, where they were overwhelmed by the scale and imaginative power of the huge canvasses, above all the *Crucifixion* [plate 14]. Writing home to his father Ruskin said: 'I have had a draught of pictures today enough to drown me. I never was so utterly crushed to the earth before any human intellect as I was today, before Tintoret.'

Ruskin's reading of Rio and the discoveries which he made on his Italian journey in 1845 had a profound influence on the contents of Volume II. The works of the Italian primitives and of Tintoretto are again and again cited as examples of the highest artistic achievement. Ruskin's apocalyptic encounter with Tintoretto seems, in particular, to have deepened his awareness of the importance of the imagination in art, a subject which he explores in the second half of the volume largely by means of a detailed examination of several works in the Scuola di San Rocco. But the chapters relating to the imagination are exploratory and not altogether consistent.

By contrast, Ruskin's bold analysis of beauty is both passionate and coherent. He insists that the perception and appreciation of beauty is not 'a mere operation of sense' (page 189) and divides the sources of beauty into two categories: Typical ('that external quality of bodies...which...

fig.4   John Ruskin, *Guinigi Palace, Lucca,* 1845

fig.5   John Ruskin, *Interior of San Frediano, Lucca,* 1845

may be shown to be in some sort typical of the Divine attributes'—page 198) and Vital ('the appearance of felicitous fulfilment of function in living things' — ibid.). All beauty is, however, of divine origin and the 'sensation of beauty' is 'dependent on a pure, right, and open state of the heart' (page 192). I will not attempt to summarise the details of Ruskin's argument. It will, however, be obvious that his account of beauty and of the 'theoretic faculty' through which it is perceived is essentially religious.

If the contents of Volume II differ markedly from those of its predecessor, so too do the tone and style. Ruskin's reverence for his parents can hardly be exaggerated, so it is perhaps not altogether fanciful to suppose that having produced in Volume I a work which, with its dazzling poetic descriptions, had gratified his father, he now felt obliged to write a book designed to appeal to the piety of his mother. There can certainly be no doubt that in writing Volume II, he consciously sought to achieve a dignity and solemnity that would be in keeping with the seriousness of his subject matter, and modelled his prose, in part at least, on that of the Elizabethan theologian, Richard Hooker, whose *Ecclesiastical Polity* he had recently read.

In his middle age Ruskin reacted strongly against Volume II, partly because he had by then rejected the dogmatic religious views which colour it and partly also because he disliked the mannered style in which it was written. He even decided at one point never to republish it. But later, as he emerged from the deep religious doubt that affected him after 1858, he revised his opinion. In 1877 he wrote that the main value of *Modern Painters* now seemed to him to lie 'exactly in that systematic scheme' which he had despised, and in the 'adoption and insistence upon the Greek term Theoria, instead of sight or perception', in which he had thought himself 'perhaps uselessly or affectedly refined'. He then felt that in writing about the 'theoretic faculty' he had been 'as a faithful scribe, writing words I knew not the force of, or the final intent'.

Following the publication of Volume II in 1846 ten years passed before the next two volumes appeared. During this time Ruskin devoted himself to the pursuit of his architectural interests. In 1849 he published *The Seven Lamps of Architecture*, a work which reflects much the same religious and intellectual preoccupations as Volume II. It established Ruskin as a leading propagandist of the Gothic Revival. In 1851 the first volume of *The Stones of Venice* appeared, to be followed by the second and third volumes two years later. *The Stones of Venice* consolidated Ruskin's reputation as one of the foremost writers and critics of the day, but the period of its composition coincided with the breakdown of his marriage.

Ruskin's disastrous relationship with Euphemia (Effie) Gray, whom he married in 1848, has been exhaustively documented and analysed. The marriage was probably doomed to failure from the start. Ruskin's attachment to his parents was unhealthily close and Effie's attempts to wean him away from them immediately embroiled her in conflict both with him and with them. Perhaps this problem could have been overcome if he had entered into a sexual relationship with Effie, but he did not. He may have been impotent — as Effie later claimed when seeking an annulment — though Ruskin privately denied this. He himself hinted darkly that there were 'certain circumstances in her person' which 'completely checked' sexual passion. Whatever these may have been, they certainly did not discourage Effie's second husband, the Pre-Raphaelite painter John Everett Millais, by whom she had a number of children. For a long time it has been believed that Ruskin was indeed rendered impotent by the discovery that his wife's body differed from a statue of a classical goddess in having pubic hair. A more recent theory is that she was menstruating on their wedding night and that this disgusted him. But these explanations strike me as superficial. It is clear from Ruskin's writings that at this stage in his life he deeply distrusted all forms of sensuality. Ruskin himself claimed that Effie willingly agreed to delay having children so as to enable them to travel freely. He would certainly have been determined not to allow his marriage to interfere with his career as a writer.

Sexual frustration and the lack of children were not the only problems confronting Effie. She was a good deal younger than Ruskin and she was unable to share fully in his rather esoteric pursuits: her interests were very different from his. While he was contemptuous of polite society, she was socially ambitious and a lover of parties. At the same time, Effie was not physically strong and had difficulty in keeping up with Ruskin when they went walking or climbing together. To make matters worse, she was soon on bad terms with Ruskin's formidable and domineering mother. There were also tensions between the elder Ruskins and Effie's parents. Effie was really only happy when, on two occasions, she and Ruskin spent long periods in Venice to enable him to research *The Stones of Venice*. Ruskin took very little notice of her, but in Venice at least she was able to lead an active social life, away from the disapproving gaze of her parents-in-law.

The marriage finally broke down when Effie fell in love with Millais. Though Ruskin's influence on the Pre-Raphaelites — and particularly Holman Hunt — was considerable, his first personal contact with any members of the Brotherhood came in 1851, two years after the first works carrying the initials 'PRB' had appeared on the walls of the Royal Academy. Ruskin was not at first particularly attracted to the work of the artists whom he was later to champion. But he was persuaded to speak up on their behalf by the poet Coventry Patmore when Millais and Holman Hunt were subjected to a savage critical assault reminiscent of those which Turner had earlier endured. He wrote two letters to *The Times* in which he approved their evident determination to 'represent stern facts' rather than 'paint fair pictures' and expressed the hope that they might lay the foundations of a school of art 'nobler than the world has seen for three hundred years'. Soon afterwards Ruskin and his wife accepted an invitation to call on Millais. They were both much taken with the handsome and brilliant young painter, and Millais for his part eagerly seized the opportunity of advancing his career which acquaintance with the famous critic offered.

Before the Ruskins set off for Venice in September 1851, they invited Millais to accompany them as far as Switzerland where Ruskin hoped that his new protégé would try his hand at the depiction of mountain scenery. Millais was unable to take up the offer but soon after their return in September 1852, Millais persuaded Effie to sit for *The Order of Release*. While Ruskin worked hard on *The Stones of Venice*, Effie spent many hours in the company of the painter who worked on the canvas at the Ruskins' house in Herne Hill. The following summer Millais and his brother accompanied the Ruskins on a long working holiday in the Scottish highlands. Ruskin paid little attention to his wife and spent most of his time either writing the lectures which he was due to deliver in Edinburgh in the autumn or trying to impose his artistic theories on Millais. The latter found himself in an extremely uncomfortable situation as he became increasingly besotted with Effie and she in turn began to fall in love with him. It was not until the following March, however, that Effie finally precipitated a scandal by walking out on her husband and demanding the annulment of their marriage. Despite the indignity and embarrassment to which he was exposed, Ruskin was glad to bring the unhappy marriage to an end and offered no defence. While the lawyers sorted matters out, Ruskin, alone again with his parents, retreated to the Swiss Alps where he spent an idyllic summer back in his favourite haunts. It is a measure of Ruskin's critical detachment that even after this humiliating episode, he was still able not only to see merit in Millais' work, but even on one occasion to compare him with his hero Titian.

During the next few years Ruskin threw himself into a variety of activities — teaching art at the newly founded Working Men's College with D.G. Rossetti (who took Millais' place as his artistic protégé), involving himself in the design and building of the new University Museum in Oxford, writing commentaries on the works displayed in the Royal Academy annual exhibitions, and delivering public lectures. There were also other books, such as *The Elements of Drawing* and *The Political Economy of Art*, both of which appeared in 1857.

Volumes III and IV of *Modern Painters* were written largely in the winter of 1855 and published in quick succession early in 1856. In the ten years which had passed since the appearance of Volume II, Ruskin's outlook had undergone profound changes. Not only had the evangelical faith on which he had depended since his childhood begun to crumble, but the ecstatic delight in nature which he had so often experienced in his youth, now visited him rarely. His unhappy marriage may well have been partly responsible for these changes, but there were other factors at work. He was becoming increasingly aware of the growing volume of scientific evidence that challenged traditional religious certainties. In a frequently quoted letter of 1851, Ruskin complained that his faith had been beaten into mere gold leaf: 'If only,' he went on, 'the geologists would let me alone, I could do very well, but those dreadful hammers! I hear the chink of them at the end of every cadence of the Bible verse . . .'. It was not however just the men of science, but the new generation of Biblical scholars who were undermining the foundations of Ruskin's childhood faith. In the face of critical evidence which showed that the text of the Bible was often corrupt and unreliable, it was no longer possible calmly to believe that the Scriptures were the literal word of God.

Although it was to be another two years before he finally abandoned the evangelical beliefs which he had absorbed from his mother, Volumes III and IV reveal signs of Ruskin's growing religious doubt. They also reflect the influence of the historian and social critic Carlyle, whose works Ruskin had long admired and whom he had come to know well following the break-up of his marriage. This can be detected in the greater informality and terseness of Ruskin's prose style and in his increasingly vehement denunciations of the social and economic structures that, in his view, not only permitted but actually promoted human suffering and the destruction of beauty, whether natural or man-made.

But Ruskin's growing concern with the world of practical affairs and his gradual espousal of the radical political and economic theories which, when explicitly enunciated later in his career, were to outrage the propertied classes, were not due only to Carlyle's influence. When Ruskin began to doubt whether there was a life to come in which transient earthly pain and hardships might be rewarded with eternal heavenly bliss, he felt bound to do whatever he could to alleviate human suffering here and now. This feeling must have been accentuated by his awareness of the contrast between his own cosseted existence and the misery and degradation endured by the poor. Around this time he became increasingly sceptical not only about the usefulness of his own art criticism, but about the value of art itself. The last three volumes of *Modern Painters* are therefore marked by a deepening mood of doubt and despondency which in Volume V comes close to despair.

Ruskin's spiritual crisis reached a climax in the summer of 1858 when he was staying alone in Turin. It was there that he finally abandoned the faith in which he had been reared. In *Fors Clavigera* and again, later, in *Praeterita*, Ruskin speaks of his 'unconversion' and relates this momentous decision to his discovery of a gorgeous painting by Veronese in the Turin Gallery – *The Presentation of the Queen of Sheba* [fig.52] – and to his attendance at a grim Waldensian church service. Just as he was repelled by the bitter puritanism of the Waldensian preacher, so he was drawn to the rich sensuality of Veronese. Whether or not this account should be taken literally, Ruskin's release from the sectarian straitjacket of his upbringing certainly resulted in a change in his aesthetic outlook – in Volume V for the first time Ruskin acknowledges that 'worldliness' has a proper place in art.

The mood of the final volume of *Modern Painters* is nonetheless profoundly dark. Ruskin no longer regards the Bible as a unique source of wisdom and in fact looks back to the pagan mythologies of the ancient Greeks with almost equal respect. Man now occupies the central place in his aesthetic scheme. 'Man,' he says, 'is the sun of the world' and later, 'all art which involves no reference to man is inferior or nugatory' (pages 524/5). But Ruskin's outlook was still profoundly religious. His loss of faith, though in some respects liberating, was a keenly felt spiritual privation. In Volume V he repeatedly affirms the essential importance of man's spirituality: man's nature is, he says, 'nobly animal', but it is also 'nobly spiritual' (pages 525/6). Furthermore, in the moving chapter entitled 'The Dark Mirror' in which he explicitly addresses the question of man's relationship with God, he offers a spiritual vision which, though desolate, still leaves room for God. The precise nature of his religious convictions at this point in his career is obscure; one thing however is clear – he could no longer find in religion grounds either for hope or consolation.

The contents of Volume V are as varied as those of its immediate predecessors but it is dominated by Ruskin's growing preoccupation with the state of society. By now he no longer believed that his time was best employed in art criticism. He might well have abandoned *Modern Painters* after Volume IV had his father not badgered him to complete his magnum opus while he was still alive to read it. In any event, as soon as Volume V was published, he embarked on a series of articles excoriating the practitioners and apologists of laissez-faire capitalism. These were published in book form as *Unto This Last*. Thereafter, much of his energy was devoted to the denunciation in increasingly apocalyptic terms of contemporary economic, social and environmental evils.

Ruskin's new willingness to tolerate 'sensuality' in art was made possible by his liberation from the puritanism of his upbringing and was precipitated by his revelatory encounter with Veronese. But it is worth mentioning that when Ruskin was engaged in the exhausting task of cataloguing Turner's drawings during the winter of 1857–8 – a task which, as he said, enabled him to review 'the whole career of Turner's mind during his life' — he came across some obscene sketches which he saw fit to destroy. His espousal of sensuality may, in part at least, have been a consequence of his need to accommodate this new and disturbing evidence about the nature of Turner's character without demoting him in his aesthetic hierarchy.

In bringing *Modern Painters* to a close, Ruskin returns to his original source of inspiration — the works of Turner. But although he maintains that his regard for Turner is undiminished, his interpretation of him is radically different from that which he had put forward in Volume I. Turner is no longer seen as a celebrant of the glories of God and nature, but as a faithless and desolate spirit. The climax of the volume comes with Ruskin's detailed examination of two paintings, *The Garden of the Hesperides* and *Apollo and Python* [plates 19 & 20]. At first sight, his complex and highly wrought interpretations of the symbolic significance of these two works may well seem far-fetched. But it is worth bearing in mind that Turner, though lacking a proper formal education, was a highly intelligent, self-taught man. He was undoubtedly familiar with some classical authors in translation and probably also made use of Lemprière's *Classical Dictionary*. It is therefore quite possible that he had in mind when working on these paintings some, if not all, of the classical texts to which Ruskin refers. Moreover, as Ruskin well knew, Turner revelled in the use of arcane symbolism and took a deeply serious view of his artistic responsibilities. Ruskin's interpretations may shed as much light on his own convictions about the faithlessness and materialism of Victorian society as they do on Turner's artistic intentions, but it is inconceivable that Turner painted these works simply as bald illustrations of classical myths. At the very least, Ruskin's close personal acquaintance with the artist, coupled with his determination to understand and explain the deeper significance of his works, obliges us to treat his views with respect.

The completion of *Modern Painters* marked the end of the first half of Ruskin's career. Volume V reveals signs of the mental turmoil which was to disturb him increasingly in the coming years and which finally overwhelmed him. By 1860 Ruskin was already falling in love with Rose La Touche, whom he had first met two years before when she was only ten years old. Ruskin's frequent use of the word 'rose' in Volume V may even reveal some half-conscious awareness of his growing attachment to this gifted but highly strung child. His relationship with her was to prove even more heart-breaking than his earlier doomed romances with Adèle Domecq and Effie Gray. As the years passed he became more and more obsessed with her and she with him. But she refused to marry him and her eventual death, insane, in 1875 left him distraught.

During the 1860s Ruskin devoted his time to a series of relatively minor works with obscure symbolic titles like *The Crown of Wild Olive* and *The Queen of the Air*. His father died in 1864 leaving him £120,000, an enormous sum in those days, which Ruskin disposed of largely by acts of lavish generosity long before his own death in 1900. Luckily for him, his books were by then earning him a good living. In 1869 Ruskin was appointed as the first Slade Professor of Fine Art at Oxford, a position which he held until 1879. By that time he had suffered at least one serious episode of mental illness which prevented him from testifying when, in 1879, the artist Whistler sued him for libel, winning damages of a farthing. Ruskin used this legal defeat as a pretext for resigning the Slade Professorship but he was persuaded to resume the chair in 1883. The 1870s saw the appearance of the long series of letters addressed to the working men of England entitled *Fors Clavigera*. In 1878 he founded the utopian Guild of St George which was quixotically intended to transform English society in accordance with Ruskinian precepts. Ruskin continued working and writing intermittently until his final complete mental collapse in 1889. The main product of these last years was *Praeterita*. He died at Brantwood, his home on Coniston Water in the Lake District on 20 January 1900.

Main Themes

It would be wrong to give the impression that *Modern Painters* is a totally chaotic work, though it is certainly far from systematic. It may therefore be useful to highlight very briefly some of the recurrent themes which provide it with a kind of loose structural unity.

Firstly, *Modern Painters* presents Ruskin's evolving ideas about what constitutes 'greatness' in art. In Volume I Ruskin puts forward a rather crude thesis — that the greatest art is that which 'conveys to the mind of the spectator...the greatest number of the greatest ideas' (page 8). Underlying this definition is his belief that painting is a poetic language and that, like a poem, a picture is capable of expressing a wide range of facts, feelings and thoughts. Every painting is to be judged by reference to the 'ideas' which it expresses. Foremost amongst these are ideas of 'truth', of 'beauty' and of 'relation' (the last named being propositions addressed to the intellect — i.e. thoughts). But he leaves many crucial questions unanswered — for example: how are these ideas to be numbered? how are they to be ranked? how indeed are they 'conveyed' into the spectator's mind?

In Volume I Ruskin postpones any detailed discussion of ideas of beauty and relation. Instead he focusses his attention on ideas of truth. This is sensible since his whole thesis only appears plausible when applied to the basic function of pictorial representation. So long as one is only interested in whether trees are drawn with botanical accuracy or reflections with due regard to the laws of optics, it makes sense to rank paintings in accordance with the 'amount' of 'truth' they convey. It is this notion of representational accuracy which underpins Ruskin's hymn of praise to Turner in Volume I. It is however much more difficult to accommodate within this straitjacket the less tangible properties which Ruskin subsumes under the headings of 'beauty' and 'relation'. It was perhaps his recognition of this fact which prompted him to amend his definition of 'great art' when he came to write Volume III. Nonetheless it is easy to see why Ruskin was attracted to this simple aesthetic calculus: not only did it appear to offer an *objective* standard of judgement; it also confirmed his own artistic preferences. Nor did he abandon the theory completely, for even in Volume IV he argues that there is an increase in the 'calculable sum of elements of beauty' in proportion to the increase in the mountainous character of natural scenery (page 470).

Ruskin also has much to say about style and handling. He is often supposed to have been the high priest of a kind of photographic realism and it is certainly true that he was strongly drawn towards artists who shared the passion for minute detail which is apparent in many of his own drawings; conversely, he detested the 'idealisation' of Reynolds's 'grand style'. But it has equally often been forgotten that the famous passage at the end of Volume I in which he calls for 'simple *bonâ fide imitation* of nature' (page 178) was exclusively addressed to *young* artists, and that the same passage concludes by saying that 'when their memories are stored' they can give rein to their fancy and 'show us what their heads are made of'.

In fact, Ruskin makes it clear early in Volume I that he has nothing but contempt for deceptive imitation, mainly because he regards it as a kind of trickery (page 12). But the distinction which he tries to make between bona fide naturalism and shallow jugglery is less than satisfactory. Why, for example, is the minuteness of Holman Hunt to be admired while the same quality in Gerard Dou is to be condemned? After all, they are both eminently realistic. This is another argument which Ruskin was later to modify. The difference between 'great and mean art', he says in Volume III, lies 'not in definable methods of handling, or styles of representation, or choices of subjects, but wholly in the nobleness of the end to which the effort of the painter is addressed' (page 295). Later on the new precedence which he accords to the expressive properties of a work of art becomes even clearer when he argues that it is precisely because a picture *differs* from reality that it becomes 'the expression of the power and intelligence of a companionable human soul' (page 355). As Sir Herbert Read first observed, *Modern Painters* reveals Ruskin as one of the most eloquent proponents of the theory of expressionism, even though the term itself was not coined for another forty years or so (*The Philosophy of Art*, 1964, p.81 ff).

One of the greatest mysteries for Ruskin was the qualitative difference between truly imaginative art (in which, he came to realise, representational accuracy was in itself of little importance) and the work of the skilful but uninspired plodder (which is how he tended to regard himself). He could find no explanation for the kind of imaginative transformations which he discovered even in purely topographical works by an artist of Turner's creative stature. He did however believe that the imaginative powers of a great artist depended on the possession of an exceptionally retentive visual memory and revealed the working of unconscious processes of selection and combination which he described as 'dream vision' (e.g. p.445). There are striking parallels between Ruskin's theory of the imagination and some psychoanalytic doctrines, in particular, Jung's concept of the 'collective unconscious' and his theories about the rôle of 'archetypal' symbols in myth and art.

The reader should perhaps be warned that Ruskin was in the habit of using the word 'truth' very freely. In fact he came to regard the products of high imagination as the most profound truths of all, even though they might bear little relation to everyday reality. But it is important to note that in Volume III Ruskin sets limits on the kinds of imaginative transformation that are acceptable in art of the highest rank. He regards any distortion of reality that results from the influence of the artist's emotions as a sign of weakness and coins the term 'pathetic fallacy' to condemn it. It is, he believes, the mark of the really great artist, such as Homer or Dante, that although subject to intense feelings, he remains firmly in command of them and is therefore always able to 'perceive rightly'. He does, however, make an exception for those who, 'strong as human creatures can be, are yet submitted to influences stronger than they, and see in a sort untruly, because what they see is inconceivably above them'. 'This last,' he says, 'is the usual condition of prophetic inspiration' (page 366).

The crucial importance of symbolism in Ruskin's theory of artistic expression emerges more and more clearly with each successive volume of *Modern Painters*. In Volume I its role is largely restricted to the interpretation of natural phenomena as evidence of divine creative power, but in the later volumes it occupies a central position. Indeed, by the time he came to compose Volume V, he had himself adopted a richly symbolic style of writing in which several layers of meaning are often embedded.

The term which Ruskin rather confusingly uses for any kind of symbolic or allegorical device is 'a grotesque'. He distinguishes several different forms of grotesque and claims that 'The greater and more thoughtful the artists, the more they delight in symbolism, and the more fearlessly they employ it' (page 330). For Ruskin the value of symbols lies in the fact that they enable the artist not only to compress complex ideas into a single, vivid and memorable image but also to encode ideas which it would be impossible to express directly. 'No element of imagination,' he argues, 'has a wider range, a more magnificent use, or so colossal a grasp of sacred truth' than the 'grotesque' (ibid.). In placing such emphasis on the importance of symbolism in art, Ruskin was out of step with most contemporary critics and his own brilliant explorations of the symbolic content of paintings (notably those of Tintoretto and Turner) foreshadow the iconographic analyses of scholars like Emile Mâle and Erwin Panofsky.

Modern Painters is remarkable for its penetrating insights into the psychological processes underlying both the creation and the appreciation of works of art. Although he coined the term 'the innocent eye' and strongly encouraged painters to try to discard conventional ways of seeing, he well understood how difficult this process could be. In Volume I, for example, he laments the fact that 'We are constantly supposing that we see what experience only has shown us, or can show us, to have existence, constantly missing the sight of what we do not know beforehand to be visible.' He then goes on to complain that 'painters, to the last hour of their lives, are apt to fall in some degree into the error of painting what exists, rather than what they can see' (page 30). Ruskin also recognises the way in which art itself can influence perception: 'if we could examine the conception formed in the minds of most educated persons when we talk of clouds, it would frequently be found composed of fragments of blue and white reminiscences of the old masters' (page 89). Moreover, Volume III includes a brilliant analysis of the rôle of the spectator's imagination (page 348ff) which shows how clearly Ruskin understood that the appreciation of a work of art is anything but a passive process. It was not until Sir Ernst Gombrich's classic study *Art and Illusion* appeared a hundred years or so later that insights such as these were developed and substantiated by reference to the findings of experimental psychologists.

In the end, however, the essential message of *Modern Painters* lies in its consistent declaration of 'the perfectness and eternal beauty of the work of God' (Preface to Volume V). Though, as we have seen, Ruskin's personal religious convictions changed dramatically during the course of the composition of *Modern Painters*, and though he came to regret deeply the 'Protestant egotism and insolence' of his earlier works, he was prepared at the end of his career to affirm that 'the Personal relation of God to man' was 'the source of all human...virtue and art'. This quotation comes from the Epilogue to *Modern Painters*, written in 1888, in which he also says that he never wished to define his beliefs further than in Volume II: 'Man's use and function (and let him who will not grant me this follow me no farther, for this I purpose always to assume) are, to be the witness of the glory of God, and to advance that glory by his reasonable obedience and resultant happiness' (page 186). 'Nothing is here said,' he reminds us, 'of any tradition of Fall, or of any scheme of Redemption; nothing of Eternal Punishment, nothing of Immortal Life. It is assumed only that man can love and obey a living Spirit, and can be happy in the presence and guidance of a Personal Deity . . .'

Conclusion

In a short introduction it would be futile to attempt to examine thoroughly the astonishingly diverse array of ideas and images contained in *Modern Painters*. Quite apart from its size and complexity, there is something Protean about it. Ruskin was a self-indulgent writer and, though he had a powerful analytical mind, he cared less and less for argumentative tidiness and rigour as he grew older. Like that other great nineteenth century prophet, Nietzsche (to whom he bears more than a passing resemblance), he was not ashamed to contradict himself. In the preface to Volume V, he excused himself by claiming that 'all true opinions are living, and show their life by being capable of nourishment; therefore of change.' But, he added, 'their change is that of a tree — not of a cloud.' Whether or not one accepts the validity of this metaphor, it would be unreasonable to expect any writer dealing with issues as profound as those tackled in *Modern Painters* not to modify his ideas over the course of seventeen years.

Any work of criticism reflects not only the individuality of its author but the intellectual and artistic climate in which it was written, and this is abundantly true of *Modern Painters*. In fact, as John Dixon Hunt has aptly observed in his biographical study *The Wider Sea: A Life of John Ruskin* (New York, 1982), it can be regarded as 'an oblique but nonetheless sharply focused autobiographical essay' in which the development of Ruskin's artistic and social theories and the evolution of his spiritual outlook can all be clearly traced.

But *Modern Painters* is also a literary achievement of a very high order. Ruskin himself regretted that he came to be known mainly as a 'fine writer', believing that those who saw him in this light were not taking him sufficiently seriously as a thinker. It is certainly true that the grace and fluency of his prose can be beguiling but it is hard to imagine that a book like *Modern Painters* would have attracted many readers or exerted such influence had it not been so beautifully written. As Virginia Woolf said: 'The style in which page after page of *Modern Painters* is written takes our breath away. We find ourselves marvelling at the words, as if all the fountains of the English language had been set playing in the sunlight for our pleasure' ('The Captain's Deathbed', article on Ruskin).

It is, of course, difficult to isolate the influence of *Modern Painters* from that of Ruskin's other writings. But it was undoubtedly enormous. I have already mentioned the dramatic effect which the reading of the second volume had on Holman Hunt, whose whole artistic career exemplifies Ruskin's theories. Ruskin's enthusiasm for minuteness of handling and complete naturalism reached out through him to the other Pre-Raphaelites and beyond, as did his conviction that great art ought to serve a high moral or spiritual purpose. During the 1850s, when Ruskin's critical reputation stood at its highest point, his opinions on artistic matters were treated almost as Gospel. In his Academy Notes for 1858, for example, Ruskin had only to lament the fact that no one had tried to paint an English spring with its blossom and fresh leaves, for a series of paintings on this theme to appear, including even one by Millais who had, of course, long ceased to be one of his devotees. Nevertheless, though he tried repeatedly to impose his views on a succession of gifted artists, no one of any real stature fell under his sway for very long, apart perhaps from Holman Hunt. Neither Millais nor Rossetti in the end took a great deal of notice of his strictures, and their personal styles moved steadily away from Ruskinian precepts as their careers developed. Two other painters, J.W. Inchbold and John Brett, briefly came under Ruskin's stern tuition and produced works which perfectly illustrate his naturalistic ideal [plate 1]. But they, too, rebelled against him.

Ruskin's influence on practising artists was perhaps less significant in the long term than the effect of his writings on the development of public taste. *Modern Painters* arrived on the scene at a time when the middle class (to which the Ruskins belonged) was growing rapidly in size and prosperity. Its members were eager to buy pictures but knew little about art and were anxious for advice from someone who could speak authoritatively in a language they could understand. Ruskin's writings met that need. Not only was he able to reassure such people that it was in their power to distinguish good paintings from bad, but, more importantly, he persuaded them that painting was a noble art, to be taken no less seriously than poetry. The fact that he was able to deploy the language of the Bible and the skills of an evangelical preacher in presenting his case (most notably in Volumes I and II) made his message still more persuasive to an early Victorian audience.

More specifically, *Modern Painters* was largely responsible for establishing Turner's almost mythical status as perhaps the greatest English painter. Ironically, he was almost too successful in this. As Sir Herbert Read has pointed out, 'Ruskin wrote so much and so effectively about Turner, that Turner's reputation has actually been a little overshadowed, as in a cloud of golden dust' (*The Meaning of Art*, 1949). *Modern Painters* also played an important role in securing the recognition of the Italian primitives (especially Fra Angelico) and Venetians such as Giovanni Bellini, Tintoretto and Veronese as major figures in the western artistic tradition.

However, by the time of his death in 1900 Ruskin's influence as an art critic was already waning. With the rise of Impressionism, he came to be seen by the avant-garde as the backward-looking apologist of an outmoded narrative style of art. This was ironic given that the primary goal of the Impressionists — the naturalistic representation of effects of light, especially in the open air — could well be seen as a logical development of Ruskin's own quest for greater 'truth' in art; it was certainly consistent with the practice of his hero Turner. Had Ruskin been aware of the artistic developments taking place in France in the 1870s, the story might conceivably have been different. But by the time the Impressionists had gained prominence, Ruskin was growing old and his interests had moved away from art. It is true that he still wrote and lectured on artistic subjects — this was, after all, the period of his Slade Professorship. But his critical opinions had largely ceased to develop and his inability to adjust to new ideas was demonstrated by his attack on Whistler for, as he put it, 'flinging a pot of paint in the public's face' — a comment sadly reminiscent of the critical abuse which had prompted his defence of Turner forty years earlier. The arrival of the Post-Impressionists and the series of revolutionary developments in the visual arts which followed, resulted in the almost complete eclipse of Ruskin's critical reputation. At the same time his highly wrought prose style and the profoundly religious view of art to which he was committed became increasingly unfashionable.

Ruskin was a pre-eminent victim of the general reaction against Victorian culture and values. Today, however, far from being reviled or ridiculed, Ruskin's ideas are little known outside the academic world. Yet he wrote for a much wider audience than scholars and critics and *Modern Painters* still has much to offer to the general reader. It is, at the very least, a document of great historical interest, which sheds light on many of the principal cultural and religious preoccupations of Victorian England. It also offers a vivid and moving insight into the mind of one of that period's most fascinating figures, and it remains a rich source of stimulating and suggestive insights and opinions.

It is not difficult to find fault with *Modern Painters*. It is marred by dogmatism, intolerance and overstatement. From his choice of epigraph it is clear that Ruskin himself was conscious of the risk of incurring the charge of arrogance. There is, however, little to be gained from judging *Modern Painters* by the standards demanded of present-day works of scholarship. Ruskin did not see himself as a scholar in this sense and had little time for system-building. Though he was always seeking to understand things scientifically, he never forgot that there are other kinds of truth than those discoverable by empirical means and that the ultimate sources of value lie elsewhere than in the material world. For him there were two kinds of science: the science of 'essence' (physical science as we know it) and the science of 'aspects' (typified by the imaginative grasp displayed in Turner's landscapes — see page 424). Ruskin himself was as much concerned with 'aspects' as with 'essence' and it is his constant mingling of these different kinds of truth that makes his writing so maddeningly inconsistent and imprecise. But it is exactly his willingness to grapple with reality at every level that raises him so far above the common run of critics and which lends his works their monumental grandeur. Approached with the sympathy which all great creative works demand, *Modern Painters* has the power to deepen our understanding not just of art and society but of our place in creation. It is as much a work of vision as of reason. If there have been any prophets in modern times, then Ruskin was surely one of them.

It may be well to end with Ruskin's own words, taken from the Epilogue which, though written not long before his faculties finally deserted him, are lucid and full of calm:

All that is involved in these passionate utterances of my youth was first expanded and then concentrated into the aphorism 'All great Art is Praise'; and on that aphorism, the yet bolder saying founded, 'so far from Art's being immoral, in the ultimate power of it, nothing but Art is moral: Life without Industry is sin, and Industry without Art, brutality'. . . and now, in writing beneath the cloudless peace of the snows of Chamouni [plate 2], what must be the really final words of the book which their beauty inspired and their strength guided, I am able, with yet happier and calmer heart than ever heretofore, to enforce its simplest assurance of Faith, that the knowledge of what is beautiful leads on, and is the first step, to the knowledge of the things which are lovely and of good report; and that the laws, the life, and the joy of beauty in the material world of God, are as eternal and sacred parts of his creation as, in the world of spirits, virtue; and in the world of angels, praise.

The Text

This abridgement is based on the texts of Volumes III, IV, V, VI and VII of the Library Edition of *The Works of John Ruskin*, edited by E.T. Cook and Alexander Wedderburn (George Allen, London, 1903–12). The Library Edition contains a vast amount of editorial material in the form of introductions, notes, cross-references and appendices, and also sets out the alternative versions of those passages (notably in Volumes I and II) which Ruskin heavily revised after their first publication. Though in some respects outdated, it remains indispensable and I gratefully acknowledge my debt to it.

I have not attempted to indicate where the cuts have been made since this would have been highly distracting. But since the majority of critical and biographical works refer to the page numbers of the Library Edition, I have included these in the margins. Gaps in the sequence signal any major excisions, but the reader should be warned that the amount of text on each page of the Library Edition varies; the fact that the marginal numbers sometimes appear very close together does not therefore necessarily mean that any cuts have been made. The largest single cuts have been made in Volumes IV and V where Ruskin's lengthy discussions of the structure and forms of mountains (Volume IV) and leaves and clouds (Volume V) have been omitted in their entirety. These sections serve mainly to amplify the discussion of these topics contained in Volume I and do not greatly advance the main arguments of *Modern Painters*. I have also been obliged to leave out Ruskin's Prefaces, his paragraph numbers and most of his own (often extensive) footnotes. The other major cuts are discussed in the notes.

The notes are intended primarily to elucidate passages which the modern reader may find obscure and to enable the reader to trace Ruskin's references. But this edition is not meant to provide an exhaustive commentary on *Modern Painters*. Such a work would probably fill several volumes. At the end I have included a short list of those works which I have found most useful under the heading 'Selected further reading'.

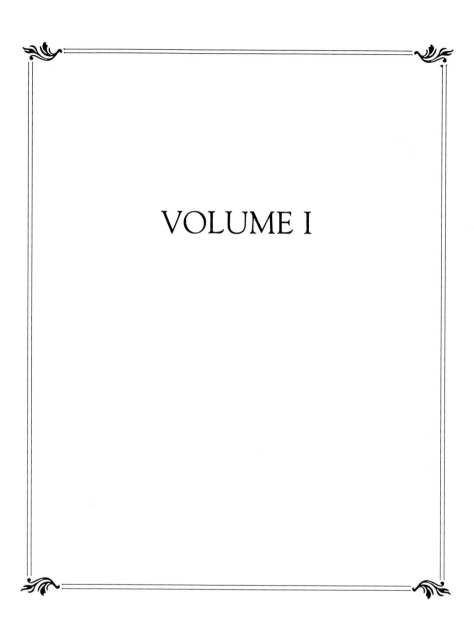

VOLUME I

PART I
Of General Principles

SECTION I
Of the Nature of the Ideas Conveyable by Art

CHAPTER I
Introductory

79   IF it be true, and it can scarcely be disputed, that nothing has been for centuries consecrated by public admiration, without possessing in a high degree some kind of sterling excellence, it is not because the average intellect and feeling of the majority of the public are competent in any way to distinguish what is really excellent, but because all erroneous opinion is inconsistent, and all ungrounded opinion transitory; so that, while the fancies and feelings which deny deserved honour, and award what is undue, have neither root nor strength sufficient to maintain consistent testimony for a length of time, the opinions formed on right grounds by those few who are in reality competent judges, being necessarily stable, communicate themselves gradually from mind to mind; descending lower as they extend wider, until they leaven the whole lump, and rule by absolute authority, even where the grounds and reasons for them cannot be understood. On this gradual victory of what is consistent over what is vacillating, depends the reputation of all that is highest in art and literature; for it is an insult to what is really great in either to suppose

80   that it in any way addresses itself to mean or uncultivated faculties. If I stand by a picture in the Academy, and hear twenty persons in succession admiring some paltry piece of mechanism or imitation in the lining of a cloak, or the satin of a slipper, it is absurd to tell me that they reprobate collectively what they admire individually; or, if they pass with apathy by a piece of the most noble conception or most perfect truth, because it has in it no tricks of the brush nor grimace of expression, it is absurd to tell me that they collectively respect what they separately scorn, or that the feelings and knowledge of such judges, by any length of time or comparison of ideas, could come to any right conclusion with respect to what is really high in art. The question is not decided by them, but for them; decided at first by few: by fewer in proportion as the merits of the work

are of a higher order. From these few the decision is communicated to the number next below them in rank of mind, and by these again to a wider and lower circle; each rank being so far cognizant of the superiority of that above it, as to receive its decision with respect; until in process of time, the right and consistent opinion is communicated to all, and held by all as a matter of faith, the more positively in proportion as the grounds of it are less perceived.

But when this process has taken place, and the work has become   81
sanctified by time in the minds of men, it is impossible that any new work of equal merit can be impartially compared with it, except by minds not only educated and generally capable of appreciating merit, but strong enough to shake off the weight of prejudice and association, which invariably incline them to the older favourite. And when, as peculiarly in   82
the case of painting, much knowledge of what is technical and practical is necessary to a right judgment, so that those alone are competent to pronounce a true verdict who are themselves the persons to be judged, and   83
who therefore can give no opinion, centuries may elapse before fair comparison can be made between two artists of different ages. It thus becomes the duty of every one capable of demonstrating any definite points of superiority in modern art, and who is in a position in which his doing so will not be ungraceful, to encounter without hesitation whatever opprobrium may fall upon him from the necessary prejudice even of the most candid minds, and from the far more virulent opposition of those who have no hope of maintaining their own reputation for discernment but in the support of that kind of consecrated merit which may be applauded without an inconvenient necessity for reasons. It is my purpose, therefore, believing that there are certain points of superiority in modern artists, and especially in one or two of their number, which have not yet been fully understood, except by those who are scarcely in a position admitting the declaration of their conviction, to institute a close comparison between the great works of ancient and modern landscape art; to raise, as far as possible, the deceptive veil of imaginary light through which we are accustomed to gaze upon the patriarchal work; and to show the real relations, whether favourable or otherwise, subsisting between it and our own.

I should scarcely have ventured to speak so decidedly, but for my full   84
conviction that we ought not to class the historical painters of the fifteenth, and landscape painters of the seventeenth, centuries together, under the general title of "old masters," as if they possessed anything like corresponding rank in their respective walks of art. I feel assured that the principles on which they worked are totally opposed, and that the landscape painters have been honoured only because they exhibited, in mechanical and technical qualities, some semblance of the manner of the nobler historical painters, whose principles of conception and composition

they entirely reversed. The course of study which has led me reverently to the feet of Michael Angelo and Da Vinci, has alienated me gradually from Claude and Gaspar;[1] I cannot, at the same time, do homage to power and pettiness—to the truth of consummate science, and the mannerism of undisciplined imagination. And let it be understood that whenever hereafter I speak depreciatingly of the old masters as a body, I refer to none of the historical painters, for whom I entertain a veneration which, though I hope reasonable in its grounds, is almost superstitious in degree. Neither, unless he be particularly mentioned, do I intend to include Nicholas Poussin, whose landscapes have a separate and elevated character, which renders it necessary to consider them apart from all others. Speaking generally of the elder masters, I refer only to Claude, Gaspar Poussin, Salvator Rosa, Cuyp, Berghem, Both, Ruysdael, Hobbima, Teniers (in his landscapes), P. Potter, Canaletto, and the various Van somethings and Back somethings, more especially and malignantly those who have libelled the sea.

It will of course be necessary for me, in the commencement of the work, to state briefly those principles on which I conceive all right judgment of art must be founded.

CHAPTER II

Definition of Greatness in Art

PAINTING, or art generally, as such, with all its technicalities, diffi-   87
culties, and particular ends, is nothing but a noble and expressive
language, invaluable as the vehicle of thought, but by itself nothing. He
who has learned what is commonly considered the whole art of painting,
that is, the art of representing any natural object faithfully, has as yet only
learned the language by which his thoughts are to be expressed. He has
done just as much towards being that which we ought to respect as a great
painter, as a man who has learnt how to express himself grammatically
and melodiously has towards being a great poet. The language is, indeed,
more difficult of acquirement in the one case than in the other, and possesses more power of delighting the sense, while it speaks to the intellect;
but it is, nevertheless, nothing more than language, and all those
excellences which are peculiar to the painter as such, are merely what   88
rhythm, melody, precision, and force are in the words of the orator and
the poet, necessary to their greatness, but not the tests of their greatness.
It is not by the mode of representing and saying, but by what is represented
and said, that the respective greatness either of the painter or the writer
is to be finally determined.

It is not, however, always easy, either in painting or literature, to deter-   89
mine where the influence of language stops, and where that of thought
begins. Many thoughts are so dependent upon the language in which they
are clothed, that they would lose half their beauty if otherwise expressed.
But the highest thoughts are those which are least dependent on language,
and the dignity of any composition, and praise to which it is entitled, are
in exact proportion to its independency of language or expression. A
composition is indeed usually most perfect, when to such intrinsic dignity
is added all that expression can do to attract and adorn; but in every case
of supreme excellence this all becomes as nothing.

There is therefore a distinction to be made between what is ornamental   90
in language and what is expressive. That part of it which is necessary to
the embodying and conveying of the thought is worthy of respect and
attention as necessary to excellence, though not the test of it. But that

6

part of it which is decorative has little more to do with the intrinsic excellence of the picture than the frame or the varnishing of it. And this caution in distinguishing between the ornamental and the expressive is peculiarly necessary in painting; for in the language of words it is nearly impossible for that which is not expressive to be beautiful, except by mere rhythm or melody, any sacrifice to which is immediately stigmatized as error. But the beauty of mere language in painting is not only very attractive and entertaining to the spectator, but requires for its attainment no small exertion of mind and devotion of time by the artist. Hence, in art, men have frequently fancied that they were becoming rhetoricians and poets when they were only learning to speak melodiously, and the judge has over and over again advanced to the honour of authors those who were never more than ornamental writing-masters.

Most pictures of the Dutch school, for instance, excepting always those of Rubens, Vandyke, and Rembrandt, are ostentatious exhibitions of the artist's power of speech, the clear and vigorous elocution of useless and senseless words; while the early efforts of Cimabue and Giotto are the burning messages of prophecy, delivered by the stammering lips of infants. It must be the part of the judicious critic carefully to distinguish what is language, and what is thought, and to rank and praise pictures chiefly for the latter, considering the former as a totally inferior excellence, and one which cannot be compared with nor weighed against thought in any way, or in any degree whatsoever. The picture which has the nobler and more numerous ideas, however awkwardly expressed, is a greater and a better picture than that which has the less noble and less numerous ideas, however beautifully expressed. No weight, nor mass nor beauty of execution, can outweigh one grain or fragment of thought. Three pen-strokes of Raffaelle are a greater and a better picture than the most finished work that ever Carlo Dolci[2] polished into inanity. Nothing but thought can pay for thought, and the instant that the increasing refinement or finish of the picture begins to be paid for by the loss of the faintest shadow of an idea, that instant all refinement or finish is an excrescence and a deformity.

Yet although in all our speculations on art, language is thus to be distinguished from, and held subordinate to, that which it conveys, we must still remember that there are certain ideas inherent in language itself, and that, strictly speaking, every pleasure connected with art has in it some reference to the intellect. The mere sensual pleasure of the eye, received from the most brilliant piece of colouring, is as nothing to that which it receives from a crystal prism, except as it depends on our perception of a certain meaning and intended arrangement of colour, which has been the subject of intellect. Nay, the term idea, according to Locke's definition of it, will extend even to the sensual impressions themselves as

far as they are "things which the mind occupies itself about in thinking;"[3]   92
that is, not as they are felt by the eye only, but as they are received by the
mind through the eye. So that, if I say that the greatest picture is that
which conveys to the mind of the spectator the greatest number of the
greatest ideas, I have a definition which will include as subjects of comparison every pleasure which art is capable of conveying. If I were to say,
on the contrary, that the best picture was that which most closely imitated
nature, I should assume that art could only please by imitating nature; and
I should cast out of the pale of criticism those parts of works of art which
are not imitative, that is to say, intrinsic beauties of colour and form, and
those works of art wholly, which, like the Arabesques of Raffaelle in the
Loggias, are not imitative at all. Now, I want a definition of art wide
enough to include all its varieties of aim. I do not say, therefore, that the
art is greatest which gives most pleasure, because perhaps there is some art
whose end is to teach, and not to please. I do not say that the art is greatest
which teaches us most, because perhaps there is some art whose end is to
please, and not to teach. I do not say that the art is greatest which imitates
best, because perhaps there is some art whose end is to create and not to
imitate. But I say that the art is greatest which conveys to the mind of the
spectator, by any means whatsoever, the greatest number of the greatest
ideas; and I call an idea great in proportion as it is received by a higher
faculty of the mind, and as it more fully occupies, and in occupying,
exercises and exalts, the faculty by which it is received.

If this, then, be the definition of great art, that of a great artist naturally
follows. He is the greatest artist who has embodied, in the sum of his
works, the greatest number of the greatest ideas.

CHAPTER III
Of Ideas of Power

93 I THINK that all the sources of pleasure, or of any other good, to be derived from works of art, may be referred to five distinct heads.

    I. Ideas of Power.—The perception or conception of the mental or bodily powers by which the work has been produced.

    II. Ideas of Imitation.—The perception that the thing produced resembles something else.

    III. Ideas of Truth.—The perception of faithfulness in a statement of facts by the thing produced.

    IV. Ideas of Beauty.—The perception of beauty, either in the thing produced, or in what it suggests or resembles.

    V. Ideas of Relation.—The perception of intellectual relations in the thing produced, or in what it suggests or resembles.

I shall briefly distinguish the nature and effects of each of these classes of ideas.

94 I. Ideas of Power.—These are the simple perception of the mental or bodily powers exerted in the production of any work of art. According to the dignity and degree of the power perceived is the dignity of the idea; but the whole class of ideas is received by the intellect, and they excite the best of the moral feelings, veneration, and the desire of exertion. As a species, therefore, they are one of the noblest connected with art; but the differences in degree of dignity among themselves are infinite, being correspondent with every order of power,—from that of the fingers to that of the most exalted intellect. Thus, when we see an Indian's paddle carved from the handle to the blade, we have a conception of prolonged manual labour, and are gratified in proportion to the supposed expenditure of time and exertion. These are, indeed, powers of a low order, yet the pleasure arising from the conception of them enters very largely into our admiration of all elaborate ornament, architectural decoration, etc. The delight with which we look on the fretted front of Rouen Cathedral depends in no small degree on the simple perception of time employed and labour expended in its production. But it is a right, that is, an ennobling pleasure, even in this its lowest phase; and even the pleasure

9

felt by those persons who praise a drawing for its "finish" or its "work,"   95
which is one precisely of the same kind, would be right, if it did not imply
a want of perception of the higher powers which render work unnecessary.
If to the evidence of labour be added that of strength or dexterity, the
sensation of power is yet increased; if to strength and dexterity be added
that of ingenuity and judgment, it is multiplied tenfold; and so on,
through all the subjects of action of body or mind, we receive the more
exalted pleasure from the more exalted power.

Men may let their great powers lie dormant, while they employ their
mean and petty powers on mean and petty objects; but it is physically
impossible to employ a great power, except on a great object. Consequently, wherever power of any kind or degree has been exerted, the   96
marks and evidence of it are stamped upon its results: it is impossible that
it should be lost or wasted, or without record, even in the "estimation of
a hair;"[4] and therefore, whatever has been the subject of a great power
bears about with it the image of that which created it, and is what is
commonly called "excellent."

The faculty of perceiving what powers are required for the production of
a thing, is the faculty of perceiving excellence. It is this faculty in which
men, even of the most cultivated taste, must always be wanting, unless
they have added practice to reflection; because none can estimate the
power manifested in victory, unless they have personally measured the
strength to be overcome. Though, therefore, it is possible, by the cultivation of sensibility and judgment, to become capable of distinguishing
what is beautiful, it is totally impossible, without practice and knowledge,
to distinguish or feel what is excellent.

CHAPTER IV
Of Ideas of Imitation

100 Whenever anything looks like what it is not, the resemblance being so great as *nearly* to deceive, we feel a kind of pleasurable surprise, an agreeable excitement of mind, exactly the same in its nature as that which we receive from juggling. Whenever we perceive this in something produced by art, that is to say, whenever the work is seen to resemble something which we know it is not, we receive what I call an idea of imitation. *Why* such ideas are pleasing, it would be out of our present purpose to inquire; we only know that there is no man who does not feel pleasure in his animal nature from gentle surprise, and that such surprise can be excited in no more distinct manner than by the evidence that a thing is not what it appears to be. Now two things are requisite to our complete and most pleasurable perception of this: first, that the resemblance be so perfect as to amount to a deception; secondly, that there be some means of proving at the same moment that it *is* a deception. The most perfect ideas and pleasures of imitation are, therefore, when one sense is contradicted by another, both bearing as positive evidence on the
101 subject as each is capable of alone; as when the eye says a thing is round, and the finger says it is flat: they are, therefore, never felt in so high a degree as in painting, where appearance of projection, roughness, hair, velvet, etc., are given with a smooth surface, or in wax-work, where the first evidence of the senses is perpetually contradicted by their experience. But the moment we come to marble, our definition checks us, for a marble figure does not look like what it is not: it looks like marble, and like the form of a man, but then it *is* marble, and it *is* the form of a man. It does not look like a man, which it is not, but like the form of a man, which it is. Form is form, *bonâ fide* and actual, whether in marble or in flesh—not an imitation or resemblance of form, but real form. The chalk outline of the bough of a tree on paper, is not an imitation; it looks like chalk and paper—not like wood, and that which it suggests to the mind is not properly said to be *like* the form of a bough, it *is* the form of a bough. Now, then, we see the limits of an idea of imitation; it extends only to the sensation of trickery and deception occasioned by a thing's intentionally

11

seeming different from what it is; and the degree of the pleasure depends on the degree of difference and the perfection of the resemblance, not on the nature of the thing resembled. The simple pleasure in the imitation would be precisely of the same degree (if the accuracy could be equal), whether the subject of it were the hero or his horse.

Ideas of imitation, then, act by producing the simple pleasure of surprise, and that not of surprise in its higher sense and function, but of the mean and paltry surprise which is felt in jugglery. These ideas and pleasures are the most contemptible which can be received from art. First, because it is necessary to their enjoyment that the mind should reject the impression and address of the thing represented, and fix itself only upon   102
the reflection that it is not what it seems to be. All high or noble emotion or thought is thus rendered physically impossible, while the mind exults in what is very like a strictly sensual pleasure. We may consider tears as a result of agony or of art, whichever we please, but not of both at the same moment. If we are surprised by them as an attainment of the one, it is impossible we can be moved by them as a sign of the other.

Ideas of imitation are contemptible in the second place, because not only do they preclude the spectator from enjoying inherent beauty in the subject, but they can only be received from mean and paltry subjects, because it is impossible to imitate anything really great. We can "paint a cat or a fiddle, so that they look as if we could take them up;"[5] but we cannot imitate the ocean, or the Alps. We can imitate fruit, but not a tree; flowers, but not a pasture; cut-glass, but not the rainbow.

Thirdly, these ideas are contemptible, because no ideas of power are associated with them. To the ignorant, imitation, indeed, seems difficult, and its success praiseworthy, but even they can by no possibility see more in the artist than they do in a juggler, who arrives at a strange end by means with which they are unacquainted. To the instructed, the juggler is by far the more respectable artist of the two, for they know sleight of hand to be an art of an immensely more difficult acquirement, and to   103
imply more ingenuity in the artist than a power of deceptive imitation in painting, which requires nothing more for its attainment than a true eye, a steady hand, and moderate industry—qualities which in no degree separate the imitative artist from a watchmaker, pin-maker, or any other neat-handed artificer.

CHAPTER V
Of Ideas of Truth

104   THE word Truth, as applied to art, signifies the faithful statement, either to the mind or senses, of any fact of nature.

We receive an idea of truth, then, when we perceive the faithfulness of such a statement.

The difference between ideas of truth and of imitation lies chiefly in the following points:

First,—Imitation can only be of something material, but truth has reference to statements both of the qualities of material things, and of emotions, impressions, and thoughts. There is a moral as well as material truth,—a truth of impression as well as of form,—of thought as well as of matter; and the truth of impression and thought is a thousand times the more important of the two. Hence, truth is a term of universal application, but imitation is limited to that narrow field of art which takes cognizance only of material things.

Secondly,—Truth may be stated by any signs or symbols which have a definite signification in the minds of those to whom they are addressed, although such signs be themselves no image nor likeness of anything. Whatever can excite in the mind the conception of certain facts, can give ideas of truth, though it be in no degree the imitation or resemblance of
105   those facts. But ideas of imitation, of course, require the likeness of the object. They speak to the perceptive faculties only: truth to the conceptive.

Thirdly, and in consequence of what is above stated, an idea of truth exists in the statement of *one* attribute of anything, but an idea of imitation requires the resemblance of as many attributes as we are usually cognizant of in its real presence.

Hence it might at first sight appear, that an idea of imitation, inasmuch as several ideas of truth are united in it, is nobler than a simple idea of truth. And if it were necessary that the ideas of truth should be perfect, or should be subjects of contemplation *as such*, it would be so. But, observe, we require to produce the effect of imitation only so many and such ideas of truth as the *senses* are usually cognizant of. Now the senses are not usually, nor unless they be especially devoted to the service, cognizant, with accuracy, of any truths but those of space and projection. It requires long study and attention before they give certain evidence of even the   106 simplest truths of form. For instance, the quay on which the figure is sitting, with his hand at his eyes, in Claude's "Seaport," No. 14 in the National Gallery, is egregiously out of perspective [plate 3]. The eye of this artist, with all his study, had thus not acquired the power of taking cognizance of the apparent form even of a simple parallelopiped: how much less of the complicated forms of boughs, leaves, or limbs?

The only facts which we are usually and certainly cognizant of, are those of distance and projection; and if these be tolerably given, with something like truth of form and colour to assist them, the idea of imitation is complete.

We shall see, in the course of our investigation of ideas of truth, that   107 ideas of imitation not only do not imply their presence, but even are in-   108 consistent with it; and that pictures which imitate so as to deceive, are never true. But this is not the place for the proof of this; at present we have only to insist on the last and greatest distinction between ideas of truth and of imitation—that the mind, in receiving one of the former, dwells upon its own conception of the fact, or form, or feeling stated, and is occupied only with the qualities and character of that fact or form, considering it as real and existing, being all the while totally regardless of the signs or symbols by which the notion of it has been conveyed. These signs have no pretence, nor hypocrisy, nor legerdemain about them;— there is nothing to be found out, or sifted, or surprised in them;—they bear their message simply and clearly, and it is that message which the mind takes from them and dwells upon, regardless of the language in which it is delivered. But the mind, in receiving an idea of imitation, is wholly occupied in finding out that what has been suggested to it is not what it appears to be: it does not dwell on the suggestion, but on the perception that it is a false suggestion: it derives its pleasure, not from the contemplation of a truth, but from the discovery of a falsehood. So that the moment ideas of truth are grouped together, so as to give rise to an idea of imitation, they change their very nature—lose their essence as ideas of truth—and are corrupted and degraded, so as to share in the treachery of what they have produced. Hence, finally, ideas of truth are the foundation, and ideas of imitation, the destruction, of all art. We shall be better able to appreciate their relative dignity after the investigation which we propose of the functions of the former; but we may as well now express the conclusion to which we shall then be led—that no picture can be good which deceives by its imitation, for the very reason that nothing can be beautiful which is not true.

CHAPTER VI

Of Ideas of Beauty

109   Any material object which can give us pleasure in the simple contemplation of its outward qualities without any direct and definite exertion of the intellect, I call in some way, or in some degree, beautiful. Why we receive pleasure from some forms and colours, and not from others, is no more to be asked or answered than why we like sugar and dislike wormwood. The utmost subtlety of investigation will only lead us to ultimate instincts and principles of human nature, for which no farther reason can be given than the simple will of the Deity that we should be so created. On these primary principles of our nature, education and accident operate to an unlimited extent; they may be cultivated or checked, directed or diverted, gifted by right guidance with the most acute and faultless sense, or subjected by neglect to every phase of error and disease. He who has followed up these natural laws of aversion and desire, rendering them more and more authoritative by constant obedience, so as to derive pleasure always from that which God originally intended should

110   give him pleasure, and who derives the greatest possible sum of pleasure from any given object, is a man of taste.

    Observe, however, I do not mean by excluding direct exertion of the intellect from ideas of beauty, to assert that beauty has no effect upon, nor connection with the intellect. All our moral feelings are so interwoven with our intellectual powers, that we cannot affect the one without in some degree addressing the other; and in all high ideas of beauty, it is more than probable that much of the pleasure depends on delicate and untraceable perceptions of fitness, propriety, and relation, which are purely intellectual, and through which we arrive at our noblest ideas of what is commonly and rightly called "intellectual beauty." But there is yet no immediate *exertion* of the intellect; that is to say, if a person receiving even the noblest ideas of simple beauty be asked *why* he likes the object exciting

111   them, he will not be able to give any distinct reason, nor to trace in his mind any formed thought, to which he can appeal as a source of pleasure.

Ideas of beauty are among the noblest which can be presented to the human mind, invariably exalting and purifying it according to their degree; and it would appear that we are intended by the Deity to be constantly under their influence, because there is not one single object in nature which is not capable of conveying them, and which, to the rightly perceiving mind, does not present an incalculably greater number of beautiful than of deformed parts; there being in fact scarcely anything, in pure undiseased nature, like positive deformity, but only degrees of beauty, or such slight and rare points of permitted contrast as may render all around them more valuable by their opposition—spots of blackness in creation, to make its colours felt.

But although everything in nature is more or less beautiful, every species of object has its own kind and degree of beauty; some being in their own nature more beautiful than others, and few, if any, individuals possessing the utmost degree of beauty of which the species is capable. This utmost degree of specific beauty, necessarily coexistent with the utmost perfection of the object in other respects, is the ideal of the object.

Ideas of beauty, then, be it remembered, are the subjects of moral, but not of intellectual perception. By the investigation of them we shall be led to the knowledge of the ideal subjects of art.

CHAPTER VII

Of Ideas of Relation

112 I USE this term rather as one of convenience than as adequately expressive of the vast class of ideas which I wish to be comprehended under it, namely, all those conveyable by art, which are the subjects of distinct intellectual perception and action, and which are therefore worthy of the name of thoughts.

Under this head must be arranged everything productive of expression, sentiment, and character, whether in figures or landscapes, (for there may be as much definite expression and marked carrying out of particular thoughts in the treatment of inanimate as of animate nature,) everything relating to the conception of the subject and to the congruity and relation of its parts; not as they enhance each other's beauty by known and constant laws of composition, but as they give each other expression and meaning, by particular application, requiring distinct thought to discover or to enjoy.

113 The principal object in the foreground of Turner's "Building of Carthage" [plate 4] is a group of children sailing toy boats. The exquisite choice of this incident, as expressive of the ruling passion which was to be the source of future greatness, in preference to the tumult of busy stonemasons or arming soldiers, is quite as appreciable when it is told as when it is seen,—it has nothing to do with the technicalities of painting; a scratch of the pen would have conveyed the idea and spoken to the intellect as much as the elaborate realizations of colour. Such a thought as this is something far above all art; it is epic poetry of the highest order. Claude, in subjects of the same kind, commonly introduces people carrying red trunks with iron locks about, and dwells, with infantine delight, on the lustre of the leather and the ornaments of the iron. The intellect can have no occupation here; we must look to the imitation or to nothing. Consequently, Turner arises above Claude in the very first instant of the conception of his picture, and acquires an intellectual superiority which no powers of the draughtsman or the artist (supposing

17

that such existed in his antagonist) could ever wrest from him.

Ideas of relation are of course, with respect to art generally, the most 114 extensive as the most important source of pleasure; and if we proposed entering upon the criticism of historical works, it would be absurd to attempt to do so without farther subdivision and arrangement. But the old landscape painters got over so much canvas without either exercise of, or appeal to, the intellect, that we shall be little troubled with the subjects as far as they are concerned; and whatever subdivision we may adopt, as it will therefore have particular reference to the works of modern artists, 115 will be better understood when we have obtained some knowledge of them in less important points.

SECTION II
Of Power

CHAPTER I
General Principles Respecting Ideas of Power

116   WE have seen in the last section what classes of ideas may be conveyed by art, and we have been able so far to appreciate their relative worth as to see, that from the list, as it is to be applied to the purposes of legitimate criticism, we may at once throw out the ideas of imitation: first, because, as we have shown, they are unworthy the pursuit of the artist; and, secondly, because they are nothing more than the result of a particular association of ideas of truth.

Ideas of power, in the same way, cannot be completely viewed as a separate class; not because they are mean or unimportant, but because they are almost always associated with, or dependent upon, some of the higher ideas of truth, beauty, or relation, rendered with decision or velocity. That power which delights us in the chalk sketch of a great painter is not like that of the writing-master, mere dexterity of hand. It is

117   the accuracy and certainty of the knowledge, rendered evident by its rapid and fearless expression, which is the real source of pleasure; and so upon each difficulty of art, whether it be to know, or to relate, or to invent, the sensation of power is attendant, when we see that difficulty totally and swiftly vanquished.

But it will be necessary at present to notice a particular form of the ideas of power, which is partially independent of knowledge of truth, or difficulty, and which is apt to corrupt the judgment of the critic, and debase the work of the artist. It is evident that the conception of power which we receive from a calculation of unseen difficulty, and an estimate of unseen strength, can never be so impressive as that which we receive from the present sensation or sight of the one resisting, and the other overwhelming. In the one case the power is imagined, and in the other felt.

There are thus two modes in which we receive the conception of power; one, the more just, when by a perfect knowledge of the difficulty to be overcome, and the means employed, we form a right estimate of the faculties exerted; the other, when without possessing such intimate and accurate knowledge, we are impressed by a sensation of power in visible action. If these two modes of receiving the impression agree in the result, and if the sensation be equal to the estimate, we receive the utmost possible idea of power. But this is the case, perhaps, with the works of only   118 one man out of the whole circle of the fathers of art—Michael Angelo. In others, the estimate and the sensation are constantly unequal, and often contradictory.

The first reason of this inconsistency is, that in order to receive a *sensation* of power, we must see it in operation. Its victory, therefore, must not be achieved, but achieving, and therefore imperfect.

Another reason is, that the sensation of power is in proportion to the apparent inadequacy of the means to the end; so that the impression is much greater from a partial success attained with slight effort, than from perfect success attained with greater proportional effort. Now, in all art, every touch or effort does individually less in proportion as the work approaches perfection. The first five chalk touches bring a head into existence out of nothing. No five touches in the whole course of the work will ever do so much as these, and the difference made by each touch is more and more imperceptible as the work approaches completion. Con-   119 sequently, the ratio between the means employed and the effect produced is constantly decreasing, and therefore the least sensation of power is received from the most perfect work.

It is thus evident that there are sensations of power about imperfect art, so that it be right art as far as it goes, which must always be wanting in its perfection; and that there are sources of pleasure in the hasty sketch and the rough-hewn block, which are partially wanting in the tinted canvas and the polished marble. But it is nevertheless wrong to prefer the sensation of power to the intellectual perception of it. There is in reality greater power in the completion than in the commencement; and though it be not so manifest to the senses, it ought to have higher influence on the mind; and therefore in praising pictures for the ideas of power they convey, we must not look to the keenest sensation, but to the highest estimate, accompanied with as much of the sensation as is compatible with it; and thus we shall consider those pictures as conveying the highest ideas of power which attain the most *perfect* end with the slightest possible means; not, observe, those in which, though much has been done with little, all has not been done, but from the picture, in which *all* has been done, and yet not a touch thrown away.

CHAPTER II
Of Ideas of Power, as They Are Dependent upon Execution

122   By the term Execution, I understand the right mechanical use of the means of art to produce a given end.

All qualities of execution, properly so called, are influenced by, and in a great degree dependent on, a far higher power that that of mere execution,—knowledge of truth. For exactly in proportion as an artist is certain of his end, will he be swift and simple in his means; and as he is accurate and deep in his knowledge, will he be refined and precise in his touch. The first merit of manipulation, then, is that delicate and ceaseless expression of refined truth which is carried out to the last touch, and shadow of a touch, and which makes every hair's-breadth of importance, and every gradation full of meaning. It is not, properly speaking, execution; but it is the only source of difference between the execution of a commonplace and that of a perfect artist. The lowest draughtsman, if he have spent the same time in handling the brush, may be equal to the highest in the other qualities of execution; but not in truth. It is in the perfection and precision of the instantaneous line that the claim to immortality is laid.

123   The second quality of execution is simplicity. The more unpretending, quiet, and retiring the means, the more impressive their effect. Any ostentation, brilliancy, or pretension of touch,—any exhibition of power or quickness, merely as such,—above all, any attempt to render lines attractive at the expense of their meaning, is vice.

The third is mystery. Nature is always mysterious and secret in her use of means; and art is always likest her when it is most inexplicable. That execution which is least comprehensible, and which therefore defies imitation (other qualities being supposed alike), is the best.

The fourth is inadequacy. The less sufficient the means appear to the end, the greater (as has been already noticed) will be the sensation of power.

The fifth is decision: the appearance, that is, that whatever is done, has been done fearlessly and at once; because this gives us the impression that both the fact to be represented, and the means necessary to its representation, were perfectly known.

The sixth is velocity. Not only is velocity, or the appearance of it, agreeable as decision is, because it gives ideas of power and knowledge; but of two touches, as nearly as possible the same in other respects, the quickest will invariably be the best. Truth being supposed equally present in the shape and direction of both, there will be more evenness, grace, and variety, in the quick one, than in the slow one. It will be more agreeable to the eye as a touch or line, and will possess more of the qualities of the lines of nature—gradation, uncertainty, and unity.

These six qualities are the only perfectly legitimate sources of pleasure in execution, but I might have added a seventh—strangeness, which in many cases is productive of a pleasure not altogether mean or degrading, though scarcely right. Supposing the other higher qualities first secured, it adds in no small degree to our impression of the artist's knowledge, if the means used be such as we should never have thought of, or should have   124
thought adapted to a contrary effect. Yet strangeness is not to be con-   125
sidered as a legitimate source of pleasure. That means which is most conducive to the end, should always be the most pleasurable; and that which is most conducive to the end, can be strange only to the ignorance of the spectator. This kind of pleasure is illegitimate, therefore, because it implies and requires, in those who feel it, ignorance of art.

The legitimate sources of pleasure in execution are therefore truth, simplicity, mystery, inadequacy, decision, and velocity. But of these, be it observed, some are so far inconsistent with others, that they cannot be united in high degrees. Mystery with inadequacy, for instance; since to see that the means are inadequate, we must see what they are. Now the first three are the great qualities of execution, and the last three are the attractive ones, because on them are chiefly attendant the ideas of power. By the first three the attention is withdrawn from the means and fixed on the result: by the last three, withdrawn from the result, and fixed on the means. Hence the danger of too great fondness for those sensations of power which are associated with the last three qualities of execution; for, although it is most desirable that these should be present as far as they are consistent with the others, and though their visible absence is always painful and wrong, yet the moment the higher qualities are sacrificed to them in the least degree, we have a brilliant vice. There is perhaps no greater stumbling-block in the artist's way, than the tendency to sacrifice truth and simplicity to decision and velocity, captivating qualities, easy   126
of attainment, and sure to attract attention and praise, while the delicate degree of truth which is at first sacrificed to them is so totally unappreciable by the majority of spectators, so difficult of attainment to the artist, that it is no wonder that effects so arduous and unrewarded should be abandoned. But if the temptation be once yielded to, its consequences are fatal; there is no pause in the fall.

PART II
Of Truth

SECTION I
General Principles Respecting Ideas of Truth

CHAPTER I
Of Ideas of Truth in Their Connection with Those of Beauty and Relation

IT cannot but be evident from the above division of the ideas convey- 133
able by art, that the landscape painter must always have two great and
distinct ends: the first, to induce in the spectator's mind the faithful
conception of any natural objects whatsoever; the second, to guide the
spectator's mind to those objects most worthy of its contemplation, and to
inform him of the thoughts and feelings with which these were regarded
by the artist himself.

In attaining the first end the painter only places the spectator where he
stands himself; he sets him before the landscape and leaves him. The
spectator is alone. He may follow out his own thoughts as he would in the
natural solitude; or he may remain untouched, unreflecting and regardless, as his disposition may incline him; but he has nothing of thought
given to him; no new ideas, no unknown feelings, forced on his attention
or his heart. The artist is his conveyance, not his companion,—his horse,
not his friend. But in attaining the second end, the artist not only *places* 134
the spectator, but *talks* to him; makes him a sharer in his own strong
feelings and quick thoughts; hurries him away in his own enthusiasm;
guides him to all that is beautiful; snatches him from all that is base; and
leaves him more than delighted,—ennobled and instructed, under the
sense of having not only beheld a new scene, but of having held communion with a new mind, and having been endowed for a time with the
keen perception and the impetuous emotions of a nobler and more penetrating intelligence.

Each of these different aims of art will necessitate a different system of
choice of objects to be represented. The first does not indeed imply choice
at all, but it is usually united with the selection of such objects as may be

naturally and constantly pleasing to all men, at all times; and this selection, when perfect and careful, leads to the attainment of the pure ideal. But the artist aiming at the second end, selects his objects for their meaning and character, rather than for their beauty; and uses them rather to throw light upon the particular thought he wishes to convey, than as in themselves objects of unconnected admiration.

Now, although the first mode of selection, when guided by deep reflection, may rise to the production of works possessing a noble and ceaseless influence on the human mind, it is likely to degenerate into, or rather, in nine cases out of ten, it never goes beyond, a mere appeal to such parts of our animal nature as are constant and common,—shared by all, and perpetual in all; such, for instance, as the pleasure of the eye in the opposition of a cold and warm colour, or of a massy form with a delicate one. It also tends to induce constant repetition of the same ideas, and reference to the same principles; it gives rise to those *rules* of art which properly excited Reynolds's indignation when applied to its higher efforts; it is the source of, and the apology for, that host of technicalities and

135 absurdities which in all ages have been the curse of art and the crown of the connoisseur.

But art, in its second and highest aim, is not an appeal to constant animal feelings, but an expression and awakening of individual thought: it is therefore as various and as extended in its efforts as the compass and grasp of the directing mind; and we feel, in each of its results, that we are looking, not at a specimen of a tradesman's wares, of which he is ready to make us a dozen to match, but at one coruscation of a perpetually active mind, like which there has not been, and will not be another.

Hence, although there can be no doubt which of these branches of art is the higher, it is equally evident that the first will be the more generally felt and appreciated. But the highest art, being based on sensations of peculiar minds, sensations occurring to *them* only at particular times, and to a plurality of mankind perhaps never, and being

136 expressive of thoughts which could only rise out of a mass of the most extended knowledge, and of dispositions modified in a thousand ways by peculiarity of intellect, can only be met and understood by persons having some sort of sympathy with the high and solitary minds which produced it—sympathy only to be felt by minds in some degree high and solitary themselves. He alone can appreciate the art, who could comprehend the conversation of the painter, and share in his emotion, in moments of his most fiery passion and most original thought. And whereas the true meaning and end of his art must thus be sealed to thousands, or misunderstood by them; so also, as he is sometimes obliged, in working out his own peculiar end, to set at defiance those constant laws which have arisen out of our lower and changeless desires,

that, whose purpose is unseen, is frequently in its means and parts displeasing.

But this want of extended influence in high art, be it especially observed, proceeds from no want of truth in the art itself, but from a want of sympathy in the spectator with those feelings in the artist which prompt him to the utterance of one truth rather than of another. For although it is possible to reach what I have stated to be the first end of art, the representation of facts, without reaching the second, the representation of thoughts, yet it is altogether impossible to reach the second without having previously reached the first. I do not say that a man cannot think, having false basis and material for thought; but that a false thought is worse than the want of thought, and therefore is not art. And this is the reason why, though I consider the second as the real and only important end of all art, I call the representation of facts the first end; because it is necessary to the other and must be attained before it. It is the foundation of all art; like real foundations, it may be little thought of when a brilliant   137 fabric is raised on it; but it must be there. And thus, though we want the thoughts and feelings of the artist as well as the truth, yet they must be thoughts arising out of the knowledge of truth, and feelings arising out of the contemplation of truth. We do not want his mind to be like a badly blown glass, that distorts what we see through it, but like a glass of sweet and strange colour, that gives new tones to what we see through it; and a glass of rare strength and clearness too, to let us see more than we could ourselves, and bring nature up to us and near to us. Nothing can atone for the want of truth, not the most brilliant imagination, the most playful fancy, the most pure feeling (supposing that feeling *could* be pure and false at the same time); not the most exalted conception, nor the most comprehensive grasp of intellect, can make amends for the want of truth, and that for two reasons: first, because falsehood is in itself revolting and degrading; and secondly, because nature is so immeasurably superior to all that the human mind can conceive, that every departure from her is a fall beneath her, so that there can be no such thing as an ornamental falsehood. All falsehood must be a blot as well as a sin, an injury as well as a deception.

We shall, in consequence, find that no artist can be graceful,   138 imaginative, or original, unless he be truthful; and that the pursuit of beauty, instead of leading us away from truth, increases the desire for it and the necessity of it tenfold; so that those artists who are really great in imaginative power, will be found to have based their boldness of conception on a mass of knowledge far exceeding that possessed by those who pride themselves on its accumulation without regarding its use. Coldness and want of passion in a picture are not signs of the accuracy, but of the paucity of its statements: true vigour and brilliancy are not signs of audacity, but of knowledge.

Hence it follows that it is in the power of all, with care and time, to form something like a just judgment of the relative merits of artists; for although with respect to the feeling and passion of pictures, it is often as impossible to criticize as to appreciate, except to such as are in some degree equal in powers of mind, and in some respects the same in modes of mind, with those whose works they judge; yet, with respect to the representation of facts, it is possible for all, by attention, to form a right judgment of the respective powers and attainments of every artist. Truth is a bar of comparison at which they may all be examined, and according to the rank they take in this examination will almost invariably be that which, if capable of appreciating them in every respect, we should be just in assigning them; so strict is the connection, so constant the relation, between the sum of knowledge and the extent of thought, between accuracy of perception and vividness of idea.

139   I shall endeavour, therefore, in the present portion of the work, to enter with care and impartiality into the investigation of the claims of the schools of ancient and modern landscape to faithfulness in representing nature. I shall pay no regard whatsoever to what may be thought beautiful, or sublime, or imaginative. I shall look only for truth; bare, clear, downright statement of facts; showing in each particular, as far as I am able, what the truth of nature is, and then seeking for the plain expression of it, and for that alone. And I shall thus endeavour, totally regardless of fervour of imagination or brilliancy of effect, or any other of their more captivating qualities, to examine and to judge the works of the great living painter, who is, I believe, imagined by the majority of the public, to paint more falsehood and less fact than any other known master. We shall see with what reason.

CHAPTER II

That the Truth of Nature Is Not to Be Discerned by the Uneducated Senses

Now I have just said that it is possible for all men, by care and attention, to form a just judgment of the fidelity of artists to nature. To do this no peculiar powers of mind are required, no sympathy with particular feelings, nothing which every man of ordinary intellect does not in some degree possess,—powers, namely, of observation and intelligence, which by cultivation may be brought to a high degree of perfection and acuteness. But until this cultivation has been bestowed, and until the instrument thereby perfected has been employed in a consistent series of careful observations, it is as absurd as it is audacious to pretend to form any judgment whatsoever respecting the truth of art: and my first business, before going a step farther, must be to combat the nearly universal error of belief among the thoughtless and unreflecting, that they know either what nature is, or what is like her; that they can discover truth by instinct, and that their minds are such pure Venice glass as to be shocked by all treachery. I have to prove to them that there are more things in heaven and earth than are dreamed of in their philosophy, and that the truth of nature is a part of the truth of God; to him who does not search it out, darkness, as it is to him who does, infinity.

The first great mistake that people make in the matter, is the supposition that they must *see* a thing if it be before their eyes. They forget the great truth told them by Locke, book ii. chap. 9. §3.—"This is certain, that whatever alterations are made in the body, if they reach not the mind; whatever impressions are made on the outward parts, if they are not taken notice of within; there is no perception. Fire may burn our bodies, with no other effect than it does a billet, unless the motion be continued to the brain, and there the sense of heat or idea of pain be produced in the mind, wherein consists actual perception."

The degree of ignorance of external nature in which men may thus remain depends partly on the number and character of the subjects with which their minds may be otherwise occupied, and partly on a natural want of sensibility to the power of beauty of form, and the other attributes of external objects. So that while in those whose sensations are naturally acute and vivid, the call of external nature is so strong that it must be obeyed, and is ever heard louder as the approach to her is nearer,—in those whose sensations are naturally blunt, the call is overpowered at once by other thoughts, and their faculties of perception, weak originally, die of disuse. With this kind of bodily sensibility is intimately connected that

143 higher sensibility which we revere as one of the chief attributes of all noble minds, and as the chief spring of real poetry. I believe this kind of sensibility may be entirely resolved into the acuteness of bodily sense of which I have been speaking, associated with love, love I mean in its infinite and holy functions, as it embraces divine and human and brutal intelligences, and hallows the physical perception of external objects by association, gratitude, veneration, and other pure feelings of our moral nature. And although the discovery of truth is in itself altogether intellectual, and dependent merely on our powers of physical perception and abstract intellect, wholly independent of our moral nature, yet these instruments (perception and judgment) are so sharpened and brightened, and so far more swiftly and effectively used, when they have the energy and passion of our moral nature to bring them into action—perception is so quickened by love, and judgment so tempered by veneration, that, practically, a man of deadened moral sensation is always dull in his perception of truth; and thousands of the highest and most divine truths of nature are wholly concealed from him, however constant and indefatigable may be his intellectual search. Thus, then, the farther we look, the more we are limited in the number of those to whom we should choose to appeal as judges of truth, and the more we perceive how great a number of mankind may be partially incapacitated from either discovering or feeling it.

Next to sensibility, which is necessary for the perception of facts, come reflection and memory, which are necessary for the retention of them, and recognition of their resemblances. For a man may receive impression after impression, and that vividly and with delight, and yet, if he take no care to reason upon those impressions, and trace them to their sources, he may remain totally ignorant of the facts that produced them; nay, may attribute them to facts with which they have no connection, or may coin causes for them that have no existence at all. And the more sensibility and imagination a man possesses, the more likely will he be to fall into error;

144 for then he will see whatever he expects, and admire and judge with his heart, and not with his eyes. And this influence of the imagination over the senses, is peculiarly observable in the perpetual disposition of mankind to suppose that they *see* what they *know*, and *vice versâ* in their not seeing what they do not know. Thus, if a child be asked to draw the corner of a house, he will lay down something in the form of the letter T. He has no conception that the two lines of the roof, which he knows to

be level, produce on his eye the impression of a slope. It requires repeated
and close attention before he detects this fact, or can be made to feel that
the lines on his paper are false. We are constantly supposing that we see   145
what experience only has shown us, or can show us, to have existence,
constantly missing the sight of what we do not know beforehand to be
visible: and painters, to the last hour of their lives, are apt to fall in some
degree into the error of painting what exists, rather than what they can
see.

Be it also observed, that all these difficulties would lie in the way, even
if the truths of nature were always the same, constantly repeated and
brought before us. But the truths of nature are one eternal change—one
infinite variety. There is no bush on the face of the globe exactly like   146
another bush;—there are no two trees in the forest whose boughs bend
into the same network, nor two leaves on the same tree which could not
be told one from the other, nor two waves in the sea exactly alike. And
out of this mass of various, yet agreeing beauty, it is by long attention only
that the conception of the constant character—the ideal form—hinted at
by all, yet assumed by none, is fixed upon the imagination for its standard
of truth.

It is not singular, therefore, nor in any way disgraceful, that the
majority of spectators are totally incapable of appreciating the truth of
nature, when fully set before them; but it is both singular and disgraceful
that it is so difficult to convince them of their own incapability. Ask a
connoisseur who has scampered over all Europe, the shape of the leaf of
an elm, and the chances are ninety to one that he cannot tell you; and
yet he will be voluble of criticism on every painted landscape from
Dresden to Madrid, and pretend to tell you whether they are like nature
or not. Ask an enthusiastic chatterer in the Sistine Chapel how many ribs
he has, and you get no answer: but it is odds that you do not get out of
the door without his informing you that he considers such and such a
figure badly drawn.

A few such interrogations as these might indeed convict, if not convince the mass of spectators of incapability, were it not for the universal
reply, that they can recognize what they cannot describe, and feel what is
truthful, though they do not know what is truth. And this is, to a certain
degree, true. A man may recognize the portrait of his friend, though he
cannot, if you ask him apart, tell you the shape of his nose, or the height
of his forehead: and every one could tell nature herself from an imitation;
why not then, it will be asked, what is like her from what is not? For this
simple reason; that we constantly recognize things by their least important
attributes, and by help of very few of those: and if these attributes exist not
in the imitation, though there may be thousands of others far higher and   147
more valuable, yet if those be wanting, or imperfectly rendered, by which

we are accustomed to recognize the object, we deny the likeness; while if these be given, though all the great and valuable and important attributes may be wanting, we affirm the likeness. Recognition is no proof of real and intrinsic resemblance. One portrait of a man may possess exact accuracy of feature, and no atom of expression; it may be, to use the ordinary terms of admiration bestowed on such portraits by those whom they please, "as like as it can stare." Everybody, down to his cat, would know this. Another portrait may have neglected or misrepresented the features, but may have given the flash of the eye, and the peculiar radiance of the lip, seen on him only in his hours of highest mental excitement. None but his friends would know this. Another may have given none of his ordinary expressions, but one which he wore in the most excited instant of his life, when all his secret passions and all his highest powers were brought into play at once. None but those who had then seen him might recognize *this* as like. But which would be the most truthful portrait of the *man*? The first gives the accidents of body—the sport of climate, and food, and time,—which corruption inhabits, and the worm waits for. The second gives the stamp of the soul upon the flesh; but it is the soul seen in the emotions which it shares with many, which may not be characteristic of its essence—the results of habit, and education, and accident,—a gloze,[6] whether purposely worn or unconsciously assumed, perhaps totally contrary to all that is rooted and real in the mind which it conceals. The third has caught the trace of all that was most hidden and most mighty, when all hypocrisy and all habit, and all petty and passing emotion,—the ice, and the bank, and the foam of the immortal river,—were shivered, and broken, and swallowed up in the awakening of its inward strength; when the call and claim of some divine motive had brought into visible being those latent forces and feelings which the spirit's own volition could not summon, nor its consciousness comprehend, which God only knew, and God only could awaken,—the depth and the mystery of its peculiar and separating attributes. And so it is with external nature: she has a body and a soul like man; but her soul is the Deity. It is possible to represent the body without the spirit; and this shall be like, to those whose senses are only cognizant of body. It is possible to represent the spirit in its ordinary and inferior manifestations; and this shall be like, to those who have not watched for its moments of power. It is possible to represent the spirit in its secret and high operations; and this shall be like, only to those to whose watching they have been revealed. All these are truth; but according to the dignity of the truths he can represent or feel, is the power of the painter,—the justice of the judge.

148

Of the Relative Importance of Truths:—Thirdly, That Truths of Colour Are the Least Important of All Truths

ACCORDING to Locke, book ii. chap. 8, there are three sorts of qualities   158
in bodies: first, the "bulk, figure, number, situation, and motion or
rest of their solid parts: those" that "are in them, whether we perceive
them or no." These he calls primary qualities. Secondly, "the power that
is in any body to operate after a peculiar manner on any of our senses"
(sensible qualities). And thirdly, "the power that is in any body to make
such a change in another body as that it shall operate on our senses
differently from what it did before:" these last being "usually called
powers."

Hence he proceeds to prove that those which he calls primary qualities
are indeed part of the essence of the body, and characteristic of it; but that
the two other kinds of qualities which together he calls secondary, are
neither of them more than *powers* of producing on other objects, or in us,
certain effects and sensations.

Now, by Locke's definition above given, only bulk, figure, situation,   159
and motion or rest of solid parts, are primary qualities. Hence all truths of
colour sink at once into the second rank. He, therefore, who has
neglected a truth of form for a truth of colour has neglected a greater truth
for a less one.[8]

And that colour is indeed a most unimportant characteristic of objects,
will be farther evident on the slightest consideration. The colour of plants
is constantly changing with the season, and of everything with the quality
of light falling on it; but the nature and essence of the thing are
independent of these changes. An oak is an oak, whether green with
spring or red with winter; a dahlia is a dahlia, whether it be yellow or
crimson; and if some monster-hunting florist should ever frighten the
flower blue, still it will be a dahlia; but not so if the same arbitrary changes
could be effected in its form. Again, colour is hardly ever even a *possible*
distinction between two objects of the same species. Two trees, of the
same kind, at the same season, and of the same age, are of absolutely the   160
same colour; but they are not of the same form, nor anything like it. There

32

can be no difference in the colour of two pieces of rock broken from them same place; but it is impossible they should be of the same form. So that form is not only the chief characteristic of species, but the only characteristic of individuals of a species.

Again, a colour, in association with other colours, is different from the same colour seen by itself. It has a distinct and peculiar power upon the retina dependent on its association. Consequently, the colour of any object is not more dependent upon the nature of the object itself, and the eye beholding it, than on the colour of the objects near it; in this respect also, therefore, it is no characteristic.

161   Before going farther, however, I must explain the sense in which I have used the word "form," because painters have a most inaccurate and careless habit of confining this term to the *outline* of bodies, whereas it necessarily implies light and shade. It is true that the outline and the chiaroscuro must be separate subjects of investigation with the student; but no form whatsoever can be known to the eye in the slightest degree without its chiaroscuro; and, therefore, in speaking of form generally as an element of landscape, I mean that perfect and harmonious unity of outline with light and shade, by which all the parts and projections and proportions of a body are fully explained to the eye; being nevertheless perfectly independent of sight or power in other objects, the presence of light upon a body being a positive existence, whether we are aware of it or not, and in no degree dependent upon our senses. This being understood, the most convincing proof of the unimportance of colour lies in the accurate observation of the way in which any material object impresses itself on the mind. If we look at nature carefully, we shall find that her colours are in a state of perpetual confusion and indistinctness, while her forms, as told by light and shade, are invariably clear, distinct, and speaking. The stones and gravel of the bank catch green reflections from the boughs above; the bushes receive greys and yellows from the ground; every hair's breadth of polished surface gives a little bit of the blue of the sky, or the gold of the sun, like a star upon the local colour; this local colour, changeful and uncertain in itself, is again disguised and modified by the hue of the light, or quenched in the grey of the shadow; and the confusion and blending of

162   tint are altogether so great, that were we left to find out what objects were by their colours only, we could scarcely in places distinguish the boughs of a tree from the air beyond them, or the ground beneath them.

CHAPTER VI
Recapitulation

It ought farther to be observed respecting truths in general, that those are always most valuable which are most historical; that is, which tell us most about the past and future states of the object to which they belong. In a tree, for instance, it is more important to give the appearance of energy and elasticity in the limbs which is indicative of growth and life, than any particular character of leaf, or texture of bough. It is more important that we should feel that the uppermost sprays are creeping higher and higher into the sky, and be impressed with the current of life and motion which is animating every fibre, than that we should know the exact pitch of relief with which those fibres are thrown out against the sky. For the first truths tell us tales about the tree, about what it has been, and will be, while the last are characteristic of it only in its present state, and are in no way talkative about themselves. Talkative facts are always more interesting and more important than silent ones. So again the lines in a crag which mark its stratification, and how it has been washed and rounded by water, or twisted and drawn out in fire, are more important, because they tell more than the stains of the lichens which change year by year, and the accidental fissures of frost or decomposition; not but that both of these are historical, but historical in a less distinct manner, and for shorter periods.

Hence in general the truths of specific form are the first and most important of all; and next to them, those truths of chiaroscuro which are necessary to make us understand every quality and part of forms, and the relative distances of objects among each other, and in consequence their relative bulks. Altogether lower than these as truths, though often most important as beauties, stand all effects of chiaroscuro which are productive merely of imitations of light and tone, and all effects of colour. To make us understand the *space* of the sky, is an end worthy of the artist's highest powers; to hit its particular blue or gold is an end to be thought of when we have accomplished the first, and not till then.

Finally, far below all these come those particular accuracies or tricks of chiaroscuro which cause objects to look projecting from the canvas, not worthy of the name of truths, because they require for their attainment the sacrifice of all others; for not having at our disposal the same intensity of light by which nature illustrates her objects, we are obliged, if we would have perfect deception in one, to destroy its relation to the rest. And thus he who throws one object out of his picture, never lets the spectator into it. Michael Angelo bids you follow his phantoms into the abyss of heaven, but a modern French painter drops his hero out of the picture frame.

This solidity or projection, then, is the very lowest truth that art can give; it is the painting of mere matter, giving that as food for the eye which is properly only the subject of touch; it can neither instruct nor exalt; nor can it please, except as jugglery; it addresses no sense of beauty nor of power; and wherever it characterizes the general aim of a picture, it is the sign and the evidence of the vilest and lowest mechanism which art can be insulted by giving name to.

CHAPTER VII

General Application of
the Foregoing Principles

W E have seen, in the preceding chapters, some proof of what was   165
before asserted, that the truths necessary for deceptive imitation
are not only few, but of the very lowest order. We thus find painters
ranging themselves into two great classes: one aiming at the development
of the exquisite truths of specific form, refined colour, and ethereal space,
and content with the clear and impressive suggestion of any of these, by
whatsoever means obtained; and the other casting all these aside, to attain
those particular truths of tone and chiaroscuro, which may trick the
spectator into a belief of reality. The first class, if they have to paint a tree,
are intent upon giving the exquisite designs of intersecting undulation in
its boughs, the grace of its leafage, the intricacy of its organization, and all
those qualities which make it lovely or affecting of its kind. The second
endeavour only to make you believe that you are looking at wood.

To which of these classes the great body of the old landscape painters
belonged, may be partly gathered from the kind of praise which is
bestowed upon them by those who admire them most, which either refers
to technical matters, dexterity of touch, clever oppositions of colour, etc.,
or is bestowed on the power of the painter to *deceive*. M. de Marmontel,
going into a connoisseur's gallery, pretends to mistake a fine Berghem for
a window. This, he says, was affirmed by its possessor to be the greatest   166
praise the picture had ever received.[9] Such is indeed the notion of art
which is at the bottom of the veneration usually felt for the old landscape
painters; it is of course the palpable, first idea of ignorance; it is the only
notion which people unacquainted with art can by any possibility have of
its ends; the only test by which people unacquainted with nature can
pretend to form anything like judgment of art. It is strange, that, with the
great historical painters of Italy before them, who had broken so boldly
and indignantly from the trammels of this notion, and shaken the very
dust of it from their feet, the succeeding landscape painters should have
wasted their lives in jugglery: but so it is, and so it will be felt, the more
we look into their works, that the deception of the senses was the great

36

and first end of all their art. To attain this they paid deep and serious attention to effects of light and tone, and to the exact degree of relief which material objects take against light and atmosphere; and sacrificing every other truth to these, not necessarily, but because they required no others for deception, they succeeded in rendering these particular facts with a fidelity and force which, in the pictures that have come down to us uninjured, are as yet unequalled, and never can be surpassed. They painted their foregrounds with laborious industry, covering them with details so as to render them deceptive to the ordinary eye, regardless of beauty or truth in the details themselves; they painted their trees with careful attention to their pitch of shade against the sky, utterly regardless of all that is beautiful or essential in the anatomy of their foliage and boughs; they painted their

167   distances with exquisite use of transparent colour and aërial tone, totally neglectful of all facts and forms which nature uses such colour and tone to relieve and adorn. They had neither love of nature, nor feeling of her beauty; they looked for her coldest and most commonplace effects, because they were easiest to imitate; and for her most vulgar forms, because they were most easily to be recognized by the untaught eyes of those whom alone they could hope to please; they did it, like the Pharisee of old, to be seen of men, and they had their reward. They do deceive and delight the unpractised eye. They will to all ages, as long as their colours endure, be the standards of excellence with all who, ignorant of nature, claim to be thought learned in art: and they will to all ages be, to those who have thorough love and knowledge of the creation which they libel, instructive proofs of the limited number and low character of the truths which are necessary, and the accumulated multitude of pure, broad, bold falsehoods which are admissible, in pictures meant only to deceive.

There is, of course, more or less accuracy of knowledge and execution combined with this aim at effect, according to the industry and precision of eye possessed by the master, and more or less of beauty in the forms selected, according to his natural taste; but both the beauty and truth are sacrificed unhesitatingly where they interfere with the great effort of deception. Claude had, if it had been cultivated, a fine feeling for beauty of form, and is seldom ungraceful in his foliage; but his picture, when examined with reference to essential truth, is one mass of error from beginning to end. Cuyp, on the other hand, could paint close truth of everything except ground and water, with decision and success, but he had no sense of beauty. Gaspar Poussin, more ignorant of truth than Claude, and almost as dead to beauty as Cuyp, has yet a perception of

168   feeling and moral truth of nature, which often redeems the picture; but yet in all of them, everything that they can do is done for deception, and nothing for the sake or love of what they are painting.

Modern landscape painters have looked at nature with totally different eyes, seeking not for what is easier to imitate, but for what is most important to tell. Rejecting at once all idea of *bonâ fide* imitation, they think only of conveying the impression of nature into the mind of the spectator. And there is, in consequence, a greater sum of valuable, essential, and impressive truth in the works of two or three of our leading modern landscape painters, than in those of all the old masters put together, and of truth too, nearly unmixed with definite or avoidable falsehood; while the unimportant and feeble truths of the old masters are choked with a mass of perpetual defiance of the most authoritative laws of nature.

I do not expect this assertion to be believed at present: it must rest for demonstration on the examination we are about to enter upon; yet, even without reference to any intricate or deep-seated truths, it appears strange to me, that any one familiar with nature, and fond of her, should not grow weary and sick at heart among the melancholy and monotonous transcripts of her which alone can be received from the old school of art. A man accustomed to the broad wild sea-shore, with its bright breakers, and free winds, and sounding rocks, and eternal sensation of tameless power, can scarcely but be angered when Claude bids him stand still on some paltry chipped and chiselled quay, with porters and wheelbarrows running against him, to watch a weak, rippling, bound and barriered water, that has not strength enough in one of its waves to upset the flower-pots on the wall, or even to fling one jet of spray over the confining stone. 169 A man accustomed to the strength and glory of God's mountains, with their soaring and radiant pinnacles, and surging sweeps of measureless distance, kingdoms in their valleys, and climates upon their crests, can scarcely but be angered when Salvator bids him stand still under some contemptible fragment of splintery crag, which an Alpine snow-wreath would smother in its first swell, with a stunted bush or two growing out of it, and a volume of manufactory smoke for a sky. A man accustomed to the grace and infinity of nature's foliage, with every vista a cathedral, and every bough a revelation, can scarcely but be angered when Poussin mocks him with a black round mass of impenetrable paint, diverging into feathers instead of leaves, and supported on a stick instead of a trunk.[10] The fact is, there is one thing wanting in all the doing of these men, and that is the very virtue by which the work of human mind chiefly rises above that of the daguerreotype or calotype, or any other mechanical means that ever have been or may be invented, Love. There is no evidence of their ever having gone to nature with any thirst, or received from her such emotion as could make them, even for an instant, lose sight of themselves; there is in them neither earnestness nor humility; there is no simple or honest record of any single truth; none of the plain words or straight efforts that men speak and make when they once feel.

170   Nor is it only by the professed landscape painters that the great verities of the material world are betrayed. Grand as are the motives of landscape in the works of the earlier and mightier men, there is yet in them nothing approaching to a general view or complete rendering of natural phenomena; not that they are to be blamed for this; for they took out of nature that which was fit for their purpose, and their mission was to do no more; but we must be cautious to distinguish that imaginative abstraction of landscape which alone we find in them, from the entire statement of truth which has been attempted by the moderns. From the window of Titian's

171   house at Venice, the chain of the Tyrolese Alps is seen lifted in spectral power above the tufted plain of Treviso; every dawn that reddens the towers of Murano lights also a line of pyramidal fires along that colossal ridge; but there is, so far as I know, no evidence in any of the master's works of his ever having beheld, much less felt, the majesty of their burning. The dark firmament and saddened twilight of Tintoret are sufficient for their end: but the sun never plunges behind San Giorgio in Aliga without such retinue of radiant cloud, such rest of zoned light on the green lagoon, as never received image from his hand. More than this, of that which they loved and rendered much is rendered conventionally: by noble conventionalities indeed, but such nevertheless as would be inexcusable if the landscape became the principal subject instead of an accompaniment. I will instance only the San Pietro Martire,[11] which, if not the most perfect, is at least the most popular of Titian's landscapes; in which, to obtain light on the flesh of the near figures, the sky is made as dark as deep sea, the mountains are laid in with violent and impossible blue, except one of them on the left, which, to connect the distant light with the foreground, is thrown into light relief, unexplained by its materials, unlikely in its position, and, in its degree, impossible under any circumstances.

    I do not instance these as faults in the picture: there are no works of very powerful colour which are free from conventionality concentrated or diffused, daring or disguised; but as the conventionality of this whole picture is mainly thrown into the landscape, it is necessary, while we acknowledge the virtue of this distance as a part of the great composition, to be on our guard against the license it assumes and the attractiveness of its overcharged colour. Fragments of far purer truth occur in the works of Tintoret; and in the drawing of foliage, whether rapid or elaborate, of

172   masses or details, the Venetian painters, taken as a body, may be considered almost faultless models. But the whole field of what they have done is so narrow, and therein is so much of what is only relatively right, and in itself false or imperfect, that the young and inexperienced painter could run no greater risk than the too early taking them for teachers; and to the general spectator their landscape is valuable rather as a means of

peculiar and solemn emotion, than as ministering to or inspiring the universal love of nature. Hence while men of serious mind, especially those whose pursuits have brought them into continued relations with the peopled rather than the lonely world, will always look to the Venetian painters as having touched those simple chords of landscape harmony which are most in unison with earnest and melancholy feeling; those whose philosophy is more cheerful and more extended, as having been trained and coloured among simple and solitary nature, will seek for a wider and more systematic circle of teaching: they may grant that the barred horizontal gloom of the Titian sky, and the massy leaves of the Titian forest, are among the most sublime of the conceivable forms of material things; but they know that the virtue of these very forms is to be learned only by right comparison of them with the cheerfulness, fulness, and comparative unquietness of other hours and scenes; that they are not intended for the continual food, but the occasional soothing of the human heart; that there is a lesson of not less value in its place, though of less concluding and sealing authority, in every one of the more humble phases of material things; and that there are some lessons of equal or greater authority which these masters neither taught nor received. And until the school of modern landscape arose, Art had never noted the links of this mighty chain; it mattered not that a fragment lay here and there, no heavenly lightning could descend by it; the landscape of the Venetians was without effect on any contemporary or subsequent schools; it still remains on the continent as useless as if it had never existed; and at this moment German and Italian landscapes, of which no words are scornful enough to befit the utter degradation, hang in the   173
Venetian Academy in the next room to the Desert of Titian and the Paradise of Tintoret.

That then which I would have the reader inquire respecting every work of art of undetermined merit submitted to his judgment, is, not whether it be a work of especial grandeur, importance, or power, but whether it have *any* virtue or substance as a link in this chain of truth; whether it have recorded or interpreted anything before unknown; whether it have added one single stone to our heaven-pointing pyramid, cut away one dark bough, or levelled one rugged hillock in our path. This, if it be an honest work of art, it must have done, for no man ever yet worked honestly without giving some such help to his race. God appoints to every one of His creatures a separate mission, and if they discharge it honourably, if they quit themselves like men and faithfully follow that light which is in them, withdrawing from it all cold and quenching influence, there will assuredly come of it such burning as, in its appointed mode and measure, shall shine before men, and be of service constant and holy. Degrees infinite of lustre there must always be, but the weakest

174   among us has a gift, however seemingly trivial, which is peculiar to him,
and which worthily used will be a gift also to his race for ever—
"Fool not," says George Herbert,

> "For all may have,
> If they dare choose, a glorious life or grave." [12]

If, on the contrary, there be nothing of this freshness achieved, if there
be neither purpose nor fidelity in what is done, if it be an envious or
powerless imitation of other men's labours, if it be a display of mere
manual dexterity or curious manufacture, or if in any other mode it show
itself as having its origin in vanity,—Cast it out. It matters not what
powers of mind may have been concerned or corrupted in it, all have lost
their savour, it is worse than worthless—perilous,—Cast it out.

Works of art are indeed always of mixed kind, their honesty being more
or less corrupted by the various weaknesses of the painter, by his vanity,
his idleness, or his cowardice. The fear of doing right has far more
influence on art than is commonly thought. That only is altogether to be
rejected which is altogether vain, idle, and cowardly; of the rest the rank
is to be estimated rather by the purity of their metal than the coined value
of it.

To the ideal landscape of the early religious painters of Italy I have
alluded in the concluding chapter of the second volume. [13] It is absolutely
right and beautiful in its peculiar application; but its grasp of nature is
narrow, and its treatment in most respects too severe and conventional to
form a profitable example when the landscape is to be alone the subject
175   of thought. The great virtue of it is its entire, exquisite, and humble
realization of those objects it selects; in this respect differing from such
German imitations of it as I have met with, that there is no effort at any
fanciful or ornamental modifications, but loving fidelity to the thing
studied. The foreground plants are usually neither exaggerated nor
stiffened; they do not form arches or frames or borders; their grace is
unconfined, their simplicity undestroyed. Cima da Conegliano, in his
picture in the church of the Madonna dell' Orto at Venice [fig.6], has
given us the oak, the fig, the beautiful "Erba della Madonna" on the wall,
precisely such a bunch of it as may be seen growing at this day on the
marble steps of that very church; ivy and other creepers, and a strawberry
plant in the foreground, with a blossom, and a berry just set, and one half
ripe and one ripe, all patiently and innocently painted from the real thing,
and therefore most divine. Fra Angelico's use of the Oxalis Acetosella is
as faithful in representation as touching in feeling. The ferns that grow on
the walls of Fiesole may be seen in their simple verity on the architecture
176   of Ghirlandajo. The rose, the myrtle, and the lily, the olive and orange,

fig.6   Cima da Conegliano, *St John the Baptist*, in the Madonna dell'Orto, Venice

pomegranate and vine, have received their fairest portraiture where they
bear a sacred character; even the common plantains and mallows of the
waysides are touched with deep reverence by Raffaelle; and indeed for the
perfect treatment of details of this kind, treatment as delicate and
affectionate as it is elevated and manly, it is to the works of these schools
alone that we can refer.

It is a misfortune for all honest critics, that hardly any quality of art is independently to be praised, and without reference to the motive from which it resulted, and the place in which it appears; so that no principle can be simply enforced but it shall seem to countenance a vice. Thus I hardly dare insist upon the virtue of completion, lest I should be supposed a defender of Wouvermans or Gerard Dow; neither can I adequately praise the power of Tintoret, without fearing to be thought adverse to Holbein or Perugino. The fact is, that both finish and impetuosity, specific minuteness and large abstraction, may be the signs of passion, or of its reverse;

177   may result from affection or indifference, intellect or dulness. Now both the finish and incompletion are right where they are the signs of passion or of thought, and both are wrong, when they cease to be so. On the whole, I conceive that the extremes of good and evil lie with the finishers, and that whatever glorious power we may admit in men like Tintoret, whatever attractiveness of method in Rubens, Rembrandt, or, though in far less degree, our own Reynolds, still the thoroughly great men are those who have done everything thoroughly, and who, in a word, have never despised anything, however small, of God's making. And this is the chief fault of our English landscapists, that they have not the intense all-observing penetration of well-balanced mind; they have not, except in one or two instances, anything of that feeling which Wordsworth shows in the following lines:—

> "So fair, so sweet, withal so sensitive;—
> Would that the little flowers were born to live
> Conscious of half the pleasure which they give.
> That to this mountain daisy's self were known
> *The beauty of its star-shaped shadow, thrown*
> *On the smooth surface of this naked stone.*"[14]

178   That is a little bit of good, downright, foreground painting—no mistake about it; daisy, and shadow, and stone texture and all. Our painters must come to this before they have done their duty; and yet, on the other hand, let them beware of finishing, for the sake of finish, all over their picture. The ground is not to be all over daisies, nor is every daisy to have its star-shaped shadow; there is as much finish in the right concealment of things as in the right exhibition of them; and while I demand this amount of specific character where nature shows it, I demand equal fidelity to her where she conceals it. To paint mist rightly, space rightly, and light rightly, it may be often necessary to paint nothing else rightly, but the rule is simple for all that; if the artist is painting something that he knows and loves, as he knows it, because he loves it, whether it be the fair strawberry of Cima, or the clear sky of Francia, or the blazing incomprehensible mist of Turner, he is all right; but the moment he does anything as he thinks

it ought to be, because he does not care about it, he is all wrong. He has only to ask himself whether he cares for anything except himself; so far as he does he will make a good picture; so far as he thinks of himself, a vile one.

Returning to the pictures of the religious schools, we find that their open skies are also of the highest value. Their preciousness is such that no subsequent schools can by comparison be said to have painted sky at all, but only clouds, or mist, or blue canopies. The dignified and simple forms   179 of cloud in repose are often by these painters sublimely expressed, but of changeful cloud form they show no examples. The architecture, mountains, and water of these distances are commonly conventional; motives are to be found in them of the highest beauty, and especially remarkable for quantity and meaning of incident; but they can only be studied or accepted in the particular feeling that produced them. It may generally be observed that whatever has been the result of strong emotion is ill seen unless through the medium of such emotion, and will lead to conclusions utterly false and perilous, if it be made a subject of cold-hearted observance, or an object of systematic imitation. One piece of genuine mountain drawing, however, occurs in the landscape of Masaccio's Tribute Money.[15] It is impossible to say what strange results might have taken place in this particular field of art, or how suddenly a   180 great school of landscape might have arisen, had the life of this great painter been prolonged. The two brothers Bellini gave a marked and vigorous impulse to the landscape of Venice. Giovanni's is in refinement of realization, I suppose, quite unrivalled, especially in passages requiring pure gradation, as the hollows of vaultings. His landscape is occasionally quaint and strange like Giorgione's and as fine in colour, as that behind the Madonna in the Brera gallery at Milan; but in the picture of St. Jerome in the church of San Crisostomo [fig.7], the landscape is as perfect and beautiful as any background may legitimately be, and, as far as it goes, finer than anything of Titian's. It is remarkable for the absolute truth of its sky, whose blue, clear as crystal, and, though deep in tone, bright as the open air, is gradated to the horizon with a cautiousness and finish almost inconceivable; and to obtain light at the horizon without contradicting   181 the system of chiaroscuro adopted in the figures, which are lighted from the right hand, it is barred across with some glowing white cirri, which, in their turn, are opposed by a single dark horizontal line of lower cloud; and to throw the whole further back, there is a wreath of rain cloud of warmer colour floating above the mountains, lighted on its under edge, whose faithfulness to nature, both in hue, and in its irregular and shattered form, is altogether exemplary. The wandering of the light among the hills is equally studied, and the whole is crowned by the grand realization of the leaves of the fig-tree, as well as of the herbage upon the rocks. Considering

fig.7   Giovanni Bellini, *St Jerome*, in San Crisostomo, Venice

that with all this care and completeness in the background, there is nothing that is not of meaning and necessity in reference to the figures, and that in the figures themselves the dignity and heavenliness of the highest religious painters are combined with a force and purity of colour, greater, I think, than Titian's, it is a work which may be set before the young artist as in every respect a nearly faultless guide.

Of Titian and Tintoret I have spoken already. The latter is every way the greater master, never indulging in the exaggerated colour of Titian, and attaining far more perfect light: his grasp of nature is more extensive, and his view of her more imaginative (incidental notices of his landscape will be found in the chapter on Imagination penetrative, of the second volume), but his impatience usually prevents him from carrying out his thoughts as clearly, or realizing with as much substantiality as Titian. In the St. Jerome of the latter in the gallery of the Brera, there is a superb 182 example of the modes in which the objects of landscape may be either suggested or elaborated according to their place and claim. The larger features of the ground, foliage, and drapery, as well as the lion in the lower angle, are executed with a slightness which admits not of close examination, and which if not in shade, would be offensive to the generality of observers. But on the rock above the lion, where it turns towards the light, and where the eye is intended to dwell, there is a wreath of ivy, of which every leaf is separately drawn with the greatest accuracy and care, and beside it a lizard, studied with equal earnestness, yet always with that right grandeur of manner to which I have alluded in the preface.[16] Tintoret seldom reaches or attempts the elaboration in substance and colour of these objects, but he is even more truth-telling and certain in his rendering of all the great characters of specific form; and as the painter of Space he stands altogether alone among dead masters; being the first who introduced the slightness and confusion of touch which are expressive of the effects of luminous objects seen through large spaces of air, and the principles of aerial colour which have been since carried out in other fields by Turner. I conceive him to be the most powerful painter whom the world has seen, and that he was prevented from being also the most perfect, partly by untoward circumstances in his position and education, partly by the very fulness and impetuosity of his own mind, partly by the want of religious feeling and its accompanying perception of beauty; for his noble treatment of religious subjects, of which I shall give several examples in the third part, appears to be the result only of that grasp which a great and well-toned intellect necessarily takes of any subject submitted to it, and is wanting in the signs of the more withdrawn and sacred sympathies.

But whatever advances were made by Tintoret in modes of artistical 183 treatment, he cannot be considered as having enlarged the sphere of landscape conception. He took no cognizance even of the materials and motives, so singularly rich in colour, which were for ever around him in his own Venice. All portions of Venetian scenery introduced by him are treated conventionally and carelessly, the architectural characters lost altogether, the sea distinguished from the sky only by a darker green, while of the sky itself only those forms were employed by him which had been repeated again and again for centuries, though in less tangibility and completion. Of mountain scenery he has left, I believe, no example so far carried as that of John Bellini above instanced.

184   No advances were made in landscape, so far as I know, after the time of Tintoret; the power of art ebbed gradually away from the derivative schools; various degrees of cleverness or feeling being manifested in more or less brilliant conventionalism.

    Though, however, at this period the general grasp of the schools was perpetually contracting, a gift was given to the world by Claude, for which we are perhaps hardly enough grateful, owing to the very frequency of our

185   after enjoyment of it. He set the sun in heaven, and was, I suppose, the first who attempted anything like the realization of actual sunshine in misty air. He gives the first example of the study of nature for her own sake, and allowing for the unfortunate circumstances of his education, and for his evident inferiority of intellect, more could hardly have been expected from him. His false taste, forced composition, and ignorant rendering of detail have perhaps been of more detriment to art than the gift he gave was of advantage. The character of his own mind is singular; I know of no other instance of a man's working from nature continually with the desire of being true, and never attaining the power of drawing so much as a bough of a tree rightly. Salvator, a man originally endowed with far higher power of mind than Claude, was altogether unfaithful to his mission, and has left us, I believe, no gift. Everything that he did is evidently for the sake of exhibiting his own dexterity; there is no love of any kind for any thing; his choice of landscape features is dictated by no delight in the sublime, but by mere animal restlessness or ferocity, guided by an imaginative power of which he could not altogether deprive himself. He has done nothing which others have not done better, or which it would not have been better not to have done; in nature he mistakes distortion for energy, and savageness for sublimity; in man, mendicity for sanctity, and conspiracy for heroism.

    The landscape of Nicolo Poussin shows much power, and is usually composed and elaborated on right principles, but I am aware of nothing that it has attained of new or peculiar excellence; it is a graceful mixture of qualities to be found in other masters in higher degrees. In finish it is inferior to Leonardo's, in invention to Giorgione's, in truth to Titian's, in grace to Raffaelle's. The landscapes of Gaspar have serious feeling and often valuable and solemn colour; virtueless otherwise, they are full of the most degraded mannerism, and I believe the admiration of them to have   186 been productive of extensive evil among recent schools.

The development of landscape north of the Alps presents us with the same general phases, under modifications dependent partly on less intensity of feeling, partly on diminished availableness of landscape material. That of the religious painters is treated with the same affectionate completion; but exuberance of fancy sometimes diminishes the influence of the imagination, and the absence of the Italian force of passion admits of more patient and somewhat less intellectual elaboration. A morbid habit of mind is evident in many, seeming to lose sight of the balance and relations of things, so as to become intense in trifles, gloomily minute, as in Albert Dürer; and this mingled with a feverish operation of the fancy, which appears to result from certain habitual conditions of bodily health rather than of mental culture; but with all this there are virtues of the very highest order in those schools, and I regret that my knowledge is insufficient to admit of my giving any detailed account of them.

In the landscape of Rembrandt and Rubens, we have the northern parallel to the power of the Venetians. Among the etchings and drawings of Rembrandt, landscape thoughts may be found not unworthy of Titian, and studies from nature of sublime fidelity; but his system of chiaroscuro was inconsistent with the gladness, and his peculiar modes of feeling with the grace, of nature; nor, from my present knowledge, can I name any work on canvas in which he has carried out the dignity of his etched conceptions, or exhibited any perceptiveness of new truths.

Not so Rubens, who perhaps furnishes us with the first instances of   187 complete, unconventional, unaffected landscape. His treatment is healthy, manly, and rational, not very affectionate, yet often condescending to minute and multitudinous detail; always, as far as it goes, pure, forcible, and refreshing, consummate in composition, and marvellous in colour.

Among the professed landscapists of the Dutch school, we find much   188 dexterous imitation of certain kinds of nature, remarkable usually for its persevering rejection of whatever is great, valuable, or affecting in the object studied. Where, however, they show real desire to paint what they saw as far as they saw it, there is of course much in them that is instructive, as in Cuyp and in the etchings of Waterloo,[17] which have even very sweet and genuine feeling; and so in some of their architectural painters. But the object of the great body of them is merely to display manual dexterities of one kind or another; and their effect on the public mind is so totally for evil, that though I do not deny the advantage an artist of real judgment may derive from the study of some of them, I conceive the best patronage   189 that any monarch could possibly bestow upon the arts, would be to collect the whole body of them into one gallery and burn it to the ground.

Passing to the English school, we find a connecting link between them and the Italians formed by Richard Wilson. Had this artist studied under favourable circumstances, there is evidence of his having possessed power enough to produce an original picture; but corrupted by study of the Poussins, and gathering his materials chiefly in their field, the district about Rome—a district especially unfavourable, as exhibiting no pure or healthy nature, but a diseased and overgrown flora, among half-developed volcanic rocks, loose calcareous concretions, and mouldering wrecks of buildings, and whose spirit I conceive to be especially opposed to the natural tone of the English mind,—his originality was altogether overpowered; and, though he paints in a manly way and occasionally reaches exquisite tones of colour, and sometimes manifests some freshness of feeling, yet his pictures are in general mere diluted adaptations from Poussin and Salvator, without the dignity of the one, or the fire of the other.

Not so Gainsborough; a great name his, whether of the English or any other school. The greatest colourist since Rubens, and the last, I think, of legitimate colourists; that is to say, of those who were fully acquainted with the power of their material; pure in his English feeling, profound in 190 his seriousness, graceful in his gaiety. There are nevertheless certain deductions to be made from his worthiness which yet I dread to make, because my knowledge of his landscape works is not extensive enough to justify me in speaking of them decisively; but this is to be noted of all that I know, that they are rather motives of feeling and colour than earnest studies; that their execution is in some degree mannered, and always hasty; that they are altogether wanting in the affectionate detail of which I have already spoken; and that their colour is in some measure dependent on a bituminous brown and conventional green, which have more of science than of truth in them. With Gainsborough terminates the series of painters connected with the elder schools. By whom, among those yet living or lately lost, the impulse was first given to modern landscape, I attempt not to decide. Such questions are rather invidious than interest-191 ing; the particular tone or direction of any school seems to me always to have resulted rather from certain phases of national character, limited to particular periods, than from individual teaching, and, especially among moderns, what has been good in each master has been commonly original.

I have already alluded[18] to the simplicity and earnestness of the mind of Constable; to its vigorous rupture with school laws, and to its unfortunate error on the opposite side. Unteachableness seems to have been a main feature of his character, and there is corresponding want of veneration in the way he approaches nature herself. His early education and associations were also against him; they induced in him a morbid preference of subjects of a low order. I have never seen any work of his in which there were any signs of his being able to draw, and hence even the most necessary details are painted by him inefficiently. His works are also eminently wanting both in rest and refinement: and Fuseli's jesting compliment[19] is too true; for the showery weather, in which the artist delights, misses alike the majesty of storm and the loveliness of calm weather; it is great-coat weather, and nothing more. There is strange want of depth in the mind which has no pleasure in sunbeams but when piercing painfully through clouds, nor in foliage but when shaken by the wind, nor in light itself but when flickering, glistening, restless and feeble. Yet, with all these deductions, his works are to be deeply respected, as thoroughly original, thoroughly honest, free from affectation, manly in manner, frequently successful in cool colour, and realizing certain motives of English scenery with perhaps as much affection as such scenery, unless when regarded through media of feeling derived from higher sources, is calculated to inspire.

Throughout the range of elder art, it will be remembered we have found   192
no instance of the faithful painting of mountain scenery, except in a faded background of Masaccio's; nothing more than rocky eminences, undulating hills, or fantastic crags, and even these treated altogether under typical forms. The more specific study of mountains seems to have coincided with the more dexterous practice of water-colour; but it admits of doubt whether the choice of subject has been directed by the vehicle, or whether, as I rather think, the tendency of national feeling has not been followed in the use of the most appropriate means. Something is to be attributed to the increased demand for slighter works of art, and much to the sense of the quality of objects now called picturesque, which appears to be exclusively of modern origin. From what feeling the character of middle-age architecture and costume arose, or with what kind of affection their forms were regarded by the inventors, I am utterly unable to guess; but of this I think we may be assured, that the natural instinct and childlike wisdom of those days were altogether different from the modern feeling which appears to have taken its origin in the absence of such objects, and to be based rather on the strangeness of their occurrence than on any real affection for them; and which is certainly so shallow and ineffective as to be instantly and always sacrificed by the majority to   193
fashion, comfort, or economy. Yet I trust that there is a healthy though feeble love of nature mingled with it; nature pure, separate, felicitous, which is also peculiar to the moderns; and as signs of this feeling, or ministers to it, I look with veneration upon many works which, in a technical point of view, are of minor importance.[20]

The name I have last to mention is that of J. M. W. Turner. I shall here   228
confine myself to a rapid glance at the relations of his past and present   229
works, and to some notice of what he has failed of accomplishing: the

greater part of the subsequent chapters will be exclusively devoted to the examination of the new fields over which he has extended the range of landscape art.

It is a fact more universally acknowledged than enforced or acted upon, that all great painters, of whatever school, have been great only in their rendering of what they had seen and felt from early childhood; and that the greatest among them have been the most frank in acknowledging this their inability to treat anything successfully but that with which they had been familiar. The Madonna of Raffaelle was born on the Urbino mountains, Ghirlandajo's is a Florentine, Bellini's a Venetian; there is not the slightest effort on the part of any one of these great men to paint her as a Jewess. It is not the place here to insist farther on a point so simple and so universally demonstrable. Expression, character, types of countenance, costume, colour, and accessories are, with all great painters whatsoever, those of their native land; and that frankly and entirely, without the slightest attempt at modification; and I assert fearlessly that it is impossible that it should ever be otherwise, and that no man ever painted, or ever will paint, well, anything but what he has early and long seen, early and long felt, and early and long loved. How far it is possible for the mind of one nation or generation to be healthily modified and taught by the work of another, I presume not to determine; but it depends upon whether the energy of the mind which receives the instruction be sufficient, while it takes out of what it feeds upon that which is universal and common to all nature, to resist all warping from national or temporary peculiarities. All artists who have attempted to assume, or in their weakness have been affected by, the national peculiarities of other times and countries, have instantly, whatever their original power, fallen to thirdrate rank, or fallen altogether; and have invariably lost their birthright and blessing, lost their power over the human heart, lost all capability of teaching or benefiting others. Compare the hybrid classicalism of Wilson with the rich English purity of Gainsborough; compare the sickly modern German imitations of the great Italians with Albert Dürer and Holbein; compare the vile classicality of Canova and the modern Italians with Mino da Fiesole, Luca della Robbia, and Andrea del Verrocchio. The manner of Nicolo Poussin is said to be Greek—it may be so; this only I know, that it is heartless and profitless. Whatever is to be truly great and affecting must have on it the strong stamp of the native land. Not a law this, but a necessity, from the intense hold on their country of the affections of all truly great men. All classicality, all middle-aged patent-reviving, is utterly vain and absurd; if we are now to do anything great, good, awful, religious, it must be got out of our own little island, and out of these very times, railroads and all; if a British painter, I say this in earnest seriousness, cannot make historical characters out of the British House of Peers, he cannot paint history; and if he cannot make a Madonna of a British girl of the nineteenth century, he cannot paint one at all.

The rule, of course, holds in landscape; yet so far less authoritatively, that the material nature of all countries and times is in many points actually, and in all, in principle, the same; so that feelings educated in Cumberland may find their food in Switzerland, and impressions first received amongst the rocks of Cornwall be recalled upon the precipices of Genoa. Add to this actual sameness, the power of every great mind to possess itself of the spirit of things once presented to it, and it is evident, that little limitation can be set to the landscape painter as to the choice of his field; and that the law of nationality will hold with him only so far as a certain joyfulness and completion will be by preference found in those parts of his subject which remind him of his own land. But if he attempt to impress on his landscapes any other spirit than that he has felt, and to make them landscapes of other times, it is all over with him, at least, in the degree in which such reflected moonshine takes the place of the genuine light of the present day.   232

The reader will at once perceive how much trouble this simple principle will save both the painter and the critic; it at once sets aside the whole school of common composition, and exonerates us from the labour of minutely examining any landscape which has nymphs or philosophers in it.   233

I do not know in what district of England Turner first or longest studied, but the scenery whose influence I can trace most definitely throughout his works, varied as they are, is that of Yorkshire. Of all his drawings, I think, those of the Yorkshire series have the most heart in them, the most affectionate, simple, unwearied, serious finishing of truth. There is in them little seeking after effect, but a strong love of place; little exhibition of the artist's own powers or peculiarities, but intense appreciation of the smallest local minutiae. It is, I believe, to those broad wooded steeps and swells of the Yorkshire downs that we in part owe the singular massiveness that prevails in Turner's mountain drawing, and gives it one of its chief elements of grandeur.   234

I am in the habit of looking to the Yorkshire drawings [plate 5], as indicating one of the culminating points in Turner's career. In these he attained the highest degree of what he had up to that time attempted, namely, finish and quantity of form united with expression of atmosphere, and light without colour. His early drawings are singularly instructive in this definiteness and simplicity of aim. No complicated or brilliant colour is ever thought of in them; they are little more than exquisite studies in light and shade, very green blues being used for the shadows, and golden browns for the lights. The difficulty and treachery of colour being thus avoided, the artist was able to bend his whole mind upon the drawing, and thus to attain such decision, delicacy, and completeness as have never in any wise been equalled, and as might serve him for a secure foundation in all after experiments.

235   About the time of their production, the artist seems to have felt that he had done either all that could be done, or all that was necessary, in that manner, and began to reach after something beyond it. The element of colour begins to mingle with his work, and in the first efforts to reconcile his intense feeling for it with his careful form, several anomalies begin to be visible, and some unfortunate or uninteresting works necessarily belong to the period. The England drawings,[21] which are very characteristic of it, are exceedingly unequal,—some, as the Oakhampton, Kilgarren, Alnwick, and Llanthony [fig.8], being among his finest works; others, as the Windsor from Eton, the Eton College, and the Bedford, showing coarseness and conventionality.

I do not know at what time the painter first went abroad,[22] but some of the Swiss drawings above named were made in 1804 or 1806; and among the earliest of the series of the Liber Studiorum[23] (dates 1808, 1809), occur the magnificent Mont St. Gothard [fig.9], and Little Devil's Bridge. Now it is remarkable that after his acquaintance with this scenery, so congenial in almost all respects with the energy of his mind, and supplying him with materials of which in these two subjects, he showed both his entire

236   appreciation and command, the proportion of English to foreign subjects should in the rest of the work be more than two to one; and that those English subjects should be, many of them, of a kind peculiarly simple, and of every-day occurrence; and that the architectural subjects, instead of being taken, as might have been expected of an artist so fond of treating effects of extended space, from some of the enormous continental masses, are almost exclusively British; and, farther, not only is the preponderance of subject British, but of affection also; for it is strange with what fulness and completion the home subjects are treated in comparison with the greater part of the foreign ones.

237   I adduce these evidences of Turner's nationality, not as proofs of weakness, but of power; not so much as testifying want of perception in foreign lands, as strong hold on his own; for I am sure that no artist who has not this hold upon his own will ever get good out of any other. Keeping this principle in mind, it is instructive to observe the depth and solemnity which Turner's feeling acquired from the scenery of the continent, the keen appreciation up to a certain point of all that is locally characteristic, and the ready seizure for future use of all valuable material.

Of all foreign countries he has most entirely entered into the spirit of France; partly because here he found more fellowship of scene with his own England; partly because an amount of thought which will miss of Italy or Switzerland will fathom France; partly because there is in the

fig.8   J.M.W. Turner, *Llanthony Abbey, Monmouthshire*

French foliage and forms of ground much that is especially congenial with his own peculiar choice of form. To what cause it is owing I cannot tell,   238 nor is it generally allowed or felt; but of the fact I am certain, that for grace of stem and perfection of form in their transparent foliage, the French trees are altogether unmatched; and their modes of grouping and massing are so perfectly and constantly beautiful, that I think, of all countries for educating an artist to the perception of grace, France bears the bell; and that not romantic nor mountainous France, not the Vosges, nor Auvergne, nor Provence, but lowland France, Picardy and Normandy, the valleys of the Loire and Seine, and even the district, so thoughtlessly and mindlessly abused by English travellers as uninteresting, traversed between Calais and Dijon; of which there is not a single valley but is full of the most lovely pictures, nor a mile from which the artist may not receive instruction. Of this kind of beauty Turner was the first to take cognizance, and he still remains the only, but in himself the sufficient, painter of French landscape.

fig.9   J.M.W. Turner, *The Mont St Gothard,* from *Liber Studiorum*

239   The artist appears, until very lately, rather to have taken from Switzerland thoughts and general conceptions of size and of grand form and effect to be used in his after compositions, than to have attempted the seizing of its local character. This was beforehand to be expected from the utter physical impossibility of rendering certain effects of Swiss scenery, and the monotony and unmanageableness of others. The Hannibal passing the Alps,[24] in its present state, exhibits nothing but a heavy shower, and a crowd of people getting wet; another picture in the artist's gallery, of a Bergfall, is most masterly and interesting, but more daring than agreeable. The "Snow-storm, avalanche, and inundation,"[25] is one of his mightiest works, but the amount of mountain drawing in it is less than of cloud and effect.

240   The effect of Italy upon his mind is very puzzling. On the one hand it gave him the solemnity and power which are manifested in the historical compositions of the Liber Studiorum; on the other, he seems never to have entered thoroughly into the spirit of Italy, and the materials he obtained there were afterwards but awkwardly introduced in his large compositions.

244   The chief reason of these failures I imagine to be the effort of the artist to put joyousness and brilliancy of effect upon scenes eminently pensive,

to substitute radiance for serenity of light, and to force the freedom and breadth of line which he learned to love on English downs and Highland moors, out of a country dotted by campaniles and square convents, bristled with cypresses, partitioned by walls, and gone up and down by steps.

In one of the cities of Italy he had no such difficulties to encounter. At Venice he found freedom of space, brilliancy of light, variety of colour, massive simplicity of general form; and to Venice we owe many of the motives in which his highest powers of colour have been displayed, after that change in his system of which we must now take note.

Among the earlier *paintings* of Turner, the culminating period, marked by the Yorkshire series in his *drawings*, is distinguished by great solemnity and simplicity of subject, prevalent gloom in chiaroscuro, and brown in the hue, the drawing manly but careful, the minutiae sometimes exquisitely delicate. All the finest works of this period are, I believe, without exception, views, or quiet single thoughts. There is nothing in   245
the range of landscape art equal to them in their way, but the full character and capacity of the painter are not in them. Grand as they are in their sobriety, they still leave much to be desired; there is great heaviness in their shadows, the material is never thoroughly vanquished (though this partly for a very noble reason, that the painter is always thinking of and referring to nature, and indulges in no artistical conventionalities), and sometimes the handling appears feeble. In warmth, lightness, and transparency, they have no chance against Gainsborough; in clear skies and air tone they are alike unfortunate when they provoke comparison with Claude; and in force and solemnity they can in no wise stand with the landscape of the Venetians.

The painter evidently felt that he had farther powers, and pressed forward into the field where alone they could be brought into play. It was impossible for him, with all his keen and long disciplined perceptions, not to feel that the real colour of nature had never been attempted by any   246
school; and that though conventional representations had been given by the Venetians of sunlight and twilight by invariably rendering the whites golden and the blues green, yet of the actual, joyous, pure, roseate hues of the external world no record had ever been given. He saw also that the finish and specific grandeur of nature had been given, but her fulness, space, and mystery never; and he saw that the great landscape painters had always sunk the lower middle tints of nature in extreme shade, bringing the entire melody of colour as many degrees down as their possible light was inferior to nature's; and that in so doing a gloomy principle had influenced them even in their choice of subject.

For the conventional colour he substituted a pure straightforward rendering of fact, as far as was in his power; and that not of such fact as had been before even suggested, but of all that is *most* brilliant, beautiful, and inimitable; he went to the cataract for its iris, to the conflagration for its flames, asked of the sea its intensest azure, of the sky its clearest gold. For the limited space and defined forms of elder landscape he substituted the quantity and the mystery of the vastest scenes of earth; and for the sub-dued chiaroscuro he substituted first a balanced diminution of opposition throughout the scale, and afterwards, in one or two instances, attempted the reverse of the old principle, taking the lowest portion of the scale truly, and merging the upper part in high light.

Innovations so daring and so various could not be introduced without corresponding peril: the difficulties that lay in his way were more than any human intellect could altogether surmount. In his time there has been no one system of colour generally approved; every artist has his own method and his own vehicle; how to do what Gainsborough did, we know not; much less what Titian; to invent a new system of colour can hardly be expected of those who cannot recover the old. To obtain perfectly satis-factory results in colour under the new conditions introduced by Turner would at least have required the exertion of all his energies in that sole direction. But colour has always been only his second object. The effects of space and form, in which he delights, often require the employment of means and method totally at variance with those necessary for the obtaining of pure colour. It is physically impossible, for instance, rightly to draw certain forms of the upper clouds with the brush; nothing will do it but the pallet knife with loaded white after the blue ground is prepared. Now it is impossible that a cloud so drawn, however glazed afterwards, should have the virtue of a thin warm tint of Titian's, showing the canvas throughout. So it happens continually. Add to these difficulties, those of the peculiar subjects attempted, and to these again, all that belong to the altered system of chiaroscuro, and it is evident that we must not be sur-prised at finding many deficiencies or faults in such works, especially in the earlier of them, nor even suffer ourselves to be withdrawn by the pursuit of what seems censurable from our devotion to what is mighty.

Notwithstanding, in some chosen examples of pictures of this kind (I will name three: Juliet and her Nurse;[26] the Old Téméraire [fig.10]; and the Slave Ship [plate 6]), I do not admit that there are at the time of their first appearing on the walls of the Royal Academy, any demonstrably avoidable faults; I do not deny that there may be, nay, that it is likely there are: but there is no living artist in Europe whose judgment might safely be taken on the subject, or who could without arrogance affirm of any part of such a picture, that it was *wrong*. I am perfectly willing to allow, that the lemon yellow is not properly representative of the yellow of the sky, that the loading of the colour is in many places disagreeable, that many of the details are drawn with a kind of imperfection different from what they would have in nature, and that many of the parts fail of imitation,

247

248

fig.10   J.M.W. Turner, *The 'Fighting Téméraire' tugged to her Last Berth to be broken up*, 1838

especially to an uneducated eye. But no living authority is of weight enough to prove that the virtues of the picture could have been obtained at a less sacrifice, or that they are not worth the sacrifice: and though it is perfectly possible that such may be the case, and that what Turner has done may hereafter in some respects be done better, I believe myself that these works are at the time of their first appearing as perfect as those of Phidias or Leonardo; that is to say, incapable, in their way, of any improvement conceivable by human mind.

Also, it is only by comparison with such that we are authorized to affirm definite faults in any of his others, for we should have been bound to speak, at least for the present, with the same modesty respecting even his worst pictures of this class, had not his more noble efforts given us canons of criticism.

On such instances I shall not insist, for the finding fault with Turner is not, I think, either decorous in myself or likely to be beneficial to the

249

reader. The greater number of failures took place in the period of transition, when the artist was feeling for the new qualities, and endeavouring to reconcile them with more careful elaboration of form than was properly consistent with them. Gradually his hand became more free, his perception and grasp of the new truths more certain, and his choice of subject more adapted to the exhibition of them.

250
251
252

    In conclusion of our present sketch of the course of landscape art, it may be generally stated that Turner is the only painter, so far as I know, who has ever drawn the sky, not the clear sky, which we before saw belonged exclusively to the religious schools, but the various forms and phenomena of the cloudy heavens; all previous artists having only represented it typically or partially, but he absolutely and universally. He is the only painter who has ever drawn a mountain, or a stone; no other man ever having learned their organization, or possessed himself of their spirit, except in part and obscurely. He is the only painter who ever drew the stem of a tree, Titian having come the nearest before him, and excelling him in the muscular development of the larger trunks (though sometimes losing the woody strength in a serpent-like flaccidity), but missing the grace and character of the ramifications. He is the only painter who has ever represented the surface of calm, or the force of agitated water; who has represented the effects of space on distant objects, or who has rendered the abstract beauty of natural colour. These assertions I make deliberately, after careful weighing and consideration, in no spirit of dispute, or momentary zeal; but from strong and convinced feeling, and with the consciousness of being able to prove them.

SECTION II
Of General Truths

CHAPTER I
Of Truth of Tone

As I have already allowed, that in effects of tone, the old masters have never yet been equalled; and as this is the first, and nearly the last, concession I shall have to make to them, I wish it at once to be thoroughly understood how far it extends.

I understand two things by the word Tone: first, the exact relief and relation of objects against and to each other in substance and darkness, as they are nearer or more distant, and the perfect relation of the shades of all of them to the chief light of the picture, whether that be sky, water, or anything else; secondly, the exact relation of the colours of the shadows to the colours of the lights, so that they may be at once felt to be merely different degrees of the same light; and the accurate relation among the illuminated parts themselves, with respect to the degree in which they are influenced by the colour of the light itself, whether warm or cold; so that the whole of the picture (or, where several tones are united, those parts of it which are under each) may be felt to be in one climate, under one kind of light, and in one kind of atmosphere; this being chiefly dependent on that peculiar and inexplicable quality of each colour laid on, which makes the eye feel both what is the actual colour of the object represented, and that it is raised to its apparent pitch by illumination.

The first of these meanings of the word Tone is liable to be confounded with what is commonly called "aërial perspective." But aërial perspective is the expression of space by any means whatsoever, sharpness of edge, vividness of colour, etc., assisted by greater pitch of shadow, and requires only that objects should be detached from each other by degrees of intensity in *proportion* to their distance, without requiring that the difference between the farthest and nearest should be in positive quantity the same that nature has put. But what I have called "tone" requires that there should be the same sum of difference, as well as the same division of differences.

Now the finely-toned pictures of the old masters are, in this respect, some of the notes of nature played two or three octaves below her key; the dark objects in the middle distance having precisely the same relation to the light of the sky which they have in nature, but the light being necessarily infinitely lowered, and the mass of the shadow deepened in the same degree.

261 Now if this could be done consistently, and all the notes of nature given in this way an octave or two down, it would be right and necessary so to do: but be it observed, not only does nature surpass us in power of obtaining light as much as the sun surpasses white paper, but she also infinitely surpasses us in her power of shade. Her deepest shades are void spaces from which no light whatever is reflected to the eye; ours are black surfaces from which, paint as black as we may, a great deal of light is still reflected, and which, placed against one of nature's deep bits of gloom, would tell as distinct light. Here we are, then, with white paper for our highest light, and visible illumined surface for our deepest shadow, set to run the gauntlet against nature, with the sun for her light, and vacuity for her gloom. It is evident that *she* can well afford to throw her material objects dark against the brilliant aërial tone of her sky, and yet give in those objects themselves a thousand intermediate distances and tones before she comes to black, or to anything like it—all the illumined surfaces of her objects being as distinctly and vividly brighter than her nearest and darkest shadows, as the sky is brighter than those illumined surfaces. But if we, against our poor dull obscurity of yellow paint, instead of sky, insist on having the same relation of shade in material objects, we go down to the bottom of our scale at once; and what in the world are we to do then? Where are all our intermediate distances to come from?—how are we to express the aërial relations among the parts themselves; for instance, of foliage, whose most distant boughs are already almost black?—how are we to come up from this to the foreground; and when we have done so, how are we to express the distinction between its solid parts, already as dark as we can make them, and its vacant hollows, which nature has marked sharp and clear and black, among its lighted surfaces? It cannot but be evident at a glance, that if to any one of the steps from one distance to

262 another, we give the same quantity of difference in pitch of shade which nature does, we must pay for this expenditure of our means by totally missing half a dozen distances, not a whit less important or marked, and so sacrifice a multitude of truths, to obtain one. And this accordingly was the means by which the old masters obtained their truth (?) of tone. They chose those steps of distance which are the most conspicuous and notice-able, that for instance from sky to foliage, or from clouds to hills; and they gave these their precise pitch of difference in shade with exquisite accuracy of imitation. Their means were then exhausted, and they were

obliged to leave their trees flat masses of mere filled-up outline, and to omit the truths of space in every individual part of their picture by the thousand. But this they did not care for; it saved them trouble; they reached their grand end, imitative effect; they thrust home just at the places where the common and careless eye looks for imitation, and they attained the broadest and most faithful appearance of truth of tone which art can exhibit.

But they are prodigals, and foolish prodigals in art; they lavish their whole means to get one truth, and leave themselves powerless when they should seize a thousand.

Turner starts from the beginning with a totally different principle. He boldly takes pure white (and justly, for it is the sign of the most intense sunbeams) for his highest light, and lampblack for his deepest shade; and between these he makes every degree of shade indicative of a separate   263 degree of distance, giving each step of approach, not the exact difference in pitch which it would have in nature, but a difference bearing the same proportion to that which his sum of possible shade bears to the sum of nature's shade; so that an object half-way between his horizon and his foreground, will be exactly in half tint of force, and every minute division of intermediate space will have just its proportionate share of the lesser sum, and no more. Hence where the old masters expressed one distance, he expresses a hundred, and where they said furlongs, he says leagues. Which of these modes of procedure be the more agreeable with truth, I think I may safely leave the reader to decide for himself. He will see, in this very first instance, one proof of what we above asserted, that the deceptive imitation of nature is inconsistent with real truth; for the very means by which the old masters attained the apparent accuracy of tone which is so satisfying to the eye, compelled them to give up all idea of real relations of retirement, and to represent a few successive and marked stages of distance, like the scenes of a theatre, instead of the imperceptible, multitudinous, symmetrical retirement of nature, who is not more careful to separate her nearest bush from her farthest one, than to separate the nearest bough of that bush from the one next to it.

Take, for instance, one of the finest landscapes that ancient art has produced—the work of a really great and intellectual mind, the quiet Nicolas Poussin in our own National Gallery, with the traveller washing his feet [fig.11]. The first idea we receive from this picture is that it is evening, and all the light coming from the horizon. Not so. It is full noon, the light coming steep from the left, as is shown by the shadow of the stick   264 on the right-hand pedestal; for if the sun were not very high, that shadow could not lose itself half-way down, and if it were not lateral, the shadow would slope, instead of being vertical. Now ask yourself, and answer candidly, if those black masses of foliage, in which scarcely any form is

fig.11 (attributed to) Nicolas Poussin, *A Man Washing His Feet*

seen but the outline, be a true representation of trees under noon-day sunlight, sloping from the left, bringing out, as it necessarily would do, their masses into golden green, and marking every leaf and bough with sharp shadow and sparkling light. The only truth in the picture is the exact pitch of relief against the sky of both trees and hills; and to this the organization of the hills, the intricacy of the foliage, and everything indicative either of the nature of the light, or the character of the objects, are unhesitatingly sacrificed. So much falsehood does it cost to obtain two apparent truths of tone!

Compare Turner's treatment of his materials in the Mercury and Argus [fig.12]. He has here his light actually coming from the distance, the sun being nearly in the centre of the picture, and a violent relief of objects against it would be far more justifiable than in Poussin's case. But this dark relief is used in its full force only with the nearest *leaves* of the nearest group of foliage overhanging the foreground from the left; and between these and the more distant members of the same group, though only three or four yards separate, distinct aërial perspective and intervening mist and light are shown; while the large tree in the centre, though very dark, as being very near, compared with

fig.12   J.M.W. Turner, *Mercury and Argus*

all the distance, is much diminished in intensity of shade from this nearest group of leaves, and is faint compared with all the foreground. It is true that this tree has not, in consequence, the actual pitch of shade against the sky which it would have in nature; but it has precisely as much as it possibly can have, to leave it the same proportionate relation to the objects near at hand. And it cannot but be evident to the thoughtful reader, that whatever trickery or deception may be the result of a contrary mode of treatment, this is the only scientific or essentially truthful system, and that what it loses in tone it gains in aërial perspective.

Observe, I am not at present speaking of the beauty or desirableness of the system of the old masters; it may be sublime, and affecting, and ideal, and intellectual, and a great deal more; but all I am concerned with at present is, that it is not *true*; while Turner's is the closest and most studied approach to truth of which the materials of art admit.

266   It was not, therefore, with reference to this division of the subject that I admitted inferiority in our great modern master to Claude or Poussin; but with reference to the second and more usual meaning of the word Tone,—the exact relation and fitness of shadow and light, and of the hues of all objects under them; and more especially that precious quality of each colour laid on, which makes it appear a quiet colour illuminated, not a bright colour in shade. But I allow this inferiority only with respect to the paintings of Turner, not to his drawings.

268   Light, with reference to the tone it induces on objects, is either to be considered as neutral and white, bringing out local colours with fidelity; or coloured, and consequently modifying these local tints with its own. But the power of pure white light to exhibit local colour is strangely variable. The morning light of about nine or ten is usually very pure; but the difference of its effect on different days, independently of mere brilliancy, is as inconceivable as inexplicable. Every one knows how capriciously the colours of a fine opal vary from day to day, and how rare the lights are which bring them fully out. Now the expression of the strange, penetrating, deep, neutral light, which, while it *alters* no colour, brings every colour up to the highest possible pitch and key of pure harmonious intensity, is the chief attribute of finely toned pictures by the great *colourists*, as opposed to pictures of equally high tone, by masters who, careless of colour, are content, like Cuyp, to lose local tints in the golden blaze of absorbing light.

Falsehood, in this neutral tone, if it may be so called, is a matter far more of feeling than of proof, for any colour is *possible* under such lights; it is meagreness and feebleness only which are to be avoided; and these are rather matters of sensation than of reasoning. But it is yet easy enough to prove by what exaggerated and false means the pictures most celebrated for this quality are endowed with their richness and solemnity of colour. In the Bacchus and Ariadne of Titian,[27] it is difficult to imagine anything

269   more magnificently impossible than the blue of the distant landscape; impossible, not from its vividness, but because it is not faint and aërial enough to account for its purity of colour; it is too dark and blue at the

same time; and there is indeed so total a want of atmosphere in it, that, but for the difference of form, it would be impossible to tell the mountains intended to be ten miles off, from the robe of Ariadne close to the spectator. Yet make this blue faint, aërial, and distant; make it in the slightest degree to resemble the truth of nature's colour; and all the tone of the picture, all its intensity and splendour, will vanish on the instant.

Now, as much of this kind of richness of tone is always given by Turner as is compatible with truth of aërial effect; but he will not sacrifice the higher truths of his landscape to mere pitch of colour, as Titian does. He infinitely prefers having the power of giving extension of space, and fulness of form, to that of giving deep melodies of tone; he feels too much the incapacity of art, with its feeble means of light, to give the abundance of nature's gradations; and therefore it is, that taking pure white for his highest expression of light, that even pure yellow may give him one more step in the scale of shade, he becomes necessarily inferior in richness of effect to the old masters of tone who always used a golden highest light, but gains by the sacrifice a thousand more essential truths. For, though we all know how much more like light, in the abstract, a finely toned warm hue will be to the feelings than white, yet it is utterly impossible   270 to mark the same number of gradations between such a sobered high light and the deepest shadow, which we can between this and white; and as these gradations are absolutely necessary to give the facts of form and distance, which, as we have above shown, are more important than any truths of tone, Turner sacrifices the richness of his picture to its completeness, the manner of the statement to its matter. And not only is he right in doing this for the sake of space, but he is right also in the abstract question of colour; for as we observed above, it is only the white light, the perfect unmodified group of rays, which will bring out local colour perfectly; and if the picture, therefore, is to be complete in its system of colour, that is, if it is to have each of the three primitives in their purity, it *must* have white for its highest light, otherwise the purity of one of them at least will be impossible. And this leads us to notice the second and more frequent quality of light (which is assumed if we make our highest representation of it yellow), the positive hue, namely, which it may itself possess, of course modifying whatever local tints it exhibits, and thereby rendering certain colours necessary, and certain colours impossible. Under the direct yellow light of a descending sun, for instance, pure white and pure blue are both impossible; because the purest whites and blues that nature could produce would be turned in some degree into gold or green by it; and when the sun is within half a degree of the horizon, if the sky be clear, a rose light supersedes the golden one, still more overwhelming in its effect on local colour. And   271 so under all coloured lights (and there are few, from dawn to twilight, which are not slightly tinted by some accident of atmosphere), there is a change of local colour, which, when in a picture it is so exactly proportioned that we feel at once both what the local colours are in themselves, and what are the colour and strength of the light upon them, gives us truth of tone.

For expression of effects of yellow sunlight, parts might be chosen out of the good pictures of Cuyp, which have never been equalled in art. But I much doubt if there be a single *bright* Cuyp in the world, which, taken as a whole, does not present many glaring solecisms in tone. I have not seen many fine pictures of his, which were not utterly spoiled by the vermilion dress of some principal figure, a vermilion totally unaffected and un-warmed by the golden hue of the rest of the picture; and, what is worse, with little distinction between its own illumined and shaded parts, so that it appears altogether out of sunshine, the colour of a bright vermilion in dead cold daylight.

272 Now, there is no instance in the works of Turner of anything so faithful and imitative of sunshine as the best parts of Cuyp; but, at the same time,
273 there is not a single vestige of the same kind of solecism. It is true, that in his fondness for colour, Turner is in the habit of allowing excessively cold fragments in his warmest pictures; but these are never, observe, warm colours with no light upon them, useless as contrasts, while they are discords in the tone; but they are bits of the very coolest tints, partially removed from the general influence, and exquisitely valuable as colour, though, with all deference be it spoken, I think them sometimes slightly destructive of what would otherwise be perfect tone.

274 The comparison of Turner with Cuyp may sound strange in most ears; but this is chiefly because we are not in the habit of analysing and dwelling upon those difficult and daring passages of the modern master which do not at first appeal to our ordinary notions of truth, owing to his habit of uniting two, three, or even more separate tones in the same composition. In this also he strictly follows nature, for wherever climate changes, tone changes, and the climate changes with every 200 feet of elevation, so that the upper clouds are always different in tone from the lower ones; these from the rest of the landscape, and in all probability, some part of the horizon from the rest. And when nature allows this in a high degree, as in her most gorgeous effects she always will, she does not herself impress at once with intensity of tone, as in the deep and quiet yellows of a July evening, but rather with the magnificence and variety of associated colour, in which, if we give time and attention to it, we shall gradually find the solemnity and the depth of twenty tones instead of one. Now, in Turner's power of associating cold with warm light no one has ever approached or even ventured into the same field with him. The old masters, content with one simple tone, sacrificed to its unity all the

exquisite gradations and varied touches of relief and change by which nature unites her hours with each other. They give the warmth of the sinking sun, overwhelming all things in its gold, but they did not give those grey passages about the horizon where, seen through its dying light, the cool and the gloom of night gather themselves for their victory. Whether it was in them impotence or judgment, it is not for me to decide. I have only to point to the daring of Turner in this respect as something 275 to which art affords no matter of comparison, as that in which the mere attempt is, in itself, superiority. Take the evening effect with the Téméraire [fig.10]. That picture will not, at the first glance, deceive as a piece of actual sunlight; but this is because there is in it more than sunlight, because under the blazing veil of vaulted fire which lights the vessel on her last path, there is a blue, deep, desolate hollow of darkness, out of which you can hear the voice of the night wind, and the dull boom of the disturbed sea; because the cold deadly shadows of the twilight are gathering through every sunbeam, and moment by moment as you look, you will fancy some new film and faintness of the night has risen over the vastness of the departing form.

CHAPTER II

Of Truth of Colour

277   THERE is, in the first room of the National Gallery, a landscape attributed to Gaspar Poussin, called sometimes Aricia, sometimes Le or La
Riccia, according to the fancy of catalogue printers [plate 7]. Whether it
can be supposed to resemble the ancient Aricia, now La Riccia, close to
Albano, I will not take upon me to determine, seeing that most of the
towns of these old masters are quite as like one place as another; but, at
any rate, it is a town on a hill, wooded with two-and-thirty bushes, of very
uniform size, and possessing about the same number of leaves each. These
bushes are all painted in with one dull opaque brown, becoming very
slightly greenish towards the lights, and discover in one place a bit of rock,
278   which of course would in nature have been cool and grey beside the
lustrous hues of foliage, and which, therefore, being moreover completely
in shade, is consistently and scientifically painted of a very clear, pretty,
and positive brick red, the only thing like colour in the picture. The
foreground is a piece of road which, in order to make allowance for its
greater nearness, for its being completely in light, and, it may be
presumed, for the quantity of vegetation usually present on carriage-roads,
is given in a very cool green grey; and the truth of the picture is completed
by a number of dots in the sky on the right, with a stalk to them, of a sober
and similar brown.

Not long ago, I was slowly descending this very bit of carriage-road, the
first turn after you leave Albano, not a little impeded by the worthy
successors of the ancient prototypes of Veiento.* It had been wild weather
279   when I left Rome, and all across the Campagna the clouds were sweeping
in sulphurous blue, with a clap of thunder or two, and breaking gleams of
sun along the Claudian aqueduct lighting up the infinity of its arches like
the bridge of chaos. But as I climbed the long slope of the Alban Mount,

*"C⅛cus adulator . . .
    Dignus Aricinos qui mendicaret ad axes,
    Blandaque devex⅛ jactaret basia rhed⅛."[28]

69

Albano, and graceful darkness of its ilex grove, rose against pure streaks of alternate blue and amber; the upper sky gradually flushing through the last fragments of rain-cloud in deep palpitating azure, half ¹⁄₈ther and half dew. The noonday sun came slanting down the rocky slopes of La Riccia, and their masses of entangled and tall foliage, whose autumnal tints were mixed with the wet verdure of a thousand evergreens, were penetrated with it as with rain. I cannot call it colour, it was conflagration. Purple, and crimson, and scarlet, like the curtains of God's tabernacle, the rejoicing trees sank into the valley in showers of light, every separate leaf quivering with buoyant and burning life; each, as it turned to reflect or to transmit the sunbeam, first a torch and then an emerald. Far up into the recesses of the valley, the green vistas arched like the hollows of mighty waves of some crystalline sea, with the arbutus flowers dashed along their flanks for foam, and silver flakes of orange spray tossed into the air around them, breaking over the grey walls of rock into a thousand separate stars, fading and kindling alternately as the weak wind lifted and let them fall. Every glade of grass burned like the golden floor of heaven, opening in sudden gleams as the foliage broke and closed above it, as sheet-lightning opens in a cloud at sunset; the motionless masses of dark rock—dark though flushed with scarlet lichen, casting their quiet shadows across its restless radiance, the fountain underneath them filling its marble hollow with blue mist and fitful sound; and over all, the multitudinous bars of amber and rose, the sacred clouds that have no   280 darkness, and only exist to illumine, were seen in fathomless intervals between the solemn and orbed repose of the stone pines, passing to lose themselves in the last, white, blinding lustre of the measureless line where the Campagna melted into the blaze of the sea.

Tell me who is likest this, Poussin or Turner? Not in his most daring and dazzling efforts could Turner himself come near it; but you could not at the time have thought of or remembered the work of any other man as having the remotest hue or resemblance of what you saw. Nor am I speaking of what is uncommon or unnatural; there is no climate, no place, and scarcely an hour, in which nature does not exhibit colour which no mortal effort can imitate or approach. For all our artificial pigments are, even when seen under the same circumstances, dead and lightless beside her living colour; the green of a growing leaf, the scarlet of a fresh flower, no art nor expedient can reach; but in addition to this, nature exhibits her hues under an intensity of sunlight which trebles their brilliancy; while the painter, deprived of this splendid aid, works still with what is actually a grey shadow compared with the force of nature's colour. Take a blade of grass and a scarlet flower, and place them so as to receive sunlight beside the brightest canvas that ever left Turner's easel, and the picture will be extinguished. So far from outfacing nature, he does not, as far as mere vividness of colour goes, one half reach her. But does he use this brilliancy of colour on objects to which it does not properly belong? Let us compare his works in this respect with a few instances from the old masters.

There is, on the left-hand side of Salvator's Mercury and the Woodman [plate 8] in our National Gallery, something without doubt intended for a rocky mountain, in the middle distance, near enough for all its fissures and crags to be distinctly visible, or, rather, for a great many awkward scratches of the brush over it to be visible, which, though not particularly representative either of one thing or another, are without doubt intended to be symbolical of rocks. Now no mountain in full light, and near enough for its details of crag to be seen, is without great variety of delicate colour. Salvator has painted it throughout without one instant of variation; but this, I suppose, is simplicity and generalization;—let it pass: but what is the colour? *Pure sky blue*, without one grain of grey or any modifying hue whatsoever; the same brush which had just given the bluest parts of the sky has been more loaded at the same part of the pallet, and the whole mountain thrown in with unmitigated ultramarine. Now mountains only can become pure blue when there is so much air between us and them that they become mere flat dark shades, every detail being totally lost: they become blue when they become air, and not till then. Consequently this part of Salvator's painting, being of hills perfectly clear and near, with all their details visible, is, as far as colour is concerned, broad bold falsehood, the direct assertion of direct impossibility.

In the whole range of Turner's works, recent or of old date, you will not find an instance of anything near enough to have details visible, painted in sky blue. Wherever Turner gives blue, there he gives atmosphere; it is air, not object. Blue he gives to his sea; so does nature;—blue he gives, sapphire-deep, to his extreme distance; so does nature;—blue he gives to the misty shadows and hollows of his hills; so does nature; but blue he gives *not*, where detail and illumined surface are visible; as he comes into light and character, so he breaks into warmth and varied hue: nor is there in one of his works —and I speak of the Academy pictures especially—one touch of cold colour which is not to be accounted for, and proved right and full of meaning.

Again, in the upper sky of the picture of Nicholas Poussin, before noticed, the clouds are of a very fine clear olive green, about the same tint as the brightest parts of the trees beneath them. They cannot have altered (or else the trees must have been painted in grey), for the hue is har-monious and well united with the rest of the picture, and the blue and white in the centre of the sky are still fresh and pure. Now a green sky in open and illumined distance is very frequent, and very beautiful; but rich olive-green clouds, as far as I am acquainted with nature, are a piece of colour in which she is not apt to indulge. You will be puzzled to show me such a thing in the recent works of Turner. Again, take any important

fig.13   Claude Gellée, *Landscape with the Marriage of
Isaac and Rebekah ('The Mill')*

group of trees, I do not care whose—Claude's, Salvator's, or Poussin's—
with lateral light (that in the Marriage of Isaac and Rebecca [fig.13], or
Gaspar's Sacrifice of Isaac [fig.14], for instance):[29] can it be seriously
supposed that those murky browns and melancholy greens are
representative of the tints of leaves under full noonday sun? I know that   283
you cannot help looking upon all these pictures as pieces of dark relief
against a light wholly proceeding from the distances; but they are nothing
of the kind, they are noon and morning effects with full lateral light. Be
so kind as to match the colour of a leaf in the sun (the darkest you like) as
nearly as you can, and bring your matched colour and set it beside one of
these groups of trees, and take a blade of common grass, and set it beside
any part of the fullest light of their foregrounds, and then talk about the
truth of colour of the old masters!

And let not arguments respecting the sublimity or fidelity of *impression*
be brought forward here. I have nothing whatever to do with this at

fig.14　Gaspar Dughet, *Landscape with Abraham and Isaac
approaching the Place of Sacrifice*

present. I am not talking about what is sublime, but about what is true.
People attack Turner on this ground; they never speak of beauty or
sublimity with respect to him, but of nature and truth, and let them
support their own favourite masters on the same grounds. Perhaps I may
have the very deepest veneration for the *feeling* of the old masters; but I
must not let it influence me now,—my business is to match colours, not
to talk sentiment. Neither let it be said that I am going too much into
details, and that general truth may be obtained by local falsehood. Truth
is only to be measured by close comparison of actual facts; we may talk for
ever about it in generals, and prove nothing. We cannot tell what effect
falsehood may produce on this or that person, but we can very well tell
what is false and what is not; and if it produce on our senses the effect of
truth, that only demonstrates their imperfection and inaccuracy, and
284　need of cultivation. Turner's colour is glaring to one person's sensations,

and beautiful to another's. This proves nothing. Poussin's colour is right to one, soot to another. This proves nothing. There is no means of arriving at any conclusion but by close comparison of both with the known and demonstrable hues of nature, and this comparison will invariably turn Claude or Poussin into blackness, and even Turner into grey.

Whatever depth of gloom may seem to invest the objects of a real landscape, yet a window with that landscape seen through it will invariably appear a broad space of light as compared with the shade of the room walls; and this single circumstance may prove to us both the intensity and the diffusion of daylight in open air, and the necessity, if a picture is to be truthful in effect of colour, that it should tell as a broad space of graduated illumination,—not, as do those of the old masters, as a patchwork of black shades. Their works are nature in mourning weeds,—*οὐδ ἐν ἡλίῳ καθαρᾳ τεθραμμένοι, ἀλλ' ὑπὸ συμμιγεῖ σκιᾷ.* [30]

It is singular enough that the chief attacks on Turner for overcharged brilliancy are made, not when there could by any possibility be any chance of his outstepping nature, but when he has taken subjects which no colours of earth could ever vie with or reach, such, for instance, as his sunsets among the high clouds. When I come to speak of skies, I shall point out what divisions, proportioned to their elevation, exist in the character of clouds. It is the highest region, that exclusively characterized by white, filmy, multitudinous, and quiet clouds, arranged in bars, or streaks, or flakes, of which I speak at present; a region which no landscape painters have ever made one effort to represent, except Rubens and Turner, the latter taking it for his most favourite and frequent study. Now we have been speaking hitherto of what is constant and necessary in nature, of the ordinary effects of daylight on ordinary colours, and we repeat again, that no gorgeousness of the pallet can reach even these. But it is a widely different thing when nature herself takes a colouring fit, and does something extraordinary, something really to exhibit her power. She has a thousand ways and means of rising above herself, but incomparably the noblest manifestations of her capability of colour are in these sunsets among the high clouds. I speak especially of the moment before the sun sinks, when his light turns pure rose-colour, and when this light falls upon a zenith covered with countless cloud-forms of inconceivable delicacy, threads and flakes of vapour, which would in common daylight be pure snow-white, and which give therefore fair field to the tone of light. There is then no limit to the multitude, and no check to the intensity, of the hues assumed. The whole sky from the zenith to the horizon becomes one molten mantling sea of colour and fire; every black bar turns into massy gold, every ripple and wave into unsullied shadowless crimson, and purple, and scarlet, and colours for which there are no words in language, and no ideas in the mind,—things which can only be conceived while

285

286

they are visible; the intense hollow blue of the upper sky melting through it all, showing here deep, and pure, and lightless; there, modulated by the filmy formless body of the transparent vapour, till it is lost imperceptibly in its crimson and gold. Now there is no connection, no one link of association or resemblance, between those skies and the work of any mortal hand but Turner's. But there are a thousand reasons why this should not be believed. The concurrence of circumstances necessary to produce the sunsets of which I speak does not take place above five or six times in a summer, and then only for a space of from five to ten minutes, just as the sun reaches the horizon. Considering how seldom people think of looking for a sunset at all, and how seldom, if they do, they are in a position from which it can be fully seen, the chances that their attention should be awake, and their position favourable, during these few flying instants of the year, are almost as nothing. What can the citizen, who can see only the red light on the canvas of the waggon

287 at the end of the street, and the crimson colour of the bricks of his neighbour's chimney, know of the flood of fire which deluges the sky from the horizon to the zenith? What can even the quiet inhabitant of the English lowlands, whose scene for the manifestation of the fire of heaven is limited to the tops of hayricks, and the rooks' nests in the old elm trees, know of the mighty passages of splendour which are tossed from Alp to Alp over the azure of a thousand miles of champaign? Even granting the constant vigour of observation, and supposing the possession of such impossible knowledge, it needs but a moment's reflection to prove how incapable the memory is of retaining for any time the distinct image of the sources even of its most vivid impressions. What recollection have we of the sunsets which delighted us last year? We may know that they were magnificent, or glowing, but no distinct image of colour or form is retained—nothing of whose *degree* (for the great difficulty with the memory is to retain, not facts, but *degrees* of fact) we could be so certain as to say of anything now presented to us, that it is

288 like it. And so, when we enter an Exhibition, as we have no definite standard of truth before us, our feelings are toned down and subdued to the quietness of colour, which is all that human power can ordinarily attain to; and when we turn to a piece of higher and closer truth, approaching the pitch of the colour of nature, but to which we are not guided, as we should be in nature, by corresponding gradations of light everywhere around us, but which is isolated and cut off suddenly by a frame and a wall, and surrounded by darkness and coldness, what can we expect but that it should surprise and shock the feelings?

289 It is to be observed, however, in general, that wherever in brilliant effects of this kind, we approach to anything like a true statement of nature's colour, there must yet be a distinct difference in the impression

we convey, because we cannot approach her *light*. All such hues are usually given by her with an accompanying intensity of sunbeams which dazzles and overpowers the eye, so that it cannot rest on the actual colours, nor understand what they are; and hence in art, in rendering all effects of this kind, there must be a want of the ideas of *imitation*, which are the great source of enjoyment to the ordinary observer; because we can only give one series of truths, those of colour, and are unable to give the accompanying truths of light; so that the more true we are in colour, the greater, ordinarily, will be the discrepancy felt between the intensity of hue and the feebleness of light. But the painter who really loves nature will not, on this account, give you a faded and feeble image, which indeed may appear to you to be right, because your feelings can detect no discrepancy in its parts, but which he knows to derive its apparent truth from a systematized falsehood. No; he will make you understand and feel that art *cannot* imitate nature; that where it appears to do so, it must malign her and mock her. He will give you, or state to you, such truths as are in his power, completely and perfectly; and those which he cannot give, he will leave to your imagination.

Nevertheless the aim and struggle of the artist must always be to do away   290
with this discrepancy as far as the powers of art admit, not by lowering his colour, but by increasing his light. And it is indeed by this that the works of Turner are peculiarly distinguished from those of all other colourists, by the dazzling intensity, namely, of the light which he sheds through every hue, and which, far more than their brilliant colour, is the real source of their overpowering effect upon the eye, an effect so *reasonably* made the subject of perpetual animadversion; as if the sun which they represent, were quite a quiet, and subdued, and gentle, and manageable luminary, and never dazzled anybody, under any circumstances whatsoever. I am fond of standing by a bright Turner in the Academy, to listen to the unintentional compliments of the crowd—"What a glaring thing!" "I declare I can't look at it!" "Don't it hurt your eyes?"—expressed as if they were in the constant habit of looking the sun full in the face with the most perfect comfort and entire facility of vision.

Hitherto, however, we have been speaking of vividness of pure colour,   291
and showing that it is used by Turner only where nature uses it, and in less degree. But we have hitherto, therefore, been speaking of a most limited and uncharacteristic portion of his works; for Turner, like all great colourists, is distinguished not more for his power of dazzling and overwhelming the eye with intensity of effect, than for his power of doing so by the use of subdued and gentle means. There is no man living more cautious and sparing in the use of pure colour than Turner. Every picture   292
of this great colourist has, in one or two parts of it (keynotes of the whole), points where the system of each individual colour is concentrated by a

single stroke, as pure as it can come from the pallet; but throughout the great space and extent of even the most brilliant of his works, there will not be found a raw colour; that is to say, there is no warmth which has not grey in it, and no blue which has not warmth in it; and the tints in which he most excels and distances all other men, the most cherished and inimitable portions of his colour, are, as with all perfect colourists they must be, his greys.

293
294 Intimately associated with this toning down and connection of the colours actually used, is his inimitable power of varying and blending them, so as never to give a quarter of an inch of canvas without a change in it, a melody as well as a harmony of one kind or another. Observe, I am not at present speaking of this as artistical or desirable in itself, not as a characteristic of the great colourist, but as the aim of the simple follower of nature. For it is strange to see how marvellously nature varies the most general and simple of her tones. A mass of mountain seen against the light, may at first appear all of one blue; and so it is, blue as a whole, by comparison with other parts of the landscape. But look how that blue is made up. There are black shadows in it under the crags, there are green shadows along the turf, there are grey half-lights upon the rocks, there are faint touches of stealthy warmth and cautious light along their edges; every bush, every stone, every tuft of moss has its voice in the matter, and joins with individual character in the universal will. Who is there who can do this as Turner will? The old masters would have settled the matter at once with a transparent, agreeable, but monotonous grey. Many among the moderns would probably be equally monotonous with absurd and false colours. Turner only would give the uncertainty; the palpitating, perpetual change; the subjection of all to a great influence, without one part or portion being lost or merged in it; the unity of action with infinity of agent. And I wish to insist on this the more particularly, because it is one of the eternal principles of nature, that she will not have one line or colour, nor one portion or atom of space, without a change in it. There is not one of her shadows, tints, or lines that is not in a state of perpetual variation: I do not mean in time, but in space. There is not a leaf in the world which has the *same colour* visible over its whole surface; it has a white high light somewhere; and in proportion as it curves to or from that focus, the colour is brighter or greyer. Pick up a common flint from the roadside, and count, if you can, its changes and hues of colour. Every bit of bare ground under your feet has in it a thousand such; the grey pebbles, the warm ochre, the green

295 of incipient vegetation, the greys and blacks of its reflexes and shadows, might keep a painter at work for a month, if he were obliged to follow them touch for touch: how much more when the same infinity of change is carried out with vastness of object and space. The extreme of distance

may appear at first monotonous; but the least examination will show it to be full of every kind of change; that its outlines are perpetually melting and appearing again,—sharp here, vague there,—now lost altogether, now just hinted and still confused among each other; and so for ever in a state and necessity of change. Hence, wherever in a painting we have unvaried colour extended even over a small space, there is falsehood. Nothing can be natural which is monotonous; nothing true which only tells one story.

One point only remains to be noted respecting his system of colour generally—its entire subordination to light and shade—a subordination 298 299 which there is no need to prove here, as every engraving from his works (and few are unengraved) is sufficient demonstration of it. I have before shown the inferiority and unimportance in nature of colour, as a truth, compared with light and shade. That inferiority is maintained and asserted by all really great works of colour; but most by Turner's, as their colour is most intense. Whatever brilliancy he may choose to assume, is subjected to an inviolable law of chiaroscuro, from which there is no appeal. No richness nor depth of tint is considered of value enough to atone for the loss of one particle of arranged light. No brilliancy of hue is permitted to interfere with the depth of a determined shadow. Were it 301 necessary, rather than lose one line of his forms, or one ray of his sunshine, he would, I apprehend, be content to paint in black and white to the end of his life. It is by mistaking the shadow for the substance, and aiming at the brilliancy and the fire, without perceiving of what deep-studied shade and inimitable form it is at once the result and the illustration, that the host of his imitators sink into deserved disgrace. With him, the hue is a beautiful auxiliary in working out the great impression to be conveyed, but is not the chief source of that impression; it is little more than a visible melody, given to raise and assist the mind in the reception of nobler ideas,—as sacred passages of sweet sound, to prepare the feelings for the reading of the mysteries of God.

CHAPTER III
Of Truth of Chiaroscuro

303 I⊤ is not my intention to enter, in the present portion of the work, upon any examination of Turner's particular effects of light. We must know something about what is beautiful before we speak of these.

At present I wish only to insist upon two great principles of chiaroscuro, which are observed throughout the works of the great modern master, and set at defiance by the ancients; great general laws, which may, or may not, be sources of beauty, but whose observance is indisputably necessary to truth.

Go out some bright sunny day in winter, and look for a tree with a broad trunk, having rather delicate boughs hanging down on the sunny side, near the trunk. Stand four or five yards from it, with your back to the sun. You will find that the boughs between you and the trunk of the tree are very indistinct, that you confound them in places with the trunk itself, and cannot possibly trace one of them from its insertion to its extremity. But the shadows which they cast upon the trunk, you will find clear, dark, and distinct, perfectly traceable through their whole course, except when they are interrupted by the crossing boughs. And if you retire backwards,

304 you will come to a point where you cannot see the intervening boughs at all, or only a fragment of them here and there, but can still see their shadows perfectly plain. Now, this may serve to show you the immense prominence and importance of shadows where there is anything like bright light. They are, in fact, commonly far more conspicuous than the thing which casts them; for being as large as the casting object, and altogether made up of a blackness deeper than the darkest part of the casting object, while that object is also broken up with positive and reflected lights, their large, broad, unbroken spaces tell strongly on the eye, especially as all form is rendered partially, often totally, invisible within them, and as they are suddenly terminated by the sharpest lines which nature ever shows. For no outline of objects whatsoever is so sharp as the edge of a close shadow.

Hence shadows are in reality, when the sun is shining, the most conspicuous things in a landscape, next to the highest lights. All forms are

understood and explained chiefly by their agency: the roughness of the
bark of a tree, for instance, is not seen in the light, nor in the shade; it is
only seen between the two, where the shadows of the ridges explain it.
And hence, if we have to express vivid light, our very first aim must be to
get the shadows sharp and visible; and this is not to be done by blackness
(though indeed chalk on white paper is the only thing which comes up to
the intensity of real shadows), but by keeping them perfectly flat, keen,
and even. Now the old masters of the Italian school, in almost all their   305
works, directly reverse this principle; they blacken their shadows till the
picture becomes quite appalling, and everything in it invisible; but they
make a point of losing their edges, and carrying them off by gradation, in
consequence utterly destroying every appearance of sunlight. All their
shadows are the faint, secondary darkness of mere *daylight*; the sun has
nothing whatever to do with them. The shadow between the pages of the
book which you hold in your hand is distinct and visible enough, though
you are, I suppose, reading it by the ordinary daylight of your room, out of
the sun; and this weak and secondary shadow is all that we ever find in the
Italian masters, as indicative of sunshine. Even Cuyp and Berghem,
though they know thoroughly well what they are about in their
foregrounds, forget the principle in their distances; and throughout the   306
works of Claude, Poussin, and Salvator, we shall find, especially in their
conventional foliage, and unarticulated barbarisms of rock, that their
whole sum and substance of chiaroscuro are merely the gradation and
variation which nature gives in the *body* of her shadows, and that all
which they do to express sunshine, she does to vary shade. They take only
one step, while she always takes two; marking, in the first place, with
violent decision, the great transition from sun to shade, and then varying
the shade itself with a thousand gentle gradations and double shadows, in
themselves equivalent, and more than equivalent, to all that the old
masters did for their entire chiaroscuro.

  Now, if there be one principle or secret more than another on which
Turner depends for attaining brilliancy of light, it is his clear and exquisite
drawing of the *shadows*. Whatever is obscure, misty, or undefined, in his
objects or his atmosphere, he takes care that the shadows be sharp and
clear; and then he knows that the light will take care of itself, and he
makes them clear, not by blackness, but by excessive evenness, unity, and
sharpness of edge. He will keep them clear and distinct, and make them
felt as shadows, though they are so faint that, but for their decisive forms,
we should not have observed them for darkness at all. He will throw them
one after another like transparent veils along the earth and upon the air,
till the whole picture palpitates with them, and yet the darkest of them
will be a faint grey, imbued and penetrated with light. Words are not   308
accurate enough, nor delicate enough, to express or trace the constant,

all-pervading influence of the finer and vaguer shadows throughout his works, that thrilling influence which gives to the light they leave its passion and its power. There is not a stone, not a leaf, not a cloud, over which light is not felt to be actually passing and palpitating before our eyes. There is the motion, the actual wave and radiation of the darted beam: not the dull universal daylight, which falls on the landscape without life, or direction, or speculation, equal on all things and dead on all things; but the breathing, animated, exulting light, which feels, and receives, and rejoices, and acts,—which chooses one thing, and rejects another,—which seeks, and finds, and loses again,—leaping from rock to rock, from leaf to leaf, from wave to wave—glowing, or flashing, or scintillating, according to what it strikes; or, in its holier moods, absorbing and enfolding all things in the deep fulness of its repose, and then again losing itself in bewilderment, and doubt, and dimness,—or perishing and passing away, entangled in drifting mist, or melted into melancholy air, but still, —kindling or declining, sparkling or serene,—it is the living light, which breathes in its deepest, most entranced rest, which sleeps, but never dies.

310   The second point to which I wish at present to direct attention has reference to the *arrangement* of light and shade. It is the constant habit of nature to use both her highest lights and deepest shadows in exceedingly small quantity; always in points, never in masses. She will give a large mass of tender light in sky or water, impressive by its quantity, and a large mass of tender shadow relieved against it, in foliage, or hill, or building; but the light is always subdued if it be extensive, the shadow always feeble if it be broad. She will then fill up all the rest of her picture with middle tints and pale greys of some sort or another, and on this quiet and harmonious whole she will touch her high lights in spots: the foam of an isolated wave, the sail of a solitary vessel, the flash of the sun from a wet roof, the gleam of a single white-washed cottage, or some such sources of local brilliancy, she will use so vividly and delicately as to throw every-

311 thing else into definite shade by comparison. And then taking up the gloom, she will use the black hollows of some overhanging bank, or the black dress of some shaded figure, or the depth of some sunless chink of wall or window, so sharply as to throw everything else into definite light by comparison; thus reducing the whole mass of her picture to a delicate middle tint, approaching, of course, here to light, and there to gloom; but yet sharply separated from the utmost degrees either of the one or the other.

313   And it is most singular that this separation, which is the great source of brilliancy in nature, should not only be unobserved, but absolutely forbidden, by our great writers on art, who are always talking about connecting the light with the shade by *imperceptible gradations*. Now so surely as this is done, all sunshine is lost, for imperceptible gradation from light to dark

is the characteristic of objects seen out of sunshine, in what is, in landscape, shadow. Nature's principle of getting light is the direct reverse. She will cover her whole landscape with middle tint, in which she will have as many gradations as you please, and a great many more than you can paint; but on this middle tint she touches her extreme lights, and extreme darks, isolated and sharp, so that the eye goes to them directly, and feels them to be keynotes of the whole composition. And although the dark touches are less attractive than the light ones, it is not because 314 they are less distinct, but because they exhibit nothing; while the bright touches are in parts where everything is seen, and where in consequence the eye goes to rest. But yet the high lights do not exhibit anything in themselves, they are too bright and dazzle the eye; and having no shadows in them, cannot exhibit form, for form can only be seen by shadow of some kind or another. Hence the highest lights and deepest darks agree in this, that nothing is seen in either of them; that both are in exceedingly small quantity, and both are marked and distinct from the middle tones of the landscape, the one by their brilliancy, the other by their sharp edges, even though many of the more energetic middle tints may approach their intensity very closely.

I need scarcely do more than tell you to glance at any one of the works of Turner, and you will perceive in a moment the exquisite observation of all these principles; the sharpness, decision, conspicuousness, and exces-sively small quantity, both of extreme light and extreme shade, all the mass of the picture being graduated and delicate middle tint.

Of Truth of Space:—Secondly, as Its Appearance Is Dependent on the Power of the Eye

327   WE have now to examine that kind of indistinctness which is dependent on real retirement of the object, even when the focus of the eye is fully concentrated upon it. The first kind of indecision is that which belongs to all objects which the eye is not adapted to, whether near or far off: the second is that consequent upon the want of power in the eye to receive a clear image of objects at a great distance from it, however attentively it may regard them.

Draw on a piece of white paper a square and a circle, each about a twelfth or eighth of an inch in diameter, and blacken them so that their forms may be very distinct; place your paper against the wall at the end of the room, and retire from it a greater or less distance accordingly as you have drawn the figures larger or smaller. You will come to a point where, though you can see both the spots with perfect plainness, you cannot tell which is the square and which the circle.

Now this takes place of course with every object in a landscape, in proportion to its distance and size. Now if the character of an object, say

328   the front of a house, be explained by a variety of forms in it, as the shadows in the tops of the windows, the lines of the architraves, the seams of the masonry, etc.; these lesser details, as the object falls into distance, become confused and undecided, each of them losing its definite form, but all being perfectly visible as something, a white or a dark spot or stroke, not lost sight of, observe, but yet so seen that we cannot tell what they are. As the distance increases, the confusion becomes greater, until at last the whole front of the house becomes merely a flat pale space, in which, however, there is still observable a kind of richness and chequering, caused by the details in it, which, though totally merged and lost in the mass, have still an influence on the texture of that mass; until at last the whole house itself becomes a mere light or dark spot which we can plainly see, but cannot tell what it is, nor distinguish it from a stone or any other object.

Now what I particularly wish to insist upon, is the state of vision in which all the details of an object are seen, and yet seen in such confusion and disorder that we cannot in the least tell what they are, or what they mean. It is not mist between us and the object, still less is it shade, still less is it want of character; it is a confusion, a mystery, an interfering of undecided lines with each other, not a diminution of their number; window and door, architrave and frieze, all are there: it is no cold and vacant mass, it is full and rich and abundant, and yet you cannot see a single form so as to know what it is.

Changes like these, and states of vision corresponding to them, take place with each and all of the objects of nature, and two great principles of truth are deducible from their observation. First, place an object as close to the eye as you like, there is always something in it which you *cannot* see, except in the hinted and mysterious manner above described. Secondly, place an object as far from the eye as you like, and until it becomes itself a mere spot, there is always something in it which you *can* see, though only in the hinted manner above described. And thus nature is never distinct and never vacant, she is always mysterious, but always abundant; you always see something, but you never see all.   329

And hence in art, every space or touch in which we can see everything, or in which we can see nothing, is false. Nothing can be true which is either complete or vacant; every touch is false which does not suggest more than it represents, and every space is false which represents nothing.   330

Now, I would not wish for any more illustrative or marked examples of the total contradiction of these two great principles, than the landscape works of the old masters, taken as a body; the Dutch masters furnishing the cases of seeing everything, and the Italians of seeing nothing. The rule with both is indeed the same, differently applied—"You shall see the bricks in the wall, and be able to count them, or you shall see nothing but a dead flat:" but the Dutch give you the bricks, and the Italians the flat. Nature's rule being the precise reverse—"You shall never be able to count the bricks, but you shall never see a dead space."

Take, for instance, the street in the centre of the really great landscape of Poussin (great in feeling at least) in the Dulwich Gallery.[32] The houses are dead square masses with a light side and a dark side, and black touches for windows. There is no suggestion of anything in any of the spaces; the light wall is dead grey, the dark wall dead grey, and the windows dead black. How differently would nature have treated us! She would have let us see the Indian corn hanging on the walls, and the image of the Virgin at the angles, and the sharp, broken, broad shadows of the tiled eaves, and the deep-ribbed tiles with the doves upon them, and the carved Roman capital built into the wall, and the white and blue stripes of the mattresses stuffed out of the windows, and the flapping corners of the mat blinds. All would have been there; not as such, not like the corn, or blinds or tiles, not to be comprehended or understood, but a confusion of yellow and black spots and strokes, carried far too fine for the eye to follow,

331   microscopic in its minuteness, and filling every atom and part of space with mystery, out of which would have arranged itself the general impression of truth and life.

332   Or take one of Poussin's extreme distances, such as that in the Sacrifice of Isaac [fig.14]. It is luminous, retiring, delicate and perfect in tone, and is quite complete enough to deceive and delight the careless eye to which all distances are alike; nay, it is perfect and masterly, and absolutely right, if we consider it as a sketch,—as a first plan of a distance, afterwards to be carried out in detail. But we must remember that all these alternate spaces of grey and gold are not the landscape itself, but the treatment of it; not its substance, but its light and shade. They are just what nature would cast over it, and write upon it with every cloud, but which she would cast in play, and without carefulness, as matters of the very smallest possible importance. All her work and her attention would be given to bring out from underneath this, and through this, the forms and the material character which this can only be valuable to illustrate, not to conceal. Every one of those broad spaces she would linger over in protracted delight, teaching you fresh lessons in every hair's breadth of it, and pouring her fulness of invention into it, until the mind lost herself in following her: now fringing the dark edge of the shadow with a tufted line of level forest; now losing it for an instant in a breath of mist; then breaking it with the white gleaming angle of a narrow brook; then dwelling upon it again in a gentle, mounded, melting undulation, over the other side of which she would carry you down into a dusty space of soft crowded light, with the hedges and the paths and the sprinkled cottages and scattered trees mixed up and mingled together in one beautiful,

333   delicate, impenetrable mystery, sparkling and melting, and passing away into the sky, without one line of distinctness, or one instant of vacancy.

   Now it is, indeed, impossible for the painter to follow all this; he cannot come up to the same degree and order of infinity, but he can give us a lesser kind of infinity. He has not one thousandth part of the space to occupy which nature has; but he can, at least, leave no part of that space vacant and unprofitable. If nature carries out her minutiæ over miles, he has no excuse for generalizing in inches. And if he will only give us all he can, if he will give us a fulness as complete and as mysterious as nature's, we will pardon him for its being the fulness of a cup instead of an ocean. But we will not pardon him, if, because he has not the mile to occupy, he will not occupy the inch, and because he has fewer means at his command, will leave half of those in his power unexerted. Still less will we pardon him for mistaking the sport of nature for her labour, and for following her only in her hour of rest, without observing how she has worked for it. After spending centuries in raising the forest, and guiding the river, and modelling the mountain, she exults over her work in buoyancy of spirit, with playful sunbeam and flying cloud; but the painter must go through the same labour, or he must not have the same recreation. Let him chisel his rock faithfully, and tuft his forest delicately, and then we will allow him his freaks of light and shade, and thank him for them; but we will not be put off with the play before the lesson, with the adjunct instead of the essence, with the illustration instead of the fact.

And now, take up one of Turner's distances, and look if every fact   335
which I have just been pointing out in nature be not carried out in it. Abundant beyond the power of the eye to embrace or follow, vast and various beyond the power of the mind to comprehend, there is yet not one atom in its whole extent and mass which does not suggest more than it represents; nor does it suggest vaguely, but in such a manner as to prove that the conception of each individual inch of that distance is absolutely clear and complete in the master's mind, a separate picture fully worked out: but yet, clearly and fully as the idea is formed, just so much of it is given, and no more, as nature would have allowed us to feel or see; just so much as would enable a spectator of experience and knowledge to understand almost every minute fragment of separate detail, but appears, to the unpractised and careless eye, just what a distance of nature's own would appear, an unintelligible mass. Not one line out of the millions there is without meaning, yet there is not one which is not affected and disguised by the dazzle and indecision of distance. No form is made out, and yet no form is unknown.

Nor is this mode of representation true only with respect to distances.   337
Every object, however near the eye, has something about it which you cannot see, and which brings the mystery of distance even into every part and portion of what we suppose ourselves to see most distinctly. Stand in the Piazza di San Marco, at Venice, as close to the church as you can, without losing sight of the top of it. Look at the capitals of the columns on the second story. You see that they are exquisitely rich, carved all over. Tell me their patterns: You cannot. Tell me the direction of a single line in them: You cannot. Yet you see a multitude of lines, and you have so much feeling of a certain tendency and arrangement in those lines, that you are quite sure the capitals are beautiful, and that they are all different from each other. But I defy you to make out one single line in any one of them.

But if there be this mystery and inexhaustible finish merely in the more   338
delicate instances of architectural decoration, how much more in the ceaseless and incomparable decoration of nature. The detail of a single weedy bank laughs the carving of ages to scorn. Every leaf and stalk has a design and tracery upon it; every knot of grass an intricacy of shade which the labour of years could never imitate, and which, if such labour could follow it out even to the last fibres of the leaflets, would yet be falsely

represented, for, as in all other cases brought forward, it is not clearly seen, but confusedly and mysteriously. That which is nearness for the bank, is distance for its details; and however near it may be, the greater part of those details are still a beautiful incomprehensibility.

339   Hence, throughout the picture, the expression of space and size is dependent upon obscurity, united with, or rather resultant from, exceeding fulness. We destroy both space and size, either by the vacancy which affords us no measure of space, or by the distinctness which gives us a false one. The distance of Poussin, having no indication of trees, nor of meadows, nor of character of any kind, may be fifty miles off, or may be five: we cannot tell; we have no measure, and in consequence, no vivid impression. But a middle distance of Hobbima's involves a contradiction in terms; it states a distance by perspective, which it contradicts by distinctness of detail.

    A single dusty roll of Turner's brush is more truly expressive of the infinity of foliage, than the niggling of Hobbima could have rendered his

340 canvas, if he had worked on it till doomsday. But it should be observed that much of harm and error has arisen from the supposition and assertions of swift and brilliant historical painters, that the same principles of execution are entirely applicable to landscape, which are right for the figure. The artist who falls into extreme detail in drawing the human

341 form, is apt to become disgusting rather than pleasing. But the exclusively generalizing landscape painter omits the whole of what is valuable in his subject; omits thoughts, designs, and beauties by the million, everything indeed, which can furnish him with variety or expression. And so in every part of the subject, I have no hesitation in asserting that it is *impossible* to go too finely or think too much about details in landscape, so that they be rightly arranged and rightly massed; but that it is equally impossible to render anything like the fulness or the space of nature, except by that mystery or obscurity of execution which she herself uses, and in which Turner only has followed her.

SECTION III
Of Truth of Skies

CHAPTER I
Of the Open Sky

IT is a strange thing how little in general people know about the sky. It 343
is the part of creation in which nature has done more for the sake of
pleasing man, more for the sole and evident purpose of talking to him and
teaching him, than in any other of her works, and it is just the part in
which we least attend to her. There are not many of her other works in
which some more material or essential purpose than the mere pleasing of
man is not answered by every part of their organization; but every essential
purpose of the sky might, so far as we know, be answered, if once in three
days, or thereabouts, a great, ugly, black rain-cloud were brought up over
the blue, and everything well watered, and so all left blue again till next
time, with perhaps a film of morning and evening mist for dew. And
instead of this, there is not a moment of any day of our lives, when nature
is not producing scene after scene, picture after picture, glory after glory,
and working still upon such exquisite and constant principles of the most
perfect beauty, that it is quite certain it is all done for us, and intended for
our perpetual pleasure.[33] And every man, wherever placed, however far 344
from other sources of interest or of beauty, has this doing for him
constantly. The noblest scenes of the earth can be seen and known but by
few; it is not intended that man should live always in the midst of them;
he injures them by his presence, he ceases to feel them if he be always with
them: but the sky is for all; bright as it is, it is not

"Too bright or good
For human nature's daily food;"[34]

it is fitted in all its functions for the perpetual comfort and exalting of the heart, for soothing it and purifying it from its dross and dust. Sometimes gentle, sometimes capricious, sometimes awful, never the same for two moments together; almost human in its passions, almost spiritual in its tenderness, almost divine in its infinity, its appeal to what is immortal in us is as distinct, as its ministry of chastisement or of blessing to what is mortal is essential. And yet we never attend to it, we never make it a subject of thought, but as it has to do with our animal sensations: we look upon all by which it speaks to us more clearly than to brutes, upon all which bears witness to the intention of the Supreme that we are to receive more from the covering vault than the light and the dew which we share with the weed and the worm, only as a succession of meaningless and monotonous accident, too common and too vain to be worthy of a moment of watchfulness, or a glance of admiration. If in our moments of utter idleness and insipidity, we turn to the sky as a last resource, which of its phenomena do we speak of? One says it has been wet; and another, it has been windy; and another, it has been warm. Who, among the whole chattering crowd, can tell me of

345   the forms and the precipices of the chain of tall white mountains that girded the horizon at noon yesterday? Who saw the narrow sunbeam that came out of the south and smote upon their summits until they melted and mouldered away in a dust of blue rain? Who saw the dance of the dead clouds when the sunlight left them last night, and the west wind blew them before it like withered leaves? All has passed, unregretted as unseen; or if the apathy be ever shaken off, even for an instant, it is only by what is gross, or what is extraordinary; and yet it is not in the broad and fierce manifestations of the elemental energies, not in the clash of the hail, nor the drift of the whirlwind, that the highest characters of the sublime are developed. God is not in the earthquake, nor in the fire, but in the still, small voice. They are but the blunt and the low faculties of our nature, which can only be addressed through lamp-black and lightning. It is in quiet and subdued passages of unobtrusive majesty, the deep, and the calm, and the perpetual; that which must be sought ere it is seen, and loved ere it is understood; things which the angels work out for us daily, and yet vary eternally: which are never wanting, and never repeated; which are to be found always, yet each found but once; it is through these that the lesson of devotion is chiefly taught, and the blessing of beauty given. These are what the artist of highest aim must study; it is these, by the combination of which his ideal is to be created; these, of which so little notice is ordinarily taken by common observers, that I fully believe, little as people in general are concerned with art, more of their ideas of sky are derived from pictures than from reality; and that if we could examine the conception formed in the minds of most educated persons when we talk of clouds, it would frequently

346   be found composed of fragments of blue and white reminiscences of the old masters.

Let us begin then with the simple open blue of the sky. This is of course
the colour of the pure atmospheric air, not the aqueous vapour, but the
pure azote[35] and oxygen, and it is the total colour of the whole mass of
that air between us and the void of space. It is modified by the varying
quantity of aqueous vapour suspended in it, whose colour, in its most
imperfect and therefore most visible state of solution, is pure white (as in
steam); which receives, like any other white, the warm hues of the rays of
the sun, and, according to its quantity and imperfect solution, makes the
sky paler, and at the same time more or less grey, by mixing warm tones
with its blue. This grey aqueous vapour, when very decided, becomes mist,
and when local, cloud. Hence the sky is to be considered as a transparent
blue liquid, in which, at various elevations, clouds are suspended, those
clouds being themselves only particular visible spaces of a substance with
which the whole mass of this liquid is more or less impregnated. Now, we
all know this perfectly well, and yet we so far forget it in practice, that we   347
little notice the constant connection kept up by nature between her blue
and her clouds; and we are not offended by the constant habit of the old
masters, of considering the blue sky as totally distinct in its nature, and far
separated from the vapours which float in it. With them, cloud is cloud,
and blue is blue, and no kind of connection between them is ever hinted
at. The sky is thought of as a clear, high, material dome, the clouds as
separate bodies suspended beneath it; and in consequence, however
delicate and exquisitely removed in tone their skies may be, you always
look *at* them, not *through* them. And if you look intensely at the pure blue
of a serene sky, you will see that there is a variety and fulness in its very
repose. It is not flat dead colour, but a deep, quivering, transparent body
of penetrable air, in which you trace or imagine short falling spots of
deceiving light, and dim shades, faint veiled vestiges of dark vapour; and
it is this trembling transparency which our great modern master has
especially aimed at and given. His blue is never laid on in smooth coats,
but in breaking, mingling, melting hues, a quarter of an inch of which, cut   348
off from all the rest of the picture, is still *spacious*, still infinite and
immeasurable in depth. It is a painting of the air, something into which
you can see, through the parts which are near you, into those which are
far off; something which has no surface and through which we can plunge
far and farther, and without stay or end, into the profundity of space;—
whereas, with all the old landscape painters except Claude, you may
indeed go a long way before you come to the sky, but you will strike hard
against it at last. A perfectly genuine and untouched sky of Claude is
indeed most perfect, and beyond praise, in all qualities of air; though even
with him, I often feel rather that there is a great deal of pleasant air
between me and the firmament, than that the firmament itself is only air.
With the Poussins, there are no favourable exceptions. Their skies are

systematically wrong; take, for instance, the sky of the Sacrifice of Isaac
349 [Fig.14]. It is here high noon, as is shown by the shadow of the figures; and
what sort of colour is the sky at the top of the picture? Is it pale and grey
with heat, full of sunshine, and unfathomable in depth? On the contrary,
it is of a pitch of darkness which, except on Mont Blanc or Chimborazo,
is as purely impossible as colour can be. He might as well have painted it
coal black; and it is laid on with a dead coat of flat paint, having no one
quality or resemblance of sky about it. It cannot have altered, because the
land horizon is as delicate and tender in tone as possible, and is evidently
unchanged; and to complete the absurdity of the whole thing, this colour
holds its own, without graduation or alteration, to within three or four
degrees of the horizon, where it suddenly becomes bold and unmixed
yellow. Now the horizon at noon may be yellow when the whole sky is
covered with dark clouds, and only *one* open streak of light left in the
distance from which the whole light proceeds; but with a clear open sky,
and opposite the sun, at noon, such a yellow horizon as this is physically
impossible. Even supposing that the upper part of the sky were pale and
warm, and that the transition from the one hue to the other were effected
imperceptibly and gradually, as is invariably the case in reality, instead of
taking place within a space of two or three degrees; even then, this gold
yellow would be altogether absurd: but as it is, we have in this sky (and it
is a fine picture, one of the best of Gaspar's that I know) a notable example
of the truth of the old masters, two impossible colours impossibly united!
Find such a colour in Turner's noon-day zenith as the blue at the top, or
such a colour at a noon-day horizon as the yellow at the bottom, or such
a connection of any colours whatsoever as that in the centre, and then you
may talk about his being false to nature if you will. Again, look at the large
350 Cuyp in the Dulwich Gallery [plate 9], which Mr. Hazlitt considers the
"finest in the world," and of which he very complimentarily says, "The
tender green of the valleys, the gleaming lake, the purple light of the hills,
have an effect like the *down* on an unripe nectarine"![36] I ought to have
apologized before now, for not having studied sufficiently in Covent
Garden to be provided with terms of correct and classical criticism. One
of my friends begged me to observe the other day, that Claude was
"pulpy;" another added the yet more gratifying information that he was
"juicy;" and it is now happily discovered that Cuyp is "downy." Now I
dare say that the sky of this first-rate Cuyp is very like an unripe nectarine:
all that I have to say about it is, that it is exceedingly unlike a sky. The
blue remains unchanged and ungraduated over three-fourths of it, down to
the horizon; while the sun, in the left-hand corner, is surrounded with a
halo, first of yellow, and then of crude pink, both being separated from
each other, and the last from the blue, as sharply as the belts of a rainbow,
and both together not ascending ten degrees in the sky. Now it is difficult

to conceive how any man calling himself a painter could impose such a thing on the public, and still more how the public can receive it, as a representation of that sunset purple which invariably extends its influence to the zenith, so that there is no pure blue anywhere, but a purple increasing in purity gradually down to its point of greatest intensity (about forty-five degrees from the horizon), and then melting imperceptibly into the gold, the three colours extending their influence over the whole sky; so that throughout the whole sweep of the heaven, there is no one spot where the colour is not in an equal state of transition, passing from gold into orange, from that into rose, from that into purple, from that into blue, with absolute equality of change, so that in no place can it be said, "Here it changes," and in no place, "Here it is unchanging." This is invariably the case. There is no such thing—there never was, and never 351 will be such a thing, while God's heaven remains as it is made—as a serene, sunset sky, with its purple and rose in *belts* about the sun.

CHAPTER II
Of Truth of Clouds:—
First of the Region of the Cirrus

358   THE first and most important character of clouds is dependent on the different altitudes at which they are formed. The atmosphere may be conveniently considered as divided into three spaces, each inhabited by clouds of specific character altogether different, though, in reality, there is no distinct limit fixed between them by nature, clouds being formed at *every* altitude, and partaking, according to their altitude, more or less of the characters of the upper or lower regions. The scenery of the

359   sky is thus formed of an infinitely graduated series of systematic forms of cloud, each of which has its own region in which alone it is formed, and each of which has specific characters which can only be properly determined by comparing them as they are found clearly distinguished by intervals of considerable space. I shall therefore consider the sky as divided into three regions: the upper region, or region of the cirrus; the central region, or region of the stratus; the lower region, or the region of the rain-cloud.

    The clouds which I wish to consider as included in the upper region, never touch even the highest mountains of Europe, and may therefore be looked upon as never formed below an elevation of at least 15,000 feet; they are the motionless multitudinous lines of delicate vapour with which the blue of the open sky is commonly streaked or speckled after several days of fine weather. Their chief characters are:

    First, Symmetry. They are nearly always arranged in some definite and evident order, commonly in long ranks reaching sometimes from the zenith to the horizon, each rank composed of an infinite number of transverse bars of about the same length, each bar thickest in the middle, and terminating in a traceless vaporous point at each side; the ranks are in the direction of the wind, and the bars of course at right angles to it;

360   these latter are commonly slightly bent in the middle. The upper clouds always fall into some modification of one or other of these arrangements. They thus differ from all other clouds, in having a plan and system; whereas other clouds, though there are certain laws which they cannot

break, have yet perfect freedom from anything like a relative and general system of government.

Secondly, Sharpness of Edge. The edges of the bars of the upper clouds which are turned to the wind, are often the sharpest which the sky shows; no outline whatever of any other kind of cloud, however marked and energetic, ever approaches the delicate decision of these edges. On the other hand, the edge of the bar turned away from the wind is always soft, often imperceptible, melting into the blue interstice between it and its next neighbour.

Thirdly, Multitude. The delicacy of these vapours is sometimes carried into such an infinity of division, that no other sensation of number that the earth or heaven can give is so impressive. Number is always most felt when it is symmetrical, and, therefore, no sea-waves nor fresh leaves make their number so evident or so impressive as these vapours.   361

Fourthly, Purity of Colour. The nearest of these clouds, those over the observer's head, being at least three miles above him, and the greater number of those which enter the ordinary sphere of vision, farther from him still, their dark sides are much greyer and cooler than those of other clouds, owing to their distance. They are composed of the purest aqueous vapour, free from all foulness of earthy gases, and of this in the lightest and most ethereal state in which it can be, to be visible. Farther, they receive the light of the sun in a state of far greater intensity than lower objects, the beams being transmitted to them through atmospheric air far less dense, and wholly unaffected by mist, smoke, or any other impurity. Hence their colours are more pure and vivid, and their white less sullied than those of any other clouds.

Lastly, Variety. Variety is never so conspicuous, as when it is united with symmetry. The perpetual change of form in other clouds is monotonous in its very dissimilarity, nor is difference striking where no connection is implied; but if through a range of barred clouds crossing half the heaven, all governed by the same forces and falling into one general form, there be yet a marked and evident dissimilarity between each member of the great mass,—one more finely drawn, the next more delicately moulded, the next more gracefully bent, each broken into differently modelled and variously numbered groups,—the variety is doubly striking, because contrasted with the perfect symmetry of which it forms a part.   362

There is scarcely a painting of Turner's in which serenity of sky and intensity of light are aimed at together, in which these clouds are not used, though there are not two cases in which they are used altogether alike. But in all cases the exquisite manipulation of the master gives to each atom of the multitude its own character and expression. Though they be countless as leaves, each has its portion of light, its shadow, its reflex, its peculiar and separating form.   363

    364

fig.15   engraving after J.M.W.Turner, *Tornaro*, from Samuel Rogers' *Poems*

Take, for instance, the illustrated edition of Roger's Poems, and open it at the 80th page [fig.15], and observe how every attribute which I have pointed out in the upper sky is there rendered with the faithfulness of a mirror; the long lines of parallel bars, the delicate curvature from the wind, which the inclination of the sail shows you to be from the west; the excessive sharpness of every edge which is turned to the wind, the faintness of every opposite one, the breaking up of each bar into rounded masses; and finally, the inconceivable variety with which individual form has been given to every member of the multitude, and not only individual form, but roundness and substance even where there is scarcely a hair's-breadth of cloud to express them in. Observe above everything the varying indication of space and depth in the whole, so that you may look through and through from one cloud to another, feeling not merely how they retire to the horizon, but how they melt back into the recesses of the

365

sky; every interval being filled with absolute air, and all its spaces so melting and fluctuating, and fraught with change as with repose, that as you look, you will fancy that the rays shoot higher and higher into the vault of light, and that the pale streak of horizontal vapour is melting away from the cloud that it crosses. Now watch for the next barred sunrise, and take this vignette to the window, and test it by nature's own clouds, among which you will find forms and passages, I do not say merely *like*, but apparently the actual originals of parts of this very drawing. And with whom will you do this, except with Turner? Will you do it with Claude, and set that blank square yard of blue, with its round, white, flat fixtures of similar cloud, beside the purple infinity of nature, with her countless multitudes of shadowy lines, and flaky waves, and folded veils of variable mist? Will you do it with Poussin, and set those massy steps   366 of unyielding solidity, with the chariot and four driving up them, by the side of the delicate forms which terminate in threads too fine for the eye to follow them, and of texture so thin woven that the earliest stars shine through them? Will you do it with Salvator, and set that volume of violent and restless manufactory smoke beside those calm and quiet bars, which pause in the heaven as if they would never leave it more?

Of the colours of these clouds I have spoken before; but though I then   368 alluded to their purity and vividness, I scarcely took proper notice of their variety; there is indeed in nature variety in all things, and it would be absurd to insist on it in each case, yet the colours of these clouds are so marvellous in their changefulness, that they require particular notice. If you watch for the next sunset when there are a considerable number of these cirri in the sky, you will see, especially at the zenith, that the sky does not remain of the same colour for two inches together. One cloud has a dark side of cold blue, and a fringe of milky white; another, above it, has a dark side of purple and an edge of red; another, nearer the sun, has an under side of orange and an edge of gold: these you will find mingled with, and passing into, the blue of the sky, which in places you will not be able to distinguish from the cool grey of the darker clouds, and which will be itself full of gradation, now pure and deep, now faint and feeble. And all this is done, not in large pieces, nor on a large scale, but over and over again in every square yard, so that there is no single part nor portion of the whole sky which has not in itself variety of colour enough for a separate picture, and yet no single part which is like another, or which has not some peculiar source of beauty, and some peculiar arrangement of colour of its own. Now instead of this you get in the old masters,—Cuyp, or Claude, or whoever they may be,—a field of blue, delicately, beautifully, and uniformly shaded down to the yellow sun, with a certain number of similar clouds, each with a dark side of the same grey, and an edge of the same yellow. I do not say that nature never does anything like this, but I say that her *principle* is to do a great deal more; and that what she does more than this,—what I have above described, and what you may see in nine sunsets out of ten,—has been observed, attempted, and rendered by 369 Turner only, and by him with a fidelity and force which present us with more essential truth, and more clear expression and illustration of natural laws, in every wreath of vapour, than composed the whole stock of heavenly information which lasted Cuyp and Claude their lives.

CHAPTER III
Of Truth of Clouds:—Secondly, of the Central Cloud Region

W E have next to investigate the character of the Central Cloud 370
Region, which may be considered as occupying a space of air ten
thousand feet in height, extending from five to fifteen thousand feet
above the sea.

These clouds, according to their elevation, appear with great variety of
form, often partaking of the streaked or mottled character of the higher
region, and as often, when the precursors of storm, manifesting forms
closely connected with the lowest rain-clouds; but the species especially
characteristic of the central region is a white, ragged, irregular, and
scattered vapour, which has little form and less colour. When this vapour
collects into masses, it is partially rounded, clumsy, and ponderous, as if it
would tumble out of the sky, shaded with a dull grey, and totally devoid
of any appearance of energy or motion.

But although this kind of cloud is typical of the central region, it is not 371
one which nature is fond of. She scarcely ever lets an hour pass without
some manifestation of finer forms, sometimes approaching the upper cirri,
sometimes the lower cumulus. I shall, as before, glance rapidly at the great
laws of specific form, and so put it in the power of the reader to judge for
himself of the truth of representation.

Clouds, it is to be remembered, are not so much local vapour, as vapour
rendered locally visible by a fall of temperature.[37] Thus a cloud, whose
parts are in constant motion, will hover on a snowy mountain, pursuing
constantly the same track upon its flanks, and yet remaining of the same 372
size, the same form, and in the same place, for half a day together. No
matter how violent or how capricious the wind may be, the instant it
approaches the spot where the chilly influence of the snow extends, the
moisture it carries becomes visible, and then and there the cloud forms on
the instant, apparently maintaining its shape against the wind, though the
careful and keen eye can see all its parts in the most rapid motion across
the mountain. The outlines of such a cloud are of course not determined
by the irregular impulses of the wind, but by the fixed lines of radiant heat

which regulate the temperature of the atmosphere of the mountain. Another resultant phenomenon is the formation of cloud in the calm air to leeward of a steep summit; cloud whose edges are in rapid motion, where they are affected by the current of the wind above, and stream from the peak like the smoke of a volcano, yet always vanish at a certain distance from it as steam issuing from a chimney. When wet weather of some duration is approaching, a small white spot of cloud will sometimes appear low on the hill flanks; it will not move, but will increase gradually for some little time, then diminish, still without moving; disappear altogether, reappear ten minutes afterwards, exactly in the same spot: increase to a greater extent than before, again disappear, again return, and at last permanently; other similar spots of cloud forming simultaneously, with various fluctuations, each in its own spot, and at the same level on the hill-side, until all expand, join together, and form an unbroken veil of threatening

373 grey, which darkens gradually into storm. What in such cases takes place palpably and remarkably, is more or less a law of formation in all clouds whatsoever; they being bounded rather by lines expressive of changes of temperature in the atmosphere, than by the impulses of the currents of wind in which those changes take place. Even when in rapid and visible motion across the sky, the variations which take place in their outlines are not so much alterations of position and arrangement of parts, as they are the alternate formation and disappearance of parts. There is, therefore, usually a parallelism and consistency in their great outlines, which give system to the smaller curves of which they are composed; and if these great lines be taken, rejecting the minutiæ of variation, the resultant form will almost always be angular, and full of character and decision. In the flock-like fields of equal masses, each individual mass has the effect, not of an ellipse or circle, but of a rhomboid; the sky is crossed and chequered, not honey-combed; in the lower cumuli, even though the most rounded of all clouds, the groups are not like balloons or bubbles, but like towers or mountains. And the result of this arrangement in masses more or less angular, varied with, and chiefly constructed of, curves of the utmost freedom and beauty, is that appearance of exhaustless and fantastic energy which gives every cloud a marked character of its own, suggesting resemblances to the specific outlines of organic objects.

374 The minor contours, out of which the larger outlines are composed, are indeed beautifully curvilinear; but they are never monotonous in their curves. First comes a concave line, then a convex one, then an angular jag breaking off into spray, then a downright straight line, then a curve again, then a deep gap, and a place where all is lost and melted away, and so on; displaying in every inch of the form renewed and ceaseless invention, setting off grace with rigidity, and relieving flexibility with force, in a manner scarcely less admirable, and far more changeful, than even in the

muscular forms of the human frame.

Now it may, perhaps, for anything we know, or have yet proved, be highly expedient and proper, in art, that this variety, individuality, and angular character should be changed into a mass of convex curves, each precisely like its neighbour in all respects, and unbroken from beginning to end; it may be highly original, masterly, bold, whatever you choose to call it; but it is *false*. The clouds which God sends upon His earth as the minis-   375 ters of dew, and rain, and shade, and with which He adorns His heaven, setting them in its vault for the thrones of His spirits, have not, in one instant or atom of their existence, one feature in common with such conceptions and creations. And there are, beyond dispute, more direct and unmitigated falsehoods told, and more laws of nature set at open defiance, in *one* of the "rolling" skies of Salvator, such as that marked 159 in the Dulwich Gallery,[38] than were ever attributed, even by the ignorant and unfeeling, to all the wildest flights of Turner put together.

And it is not as if the error were only occasional. It is systematic and constant in all the Italian masters of the seventeenth century, and in most of the Dutch. They looked at clouds, as at everything else which did not particularly help them in their great end of deception, with utter carelessness and bluntness of feeling; saw that there were a great many rounded passages in them; found it much easier to sweep circles than to design beauties, and sat down in their studies, contented with perpetual repetitions of the same spherical conceptions, having about the same relation to the clouds of nature, that a child's carving of a turnip has to the head of the Apollo.

But it is not the outline only which is thus systematically false. The   376 drawing of the solid form is worse still, for it is to be remembered that although clouds of course arrange themselves more or less into broad masses, with a light side and dark side, both their light and shade are invariably composed of a series of divided masses, each of which has in its outline as much variety and character as the great outline of the cloud; presenting therefore, a thousand times repeated, all that I have described as characteristic of the general form. Nor are these multitudinous divisions a truth of slight importance in the character of sky, for they are dependent on, and illustrative of, a quality which is usually in a great degree overlooked,—the enormous retiring spaces of solid clouds. Between the illumined edge of a heaped cloud, and that part of its body which turns into shadow, there will generally be a clear distance of several miles, more or less, of course, according to the general size of the cloud; but, in such large masses as in Poussin and others of the old masters occupy the fourth or fifth of the visible sky, the clear illumined breadth of vapour, from the edge to the shadow, involves at least a distance of five or six miles. We are little apt, in watching the changes of a mountainous range

plate 1   John Brett, *The Glacier of Rosenlaui*, 1856

plate 2   John Ruskin, *La Cascade de la Folie, Chamouni*, 1849

plate 3 Claude Gellée, *Seaport with the Embarkation of the Queen of Sheba*

plate 4   J.M.W. Turner, *Dido building Carthage*

plate 5 J.M.W. Turner, *Richmond, Yorkshire*

plate 6 J.M.W. Turner, *The Slave Ship (Slavers throwing overboard the dead and the dying, Typhon coming on)*

377   of cloud, to reflect that the masses of vapour which compose it are huger and higher than any mountain range of the earth; and the distances between mass and mass are not yards of air traversed in an instant by the flying form, but valleys of changing atmosphere leagues over; that the slow motion of ascending curves, which we can scarcely trace, is a boiling energy of exulting vapour, rushing into the heaven a thousand feet in a minute; and that the toppling angle, whose sharp edge almost escapes notice in the multitudinous forms around it, is a nodding precipice of storms 3000 feet from base to summit. It is not until we have actually compared the forms of the sky with the hill ranges of the earth, and seen the soaring Alp overtopped and buried in one surge of the sky, that we begin to conceive or appreciate the colossal scale of the phenomena of the latter. But of this there can be no doubt in the mind of any one accustomed to trace the forms of clouds among hill ranges, as it is there a demonstrable and evident fact, that the space of vapour visibly extended over an ordinarily clouded sky is not less, from the point nearest to the observer to the horizon, than twenty leagues; that the size of every mass of separate form, if it be at all largely divided, is to be expressed in terms of *miles*; and that every boiling heap of illuminated mist in the nearer sky is an enormous mountain, fifteen or twenty thousand feet in height, six or seven miles over in illuminated surface, furrowed by a thousand colossal ravines, torn by local tempests into peaks and promontories, and changing its features with the majestic velocity of the volcano.

378   Now if an artist, taking for his subject a chain of vast mountains several leagues long, were to unite all their varieties of ravine, crag, chasm, and precipice, into one solid unbroken mass, with one light side and one dark side, looking like a white ball or parallelopiped two yards broad, the words "breadth," "boldness," "generalization," would scarcely be received as a sufficient apology for a proceeding so glaringly false, and so painfully degrading.

379   This is done, more or less, by all the old masters, without an exception. Their idea of clouds was altogether similar; more or less perfectly carried out, according to their power of hand and accuracy of eye, but universally the same in conception. It was the idea of a comparatively small, round, puffed-up white body, irregularly associated with other round and puffed-up white bodies, each with a white light side, and a grey dark side, and a soft reflected light, floating a great way below a blue dome. Such is the idea of a cloud formed by most people; it is the first, general, uncultivated notion of what we see every day.

380   But perhaps the most grievous fault of all, in the clouds of these painters, is the utter want of transparency. Not in her most ponderous and lightless masses will nature ever leave us without some evidence of transmitted sunshine; and she perpetually gives us passages in which the vapour

becomes visible only by the sunshine which it arrests and holds within itself, not caught on its surface, but entangled in its mass,—floating fleeces, precious with the gold of heaven; and this translucency is especially indicated on the dark sides even of her heaviest wreaths, which possess opalescent and delicate hues of partial illumination, far more dependent upon the beams which pass through them than on those which are reflected upon them. Nothing, on the contrary, can be more painfully and ponderously opaque than the clouds of the old masters universally. However far removed in aërial distance, and however brilliant in light, they never appear filmy or evanescent, and their light is always *on* them, not *in* them.

And be it remembered that all these faults and deficiencies are to be found in their drawing merely of the separate masses of the solid cumulus, the easiest drawn of all clouds. But nature scarcely ever confines herself to   381
such masses; they form but the thousandth part of her variety of effect. She builds up a pyramid of their boiling volumes, bars this across like a mountain with the grey cirrus, envelopes it in black, ragged, drifting vapour, covers the open part of the sky with mottled horizontal fields, breaks through these with sudden and long sunbeams, tears up their edges with local winds, scatters over the gaps of blue the infinity of multitude of the high cirri, and melts even the unoccupied azure into palpitating shades. And all this is done over and over again in every quarter of a mile. Now let us, keeping in memory what we have seen of Poussin and   382
Salvator, take up one of Turner's skies, and see whether *he* is as narrow in his conception, or as niggardly in his space. It does not matter which we take; his sublime Babylon [fig.16] is a fair example for our present purpose. Ten miles away, down the Euphrates, where it gleams last along the plain, he gives us a drift of dark elongated vapour, melting beneath into a dim haze which embraces the hills on the horizon. It is exhausted with its own motion, and broken up by the wind in its own mass into numberless groups of billowy and tossing fragments, which, beaten by the weight of storm down to the earth, are just lifting themselves again on wearied wings, and perishing in the effort. Above these, and far beyond them, the eye goes back to a broad sea of white illuminated mist, or rather cloud melted into rain, and absorbed again before that rain has fallen, but penetrated throughout, whether it be vapour or whether it be dew, with soft sunshine, turning it as white as snow. Gradually, as it rises, the rainy fusion ceases. You cannot tell where the film of blue on the left begins, but it is deepening, deepening still; and the cloud, with its edge first invisible, then all but imaginary, then just felt when the eye is *not* fixed on it, and lost when it is, at last rises, keen from excessive distance, but soft and mantling in its body as a swan's bosom fretted by faint wind; heaving fitfully against the delicate deep blue, with white waves, whose forms are traced by the pale lines of opalescent shadow, shade only because the light

fig.16 engraving after J.M.W. Turner, *Babylon*, from Finden's Bible

is within it, and not upon it, and which break with their own swiftness into a driven line of level spray, winnowed into threads by the wind, and flung before the following vapour like those swift shafts of arrowy water which a great cataract shoots into the air beside it, trying to find the earth. Beyond these, again, rises a colossal mountain of grey cumulus, through whose shadowed sides the sunbeams penetrate in dim, sloping, rain-like shafts; and over which they fall in a broad burst of streaming light, sinking to the earth, and showing through their own visible radiance the three successive ranges of hills which connect its desolate plain with space. Above, the edgy summit of the cumulus, broken into fragments, recedes into the sky, which is peopled in its serenity with quiet multitudes of the white, soft, silent cirrus; and, under these, again, drift near the zenith disturbed and impatient shadows of a darker spirit, seeking rest and finding none.

Now this is nature! It is the exhaustless living energy with which the universe is filled; and what will you set beside it of the works of other men? Show me a single picture, in the whole compass of ancient art, in which I can pass from cloud to cloud, from region to region, from first to second and third heaven, as I can here, and you may talk of Turner's want of truth.

383

CHAPTER IV
Of Truth Of Clouds:—Thirdly, of the Region of the Rain-Cloud

THE clouds which I wish to consider as characteristic of the lower, or 393
rainy region, differ not so much in their real nature from those of the
central and uppermost regions, as in appearance, owing to their greater
nearness.

In the first place, the clouds of the central region have, as has been
before observed, pure and aërial greys for their dark sides, owing to their
necessary distance from the observer; and as this distance permits a
multitude of local phenomena capable of influencing colour, such as
accidental sunbeams, refractions, transparencies, or local mists and
showers, to be collected into a space apparently small, the colours of these
clouds are always changeful and palpitating; and whatever degree of grey
or of gloom may be mixed with them is invariably pure and aërial. But 394
the nearness of the rain-cloud rendering it impossible for a number of
phenomena to be at once visible, makes its hue of grey monotonous, and
(by losing the blue of distance) warm and brown compared with that of the
upper clouds. This is especially remarkable on any part of it which may
happen to be illumined, such part being of a brown, bricky, ochreous tone,
never bright, always coming in dark outline on the lights of the central
clouds.

With these striking differences in colour, it presents no fewer nor less
important in form, chiefly from losing almost all definiteness of character
and outline. It is sometimes nothing more than a thin mist, whose outline
cannot be traced, rendering the landscape locally indistinct or dark; if its
outline be visible, it is ragged and torn, rather a spray of cloud, taken off
its edge and sifted by the wind, than an edge of the cloud itself. In fact, it
rather partakes of the nature, and assumes the appearance, of real water in
the state of spray, than of elastic vapour. This appearance is enhanced by
the usual presence of formed rain, carried along with it in a columnar
form, ordinarily of course reaching the ground like a veil, but very often
suspended with the cloud, and hanging from it like a jagged fringe, or over
it, in light, rain being always lighter than the cloud it falls from. These

columns or fringes of rain are often waved and bent by the wind, or twisted, sometimes even swept upwards from the clouds. The velocity of these vapours, though not necessarily in reality greater than that of the central clouds, appears greater, owing to their proximity, and, of course, also to the usual presence of a more violent wind. They are also apparently much more in the power of the wind, having less elastic force in themselves; but they are precisely subject to the same great laws of form which regulate the upper clouds. They are not solid bodies borne about with the wind, but they carry the wind with them, and cause it. Every one knows, who has ever been out in a storm, that the time when it rains heaviest is precisely the time when he cannot hold up his umbrella; that the wind is carried with the cloud, and lulls when it has passed. Every one who has ever seen rain in a hill country knows that a rain-cloud, like any other, may have all its parts in rapid motion, and yet, as a whole, remain in one spot. I remember once, when in crossing the Tête Noire, I had turned up the valley towards Trient, I noticed a rain-cloud forming on the Glacier de Trient. With a west wind, it proceeded towards the Col de Balme, being followed by a prolonged wreath of vapour, always forming exactly at the same spot over the glacier. This long, serpent-like line of cloud went on at a great rate till it reached the valley leading down from the Col de Balme, under the slate rocks of the Croix de Fer. There it turned sharp round, and came down this valley, at right angles to its former progress, and finally directly contrary to it, till it came down within five hundred feet of the village, where it disappeared; the line behind always advancing, and always disappearing, at the same spot. This continued for half an hour, the long line describing the curve of a horse-shoe; always coming into existence and always vanishing at exactly the same places; traversing the space between with enormous swiftness. This cloud, ten miles off, would have looked like a perfectly motionless wreath, in the form of a horse-shoe, hanging over the hills.

To the region of the rain-cloud belong also all the phenomena of drifted smoke, heat-haze, local mists in the morning or evening, in valleys or over water, mirage, white steaming vapour rising in evaporation from moist and open surfaces, and everything which visibly affects the condition of the atmosphere without actually assuming the form of cloud. These phenomena are as perpetual in all countries as they are beautiful, and afford by far the most effective and valuable means which the painter possesses, for modification of the forms of fixed objects. It is therefore matter of no little marvel to me, and I conceive that it can scarcely be otherwise to any reflecting person, that throughout the whole range of ancient landscape art there occurs no instance of the painting of a real rain-cloud, still less of any of the more delicate phenomena characteristic of the region. "Storms" indeed, as the innocent public persist in calling

fig.17   Gaspar Dughet, *Landscape with a Storm*

such abuses of nature and abortions of art as the two windy Gaspars in our
National Gallery [fig.17],[39] are common enough; massive concretions of
ink and indigo, wrung and twisted very hard, apparently in a vain effort
to get some moisture out of them; bearing up courageously and successfully
against a wind whose effects on the trees in the foreground can be
accounted for only on the supposition that they are all of the India-rubber
species. Enough of this, in all conscience, we have, and to spare; but for
the legitimate rain-cloud, with its ragged and spray-like edge, its veily   397
transparency, and its columnar burden of blessing, neither it, nor anything like it or approaching it, occurs in any painting of the old masters
that I have ever seen; and I have seen enough to warrant my affirming that
if it occur anywhere, it must be through accident rather than intention.

In passing to the works of our greatest modern master, it must be   400
premised that the qualities which constitute a most essential part of the
truth of the rain-cloud are in no degree to be rendered by engraving. What
we say of his works, therefore, must be understood as referring only to the
original drawings.

Jumièges [fig.18], in the Rivers of France, ought, perhaps, to be our first
object of attention. The haze of sunlit rain of this most magnificent   401
picture, the gradual retirement of the dark wood into its depth, and the

fig.18 J.M.W. Turner, *Jumièges*

sparkling and evanescent light which sends its variable flashes on the abbey, figures, foliage, and foam, require no comment; they speak home at once.

402   From this picture we should pass to the Llanthony [fig.8],[40] which is the rendering of the moment immediately following that given in the Jumièges. The shower is here half exhausted, half passed by, the last drops are rattling faintly through the glimmering hazel boughs, the white torrent, swelled by the sudden storm, flings up its hasty jets of springing spray to meet the returning light; and these, as if the heaven regretted what it had given, and were taking it back, pass as they leap, into vapour, and fall not again, but vanish in the shafts of the sunlight; hurrying, fitful, wind-woven sunlight, which glides through the thick leaves, and paces along the pale rocks like rain; half conquering, half quenched by the very mists which it summons itself from the lighted pastures as it passes, and gathers out of the drooping herbage and from the streaming crags; sending them with messages of peace to the far summits of the yet unveiled mountains, whose silence is still broken by the sound of the rushing rain.

403   In the Long Ships Lighthouse, Land's End [fig.19], we have clouds
404   without rain, at twilight, enveloping the cliffs of the coast, but concealing nothing, every outline being visible through their gloom; and not only the

fig.19   engraving after J.M.W. Turner, *Longships lighthouse, Land's End*

outline, for it is easy to do this, but the *surface*. The bank of rocky coast approaches the spectator inch by inch, felt clearer and clearer as it withdraws from the garment of cloud; not by edges more and more defined, but by a surface more and more unveiled. We have thus the painting, not of a mere transparent veil, but of a solid body of cloud, every inch of whose increasing distance is marked and felt. But the great wonder of the picture is the intensity of gloom which is attained in pure warm grey, without either blackness or blueness. It is a gloom dependent rather on the enormous space and depth indicated, than on actual pitch of colour; distant by real drawing, without a grain of blue; dark by real substance, without a stroke of blackness: and with all this, it is not formless, but full of indications of character, wild, irregular, shattered, and indefinite; full of the energy of storm, fiery in haste, and yet flinging back out of its motion the fitful swirls of bounding drift, of tortured vapour tossed up like men's hands, as in defiance of the tempest, the jets of resulting whirlwind, hurled back from the rocks into the face of the coming darkness, which, beyond all other characters, mark the raised passion of the elements. It is this untraceable, unconnected, yet perpetual form, this fulness of character absorbed in universal energy, which distinguish nature and Turner from all their imitators.

The drawing of Coventry [fig.20] may be particularized as a farther   405
example of this fine suggestion of irregularity and fitfulness, through very

fig.20   J.M.W. Turner, *Coventry*

constant parallelism of direction, both in rain and clouds. The great mass of cloud which traverses the whole picture is characterized throughout by severe right lines, nearly parallel with each other, into which every one of its wreaths has a tendency to range itself; but no one of these right lines is actually and entirely parallel to any other, though all have a certain tendency, more or less defined in each, which impresses the mind with the most distinct *idea* of parallelism. Neither are any of the lines actually straight and unbroken; on the contrary, they are all made up of the most exquisite and varied curves, and it is the imagined line which joins the apices of these, a tangent to them all, which is in reality straight. They are suggested, not represented, right lines: but the whole volume of cloud is visibly and totally bounded by them; and, in consequence, its whole body is felt to be dragged out and elongated by the force of the tempest which it carries with it, and every one of its wreaths to be (as was before explained) not so much something borne *before* or *by* the wind, as the visible form and presence of the wind itself.

406   But there is yet more to be noticed in this noble sky of Turner's. Not only are the lines of the rolling cloud thus irregular in their parallelism, but those of the falling rain are equally varied in their direction,

indicating the gusty changefulness of the wind, and yet kept so straight and stern in their individual descent, that we are not suffered to forget its strength. This impression is still farther enhanced by the drawing of the smoke, which blows every way at once, yet turning perpetually in each of its swirls back in the direction of the wind, but so suddenly and violently as almost to assume the angular lines of lightning. Farther, to complete the impression, be it observed that all the cattle, both upon the near and distant hill-side, have left off grazing, and are standing stock still and stiff, with their heads down and their backs to the wind; and finally, that we may be told not only what the storm is, but what it has been, the gutter at the side of the road is gushing in a complete torrent, and particular attention is directed to it by the full burst of light in the sky being brought just above it, so that all its waves are bright with the reflection.

But I have not quite done with this noble picture yet. Impetuous clouds,   407 twisted rain, flickering sunshine, fleeting shadow, gushing water, and oppressed cattle, all speak the same story of tumult, fitfulness, power, and velocity. Only one thing is wanted, a passage of repose to contrast with it all; and it is given. High and far above the dark volumes of the swift rain-cloud, are seen on the left, through their opening, the quiet, horizontal, silent flakes of the highest cirrus, resting in the repose of the deep sky. Of all else that we have noticed in this drawing, some faint idea can be formed from the engraving; but of the delicate and soft forms of these pausing vapours not the slightest, and still less of the exquisite depth and palpitating tenderness of the blue with which they are islanded.

To appreciate the full truth of this passage, we must understand another effect peculiar to the rain-cloud, that its openings exhibit the purest blue which the sky ever shows. For as we saw, in the first chapter in this section, that aqueous vapour always turns the sky more or less grey, it follows that we never can see the azure so intense as when the greater part of this vapour has just fallen in rain. Then, and then only, pure blue sky becomes visible in the first openings, distinguished especially by the manner in which the clouds melt into it; their edges passing off in faint white threads and fringes, through which the blue shines more and more intensely, till the last trace of vapour is lost in its perfect colour. It is only the upper white clouds, however, which do this, or the last fragments of   408 rain-clouds becoming white as they disappear, so that the blue is never *corrupted* by the cloud, but only paled and broken with pure white, the purest white which the sky ever shows. Thus we have a melting and palpitating colour, never the same for two inches together, deepening and broadening here and there into intensity of perfect azure, then drifting and dying away, through every tone of pure pale sky, into the snow white of the filmy cloud. Over this roll the determined edges of the rain-clouds, throwing it all far back, as a retired scene, into the upper sky. Of this effect the old masters, as far as I remember, have taken no cognizance whatsoever; all with them is, as we partially noticed before, either white cloud or pure blue: they have no notion of any double dealing or middle measures. They bore a hole in the sky, and let you up into a pool of deep stagnant blue, marked off by the clear round edges of imperturbable impenetrable cloud on all sides; beautiful in positive colour, but totally destitute of that exquisite gradation and change, that fleeting, panting, hesitating effort, with which the first glance of the natural sky is shed through the turbulence of the earth-storm.

They have some excuse, however, for not attempting this, in the nature of their material, as one accidental dash of the brush with water-colour, on a piece of wet or damp paper, will come nearer the truth and transparency of this rain-blue than the labour of a day in oils; and the purity and felicity of some of the careless, melting, water-colour skies of Cox and Tayler[41] may well make us fastidious in all effects of this kind. It is, however, only in the drawings of Turner that we have this perfect transparency and variation of blue given, in association with the perfection of considered form. In Tayler and Cox the forms are always partially accidental and unconsidered, often

409 essentially bad, and always incomplete: in Turner the dash of the brush is as completely under the rule of thought and feeling as its slowest line; all that it does is perfect, and could not be altered even in a hair's-breadth without injury; in addition to this, peculiar management and execution are used in obtaining quality in the colour itself, totally different from the manipulation of any other artist; and none, who have ever spent so much as one hour of their lives over his drawing, can forget those dim passages of dreamy blue, barred and severed with a thousand delicate and soft and snowy forms, which, gleaming in their patience of hope between the troubled rushings of the racked earth-cloud, melt farther and farther back into the height of heaven until the eye is bewildered and the heart lost in the intensity of their peace. I do not say that this is beautiful, I do not say it is ideal or refined, I only ask you to watch for the first opening of the clouds after the next south rain, and tell me if it be not *true*.

415 The conclusion, then, to which we are led by our present examination of the truth of clouds is, that the old masters attempted the representation of only one among the thousands of their systems of scenery, and were altogether false in the little they attempted; while we can find records in modern art of every form or phenomenon of the heavens from the highest film that glorifies the aether to the wildest vapour that darkens the dust, and in all these records, we find the most clear language and close thought, firm words and true message, unstinted fulness and unfailing faith.

And indeed it is difficult for us to conceive how, even without such laborious investigation as we have gone through, any person can go to nature for a single day or hour, when she is really at work in any of her nobler spheres of action, and yet retain respect for the old masters; finding, as find he will, that every scene which rises, rests, or departs before him, bears with it a thousand glories of which there is not one shadow, one image, one trace or line, in any of their works; but which will illustrate to him, at every new instant, some passage which he had not before understood in the high works of modern art. Stand upon the peak of some isolated mountain at daybreak, when the night mists first rise from off the plains, and watch their white and lake-like fields, as they float in   416 level bays and winding gulfs about the islanded summits of the lower hills, untouched yet by more than dawn, colder and more quiet than a windless sea under the moon of midnight; watch when the first sunbeam is sent upon the silver channels, how the foam of their undulating surface parts and passes away, and down under their depths the glittering city and green pasture lie like Atlantis, between the white paths of winding rivers; the flakes of light falling every moment faster and broader among the starry spires, as the wreathed surges break and vanish above them, and the confused crests and ridges of the dark hills shorten their grey shadows upon the plain. Has Claude given this? Wait a little longer, and you shall see those scattered mists rallying in the ravines, and floating up towards you, along the winding valleys, till they crouch in quiet masses, iridescent with the morning light, upon the broad breasts of the higher hills, whose leagues of massy undulation will melt back and back into that robe of material light, until they fade away, lost in its lustre, to appear again above, in the serene heaven, like a wild, bright, impossible dream, foundationless and inaccessible, their very bases vanishing in the unsubstantial and mocking blue of the deep lake below. Has Claude given this? Wait yet a little longer, and you shall see those mists gather themselves into white towers, and stand like fortresses along the promontories, massy and motionless, only piled with every instant higher and higher into the sky, and casting longer shadows athwart the rocks;   417 and out of the pale blue of the horizon you will see forming and advancing a troop of narrow, dark, pointed vapours, which will cover the sky, inch by inch, with their grey network, and take the light off the landscape with an eclipse which will stop the singing of the birds and the motion of the leaves, together; and then you will see horizontal bars of black shadow forming under them, and lurid wreaths create themselves, you know not how, along the shoulders of the hills; you never see them form, but when you look back to a place which was clear an instant ago, there is a cloud on it, hanging by the precipices, as a hawk pauses over his prey. Has Claude given this? And then you will hear the sudden rush of the awakened wind, and you will see those watch-towers of vapour swept away from their foundations, and waving curtains of opaque rain let down to the valleys, swinging from the burdened clouds in black bending fringes, or pacing in pale columns along the lake level, grazing its surface into foam as they go. And then, as the sun sinks, you shall see the storm drift for an instant from off the hills, leaving their broad sides smoking, and loaded yet with snow-white, torn, steam-like rags of capricious vapour, now gone, now gathered again; while the smouldering sun, seeming not far away, but burning like a red-hot ball beside you, and as if you could reach it, plunges through the rushing wind and rolling cloud with headlong fall, as if it meant to rise no more, dyeing all the air about it with blood. Has Claude given this? And then you shall hear the fainting tempest die in the hollow of the night, and you shall see a green halo kindling on the summit of the eastern hills, brighter—brighter yet, till the large white circle of the slow moon is lifted up among the barred clouds, step by step, line by line; star after star she quenches with her kindling light, setting in their stead an army of pale, penetrable, fleecy wreaths in the heaven, to give light upon the earth, which move together, hand in hand, company by company, troop by troop, so measured in their unity of motion, that the whole heaven seems to roll with them, and the earth to reel under them. Ask Claude, or his brethren, for that. And then wait yet for one hour, until the east again becomes purple, and the heaving mountains, rolling against it in darkness, like waves of a wild sea, are drowned one by one in the glory of its burning: watch the white glaciers blaze in their winding paths about the mountains, like mighty serpents with scales of fire: watch the columnar peaks of solitary snow, kindling downwards, chasm by chasm, each in itself a new morning; their long avalanches cast down in keen streams brighter than the lightning, sending each his tribute of driven snow, like altar-smoke, up to the heaven; the rose-light of their silent domes flushing that heaven about them and above them, piercing with purer light through its purple lines of lifted cloud, casting a new glory on every wreath as it passes by, until the whole heaven, one scarlet canopy, is interwoven with a roof of waving flame, and tossing, vault beyond vault, as with the drifted wings of many companies of angels: and then, when you can look no more for gladness, and when you are bowed down with fear and love of the Maker and Doer of this, tell me who has best delivered this His message unto men!

SECTION IV
Of Truth of Earth

CHAPTER I
Of General Structure

B Y truth of earth, we mean the faithful representation of the facts   425
and forms of the bare ground, considered as entirely divested of vegetation, through whatever disguise, or under whatever modification the
clothing of the landscape may occasion. Ground is to the landscape
painter what the naked human body is to the historical. The growth of
vegetation, the action of water and even of clouds upon it and around it,
are so far subject and subordinate to its forms, as the folds of the dress and
the fall of the hair are to the modulation of the animal anatomy. Nor is
this anatomy always so concealed, but in all sublime compositions,
whether of nature or art, it must be seen in its naked purity. The laws of
the organization of the earth are distinct and fixed as those of the animal
frame, simpler and broader, but equally authoritative and inviolable.
Their results may be arrived at without knowledge of the interior mechanism; but for that very reason ignorance of them is the more disgraceful,
and violation of them more unpardonable. They are in the landscape the
foundation of all other truths, the most necessary, therefore, even if they
were not in themselves attractive; but they are as beautiful as they are
essential, and every abandonment of them by the artist must end in
deformity as it begins in falsehood.

Mountains are to the rest of the body of the earth, what violent   427
muscular action is to the body of man. The muscles and tendons of its
anatomy are, in the mountain, brought out with force and convulsive
energy, full of expression, passion, and strength; the plains and the lower
hills are the repose and the effortless motion of the frame, when its
muscles lie dormant and concealed beneath the lines of its beauty, yet
ruling those lines in their every undulation. This, then, is the first grand
principle of the truth of the earth. The spirit of the hills is action, that of
the lowlands repose; and between these there is to be found every variety

of motion and of rest, from the inactive plain, sleeping like the firmament, with cities for stars, to the fiery peaks, which, with heaving bosoms and exulting limbs, with the clouds drifting like hair from their bright foreheads, lift up their Titan hands to heaven, saying, "I live for ever!"

But there is this difference between the action of the earth, and that of a living creature; that while the exerted limb marks its bones and tendons through the flesh, the excited earth casts off the flesh altogether, and its bones come out from beneath. Mountains are the bones of the earth, their highest peaks are invariably those parts of its anatomy which in the plains lie buried under five and twenty thousand feet of solid thickness of superincumbent soil, and which spring up in the mountain ranges in vast pyramids or wedges, flinging their garment of earth away from them on each side. The masses of the lower hills are laid over and against their sides, like the masses of lateral masonry against the skeleton arch of an unfinished bridge, except that they slope up to and lean against the central ridge: and, finally, upon the slopes of these lower hills are strewed the level beds of sprinkled gravel, sand, and clay, which form the extent of the champaign. Here then is another grand principle of the truth of earth, that the mountains must come from under all, and be the support of all; and that everything else must be laid in their arms, heap above heap, the plains being the uppermost.

We find, according to this its internal structure, that the earth may be considered as divided into three great classes of formation, which geology has already named for us. Primary: the rocks, which, though in position lower than all others, rise to form the central peaks, or interior nuclei of all mountain ranges. Secondary: the rocks which are laid in beds above these, and which form the greater proportion of all hill scenery. Tertiary: the light beds of sand, gravel, and clay, which are strewed upon the surface of all, forming plains and habitable territory for man. We shall find it convenient, in examining the truth of art, to adopt, with a little modification, the geological arrangement, considering, first, the formation and character of the highest or central peaks; next, the general structure of the lower mountains, including in this division those composed of the various slates which a geologist would call primary; and, lastly, the minutiae and most delicate characters of the beds of these hills, when they are so near as to become foreground objects, and the structure of the common soil which usually forms the greater space of an artist's foreground.

CHAPTER II
Of the Central Mountains

IT does not always follow, because a mountain is the highest of its group,   431
that it is in reality one of the central range. But the central peaks are
usually the highest, and may be considered as the chief components of all
mountain scenery in the snowy regions. Being composed of the same rocks
in all countries, their external character is the same everywhere.

Their summits are almost invariably either pyramids or wedges. Domes
may be formed by superincumbent snow, or appear to be formed by the
continuous outline of a sharp ridge seen transversely, with its precipice to
the spectator; but wherever a rock appears, the uppermost termination of
that rock will be a steep edgy ridge, or a sharp point, very rarely presenting
even a gentle slope on any of its sides, but usually inaccessible unless
encumbered with snow.

These pyramids and wedges split vertically, or nearly so, giving smooth
faces of rock, either perpendicular, or very steeply inclined, which appear
to be laid against the central wedge or peak, like planks upright against a
wall.

Hence, however the light may fall, these peaks are seen marked with   432
sharp and defined shadows, indicating the square edges of the planks of
which they are made up. Where there has been much disintegration, the
peak is often surrounded with groups of lower ridges or peaks, like the
leaves of an artichoke or a rose, all evidently part and parcel of the great
peak; but falling back from it, as if it were a budding flower, expanding its
leaves one by one.

Now, whenever these vast peaks, rising from 12,000 to 24,000 feet   434
above the sea, form part of anything like a landscape; that is to say,
whenever the spectator beholds them from the region of vegetation, or
even from any distance at which it is possible to get something like a view
of their whole mass, they must be at so great a distance from him as to
become aërial and faint in all their details. Most artists would treat a
horizon fifteen miles off very much as if it were mere air; and though the
greater clearness of the upper air permits the high summits to be seen with
extraordinary distinctness, yet they never can by any possibility have dark

435   or deep shadows, or intense dark relief against a light. Clear they may be, but faint they must be; and their great and prevailing characteristic, as distinguished from other mountains, is want of apparent solidity.

Now, let me once more ask, though I am sufficiently tired of asking, what record have we of anything like this in the works of the old masters? There is no vestige, in any existing picture, of the slightest effort to represent the high hill ranges; and as for such drawing of their forms as we have found in Turner, we might as well look for them among the Chinese. Very possibly it may be all quite right; very probably these men showed the most cultivated taste, and most unerring judgment, in filling their pictures with mole-hills and sand-heaps. Very probably the withered and poisonous banks of Avernus, and the sand and cinders of the Campagna, are much more sublime things than the Alps; but still what limited truth it is, if truth it be, when through the last fifty pages we have been pointing out fact after fact, scene after scene, in clouds and hills (and not individual facts or scenes, but great and important classes of them), and still we have nothing to say when we come to the old masters; but "they are not here." Yet this is what we hear so constantly called painting "general" nature.

436   Although, however, there is no vestige among the old masters of any effort to represent the attributes of the higher mountains seen in comparative proximity, we are not altogether left without evidence of their having thought of them as sources of light in the extreme distance; as for example, in that of the reputed Claude in our National Gallery,

437   called the Marriage of Isaac and Rebecca [fig.13].[42] In the distance of that picture is something white, which I believe must be intended for a snowy mountain, because I do not see that it can well be intended for anything else. Now no mountain of elevation sufficient to be so sheeted with perpetual snow can, by any possibility, sink so low on the horizon as this something of Claude's, unless it be at a distance of from fifty to seventy miles. At such distances, though the outline is invariably sharp and edgy to an excess, yet all the circumstances of aërial perspective, faintness of shadow, and isolation of light, which I have described as characteristic of the Alps fifteen miles off, take place, of course, in a three-fold degree; the mountains rise from the horizon like transparent films, only distinguishable from mist by their excessively keen edges, and their brilliant flashes of sudden light; they are as unsubstantial as the air itself, and impress their enormous size by means of this aërialness, in a far greater degree at these vast distances, than even when towering above the spectator's head. Now, I ask of the candid observer, if there be the smallest vestige of an effort to attain, if there be the most miserable, the most contemptible, shadow of attainment of such an effect by Claude. Does that white thing on the horizon look seventy miles off? Is it faint, or fading, or to be looked for by the

eye before it can be found out? Does it look high? does it look large? does
it look impressive? You cannot but feel that there is not a vestige of any
kind or species of truth in that horizon; and that, however artistical it may
be, as giving brilliancy to the distance (though, as far as I have any feeling
in the matter, it only gives coldness), it is, in the very branch of art on   438
which Claude's reputation chiefly rests, aërial perspective, hurling
defiance to nature in her very teeth.

But there are worse failures yet in this unlucky distance. No mountain
was ever raised to the level of perpetual snow, without an infinite
multiplicity of form. Its foundation is built of a hundred minor mountains,
and, from these, great buttresses run in converging ridges to the central
peak. There is no exception to this rule; no mountain 15,000 feet high
is ever raised without such preparation and variety of outwork. Consequently, in distant effect, when chains of such peaks are visible at once,
the multiplicity of form is absolutely oceanic; and though it is possible in
near scenes to find vast and simple masses composed of lines which run
unbroken for a thousand feet or more, it is physically impossible when
these masses are thrown seventy miles back to have simple outlines, for
then these large features become mere jags and hillocks, and are heaped
and huddled together in endless confusion. Hence these mountains of
Claude, having no indication of the steep vertical summits which we have
shown to be the characteristic of the central ridges, having soft edges
instead of decisive ones, simple forms (one line to the plain on each side)
instead of varied and broken ones, and being painted with a crude raw
white, having no transparency, nor filminess, nor air in it, instead of
rising in the opalescent mystery which invariably characterizes the distant
snows, have the forms and the colours of heaps of chalk in a lime-kiln, not
of Alps. They are destitute of energy, of height, of distance, of splendour,
and of variety, and are the work of a man, whether Claude or not, who had
neither feeling for nature, nor knowledge of art.

The multiplicity of form which I have shown to be necessary in the   439
outline, is not less felt in the body of the mass. For, in all extensive hill
ranges, there are five or six lateral chains separated by deep valleys, which
rise between the spectator and the central ridge, showing their tops one
over another, wave beyond wave, until the eye is carried back to the
faintest and highest forms of the principal chain. These successive ridges,
and I speak now not merely of the Alps, but of mountains generally, show
themselves, in extreme distance, merely as vertical shades, with very
sharp outlines, detached from one another by greater intensity, according
to their nearness. It is with the utmost difficulty that the eye can discern
any solidity or roundness in them; the lights and shades of solid form are
both equally lost in the blue of the atmosphere, and the mountain tells
only as a flat sharp-edged film, of which multitudes intersect and overtop

each other, separated by the greater faintness of the retiring masses. This is the most simple and easily imitated arrangement possible, and yet, both in nature and art, it expresses distance and size in a way otherwise quite unattainable.

440   I may point out, in illustration of these facts, the engravings of two drawings of precisely the same chain of distant hills; Stanfield's Borromean Islands [fig.21],[43] with the St. Gothard in the distance; and
441   Turner's Arona [plate 10], also with the St. Gothard in the distance. The former of these plates is an example of everything which a hill distance is not, and the latter of everything which it is. In the former, we have the mountains covered with patchy lights, which being of equal intensity, whether near or distant, confuse all the distances together; while the eye,

fig.21   engraving after Clarkson Stanfield, *Lago Maggiore* from
Heath's Picturesque Annual, 1832

perceiving that the light falls so as to give details of solid form, yet finding nothing but insipid and formless spaces displayed by it, is compelled to suppose that the whole body of the hills is equally monotonous and devoid of character; and the effect upon it is not one whit more impressive and agreeable than might be received from a group of sand-heaps, washed into uniformity by recent rain.

Compare with this the distance of Turner in Arona. It is totally impossible here to say which way the light falls on the distant hills, except by the slightly increased decision of their edges turned towards it, but the greatest attention is paid to get these edges decisive, yet full of gradation, and perfectly true in character of form. All the rest of the mountain is then undistinguishable haze; and by the bringing of these edges more and more decisively over one another, Turner has given us, between the right-hand side of the picture and the snow, fifteen distinct distances, yet every one of these distances in itself palpitating, changeful, and suggesting sub-division into countless multitude.

These truths are invariably given in every one of Turner's distances,   442 that is to say, we have always in them two principal facts forced on our notice: transparency, or filminess of mass, and excessive sharpness of edge.

CHAPTER III
Of The Inferior Mountains

450 WE have next to investigate the character of those intermediate masses which constitute the greater part of all hill scenery, forming the outworks of the high ranges, and being almost the sole constituents of such lower groups as those of Cumberland, Scotland, or South Italy.

All mountains whatsoever, not composed of granite or gneiss rocks, nor volcanic (these latter being comparatively rare), are composed of beds, not of homogeneous, heaped materials, but of accumulated layers, whether of rock or soil. It may be slate, sandstone, limestone, gravel, or clay; but whatever the substance, it is laid in layers, not in a mass. In consequence of this division into beds, every mountain will have two great sets of lines more or less prevailing in its contours: one indicative of the surfaces of the beds, where they come out from under each other; and the other indicative of the extremities or edges of the beds, where their continuity has been interrupted.

Farther, in almost all rocks there is a third division of substance, which gives to their beds a tendency to split transversely in some directions rather than others, giving rise to what geologists call "joints," and throw-451 ing the whole rock into blocks more or less rhomboidal; so that the beds are not terminated by torn or ragged edges, but by faces comparatively smooth and even, usually inclined to each other at some definite angle. The whole arrangement may be tolerably represented by the bricks of a wall, whose tiers may be considered as strata, and whose sides and extremities will represent the joints by which those strata are divided, varying, however, their direction in different rocks, and in the same rock under differing circumstances.

Finally, in the greater number of *mountain* rocks, we find another most conspicuous feature of general structure, the lines of lamination, which divide the whole rock into an infinite number of delicate plates or layers, sometimes parallel to the direction or "strike" of the strata, oftener obliquely crossing it, and sometimes, apparently, altogether independent of it, maintaining a consistent and unvarying slope through a series of beds contorted and undulating in every conceivable direction.

This then is the broad organization of all hills, modified afterwards by   452
time and weather, concealed by superincumbent soil and vegetation, and
ramified into minor and more delicate details in a way presently to be
considered, but nevertheless universal in its great first influence, and
giving to all mountains a particular cast and inclination; like the exertion
of voluntary power in a definite direction, an internal spirit, manifesting
itself in every crag, and breathing in every slope, flinging and forcing the
mighty mass towards the heaven with an expression and an energy like
that of life.

Now, if I had to give a clear idea of this organization of the lower hills,   453
where it is seen in its greatest perfection, with a mere view to geological
truth, I should not refer to any geological drawings, but I should take the
Loch Coriskin of Turner [plate 11]. Looking at any group of the multitudinous lines which make up this mass of mountain, they appear to be
running anywhere and everywhere; there are none parallel to each other,
none resembling each other for a moment; yet the whole mass is felt at
once to be composed with the most rigid parallelism, the surfaces of the
beds towards the left, their edges or escarpments towards the right. In the
centre, near the top of the ridge, the edge of a bed is beautifully defined,
casting its shadow on the surface of the one beneath it; this shadow
marking, by three jags, the chasms caused in the inferior one by three of
its parallel joints. Every peak in the distance is evidently subject to the
same great influence, and the evidence is completed by the flatness and
evenness of the steep surfaces of the beds which rise out of the lake on the
extreme right, parallel with those in the centre.

Now compare with this the second mountain from the left in the picture   454
of Salvator, in the Dulwich Gallery.[44] The whole is first laid in with a very
delicate and masterly grey, right in tone, agreeable in colour, quite
unobjectionable for a beginning. But how is this made into rock? On the   455
light side Salvator gives us a multitude of touches, all exactly like one
another, and therefore, it is to be hoped, quite patterns of perfection in
rock drawing, since they are too good to be even varied. Every touch is a
dash of the brush, as nearly as possible in the shape of a comma, round and
bright at the top, convex on its right side, concave on its left, and melting
off at the bottom into the grey. These are laid in confusion one above
another, some paler, some brighter, some scarcely discernible, but all alike
in shape. Now, I am not aware myself of any particular object, either in
earth or heaven, which these said touches do at all resemble or portray. I
do not, however, assert that they may not resemble something; feathers,
perhaps; but I do say, and say with perfect confidence, that they may be
Chinese for rocks, or Sanscrit for rocks, or symbolical of rocks in some
mysterious and undeveloped character; but that they are no more *like*
rocks than the brush that made them. The dark sides appear to embrace

and overhang the lights; they cast no shadows, are broken by no fissures, and furnish, as food for contemplation, nothing but a series of concave curves.

Yet if we go on we shall find something a great deal worse.[45] I can believe Gaspar Poussin capable of committing as much sin against nature as most people; but I certainly do not suspect him of having had any hand in this thing, at least after he was ten years old. Nevertheless, it shows what he is supposed capable of by his admirers, and will serve for a broad illustration of all those absurdities which he himself in a less degree, and with feeling and thought to atone for them, perpetually commits. Take the white bit of rock on the opposite side of the river, just above the right

456   arm of the Niobe, and tell me of what the square green daubs of the brush at its base can be conjectured to be typical. There is no cast shadow, no appearance of reflected light, of substance, or of character on the edge; nothing, in short, but pure staring green paint, scratched heavily on a white ground. Nor is there a touch in the picture more expressive. All are the mere dragging of the brush here and there and everywhere, without meaning or intention; winding, twisting, zigzagging, doing anything in fact which may serve to break up the light and destroy its breadth, without bestowing in return one hint or shadow of anything like form. This picture is, indeed, an extraordinary case, but the Salvator above mentioned is a characteristic and exceedingly favourable example of the usual mode of mountain drawing among the old landscape painters. Their admirers may

457   be challenged to bring forward a single instance of their expressing, or even appearing to have noted, the great laws of structure above explained.

We ought, when speaking of their stratification, to have noticed another great law, which must, however, be understood with greater latitude of application than any of the others, as very far from imperative or constant in particular cases, though universal in its influence on the aggregate of all. It is that the lines by which rocks are terminated, are always steeper and more inclined to the vertical as we approach the summit of the mountain. Thousands of cases are to be found in every group, of rocks and lines horizontal at the top of the mountain and vertical at the bottom; but they are still the exceptions, and the average out of a given number of lines in any rock formation whatsoever will be found increasing in perpendicularity as they rise. Consequently the great skeleton lines of rock outline are always concave; that is to say, all distant ranges of rocky mountain approximate more or less to a series of concave curves, meeting in peaks, like a range of posts with chains hanging between.

458   But, although this is the primary form of all hills, and that which will always cut against the sky in every distant range, there are two great influences whose tendency is directly the reverse, and which modify, to a

great degree, both the evidences of stratification and this external form. These are aqueous erosion and disintegration. The latter only is to be taken into consideration when we have to do with minor features of crag: but the former is a force in constant action, of the very utmost importance; a force to which one half of the great outlines of all mountains is entirely owing, and which has much influence upon every one of their details.

Now the tendency of aqueous action over a large elevated surface is *always* to make that surface symmetrically and evenly convex and dome-like, sloping gradually more and more as it descends, until it reaches an inclination of about 40°, at which slope it will descend perfectly straight to the valley; for at that slope the soil washed from above will accumulate upon the hill-side, as it cannot lie in steeper beds. This influence, then, is exercised more or less on all mountains, with greater or less effect in proportion as the rock is harder or softer, more or less liable to decomposition, more or less recent in date of elevation, and more or less characteristic in its original forms; but it universally induces, in the lower parts of mountains, a series of the most exquisitely symmetrical convex curves, terminating, as they descend to the valley, in uniform and uninterrupted slopes; this symmetrical structure being perpetually interrupted by cliffs and projecting masses, which give evidence of the interior parallelism of the mountain anatomy, but which interrupt the convex forms more frequently by rising out of them, than by indentation.

There remains but one fact more to be noticed. All mountains, in some degree, but especially those which are composed of soft or decomposing 459 substance, are delicately and symmetrically furrowed by the descent of streams. The traces of their action commence at the very summits, fine as threads, and multitudinous, like the uppermost branches of a delicate tree. They unite in groups as they descend, concentrating gradually into dark undulating ravines, into which the body of the mountain descends on each side, at first in a convex curve, but at the bottom with the same uniform slope on each side which it assumes in its final descent to the plain, unless the rock be very hard, when the stream will cut itself a vertical chasm at the bottom of the curves, and there will be no even slope. If, on the other hand, the rock be very soft, the slopes will increase rapidly in height and depth from day to day; washed away at the bottom and crumbling at the top, until, by their reaching the summit of the masses of rock which separate the active torrents, the whole mountain is divided into a series of pent-house-like ridges, all guiding to its summit, and becoming steeper and narrower as they ascend; these in their turn being divided by similar but smaller ravines, caused in the same manner, into the same kind of ridges; and these again by another series, the arrangement being carried finer and farther according to the softness of the rock.

460   Now we wish to draw especial attention to the broad and bold simplicity of mass, and the excessive complication of details, which influences like these, acting on an enormous scale, must inevitably produce in all mountain groups: because each individual part and promontory, being compelled to assume the same symmetrical curves as its neighbours, and to descend at precisely the same slope to the valley, falls in with their prevailing lines, and becomes a part of a great and harmonious whole, instead of an unconnected and discordant individual. Hence we see that

461   the same imperative laws which require perfect simplicity of mass, require infinite and termless complication of detail; that there will not be an inch nor a hair's-breadth of the gigantic heap which has not its touch of separate character, its own peculiar curve, stealing out for an instant and then melting into the common line; felt for a moment by the blue mist of the hollow beyond, then lost when it crosses the enlightened slope; that all this multiplicity will be grouped into larger divisions, each felt by its increasing aërial perspective, and its instants of individual form, these into larger, and these into larger still, until all are merged in the great impression and prevailing energy of the two or three vast dynasties which divide the kingdom of the scene.

There is no vestige nor shadow of approach to such treatment as this in the whole compass of ancient art. Whoever the master, his hills, wherever he has attempted them, have not the slightest trace of association or connection; they are separate, conflicting, confused, petty and paltry heaps of earth; there is no marking of distances or divisions in their body; they may have holes in them, but no valleys,—protuberances and excrescences, but no parts; and, in consequence, are invariably diminutive and contemptible in their whole appearance and impression.

But look at the mass of mountain on the right in Turner's Daphne hunting with Leucippus [fig.22].[46] It is simple, broad, and united as one surge of a swelling sea; it rises in an unbroken line along the valley, and lifts its promontories with an equal slope. But it contains in its body ten thousand hills. There is not a quarter of an inch of its surface without its suggestion of increasing distance and individual form. First, on the right, you have a range of tower-like precipices, the clinging wood climbing along their ledges and cresting their summits, white waterfalls

462   gleaming through its leaves; not, as in Claude's scientific ideals, poured in vast torrents over the top, and carefully keeping all the way down on the most projecting parts of the sides; but stealing down, traced from point to point, through shadow after shadow, by their evanescent foam and flashing light,—here a wreath, and there a ray,—through the deep chasms and hollow ravines, out of which rise the soft rounded slopes of mightier mountain, surge beyond surge, immense and numberless, of delicate and gradual curve, accumulating in the sky until their garment

fig.22   J.M.W. Turner, *Apollo and Daphne*

of forest is exchanged for the shadowy fold of slumbrous morning cloud,
above which the utmost silver peak shines islanded and alone. Put what
mountain painting you will beside this, of any other artist, and its heights
will look like mole-hills in comparison, because it will not have the unity
and the multiplicity which are in nature, and with Turner, the signs of
size.

Again, in the Avalanche and Inundation,[47] we have for the whole
subject nothing but one vast bank of united mountain, and one stretch of
uninterrupted valley. Though the bank is broken into promontory beyond
promontory, peak above peak, each the abode of a new tempest, the
arbiter of a separate desolation, divided from each other by the rushing of
the snow, by the motion of the storm, by the thunder of the torrent; the
mighty unison of their dark and lofty line, the brotherhood of ages, is
preserved unbroken: and the broad valley at their feet, though measured
league after league away by a thousand passages of sun and darkness, and
marked with fate beyond fate of hamlet and of inhabitant, lies yet but as
a straight and narrow channel, a filling furrow before the flood. Whose
work will you compare with this? Salvator's grey heaps of earth, seven
yards high, covered with bunchy brambles that we may be under no
mistake about the size, thrown about at random in a little plain, beside a
zigzagging river just wide enough to admit of the possibility of there being   463
fish in it, and with banks just broad enough to allow the respectable angler
or hermit to sit upon them conveniently in the foreground? Is there more
of nature in such paltriness, think you, than in the valley and the
mountain which bend to each other like the trough of the sea; with the

flank of the one swept in one surge into the height of heaven, until the pine forests lie on its immensity like the shadows of narrow clouds, and the hollow of the other laid league by league into the blue of the air, until its white villages flash in the distance only like the fall of a sunbeam?

465   I do not mean to assert that this great painter is acquainted with the geological laws and facts he has thus illustrated; I am not aware whether he be or not; I merely wish to demonstrate, in points admitting of demonstration, that intense observation of, and strict adherence to, truth, which it is impossible to demonstrate in its less tangible and more delicate mani-

466 festations. However I may *feel* the truth of every touch and line, I cannot *prove* truth, except in large and general features; and I leave it to the arbitration of every man's reason, whether it be not likely that the painter who is thus so rigidly faithful in great things that every one of his pictures might be the illustration of a lecture on the physical sciences, is not likely to be faithful also in small.

CHAPTER IV

Of the Foreground

WE have now only to observe the close characteristics of the rocks   473
and soils to which the large masses of which we have been speaking
owe their ultimate characters.

We have already seen that there exists a marked distinction between
those stratified rocks whose beds are amorphous and without subdivision,
as many limestones and sandstones, and those which are divided by lines
of lamination, as all slates. The last kind of rock is the more frequent in
nature, and forms the greater part of all hill scenery. It has, however, been
successfully grappled with by few, even of the moderns, except Turner;
while there is no single example of any aim at it or thought of it among
the ancients, whose foregrounds, as far as it is possible to guess at their
intention through their concentrated errors, are chosen from among the
tufa and travertin of the lower Apennines (the ugliest as well as the least
characteristic rocks of nature), and whose larger features of rock scenery,
if we look at them with a predetermination to find in them a resemblance
of *something*, may be pronounced at least liker the mountain limestone
than anything else. I shall glance, therefore, at the general characters of
these materials first, in order that we may be able to appreciate the fidelity
of rock-drawing on which Salvator's reputation has been built.

The massive limestones separate generally into irregular blocks, tending
to the form of cubes or parallelopipeds, and terminated by tolerably
smooth planes. The weather, acting on the edges of these blocks, rounds
them off; but the frost, which, while it cannot penetrate nor split the body   474
of the stone, acts energetically on the angles, splits off the rounded
fragments, and supplies sharp, fresh, and complicated edges. Thus, as a
general principle, if a rock have character anywhere, it would be on the
angle; and however even and smooth its great planes may be, it will
usually break into variety where it turns a corner. It follows from this
structure that the edges of all rock being partially truncated, first by large
fractures, and then by the rounding of the fine edges of these by the
weather, perpetually present *convex* transitions from the light to the dark
side, the planes of the rock almost always swelling a little *from* the angle.

Now it will be found throughout the works of Salvator, that his most usual practice was to give a *concave* sweep of the brush for his first expression of the dark side, leaving the paint darkest towards the light; by which daring and original method of procedure he has succeeded in covering his foregrounds with forms which approximate to those of drapery, of ribands, of crushed cocked hats, of locks of hair, of waves, leaves, or anything, in short, flexible or tough, but which of course are not only unlike, but directly contrary to, the forms which nature has impressed on rocks. And the circular and sweeping strokes or stains which are dashed at random over their surfaces, only fail of destroying all resemblance whatever to rock structure from their frequent want of any meaning at all, and from the impossibility of our supposing any of them to be representative of shade. Now, if there be any part of landscape in which nature develops her principles of light and shade more clearly than another, it is rock; for the dark sides of fractured stone receive brilliant reflexes from the lighted surfaces, on which the shadows are marked with the most exquisite precision, especially because, owing to the parallelism of cleavage, the surfaces lie usually in directions nearly parallel. So far are the works of the old landscape painters from rendering this, that it is exceedingly rare to find a single passage in which the shadow can even be distinguished from the dark side—they scarcely seem to know the one to be darker than the other; and the strokes of the brush are not used to explain or express a form known or conceived, but are dashed and daubed about without any aim beyond the covering of the canvas. "A rock," the old masters appear to say to themselves, "is a great, irregular, formless, characterless lump; but it must have shade upon it, and any grey marks will do for that shade."

Finally, while few, if any, of the rocks of nature are untraversed by delicate and slender fissures, whose black sharp lines are the only means by which the peculiar quality in which rocks most differ from the other objects of the landscape, brittleness, can be effectually suggested, we look in vain among the blots and stains with which the rocks of ancient art are loaded, for any vestige or appearance of fissure or splintering. Toughness and malleability appear to be the qualities whose expression is most aimed at; sometimes sponginess, softness, flexibility, tenuity, and occasionally transparency.

Before passing to Turner, let us take one more glance at the foregrounds of the old masters, with reference, not to their management of rock, which is comparatively a rare component part of their foregrounds, but to the common soil which they were obliged to paint constantly, and whose forms and appearances are the same all over the world. A steep bank of loose earth of any kind, that has been at all exposed to the weather, contains in it, though it may not be three feet high, features capable of giving high gratification to a careful observer. It is almost a facsimile of a mountain slope of soft and decomposing rock; it possesses nearly as much variety of character, and is governed by laws of organization no less rigid. It is furrowed in the first place by undulating lines, caused by the descent of the rain; little ravines, which are cut precisely at the same slope as those of the mountain, and leave ridges scarcely less graceful in their contour, and beautifully sharp in their chiselling. Where a harder knot of ground or a stone occurs, the earth is washed from beneath it, and accumulates above it, and there we have a little precipice connected by a sweeping curve at its summit with the great slope, and casting a sharp dark shadow; where the soil has been soft, it will probably be washed away underneath until it gives way, and leaves a jagged, hanging, irregular line of fracture: and all these circumstances are explained to the eye in sunshine with the most delicious clearness; every touch of shadow being expressive of some particular truth of structure, and bearing witness to the symmetry into which the whole mass has been reduced. Where this operation has gone on long, and vegetation has assisted in softening the outlines, we have our ground brought into graceful and irregular curves, of infinite variety, but yet always so connected with each other, and guiding to each other, that the eye never feels them as *separate* things, nor feels inclined to count them, nor perceives a likeness in one to the other; they are not repetitions of each other, but are different parts of one system. Each would be imperfect without the one next to it.   481

Let not these points be deemed unimportant: the truths of form in common ground are quite as valuable (let me anticipate myself for a moment), quite as beautiful, as any others which nature presents; and in lowland landscape they furnish a species of line which it is quite impossible to obtain in any other way, the alternately flowing and broken line of mountain scenery, which, however small its scale, is always of inestimable value, contrasted with the repetitions of organic form which we are compelled to give in vegetation. A really great artist dwells on every inch of exposed soil with care and delight, and renders it one of the most essential, speaking, and pleasurable parts of his composition. Nor do I myself see wherein the great difference lies between a master and a novice, except in the rendering of the finer truths of which I am at present speaking. To handle the brush freely, and to paint grass and weeds with accuracy enough to satisfy the eye, are accomplishments which a year or two's practice will give any man: but to trace among the grass and weeds those mysteries of invention and combination by which nature appeals to the intellect; to render the delicate fissure, and descending curve, and undulating shadow of the mouldering soil, with gentle and fine finger, like the touch of the rain itself; to find even in all that appears most trifling or contemptible, fresh evidence of the constant working of the Divine power "for glory and for beauty," and to teach it and proclaim it to the unthinking and the unregarding; this, as it is the peculiar province and faculty of the master-mind, so it is the peculiar duty which is demanded of it by the Deity.

It would take me no reasonable or endurable time, if I were to point out one half of the various kinds and classes of falsehood which the inventive faculties of the old masters succeeded in originating, in the drawing of foregrounds. It is not this man nor that man, nor one school nor another; all agree in entire repudiation of everything resembling facts, and in the high degree of absurdity of what they substitute for them. Perhaps, however, the foregrounds of Claude afford the most remarkable instances of childishness and incompetence of all. That of his morning landscape, with the large group of trees and high single-arched bridge, in the National Gallery,[48] is a fair example of the kind of error into which he constantly falls. I will not say anything of the agreeable composition of the three banks, rising one behind another from the water, except only that it amounts to a demonstration that all three were painted in the artist's study, without any reference to nature whatever. In fact, there is quite enough intrinsic evidence in each of them to prove this, seeing that what appears to be meant for vegetation upon them, amounts to nothing more than a green stain on their surfaces, the more evidently false because the leaves of the trees twenty yards farther off are all perfectly visible and distinct; and that the sharp lines with which each cuts against that beyond it are not only such as crumbling earth could never show or assume, but are maintained through their whole progress ungraduated, unchanging, and unaffected by any of the circumstances of varying shade to which every one of nature's lines is inevitably subjected. In fact, the whole arrangement is the impotent struggle of a tyro to express by successive edges that approach of earth which he finds himself incapable of expressing by drawing of the surface. Claude wished to make you understand that the edge of his pond came nearer and nearer; he had probably often tried to do this with an unbroken bank, or a bank only varied by the delicate and harmonized anatomy of nature; and he had found that owing to his total ignorance of the laws of perspective such efforts on his part invariably ended in his reducing his pond to the form of a round O, and making it look perpendicular. Much comfort and solace of mind, in such unpleasant circumstances, may be derived from instantly dividing the obnoxious bank into a number of successive promontories, and developing their edges with completeness and intensity. Every school-girl's drawing, as soon as her mind has arrived at so great a degree of enlightenment as to perceive that perpendicular water is objectionable, will supply us with edifying instances of this unfailing resource; and this foreground of Claude's is only one out of the thousand cases in which he has been reduced to it. And if it be asked, how the proceeding differs from that of nature, I have only to point to nature herself, as she is drawn in the foreground of Turner's Mercury and Argus [fig.12], a case precisely similar to Claude's, of earthy crumbling banks cut away by water. It will be found in this picture (and I am now describing nature's work and Turner's with the same words) that the whole distance is given by retirement of solid surface; and that if ever an edge is expressed, it is only felt for an instant, and then lost again; so that the eye cannot stop at it and prepare for a long jump to another like it, but is guided over it, and round it into the hollow beyond; and thus the whole receding mass of ground, going back for more than a quarter of a mile, is made completely *one*, no part of it is separated from the rest for an instant, it is all united, and its modulations are *members*, not *divisions* of its mass. But these modulations are countless; heaving here, sinking there; now swelling, now mouldering; now blending, now breaking; giving, in fact, to the foreground of this universal master precisely the same qualities which we have before seen in his hills, as Claude gave to his foreground precisely the same qualities which we   486 had before found in *his* hills,—infinite unity in the one case, finite division in the other.

Let us, then, having now obtained some insight into the principles of the old masters in foreground drawing, contrast them throughout with those of our great modern master. The investigation of the excellence of Turner's drawing becomes shorter and easier as we proceed, because the great distinctions between his work and that of other painters are the same, whatever the object or subject may be; and after once showing the general characters of the particular specific forms under consideration, we have only to point, in the works of Turner, to the same principles of infinity and variety in carrying them out, which we have before insisted upon with reference to other subjects.

The Upper Fall of the Tees, Yorkshire [fig.23], may be given as a standard example of rock-drawing to be opposed to the work of Salvator. We have, in the great face of rock which divides the two streams, horizontal lines which indicate the real direction of the strata, and the same lines are given in ascending perspective all along the precipice on the right. But we see also on the central precipice fissures absolutely vertical, which inform us of one series of joints dividing these horizontal strata; and the exceeding smoothness and evenness of the precipice itself inform us that it has been caused by a great separation of substance in the direction of another more important line of joints, running across the river. Accordingly we see on the left that the whole summit of the precipice is divided again and again by this great series of joints into vertical beds, which lie against each other with their sides toward us, and are traversed downwards by the same vertical lines traceable on the face of the

fig.23   engraving after J.M.W. Turner, *The Upper Fall of Tees*

central cliff. Now, let me direct especial attention to the way in which
487   Turner has marked, over this general and grand unity of structure, the
modifying effects of the weather and the torrent. Observe how the whole
surface of the hill above the precipice on the left is brought into one
smooth unbroken curvature of gentle convexity, until it comes to the edge
of the precipice, and then, just on the angle, breaks into the multiplicity
of fissure which marks its geological structure. Observe how every one of
the separate blocks into which it divides is rounded and convex in its
salient edges turned to the weather, and how every one of their inward
angles is marked clearly and sharply by the determined shadow and transparent reflex. Observe how exquisitely graceful are all the curves of the
convex surfaces, indicating that every one of them has been modelled by
the winding and undulating of running water; and how gradually they
become steeper as they descend, until they are torn down into the face of
the precipice. Finally, observe the exquisite variety of all the touches
which express fissure or shade; every one in varying direction and with
new form, and yet of which one deep and marked piece of shadow indicates the greatest proximity; and from this every shade becomes fainter
and fainter, until all are lost in the obscurity and dimness of the hanging
precipice and the shattering fall. Again, see how the same fractures just

upon the edge take place with the central cliff above the right-hand fall, and how the force of the water is told us by the confusion of débris accumulated in its channel. In fact, the great quality about Turner's drawings which more especially proves their transcendent truth is, the capability they afford us of reasoning on past and future phenomena, just as if we had the actual rocks before us; for this indicates not that one truth is given, or another, not that a pretty or interesting morsel has been   488 selected here and there, but that the whole truth has been given, with all the relations of its parts; so that we can pick and choose our points of pleasure or of thought for ourselves, and reason upon the whole with the same certainty which we should after having climbed and hammered over the rocks bit by bit. With this drawing before him, a geologist could give a lecture upon the whole system of aqueous erosion, and speculate as safely upon the past and future states of this very spot, as if he were standing and getting wet with the spray. He would tell you at once, that the waterfall was in a state of rapid recession; that it had once formed a wide cataract just at the place where the figure is sitting on the heap of débris; and that when it was there, part of it came down by the channel on the left, its bed being still marked by the delicately chiselled lines of fissure. He would tell you that the foreground had also once been the top of the fall, and that the vertical fissures on the right of it were evidently then the channel of a side stream. He would tell you that the fall was then much lower than it is now, and that being lower, it had less force, and cut itself a narrower bed; and that the spot where it reached the higher precipice is marked by the expansion of the wide basin which its increased violence has excavated, and by the gradually increasing concavity of the rocks below, which we see have been hollowed into a complete vault by the elastic bound of the water. But neither he nor I could tell you with what exquisite and finished marking of every fragment and particle of soil or rock, both in its own structure and the evidence it bears of these great influences, the whole of this is confirmed and carried out.

The blocks of stone which form the foreground of the Ulleswater [plate   489 12] are, I believe, the finest example in the world of the finished drawing   90 of rocks which have been subjected to violent aqueous action. Their surfaces seem to palpitate from the fine touch of the waves, and every part of them is rising or falling, in soft swell or gentle depression, though the eye can scarcely trace the fine shadows on which this chiselling of the surface depends. And with all this, every block of them has individual character, dependent on the expression of the angular lines of which its contours were first formed, and which is retained and felt through all the modulation and melting of the water-worn surface.

I consider cases like these, of perfect finish and new conception, applied and exerted in the drawing of every member of a confused and almost countlessly divided system, about the most wonderful, as well as the most characteristic, passages of Turner's foregrounds.

491   The higher the mind, it may be taken as a universal rule, the less it will scorn that which appears to be small or unimportant; and the rank of a painter may always be determined by observing how he uses, and with what respect he views the minutiæ of nature. Greatness of mind is not shown by admitting small things, but by making small things great under its influence. He who can take no interest in what is small, will take false interest in what is great; he who cannot make a bank sublime will make a mountain ridiculous.

SECTION V
Of Truth of Water

CHAPTER I
Of Water, as Painted by the Ancients

O F all inorganic substances, acting in their own proper nature, and 494 without assistance or combination, water is the most wonderful. If we think of it as the source of all the changefulness and beauty which we have seen in clouds; then as the instrument by which the earth we have contemplated was modelled into symmetry, and its crags chiselled into grace; then as, in the form of snow, it robes the mountains it has made with that transcendent light which we could not have conceived if we had not seen; then as it exists in the foam of the torrent, in the iris which spans it, in the morning mist which rises from it, in the deep crystalline pools which mirror its hanging shore, in the broad lake and glancing river; finally, in that which is to all human minds the best emblem of unwearied unconquerable power, the wild, various, fantastic, tameless unity of the sea; what shall we compare to this mighty, this universal element, for glory and for beauty? or how shall we follow its eternal changefulness of feeling? It is like trying to paint a soul.

To suggest the ordinary appearance of calm water, to lay on canvas as 495 much evidence of surface and reflection as may make us understand that water is meant, is perhaps, the easiest task of art; and even ordinary running or falling water may be sufficiently rendered, by observing careful curves of projection with a dark ground, and breaking a little white over it, as we see done with judgment and truth by Ruysdael. But to paint the actual play of hue on the reflective surface, or to give the forms and fury of water when it begins to show itself; to give the flashing and rocket-like velocity of a noble cataract, or the precision and grace of the sea wave, so exquisitely modelled, though so mockingly transient, so mountainous in its form, yet so cloud-like in its motion, with its variety and delicacy of colour, when every ripple and wreath has some peculiar passage of reflection upon itself alone, and the radiating and scintillating sunbeams are mixed with the dim hues of transparent depth and dark rock below; to do this perfectly is beyond the power of man; to do it even partially has been granted to but one or two, even of those few who have dared to attempt it.[49]

496   What I shall here state are a few only of the broadest laws verifiable by the reader's immediate observation, but of which, nevertheless, I have found artists frequently ignorant; owing to their habit of sketching from nature without thinking or reasoning, and especially of finishing at home. It is not often, I believe, that an artist draws the reflections in water as he sees them; over large spaces, and in weather that is not very calm, it is nearly impossible to do so; when it is possible, sometimes in haste, and sometimes in idleness, and sometimes under the idea of improving nature, they are slurred or misrepresented. It is so easy to give something like a suggestive resemblance of calm water, that, even when the landscape is finished from nature, the water is merely indicated as something that may be done at any time; and then, in the home work, come the cold leaden greys with some, and the violent blues and greens with others, and the horizontal lines with the feeble, and the bright touches and sparkles with the dexterous, and everything that is shallow and commonpace with all. Now, the fact is that there is hardly a road-side pond or pool which has not as much landscape *in* it as above it. It is not the brown, muddy, dull thing we suppose it to be; it has a heart like ourselves, and in the bottom of that there are the boughs of the tall trees, and the blades of the shaking grass, and all manner of hues of variable pleasant light out of the sky. Nay, the

497   ugly gutter, that stagnates over the drain-bars in the heart of the foul city, is not altogether base; down in that, if you will look deep enough, you may see the dark serious blue of far-off sky, and the passing of pure clouds. It is at your own will that you see, in that despised stream, either the refuse of the street, or the image of the sky. So it is with almost all other things that we unkindly despise. Now, this far-seeing is just the difference between the great and the vulgar painter: the common man *knows* the roadside pool is muddy, and draws its mud; the great painter sees beneath and behind the brown surface what will take him a day's work to follow, but he follows it, cost what it will. And if painters would only go out to the nearest common, and take the nearest dirty pond among the furze, and draw that thoroughly; not considering that it is water that they are drawing, and that water must be done in a certain way, but drawing determinedly what they *see*;—that is to say, all the trees, and their shaking leaves, and all the hazy passages of disturbing sunshine; and the bottom seen in the clearer little bits at the edge, and the stones of it; and all the sky, and the clouds far down in the middle, drawn as completely as the real clouds above;—they would come home with such a notion of water-painting as might save me and every one else all trouble of writing about

the matter. But now they do nothing of the kind, but take the ugly, round, yellow surface for granted, or else "improve" it at home; and, instead of giving that refined, complex, delicate, but saddened and gloomy reflection in the polluted water, they clear it up with coarse flashes of yellow, and green, and blue, and spoil their own eyes, and hurt ours; failing, of course still more hopelessly in reaching the pure light of waves thrown loose. And so Canaletto is still thought to have painted canals, and Vandevelde and Backhuysen to have painted sea; and the uninterpreted streams and maligned sea hiss shame upon us from all their rocky beds and hollow shores.

I approach this part of my subject with more despondency than any other, and that for several reasons; first, the water-painting of all the elder landscape painters, except a few of the better passages of Claude and Ruysdael, is so execrable, so beyond all expression and explanation bad, and Claude's and Ruysdael's best so cold and valueless, that I do not know how to address those who like such painting; I do not know what their sensations are respecting sea. I can perceive nothing in Vandevelde or Backhuysen of the lowest redeeming merit: no power, no presence of intellect, or evidence of perception of any sort or kind; no resemblance, even the feeblest, of anything natural; no invention, even the most sluggish, of anything agreeable. Had they given us staring green seas with hatchet edges, such as we see Her Majesty's ships so-and-so fixed into by the heads or sterns, in the Royal Academy, the admiration of them would have been comprehensible; there being a natural predilection in the mind of man for green waves with curling tops, but not for clay and wool: so that though I can understand, in some sort, why people admire everything else in the old art, why they admire Salvator's rocks, and Claude's foregrounds, and Hobbima's trees, and Paul Potter's cattle, and Jan Steen's pans; and while I can perceive in all these likings a root which seems right and legitimate, and to be appealed to; yet when I find they can even *endure* the *sight* of a Backhuysen on their room walls (I speak seriously) it makes me hopeless at once. I may be wrong, or they may be wrong, or at least I can conceive of no principle or opinion common between us, which either can address or understand in the other; and yet I am wrong in this want of conception, for I know that Turner once liked Vandevelde, and I can trace the evil influence of Vandevelde on most of his early sea-painting, but Turner certainly could not have liked Vandevelde without *some* legitimate cause. Another discouraging point is, that I cannot catch a wave, nor daguerreotype it, and so there is no coming to pure demonstration; but the forms and hues of water must always be in some measure a matter of dispute and feeling, and the more so because there is no perfect or even tolerably perfect sea-painting to refer to. The sea never has been, and I fancy never will be nor can be painted; it is only suggested

498

499

by means of more or less spiritual and intelligent conventionalism: and though Turner has done enough to suggest the sea mightily and gloriously, after all it is by conventionalism still, and there remains so much that is unlike nature, that it is always possible for those who do not feel his power to justify their dislike, on very sufficient and reasonable grounds; and to maintain themselves obstinately unreceptant of the good, by insisting on the deficiency which no mortal hand can supply, and which commonly is most manifest on the one hand, where most has been achieved on the other.

With calm water the case is different. Facts are ascertainable and demonstrable there, and, by the notice of one or two of the simplest, we may obtain some notion of the little success and intelligence of the elder painters in this easier field, and so prove their probable failure in contending with greater difficulties.

I. Water, of course, owing to its transparency, possesses not a perfectly reflective surface, like that of speculum metal, but a surface whose reflective power is dependent on the angle at which the rays to be reflected fall. The smaller this angle, the greater are the number of rays reflected. Now, according to the number of rays reflected is the force of the image of objects above, and according to the number of rays transmitted is the perceptibility of objects below, the water. Hence the visible transparency and reflected power of water are in inverse ratio. In looking down into it from above, we receive transmitted rays which exhibit either the bottom or the objects floating in the water; or else if the water be deep and clear, we receive very few rays, and the water looks black. In looking along water we receive reflected rays, and therefore the image of objects above it. Hence, in shallow water on a level shore the bottom is seen at our feet, clearly; it becomes more and more obscure as it retires, even though the water do not increase in depth; and at a distance of twelve or twenty yards, more or less according to our height above the water, becomes entirely invisible, lost in the lustre of the reflected surface.

II. The brighter the objects reflected, the larger the angle at which reflection is visible. It is always to be remembered that, strictly speaking, only light objects are reflected, and that the darker ones are seen only in proportion to the number of rays of light that they can send; so that a dark object comparatively loses its power to affect the surface of water, and the water in the space of a dark reflection is seen partially with the image of the object, and partially transparent. It will be found on observation that under a bank, suppose with dark trees above showing spaces of bright sky, the bright sky is reflected distinctly, and the bottom of the water is in those spaces not seen; but in the dark spaces of reflection we see the bottom of the water, and the colour of that bottom and of the water itself mingles with and modifies that of the colour of the trees casting the dark reflection.

This is one of the most beautiful circumstances connected with water surface, for by these means a variety of colour and a grace and evanescence are introduced in the reflection otherwise impossible. Of course, at great distances, even the darkest objects cast distinct images, and the hue of the water cannot be seen; but, in near water, the occurrence of its own colour modifying the dark reflections while it leaves light ones unaffected is of infinite value.

III. Clear water takes no shadow, and that for two reasons: a perfect   501
surface of speculum metal takes no shadow (this the reader may instantly demonstrate for himself), and a perfectly transparent body, as air, takes no shadow, hence water, whether transparent or reflective, takes no shadow.

But shadows, or the forms of them, appear on water frequently and   502
sharply: it is necessary carefully to explain the causes of these, as they form one of the most eminent sources of error in water-painting.

First, water in shade is much more reflective than water in sunlight. Under sunlight the local colour of the water is commonly vigorous and active, and forcibly affects, as we have seen, all the dark reflections, commonly diminishing their depth. Under shade, the reflective power is in a high degree increased, and it will be found most frequently that the forms of shadows are expressed on the surface of water, not by actual shade, but by more genuine reflection of objects above. This is another most important and valuable circumstance, and we owe to it some phenomena of the highest beauty.

A very muddy river, as the Arno for instance at Florence, is seen during sunshine of its own yellow colour, rendering all reflections discoloured and feeble. At twilight it recovers its reflective power to the fullest extent, and the mountains of Carrara are seen reflected in it as clearly as if it were a crystalline lake. The Mediterranean, whose determined blue yields to hardly any modifying colour in day-time, receives at evening the image of its rocky shores. On our own seas, seeming shadows are seen constantly cast in purple and blue, upon pale green. These are no shadows, but the pure reflection of dark or blue sky above, seen in the shadowed space, refused by the local colour of the sea in the sunlighted spaces, and turned more or less purple by the opposition of the vivid green.

Farther, on whatever dust and other foulness may be present in water,   503
real shadow of course falls clear and dark in proportion to the quantity of solid substance present. On very muddy rivers, real shadow falls in sunlight nearly as sharply as on land; on our own sea, the apparent shadow caused by increased reflection is much increased in depth by the chalkiness and impurity of the water.

Farther, when surface is rippled, every ripple, up to a certain variable distance on each side of the spectator, and at a certain angle between him and the sun varying with the size and shape of the ripples, reflects to him a small image of the sun. Hence those dazzling fields of expanding light so

504   often seen upon the sea. Any object that comes between the sun and these ripples takes from them the power of reflecting the sun, and, in consequence, all their light; hence any intervening objects cast upon such spaces seeming shadows of intense force, and of the exact shape, and in the exact place, of real shadows, and yet which are no more real shadows than the withdrawal of an image of a piece of white paper from a mirror is a shadow on the mirror.

Farther, in all shallow water, more or less in proportion to its shallowness, but in some measure, I suppose, up to depths of forty or fifty fathoms, and perhaps more, the local colour of the water depends in great measure on light reflected from the bottom.

505   One more case must be stated belonging to rough water. Every large wave of the sea is in ordinary circumstances divided into, or rather covered by, innumerable smaller waves, each of which, in all probability, from some of its edges or surfaces reflects the sunbeams; and hence result a glitter, polish, and vigorous light over the whole flank of the waves, which are, of course, instantly withdrawn within the space of a cast shadow, whose form, therefore, though it does not affect the great body or ground of the water in the least, is sufficiently traceable by the withdrawal of the high lights; also every string and wreath of foam above or within the wave takes real shadow, and thus adds to the impression.

I have not stated one half of the circumstances which produce or influence effects of shadow on water; but, lest I should confuse or weary the reader, I leave him to pursue the subject for himself; enough having been stated to establish this general principle, that whenever shadow is seen on clear water, and, in a measure, even on foul water, it is not, as on land, a dark shade subduing the sunny general hue to a lower tone, but it is a space of an entirely different colour, subject itself, by its susceptibility of reflection, to infinite varieties of depth and hue, and liable, under certain circumstances, to disappear altogether; and that, therefore, whenever we have to paint such shadows, it is not only the hue of the

506   water itself that we have to consider, but all the circumstances by which in the position attributed to them such shaded spaces could be affected.

IV. If water be rippled, the side of every ripple next to us reflects a piece of the sky, and the side of every ripple farthest from us reflects a piece of the opposite shore, or of whatever objects may be beyond the ripple. But as we soon lose sight of the farther sides of the ripples on the retiring surface, the whole rippled space will then be reflective of the sky only. Thus, where calm distant water receives reflections of high shores, every extent of rippled surface appears as a bright line interrupting that reflection with the colour of the sky.

V. When a ripple or swell is seen at such an angle as to afford a view of its farther side, it carries the reflection of objects farther down than calm water would. Therefore all motion in water elongates reflections, and throws them into confused vertical lines. The real amount of this elongation is not distinctly visible, except in the case of very bright objects, and especially of lights, as of the sun, moon, or lamps by a river shore, whose reflections are hardly ever seen as circles or points, which of course they are on perfectly calm water, but as long streams of tremulous light.

But it is strange that while we are constantly in the habit of seeing the reflection of the sun, which ought to be a mere circle, elongated into a stream of light, extending from the horizon to the shore, the elongation of the reflection of a sail or other object to one half of this extent is received, if represented in a picture, with incredulity by the greater number of spectators.

VI. Rippled water, of which we can see the farther side of the waves, will reflect a perpendicular line clearly, a bit of its length being given on the side of each wave, and easily joined by the eye. But if the line slope, its reflection will be excessively confused and disjointed; and if horizontal, nearly invisible.   507

VII. Every reflection is the image in reverse of just so much of the objects beside the water, as we could see if we were placed as much under the level of the water as we are actually above it. If an object be so far back   508 from the bank, that if we were five feet under the water level we could not see it over the bank, then, standing five feet above the water, we shall not be able to see its image under the reflected bank. Hence the reflection of all objects that have any slope back from the water is shortened, and at last disappears as we rise above it. Lakes seen from a great height appear like plates of metal set in the landscape, reflecting the sky, but none of their shores.

VIII. Any given point of the object above the water is reflected, if reflected at all, at some spot in a vertical line beneath it, so long as the plane of the water is horizontal. On rippled water a slight deflection sometimes takes place, and the image of a vertical tower will slope a little away from the wind, owing to the casting of the image on the sloping sides of the ripples. On the sloping sides of large waves the deflection is in proportion to the slope.

Such are the most common and general optical laws which are to be taken into consideration in the painting of water. Yet, in the application of them as tests of good or bad water-painting, we must be cautious in the extreme. An artist may know all these laws, and comply with them, and yet paint water execrably; and he may be ignorant of every one of them, and, in their turn, and in certain places, violate every one of them, and yet paint water gloriously. Thousands of exquisite effects take place in nature, utterly inexplicable, and which can be believed only while they are seen; the combinations and applications of the above laws are so varied and complicated that no knowledge or labour could, if applied analytically, keep pace with them. Constant and eager watchfulness, and portfolios filled with actual statements of water-effect, drawn on the spot and on the instant, are worth more to the painter than the most extended optical knowledge. Without these all his knowledge will end in a pedantic falsehood; with these it does not matter how gross or how daring here and there may be his violations of this or that law; his very transgressions will be admirable.

It may be said, that this is a dangerous principle to advance in these days of idleness. I cannot help it; it is true, and must be affirmed. Of all contemptible criticism, that is most to be contemned which punishes great works of art when they fight without armour, and refuses to feel or acknowledge the great spiritual refracted sun of their truth, because it has risen at a false angle, and burst upon them before its appointed time. And yet, on the other hand, let it be observed, that it is not feeling, nor fancy, nor imagination, so called, that I have put before science, but watchfulness, experience, affection, and trust in nature; and farther let it be observed, that there is a difference between the license taken by one man and another, which makes one license admirable, and the other punishable; and that this difference is of a kind sufficiently discernible by every earnest person, though it is not so explicable as that we can before-hand say where and when, or even to whom, the license is to be forgiven.

In Turner's Pas de Calais[50] there is a buoy poised on the ridge of a near wave. It casts its reflection vertically down the flank of the wave, which slopes steeply. I cannot tell whether this is license or mistake; I suspect the latter, for the same thing occurs not unfrequently in Turner's seas; but I am almost certain that it would have been done wilfully in this case, even had the mistake been recognized, for the vertical line is necessary to the picture, and the eye is so little accustomed to catch the real bearing of the reflections on the slopes of waves that it does not feel the fault.

In the picture of Cuyp, No. 83 in the Dulwich Gallery,[51] the post at the end of the bank casts three or four radiating reflections. This is visibly neither license nor half-science, but pure ignorance. Again, in the picture attributed to Paul Potter, No. 176 Dulwich Gallery,[52] I believe most people must feel, the moment they look at it, that there is something wrong with the water, that it looks odd, and hard, and like ice or lead; and though they may not be able to tell the reason of the impression, for when they go near they will find it smooth and lustrous, and prettily painted, yet they will not be able to shake off the unpleasant sense of its being like a plate of bad mirror set in a model landscape among moss, rather than like a pond. The reason is, that while this water receives clear reflections from the fence and hedge on the left, and is everywhere smooth and evidently capable of giving true images, it yet reflects none of the cows.

Among all the pictures of Canaletto, which I have ever seen, and they   513 are not a few, I remember but one or two where there is any variation from one method of treatment of the water. He almost always covers the whole space of it with one monotonous ripple, composed of a coat of well chosen, but perfectly opaque and smooth sea-green, covered with a certain number, I cannot state the exact average, but it varies from three hundred and fifty to four hundred and upwards, according to the extent of canvas to be covered, of white concave touches, which are very properly symbolical of ripple.

And, as the canal retires back from the eye, he very geometrically diminishes the size of his ripples, until he arrives at an even field of apparently smooth water. By our sixth rule, this rippling water, as it retires, should show more and more reflection of the sky above it, and less and less of that of objects beyond it, until, at two or three hundred yards down the canal, the whole field of water should be one even grey or blue, the colour of the sky, receiving no reflections whatever of other objects. What does Canaletto do? Exactly in proportion as he retires, he displays *more* and *more* of the reflection of objects, and less and less of the sky, until, three hundred yards away, all the houses are reflected as clear and sharp as in a quiet lake.

This, again, is wilful and inexcusable violation of truth, of which the   514 reason, as in the last case, is the painter's consciousness of weakness. It is one of the most difficult things in the world to express the light reflection of the blue sky on a distant ripple, and to make the eye understand the cause of the colour, and the motion of the apparently smooth water, especially where there are buildings above to be reflected, for the eye never understands the want of the reflection. But it is the easiest and most agreeable thing in the world to give the inverted image; it occupies a vast space of otherwise troublesome distance in the simplest way possible, and is understood by the eye at once. Hence Canaletto is glad, as any other inferior workman would be, not to say obliged, to give the reflections in the distance. But when he comes up close to the spectator, he finds the smooth surface just as troublesome near, as the ripple would have been far off. It is a very nervous thing for an ignorant artist to have a great space of vacant smooth water to deal with, close to him, too far down to take reflections from buildings, and yet which must be made to look flat and retiring and transparent. Canaletto, with his sea-green, did not at all feel himself equal to anything of this kind, and had therefore no resource but in the white touches above described, which occupy the alarming space without any troublesome necessity for knowledge or invention, and supply by their gradual diminution some means of expressing retirement of surface.

Now in all these cases it is not the mistake or the license itself, it is not the infringement of this or that law, which condemns the picture, but it is the habit of mind in which the license is taken, the cowardice or bluntness of feeling, which infects every part alike, and deprives the whole picture of vitality. Canaletto, had he been a great painter, might have cast his reflections wherever he chose, and rippled the water wherever he chose, and painted his sea sloping if he chose, and neither I nor any one else should have dared to say a word against him; but he is a little and a bad painter, and so continues everywhere multiplying and magnifying mistakes, and adding apathy to error, until nothing can any more be pardoned in him. If it be but remembered that every one of the surfaces of those multitudinous ripples is in nature a mirror which catches, according to its position, either the image of the sky or of the silver beaks of the gondolas, or of their black bodies and scarlet draperies, or of the white marble, or the green seaweed on the low stones, it cannot but be felt that those waves would have something more of colour upon them than that opaque dead green. Green they are by their own nature, but it is a transparent and emerald hue, mixing itself with the thousand reflected tints without overpowering the weakest of them; and thus, in every one of those individual waves, the truths of colour are contradicted by Canaletto by the thousand.

Venice is sad and silent now, to what she was in his time; the canals are choked gradually one by one, and the foul water laps more and more sluggishly against the rent foundations: but even yet, could I but place the reader at early morning on the quay below the Rialto, when the market boats, full laden, float into groups of golden colour, and let him watch the dashing of the water about their glittering steely heads, and under the shadows of the vine leaves; and show him the purple of the grapes and the figs, and the glowing of the scarlet gourds carried away in long streams upon the waves; and among them, the crimson fish baskets, plashing and sparkling, and flaming as the morning sun falls on their wet tawny sides: and above, the painted sails of the fishing-boats, orange and white, scarlet and blue; and better than all such florid colour, the naked, bronzed, burning limbs of the seamen, the last of the old Venetian race, who yet keep the right Giorgione colour on their brows and bosoms, in strange contrast with the sallow sensual degradation of the creatures that live in the cafés of the Piazza, he would not be merciful to Canaletto any more.

Yet even Canaletto, in relation to the truths he had to paint, is spiritual, faithful, powerful, compared with the Dutch painters of sea. It is easily understood why his green paint and concave touches should be thought expressive of the water on which the real colours are not to be discerned but by attention, which is never given; but it is not so easily understood, considering how many there are who love the sea, and look at it, that Vandevelde and such others should be tolerated. As I before said, I feel utterly hopeless in addressing the admirers of these men, because I do not know what it is in their works which is supposed to be like nature. Foam appears to me to curdle and cream on the wave sides, and to fly flashing from their crests, and not to be set astride upon them like a peruke; and waves appear to me to fall, and plunge, and toss, and nod, and crash over, and not to curl up like shavings; and water appears to me, when it is grey, to have the grey of stormy air mixed with its own deep, heavy, thunderous, threatening blue, and not the grey of the first coat of cheap paint on a deal door; and many other such things appear to me, which, as far as I can conjecture by what is admired of marine painting, appear to few else.

The seas of Claude are the finest pieces of water-painting in ancient art.   517
I do not say that I like them, because they appear to me selections of the particular moment when the sea is most insipid and characterless; but I think that they are exceedingly true to the forms and times selected, or at least that the fine instances of them are so, of which there are exceedingly few.

The merits of Poussin as a sea or water painter may, I think, be   518
sufficiently determined by the Deluge in the Louvre,[53] where the breaking up of the fountains of the deep is typified by the capsizing of a wherry over a weir.

It seems exceedingly strange that the great Venetian painters should   519
have left us no instance, as far as I know, of any marine effects carefully studied. As already noted, whatever passages of sea occur in their backgrounds are merely broad extents of blue or green surface, fine in colour, and coming dark usually against the horizon, well enough to be   520
understood as sea (yet even that not always without the help of a ship), but utterly unregarded in all questions of completion and detail. Among the religious schools very sweet motives occur, but nothing which for a moment can be considered as real water-painting. On the whole, I suppose that the best imitations of level water surface to be found in ancient art are in the clear Flemish landscapes. Of any tolerable representation of water in agitation, or under any circumstances that bring out its power and character, I know no instance; and the more capable of noble treatment the subject happens to be, the more manifest invariably is the painter's want of feeling in every effort, and of knowledge in every line.

CHAPTER III[54]
Of Water as Painted by Turner

545 THERE is more in Turner's painting of water surface than any philosophy of reflection, or any peculiarity of means can account for or accomplish;[55] there is a might and wonder about it which will not admit of our whys and hows. Take, for instance, the picture of the Sun of Venice going to Sea [fig.24], of 1843; respecting which, however, there are one or two circumstances which may as well be noted besides its water-painting. The reader, if he has not been at Venice, ought to be made aware that the Venetian fishing-boats, almost without exception, carry canvas painted with bright colours; the favourite design for the centre being either a cross or a large sun with many rays, the favourite colours being red, orange, and black, blue occurring occasionally. The radiance of

fig.24   J.M.W. Turner, *The Sun of Venice Going to Sea*

147

these sails and of the bright and grotesque vanes at the mast-heads under
sunlight is beyond all painting; but it is strange that, of constant
occurrence as these boats are on all the lagoons, Turner alone should
have availed himself of them. Nothing could be more faithful than the
boat, which was the principal object in this picture, in the cut of the
sail, the filling of it, the exact height of the boom above the deck, the
quartering of it with colour; finally and especially, the hanging of the
fish-baskets about the bows. All these, however, are comparatively
minor merits (though not the blaze of colour which the artist elicited
from the right use of these circumstances); but the peculiar power of the
picture was the painting of the sea surface, where there were no reflections
to assist it. A stream of splendid colour fell from the boat, but that
occupied the centre only; in the distance the city and crowded boats
threw down some playing lines, but these still left on each side of the   546
boat a large space of water reflecting nothing but the morning sky. This
was divided by an eddying swell, on whose continuous sides the local
colour of the water was seen, pure aquamarine (a beautiful occurrence
of closely observed truth); but still there remained a large blank space of
pale water to be treated, the sky above had no distinct details, and was
pure faint grey, with broken white vestiges of cloud; it gave no help
therefore. But there the water lay, no dead grey flat paint, but downright clear, playing, palpable surface, full of indefinite hue, and retiring
as regularly and visibly back and far away, as if there had been objects
all over it to tell the story by perspective. Now it is the doing of this
which tries the painter, and it is his having done this which made me say
above that "no man had ever painted the surface of calm water but
Turner."

But Turner is not satisfied with this. He is never altogether content
unless he can, at the same time that he takes advantage of all the placidity
of repose, tell us something either about the past commotion of the water,
or of some present stirring of tide or current which its stillness does not   547
show; or give us something or other to think about and reason upon, as
well as to look at. Take a few instances. His Cowes, Isle of Wight
[fig.25],[56] is a summer twilight, about half an hour, or more, after sunset.
Intensity of repose is the great aim throughout, and the unity of tone of
the picture is one of the finest things that Turner has ever done. But there
is not only quietness, there is the very deepest solemnity in the whole of
the light, as well as in the stillness of the vessels; and Turner wishes to
enhance this feeling by representing not only repose, but *power* in repose,
the emblem, in the sea, of the quiet ships of war. Accordingly, he takes the
greatest possible pains to get his surface polished, calm, and smooth; but
he indicates the reflection of a buoy floating a full quarter of a mile off by
three black strokes with wide intervals between them, the last of which

fig.25   engraving after J.M.W. Turner, *West Cowes, Isle of Wight*

touches the water within twenty yards of the spectator. Now these three
reflections can only indicate the farther sides of three rises of an enormous
swell, and give by their intervals of separation, a space of from twelve to
twenty yards for the breadth of each wave, including the sweep between
them; and this swell is farther indicated by the reflection of the new moon
falling in a wide zigzag line. The exceeding majesty which this single
circumstance gives to the whole picture, the sublime sensation of power
and knowledge of former exertion which we instantly receive from it, if we
have but acquaintance with nature enough to understand its language,
render this work not only a piece of the most refined truth (as which I have
at present named it), but, to my mind, one of the highest pieces of
intellectual art existing.

Again, in the scene on the Loire, with the square precipice and fiery
548   sunset, in the Rivers of France,[57] repose has been aimed at in the same
way, and most thoroughly given; but the immense width of the river at
this spot makes it look like a lake or sea, and it was therefore necessary
that we should be made thoroughly to understand and feel that this is not
the calm of still water, but the tranquillity of a majestic current.
Accordingly, a boat swings at anchor on the right; and the stream,
dividing at its bow, flows towards us in two long, dark waves, especial
attention to which is enforced by the one on the left being brought across

the reflected stream of sunshine, which is separated and broken by the general undulation and agitation of the water in the boat's wake; a wake caused by the water's passing it, not by *its* going through the water.

And thus there will scarcely ever be found a piece of quiet water by Turner, without some story in it of one kind or another; sometimes a slight but beautiful incident; oftener, as in the Cowes, something on which the whole sentiment and intention of the picture in a great degree depends; but invariably presenting some new instance of varied knowledge and observation, some fresh appeal to the highest faculties of the mind.

Early works of the artist have been eclipsed by some recent drawings of Switzerland. These latter are not to be described by any words; but they must be noted here, not only as presenting records of lake effect on a grander scale, and of more imaginative character, than any other of his works, but as combining effects of the surface of mist with the surface of water. Two or three of the Lake of Lucerne, seen from above, give the melting of the mountain promontories beneath into the clear depth, and above into the clouds; one of Constance shows the vast lake at evening, seen not as water, but its surface covered with low white mist, lying, league beyond league, in the twilight, like a fallen space of moony cloud; one of Goldau shows the Lake of Zug appearing through the chasm of a thunder-cloud under sunset, its whole surface one blaze of fire, and the promontories of the hills thrown out against it like spectres; another of Zurich gives the playing of the green waves of the river among white streams of moonlight; a purple sunset on the Lake of Zug is distinguished for the glow obtained without positive colour, the rose and purple tints being in great measure brought by opposition out of brown; finally, a drawing executed in 1845, of the town of Lucerne from the lake, is unique for its expression of water surface reflecting the clear green hue of sky at twilight. [58]

It will be remembered that it was said above, that Turner was the only painter who had ever represented the surface of calm or the *force* of agitated water. He obtains this expression of force in falling or running water by fearless and full rendering of its forms. He never loses himself and his subject in the splash of the fall, his presence of mind never fails as he goes down; he does not blind us with the spray, or veil the countenance of his fall with its own drapery. A little crumbling white, or lightly rubbed paper, will soon give the effect of indiscriminate foam; but nature gives more than foam, she shows beneath it, and through it, a peculiar character of exquisitely studied form bestowed on every wave and line of fall; and it is this variety of definite character which Turner always aims at, rejecting, as much as possible, everything that conceals or overwhelms it. Thus, in the Upper Fall of the Tees [fig.23], though the whole basin of the fall is blue and dim with the rising vapour, yet the attention of the spectator is

549

551

552

553

chiefly directed to the concentric zones and delicate curves of the falling water itself; and it is impossible to express with what exquisite accuracy these are given. They are the characteristic of a powerful stream descending without impediment or break, but from a narrow channel, so as to expand as it falls. They are the constant form which such a stream assumes as it descends; and yet I think it would be difficult to point to another instance of their being rendered in art. You will find nothing in the waterfalls even of our best painters, but springing lines of parabolic descent, and splashing shapeless foam; and, in consequence, though they may make you understand the swiftness of the water, they never let you feel the weight of it; the stream in their hands looks *active*, not *supine*, as if it leaped, not as if it fell. Now water will leap a little way, it will leap down a weir or over a stone, but it *tumbles* over a high fall like this; and it is when we have lost the parabolic line, and arrived at the catenary, when we have lost the *spring* of the fall, and arrived at the *plunge* of it, that we begin really to feel its weight and wildness. Where water takes its first leap from the top, it is cool, and collected, and uninteresting, and mathematical; but it is when it finds that it has got into a scrape, and has farther to go than it thought, that its character comes out: it is then that it begins to writhe, and twist, and sweep out, zone after zone, in wilder stretching as it falls; and to send down the rocket-like, lance-pointed, whizzing shafts at its sides, sounding for the bottom. And it is this prostration, this hopeless abandonment of its ponderous power to the air, which is always peculiarly expressed by Turner, and especially in the case before us; while our other artists, keeping to the parabolic line, where they do not lose themselves in smoke and foam, make their cataract look muscular and wiry, and may consider themselves fortunate if they can keep it from stopping. I believe the majesty of motion which Turner has given by these concentric catenary lines must be felt even by those who have never seen a high waterfall, and therefore cannot appreciate their exquisite fidelity to nature.

554

When water, not in very great body, runs in a rocky bed much interrupted by hollows, so that it can rest every now and then in a pool as it goes along, it does not acquire a continuous velocity of motion. It pauses after every leap, and curdles about, and rests a little and then goes on again; and if in this comparatively tranquil and rational state of mind it meets with any obstacle, as a rock or stone, it parts on each side of it with a little bubbling foam, and goes round; if it comes to a step in its bed, it leaps it lightly, and then after a little splashing at the bottom, stops again to take breath. But if its bed be on a continuous slope, not much interrupted by hollows, so that it cannot rest, or if its own mass be so increased by flood that its usual resting-places are not sufficient for it, but that it is perpetually pushed out of them by the following current, before it has had time to tranquillize itself, it of course gains velocity with every

555

yard that it runs; the impetus got at one leap is carried to the credit of the next, until the whole stream becomes one mass of unchecked accelerating motion. Now when water in this state comes to an obstacle, it does not part at it, but clears it, like a race-horse; and when it comes to a hollow, it does not fill it up and run out leisurely at the other side, but it rushes down into it and comes up again on the other side, as a ship into the hollow of the sea. Hence the whole appearance of the bed of the stream is changed, and all the lines of the water altered in their nature. The quiet stream is a succession of leaps and pools; the leaps are light and springy, and parabolic, and make a great deal of splashing when they tumble into the pools; then we have a space of quiet curdling water and another similar leap below. But the stream when it has gained an impetus, *takes the shape* of its bed, goes down into every hollow, not with a leap, but with a swing, not foaming, nor splashing, but in the bending line of a strong sea-wave, and comes up again on the other side, over rock and ridge, with the ease of a bounding leopard; if it meet a rock three or four feet above the level of its bed, it will often neither part nor foam, nor express any concern about the matter, but clear it in a smooth dome of water, without apparent exertion, the whole surface of the surge being drawn into parallel lines by its extreme velocity, so that the whole river has the appearance of a deep and raging sea, with this only difference, that the torrent-waves always 556 break backwards, and sea-waves forwards. Thus, then, in the water which has gained an impetus, we have the most exquisite arrangements of curved lines, perpetually changing from convex to concave, and *vice versâ*, following every swell and hollow of the bed with their modulating grace, and all in unison of motion, presenting perhaps the most beautiful series of inorganic forms which nature can possibly produce; for the sea runs too much into similar and concave curves with sharp edges, but every motion of the torrent is united, and all its curves are modifications of beautiful line.

We see, therefore, why Turner seizes on these curved lines of the torrent, not only as being among the most beautiful forms of nature, but because they are an instant expression of the utmost power and velocity, and tell us how the torrent has been flowing before we see it. For the leap and splash might be seen in the sudden freakishness of a quiet stream, or the fall of a rivulet over a mill-dam; but the undulating line is the attribute 557 of the mountain-torrent, whose fall and fury have made the valleys echo for miles; and thus the moment we see one of its curves over a stone in the foreground, we know it has come far and fiercely. And we shall find the most exquisite instance of the use of such lines in the Llanthony Abbey [fig.8], which may be considered as the standard of torrent-drawing. The chief light of the picture here falls upon the surface of the stream, swelled by recent rain; and its mighty waves come rolling down close to the spectator, green and clear, but pale with anger, in broad, unbroken, oceanic curves, bending into each other without break, though jets of

558   fiery spray are cast into the air along the rocky shore, and rise in the sunshine in dusty vapour. The whole surface is one united race of mad motion; all the waves dragged, as I have described, into lines and furrows by their swiftness; and every one of those fine forms is drawn with the most studied chiaroscuro of delicate colour, greys and greens, as silvery and pure as the finest passages of Paul Veronese, and with a refinement of execution which the eye strains itself in looking into. The rapidity and gigantic force of this torrent, the exquisite refinement of its colour, and the vividness of foam which is obtained through a general middle tint, render it about the most perfect piece of painting of running water in existence.

559   More determined efforts have at all periods been made in sea-painting than in torrent-painting, yet less successful. As above stated, it is easy to obtain a resemblance of broken running water by tricks and dexterities, but the sea *must* be legitimately drawn; it cannot be given as utterly disorganised and confused, its weight and mass must be expressed, and the

560   efforts at expression of it end in failure with all but the most powerful men; even with these few a partial success must be considered worthy of the highest praise.

As the right rendering of the Alps depends on power of drawing snow, so the right painting of the sea must depend, at least in all coast scenery, in no small measure on the power of drawing foam. Yet there are two conditions of foam of invariable occurrence on breaking waves, of which I have never seen the slightest record attempted; first, the thick, creamy, curdling, overlapping, massy foam, which remains for a moment only after the fall of the wave, and is seen in perfection in its running up the beach; and, secondly, the thin white coating into which this subsides, which opens into oval gaps and clefts, marbling the waves over their whole surface, and connecting the breakers on a flat shore by long dragging streams of white.

It is evident that the difficulty of expressing either of these two conditions must be immense. The lapping and curdling foam is difficult enough to catch, even when the lines of its undulation alone are considered; but the lips, so to speak, which lie along these lines, are full, projecting, and marked by beautiful light and shade; each has its high light, a gradation into shadow of indescribable delicacy, a bright reflected light, and a dark cast shadow: to draw all this requires labour and care, and firmness of work, which, as I imagine, must always, however skilfully bestowed, destroy all impressions of wildness, accidentalism, and evan-escence, and so kill the sea. Again, the openings in the thin subsided foam, in their irregular modifications of circular and oval shapes dragged hither and thither, would be hard enough to draw, even if they could be seen on a flat surface; instead of which, every one of the openings is seen in undulation on a tossing surface, broken up over small surges and ripples, and so thrown into perspectives of the most hopeless intricacy. Now it is not easy to express the fall of a pattern with oval openings on the folds of drapery. I do not know that any one under the mark of Veronese or Titian   561 could even do this as it ought to be done, yet in drapery much stiffness and error may be overlooked: not so in sea; the slightest inaccuracy, the slightest want of flow and freedom in the line, is attached by the eye, in a moment, of high treason, and I believe success to be impossible.

Yet there is not a wave, nor any violently agitated sea, on which both these forms do not appear; the latter especially, after some time of storm, extends over their whole surfaces: the reader sees, therefore, why I said that sea could only be painted by means of more or less dexterous conventionalism, since two of its most enduring phenomena cannot be represented at all.

Again, as respects the form of breakers on an even shore, there is difficulty of no less formidable kind. There is in them an irreconcilable mixture of fury and formalism. Their hollow surface is marked by parallel lines, like those of a smooth mill-weir, and graduated by reflected and transmitted lights of the most wonderful intricacy, its curve being at the same time necessarily of mathematical purity and precision; yet at the top of this curve, when it nods over, there is a sudden laxity and giving way, the water swings and jumps along the ridge like a shaken chain, and the motion runs from part to part as it does through a serpent's body. Then the wind is at work on the extreme edge, and instead of letting it fling itself off naturally, it supports it, and drives it back, or scrapes it off, and carries it bodily away; so that the spray at the top is in a continual transition between forms projected by their own weight, and forms blown and carried off with their weight overcome. Then at last, when it has come down, who shall say what shape that may be called, which "shape has none," of the great crash where it touches the beach?

I think it is that last crash which is the great taskmaster. Nobody can do anything with it. I have seen Copley Fielding come very close to the jerk   562 and nod of the lifted threatening edge, curl it very successfully, and without any look of its having been in papers, down nearly to the beach, but the final fall has no thunder in it. Turner has tried hard for it once or twice, but it will not do.

It is not, however, from the shore that Turner usually studies his sea. Seen from the land, the curl of the breakers, even in nature, is somewhat uniform and monotonous; the size of the waves out at sea is uncomprehended; and those nearer the eye seem to succeed and resemble each   563 other, to move slowly to the beach, and to break in the same lines and forms.

Afloat even twenty yards from the shore, we receive a totally different impression. Every wave around us appears vast, every one different from all the rest; and the breakers present, now that we see them with their backs towards us, the grand, extended, and varied lines of long curvature which are peculiarly expressive both of velocity and power. Recklessness, before unfelt, is manifested in the mad, perpetual, changeful, undirected motion, not of wave after wave, as it appears from the shore, but of the very same water rising and falling. Of waves that successively approach and break, each appears to the mind a separate individual, whose part being performed, it perishes, and is succeeded by another; and there is nothing in this to impress us with the idea of restlessness, any more than in any successive and continuous functions of life and death. But it is when we perceive that it is no succession of wave, but the same water, constantly rising, and crashing, and recoiling, and rolling in again in new forms and with fresh fury, that we perceive the perturbed spirit, and feel the intensity of its unwearied rage. The sensation of power is also trebled; for not only is the vastness of apparent size much increased, but the whole action is different; it is not a passive wave, rolling sleepily forward until it tumbles heavily, prostrated upon the beach; but a sweeping exertion of tremendous and living strength, which does not now appear to *fall*, but to *burst* upon the shore; which never perishes but recoils and recovers.

564   Aiming at these grand characters of the sea, Turner almost always places the spectator, not on the shore, but twenty or thirty yards from it, beyond the first range of the breakers, as in the Land's End [fig.19], Fowey, Dunbar, and Laugharne [fig.26]. The latter has been well engraved, and may be taken as a standard of the expression of fitfulness and power. The grand division of the whole space of the sea by a few dark continuous furrows of tremendous swell (the breaking of one of which alone has strewed the rocks in front with ruin) furnishes us with an estimate of space and strength, which at once reduces the men upon the shore to insects; and yet through this terrific simplicity there are indicated a fitfulness and fury in the tossing of the individual lines, which give to the whole sea a wild, unwearied, reckless incoherency, like that of an enraged multitude, whose masses act together in phrensy, while not one individual feels as another. Especial attention is to be directed to the flatness of all the lines, for the same principle holds in sea which we have seen in mountains. All the size and sublimity of nature are given, not by the height, but by the breadth, of her masses; and Turner, by following her in her sweeping lines, while he does not lose the elevation of its surges, adds in a tenfold degree to their power. Farther, observe the peculiar expression of *weight* which there is in Turner's waves, precisely of the same kind which we saw in his

fig.26   engraving after J.M.W. Turner, *Laugharne Castle*

waterfall. We have not a cutting, springing, elastic line; no jumping or leaping in the waves: *that* is the characteristic of Chelsea Reach or Hampstead Ponds in a storm. But the surges roll and plunge with such prostration and hurling of their mass against the shore, that we feel the rocks are shaking under them. And, to add yet more to this impression, observe how little, comparatively, they are broken by the wind: above the floating wood, and along the shore, we have indication of a line of torn spray; but it is a mere fringe along the ridge of the surge, no interference with its gigantic body. The wind has no power over its tremendous unity of force and weight. Finally, observe how, on the rocks on the left, the violence and swiftness of the rising wave are indicated by precisely the same lines which we saw were indicative of fury in the torrent. The water on these rocks is the body of the wave which has just broken, rushing up over them; and in doing so, like the torrent, it does not break, nor foam, nor part upon the rock, but accommodates itself to every one of its swells and hollows with undulating lines, whose grace and variety might alone serve us for a day's study; and it is only where two streams of this rushing water meet in the hollow of the rock, that their force is shown by the vertical bound of the spray.

In the distance of this grand picture there are two waves which entirely depart from the principle observed by all the rest, and spring high into the

565

air. They have a message for us which it is important that we should understand. Their leap is not a preparation for breaking, neither is it caused by their meeting with a rock. It is caused by their encounter with the recoil of the preceding wave. When a large surge, in the act of breaking, just as it curls over, is hurled against the face either of a wall or of a vertical rock, the sound of the blow is not a crash, nor a roar, it is a report as loud as, and in every respect similar to, that of a great gun, and the wave is dashed back from the rock with force scarcely diminished, but reversed in direction; it now recedes from the shore, and at the instant that it encounters the following breaker, the result is the vertical bound of both which is here rendered by Turner. Such a recoiling wave will 566 proceed out to sea through ten or twelve ranges of following breakers, before it is overpowered. But the effect of the blow at the shore itself is given in the Land's End [fig.19]. Under favourable circumstances with an advancing tide under a heavy gale, where the breakers feel the shore underneath them a moment before they touch the rock, so as to nod over when they strike, the effect is nearly incredible except to an eye-witness. I have seen the whole body of the wave rise in one white vertical broad fountain, eighty feet above the sea, half of it beaten so fine as to be borne away by the wind, the rest turning in the air when exhausted, and falling back with a weight and crash like that of an enormous waterfall. The Laugharne [fig.26] gives the surge and weight of the ocean in a gale, on a comparatively level shore; but the Land's End, the entire disorder of the surges when every one of them, divided and entangled among promontories as it rolls in, and beaten back part by part from walls of rock on this side and that side, recoils like the defeated division of a great army, throwing all behind it into disorder, breaking up the succeeding waves into vertical ridges, which in their turn, yet more totally shattered upon the shore, retire in more hopeless confusion; until the whole surface of the sea becomes one dizzy whirl of rushing, writhing, tortured, undirected 567 rage, bounding, and crashing, and coiling in an anarchy of enormous power; subdivided into myriads of waves, of which every one is not, be it remembered, a separate surge, but part and portion of a vast one, actuated by internal power, and giving in every direction the mighty undulation of impetuous line which glides over the rocks and writhes in the wind, overwhelming the one, and piercing the other with the form, fury, and swiftness of a sheet of lambent fire. And throughout the rendering of all this there is not one false curve given, not one which is not the perfect expression of visible motion; and the forms of the infinite sea are drawn throughout with that utmost mastery of art which, through the deepest study of every line, makes every line appear the wildest child of chance, while yet each is in itself a subject and a picture different from all else around. Of the colour of this magnificent sea I have before spoken; it is a solemn green grey (with its foam seen dimly through the darkness of twilight), modulated with the fulness, changefulness, and sadness of a deep wild melody.

Few people, comparatively, have ever seen the effect on the sea of a 569 powerful gale continued without intermission for three or four days and nights; and to those who have not, I believe it must be unimaginable, not from the mere force or size of surge, but from the complete annihilation of the limit between sea and air. The water from its prolonged agitation is beaten, not into mere creaming foam, but into masses of accumulated yeast, which hang in ropes and wreaths from wave to wave, and, where 570 one curls over to break, form a festoon like a drapery from its edge: these are taken up by the wind, not in dissipating dust, but bodily, in writhing, hanging, coiling masses, which make the air white and thick as with snow, only the flakes are a foot or two long each: the surges themselves are full of foam in their very bodies, underneath, making them white all through, as the water is under a great cataract; and their masses, being thus half water and half air, are torn to pieces by the wind whenever they rise, and carried away in roaring smoke, which chokes and strangles like actual water. Add to this, that when the air has been exhausted of its moisture by long rain, the spray of the sea is caught by it and covers its surface not merely with the smoke of finely divided water, but with boiling mist; imagine also the low rain-clouds brought down to the very level of the sea, as I have often seen them, whirling and flying in rags and fragments from wave to wave; and finally, conceive the surges themselves in their utmost pitch of power, velocity, vastness, and madness, lifting themselves in precipices and peaks, furrowed with their whirl of ascent, through all this chaos; and you will understand that there is indeed no distinction left between the sea and air; that no object, nor horizon, nor any land-mark or natural evidence of position is left; that the heaven is all spray, and the ocean all cloud, and that you can see no farther in any direction than you could see through a cataract. Suppose the effect of the first sunbeam sent 571 from above to show this annihilation to itself, and you have the sea picture of the Academy, 1842, the Snowstorm [fig.27], one of the very grandest statements of sea-motion, mist, and light, that has ever been put on canvas, even by Turner. Of course it was not understood; his finest works never are: but there was some apology for the public's not comprehending this, for few people have had the opportunity of seeing the sea at such a time, and when they have, cannot face it. To hold by a mast or a rock, and watch it, is a prolonged endurance of drowning which few people have courage to go through. To those who have, it is one of the noblest lessons of nature.

But, I think, the noblest sea that Turner has ever painted, and, if so, the noblest certainly ever painted by man, is that of the Slave Ship, the chief

fig.27   J.M.W. Turner, *Snowstorm: Steamboat Off a Harbour's Mouth*

Academy picture of the Exhibition of 1840 [plate 6].[59] It is a sunset on the Atlantic, after prolonged storm; but the storm is partially lulled, and the torn and streaming rain-clouds are moving in scarlet lines to lose themselves in the hollow of the night. The whole surface of sea included in the picture is divided into two ridges of enormous swell, not high, nor local, but a low broad heaving of the whole ocean, like the lifting of its bosom by deep-drawn breath after the torture of the storm. Between these two ridges the fire of the sunset falls along the trough of the sea, dyeing it with an awful but glorious light, the intense and lurid splendour which burns like gold, and bathes like blood. Along this fiery path and valley, the tossing waves by which the swell of the sea is restlessly divided, lift themselves in dark, indefinite, fantastic forms, each casting a faint and ghastly shadow behind it along the illumined foam. They do not rise everywhere, but three or four together in wild groups, fitfully and furiously, as the under strength of the swell compels or permits them; leaving between them treacherous spaces of level and whirling water, now lighted with green and lamp-like fire, now flashing back the gold of the declining sun, now fearfully dyed from above with the undistinguishable images of the burning clouds, which fall upon them in flakes of crimson and scarlet, and give to the reckless waves the added motion of their own

572

fiery flying. Purple and blue, the lurid shadows of the hollow breakers are cast upon the mist of night, which gathers cold and low, advancing like the shadow of death upon the guilty* ship as it labours amidst the light-ning of the sea, its thin masts written upon the sky in lines of blood, girded with condemnation in that fearful hue which signs the sky with horror, and mixes its flaming flood with the sunlight, and, cast far along the deso-late heave of the sepulchral waves, incarnadines the multitudinous sea.[60]

I believe, if I were reduced to rest Turner's immortality upon any single work, I should choose this. Its daring conception, ideal in the highest sense of the word, is based on the purest truth, and wrought out with the concentrated knowledge of a life; its colour is absolutely perfect, not one false or morbid hue in any part or line, and so modulated that every square inch of canvas is a perfect composition; its drawing as accurate as fearless; the ship buoyant, bending, and full of motion; its tones as true as they are 573 wonderful; and the whole picture dedicated to the most sublime of sub-jects and impressions (completing thus the perfect system of all truth, which we have shown to be formed by Turner's works)—the power, majesty, and deathfulness of the open, deep, illimitable sea.

* She is a slaver, throwing her slaves overboard. The near sea is encumbered with corpses.

SECTION VI
Of Truth of Vegetation.—Conclusion

CHAPTER I
Of Truth of Vegetation

574 WE have now arrived at the consideration of what was, with the old masters, the subject of most serious and perpetual study. If they do not give us truth here, they cannot have the faculty of truth in them: for foliage is the chief component part of all their pictures, and is finished by them with a care and labour which, if bestowed without attaining truth, must prove either their total bluntness of perception, or total powerlessness of hand.

575 It will be best to begin as nature does, with the stems and branches, and then to put the leaves on. And in speaking of trees generally, be it observed, when I say *all* trees, I mean only those ordinary forest or copse trees of Europe, which are the chief subjects of the landscape painter. I do not purpose to examine the characteristics of each tree; it will be enough to observe the laws common to all. First, then, neither the stems nor the boughs of any of the above trees *taper*, except where they fork. Wherever a stem sends off a branch, or a branch a lesser bough, or a lesser bough a bud, the stem of the branch is, on the instant, less in diameter by the exact quantity of the branch or the bough they have sent off, and they remain of the same diameter; or if there be any change, rather increase than diminish until they send off another branch or bough. This law is imperative and without exception; no bough, nor stem, nor twig, ever tapering or becoming narrower towards its extremity by a hair's-breadth, save where it parts with some portion of its substance at a fork or bud, so that if all the twigs and sprays at the top and sides of the tree, which are, and *have been*, could be united without loss of space, they would form a

576 round log of at least the diameter of the trunk from which they spring.

But nature takes great care and pains to conceal this uniformity in her boughs. They are perpetually parting with little sprays here and there, which steal away their substance cautiously and where the eye does not perceive the theft, until, a little way above, it feels the loss; and in the upper parts of the tree, the ramifications take place so constantly and delicately, that the effect upon the eye is precisely the same as if the boughs actually tapered, except here and there, where some avaricious one, greedy of substance, runs on for two or three yards without parting with anything, and becomes ungraceful in so doing.

Hence we see that although boughs may and must be represented as actually tapering, they must only be so when they are sending off foliage and sprays, and when they are at such a distance that the particular forks   577 and divisions cannot be evident to the eye; and farther, even in such circumstances, the tapering never can be sudden or rapid.

And therefore we see at once that the stem of Gaspar Poussin's tall tree, on the right of the La Riccia, in the National Gallery [plate 7], is a painting of a carrot or a parsnip, not of the trunk of a tree. For, being so near that every individual leaf is visible, we should not have seen, in nature, one branch or stem actually tapering. We should have received an *impression* of graceful diminution; but we should have been able, on examination, to trace it joint by joint, fork by fork, into the thousand minor supports of the leaves. Gaspar Poussin's stem, on the contrary, only sends off four or five minor branches altogether, and both it and they taper violently, and without showing why or wherefore; without parting with a single twig, without showing one vestige of roughness or excrescence; and leaving, therefore, their unfortunate leaves to hold on as best they may. The latter, however, are clever leaves, and support themselves as swarming bees do, hanging on by each other.

But even this piece of work is a jest to the perpetration of the bough at the left-hand upper corner of the picture opposite to it, the View near Albano [fig.28]. This latter is a representation of an ornamental group of elephants' tusks, with feathers tied to the ends of them. Not the wildest imagination could ever conjure up in it the remotest resemblance to the   578 bough of a tree. It might be the claws of a witch, the talons of an eagle, the horns of a fiend; but it is a full assemblage of every conceivable false-hood which can be told respecting foliage, a piece of work so barbarous in every way, that one glance at it ought to prove the complete charlatanism and trickery of the whole system of the old landscape painters. For I will depart for once from my usual plan, of abstaining from all assertion of a thing's being beautiful or otherwise; I will say here, at once, that such drawing as this is as ugly as it is childish, and as painful as it is false; and that the man who could tolerate, much more, who could deliberately set down such a thing on his canvas, had neither eye nor feeling for one single attribute or excellence of God's works. He might have drawn the other stem in excusable ignorance, or under some false impression of being able to improve upon nature; but *this* is conclusive and unpardonable.

fig.28 Gaspar Dughet, *Landscape Near Albano*(?)

579   But the old masters are not satisfied with drawing carrots for boughs. Nature can be violated in more ways than one, and the industry with which they seek out and adopt every conceivable mode of contradicting her is matter of no small interest. It is evident from what we have above stated of the structure of all trees, that as no boughs diminish where they do not fork, so they cannot fork without diminishing. It is impossible that the smallest shoot can be sent out of the bough without a diminution of the diameter above it; and wherever a branch goes off it must not only be less in diameter than the bough from which it springs, but the bough beyond the fork must be less by precisely the quantity of the branch it has
580   sent off. Now observe the bough underneath the first bend of the great stem in Claude's Narcissus;[61] it sends off four branches like the ribs of a leaf. The two lowest of these are both quite as thick as the parent stem, and the stem itself is much thicker after it has sent off the first one than it was before.

But there are farther conclusions to be drawn from this great principle in trees. As they only diminish where they divide, their increase of number is in precise proportion to their diminution of size; so that whenever we come to the extremities of boughs, we must have a multitude of sprays sufficient to make up, if they were united, the bulk of that from which they spring. Precision in representing this is neither desirable nor possible. All that is required is just so much observance of the general principle as may make the eye feel satisfied that there is something like the same quantity of wood in the sprays which there is in the stem. But to do this there must be, what there always is in nature, an exceeding complexity of the outer sprays. Now it will be found universally, in the works of Claude, Gaspar, and Salvator, that the boughs do *not* get in the least complex or multiplied towards the extremities; that each large limb forks only into two or three smaller ones, each of which vanishes into the air without any cause or reason for such unaccountable conduct, unless that the mass of leaves transfixed upon it or tied to it, entirely dependent on its single strength, have been too much, as well they may be, for its powers of solitary endurance. This total ignorance of tree-structure is shown throughout their works.

581

The landscape of Poussin with the storm [fig.17], the companion to the Dido and Æneas, in the National Gallery, presents us, in the foreground tree, with a piece of atrocity which I think, to any person who candidly considers it, may save me all further trouble of demonstrating the errors of ancient art. I do not in the least suspect the picture; the tones of it, and much of the handling, are masterly; yet that foreground tree comprises every conceivable violation of truth which the human hand can commit, or head invent, in drawing a tree, except only that it is not drawn root uppermost. It has no bark, no roughness nor character of stem; its boughs do not grow out of each other, but are stuck into each other; they ramify without diminishing, diminish without ramifying, are terminated by no complicated sprays, have their leaves tied to their ends, like the heads of Dutch brooms; and finally, and chiefly, they are evidently not made of wood, but of some soft elastic substance, which the wind can stretch out as it pleases, for there is not a vestige of an angle in any one of them. *Now the fiercest wind that ever blew upon the earth could not take the angles out of the bough of a tree an inch thick.* The whole bough bends together, retaining its elbows, and angles, and natural form, but affected throughout with curvature in each of its parts and joints. That part of it which was before perpendicular being bent aside, and that which was before sloping being bent into still greater inclination, the angle at which the two parts meet remains the same; or, if the strain be put in the opposite direction, the bough will break long before it loses its angle. You will find it difficult to bend the angles out of the youngest sapling, if they be marked; and absolutely impossible with a strong bough. You may break it, but you will not destroy its angles. And if you watch a tree in the wildest storm, you will find that though all its boughs are bending, none lose their character, but the utmost shoots and sapling spray. Hence Gaspar Poussin, by his bad drawing, does not make his storm strong, but his tree weak; he does not

583

584

make his gust violent, but his boughs of India-rubber.

These laws respecting vegetation are so far more imperative than those which were stated respecting water, that the greatest artist cannot violate them without danger, because they are laws resulting from organic structure which it is always painful to see interrupted; on the other hand, they have this in common with all laws, that they may be observed with mathematical precision, yet with no right result; the disciplined eye and the life in the woods are worth more than all botanical knowledge. For there is that about the growing of the tree trunk, and that grace in its upper ramification, which cannot be taught, and which cannot even be seen but by eager watchfulness.

585

Generally, I think the perception of the muscular qualities of the tree trunk incomplete, except in men who have studied the human figure; and in loose expression of those characters, the painter who can draw the living muscle seldom fails; but the thoroughly peculiar lines belonging to woody fibre can only be learned by patient forest study. And hence in all the trees of the merely historical painters, there is fault of some kind or another; commonly exaggeration of the muscular swellings, or insipidity and want of spring in curvature, or fantasticism and unnaturalness of arrangement, and especially a want of the peculiar characters of bark which express the growth and age of the tree; for bark is no mere excrescence, lifeless and external, it is a skin of especial significance in its indications of the organic form beneath; in places under the arms of the tree it wrinkles up and forms fine lines *round* the trunk, inestimable in their indication of the direction of its surface; in others, it bursts or peels longitudinally, and the rending and bursting of it are influenced in direction and degree by the undergrowth and swelling of the woody fibre, and are not a mere roughness and granulated pattern of the hide. Farther, the modes of ramification of the upper branches are so varied, inventive, and graceful, that the least alteration of them, even the measure of a hair's-breadth, spoils them; and though it is sometimes possible to get rid of a troublesome bough, accidentally awkward, or in some minor respects to assist the arrangement, yet so far as the real branches are copied, the hand libels their lovely curvatures even in its best attempts to follow them.

586

These two characters, the woody stiffness hinted through muscular line, and the inventive grace of the upper boughs, have never been rendered except by Turner; he does not merely draw them better than others, but he is the only man who has ever drawn them at all.

588

Let us, however, pass to the leafage of the elder landscape painters, and see if it atones for the deficiencies of the stems. One of the most remarkable characters of natural leafage is the constancy with which, while the leaves are arranged on the spray with exquisite regularity, that regularity is modified in their actual effect. For as in every group of leaves some are seen sideways, forming merely long lines, some foreshortened, some crossing each other, every one differently turned and placed from all the others, the forms of the leaves, though in themselves similar, give rise to a thousand strange and differing forms in the group; and the shadows of some, passing over the others, still further disguise and confuse the   589 mass, until the eye can distinguish nothing but a graceful and flexible disorder of innumerable forms, with here and there a perfect leaf on the extremity, or a symmetrical association of one or two, just enough to mark the specific character and to give unity and grace, but never enough to repeat in one group what was done in another, never enough to prevent the eye from feeling that, however regular and mathematical may be the structure of parts, what is composed out of them is as various and infinite as any other part of nature. Nor does this take place in general effect only. Break off an elm bough three feet long, in full leaf, and lay it on the table before you, and try to draw it, leaf for leaf. It is ten to one if in the whole bough you find one form of a leaf exactly like another; perhaps you will not even have *one* complete. Every leaf will be oblique, or foreshortened, or curled, or crossed by another, or shaded by another, or have something or other the matter with it; and though the whole bough will look graceful and symmetrical, you will scarcely be able to tell how or why it does so, since there is not one line of it like another. Now go to Gaspar Poussin and take one of his sprays where they come against the sky; you may count it all round: one, two, three, four, one bunch; five, six, seven, eight, two bunches; nine, ten, eleven, twelve, three bunches; with four leaves each; and such leaves! every one precisely the same as its neighbour, blunt and round at the end (where every forest leaf is sharp, except that of the fig-tree), tied together by the stalks, and so fastened on to the demoniacal claws above described, one bunch to each claw.

But if nature is so various when you have a bough on the table before you, what must she be when she retires from you, and gives you her whole mass and multitude? The leaves then at the extremities become as fine as dust, a mere confusion of points and lines between you and the sky, a confusion which, you might as well hope to draw sea-sand particle by   590 particle, as to imitate leaf for leaf. This, as it comes down into the body of the tree, gets closer, but never opaque; it is always transparent with crumbling lights in it letting you through to the sky; then out of this, come, heavier and heavier, the masses of illumined foliage, all dazzling and inextricable, save here and there a single leaf on the extremities: then, under these, you get deep passages of broken irregular gloom, passing into transparent, green-lighted, misty hollows; the twisted stems glancing through them in their pale and entangled infinity, and the shafted sunbeams, rained from above, running along the lustrous leaves for an instant; then lost, then caught again on some emerald bank or knotted root, to be sent up again with a faint reflex on the white under-sides of dim groups of drooping foliage, the shadows of the upper boughs running in grey network down the glossy stems, and resting in quiet chequers upon the glittering earth; but all penetrable and transparent, and, in proportion, inextricable and incomprehensible, except where across the labyrinth and the mystery of the dazzling light and dream-like shadow, falls, close to us, some solitary spray, some wreath of two or three motionless large leaves, the type and embodying of all that in the rest we feel and imagine, but can never see.

Now, with thus much of nature in your mind, go to Gaspar Poussin's view near Albano, in the National Gallery [fig.28]. It is the very subject to unite all these effects, a sloping bank shaded with intertwined forest. And what has Gaspar given us? A mass of smooth, opaque, varnished brown, without one interstice, one change of hue, or any vestige of leafy structure, in its interior, or in those parts of it, I should say, which are intended to represent interior; but out of it, over it rather, at regular intervals, we have circular groups of greenish touches, always the same in

591   size, shape, and distance from each other, containing so exactly the same number of touches each, that you cannot tell one from another. There are eight or nine and thirty of them, laid over each other like fish-scales; the shade being most carefully made darker and darker as it recedes from each until it comes to the edge of the next, against which it cuts in the same sharp circular line, and then begins to decline again, until the canvas is covered, with about as much intelligence or feeling of art as a house-painter has in marbling a wainscot, or a weaver in repeating an ornamental pattern. What is there in this, which the most determined prejudice in favour of the old masters can for a moment suppose to resemble trees? It is exactly what the most ignorant beginner, trying to make a complete drawing, would lay down; exactly the conception of trees which we have in the works of our worst drawing-masters, where the shade is laid on with the black lead and stump, and every human power exerted to make it look like a kitchen-grate well polished.

592   But nature observes another principle in her foliage more important even than its intricacy. She always secures an exceeding harmony and repose. She is *so* intricate that her minuteness of parts becomes to the eye, at a little distance, one united veil or cloud of leaves, to destroy the evenness of which is perhaps a greater fault than to destroy its transparency.

593   It is here that Hobbima and Both fail. They can paint oak leafage faithfully, but do not know where to stop, and by doing too much, lose the truth of all, lose the very truth of detail at which they aim, for all their minute work only gives two leaves to nature's twenty. They are evidently incapable of even thinking of a tree, much more of drawing it,

except leaf by leaf; they have no notion nor sense of simplicity, mass, or obscurity, and when they come to distance, where it is totally impossible that leaves should be separately seen, being incapable of conceiving or rendering the grand and quiet forms of truth, they are reduced to paint their bushes with dots and touches expressive of leaves three feet broad each.

But let us oppose to their works the group of trees on the left in Turner's Marly [plate 13]. We have there perfect and ceaseless intricacy to oppose to Poussin, perfect and unbroken repose to oppose to Hobbima; and in the unity of these the perfection of truth. This group may be taken as a fair standard of Turner's tree-painting. We have in it the admirably drawn stems, instead of the claws or the serpents; full, transparent, boundless intricacy, instead of the shell pattern; and misty depth of intermingled light and leafage, instead of perpetual repetition of one mechanical touch.

The last and most important truth to be observed respecting trees is, 594 that their boughs always, in finely grown individuals, bear among themselves such a ratio of length as to describe with their extremities a symmetrical curve, constant for each species; and within this curve all the irregularities, segments, and divisions of the tree are included, each bough reaching the limit with its extremity, but not passing it. When a tree is 595 perfectly grown, each bough starts from the trunk with just so much wood as, allowing for constant ramification, will enable it to reach the terminal line; or if, by mistake, it start with too little, it will proceed without ramifying till within a distance where it may safely divide; if on the contrary it start with too much, it will ramify quickly and constantly; or, to express the real operation more accurately, each bough growing on so as to keep even with its neighbours, takes so much wood from the trunk as is sufficient to enable it to do so, more or less in proportion as it ramifies fast or slowly. In badly grown trees the boughs are apt to fall short of the curve, or at least there are so many jags and openings that its symmetry is interrupted; and in young trees, the impatience of the upper shoots frequently breaks the line: but, in perfect and mature trees, every bough does its duty completely, and the line of curve is quite filled up, and the mass within it unbroken, so that the tree assumes the shape of a dome as in the oak, or, in tall trees, of a pear with the stalk downmost. The old masters paid no attention whatsoever to this great principle. They swing their boughs about, anywhere and everywhere; each stops or goes on just as it likes; nor will it be possible, in any of their works, to find a single example in which any symmetrical curve is indicated by the extremities. 596

But I need scarcely tell any one in the slightest degree acquainted with the works of Turner, how rigidly and constantly he adheres to this principle of nature; taking in his highest compositions the perfect ideal form, every spray being graceful and varied in itself, but inevitably terminating at the assigned limit, and filling up the curve without break or gap; in his lower works, taking less perfect form but invariably hinting the constant tendency in all; and thus, in spite of his abundant complexity, he arranges his trees under simpler and grander forms than any other artist, even among the moderns.[62]

CHAPTER II
General Remarks Respecting the Truth
of Turner

W^E have now arrived at some general conception of the extent of   606
Turner's knowledge, and the truth of his practice, by the deliberate
examination of the characteristics of the four great elements of
landscape,—sky, earth, water, and vegetation.

All those truths which I have been able to explain and demonstrate in   609
Turner, are such as any artist of ordinary powers of observation ought to
be capable of rendering. It is disgraceful to omit them; but it is no very
great credit to observe them. I have indeed proved that they have been
neglected, and disgracefully so, by those men who are commonly
considered the Fathers of Art; but in showing that they have been
observed by Turner, I have only proved him to be *above* other men in
knowledge of truth, I have not given any conception of his own positive
rank as a Painter of Nature. But it stands to reason, that the men, who in
broad, simple, and demonstrable matters are perpetually violating truth,
will not be particularly accurate or careful in carrying out delicate and
refined and undemonstrable matters; and it stands equally to reason that
the man, who, as far as argument or demonstration can go, is found
invariably truthful, will, in all probability, be truthful to the last line, and
shadow of a line. And such is, indeed, the case with every touch of this
consummate artist; the essential excellence, all that constitutes the real
and exceeding value of his works, is beyond and above expression: it is a
truth inherent in every line, and breathing in every hue, too delicate and
exquisite to admit of any kind of proof, nor to be ascertained except by the
highest of tests, the keen feeling attained by extended knowledge and long
study. Two lines are laid on canvas; one is right and another wrong. There
is no difference between them appreciable by the compasses, none
appreciable by the ordinary eye, none which can be pointed out, if it is not
seen. One person feels it, another does not; but the feeling or sight of the   610
one can by no words be communicated to the other:—that feeling and
sight have been the reward of years of labour. There is no test of our
acquaintance with nature so absolute and unfailing, as the degree of
admiration we feel for Turner's painting. Precisely as we are shallow in our

170

knowledge, vulgar in our feeling, and contracted in our views of principles, will the works of this artist be stumbling-blocks or foolishness to us:
precisely in the degree in which we are familiar with nature, constant in
our observation of her, and enlarged in our understanding of her, will they
expand before our eyes into glory and beauty. In every new insight which
we obtain into the works of God, in every new idea which we receive from
His creation, we shall find ourselves possessed of an interpretation and a
guide to something in Turner's works which we had not before understood. We may range over Europe, from shore to shore; and from every
rock that we tread upon, every sky that passes over our heads, every local
form of vegetation or of soil, we shall receive fresh illustration of his
principles, fresh confirmation of his facts. We shall feel, wherever we go,
that he has been there before us: whatever we see, that he has seen and
seized before us: and we shall at last cease the investigation, with a well-
611 grounded trust, that whatever we have been unable to account for, and
what we still dislike in his works, has reason for it, and foundation like the
rest; and that even where he has failed or erred, there is a beauty in the
failure which none are able to equal, and a dignity in the error which none
are worthy to reprove.

There has been marked and constant progress in his mind; he has not,
like some few artists, been without childhood; his course of study has been
as evidently, as it has been swiftly, progressive; and in different stages of
the struggle, sometimes one order of truth, sometimes another, has been
aimed at or omitted. But, from the beginning to the height of his career,
he never sacrificed a greater truth to a less. As he advanced, the previous
knowledge or attainment was absorbed in what succeeded, or abandoned
only if incompatible, and never abandoned without a gain; and his last
works presented the sum and perfection of his accumulated knowledge,
delivered with the impatience and passion of one who feels too much, and
knows too much, and has too little time to say it in, to pause for expression, or ponder over his syllables. There was in them the obscurity,
but the truth, of prophecy; the instinctive and burning language which
would express less if it uttered more, which is indistinct only by its fulness,
and dark with its abundant meaning. He felt now, with long-trained
vividness and keenness of sense, too bitterly the impotence of the hand,
and the vainness of the colour, to catch one shadow or one image of the
glory which God had revealed to him. "I cannot gather the sunbeams out
of the east, or I would make *them* tell you what I have seen; but read this,
and interpret this, and let us remember together. I cannot gather the
gloom out of the night-sky, or I would make that teach you what I have
seen; but read this, and interpret this, and let us feel together. And if you
have not that within you which I can summon to my aid, if you have not
the sun in your spirit, and the passion in your heart, which my words may

awaken, though they be indistinct and swift, leave me; for I will give you 612 no patient mockery, no laborious insult of that glorious nature, whose I am and whom I serve. Let other servants imitate the voice and the gesture of their master, while they forget his message. Hear that message from me; but remember that the teaching of Divine truth must still be a mystery."

CHAPTER III
Conclusion.—Modern Art and Modern Criticism

613   WE have only, in conclusion, to offer a few general remarks respecting modern art and modern criticism.

We wish, in the first place, to remove the appearance of invidiousness and partiality which the constant prominence given in the present portion of the work to the productions of one artist, can scarcely fail of bearing in the minds of most readers. When we pass to the examination of what is beautiful and expressive in art, we shall frequently find distinctive qualities in the minds even of inferior artists, which have led them to the pursuit and embodying of particular trains of thought, altogether different from those which direct the compositions of other men, and incapable of comparison with them. Now, when this is the case, we should consider it in the highest degree both invidious and illogical, to say of such different modes of exertion of the intellect, that one is in all points greater or nobler than another. We shall probably find something in the working of all minds which has an end and a power peculiar to itself, and which is deserving of free and full admiration, without any reference whatsoever to what has, in other fields, been accomplished by other modes of thought, and directions of aim. We shall, indeed, find a wider range and grasp in one man than in another; but yet it will be our own fault if we do not discover something in the most limited range of mind which is different from, and in its way better than, anything presented to us by the more grasping intellect. We all know that the nightingale sings more nobly than the lark; but who, therefore, would wish the

614   lark not to sing, or would deny that it had a character of its own, which bore a part among the melodies of creation no less essential than that of the more richly gifted bird? And thus we shall find and feel that whatever difference may exist between the intellectual powers of one artist and another, yet wherever there is any true genius, there will be some peculiar lesson which even the humblest will teach us more sweetly and perfectly than those far above them in prouder attributes of mind; and we should be as mistaken as we should be unjust and invidious, if we refused to receive this their peculiar message with gratitude and veneration, merely because

173

it was a sentence and not a volume. But the case is different when we examine their relative fidelity to given facts. That fidelity depends on no peculiar modes of thought or habits of character; it is the result of keen sensibility, combined with high powers of memory and association. These qualities, as such, are the same in all men; character or feeling may direct their choice to this or that object, but the fidelity with which they treat either the one or the other, is dependent on those simple powers of sense and intellect which are like and comparable in all, and of which we can always say that they are greater in this man, or less in that, without reference to the character of the individual. Wherever we have, in the   615 drawing of any one object, sufficient evidence of real intellectual power, of the sense which perceives the essential qualities of a thing, and the judgment which arranges them so as to illustrate each other, we may be quite certain that the same sense and judgment will operate equally on whatever is subjected to them, and that the artist will be equally great and masterly in his drawing of all that he attempts. And thus we have been   616 compelled, however unwillingly, to pass hastily by the works of many gifted men, because, however pure their feeling, or original their conceptions, they were wanting in those faculties of the hand and mind which insure perfect fidelity to nature; it will be only hereafter, when we are at liberty to take full cognizance of the thought, however feebly it may be clothed in language, that we shall be able to do real justice to the disciples either of modern or of ancient art.

But as far as we have gone at present, and with respect only to the *material* truth, which is all that we have been able to investigate, the conclusion to which we must be led is as clear as it is inevitable: that modern artists, as a body, are far more just and full in their views of material things than any landscape painters whose works are extant; but that J. M. W. Turner is the only man who has ever given an entire transcript of the whole system of nature, and is, in this point of view, the only perfect landscape painter whom the world has ever seen.

Nor are we disposed to recede from our assertion that this material truth is indeed a perfect test of the relative rank of painters, though it does not in itself constitute that rank. We shall be able to prove that truth and beauty, knowledge and imagination, invariably are associated in art; and   617 we shall be able to show that not only in truth to nature, but in all other points, Turner is the greatest landscape painter who has ever lived. But his superiority is, in matters of feeling, one of kind, not of degree. Superiority of degree implies a superseding of others; superiority of kind implies only sustaining a more important, but not more necessary, part than others. If *truth* were all that we required from art, all other painters might cast aside their brushes in despair, for all that they have done he has done more fully and accurately; but when we pass to the higher requirements of art, beauty and character, their contributions are all equally necessary and desirable, because different, and however inferior in position or rank, are still perfect of their kind; their inferiority is only that of the lark to the nightingale, or of the violet to the rose.

Such then are the rank and standing of our modern artists. We have had, living with us, and painting for us, the greatest painter of *all* time; a man with whose supremacy of power no intellect of past ages can be put in comparison for a moment. Let us next inquire what is the rank of our critics. Public taste, I believe, as far as it is the encourager and supporter of art, has been the same in all ages; a fitful and vacillating current of vague impression, perpetually liable to change, subject to epidemic desires, and agitated by infectious passion, the slave of fashion, and the fool of fancy; but yet always distinguishing, with singular clearsightedness, between that which is best and that which is worst of the particular class of food which its morbid appetite may call for; never failing to distinguish that which is produced by intellect, from that which is not, though it may be intellect degraded by ministering to its misguided will. Public taste may thus degrade a race of men capable of the highest efforts in art into the portrait painters of ephemeral fashions, but it will yet not fail of discovering who, among these portrait painters, is the man of most mind.

618   It will separate the man who would have become Buonaroti from the man who would have become Bandinelli,[63] though it will employ both in painting curls, and feathers, and bracelets. Hence, generally speaking, there is no *comparative* injustice done, no false elevation of the fool above the man of mind, provided only that the man of mind will condescend to supply the particular article which the public chooses to want. The press, therefore, and all who pretend to lead the public taste, have not so much to direct the multitude whom to go to, as what to ask for. Their business is not to tell us which is our best painter, but to tell us whether we are making our best painter do his best.

Now none are capable of doing this, but those whose principles of judgment are based both on thorough *practical* knowledge of art, and on broad general views of what is true and right, without reference to what has been done at one time or another, or in one school or another. Nothing can be more perilous to the cause of art, than the constant ringing in our painters' ears of the names of great predecessors, as their examples or masters. But such references to former excellence are the only refuge and resource of persons endeavouring to be critics without being artists. They cannot tell you whether a thing is right or not; but they can tell you whether it is like something else or not. And the whole tone of modern criticism, so far as it is worthy of being called criticism, suf-

619   ficiently shows it to proceed entirely from persons altogether unversed in practice, and ignorant of truth, but possessing just enough of feeling to

enjoy the solemnity of ancient art; who, not distinguishing that which is really exalted and valuable in the modern school, nor having any just idea of the real ends or capabilities of landscape art, consider nothing right which is not based on the conventional principles of the ancients, and nothing true which has more of nature in it than of Claude. But it is strange that while the noble and unequalled works of modern landscape painters are thus maligned and misunderstood, our historical painters, such as we have, are permitted to pander more fatally every year to the vicious English taste, which can enjoy nothing but what is theatrical, entirely unchastised, nay, encouraged and lauded, by the very men who endeavour to hamper our great landscape painters with rules derived from consecrated blunders. The very critic who has just passed one of the noblest works of Turner,—that is to say, a masterpiece of art to which Time can show no parallel,—with a ribald jest, will yet stand gaping in admiration before the next piece of dramatic glitter and grimace, suggested by the society and adorned with the appurtenances of the green-room, [64] which he finds hung low upon the wall as a brilliant example of the ideal of English art. It is natural enough indeed, that the persons who are disgusted by what is pure and noble, should be delighted with what is vicious and degraded; but it is singular that those who are constantly   620 talking of Claude and Poussin, should never even pretend to a thought of Raffaelle. We could excuse them for not comprehending Turner, if they only would apply the same cut-and-dried criticisms where they might be applied with truth, and productive of benefit; but we endure not the paltry compound of ignorance, false taste, and pretension, which assumes the dignity of classical feeling, that it may be able to abuse whatever is above the level of its understanding, but bursts into rapture with all that is mean or meretricious, if sufficiently adapted to the calibre of its comprehension.

To notice such criticisms, however, is giving them far more importance than they deserve. They can lead none astray but those whose opinions are absolutely valueless, and we did not begin this chapter with any intent of wasting our time on these small critics, but in the hope of pointing out to the periodical press what kind of criticism is now most required by our school of landscape art; and how it may be in their power, if they will, to regulate its impulses, without checking its energies, and really to advance both the cause of the artist, and the taste of the public.

One of the most morbid symptoms of the general taste of the present day is, a too great fondness for unfinished works. Brilliancy and rapidity of execution are everywhere sought as the highest good, and so that a picture be cleverly handled as far as it is carried, little regard is paid to its imperfection as a whole. Hence some artists are permitted, and others compelled, to confine themselves to a manner of working altogether destructive of their powers, and to tax their energies, not to concentrate the greatest quantity of thought on the least possible space of canvas, but to produce the greatest quantity of glitter and clap-trap in the shortest possible time. To the idler and trickster in art, no system can be more advantageous; but to the man who is really desirous of doing something worth having lived for, to a man of industry, energy, or feeling, we believe it to be the cause of the most bitter discouragement. Now the press should especially endeavour to convince the public that by this purchase of imperfect pictures they not only prevent all progress and development of high talent, and set tricksters and mechanics on a level with men of mind, but defraud and injure themselves. For there is no doubt whatever, that, estimated merely by the quantity of pleasure it is capable of conveying, a well-finished picture is worth to its possessor half-a-dozen incomplete ones; and that a perfect drawing is, simply as a source of delight, better worth a hundred guineas than a drawing half as finished is worth thirty.* On the other hand, the body of our artists should be kept in mind, that, by indulging the public with rapid and unconsidered work, they are not only depriving themselves of the benefit which each picture ought to render to them, as a piece of practice and study, but they are destroying the refinement of general taste, and rendering it impossible for themselves ever to find a market for more careful works, supposing that they were inclined to execute them. Nor need any single artist be afraid of setting the example, and producing laboured works, at advanced prices, among the cheap quick drawings of the day. The public will soon find the value of the complete work, and will be more ready to give a large sum for that which is inexhaustible, than a portion of it for that which they are wearied of in a month. The artist who never lets the price command the picture, will soon find the picture command the price. And it ought to be a rule with every painter, never to let a picture leave his easel while it is yet capable of improvement, or of having more thought put into it. The general effect is often perfect and pleasing, and not to be improved upon,

---

* I would further insist on all that is advanced in these paragraphs, with especial reference to the admirable, though strange, pictures of Mr. Millais and Mr. Holman Hunt; and to the principles exemplified in the efforts of other members of a society which unfortunately, or rather unwisely, has given itself the name of "Pre-Raphaelite;" unfortunately, because the principles on which its members are working are neither pre- not post-Raphaelite, but everlasting. They are endeavouring to paint, with the highest possible degree of completion, what they see in nature, without reference to conventional or established rules; but by no means to imitate the style of any past epoch. Their works are, in finish of drawing, and in splendour of colour, the best in the Royal Academy; and I have great hope that they may become the foundation of a more earnest and able school of art than we have seen for centuries.[65]

when the details and facts are altogether imperfect and unsatisfactory. It may be difficult, perhaps the most difficult task of art, to complete these details, and not to hurt the general effect; but, until the artist can do this, his art is imperfect and his picture unfinished. That only is a complete picture which has both the general wholeness and effect of nature, and the inexhaustible perfection of nature's details. And it is only in the effort to unite these that a painter really improves. By aiming only at details, he becomes a mechanic; by aiming only at generals, he becomes a trickster; his fall in both cases is sure. Two questions the artist has, therefore, always to ask himself: First, "Is my whole right?" Secondly, "Can my details be added to? Is there a single space in the picture where I can crowd in another thought? Is there a curve in it which I can modulate, a line which I can vary, a vacancy I can fill? Is there a single spot which the eye, by any peering or prying, can fathom or exhaust? If so, my picture is imperfect; and if, in modulating the line or filling the vacancy, I hurt the general effect, my art is imperfect."

But, on the other hand, though incomplete pictures ought neither to be   623
produced nor purchased, careful and real *sketches* ought to be valued much more highly than they are. Studies of landscape, in chalk or sepia, should form a part of every Exhibition, and a room should be allotted to drawings and designs of figures in the Academy.

From young artists nothing ought to be tolerated but simple *bonâ fide imitation* of nature. They have no business to ape the execution of masters; to utter weak and disjointed repetitions of other men's words, and mimic the gestures of the preacher, without understanding his meaning or sharing in his emotions. We do not want their crude ideas of composition, their unformed conceptions of the Beautiful, their unsystematized experiments upon the Sublime. We scorn their velocity; for it is without direction: we reject their decision; for it is without grounds: we contemn their composition; for it is without materials: we reprobate their choice; for it is without comparison. Their duty is neither to choose, nor compose, nor imagine, nor experimentalize; but to be humble and earnest in following the steps of nature, and tracing the finger of God. Nothing is so bad a symptom, in the work of young artists, as too much dexterity of handling; for it is a sign that they are satisfied with their work, and have tried to do nothing more than they were able to do. Their work should be full of failures; for these are the signs of efforts. They should keep to quiet colours, greys and browns; and, making the early works of Turner their example, as his latest are to be their object of emulation, should go to   624
Nature in all singleness of heart, and walk with her laboriously and trustingly, having no other thoughts but how best to penetrate her meaning, and remember her instruction; rejecting nothing, selecting nothing, and scorning nothing; believing all things to be right and good,

and rejoicing always in the truth. Then, when their memories are stored, and their imaginations fed, and their hands firm, let them take up the scarlet and the gold, give the reins to their fancy, and show us what their heads are made of. We will follow them wherever they choose to lead; we will check at nothing; they are then our masters, and are fit to be so. They have placed themselves above our criticism, and we will listen to their words in all faith and humility; but not unless they themselves have before bowed, in the same submission, to a higher Authority and Master.

Among our greater artists, the chief want, at the present day, is that of *solemnity* and definite purpose. We have too much picture-manufacturing, too much making up of lay figures with a certain quantity of foliage, and a certain quantity of sky, and a certain quantity of water; a little bit of all that is pretty, a little sun and a little shade, a touch of pink and a touch of blue, a little sentiment and a little sublimity, and a little humour and a little antiquarianism, all very neatly associated in a very charming picture, but not working together for a definite end. Or if the aim be higher, we are generally put off with stale repetitions of eternal composition; a great tree, and some goats, and a bridge, and a lake, and the Temple at Tivoli, etc. Now we should like to see our artists working out, with all exertion of their concentrated powers, such marked pieces of landscape character as might bear upon them the impression of solemn, earnest, and pervading thought, definitely directed, and aided by every accessary of detail, colour, and idealized form, which the disciplined feeling, accumulated knowledge, and unspared labour of the painter could supply.

Let then every picture be painted with earnest intention of impressing on the spectator some elevated emotion, and exhibiting to him some one particular, but exalted, beauty. Let a real subject be carefully selected, in itself suggestive of, and replete with, this feeling and beauty; let an effect of light and colour be taken which may harmonize with both; and a sky not invented but recollected: in fact, all so-called invention is in landscape nothing more than appropriate recollection, good in proportion as it is distinct. Then let the details of the foreground be separately studied, especially those plants which appear peculiar to the place; if any one, however unimportant, occurs there, which occurs not elsewhere, it should occupy a prominent position: for the other details, the highest examples of the ideal forms or characters which he requires are to be selected by the artist from his former studies, or fresh studies made expressly for the purpose, leaving as little as possible—nothing, in fact, beyond their connection and arrangement—to mere imagination. Finally, when his picture is thus perfectly realized in all its parts, let him dash as much of it out as he likes; throw, if he will, mist round it, darkness, or dazzling and confused light, whatever, in fact, impetuous feeling or vigorous imagination may dictate or desire; the forms, once so laboriously realized, will come out, whenever they *do* occur, with a startling and impressive truth which the uncertainty in which they are veiled will enhance rather than diminish; and the imagination, strengthened by discipline and fed with truth, will achieve the utmost of creation that is possible to finite mind.

The artist who thus works will soon find that he cannot repeat himself if he would; and new fields of exertion, new subjects of contemplation, open to him in nature day by day; and that, while others lament the weakness of their invention, *he* has nothing to lament but the shortness of life.

And now but one word more, respecting the great artist whose works   629 have formed the chief subject of this treatise. The greatest qualities of those works have not yet been so much as touched upon. None but their imitative excellences have been proved, and, therefore, the enthusiasm with which I speak of them must necessarily appear overcharged and absurd. It might, perhaps, have been more prudent to have withheld the full expression of it till I had shown the full grounds for it: but once written, such expression must remain till I have justified it. And, indeed, I think there is enough, even in the foregoing pages, to show that these works are, as far as concerns the ordinary critics of the press, above all animadversion, and above all praise; and that, by the public, they are not to be received as in any way subjects or matters of opinion, but of faith. We are not to approach them to be pleased, but to be taught; not to form a judgment, but to receive a lesson. Our periodical writers, therefore, may save themselves the trouble either of blaming or praising: their duty is not to pronounce opinions upon the work of a man who has walked with nature threescore years; but to impress upon the public the respect with which they are to be received, and to make request to him, on the part of the people of England, that he would now touch no unimportant work, that he would not spend time on slight or small pictures, but give to the nation a series of grand, consistent, systematic, and completed poems. We desire that he should follow out his own thoughts and intents of heart, without reference to any human authority. But we request, in all humility,   630 that those thoughts may be seriously and loftily given; and that the whole power of his unequalled intellect may be exerted in the production of such works as may remain for ever, for the teaching of the nations. In all that he says, we believe; in all that he does, we trust. It is therefore that we pray him to utter nothing lightly; to do nothing regardlessly. He stands upon an eminence, from which he looks back over the universe of God and forward over the generations of men. Let every work of his hand be a history of the one, and a lesson to the other. Let each exertion of his   631 mighty mind be both hymn and prophecy; adoration to the Deity, revelation to mankind.

POSTSCRIPT

THE above passage was written in the year 1843; too late. It is true, that, soon after the publication of this work, the abuse of the press, which had been directed against Turner with unceasing virulence during the production of his noblest works, sank into timid animadversion, or changed into unintelligent praise; but not before illness, and, in some degree, mortification, had enfeebled the hand and chilled the heart of the painter.

This year (1851) he has no picture on the walls of the Academy; and the *Times* of May 3rd says, "We miss those works of INSPIRATION!"

We miss! Who misses? The populace of England rolls by to weary itself in the great bazaar of Kensington, little thinking that a day will come when those veiled vestals and prancing amazons, and goodly merchandize of precious stones and gold, will all be forgotten as though they had not been, but that the light which has faded from the walls of the Academy is one which a million of Koh-i-Noors could not rekindle, and that the year 1851 will, in the far future, be remembered less for what it has displayed than for what it has withdrawn.

DENMARK HILL,
June, 1851.

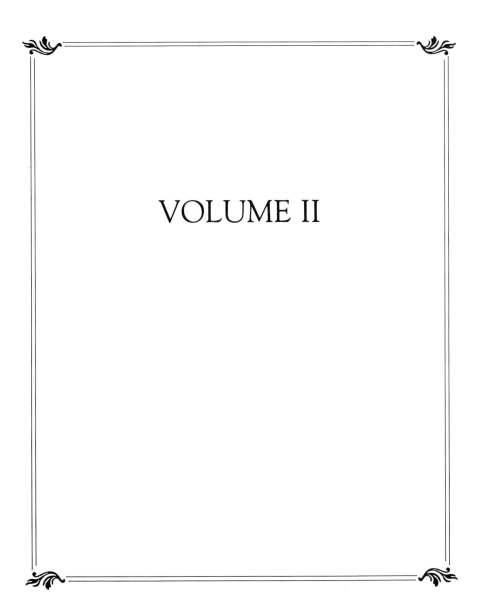

VOLUME II

PART III
Of Ideas of Beauty

SECTION I
Of the Theoretic Faculty

CHAPTER I
Of the Rank and Relations of
the Theoretic Faculty

25 ALTHOUGH the hasty execution and controversial tone of the former portions of this essay have been subjects of frequent regret to the writer, yet the one was in some measure excusable in a work referred to a temporary end, and the other unavoidable in one directed against particular opinions. Nor is either of any necessary detriment to its availableness as a foundation for more careful and extended survey, in so far as its province was confined to the assertion of obvious and visible facts, the verification of which could in no degree be dependent either on the care with which they might be classed, or the temper in which they were regarded. Not so with respect to the investigation now before us, which, being not of things outward, and sensibly demonstrable, but of the value and meaning of mental impressions, must be entered upon with a modesty and cautiousness proportioned to the difficulty of determining the likeness, or community, of such impressions, as they are

26 received by different men; and with seriousness proportioned to the importance of rightly regarding those faculties over which we have moral power, and therefore in relation to which we assuredly incur a moral responsibility.

Nor indeed have I ever, even in the preceding sections, spoken with levity, though sometimes perhaps with rashness. I have never treated the subject as other than demanding heedful and serious examination, and taking high place among those which justify, as they reward, our utmost ardour and earnestness of pursuit. That it justifies them must be my present task to prove; that it demands them has never been doubted. Art, properly so called, is no recreation; it cannot be learned at spare moments, nor pursued when we have nothing better to do. It is no handiwork for drawing-room tables, no relief of the ennui of boudoirs; it must be understood and undertaken seriously, or not at all. To advance it men's lives must be given, and to receive it, their hearts. But that this labour, the necessity of which, in all ages, has been most frankly admitted by the greatest men, is justifiable from a moral point of view, that it is not a vain devotion of the lives of men, that it has functions of usefulness addressed to the weightiest of human interests, and that the objects of it have calls upon us which it is inconsistent alike with our human dignity and our heavenward duty to disobey, has never been boldly asserted nor fairly admitted; least of all is it likely to be so in these days of despatch and display, where vanity, on the one side, supplies the place of that love of art which is the only effective patronage, and, on the other, that of *the incorruptible and earnest pride which no applause, no reprobation, can blind to its shortcomings, or beguile of its hope.*

And yet it is in the expectation of obtaining at least a partial acknowledgment of this, as a truth decisive both of aim and conduct, that I enter upon the second division of my subject. The time I have already devoted to the task I should have considered too great, and that which I fear may be yet required for its completion would have been cause to me of utter discouragement, but that the object I propose to myself is of no partial nor accidental importance. It is not now to distinguish between disputed degrees of ability in individuals, or agreeableness in canvases; it is not now to expose the ignorance or defend the principles of party or person; it is to summon the moral energies of the nation to a forgotten duty, to display the use, force, and function of a great body of neglected sympathies and desires, and to elevate to its healthy and beneficial operation that art which, being altogether addressed to them, rises or falls with their variableness of vigour, now leading them with Tyrtæan[1] fire, now singing them to sleep with baby murmurings.

It will be well in the outset that I define exactly what kind of Utility I mean to attribute to art, and especially to that branch of it which is concerned with those impressions of external Beauty, whose nature it is our present object to discover.

That is, to everything created pre-eminently useful, which enables it rightly and fully to perform the functions appointed to it by its Creator. Therefore, that we may determine what is chiefly useful to man, it is necessary first to determine the use of Man himself.

Man's use and function (and let him who will not grant me this follow me no farther, for this I purpose always to assume) are, to be the witness of the glory of God, and to advance that glory by his reasonable obedience and resultant happiness.

Whatever enables us to fulfil this function is, in the pure and first sense of the word, Useful to us: pre-eminently, therefore, whatever sets the glory of God more brightly before us. But things that only help us to exist are, (*only*) in a secondary and mean sense, useful; or rather, if they be looked for alone, they are useless, and worse, for it would be better that we should not exist, than that we should guiltily disappoint the purposes of existence.

And yet people speak in this working age, when they speak from their hearts, as if houses and lands, and food and raiment were alone useful, and as if Sight, Thought, and Admiration were all profitless, so that men insolently call themselves Utilitarians, who would turn, if they had their way, themselves and their race into vegetables; men who think, as far as such can be said to think, that the meat is more than the life, and the raiment than the body, who look to the earth as a stable, and to its fruit as fodder; vinedressers and husbandmen, who love the corn they grind, and the grapes they crush, better than the gardens of the angels upon the slopes of Eden; hewers of wood and drawers of water, who think that it is to give them wood to hew and water to draw, that the pine-forests cover the mountains like the shadow of God, and the great rivers move like His eternity. And so comes upon us that Woe of the preacher, that though God "hath made everything beautiful in his time, also He hath set the world in their heart, so that no man can find out the work that God maketh from the beginning to the end."[2]

This Nebuchadnezzar curse, that sends men to grass like oxen, seems to follow but too closely on the excess or continuance of national power and peace. In the perplexities of nations, in their struggles for existence, in their infancy, their impotence, or even their disorganization, they have higher hopes and nobler passions. Out of the suffering comes the serious mind; out of the salvation, the grateful heart; out of endurance, fortitude; out of deliverance, faith: but when they have learned to live under providence of laws and with decency and justice of regard for each other, and when they have done away with violent and external sources of suffering, worse evils seem to arise out of their rest; evils that vex less and mortify more, that suck the blood though they do not shed it, and ossify the heart though they do not torture it. And deep though the causes of thankfulness must be to every people at peace with others and at unity in itself, there are causes of fear, also, a fear greater than of sword and sedition: that dependence on God may be forgotten, because the bread is given and the water sure; that gratitude to Him may cease, because His constancy of protection has taken the semblance of a natural law; that heavenly hope may grow faint amidst the full fruition of the world; that selfishness may take place of undemanded devotion, compassion be lost in vainglory, and love in dissimulation; that enervation may succeed to strength, apathy to patience, and the noise of jesting words and foulness of dark thoughts, to the earnest purity of the girded loins and the burning

lamp. About the river of human life there is a wintry wind, though a
heavenly sunshine; the iris colours its agitation, the frost fixes upon its   31
repose. Let us beware that our rest become not the rest of stones, which,
so long as they are torrent-tossed and thunder-stricken, maintain their
majesty, but when the stream is silent, and the storm passed, suffer the
grass to cover them and the lichen to feed on them, and are ploughed
down into dust.

And though I believe that we have salt enough of ardent and holy mind
amongst us to keep us in some measure from this moral decay, yet the signs
of it must be watched with anxiety, in all matters however trivial, in all
directions however distant. And at this time, when the iron roads are
tearing up the surface of Europe, as grapeshot do the sea; when their great
net is drawing and twitching the ancient frame and strength together,
contracting all its various life, its rocky arms and rural heart, into a
narrow, finite, calculating metropolis of manufactures; when there is not
a monument throughout the cities of Europe that speaks of old years and
mighty people, but it is being swept away to build cafés and gaming-
houses; when the honour of God is thought to consist in the poverty of His   32
temple, and the column is shortened and the pinnacle shattered, the
colour denied to the casement and the marble to the altar, while ex-
chequers are exhausted in luxury of boudoirs and pride of reception-
rooms; when we ravage without a pause all the loveliness of creation
which God in giving pronounced Good, and destroy without a thought all
those labours which men have given their lives and their sons' sons' lives
to complete, and have left for a legacy to all their kind, a legacy of more
than their hearts' blood, for it is of their souls' travail;—there is need,
bitter need, to bring back into men's minds, that to live is nothing, unless
to live be to know Him by whom we live; and that He is not to be known
by marring His fair works, and blotting out the evidence of His influences
upon His creatures; nor amidst the hurry of crowds and crash of innovation, but in solitary places, and out of the glowing intelligences which
He gave to men of old. He did not teach them how to build for glory and
for beauty; He did not give them the fearless, faithful, inherited energies
that worked on and down from death to death, generation after generation, that we might give the work of their poured-out spirit to the axe and
the hammer; He has not cloven the earth with rivers, that their white wild
waves might turn wheels and push paddles, nor turned it up under as it
were fire, that it might heat wells and cure diseases; He brings not up His
quails by the east wind only to let them fall in flesh about the camp of
men; He has not heaped the rocks of the mountain only for the quarry, nor
clothed the grass of the field only for the oven.

Science and art are either subservient to life or the objects of it. As
subservient to life, or practical, their results are, in the common sense of   33

the word, Useful. As the object of life or theoretic,[3] they are, in the common sense, Useless. And yet the step between practical and theoretic science is the step between the miner and the geologist, the apothecary and the chemist; and the step between practical and theoretic art is that between the builder and the architect, between the plumber and the artist; and this is a step allowed on all hands to be from less to greater. So that the so-called useless part of each profession does, by the authoritative and right instinct of mankind, assume the more noble place; even though books be sometimes written, and that by writers of no ordinary mind, which assume that a chemist is rewarded for the years of toil which have traced the greater part of the combinations of matter to their ultimate atoms, by discovering a cheap way of refining sugar; and date the eminence of the philosopher whose life has been spent in the investigation of the laws of light, from the time of his inventing an improvement in spectacles.

34   It would appear, therefore, that those pursuits which are altogether theoretic, whose results are desirable or admirable in themselves and for

35 their own sake, and in which no farther end to which their productions or discoveries are referred can interrupt the contemplation of things as they are, by the endeavour to discover of what selfish uses they are capable (and of this order are painting and sculpture), ought to take rank above all pursuits which have any taint in them of subserviency to life, in so far as all such tendency is the sign of less eternal and less holy function. And such rank these two sublime arts would indeed assume in the minds of nations, and become objects of corresponding efforts, but for two fatal and widespread errors respecting the great faculties of mind concerned in them.

    The first of these, or the Theoretic faculty, is concerned with the moral perception and appreciation of ideas of beauty. And the error respecting it is, the considering and calling it Æsthetic, degrading it to a mere

36 operation of sense, or perhaps worse, of custom; so that the arts which appeal to it sink into a mere amusement, ministers to morbid sensibilities, ticklers and fanners of the soul's sleep.

    The second great faculty is the Imaginative, which the mind exercises in a certain mode of regarding or combining the ideas it has received from external nature, and the operations of which become in their turn objects of the theoretic faculty to other minds. And the error respecting this faculty is, in considering that its function is one of falsehood, that its operation is to exhibit things as they are *not*, and that in so doing it mends the works of God.

CHAPTER II

Of the Theoretic Faculty
as Concerned with Pleasures of Sense

Now the term "æsthesis" properly signifies mere sensual perception   42
of the outward qualities and necessary effects of bodies; in which
sense only, if we would arrive at any accurate conclusions on this difficult
subject, it should always be used. But I wholly deny that the impressions
of beauty are in any way sensual; they are neither sensual nor intellectual,
but moral: and for the faculty receiving them, no term can be more
accurate or convenient than that employed by the Greeks, "Theoretic,"
which I pray permission, therefore, always to use, and to call the operation
of the faculty itself, Theoria.

Now it is evident that the being common to brutes, or peculiar to man,
can alone be no rational test of inferiority or dignity in pleasures. We must
not assume that man is the nobler animal, and then deduce the nobleness
of his delights; but we must prove the nobleness of the delights, and   43
thence the nobleness of the animal.

The first great distinction, we observe, is that noted by Aristotle, that
men are called temperate and intemperate with regard to some, and not
so with respect to others; and that those with respect to which they are so
called, are, by common consent, held to be the vilest.

Men are held intemperate, only when their desires *overcome or*   44
prevent the action of their reason; and they are indeed intemperate in the
exact degree in which such prevention or interference takes place. And
this is evidently the case with respect to inordinate indulgence in
pleasures of touch and taste; for these, being destructive in their continuance not only of all other pleasures, but of the very sensibilities by which
they themselves are received, and this penalty being actually known and
experienced by those indulging in them, so that the reason cannot but
pronounce right respecting their perilousness, there is no palliation of the
wrong choice; and the man, as utterly incapable of Will, is called
intemperate, or ἀκόλαστος.

The primal ground of inferiority in these pleasures is that which *proves*   45
their indulgence to be contrary to reason; namely, their destructiveness

upon prolongation, and their incapability of coexisting continually with the better delights and true perfections of human nature.

And this incapability of continuance directs us to the second cause of their inferiority; namely, that they are given to us as subservient to life, as instruments of our preservation, compelling us to seek the things necessary to our being, and that, therefore, when this their function is fully performed, they ought to have an end; and can be only artificially, and under high penalty, prolonged. But the pleasures of sight and hearing are given as gifts. They answer not any purposes of mere existence; for the
46 distinction of all that is useful or dangerous to us might be made, and often is made, by the eye, without its receiving the slightest pleasure of sight. We might have learned to distinguish fruits and grain from flowers, without having any superior pleasure in the aspect of the latter; and the ear might have learned to distinguish the sounds that communicate ideas, or to recognize intimations of elemental danger, without perceiving either melody in the voice, or majesty in the thunder. And as these pleasures have no function to perform, so there is no limit to their continuance in the accomplishment of their end, for they are an end in themselves, and so may be perpetual with all of us; being in no way destructive, but rather increasing in exquisiteness by repetition.

Herein, then, we find very sufficient ground for the higher estimation of these delights; first, in their being eternal and inexhaustible, and, secondly, in their being evidently no means or instrument of life, but an object of life. And so, though we were to regard the pleasures of sight merely as the highest of sensual pleasures, and though they were of rare occurrence, and, when occurring, isolated and imperfect, there would still be a supernatural character about them, owing to their self-sufficiency.
47 But when, instead of being scattered, interrupted, or chance-distributed, they are gathered together, and so arranged to enhance each other as by chance they could not be, there is caused by them not only a feeling of strong affection towards the object in which they exist, but a perception of purpose and adaptation of it to our desires; a perception, therefore, of the immediate operation of the Intelligence which so formed us, and so feeds us.

Now the mere animal consciousness of the pleasantness I call Æsthesis; but the exulting, reverent, and grateful perception of it I call Theoria. For this, and this only, is the full comprehension and contemplation of the Beautiful as a gift of God; a gift not necessary to our being, but added to, and elevating it, and twofold: first of the desire, and secondly of the thing desired.
48 It will now be understood why it was formerly said in the chapter respecting ideas of beauty, that those ideas were the subject of moral, and not of intellectual, nor altogether of sensual perception; and why I spoke

of the pleasures connected with them as derived from "those material sources which are agreeable to our moral nature in its purity and perfection." For, as it is necessary to the existence of an idea of beauty, that the sensual pleasure which may be its basis should be accompanied first with joy, then with love of the object, then with the perception of kindness in a superior intelligence, finally, with thankfulness and veneration towards that intelligence itself; and as no idea can be at all considered as in any way an idea of beauty, until it be made up of these emotions, and as these emotions are in no way resultant from, nor obtainable by, any operation of the Intellect; it is evident that the sensation of beauty is not sensual on the one hand, nor is it intellectual on the other, but is dependent on a pure, right, and open state of the heart. Dependent both for its truth and for its intensity, insomuch that even the right after-action of the Intellect upon facts of beauty so apprehended, is dependent on the acuteness of the heart-feeling about them. For we do indeed see constantly that men having naturally acute perceptions of the beautiful, yet not receiving it with a pure heart, nor into their hearts at all, never comprehend it, nor receive good from it; but make it a mere minister to their desires, and accompaniment and seasoning of lower sensual pleasures, until all their emotions take the same earthly stamp, and the sense of beauty sinks into the servant of lust.

49

Nor is what the world commonly understands by the cultivation of 'taste,' anything more or better than this; at least in times of corrupt and overpampered civilization, when men build palaces, plant groves, and gather luxuries, that they and their devices may hang in the corners of the world like fine-spun cobwebs, with greedy, puffed-up, spider-like lusts in the middle. And this, which in Christian times is the abuse and corruption of the sense of beauty, was in that Pagan life of which St. Paul speaks, little less than the essence of it, and the best they had. But the Christian Theoria seeks not, though it accepts and touches with its own purity, what the Epicurean sought; but finds its food and the objects of its love everywhere, in what is harsh and fearful as well as in what is kind: nay, even in all that seems coarse and commonplace, seizing that which is good; and sometimes delighting more at finding its table spread in strange places, and in the presence of its enemies, and its honey coming out of the rock, than if all were harmonized into a less wondrous pleasure; hating only what is self-sighted and insolent of men's work, despising all that is not of God, unless reminding it of God, yet able to find evidence of Him still where all seems forgetful of Him, and to turn that into a witness of His working which was meant to obscure it; and so with clear and unoffended sight beholding Him for ever, according to the written promise, "Blessed are the pure in *heart*, for they shall see God."

50

CHAPTER III

Of Accuracy and Inaccuracy
in Impressions of Sense

51 HITHERTO we have observed only the distinctions of dignity among pleasures of sense, considered merely as such, and the way in which *any* of them may become theoretic in being received with right feeling.

But as we go farther, and examine the distinctive nature of ideas of beauty, we shall, I believe, perceive something in them besides æsthetic pleasure, something which attests a more important function belonging to them than attaches to other sensual ideas, and exhibits a more exalted character in the faculty by which they are received. And this was what I alluded to when I said that "we may indeed perceive, as far as we are acquainted with the nature of God, that we have been so constructed as in a healthy state of mind to derive pleasure from whatever things are illustrative of that nature."

52 Our first inquiry must evidently be, how we are authorized to affirm of any man's mind, that it is in a healthy state or otherwise, respecting impressions of sight; and what canon or test there is by which we may determine of these impressions that they are or are not *rightly* esteemed beautiful. For it does not at first appear easy to prove that men ought to like one thing rather than another; and although this is granted generally by men's speaking of 'bad' or 'good' taste, yet the right of individual opinion (sometimes claimed even in moral matters, though then palpably without foundation) does not appear altogether irrational in matters æsthetic, wherein little operation of voluntary choice is supposed possible. It would appear strange, for instance, to assert, respecting a particular person who preferred the scent of violets to that of roses, that he had no right to do so. And yet, while I have said that the sensation of beauty is intuitive and necessary, as men derive pleasure from the scent of a rose, I have assumed that there are some sources from which it is rightly derived, and others from which it is wrongly derived; in other words, that men have no right to think some things beautiful and no right to remain apathetic with regard to others.

Hence then arise two questions, according to the sense in which the word *right* is taken: the first, in what way an impression of sense may be *deceptive*, and therefore a conclusion respecting it untrue; and the second, in what way an impression of sense, or the preference of one, may be a subject of *will*, and therefore of moral duty or delinquency.

To the first of these questions I answer, that we cannot speak of the   53 immediate impression of sense as false, nor of its preference to others as mistaken: for no one can be deceived respecting the actual sensation he perceives or prefers. But falsity may attach to his assertion or supposition, that what he himself perceives is from the same object perceived by others, or is always to be by himself perceived, or is always to be by himself preferred; and when we speak of a man as wrong in his impressions of sense, we either mean that he feels differently from all, or from a majority, respecting a certain object, or that he prefers at present those of his impressions which ultimately he will not prefer.

To the second I answer, that over immediate impressions and immediate preferences we have no power, but over *ultimate* impressions, and especially ultimate preferences, we have; and that, though we can neither at once choose whether we shall see an object red, green, or blue, nor determine to like the red better than the blue, or the blue better than the red, yet we can, if we choose, make ourselves ultimately susceptible of such impressions in other degrees, and capable of pleasure in them in different measure. And seeing that wherever power of any kind is given there is responsibility attached, it is the duty of men to prefer certain impressions of sense to others, *because* they have the power of doing so.[4] And this is precisely analogous to the law of the moral world, whereby   54 men are supposed not only capable of governing their likes and dislikes, but the whole culpability or propriety of actions is dependent upon this capability; so that men are guilty or otherwise, not for what they do, but for what they desire, the command being not Thou shalt obey, but Thou shalt love, the Lord thy God; a vain command if men were not capable of governing and directing their affections.

Let us take an instance from one of the lowest of the senses, and observe the kind of power we have over the impressions of lingual taste. On the first offering of two different things to the palate, it is not in our power to prevent or command the instinctive preference. One will be unavoidably and helplessly preferred to the other. But if the same two things be submitted to judgment frequently and attentively, it will be often found that their relations change. The palate, which at first perceived only the coarse and violent qualities of either, will, as it becomes more experienced, acquire greater subtlety of discrimination, perceiving in both characters at first unnoticed, which on continued experience will probably become more influential than the first impressions; and whatever this final verdict may be, it is felt by the person who gives it, and received by others, as a more correct one than the first.

So, then, the power we have over the preference of impressions of taste is not actual nor immediate, but only a power of testing and comparing them frequently and carefully, until that which is the more permanent, the more consistently agreeable, be determined. But when the instrument of taste is thus in some degree perfected and rendered subtle, by its being practised upon a single object, its conclusions will be more rapid with respect to others; and it will be able to distinguish more quickly in other things, and even to prefer at once those qualities which are calculated finally to give it most pleasure, though more capable with respect to those on which it is more frequently exercised; whence people are called 'judges' with respect to this or that particular object of Taste.

Now, that verdicts of this kind are received as authoritative by others, proves another and more important fact; namely, that not only changes of opinion take place in consequence of experience, but that those changes are from *variation* of opinion to *unity* of opinion;—and that whatever may be the differences of estimate among unpractised or uncultivated tastes, there will be unity of taste among the experienced; and that, therefore, the result of repeated trial and experience is to arrive at principles of preference in some sort common to all, and which are a part of our nature.

But two very important points are to be observed respecting the direction and discipline of the attention in the early stages of judgment. The first, that, for beneficent purposes, the nature of man has been made reconcilable by custom to many things naturally painful to it, and even improper for it; and that therefore, though by continual experience, united with thought, we may discover that which is best of several, yet if we submit ourselves to authority or fashion, and close our eyes, we may be by custom made to tolerate, and even to love and long for, that which is naturally painful and pernicious to us; whence arise incalculable embarrassments on the subject of art.

The second, that, in order to the discovery of that which is better of two things, it is necessary that both should be equally submitted to the attention, and therefore that we should have so much faith in authority as shall make us repeatedly observe and attend to that which is said to be right, even though at present we may not feel it so. And in the right mingling of this faith with the openness of heart which proves all things, lies the great difficulty of the cultivation of the taste, as far as the spirit of the scholar is concerned; though, even when he has this spirit, he may be long retarded by having evil examples submitted to him by ignorant masters.

The temper, therefore, by which right taste is formed, is characteristically patient. It dwells upon what is submitted to it. It does not trample upon it, lest it should be pearls, even though it looks like husks. It is a good ground, soft, penetrable, retentive; it does not send up thorns of unkind thoughts, to choke the weak seed; it is hungry and thirsty too, and drinks all the dew that falls on it. It is "an honest and good heart,"[5] that shows no too ready springing before the sun be up, but fails not afterwards; it is distrustful of itself, so as to be ready to believe and to try all things, and yet so trustful of itself, that it will neither quit what it has tried, nor take anything without trying. And the pleasure which it has in things that it finds true and good is so great, that it cannot possibly be led aside by any tricks of fashion, or diseases of vanity; it cannot be cramped in its conclusions by partialities and hypocrisies; its visions and its delights are too penetrating, too living, for any whitewashed object or shallow fountain long to endure or supply. It clasps all that it loves so hard, that it crushes it if it be hollow.

Now, the conclusions of this disposition are sure to be eventually right; more and more right according to the general maturity of all the powers, but it is sure to come (*quite*)[6] right at last, because its operation is in analogy to, and in harmony with, the whole spirit of the Christian moral system, and must ultimately love and rest in the great sources of happiness common to all the human race, and based on the relations they hold to their Creator.

These common and general sources of pleasure consist, I believe, in a certain seal, or impress of divine work and character, upon whatever God has wrought in all the world; only, it being necessary for the perception of them, that their contraries should also be set before us, these divine characteristics, though inseparable from all divine works, are yet suffered to exist in such varieties of degree, that their most limited manifestation shall, in opposition to their most abundant, act as a foil or contrary; just as we conceive of cold as contrary to heat, though the most extreme cold we can produce or conceive is not inconsistent with an unknown amount of heat in the body.

Our purity of taste, therefore, is best tested by its universality; for if we can only admire this thing or that, we may be sure that our cause for liking is of a finite and false nature. But if we can perceive beauty in everything of God's doing, we may argue that we have reached the true perception of its universal laws. Hence, false taste may be known by its fastidiousness, by its demands of pomp, splendour, and unusual combination, by its enjoyment only of particular styles and modes of things, and by its pride also: for it is for ever meddling, mending, accumulating, and self-exulting; its eye is always upon itself, and it tests all things round it by the way they fit it. But true taste is for ever growing, learning, reading, worshipping, laying its hand upon its mouth because it is astonished, lamenting over itself, and testing itself by the way that it fits things. And it finds whereof to feed, and whereby to grow, in all things. The complaint so often heard from young artists, that they have not within their reach materials or

59

60

subjects enough for their fancy, is utterly groundless, and the sign only of their own blindness and inefficiency; for there is that to be seen in every street and lane of every city,—that to be felt and found in every human heart and countenance,—that to be loved in every roadside weed and moss-grown wall which, in the hands of faithful men, may convey emotions of glory and sublimity continual and exalted.

Let therefore the young artist beware of the spirit of Choice; it is an insolent spirit at the best, and commonly a base and blind one too, checking all progress and blasting all power, encouraging weaknesses, pampering partialities, and teaching us to look to accidents of nature for the help and the joy which should come from our own hearts. He draws 61 nothing well who thirsts not to draw *everything*; when a good painter shrinks, it is because he is humbled, not fastidious; when he stops, it is because he is surfeited, and not because he thinks Nature has given him unkindly food, or that he fears famine.

Hence, it becomes a more imperative duty to accustom ourselves to the enjoyment of those pleasures of sight which are most elevated in character, because these are not only the most acute, but the most easily, constantly, and unselfishly attainable. For had it been ordained by the Almighty that the highest pleasures of sight should be those of most difficult attainment, and that to arrive at them it should be necessary to accumulate gilded palaces, tower over tower, and pile artificial mountains around insinuated lakes, there would have been a direct contradiction between the unselfish duties and inherent desires of every individual. But no such contradiction exists in the system of Divine Providence; which, leaving it open to us if we will, as creatures in probation, to abuse this sense like every other, and pamper it with selfish and thoughtless vanities as we pamper the palate with deadly meats, until the appetite of tasteful 62 cruelty is lost in its sickened satiety, incapable of pleasure, unless, Caligula like, it concentrate the labour of a million of lives into the sensation of an hour, leaves it also open to us, by humble and loving ways, to make ourselves susceptible of deep delight from the meanest objects of creation;—a delight which shall not separate us from our fellows, nor require the sacrifice of any duty or occupation, but which shall bind us closer to men and to God, and be with us always, harmonized with every action, consistent with every claim, unchanging and eternal.

Seeing then that these qualities of material objects which are calculated to give us this universal pleasure, are demonstrably constant in their address to human nature, they must belong in some measure to whatever has been esteemed beautiful throughout successive ages of the world, and they are also by their definition common to all the works of God. Therefore it is evident that it must be possible to reason them out, as well as to feel them out; possible to divest every object of that which makes it accidentally or temporarily pleasant, and to strip it bare of distinctive qualities, until we arrive at those which it has in common with all other beautiful things, which we may then safely affirm to be the cause of its ultimate and true delightfulness.

Now this process of reasoning will be that which I shall endeavour to employ in the succeeding investigations, a process perfectly safe, so long as we are quite sure that we are reasoning concerning objects which produce in us one and the same sensation, but not safe if the sensation produced be of a different nature, though it may be equally agreeable; for what produces a different sensation must be a different cause. And the difficulty of reasoning respecting Beauty arises chiefly from the ambiguity of the word, which stands in different people's minds for totally different sensations, for which there can be no common cause.   63

By the term Beauty, properly are signified two things. First, that external quality of bodies already so often spoken of, and which, whether it occur in a stone, flower, beast, or in man, is absolutely identical, which, as I have already asserted, may be shown to be in some sort typical of the Divine attributes, and which therefore I shall, for distinction's sake, call Typical Beauty: and, secondarily, the appearance of felicitous fulfilment of function in living things, more especially of the joyful and right exertion of perfect life in man; and this kind of beauty I shall call Vital Beauty.   64

Any application of the word Beautiful to other appearances or qualities than these is either false or metaphorical; as, for instance, to the splendour of a discovery, the fitness of a proportion, the coherence of a chain of reasoning, or the power of bestowing pleasure which objects receive from association, a power confessedly great, and interfering, as we shall presently find, in a most embarrassing way with the attractiveness of inherent beauty.

I shall briefly glance at the four erroneous positions most frequently held upon this subject, before proceeding to examine those typical and vital properties of things, to which I conceive that all our original conceptions of beauty may be traced.   65

CHAPTER V

Of Typical Beauty:—First, of Infinity, or the Type of Divine Incomprehensibility

76   THE subject being now in some measure cleared of embarrassment,[7] let us briefly distinguish those qualities or types on whose combination is dependent the power of mere material loveliness.

77   And first, I would ask of the reader to enter upon the subject with me, as far as may be, as a little child, ridding himself of all conventional and authoritative thoughts, and especially of such associations as arise from his respect for Pagan art, or which are in any way traceable to classical readings. For there was never yet the child of any promise (so far as the Theoretic faculties are concerned) but awaked to the sense of beauty with the first gleam of reason; and I suppose there are few among those who love Nature otherwise than by profession and at second-hand, who look not back to their youngest and least-learned days as those of the most intense, superstitious, insatiable, and beatific perception of her

78   splendours. And the bitter decline of this glorious feeling, though many note it not, partly owing to the cares and weight of manhood, which leave them not the time nor the liberty to look for their lost treasure, and partly to the human and divine affections which are appointed to take its place, yet has formed the subject, not indeed of lamentation, but of holy thankfulness for the witness it bears to the immortal origin and end of our nature, to one whose authority is almost without appeal in all questions relating to the influence of external things upon the pure human soul.

> "Heaven lies about us in our infancy.
>   Shades of the prison-house begin to close
>   Upon the growing boy:
>   But he beholds the light, and whence it flows,
>   He sees it in his joy.
>   The youth, who daily farther from the east
>   Must travel, still is nature's priest,
>   And by the vision splendid
>   Is on his way attended.
>   At length the man perceives it die away
>   And fade into the light of common day."[8]

And if it were possible for us to recollect all the unaccountable and happy instincts of the careless time, and to reason upon them with the maturer judgment, we might arrive at more rapid and right results than either the philosophy or the sophisticated practice of art has yet attained. But we lose the perceptions before we are capable of methodizing or comparing them.   79

One, however, of these child instincts, I believe that few forget, the emotion, namely, caused by all open ground, or lines of any spacious kind against the sky, behind which there might be conceived the Sea. It is an emotion more pure than that caused by the sea itself, for I recollect distinctly running down behind the banks of a high beach to get their land line cutting against the sky, and receiving a more strange delight from this than from the sight of the ocean. I am not sure that this feeling is common to all children, (or would be common, if they were all in circumstances admitting it,) but I have ascertained it to be frequent among those who possess the most vivid sensibilities for nature; and I am certain that the modification of it which belongs to our after years is common to all, the love, namely, of a light distance appearing over a comparatively dark horizon. Whatever beauty there may result from effects of light on foreground objects,—from the dew of the grass, the flash of the cascade, the glitter of the birch trunk, or the fair daylight hues of darker things (and joyfulness there is in all of them), there is yet a light which the eye invariably seeks with a deeper feeling of the beautiful,—the light of the declining or breaking day, and the flakes of scarlet cloud burning like watch-fires in the green sky of the horizon; a deeper feeling, I say, not perhaps more acute, but having more of spiritual hope and longing, less   80 of animal and present life, more manifest, invariably, in those of more serious and determined mind, (I use the word serious, not as being opposed to cheerful, but to trivial and volatile,) but I think, marked and unfailing even in those of the least thoughtful dispositions. I am willing to let it rest on the determination of every reader, whether the pleasure which he has received from these effects of calm and luminous distance be not the most singular and memorable of which he has been conscious; whether all that is dazzling in colour, perfect in form, gladdening in expression, be not of evanescent and shallow appealing, when compared with the still small voice of the level twilight behind purple hills, or the scarlet arch of dawn over the dark troublous-edged sea.

Let us try to discover that which effects of this kind possess or suggest, peculiar to themselves, and which other effects of light and colour possess not. There *must* be something in them of a peculiar character, and that, whatever it be, must be one of the primal and most earnest motives of beauty to human sensation.

Do they show finer characters of form than can be developed by the broader daylight? Not so; for their power is almost independent of the forms they assume or display; it matters little whether the bright clouds be simple or manifold, whether the mountain line be subdued or majestic; the fairer forms of earthly things are by them subdued and disguised, the round and muscular growth of the forest trunks is sunk into skeleton lines of quiet shade, the purple clefts of the hill-side are labyrinthed in the darkness, the orbed spring and whirling wave of the torrent have given place to a white, ghastly, interrupted gleaming. Have they more perfection or fulness of colour? Not so; for their effect is oftentimes deeper when their hues are dim, than when they are blazoned with crimson and pale gold: and assuredly, in the blue of the rainy sky, in the many tints of morning flowers, in the sunlight on summer foliage

81 and field, there are more sources of mere sensual colour-pleasure than in the single streak of wan and dying light. It is not then by nobler form, it is not by positiveness of hue, it is not by intensity of light (for the sun itself at noonday is effectless upon the feelings), that this strange distant space possesses its attractive power. But there is one thing that it has, or suggests, which no other object of sight suggests in equal degree, and that is—Infinity. It is of all visible things the least material, the least finite, the farthest withdrawn from the earth prison-house, the most typical of the nature of God, the most suggestive of the glory of His dwelling-place. For the sky of night, though we may know it boundless, is dark; it is a studded vault, a roof that seems to shut us in and down; but the bright distance has no limit, we feel its infinity, as we rejoice in its purity of light.

Now not only is this expression of infinity in distance most precious wherever we find it, however solitary it may be, and however unassisted by other forms and kinds of beauty, but it is of that value that no such other forms will altogether recompense us for its loss; and, much as I dread the enunciation of anything that may seem like a conventional rule, I have no hesitation in asserting that no work of any art, in which this expression of infinity is possible, can be perfect, or supremely elevated, without it, and that, in proportion to its presence, it will exalt and render impressive even the most tame and trivial themes. And I think if there be any one grand division, by which it is at all possible to set the productions of painting, so far as their mere plan or system is concerned, on our right and left hands, it is this of light and dark background, of *heaven light* or of *object light*. For I know not any truly great painter of any time, who manifests not the most intense pleasure in the

82 luminous space of his backgrounds, or who ever sacrifices this pleasure where the nature of his subject admits of its attainment; as, on the other hand, I know not that the habitual use of dark backgrounds can be shown as having ever been coexistent with pure or high feeling, and, except in

the case of Rembrandt (and then under peculiar circumstances only), with any high power of intellect.

And I think I am supported in this feeling by the unanimous practice, if not the confessed opinion, of all artists. The painter of portrait is unhappy without his conventional white stroke under the sleeve, or beside the arm-chair; the painter of interiors feels like a caged bird, unless he can throw a window open, or set the door ajar; the landscapist dares not lose himself in forest without a gleam of light under its farthest branches, nor venture out in rain unless he may somewhere pierce to a better promise in the distance, or cling to some closing gap of variable blue above. Escape, Hope, Infinity, by whatever conventionalism sought, the   83 desire is the same in all, the instinct constant.

But although this narrow portal of escape be all that is absolutely necessary, I think that the dignity of the painting increases with the extent and amount of the expression. With the earlier and mightier painters of Italy, the practice is commonly to leave their distance of pure and open sky, of such simplicity that it in nowise shall interfere with, or draw the attention from, the interest of the figures; and of such purity that, especially towards the horizon, it shall be in the highest degree expressive of the infinite space of heaven. I do not mean to say that they did this with any occult or metaphysical motives. They did it, I think, with the unpretending simplicity of all earnest men; they did what they loved and felt; they sought what the heart naturally seeks, and gave what it most gratefully receives; and I look to them as in all points of principle (not, observe, of knowledge or empirical attainment) as the most irrefra-   84 gable authorities, precisely on account of the child-like innocence, which never deemed itself authoritative, but acted upon desire, and not upon dicta, and sought for sympathy, not for admiration.

And so we find the same simple and sweet treatment, the open sky, the tender, unpretending horizontal white clouds, the far winding and abundant landscape, in Giotto, Taddeo Gaddi, Laurati,[9] Angelico, Benozzo, Ghirlandajo, Francia, Perugino, and the young Raffaelle; the first symptom of conventionality appearing in Perugino, who, though with intense feeling of light and colour he carried the glory of his luminous distance far beyond all his predecessors, began at the same time to use a somewhat morbid relief of his figures against the upper sky. Raffaelle, in his fall, betrayed the faith he had received from his father   85 and his master, and substituted for the radiant sky of the Madonna del Cardellino, the chamber-wall of the Madonna della Seggiola, and the brown wainscot of the Baldacchino.[10]

That which was done by the Florentines in pure simplicity of heart, the Venetians did through love of the colour and splendour of the sky itself, even to the frequent sacrificing of their subject to the passion of its

86   distance. In Carpaccio, John Bellini, Giorgione, Titian, Veronese, and
      Tintoret, the preciousness of the luminous sky, so far as it might be at all
      consistent with their subject, is nearly constant; abandoned altogether in
      portraiture only, seldom even there, and never with advantage. Titian
      and Veronese, who had less exalted feeling than the others, afford a few
      instances of exception: the latter overpowering his silvery distances with
      foreground splendour; the former sometimes sacrificing them to a luscious
      fulness of colour, as in the Flagellation in the Louvre, by a comparison of
      which with the unequalled majesty of the Entombment opposite, the
      applicability of the general principle may at once be tested.

87   Now although I doubt not that the general value of this treatment will
      be acknowledged by all lovers of art, it is not certain that the point to
      prove which I have brought it forward will be as readily conceded; namely,
      the inherent power of all representations of infinity over the human heart.
      For there are, indeed, countless associations of pure and religious kind,
      which combine with each other to enhance the impression when
      presented in this particular form, whose power I neither deny nor am
      careful to distinguish, seeing that they all tend to the same point, and
      have reference to heavenly hopes; delights they are in seeing the narrow,
      black, miserable earth fairly compared with the bright firmament;
      reaching forward unto the things that are before, and joyfulness in the
      apparent, though unreachable, nearness and promise of them. But there
      are other modes in which infinity may be represented, which are confused
      by no associations of the kind, and which would, as being in mere matter,
      appear trivial and mean, but for their incalculable influence on the forms
      of all that we feel to be beautiful. The first of these is the curvature of
      lines and surfaces, wherein it at first appears futile to insist upon any
      resemblance or suggestion of infinity, since there is certainly, in our
      ordinary contemplation of it, no sensation of the kind.

88   That all forms of acknowledged beauty are composed exclusively of
      curves will, I believe, be at once allowed; but that which there will be
      need more especially to prove is, the subtlety and constancy of curvature
      in all natural forms whatsoever. I believe that, except in crystals, in
      certain mountain forms admitted for the sake of sublimity or contrast (as
      in the slope of débris), in rays of light, in the levels of calm water and
      alluvial land, and in some few organic developments, there are no lines
      nor surfaces of nature without curvature; though as we before saw in
      clouds, more especially in their under lines towards the horizon, and in
      vast and extended plains, right lines are often suggested which are not
      actual. Without these we could not be sensible of the value of the
      contrasting curves; and while, therefore, for the most part the eye is fed in
      natural forms with a grace of curvature which no hand nor instrument can
      follow, other means are provided to give beauty to those surfaces which

are admitted for contrast, as in water by its reflection of the gradations which it possesses not itself.

What curvature is to lines, gradation is to shades and colours. It is their   89
infinity, and divides them into an infinite number of degrees. Absolutely without gradation no natural surface can possibly be, except under circumstances of so rare conjunction as to amount to a lusus naturæ: for we have seen that few surfaces are without curvature, and every curved surface must be gradated by the nature of light; and for the gradation of the few plane surfaces that exist, means are provided in local colour, aërial perspective, reflected lights, etc., from which it is but barely conceivable that they should ever escape.

Gradation is so inseparable a quality of all natural shade, that the eye refuses in painting to understand a shadow which appears without it; while, on the other hand, nearly all the gradations of nature are so subtle, and between degrees of tint so slightly separated, that no human hand can in any wise equal, or do anything more than suggest the idea of them. In proportion to the space over which gradation extends, and to its invisible subtlety, is its grandeur: and in proportion to its narrow limits and violent degrees, its vulgarity.

Such are the expressions of infinity which we find in creation, of which   91
the importance is to be estimated rather by their frequency than by their distinctness. Let, however, the reader bear constantly in mind that I insist not on his accepting any interpretation of mine, but only on his dwelling so long on those objects which he perceives to be beautiful, as to determine whether the qualities to which I trace their beauty be necessarily there or not. Farther expressions of infinity there are in the mystery of Nature, and, in some measure, in her vastness; but these are dependent on our own imperfections, and therefore, though they produce sublimity, they are unconnected with beauty. For that which we foolishly call vastness is, rightly considered, not more wonderful, not more impressive, than that which we insolently call littleness: and the infinity of God is not mysterious, it is only unfathomable; not concealed, but incomprehensible; it is a clear infinity, the darkness of the pure unsearchable sea.

CHAPTER VI
Of Unity, or the Type of the Divine Comprehensiveness

92 " ALL things," says Hooker, "God only excepted, besides the nature which they have in themselves, receive externally some perfection from other things."[11] Hence the appearance of separation or isolation in anything, and of self-dependence, is an appearance of imperfection; and all appearances of connection and brotherhood are pleasant and right, both as significative of perfection in the things united, and as typical of that Unity which we attribute to God, which consists not in His own singleness or separation, but in the necessity of His inherence in all things that be, without which no creature of any kind could hold existence for a moment.

93 And so there is not any matter, nor any spirit, nor any creature, but it is capable of a unity of some kind with other creatures; and in that unity is its perfection and theirs, and a pleasure also for the beholding of all other creatures that can behold. So the unity of spirits is partly in their sympathy, and partly in their giving and taking, and always in their love; and these are their delight and their strength; for their strength is in their co-working and army fellowship, and their delight is in the giving and receiving of alternate and perpetual good; their inseparable dependency on each other's being, and their essential and perfect depending on their Creator's. And so the unity of earthly creatures is their power and their peace; not like the dead and cold peace of undisturbed stones and solitary mountains; but the living peace of trust, and the living power of support; of hands that hold each other and are still. And so the unity of matter is, in its noblest form, the organization of it which builds it up into temples for the spirit; and in its lower form, the sweet and strange affinity which gives to it the glory of its orderly elements, and the fair variety of change and assimilation that turns the dust into the crystal, and separates the waters that be above the firmament from the waters that be beneath: and, in its lowest form, it is the working and walking and clinging together that gives their power to the winds, and its syllables and soundings to the air, and their weight to the waves, and their burning
94 to the sunbeams, and their stability to the mountains, and to every

creature whatsoever operation is for its glory and for others' good.

Now of that which is thus necessary to the perfection of all things, all appearance, sign, type, or suggestion must be beautiful, in whatever matter it may appear; and the appearance of some species of unity is, in the most determined sense of the word, essential to the perfection of beauty in lines, colours, or forms.

But of the appearances of unity, as of unity itself, there are several kinds, which it will be found hereafter convenient to consider separately. Thus there is the Unity of different and separate things, subjected to one and the same influence, which may be called Subjectional Unity; and this is the unity of the clouds, as they are driven by the parallel winds, or as they are ordered by the electric currents; this the unity of the sea-waves, this of the bending and undulation of the forest masses; and in creatures capable of will it is the unity of will or of impulse. And there is Unity of Origin, which we may call Original Unity; which is of things arising from one spring and source, and speaking always of this their brotherhood; and this in matter is the unity of the branches of the trees, and of the petals and starry rays of flowers, and of the beams of light; and in spiritual creatures it is their filial relation to Him from whom they have their being. And there is unity of Sequence, which is that of things that form links in chains, and steps in ascents, and stages in journeys; and this, in matter, is the unity of communicable forces in their continuance from one thing to another; and it is the passing upwards and downwards of beneficent effects among all things, the melody of sounds, the continuity of lines, and   95 the orderly succession of motions and times; and in spiritual creatures it is their own constant building up, by true knowledge and continuous reasoning, to higher perfection, and the singleness and straightforwardness of their tendencies to more complete communion with God. And there is the unity of Membership, which we may call Essential Unity, which is the unity of things separately imperfect into a perfect whole; and this is the great unity of which other unities are but parts and means; it is in matter the harmony of sounds and consistency of bodies, and among spiritual creatures their love and happiness and very life in God.

Now of the nature of this last kind of unity, the most important whether in moral or in those material things with which we are at present concerned, there is this necessary to be observed; that it cannot exist between things similar to each other. Two or more equal and like things cannot be members one of another, nor can they form one, or a whole thing. Two they must remain, both in nature, and in our conception, so long as they remain alike, unless they are united by a third different from both. Thus the arms, which are like each other, remain two arms in our conception. They could not be united by a third arm; they must be united by something which is not an arm, and which, imperfect without them as they without it, shall form one perfect body. Nor is unity even thus accomplished, without a difference and opposition of direction in the setting on of the like members.

96   Hence, out of the necessity of Unity, arises that of Variety; a necessity often more vividly, though never so deeply felt, because lying at the surface of things, and assisted by an influential principle of our nature, the love of change, and by the power of contrast. But it is a mistake which has led to many unfortunate results, in matters respecting art, to insist on any inherent agreeableness of variety, without reference to a farther end. For it is not even true that variety as such, and in its highest degree, is beautiful. It is only harmonious and chordal variety, that variety which is necessary to secure and extend unity (for the greater the number of objects which by their differences become members of one another, the more

97 extended and sublime is their unity), which is rightly agreeable; and so I name not Variety as essential to beauty, because it is only so in a secondary and casual sense.

99   Receiving, therefore, variety only as that which accomplishes unity, or makes it perceived, its operation is found to be very precious, both in that which I have called Unity of Subjection, and Unity of Sequence, as well as in Unity of Membership; for although things in all respects the same may, indeed, be subjected to one influence, yet the power of the influence, and their obedience to it, are best seen by varied operation of them on their individual differences; as in clouds and waves there is a glorious unity of rolling, wrought out by the wild and wonderful differences of their absolute forms; which differences, if removed, would

100 leave in them only multitudinous and petty repetition, instead of the majestic oneness of shared passion. And so in the waves and clouds of human multitude when they are filled with one thought; as we find frequently in the works of the early Italian men of earnest purpose, who despising, or happily ignorant of, the sophistications of theories and the proprieties of composition, indicated by perfect similarity of action and gesture on the one hand, and by the infinite and truthful variation of expression on the other, the most sublime strength, because the most absorbing unity, of multitudinous passion that ever human heart conceived. Hence, in the cloister of St. Mark's, the intense, fixed, statue-like silence of ineffable adoration upon the spirits in prison at the feet of Christ, side by side, the hands lifted, and the knees bowed, and the lips

101 trembling together; and in St. Domenico of Fiesole, that whirlwind rush of the angels and the redeemed souls round about Him at His resurrection, in which we hear the blast of the horizontal trumpets mixed with the dying clangour of their ingathered wings.[12]

102   In Unity of Sequence, the effect of variety is best exemplified by the melodies of music, wherein, by the differences of the notes, they are

connected with each other in certain pleasant relations. This connection, taking place in quantities, is Proportion, respecting which certain general principles must be noted, as the subject is one open to many errors, and obscurely treated of by writers on art.

Proportion is of two distinct kinds: *Apparent* when it takes place between quantities for the sake of connection only, without any ultimate object or causal necessity; and *Constructive,* when it has reference to some function to be discharged by the quantities depending on their proportion. From the confusion of these two kinds of proportion have arisen the greater part of the erroneous conceptions of the influence of either.

(A) Apparent Proportion, or the sensible relation of quantities, is one of the most important means of obtaining unity amongst things which otherwise must have remained distinct in similarity; and as it may consist with every other kind of unity, and persist when every other means of it fails, it may be considered as lying at the root of most of our impressions   103
of the beautiful. There is no sense of rightness or wrongness connected with it; no sense of utility, propriety, or expediency. These ideas enter only where the proportion of quantities has reference to some function to be performed by them.

(B) On the other hand, Constructive Proportion, or the adaptation of quantities to functions, is agreeable, not (necessarily) to the eye, but to the mind, which is cognizant of the function to be performed. Thus the pleasantness or rightness of the proportions of a column depends not on the mere relation of diameter and height (which is not proportion at all, for proportion is between three terms at least); but on three other involved terms, the strength of materials, the weight to be borne, and the scale of the building. The proportions of a wooden column are wrong in a stone one, and of a small building wrong in a large one; and this owing solely to mechanical considerations which have no more connection with ideas of   104
beauty, than the relation between the arms of a lever adapted to the raising of a given weight; and yet it is highly agreeable to perceive that such constructive proportion has been duly observed, as it is agreeable to see that anything is fit for its purpose or for ours, and also that it has been the result of intelligence in the artificer of it; so that we sometimes feel a   105
pleasure in apparent non-adaptation, if it be a sign of ingenuity, as in the unnatural and seemingly impossible lightness of Gothic spires and roofs.

Now, the full proof of the influence of Apparent Proportion, I must   106
reserve for illustration by diagram;[13] one or two instances, however, may be given at present, for the better understanding of its nature.

We have already asserted that all curves are more beautiful than right lines. All curves, however, are not equally beautiful, and their differences of beauty depend on the different proportions borne to each other by those infinitely small right lines of which they may be conceived as composed.

When these lines are equal and contain equal angles, there can be no connection nor unity or sequence in them. The resulting curve, the circle, is therefore the least beautiful of all curves.

When the lines bear to each other some certain proportion: or when, the lines remaining equal, the angles vary; or when by any means whatsoever, and in whatever complicated modes, such differences as shall imply connection are established between the infinitely small segments, the resulting curves become beautiful. The simplest of the beautiful curves are the conic, and the various spirals; but it is difficult to trace any ground of superiority or inferiority among the infinite numbers of the higher curves. I believe that almost all are beautiful in their own nature, and that their comparative beauty depends on the constant quantities involved in their equations.

The universal forces of nature, and the individual energies of the matter submitted to them, are so appointed and balanced, that they are continually bringing out curves of this kind in all visible forms, and that circular lines become nearly impossible under any circumstances. The acceleration, for instance, of velocity, in streams that descend from hill-
107 sides, gradually increases their power of erosion, and in the same degree the rate of curvature in the descent of the slope, until at a certain degree of steepness this descent meets, and is concealed by, the straight line of the detritus. The junction of this right line with the plain is again modified by the farther bounding of the larger blocks, and by the successively diminishing scale of landslips caused by the erosion at the bottom. So that the whole contour of the hill is one of curvature; first, gradually increasing in rapidity to the maximum steepness of which the particular rock is capable, and then decreasing in a decreasing ratio, until it arrives at the plain-level. This type of form, modified of course more or less by the original boldness of the mountain, and dependent on its age, its constituent rock, and the circumstances of its exposure, is yet in its general formula applicable to all. So the curves of all things in motion, and of all organic forms, most rude and simple in the shell spirals, and most complicated in the muscular lines of the higher animals.

This influence of Apparent Proportion, a proportion, be it observed,
108 which has no reference to ultimate ends, but which is itself, seemingly, the end of operation to many of the forces of nature, is therefore at the root of all our delight in any beautiful form whatsoever. For no form can be beautiful which is not composed of curves whose unity is secured by relations of this kind.

Not only however in curvature, but in all associations of lines whatsoever, it is desirable that there should be reciprocal relation, and the eye is unhappy without perception of it. It is utterly vain to endeavour to reduce this proportion to finite rules, for it is as various as musical melody, and the laws to which it is subject are of the same general kind; so that the determination of right or wrong proportion is as much a matter of feeling and experience as the appreciation of good musical composition. Not but that there is a science of both, and principles which may not be infringed; but that within these limits the liberty of invention is infinite, and the degrees of excellence infinite also.

The argument of Burke on this subject[14] is summed up in the following words:— "Examine the head of a beautiful horse, find what proportion that bears to his body and to his limbs, and what relations these have to each other; and when you have settled these proportions as a standard of beauty, then take a dog or cat, or any other animal, and examine how   109 far the same proportions between their heads and their necks, between those and the body, and so on, are found to hold; I think we may safely say, that they differ in every species, yet that there are individuals found in a great many species so differing, that have a very striking beauty. Now if it be allowed that very different, and even contrary, forms and dispositions are consistent with beauty, it amounts, I believe, to a concession, that no certain measures operating from a natural principle are necessary to produce it, at least so far as the brute species is concerned."

In this argument there are three very palpable fallacies. The first is, the rough application of measurement to the heads, necks, and limbs, without observing the subtle differences of proportion and position of parts in the members themselves; for it would be strange if the different adjustment of the ears and brow in the dog and horse, did not require a harmonizing difference of adjustment in the head and neck. The second fallacy is the supposition that proportion cannot be beautiful if susceptible of variation; whereas the whole meaning of the term has reference to the adjustment and functional correspondence of *infinitely variable* quantities. And the third error is, the oversight of the very important fact, that, although "different and even contrary forms and dispositions are consistent with beauty," they are by no means consistent with equal *degrees* of beauty: so that, while we find in all animals such proportion and harmony of form as gift them with positive agreeableness consistent with the station and dignity of each, we perceive, also, a better proportion in some (as the   110 horse, eagle, lion, and man, for instance,) expressing the nobler functions and more exalted powers of the animal.

And this allowed superiority of some animal forms is, in itself, argument against the error of attributing the sensation of beauty to the perception of Expedient or Constructive Proportion. The megatherium is absolutely as well proportioned, in the adaptation of parts to purposes, as the horse or the swan; but by no means so handsome as either. The fact is, that the perception of expediency of proportion can but rarely affect our estimates of beauty, for it implies a knowledge which we very rarely and imperfectly possess, and the want of which we tacitly acknowledge.

Let us consider that instance of the proportion of the stalk of a plant to its head,[15] given by Burke. In order to judge of the expediency of this proportion, we must know, First, the scale of the plant; for the smaller the scale, the longer the stem may safely be: Secondly, the toughness of the materials of the stem, and the mode of their mechanical structure: Thirdly, the specific gravity of the head: Fourthly, the position of the head which the nature of fructification requires: Fifthly, the accidents and influences to which the situation for which the plant was created is exposed. Until we know all this, we cannot say that proportion or disproportion exists: and because we cannot know all this, the idea of expedient proportion enters but slightly into our impression of vegetable beauty, but rather, since the very existence of the plant proves that these proportions have been observed, and we know that nothing but our own ignorance prevents us from perceiving them, we take their accuracy on trust, and are delighted by the variety of results which the Divine intelligence has attained in the various involutions of these quantities; and perhaps most when, to outward appearance, such proportions have been neglected; more by the slenderness of the campanula than the security of the pine.

What is obscure in plants is utterly concealed in animals, owing to the greater number of means employed and functions performed. To judge of Expedient Proportion in them, we must know all that each member has to do, its bones, its muscles, and the amount of nervous energy communicable to them; and yet, as we have more experience and instinctive sense of the strength of muscles than of wood, and more practical knowledge of the use of a head or a foot than of a flower or a stem, we are much more likely to presume upon our judgment respecting proportions here; and are not afraid to assert that the plesiosaurus and camelopard have necks too long, that the turnspit[16] has legs too short, and the elephant a body too ponderous.

But the painfulness arising from the idea of this being the case is occasioned partly by our sympathy with the animal, partly by our false apprehension of incompletion in the Divine work; nor in either case has it any connection with impressions of that typical beauty of which we are at present speaking; though some, perhaps, with that vital beauty which will hereafter come under discussion.

I wish therefore the reader to hold, respecting proportion generally:

1st, That Apparent Proportion, or the melodious connection of quantities, is a cause of unity, and therefore one of the sources of all beautiful form.

2ndly, That Constructive Proportion is agreeable to the mind when it is known or supposed, and that its seeming absence is painful in a like degree; but that this pleasure and pain have nothing in common with those dependent on Ideas of Beauty.

CHAPTER VII
Of Repose, or the Type of
Divine Permanence

113   THERE is probably no necessity more imperatively felt by the artist, no test more unfailing of the greatness of artistical treatment, than that of the appearance of repose; yet there is no quality whose semblance in matter is more difficult to define or illustrate. Nevertheless, I believe that our instinctive love of it, as well as the cause to which I attribute that love, (although here also, as in the former cases, I contend not for the interpretation, but for the fact,) will be readily allowed by the reader. As opposed to passion, change, fulness, or laborious exertion, Repose is the especial and separating characteristic of the eternal mind and power. It is the "I am" of the Creator opposed to the "I become" of all creatures; it is the sign alike of the supreme knowledge which is incapable of surprise, the supreme power which is incapable of labour, the supreme volition which is incapable of change; it is the stillness of the beams of the eternal chambers laid upon the variable waters of ministering creatures. And as we saw before that the infinity which was a type of the Divine nature on the one hand, became yet more desirable on the other from its peculiar address to our prison hopes, and to the expectations of an unsatisfied and unaccomplished existence; so the types of this third attribute of the Deity might seem to have been rendered farther attractive to mortal instinct

114   through the infliction upon the fallen creature of a curse necessitating a labour once unnatural and still most painful; so that the desire of rest planted in the heart is no sensual nor unworthy one, but a longing for renovation and for escape from a state whose every phase is mere preparation for another equally transitory, to one in which permanence shall have become possible through perfection.

Repose, as it is expressed in material things, is either a simple appearance of permanence and quietness, as in the massy forms of a mountain or rock, accompanied by the lulling effect of all mighty sight and sound, which all feel and none define or else it is repose proper, the rest of things in which there is vitality or capability of motion actual or imagined: and

115   with respect to these the expression of repose is greater in proportion to the amount and sublimity of the action which is *not* taking place, as well

213

as to the intensity of the negation of it. Thus we do not speak of repose in a pebble, because the motion of a pebble has nothing in it of energy or vitality, neither its repose of stability. But having once seen a great rock come down a mountain side, we have a noble sensation of its rest, now bedded immovably among the fern; because the power and fearfulness of its motion were great, and its stability and negation of motion are now great in proportion. Hence the imagination, which delights in nothing more than in the enhancing of the characters of repose, effects this usually by either attributing to things visibly energetic an ideal stability, or to things visibly stable an ideal activity or vitality.

Thus, as we saw that Unity demanded for its expression what at first   116
might have seemed its contrary, Variety, so Repose demands for its expression the implied capability of its opposite, Energy: and this even in its lower manifestations, in rocks and stones and trees. By comparing the modes in which the mind is disposed to regard the boughs of a fair and vigorous tree, motionless in the summer air, with the effect produced by one of the same boughs hewn square and used for threshold or lintel, the reader will at once perceive the connection of vitality with repose, and the part they both bear in beauty.

But that which in lifeless things ennobles them by seeming to indicate life, ennobles higher creatures by indicating the exaltation of their earthly vitality into a Divine vitality; and raising the life of sense into the life of faith: faith, whether we receive it in the sense of adherence to resolution, obedience to law, regardfulness of promise, in which from all time it has been the test, as the shield, of the true being and life of man; or in the still higher sense of trustfulness in the presence, kindness, and word of God, in which form it has been exhibited under the Christian dispensation. For, whether in one or other form,—whether the faithfulness of men whose path is chosen and portion fixed, in the following and receiving of that path and portion, as in the Thermopylæ[17] camp; or the happier faithfulness of children in the good giving of their Father, and of subjects in the conduct of their King, as in the "Stand still and see the salvation of God"[18] of the Red Sea shore, there is rest and peacefulness, the "standing still," in both, the quietness of action determined, of spirit unalarmed, of expectation unimpatient: beautiful even when based only, as of old, on the self-command and self-possession, the persistent dignity or the uncal-   117
culating love, of the creature; but more beautiful yet when the rest is one of humility instead of pride, and the trust no more in the resolution we have taken, but in the hand we hold.

Hence I think that there is no desire more intense or more exalted than that which exists in all rightly disciplined minds for the evidences of repose in external signs: and what I cautiously said respecting infinity, I say fearlessly respecting repose; that no work of art can be great without

118 it, and that all art is great in proportion to the appearance of it.* It is the most unfailing test of beauty, whether of matter or of motion; nothing can be ignoble that possesses it, nothing right that has it not; and in strict proportion to its appearance in the work is the majesty of mind to be inferred in the artificer. Without regard to other qualities, we may look to this for our evidence; and by the search for this alone we may be led to the rejection of all that is base, and the accepting of all that is good and great, for the paths of wisdom are all peace. We shall see, by this light, three colossal images standing up side by side, looming in their great rest of spirituality above the whole world-horizon, Phidias, Michael Angelo, and

---

*This is wildly overstated; and the rest of the paragraph is nearly pure nonsense,—yet with a grain of meaning at the bottom, which is worth explanation, and, once explained, contains an apology due to the reader, and a palliation, just to myself, for the extravagance, not of this passage only, but of many subsequent ones like it.

When I was first in Rome, in the winter of 1840, my own real art pleasures were only in Turner and Prout: but I desired earnestly to profit by the opportunities round me; and when Mr. George Richmond and Mr. Joseph Severn took me to the Vatican, looked very reverently at whatever I was bid.

Of Raphael, however, I found I could make nothing whatever. The only thing clearly manifest to me in his compositions was, that everybody seemed to be pointing at everybody else, and that nobody, to my notion, was worth pointing at.

But the colossal perplexities and subtle chiaroscuro of the Sistine Chapel impressed me, like the sublimity of mountains; the authority of Reynolds, which was at that time conclusive with me, enforced the feeling of which I was already not a little vain, that I could sympathize with the greatest (so he was called by all my friends) of Italian masters. I set myself almost exclusively to the study of him, and long before I had begun writing Modern Painters, knew every figure and statue by Michael Angelo, either in Rome or Florence, very literally by heart: while I remained in total ignorance of the antecedent religious schools. When, in 1845, I worked for the first time in Santa Maria Novella, and also for the first time read Dante, it seemed to me that the entire virtue and intellectual power of the older schools had been consummated in Dante; and then the three dynasties of Greek, Christian Mystic, and Christian Naturalist, became represented to me by the three men, Phidias, Michael Angelo, and Dante, named in the text; and represented also, with a power and simplicity unqualified by relative or intermediate knowledge. The physical repose of the statues of the Theseus, and of the Dawn and Twilight,[19] and the spiritual repose of the conceptions of Paradise, by Dante and Angelico, impressed me as their distinctive character: and the apparently sudden enthusiasm of the pages I am excusing, was indeed the outcome of the eager emotions of five youthful years. Rightly expanded, or even understood as it was meant, the paragraph has a considerable measure of subtle truth in it; but as it stands, it is, as I have just confessed, nearly pure nonsense; for although great work is for the most part quiet, there is a great deal of quiet work in the world which is also extremely small, and extremely dull[1883].

Dante; and then, separated from their great religious thrones only by less
fulness and earnestness of faith, Homer and Shakespeare; and from these
we may go down step by step among the mighty men of every age, securely   119
and certainly observant of diminished lustre in every appearance of
restlessness and effort, until the last trace of true inspiration vanishes in
tottering affectation or tortured insanity. There is no art, nor pursuit
whatsoever, but its results may be classed by this test alone. Everything of
evil is betrayed and winnowed away by it; glitter, confusion, or glare of
colour; inconsistency of thought; forced expression; evil choice of subject;
redundance of materials, pretence, overcharged decoration, or excessive
division of parts; and this in everything. In architecture, in music, in
acting, in dancing, in whatsoever art, great or mean, there are yet degrees
of greatness or meanness entirely dependent on this single quality of
repose.

In Christian art, it would be well to compare the feeling of the finer   121
among the altar-tombs of the middle ages, with any monumental works
after Michael Angelo; perhaps more especially with works of Roubillac or
Canova.[20]

In the Cathedral of Lucca, near the entrance-door of the north transept,   122
there is a monument by Jacopo della Quercia[21] to Ilaria di Caretto, the
wife of Paolo Guinigi [fig.29]. I name it not as more beautiful or perfect
than other examples of the same period; but as furnishing an instance of

fig.29   Jacopo della Quercia, *Ilaria di Caretto*, in Lucca Cathedral

the exact and right mean between the rigidity and rudeness of the earlier monumental effigies, and the morbid imitation of life, sleep, or death, of
123 which the fashion has taken place in modern times. She is lying on a simple couch with a hound at her feet; not on the side, but with the head laid straight and simply on the hard pillow, in which, let it be observed, there is no effort at deceptive imitation of pressure. It is understood as a pillow, but not mistaken for one. The hair is bound in a flat braid over the fair brow, the sweet and arched eyes are closed, the tenderness of the loving lips is set and quiet; there is that about them which forbids breath; something which is not death nor sleep, but the pure image of both. The hands are not lifted in prayer, neither folded, but the arms are laid at length upon the body, and the hands cross as they fall. The feet are hidden by the drapery, and the forms of the limbs concealed, but not their tenderness.

CHAPTER VIII
Of Symmetry, or the Type of
Divine Justice

IN all perfectly beautiful objects, there is found the opposition of one   125
part to another, and a reciprocal balance, in animals commonly
between opposite sides (note the disagreeableness occasioned by the
exception in flat-fish, having the eyes on one side of the head); while in
vegetables the opposition is less distinct, as in the boughs on opposite
sides of trees, and the leaves and sprays on each side of the boughs; and in
dead matter less perfect still, often amounting only to a certain tendency
towards a balance, as in the opposite sides of valleys and alternate
windings of streams. In things in which perfect symmetry is from their
nature impossible or improper, a balance must be at least in some measure
expressed before they can be beheld with pleasure. Hence the necessity of
what artists require as opposing lines or masses in composition, the
propriety of which, as well as their value, depends chiefly on their
inartificial and natural invention. Absolute equality is not required, still
less absolute similarity. A mass of subdued colour may be balanced by a
point of a powerful one, and a long and latent line overpowered by a short
and conspicuous one.

Whether the agreeableness of symmetry be in any way referable to its   126
expression of the Aristotelian $\dot{\iota}\sigma\acute{o}\tau\eta\varsigma$, that is to say, of abstract justice, I
leave the reader to determine; I only assert respecting it, that it is
necessary to the dignity of every form, and that by the removal of it we
shall render the other elements of beauty comparatively ineffectual:
though, on the other hand, it is to be observed that it is rather a mode of
arrangement of qualities than a quality itself; and hence symmetry has
little power over the mind, unless all the other constituents of beauty be
found together with it.

CHAPTER IX
Of Purity, or the Type of Divine Energy

128 IT may at first appear strange that I have not, in my enumeration of the Types of Divine attributes, included that which is certainly the most visible and evident of all, as well as the most distinctly expressed in Scripture; "God is light, and in Him is no darkness at all."[22] But I could not logically class the presence of an actual substance or motion with mere conditions and modes of being; neither could I logically separate from any of these, that which is evidently necessary to the perception of all. And it is also to be observed, that, though the love of light is more instinctive in the human heart than any other of the desires connected with beauty, we can hardly separate its agreeableness in its own nature from the sense of its necessity and value for the purposes of life; neither the abstract painfulness of darkness from the sense of danger and powerlessness connected with it. And note also that it is not *all* light, but light possessing the universal qualities of beauty, diffused or infinite rather than in points; tranquil, not startling and variable; pure, not sullied or oppressed; which is indeed pleasant and perfectly typical of the Divine nature.

Observe, however, that there is one quality, the idea of which has been just introduced in connection with light, which might have escaped us in the consideration of mere matter, namely Purity: and yet I think that the original notion of this quality is altogether material, and has only been attributed to colour when such colour is suggestive of the condition of

129 matter from which we originally received the idea. For I see not in the abstract how one colour should be considered *purer* than another, except as more or less compounded: whereas there is certainly a sense of purity or impurity in the most compound and neutral colours, as well as in the simplest; a quality difficult to define, and which the reader will probably be surprised by my calling the type of Energy, with which it has certainly little traceable connection in the mind.

I believe, however, if we carefully analyze the nature of our ideas of impurity in general, we shall find them refer especially to conditions of matter in which its various elements are placed in a relation incapable of healthy or proper operation; and most distinctly to conditions in which

219

the negation of vital or energetic action is most evident; as in corruption and decay of all kinds, wherein particles which once, by their operation on each other, produced a living and energetic whole, are reduced to a condition of perfect passiveness, in which they are seized upon and appropriated, one by one, piecemeal, by whatever has need of them, without any power of resistance or energy of their own.

In colour, I imagine that the quality which we term purity is dependent   133
on the full energizing of the rays that compose it; of which if in compound hues any are overpowered and killed by the rest, so as to be of no value nor operation, foulness is the consequence; while so long as all act together, whether side by side, or from pigments seen one through the other, so that all the colouring matter employed may come into play in the harmony desired, and none be quenched nor killed, purity results. And so in all cases I suppose that pureness is made to us desirable, because expressive of that constant presence and energizing of the Deity by which all things live and move, and have their being; and that foulness is painful as the accompaniment of disorder and decay, and always indicative of the withdrawal of Divine support. And the practical analogies of life, the invariable connection of outward foulness with mental sloth and degradation, as well as with bodily lethargy and disease, together with the contrary indications of freshness and purity belonging to every healthy and active organic frame (singularly seen in the effort of the young leaves when first their inward energy prevails over the earth, pierces its corruption, and shakes its dust away from their own white purity of life),   134
all these circumstances strengthen the instinct by associations countless and irresistible. And then, finally, with the idea of purity comes that of spirituality; for the essential characteristic of matter is its inertia, whence, by adding to its purity of energy, we may in some measure spiritualize even matter itself. Thus in the Apocalyptic descriptions, it is the purity of every substance that fits it for its place in heaven; the river of the water of life, that proceeds out of the throne of the Lamb, is clear as crystal, and the pavement of the city is pure gold "like unto clear glass."[23]

CHAPTER XII[24]
Of Vital Beauty
I. Of Relative Vital Beauty

146   I proceed more particularly to examine the nature of that second kind of Beauty of which I spoke in the third chapter,[25] as consisting in "the appearance of felicitous fulfilment of function in living things." I have already noticed[26] the example of very pure and high typical beauty which is to be found in the lines and gradations of unsullied snow: if, passing to the edge of a sheet of it, upon the Lower Alps, early in May, we find, as we are nearly sure to find, two or three little round openings pierced in it, and through these emergent, a slender, pensive, fragile flower,* whose small, dark purple, fringed bell hangs down and shudders over the icy cleft that it has cloven, as if partly wondering at its own recent grave, and partly

147   dying of very fatigue after its hard-won victory; we shall be, or we ought to be, moved by a totally different impression of loveliness from that which we receive among the dead ice and the idle clouds. There is now uttered to us a call for sympathy, now offered to us an image of moral purpose and achievement, which, however unconscious or senseless the creature may indeed be that so seems to call, cannot be heard without affection, nor contemplated without worship, by any of us whose heart is rightly tuned, or whose mind is clearly and surely sighted.

    Throughout the whole of the organic creation every being in a perfect state exhibits certain appearances or evidences of happiness; and is in its nature, its desires, its modes of nourishment, habitation, and death, illustrative or expressive of certain moral dispositions or principles. Now, first, in the keenness of the sympathy which we feel in the happiness, real or apparent, of all organic beings, and which, as we shall presently see, invariably prompts us, from the joy we have in it, *to look upon those as most lovely which are most happy;* and, secondly, in the justness of the moral sense which rightly reads the lesson they are all intended to teach, and classes them in orders of worthiness and beauty according to the rank and nature of that lesson, whether it be of warning or example, in those that

---

*Soldanella alpina.

wallow or in those that soar;—in our right accepting and reading of all this, consists, I say, the ultimately perfect condition of that noble Theoretic faculty, whose place in the system of our nature I have already partly vindicated with respect to typical, but which can only fully be established with respect to vital beauty.

Its first perfection, therefore, relating to Vital Beauty, is the kindness 148 and unselfish fulness of heart, which receives the utmost amount of pleasure from the happiness of all things. Even the ordinary exercise of this faculty implies a condition of the whole moral being in some measure right and healthy, and to the entire exercise of it there is necessary the entire perfection of the Christian character; for he who loves not God, nor his brother, cannot love the grass beneath his feet,* and the creatures which live not for his uses, filling those spaces in the universe which he needs not; while on the other hand, none can love God, nor his human brother, without loving all things which his Father loves; nor without 149 looking upon them, every one, as in that respect his brethren also, and perhaps worthier than he, if, in the under concords they have to fill, their part is touched more truly.

As we pass from those beings of whose happiness and pain we are 150 certain, to those in which it is doubtful, or only seeming, as possibly in plants, yet our feeling for them has in it more of sympathy than of actual love, as receiving from them in delight far more than we can give; for love, I think, chiefly grows in giving; at least its essence is the desire of doing good or giving happiness. Still the sympathy of very sensitive minds usually reaches so far as to the conception of life in the plant, nor do I believe that any mind, however rude, is without some slight perception or acknowledgment of joyfulness in breathless things, as most certainly 151 there are none but feel instinctive delight in the appearances of such enjoyment.

For it is matter of easy demonstration, that setting the characters of typical beauty aside, the pleasure afforded by every organic form is in proportion to its appearance of healthy vital energy. In a rose-tree, setting aside all the considerations of gradated flushing of colour, and fair folding of line, which its flowers share with the cloud or the snow-wreath, we find, in and through all this, certain signs pleasant and acceptable as signs of life and strength in the plant. Every leaf and stalk is seen to have a function, to be constantly exercising that function, and as it *seems, solely* for the

---

*Untrue, I am sorry to say, in both clauses of the sentence. It is very possible to love grasses and ferns without loving God, and much too possible to be religious without loving either fields or beasts. The simple statement that the degree of beauty we can see, in visible things, depends on the love we can bear them, is trustworthy. [1883.]

good and enjoyment of the plant. It is true that reflection will show us that the plant is not living for itself alone, that its life is one of benefaction, that it gives as well as receives; but no sense of this whatsoever mingles with our perception of physical beauty in its forms.

152   Now I wish particularly to impress upon the reader that all these higher sensations of beauty in the plant arise from our unselfish sympathy with its happiness, and not from any view of the qualities in it which may bring good to us, nor even from our acknowledgment in it of any moral condition beyond that of mere felicity; for such an acknowledgment

153 belongs to the second operation of the Theoretic faculty and not to the sympathetic part which we are at present examining; so that we even find that in this respect, the moment we begin to look upon any creature as subordinate to some purpose out of itself, some of the sense of organic beauty is lost. Thus, when we are told that the leaves of a plant are occupied in decomposing carbonic acid, and preparing oxygen for us, we begin to look upon it with some such indifference as upon a gasometer. It has become a machine; some of our sense of its happiness is gone; its emanation of inherent life is no longer pure. The bending trunk, waving to and fro in the wind above the waterfall, is beautiful because it is happy, though it is perfectly useless to us. The same trunk, hewn down, and thrown across the stream, has lost its beauty. It serves as a bridge,—it has become useful; and its beauty is gone, or what it retains is purely typical, dependent on its lines and colours, not on its functions. Saw it into planks, and though now adapted to become permanently useful, its beauty is lost for ever, or to be regained only when decay and ruin shall have withdrawn it again from use, and left it to receive from the hand of nature the velvet moss and varied lichen, which may again suggest ideas of inherent happiness, and tint its mouldering sides with hues of life.

   There is something, I think, peculiarly beautiful and instructive in this unselfishness of the Theoretic faculty, and in its abhorrence of all utility to one creature which is based on the pain or destruction of any other; for in such services as are consistent with the essence and energy of both it

154 takes delight, as in the clothing of the rock by the herbage, and the feeding of the herbage by the stream.

   But still clearer evidence of its being indeed the expression of happiness to which we look for our first pleasure in organic form, is to be found in the way in which we regard the bodily frame of animals: of which it is to be noted first, that there is not anything which causes so intense and tormenting a sense of ugliness as any scar, wound, monstrosity, or imperfection which seems inconsistent with the animal's ease and health; and that although in vegetables, where there is no immediate sense of pain, we are comparatively little hurt by excrescences and irregularities, but are sometimes even delighted with them, and fond of them, as children of the oak-apple, and sometimes look upon them as more interesting than the uninjured conditions, as in the gnarled and knotted trunks of trees; yet the slightest approach to anything of the kind in *animal* form is regarded with intense horror, merely from the sense of pain it conveys. And, in the second place, it is to be noted that whenever we dissect the animal frame, or conceive it as dissected, and substitute in our thoughts the neatness of mechanical contrivance for the pleasure of the animal; the moment we reduce enjoyment to ingenuity, and volition to leverage, that instant all sense of beauty ceases.

If therefore it is the sense of felicity which we first desire in organic form,   155
those forms will be the most beautiful (always, observe, leaving typical beauty out of the question) which exhibit most of power, and seem capable of most quick and joyous sensation. Hence we find gradations of beauty, from the impenetrable hide and slow movement of the elephant and the rhinoceros, from the foul occupation of the vulture, from the   156
earthy struggling of the worm, to the brilliancy of the moth, the buoyancy of the bird, the swiftness of the fawn and the horse, the fair and kingly sensibility of man.

Thus far then, the Theoretic faculty is concerned with the *happiness* of animals, and its exercise depends on the cultivation of the affections only. Let us next observe how it is concerned with the *moral functions* of animals, and therefore how it is dependent on the cultivation of every moral sense. There is not any organic creature but, in its history and habits, will exemplify or illustrate to us some moral excellence or deficiency, or some point of God's providential government, which it is necessary for us to know. Thus the functions and the fates of animals are distributed to them, with a variety which exhibits to us the dignity and results of almost every passion and kind of conduct: some filthy and slothful, pining and unhappy; some rapacious, restless, and cruel; some ever earnest and laborious, and, I think, unhappy in their endless labour; creatures, like the bee, that heap up riches and cannot tell who shall gather them, and others employed, like angels, in endless offices of love and praise.

Whence, in fine, looking to the whole kingdom of organic nature, we   161
find that our full receiving of its beauty depends, first on the sensibility, and then on the accuracy and faithfulness, of the heart in its moral judgments; so that it is necessary that we should not only love all creatures well, but esteem them in that order which is according to God's laws and not according to our own human passions and predilections; not looking for swiftness, and strength, and cunning, rather than for patience and kindness; still less delighting in their animosity and cruelty one toward another: neither, if it may be avoided, interfering with the working of nature in any way; nor, when we interfere to obtain service, judging from

162 the morbid conditions of the animal or vegetable so induced; so that in all cases we are to beware of such opinions as seem in any way referable to human pride, or even to the grateful or pernicious influence of things upon ourselves; and to cast the mind free, and out of ourselves, humbly, and yet always in that noble position of pause above the other visible creatures, nearer God than they, which we authoritatively hold, thence looking down upon them, and testing the clearness of our moral vision by the extent, and fulness, and constancy of our pleasure in the light of God's love as it embraces them, and the harmony of His holy laws, that for ever bring mercy out of rapine, and religion out of wrath.

CHAPTER XIII
II.   Of Generic Vital Beauty

IN the first or sympathetic operation of the Theoretic faculty, it will be   163
remembered, we receive pleasure from the signs of mere happiness in
living things. In the second theoretic operation of comparing and judging,
we constituted ourselves such judges of the lower creatures as Adam was
made by God when they were brought to him to be named; and we
allowed of beauty in them as they reached, more or less, to that standard   164
of moral perfection by which we test ourselves. But in the third place we
are to come down again from the judgment seat, and, taking it for granted
that every creature of God is in some way good, and has a duty and specific
operation providentially accessary to the wellbeing of all, we are to look,
in this faith, to that employment and nature of each, and to derive
pleasure from their entire perfection and fitness for the duty they have to
do, and in their entire fulfilment of it; and so we are to take pleasure and
find beauty in the magnificent binding together of the jaws of the
ichthyosaurus for catching and holding, and in the adaptation of the lion
for springing, and of the locust for destroying, and of the lark for singing,
and in every creature for the doing of that which God has made it to do.
Which faithful pleasure in the perception of the perfect operation of
lower creatures I have placed last among the perceptions of the Theoretic
faculty concerning them, because it is commonly last acquired, both
owing to the humbleness and trustfulness of heart which it demands, and
because it implies a knowledge of the habits and structure of every
creature, such as we can but imperfectly possess.

The perfect *idea* of the form and condition in which all the properties
of the species are fully developed, is called the Ideal of the species. The
question of the nature of ideal conception of species, and of the mode in
which the mind arrives at it, has been the subject of so much discussion,
and source of so much embarrassment, chiefly owing to that unfortunate
distinction between Idealism and Realism which leads most people to
imagine the Ideal opposed to the Real, and therefore *false*, that I think it
necessary to request the reader's most careful attention to the following
positions.

165   Any work of art which represents, not a material object, but the mental conception of a material object, is, in the primary sense of the word, ideal. That is to say, it represents an idea and not a thing. Any work of art which represents or realizes a material object is, in the primary sense of the term, unideal.

Ideal works of art, therefore, in the first sense, represent the result of an act of imagination, and are good or bad in proportion to the healthy condition and general power of the imagination whose acts they represent.

Unideal works of art (the studious production of which is termed Realism) represent actual existing things, and are good or bad in proportion to the perfection of the representation.

All entirely bad works of art may be divided into those which, professing to be imaginative, bear no stamp of imagination, and are therefore false; and those which, professing to be representative of matter, miss of the representation, and are therefore nugatory.

It is the habit of most observers to regard art as representative of matter, and to look only for the entireness of representation; and it was to this view of art that I limited the arguments of the former sections of the present work, wherein, having to oppose the conclusions of a criticism entirely based upon the realist system, I was compelled to meet that criticism on its own grounds. But the greater parts of works of art, more especially those devoted to the expression of ideas of beauty, are the results of the agency of imagination, their worthiness depending, as above stated, on the healthy condition of the imagination.

Hence it is necessary for us, in order to arrive at conclusions respecting the worthiness of such works, to define and examine the nature of the imaginative faculty, upon which examination I shall enter in the 2nd Section of the present Part.

166   But there is another sense of the word 'Ideal' besides this, and it is that with which we are here concerned. It is evident that, so long as we apply the word to that art which represents ideas and not things, we may use it as truly of the art which represents an idea of Caliban, and not real Caliban, as of the art which represents an idea of Antinous, and not real Antinous. For that is as much imagination which conceives the monster, as which conceives the man. If, however, Caliban and Antinous be creatures of the same species, and the form of the one contain not the fully developed types or characters of the species, while the form of the other presents the greater part of them, then the latter is said to be a form more ideal than the other, as a nearer approximation to the general 'idea' or conception of the species.

Now it is evident that this use of the word Ideal is much less accurate than the other from which it is derived; for it rests on the assumption that

the assemblage of all the characters of a species in their perfect development cannot exist but in the imagination. For if it can actually and in
reality exist, it is not right to call it ideal or imaginary; it would be better
to call it characteristic or general, and to reserve the word Ideal for the
results of the operation of the imagination, either on the perfect or
imperfect forms.

Nevertheless, the word Ideal has been so long and universally accepted
in this sense, that it becomes necessary to continue the use of it, so only
that the reader will be careful to observe the distinction in the sense,
according to the subject matter under discussion. At present then, using   167
it as expressive of the noble generic form which indicates the full
perfection of the creature in all its functions, I wish to examine how far
this perfection exists, or may exist, in nature, and, if not in nature, how
it is by us discoverable or imaginable.

Let us ask, first, what kind of ideal form may be attributed to a limpet
or an oyster; that is to say, whether all oysters do or do not come up to the
entire notion or idea of an oyster. I apprehend that, of those which are of
full size and healthy condition, there will be found many which fulfil the
conditions of an oyster in every respect; and that so perfectly, that we
could not, by combining the features of two or more together, produce a
more perfect oyster than any that we see. I suppose, also, that out of a
number of healthy fish, birds, or beasts, of the same species, it would not
be easy to select an individual as superior to *all* the rest; neither, by
comparing two or more of the nobler examples together, to arrive at the
conception of a form superior to that of either; but that, though the
accidents of more abundant food or more fitting habitation may induce   168
among them some varieties of size, strength, and colour, yet the entire
generic form would be presented by many, neither would any art be able
to add to or diminish from it.

Let us next observe the conditions of ideality in vegetables. Out of a
large number of primroses or violets, I apprehend that, although one or
two might be larger than all the rest, the greater part would be very
sufficient primroses and violets; and that we could, by no study nor
combination of violets, conceive of a better violet than many in the bed.
And so generally of the blossoms and separate members of all vegetables.

But among the entire forms of the complex vegetables, as of oak trees,
for instance, there exists very large and constant difference; some being
what we hold to be fine oaks, as in parks and places where they are taken
care of, and have their own way, and some are but poor and mean oaks,
which have had no one to take care of them, but have been obliged to   169
maintain themselves.

That which we have to determine is, whether ideality be predicable of
the fine oaks only, or whether the poor and mean oaks also may be

plate 7 Gaspar Dughet, *Ariccia*

plate 8 Salvator Rosa, *Landscape with Mercury and the Dishonest Woodman*

plate 9 Aelbert Cuyp, *Herdsman with Cows*

plate 10 J.M.W. Turner, *Arona*

plate 11 J.M.W. Turner, *Loch Coruisk, Skye*

plate 12 J.M.W. Turner, *Ulleswater*

considered as ideal, that is, coming up to the conditions of oak, and the general notion of oak.

Now there is this difference between the positions held in creation by animals and plants, and thence in the dispositions with which we regard them; that the animals, being for the most part locomotive, are capable both of living where they choose, and of obtaining what food they want, and of fulfilling all the conditions necessary to their health and perfection. For which reason they are answerable for such health and perfection, and we should be displeased and hurt, if we did not find it in one individual as well as another.

But the case is evidently different with plants. They are intended fixedly to occupy many places comparatively unfit for them, and to fill up all the spaces where greenness, and coolness, and ornament, and oxygen are wanted, and that with very little reference to their comfort or convenience. Now it would be hard upon the plant, if, after being tied to a particular spot, where it is indeed much wanted, and is a great blessing, but where it has enough to do to live; whence it cannot move to obtain what it needs or likes, but must stretch its unfortunate arms here and there for bare breath and light, and split its way among rocks, and grope for sustenance in unkindly soil; it would be hard upon the plant, I say, if under all these disadvantages, it were made answerable for its appearance, and found fault with because it was not a fine plant of the kind. And it seems to be that, in order that no unkind comparisons may be drawn between one and another, there are not appointed to plants the fixed number, position, and proportion of members which are ordained in animals (and

170 any variation from which in these is unpardonable), but a continually varying number and position, even among the more freely growing examples, admitting therefore all kinds of license to those which have enemies to contend with; and that without in any way detracting from their dignity and perfection.

So then there is in trees no perfect form which can be fixed upon or reasoned out as ideal; but that is always an ideal oak which, however poverty-stricken, or hunger-pinched, or tempest-tortured, is yet seen to have done, under its appointed circumstances, all that could be expected of oak.

And herein, then, we at last find the cause of that fact that the exalted or seemingly improved condition, whether of plant or animal, induced by

171 human interference, is not the true and artistical idea of it. It has been well shown that many plants are found alone on a certain soil or subsoil in a wild state, not because such soil is favourable to them, but because they alone are capable of existing on it, and because all dangerous rivals are by its inhospitality removed. Now if we withdraw the plant from this position, which it hardly endures, and supply it with the earth, and

maintain about it the temperature, that it delights in; withdrawing from it, at the same time, all rivals, which, in such conditions, nature would have thrust upon it, we shall indeed obtain a magnificently developed example of the plant, colossal in size, and splendid in organization; but we shall utterly lose in it that moral ideal which is dependent on its right fulfilment of its appointed functions.

The first time that I saw the Soldanella alpina, before spoken of,[27] it was growing, of magnificent size, on a sunny alpine pasture, among bleating of   172
sheep and lowing of cattle, associated with a profusion of Geum montanum, and Ranunculus pyrenæus. I noticed it only because new to me, nor perceived any peculiar beauty in its cloven flower. Some days after, I found it alone, among the rack of the higher clouds, and howling of glacier winds; and, as I described it, piercing through an edge of ava-lanche, which, in its retiring, had left the new ground brown and lifeless, and as if burned by recent fire; the plant was poor and feeble, and seem-ingly exhausted with its efforts, but it was then that I comprehended its ideal character, and saw its noble function and order of glory among the constellations of the earth.

And if it be asked how this conception of the utmost beauty of ideal form is consistent with what we formerly argued respecting the pleasant-ness of the appearance of felicity in the creature, let it be observed, and for ever held, that the right and true happiness of every creature is in this very   173
discharge of its function, and in those efforts by which its strength and inherent energy are developed; and that the repose of which we also spoke as necessary to all beauty, is, as was then stated, repose not of inanition, nor of luxury, nor of irresolution, but the repose of magnificent energy and being; in action, the calmness of trust and determination; in rest, the consciousness of duty accomplished and of victory won; and this repose and this felicity can take place as well in the midst of trial and tempest, as beside the waters of comfort; they perish only when the creature is either unfaithful to itself, or is afflicted by circumstances unnatural and malig-nant to its being, and for the contending with which it was neither fitted nor ordained. Hence that rest which is indeed glorious is of the chamois crouched breathless on his granite bed, not of the stalled ox over his fodder; and that happiness which is indeed beautiful is in the bearing of those trial tests which are appointed for the proving of every creature, whether it be good, or whether it be evil; and in the fulfilment to the uttermost of every command it has received, and the outcarrying to the uttermost of every power and gift it has gotten from its God.

Therefore the task of the painter, in his pursuit of ideal form, is to attain accurate knowledge, so far as may be in his power, of the peculiar virtues, duties, and characters of every species of being; down even to the stone, for there is an ideality of stones according to their kind, an ideality of granite and slate and marble, and it is in the utmost and most exalted exhibition of such individual character, order, and use, that all ideality of art consists.*

*Extreme nonsense, I grieve to see—and say, and what is worse, unguarded nonsense; for I never really meant that "all" ideality of art consisted in specific distinctions. The passage is an impetuous slip in controversy, and meant to be conclusive against the people who had said that trees, in a painting, should be of no particular species.   [1883.]

CHAPTER XIV
III. Of Vital Beauty in Man

HAVING thus passed gradually through all the orders and fields of 176
creation, and traversed that goodly line of God's happy creatures
who "leap not, but express a feast, where all the guests sit close, and
nothing wants,"²⁸ without finding any deficiency which human invention might supply, nor any harm which human interference might mend,
we come at last to set ourselves face to face with ourselves; expecting that
in creatures made after the image of God, we are to find comeliness and
completion more exquisite than in the fowls of the air and the things that
pass through the paths of the sea.

But behold now a sudden change from all former experience. No longer
among the individuals of the race is there equality or likeness, a
distributed fairness and fixed type visible in each; but evil diversity,
and terrible stamp of various degradation: features seamed by sickness,
dimmed by sensuality, convulsed by passion, pinched by poverty, shadowed by sorrow, branded with remorse: bodies consumed with sloth,
broken down by labour, tortured by disease, dishonoured in foul uses;
intellects without power, hearts without hope, minds earthly and devilish;
our bones full of the sin of our youth, the heaven revealing our iniquity,
the earth rising up against us, the roots dried up beneath, and the branch 177
cut off above; well for us only, if, after beholding this our natural face in
a glass, we desire not straightway to forget what manner of men we be.

Herein there is at last something, and too much for that short-stopping
intelligence and dull perception of ours to accomplish, whether in earnest
fact, or in the seeking for the outward image of beauty:—to undo the
devil's work; to restore to the body the grace and the power which
inherited disease has destroyed; to restore to the spirit the purity, and to
the intellect the grasp, that they had in Paradise. Now, first of all, this
work, be it observed, is in no respect a work of imagination. Wrecked we
are, and nearly all to pieces; but that little good *by which we are to redeem
ourselves* is to be got out of the old wreck, beaten about and full of sand
though it be; and not out of that desert island of pride on which the devils
split first, and we after them: and so the only restoration of the body that

we can reach is not to be coined out of our fancies, but to be collected out of such uninjured and bright vestiges of the old seal as we can find and set together: and the ideal of the good and perfect soul, as it is seen in the features, is not to be reached by imagination, but by the seeing and reaching forth of the better part of the soul to that of which it must first know the sweetness and goodness in itself, before it can much desire, or rightly find, the signs of it in others.

178 Now, of the ordinary process by which the realization of ideal bodily form is reached, there is explanation enough in all treatises on art, and it is so far well comprehended that I need not stay long to consider it. So far as the sight and knowledge of the human form, of the purest race, exercised from infancy constantly, but not excessively, in all exercises of dignity, not in straining dexterities, but in natural exercises of running, casting, or riding; practised in endurance, not of extraordinary hardship, for that hardens and degrades the body, but of natural hardship, vicissitudes of winter and summer, and cold and heat, yet in a climate where none of these are severe; surrounded also by a certain degree of right luxury, so as to soften and refine the forms of strength; so far as the sight of all this could render the mental intelligence of what is noble in human form so acute as to be able to abstract and combine, from the best examples so produced, that which was most perfect in each, so far the Greek conceived and attained the ideal of humanity: and on the Greek modes of attaining it, chiefly dwell those writers whose opinions on this subject I have collected; wholly losing sight of what seems to me the most important branch of the inquiry, namely, the influence, for good or evil, of the mind upon the bodily shape, the wreck of the mind itself, and the modes by which we may conceive of its restoration.

The visible operation of the mind upon the body may be classed under three heads.

179 First, the operation of the intellectual powers upon the features, in the fine cutting and chiselling of them, and removal from them of signs of sensuality and sloth, by which they are blunted and deadened; and substitution of energy and intensity for vacancy and insipidity (by which wants alone the faces of many fair women are utterly spoiled and rendered valueless); and by the keenness given to the eye and fine moulding and development to the brow.

Secondly, the operation of the moral feelings conjointly with the intellectual powers on both the features and form. Now, the operation of the right moral feelings on the intellect is always for the good of the latter, 180 for *it is not possible that selfishness should reason rightly in any respect*, but must be blind in its estimation of the worthiness of all things: neither anger, for that overpowers the reason or outcries it; neither sensuality, for that overgrows and chokes it; neither agitation, for that has no time to compare things together; neither enmity, for that must be unjust; neither fear, for that exaggerates all things; neither cunning and deceit, for that which is voluntarily untrue will soon be unwittingly so; but the great reasoners are self-command, and trust unagitated, and deep-looking Love, and Faith, which as she is above Reason, so she best holds the reins of it from her high seat; so that they err grossly who think of the right development even of the intellectual type as possible, unless we look to higher sources of beauty first.

The third point to be considered with respect to the corporeal   182
expression of mental character is, that there is a certain period of the soul-culture when it begins to interfere with some of the characters of typical beauty belonging to the bodily frame, the stirring of the intellect wearing down the flesh, and the moral enthusiasm burning its way out to heaven, through the emaciation of the earthen vessel; and that there is, in this indication of subduing of the mortal by the immortal part, an ideal glory of perhaps a purer and higher range than that of the more perfect material form.

Now, be it observed that, in our statement of these three directions of mental influence, we have several times been compelled to stop short of definite conclusions, owing to the inconsistency, first, of different kinds of intellect with each other; secondly, of the moral faculties with the intellectual; and again, of the soul-culture generally with the bodily perfections. And this peculiarity of relation among the perfections of man   183
is no result of his fall or sinfulness, *but an evidence of his greater nobility*, and of the goodness of God towards him. For the individuals of each race of lower animals, being not intended to hold among each other those relations of charity which are the privilege of humanity, are not adapted to each other's assistance, admiration, or support, by differences of power and function. But the Love of the human race is increased by their individual differences, and the Unity of the creature, as before we saw of all unity, made perfect by each having something to bestow and to receive, bound to the rest by a thousand various necessities and various gratitudes; humility in each rejoicing to admire in his fellow that which he finds not in himself, and each being in some respect the complement of his race. Therefore, in investigating the signs of the ideal or perfect type   184
of humanity, we must not presume on the singleness of that type; and yet, on the other hand, we must cautiously distinguish between differences conceivably existing in a perfect state, and differences resulting from immediate and present operation of the Adamite curse. For although we can suppose the ideal or perfect human heart, and the perfect human intelligence, equally adapted to receive every right sensation, and pursue every order of truth, yet as it is appointed for some to be in authority and others in obedience, some in solitary functions and others in relative ones,

some to receive and others to give, some to teach and some to discover; so there are habits and capacities of expression induced by these various offices, which admit of many separate ideals of equal perfection. There is an ideal of Authority, of Judgment, of Affection, of Reason, and of Faith, neither can any combination of these ideals be attained; not that the just judge is to be supposed incapable of affection, nor the king incapable of obedience, but as it is impossible that any essence short of the Divine should at the same instant be equally receptive of all emotions, those

185   emotions which, by right and order, have the most usual victory, both leave the stamp of their habitual presence on the body, and render the individual more and more susceptible of them in proportion to the frequency of their prevalent recurrence. Still less can the differences of age and sex, though seemingly of more finite influence, be banished from any human conception.

186   Hence, then, it will follow, that we must not determinedly banish from the human form and countenance, in our restoration of its ideal, everything which can be ultimately traced to the Adamite Fall for its cause, but only the immediate operation and presence of the degrading power of sin. For there is not any part of our nature, nor can there be through eternity, uninfluenced or unaffected by the fall, and that not in any way of degradation, for the renewing in the divinity of Christ is a nobler condition than that of Paradise. So that we have not to banish from the ideal countenance the evidences of sorrow, nor of past suffering, nor even of past and conquered sin, but only the immediate operation of any evil, or the immediate coldness and hollowness of any good emotion. And hence in that contest before noted, between the body and the soul, we may often have to indicate the body as far conquered and outworn, and with signs of hard struggle and bitter pain upon it; and yet without ever diminishing the purity of its ideal: and since it is not in the power of any human imagination to reason out or conceive the countless modifications of experience, suffering, and separated feeling, which have modelled and written their indelible images, in various order, upon every human countenance, so no right ideal can be reached by any combination of feature nor by any moulding and melting of individual beauties together,

187   and still less without model or example at all; but *there is a perfect ideal to be wrought out of every face around us* that has on its forehead the writing and the seal of the angel ascending from the East, [29] by the earnest study and penetration of the written history thereupon, and the banishing of the blots and stains, wherein we still see, in all that is human, the visible and instant operation of unconquered Sin.

Now I see not how any of the steps of the argument by which we have arrived at this conclusion can be evaded, and yet it would be difficult to state anything more directly opposite to the general teaching and practice of artists. It is usual to hear portraiture opposed to the pursuit of ideality, and yet we find that no face can be ideal which is not a portrait. Of this general principle, however, there are certain modifications which we must presently state; but let us first pursue it a little farther and deduce its practical consequences.

These are, first, that the pursuit of idealism in humanity, as of idealism in lower nature, can be successful only when followed through the most constant, patient, and humble rendering of actual models, accompanied with that earnest mental study of each, which can interpret all that is written upon it, disentangle the hieroglyphics of its sacred history, rend the veil of the bodily temple, and rightly measure the relations of good and evil contending within it for mastery; that everything done without such study must be shallow and contemptible; that generalization or combination of individual character will end less in the mending than the losing of it, and, except in certain instances of which we shall presently take note, is valueless and vapid, even if it escape being painful from its want of truth. And that habit of the old and great painters of introducing   188 portrait into all their highest works, I look to, not as error in them, but as the very source and root of their superiority in all things; for they were too great and too humble not to see in every face about them that which was above them, and which no fancies of theirs could match nor take place of.

And therefore there is not any greater sign of want of vitality and   190 hopefulness in the schools of the present day, than that unhappy prettiness and sameness under which they mask, or rather for which they barter, in their lentil[30] thirst, all the birthright and power of nature; which prettiness, wrought out and spun fine in the study, till it hardly betters the blocks on which dresses and hair are tried in barbers' windows and milliners' books, cannot but be revolting to any man who has his eyes, even in a measure, open to the divinity of the immortal seal on the common features that he meets in the highways and hedges hourly and momentarily, outreaching all efforts of conception as all power of realization, were it Raffaelle's three times over, even when the glory of the wedding garment is not there.

If then individual humanity be taken as the basis of our conception, its right ideal is to be reached, we have asserted, only by the banishment of the immediate signs of sin upon the countenance and body. How, therefore, are the signs of sin to be known and separated?

No intellectual operation is here of any avail. There is not any reasoning by which the evidences of depravity are to be traced in movements of muscle or forms of feature; there is not any knowledge, nor experience, nor diligence of comparison that can be of avail. Here, as   191 throughout the operation of the Theoretic faculty, the perception is altogether moral, and instinctive love and clinging to the lines of light.

Nothing but love can read the letters, nothing but sympathy catch the sound; there is no pure passion that can be understood or painted except by pureness of heart; the foul or blunt feeling will see itself in everything, and set down blasphemies; it will see Baalzebub in the casting out of devils; it will find its God of flies in every alabaster box of precious ointment. The indignation of zeal toward God it will take for anger against man; faith and veneration it will miss, as not comprehending; charity it will turn into lust; compassion into pride; every virtue it will go over against, like Shimei, casting dust.[31] But the right Christian mind will, in like manner, find its own image wherever it exists; it will seek for what it loves, and draw it out of all dens and caves, and it will believe in its being, often when it cannot see it, and always turn away its eyes from beholding vanity; and so it will lie lovingly over all the faults and rough places of the human heart, as the snow from heaven does over the hard, and black, and broken mountain rocks, following their forms truly, and yet catching light for them to make them fair, and that must be a steep and unkindly crag indeed which it cannot cover.

CHAPTER XV
General Conclusions
Respecting the Theoretic Faculty

OF the sources of beauty open to us in the visible world, we have now   208
obtained a view which, however scanty in its detail, is yet general in
its range.

We have seen that this subject matter is referable to four general heads.   210
It is either the record of conscience, written in things external, or it is a
symbolizing of Divine attributes in matter, or it is the felicity of living
things, or the perfect fulfilment of their duties and functions. In all cases
it is something Divine; either the approving voice of God, the glorious
symbol of Him, the evidence of His kind presence, or the obedience to His
will by Him induced and supported.

All these subjects of contemplation are such as we may suppose will
remain sources of pleasure to the perfected spirit throughout eternity.
Divine in their nature, they are addressed to the immortal part of men.

There remain, however, two points to be noticed before I can hope that
this conclusion will be frankly accepted by the reader. If it be the moral
part of us to which Beauty addresses itself, how does it happen, it will be
asked, that it is ever found in the works of impious men, and how is it
possible for such to desire or conceive it?

On the other hand, how does it happen that men in high state of moral
culture are often insensible to the influence of material beauty: and insist
feebly upon it as an instrument of soul culture?

These two objections I shall endeavour briefly to answer; not that they
can be satisfactorily treated without that examination of the connection
between all kinds of greatness in art, on which I purpose to enter in the
following volume. For the right determination of these two questions is   211
indeed the whole end and aim of my labour (and if it could be here
accomplished, I should bestow no effort farther), namely, the proving that
no supreme power of art can be attained by impious men; and that the
neglect of art, as an interpreter of divine things, has been of evil
consequence to the Christian world. [32]

At present, however, I would only meet such objections as must
immediately arise in the reader's mind.

238

And first, it will be remembered that I have, throughout the examination of Typical beauty, asserted our instinctive sense of it; the moral *meaning* of it being only discoverable by reflection. Now this instinctive sense of it varies in intensity among men, being given, like the hearing ear of music, to some more than to others: and if those to whom it is given in large measure be unfortunately men of impious or unreflecting spirit, it is very possible that the perceptions of beauty should be by them cultivated on principles merely *æsthetic*, and so lose their hallowing power; for though the good seed in them is altogether divine, yet, there being no blessing in the spring thereof, it brings forth wild grapes in the end. And yet these wild grapes are well discernible, like the deadly gourds of Gilgal.[33] There is in all works of such men a taint and stain, and jarring discord, darker and louder exactly in proportion to the moral deficiency; of which the best proof and measure are to be found in their treatment of the human form (since in landscape it is nearly

212 impossible to introduce definite expression of evil), of which the highest beauty has been attained only once, and then by no system-taught painter, but by a most holy Dominican monk of Fiesole:[34] and beneath him all fall lower and lower in proportion to their inferior sanctity (though with more or less attainment of that which is noble, according to their intellectual power and earnestness), as Raffaelle in his St. Cecilia[35] (a mere study of a passionate, dark-eyed, large-formed Italian model); and even Perugino, in that there is about his noblest faces a short-coming, indefinable; an absence of the full outpouring of the sacred spirit that there is in Angelico; and so all other even of the sacred painters, not to speak of the lower body of men in whom, on the one hand, there is marked sensuality and impurity in all that they seek of beauty, as in Correggio and Guido;[36] or, on the other, a partial want of the sense of beauty itself, as in Rubens and Titian, exhibited in the adoption of coarse types of feature and form; sometimes,

213 also (of which I could find instances in modern times), by a want of evidence of delight in what they do; so that, after they have rendered some passage of exceeding beauty, they will suffer some discordant point to interfere with it, and it will not hurt them; and sometimes by total want of choice, for there is a choice of love in all rightly tempered men; not that ignorant and insolent choice which rejects half nature as empty of the right, but that pure choice that fetches the right out of everything; and where this is wanting, we may see men walking up and down in dry places, finding no rest; ever and anon doing something noble and yet not following it up, but dwelling the next instant on something impure or profitless with the same intensity and yet impatience, so that they are ever wondered at and never sympathized with, and while they dazzle all they lead none; and then, beneath these again, we find others on whose works there are definite signs of evil desire ill repressed, and then inability to

avoid, and at last perpetual seeking for, and feeding upon, horror and ugliness, and filthiness of sin; as eminently in Salvator and Caravaggio, and the lower Dutch schools, only in these last less painfully as they lose the villainous in the brutal, and the horror of crime in its idiocy.

But secondly, it is to be noted that it is neither by us ascertainable what moments of pure feeling or aspiration may occur to men of minds apparently cold and lost, nor by us to be pronounced through what instruments, and in what strangely occurrent voices, God may choose to communicate good to men. It seems to me that much of what is great, and to all men beneficial, has been wrought by those who neither intended 214 nor knew the good they did; and that many mighty harmonies have been discoursed by instruments that had been dumb or discordant, but that God knew their stops. It is not our part to look hardly, nor to look always, to the character or the deeds of men, but to acccept from all of them, and to hold fast, that which we can prove good, and feel to be ordained for us. We know that whatever good there is in them is itself divine; and wherever we see the virtue of ardent labour and self-surrendering to a single purpose, wherever we find constant reference made to the written scripture of natural beauty, this at least we know is great and good; this we know is not granted by the counsel of God without purpose, nor maintained without result: their interpretation we may accept, into their labour we may enter, but they themselves must look to it, if what they do has no intent of good, nor any reference to the Giver of all gifts. Selfish in their industry, unchastened in their wills, ungrateful for the Spirit that is upon them, they may yet be helmed by that Spirit whithersoever the Governor listeth; involuntary instruments they may become of others' good; unwillingly they may bless Israel, doubtingly discomfit Amalek;[37] but short-coming there will be of their glory, and sure, of their punishment.

It has been said by Schiller, in his letters on æsthetic culture, that the 215 sense of beauty never farthered the performance of a single duty.[38]

Although this gross and inconceivable falsity will hardly be accepted by any one in so many words, seeing that there are few who do not receive, and know that they receive, at certain moments strength of some kind, or rebuke, from the appealings of outward things; and that it is not possible for a Christian man to walk across so much as a rood of the natural earth, with mind unagitated and rightly poised, without receiving strength and hope from some stone, flower, leaf, or sound, nor without a sense of a dew falling upon him out of the sky; though, I say, this falsity is not wholly and 216 in terms admitted, yet it seems to be partly and practically so in much of the doing and teaching even of holy men, who in the recommending of the love of God to us, refer but seldom to those things in which it is most abundantly and immediately shown: though they insist much on His giving of bread, and raiment, and health (which He gives to all inferior creatures), they require us not to thank Him for that glory of His works which He has permitted us alone to perceive: they tell us often to meditate in the closet, but they send us not, like Isaac, into the fields at even;[39] they dwell on the duty of self-denial, but they exhibit not the duty of delight. Now there are reasons for this, manifold, in the toil and warfare of an earnest mind, which, in its efforts at the raising of men from utter loss and misery, has often but little time or disposition to take heed of anything more than the mere life, and of those so occupied it is not for us to judge; but I think that of the weaknesses, distresses, vanities, schisms, and sins, which often, even in the holiest men, diminish their usefulness, and mar their happiness, there would be fewer if, in their struggle with nature fallen, they sought for more aid from nature undestroyed. It seems to me that the real sources of bluntness in the feelings towards the splendour of the grass and glory of the flower,[40] are less to be found in ardour of occupation, in seriousness of compassion, or heavenliness of desire, than in the turning of the eye at intervals of rest too selfishly within; the want of power to shake off the anxieties of actual and near interest, and to leave results in God's hands; the scorn of all that does not seem immediately apt for our purposes, or open to our understanding, and

217 perhaps something of pride, which desires rather to investigate than to feel. At all events, whatever may be the inability, in this present life, to mingle the full enjoyment of the Divine works with the full discharge of every practical duty, and confessedly in many cases this must be, let us not attribute the inconsistency to any indignity of the faculty of contemplation, but to the sin and the suffering of the fallen state, and the change of order from the keeping of the garden to the tilling of the ground. We cannot say how far it is right or agreeable with God's will, while men

218 are perishing round about us; while grief and pain, and wrath, and impiety, and death, and all the powers of the air, are working wildly and evermore, and the cry of blood going up to heaven, that any of us should take hand from the plough; but this we know, that there will come a time when the service of God shall be the beholding of Him; and though in these stormy seas where we are now driven up and down, His Spirit is dimly seen on the face of the waters, and we are left to cast anchors out of the stern, and wish for the day, that day will come, when, with the evangelists on the crystal and stable sea, all the creatures of God shall be full of eyes within, and there shall be "no more curse, but His servants shall serve Him, and shall see His face."[41]

SECTION II
Of the Imaginative Faculty

CHAPTER I
Of the Three Forms of Imagination

WE have hitherto been exclusively occupied with those sources of pleasure which exist in the external creation, and which in any faithful copy of it must to a certain extent exist also.

These sources of beauty, however, are not presented by any very great work of art in a form of pure transcript. They invariably receive the reflection of the mind under whose influence they have passed, and are modified or coloured by its image.

This modification is the Work of Imagination.

It is neither desirable nor possible here to examine or illustrate in full the essence of this mighty faculty. Our present task is not to explain or exhibit full portraiture of this function of the mind in all its relations, but only to obtain some certain tests by which we may determine whether it be very Imagination or not, and unmask all impersonations of it; and this chiefly with respect to art.

Dugald Stewart's meagre definition may serve us for a starting point.[42] "Imagination," he says, "includes conception or simple apprehension, which enables us to form a notion of those former objects of perception or of knowledge, out of which we are to make a selection; abstraction, which separates the selected materials from the qualities and circumstances which are connected with them in nature; and judgment or taste, which selects the materials and directs their combination. To these powers we may add that particular habit of association to which I formerly gave the name of Fancy; as it is this which presents to our choice all the different materials which are subservient to the efforts of imagination, and which may therefore be considered as forming the ground-work of poetical genius."

(By Fancy in this passage, we find on referring to the chapter treating of it, that nothing more is meant than the rapid occurrence of ideas of sense to the mind.)

Now, in this definition, the very point and purpose of all the inquiry is missed. We are told that judgment or taste "directs the combination." In order that anything may be directed, an end must be previously determined; what is the faculty that determines this end? and of what frame and make, how boned and fleshed, how conceived or seen, is the end itself? Bare judgment or taste, cannot approve of what has no existence; and yet by Dugald Stewart's definition we are left to their catering among a host of conceptions, to produce a combination which, as they work for, they must see and approve before it exists. This power of prophecy is the very essence of the whole matter, and it is just that inexplicable part which the metaphysician misses.

226   Hence if we take any passage in which there is real imagination, we shall find Stewart's hypothesis not only inefficient and obscure, but utterly inapplicable.

Take one or two at random [from Milton].

> "On the other side,
> Incensed with indignation, Satan stood
> Unterrified, and like a comet burned,
> That fires the length of Ophiuchus huge
> In the arctic sky, and from his horrid hair
> Shakes pestilence and war."

227   (Note that the word incensed is to be taken in its literal and material sense, set on fire.) What taste or judgment was it that directed this combination? or is there nothing more than taste or judgment here?

> "Ten paces huge
> He back recoiled; the tenth on bended knee
> His massy spear upstaid; as if on earth
> Winds under ground, or waters forcing way,
> *Sidelong had pushed a mountain from his seat,*
> *Half-sunk with all his pines.*"

> "Together both, ere the high lawns appeared
> *Under the opening eyelids* of the morn,
> We drove afield, and both together heard
> What time the gray-fly winds her *sultry* horn."

> "Missing thee, I walk unseen
> On the dry smooth-shaven green,
> To behold the wandering moon,
> Riding near her highest noon,
> *Like one that had been led astray*
> Through the heaven's wide pathless way;
> And oft, *as if her head she bowed,*
> Stooping through a fleecy cloud."[43]

It is evident that Stewart's explanation utterly fails in all these instances; for there is in them no "combination" whatsoever, but a particular mode of regarding the qualities or appearances of a single thing, illustrated and conveyed to us by the image of another; and the act of imagination, observe, is not the selection of this image, but the mode of regarding the object.

But the metaphysician's definition fails yet more utterly, when we look at the imagination neither as regarding, nor combining, but as penetrating.

> "My gracious silence, hail!
> Wouldst thou have laugh'd, had I come coffin'd home,
> That weep'st to see me triumph? Ah, my dear,
> Such eyes the widows in Corioli wear,
> And mothers that lack sons."[44]

How did Shakespeare *know* that Virgilia could not speak?   228

This knowledge, this intuitive and penetrative perception, is still one of the forms, the highest, of imagination, but there is no combination of images here.

We find, then, that the Imagination has three totally distinct functions. It combines, and by combination creates new forms; but the secret principle of this combination has not been shown by the analysts. Again, it treats, or regards, both the simple images and its own combinations in peculiar ways; and, thirdly, it penetrates, analyzes, and reaches truths by no other faculty discoverable.

CHAPTER II

Of Imagination Associative

229   AFTER beholding and examining any material object, our knowledge respecting it exists in two different forms. Some facts exist in the brain in a verbal form, as known, but not conceived; as, for instance, that it was heavy or light, that it was eight inches and a quarter long, etc., of which length we cannot have accurate conception, but only such a conception as might attach to a length of seven inches or nine; and which fact we may recollect without any conception of the object at all. Other facts respecting it exist in the brain in a visible form, not always visible , but visible at will, as its being of such a colour, or having such and such a complicated shape: as the form of a rose-bud for instance, which it would be difficult to express verbally, neither is it retained by the brain in a verbal form, but a visible one: that is, when we wish for knowledge of its form for immediate use, we summon up a vision or image of the thing; we do not remember it in words, as we remember the fact that it took so many days to blow, or that it was gathered at such and such a time.

The knowledge of things retained in this visible form is called Conception by the metaphysicians, which term I shall retain.

230   There are many questions respecting this faculty of very great interest; such as the exact amount of aid that verbal knowledge renders to visible knowledge (as, for instance, the verbal knowledge that a flower has five, or seven, or ten petals, or that a muscle is inserted at such and such a point of the bone, aids the conception of the flower or the limb); and again, what amount of aid the visible knowledge renders to the verbal; as, for instance, whether any one, being asked a question about some animal or thing which instantly and from verbal knowledge he cannot answer, may have such power of summoning up the image of the animal or thing as to ascertain the fact by actual beholding (which I do not assert, but can conceive to be possible); and again, what is that indefinite and subtle character of the conception itself in most men, which admits not of being by themselves traced or realized, and yet is a sure test of likeness in any representation of the thing; these and many other questions it is irrelevant at present to determine, since to forward our present purpose, it will be

well to suppose the conception aided by verbal knowledge to be absolutely perfect; and we will suppose a man to retain such clear image of a large number of the material things he has seen, as to be able to set down any of them on paper, with perfect fidelity and absolute memory of their most minute features.

In thus setting them down on paper, he works, I suppose, exactly as he   231 would work from nature, only copying the remembered image in his mind, instead of the real thing. He is, therefore, still nothing more than a copyist. There is no exercise of imagination in this whatsoever.

But over these images, vivid and distinct as nature herself, he has a command which over nature he has not. He can summon any that he chooses; and if, therefore, any group of them which he received from nature be not altogether to his mind, he is at liberty to remove some of the component images, and others foreign, and re-arrange the whole.

This is composition, and is what Dugald Stewart mistook for imagination, in the kingdom of which noble faculty it has no part nor lot.

The essential acts of Composition, properly so called, are the following. The mind which desires the new feature summons up before it those images which it supposes to be the kind wanted; of these it takes the one which it supposes to be fittest, and tries it; if it will not answer, it tries another, until it has obtained such an association as pleases it.

In this operation, if it be of little sensibility, it regards only the absolute beauty or value of the images brought before it; and takes that or those which it thinks fairest or most interesting, without any regard to their sympathy with those for whose company they are destined.

If the mind be of higher feeling, it will look to the sympathy or contrast   232 of the features, to their likeness or dissimilarity: it will take, as it thinks best, features resembling or discordant; and if, when it has put them together, it be not satisfied, it will repeat the process on the features themselves, cutting away one part and putting in another; so working more and more delicately down to the lowest details, until by dint of experiment, of repeated trials and shiftings, and constant reference to principles (as that two lines must not mimic one another, that one mass must not be equal to another), etc., it has mortised together a satisfactory result.

This process will be more and more rapid and effective, in proportion to the artist's powers of conception and association, these in their turn depending on his knowledge and experience. The distinctness of his powers of conception will give value, point, and truth to every fragment that he draws from memory. His powers of association, and his knowledge of nature, will pour out before him, in greater or less number and appositeness, the images from which to choose. His experience guides him to quick discernment in the combination, when made, of the parts that are offensive and require change.

The most elevated power of mind of all these is that of association, by which images apposite or resemblant, or of whatever kind wanted, are called up quickly and in multitudes. When this power is very brilliant, it is called Fancy.[45]

Great differences of power are manifested among artists in this respect; some having hosts of distinct images always at their command, and rapidly discerning resemblance or contrast; others having few images, and obscure, at their disposal, nor readily governing those they have.

233 Where the powers of fancy are very brilliant, the picture becomes highly interesting; if her images are systematically and rightly combined, and truthfully rendered, it will become even impressive and instructive; if wittily and curiously combined, it will be captivating and entertaining.

But all this time the imagination has not once shown itself. All this (except the gift of fancy) may be taught; all this is easily comprehended and analyzed; but imagination is neither to be taught, nor by any efforts to be attained, nor by any acuteness of discernment dissected or analyzed.

It has been said that in composition the mind can only take cognizance of likeness or dissimilarity, or of abstract beauty among the ideas it brings together. But neither likeness nor dissimilarity secures harmony. We saw in the Chapter on Unity that likeness destroyed harmony or unity of membership;[46] and that difference did not necessarily secure it, but only that particular *imperfection* in each of the harmonizing parts which can only be supplied by its fellow part. If, therefore, the combination made is to be harmonious, the artist must induce in each of its component parts (suppose two only, for simplicity's sake), such imperfection as that the other shall put it right. If one of them be perfect by itself, the other will be an excrescence. Both must be faulty when separate, and each corrected by the presence of the other. If he can accomplish this, the result will be beautiful; it will be a whole, an organized body with dependent members;—he is an inventor. If not, let his separate features be as

234 beautiful, as apposite, or as resemblant as they may, they form no whole. They are two members glued together. He is only a carpenter and joiner.

Now, the conceivable imperfections of any single feature are infinite. It is impossible, therefore, to fix upon a form of imperfection in the one, and try with this all the forms of imperfection of the other until one fits; but the two imperfections must be co-relatively and simultaneously conceived.

This is Imagination, properly so called; imagination associative, the grandest mechanical power that the human intelligence possesses, and one which will appear more and more marvellous the longer we consider it. By its operation, two ideas are chosen out of an infinite mass (for it evidently matters not whether the imperfections be conceived out of the infinite number conceivable, or selected out of a number recollected), two ideas which are *separately wrong*, which together shall be right, and of whose unity, therefore, the idea must be formed at the instant they are seized, as it is only in that unity that either is good, and therefore only the *conception of that unity can prompt the preference.*

This operation of mind, so far as I can see, is absolutely inexplicable, but there is something like it in chemistry.

"The action of sulphuric acid on metallic zinc affords an instance of what was once called Disposing Affinity. Zinc decomposes pure water at   235 common temperatures with extreme slowness; but as soon as sulphuric acid is added, decomposition of the water takes place rapidly, though the acid merely unites with oxide of zinc. The former explanation was, that the affinity of the acid for oxide of zinc disposed the metal to unite with oxygen, and thus enabled it to decompose water; that is, the oxide of zinc was supposed to produce an effect previous to its existence. The obscurity of this explanation arises from regarding changes as consecutive, which are in reality simultaneous. There is no succession in the process, the oxide of zinc is not formed previously to its combination with the acid, but at the same instant. There is, as it were, but one chemical change, which consists in the combination, at one and the same moment, of zinc with oxygen, and of oxide of zinc with the acid; and this change occurs because these two affinities, acting together, overcome the attraction of oxygen and hydrogen for one another."*

Now, if the imaginative artist will permit us, with all deference, to represent his combining intelligence under the figure of sulphuric acid; and if we suppose the fragment of zinc to be embarrassed among infinitely numerous fragments of diverse metals, and the oxygen dispersed and mingled among gases countless and indistinguishable; we shall have an excellent type, in material things, of the action of the imagination on the immaterial. Both actions are, I think, inexplicable; for, however simultaneous the chemical changes may be, yet the causing power is the affinity of the acid for what has no existence. It is neither to be explained how that affinity operates on atoms uncombined, nor how the artist's desire for an unconceived whole prompts him to the selection of necessary divisions.

This operation would be wonderful enough, if it were concerned with two ideas only. But a powerfully imaginative mind seizes and combines at   236 the same instant, not only two, but all the important ideas of its poem or picture; and while it works with any one of them, it is at the same instant working with and modifying all in their relations to it, never losing sight of their bearings on each other; as the motion of a snake's body goes

* *Elements of Chemistry*, by the late Edward Turner, M.D., part ii. sec. iv.

through all parts at once, and its volition acts at the same instant in coils that go contrary ways.

This faculty is indeed something that looks as if man were made after the image of God. It is inconceivable, admirable, altogether divine; and yet, wonderful as it may seem, it is palpably evident that no less an operation is necessary for the production of any great work: for, by the definition of Unity of Membership (the essential characteristic of greatness), not only certain couples or groups of parts, but *all* the parts of a noble work must be separately imperfect; each must imply, and ask for all the rest, and the glory of every one of them must consist in its relation to the rest; neither while so much as one is wanting can any be right. And it is evidently impossible to conceive, in each separate feature, a certain want or wrongness which can only be corrected by the other features of the picture (not by one or two merely, but by all), unless, together with the want, we conceive also of what is wanted, that is, of all the rest of the work or picture.

There is, however, a limit to the power of all human imagination. When the relations to be observed are *absolutely* necessary, and highly complicated, the mind cannot grasp them; and the result is a total deprivation of all power of imagination associative in such matter. For this reason, no human mind has ever conceived a new animal.

237

The matter, therefore, in which associative imagination can be shown is that which admits of great licence and variety of arrangement, and in which a certain amount of relation only is required; as especially in the elements of landscape painting, in which best it may be illustrated.

When an unimaginative painter is about to draw a tree, (and we will suppose him, for better illustration of the point in question, to have good feeling and correct knowledge of the nature of trees,) he probably lays on his paper such a general form as he knows to be characteristic of the tree to be drawn, and such as he believes will fall in agreeably with the other masses of his picture, which we will suppose partly prepared. When this form is set down, he assuredly finds it has done something he did not intend it to do. It has mimicked some prominent line, or overpowered some necessary mass. He begins pruning and changing, and, after several experiments, succeeds in obtaining a form which does no material mischief to any other. To this form he proceeds to attach a trunk, and, working probably on a received notion or rule (for the unimaginative painter never works without a principle) that tree trunks ought to lean first one way and then the other as they go up, and ought not to stand under the middle of the tree, he sketches a serpentine form of requisite propriety; when it has gone up far enough, that is, till it looks disagreeably long, he will begin to ramify it; and if there be another tree in the picture with two large branches, he knows that this, by all laws of composition,

238

ought to have three or four, or some different number; and because he knows that if three or four branches start from the same point they will look formal, therefore he makes them start from points one above another; and because equal distances are improper, therefore they shall start at unequal distances. When they are fairly started, he knows they must undulate or go backwards and forwards, which accordingly he makes them do at random; and because he knows that all forms ought to be contrasted, he makes one bend down while the other three go up. The three that go up he knows must not go up without interfering with each other, and so he makes two of them cross. He thinks it also proper that there should be variety of character in them; so he makes the one that bends down graceful and flexible, and, of the two that cross, he splinters one and makes a stump of it. He repeats the process among the more complicated minor boughs, until coming to the smallest, he thinks farther care unnecessary, but draws them freely, and by chance. Having to put on the foliage, he will make it flow properly in the direction of the tree's growth; he will make all the extremities graceful; but will be tormented by finding them come all alike, and at last will be obliged to spoil a number of them altogether, in order to obtain opposition. They will not, however, be united in this their spoliation, but will remain uncomfortably separate and individually ill-tempered. He consoles himself by the reflection that it is unnatural for all of them to be equally perfect.

Now, I suppose that through the whole of this process, he has been able 239 to refer to his definite memory or conception of nature for every one of the fragments he has successively added; that the details, colour, fractures, insertions, etc., of his boughs, are all either actual recollections or based on secure knowledge of the tree (and herein I allow far more than is commonly the case with unimaginative painters). But, as far as the process of combination is concerned, it is evident that, from beginning to end, his laws have been his safety, and his plague has been his liberty. He has been compelled to work at random or under the guidance of feeling only, whenever there was anything left to his own decision. He has never been decided in anything except in what he *must* or *must not* do. He has walked as a drunken man on a broad road; his guides are the hedges; and, between these limits, the broader the way, the more difficult his progress.

The advance of the imaginative artist is precisely the reverse of this. He owns no laws. He defies all restraint, and cuts down all hedges. There is nothing within the limits of natural possibility that he dares not do, or that he allows the necessity of doing. The laws of nature he knows; these are to him no restraint. They are his own nature. All other laws or limits he sets at utter defiance; his journey is over an untrodden and pathless plain. But he sees his end over the waste from the first, and goes straight at it; never losing sight of it, nor throwing away a step. Nothing can stop him, nothing turn him aside; falcons and lynxes are of slow and uncertain sight compared with his. He saw his tree, trunk, boughs, foliage and all, from the first moment; not only the tree, but the sky behind it; not only that tree or sky, but all the other great features of his picture: by what intense power of instantaneous selection and amalgamation cannot be explained, but by this it may be proved and tested; that, if we examine the tree of the unimaginative painter, we shall find that on removing any part or parts of it, though the rest will indeed suffer, as being deprived of the proper development of a tree, and as involving a blank space that wants occupation, yet the portions left are not made discordant or disagreeable. They are absolutely and in themselves as valuable as they can be; every stem is a perfect stem, and every twig a graceful twig, or at least as perfect and as graceful as they were before the removal of the rest. But if we try the same experiment on the imaginative painter's work, and break off the merest stem or twig of it, it all goes to pieces like a Prince Rupert's drop.[47] There is not so much as a seed of it but it lies on the tree's life, like the grain upon the tongue of Chaucer's sainted child.[48] Take it away, and the boughs will sing to us no longer. All is dead and cold.

This, then, is the first sign of the presence of real imagination as opposed to composition. But here is another not less important.

We have seen that as each part is selected and fitted by the unimaginative painter, he renders it, in itself, as beautiful as he is able. If it be ugly it remains so; he is incapable of correcting it by the *addition of another ugliness*, and therefore he chooses all his features as fair as they may be (at least if his object be beauty). But a small proportion only of the ideas he has at his disposal will reach his standard of absolute beauty. The others will be of no use to him: and among those which he permits himself to use, there will be so marked a family likeness that he will be more and more cramped, as his picture advances, for want of material, and tormented by multiplying resemblances, unless disguised by some artifice of light and shade or other forced difference; and with all the differences he can imagine, his tree will yet show a sameness and sickening repetition in all its parts, and all his trees will be like one another, except so far as one leans east and another west, one is broadest at the top and another at the bottom: while through all this insipid repetition, the means by which he forces contrast, dark boughs opposed to light, rugged to smooth, etc., will be painfully evident, to the utter destruction of all dignity and repose. The imaginative work is necessarily the absolute opposite of all this. As all its parts are imperfect, and as there is an unlimited supply of imperfection (for the ways in which things may be wrong are infinite), the imagination is never at a loss, nor ever likely to repeat itself; nothing comes amiss to it; but whatever rude matter it receives, it instantly so arranges that it comes right; all things fall into their place, and appear in that place perfect, useful, and evidently not to be spared; so that of its combinations there is endless variety, and every intractable and seemingly unavailable fragment that we give to it, is instantly turned to some brilliant use, and made the nucleus of a new group of glory; however poor or common the gift, it will be thankful for it, treasure it up, and pay in gold; and it has that life in it, and fire, that wherever it passes, among the dead bones and dust of things, behold! a shaking, and the bones come together bone to his bone.

And now we find what noble sympathy and unity there are between the Imaginative and Theoretic faculties. Both agree in this, that they reject nothing, and are thankful for all; but the Theoretic faculty takes out of everything that which is beautiful, while the Imaginative faculty takes hold of the very imperfections which the Theoretic rejects; and, by means of these angles and roughnesses, it joints and bolts the separate stones into a mighty temple, wherein the Theoretic faculty, in its turn, does deepest homage. Thus sympathetic in their desires, harmoniously diverse in their   242
operation, each working for the other with what the other needs not, all things external to man are by one or other turned to good.

Now we have hitherto, for the sake of clearness, opposed the total absence of imagination to the perfect presence of it, in order to make the difference between composition and imagination thoroughly understood. But if we are to give examples of either the want or the presence of the Power, it is necessary to note the circumstances by which both are modified. In the first place, few artists of any standing are totally devoid of this faculty: some small measure of it most of them possess, though of all the forms of intellect, this, and its sister, penetrative imagination, are the rarest and most precious; but few painters have reached eminence without some leaven of it; whether it can be increased by practice I doubt. On the other hand, fewer still are possessed of it in very high degree; and even with the men of most gigantic power in this respect, of whom, I think, Tintoret stands far the head, there are evident limits to its exercise, and portions to be found in their works that have not been included in the original grasp of them, but have been suggested and incorporated during their progress, or added in decoration; and, with the great mass of painters, there are frequent flaws and failures in the conception, so that when they intend to produce a perfect work, they throw their thought into different experimental forms, and decorate it and discipline it long before realizing it, so that there is a certain amount of mere composition in the most imaginative works; and a grain or two of imagination commonly in the most artificial. And again, whatever portions of a picture are taken honestly and without alteration from nature, have, so far as they go, the look of imagination, because all that nature does is imaginative, that is, perfect as a whole, and made up of imperfect features; so that the painter of the meanest imaginative power may yet do grand   243 things, if he will keep to strict portraiture; and it would be well if all artists were to endeavour to do so, for if they have imagination, it will force its way in spite of them, and show itself in their every stroke; and if not, they will not get it by leaving nature, but only sink into nothingness.

245   For immediate and close illustration, it is perhaps best to refer to the Cephalus and Procris of Turner in the Liber Studiorum [fig.30] I know of no landscape more purely or magnificently imaginative, or bearing more distinct evidence of the relative and simultaneous conception of the parts. Let the reader first cover with his hand the two trunks that rise against the sky on the right, and ask himself how any termination of the central mass so *ugly* as the straight trunk which he will then painfully see, could have been conceived or admitted without *simultaneous conception* of the trunks he has taken away on the right? Let him again conceal the whole central mass, and leave these two only, and again ask himself whether anything so ugly as that bare trunk in the shape of a Y, could have been admitted without reference to the central mass? Then let him remove from this trunk its two arms, and try the effect; let him again remove the single trunk on the extreme right; then let him try the third trunk without the excrescence at the bottom of it; finally, let him con- ceal the fourth trunk from the right, with the slender boughs at the top: he will find, in each case, that he has destroyed a feature on which everything else depends; and if proof be required of the vital power of still smaller features, let him remove the sunbeam that comes through

fig.30   J.M.W. Turner, *Procris and Cephalus*, from *Liber Studiorum*

beneath the faint mass of trees on the hill in the distance.

It is useless to enter into farther particulars; the reader may be left to his own close examination of this and of the other works of Turner, in which   246 he will always find the associative imagination developed in the most profuse and marvellous modes; especially in the drawing of foliage and skies, in both of which the presence or absence of the associative power may best be tested in all artists.

I have just said that nature is always imaginative, but it does not follow that her imagination is always of high subject, or that the imagination of all the parts is of a like and sympathetic kind; the boughs of every bramble bush are imaginatively arranged, so are those of every oak and cedar; but it does not follow that there is imaginative sympathy between bramble and cedar. There are few natural scenes whose harmonies are not conceivably improvable either by banishment of some discordant point, or by addition of some sympathetic one; it constantly happens that there is a profuseness too great to be comprehended, or an inequality in the pitch, meaning, and intensity of different parts. The imagination will banish all that is extraneous; it will seize out of the many threads of different feeling which nature has suffered to become entangled, one only; and where that seems thin and likely to break, it will spin it stouter, and in doing this, it never knots, but weaves in the new thread; so that all its work looks as pure and true as nature itself, and cannot be guessed from it but by its exceeding simplicity, (*known* from it, it cannot be); so that herein we find another test of the imaginative work, that it looks always   247 as if it had been gathered straight from nature, whereas the unimaginative shows its joints and knots, and is visibly composition.

And here, then, we arrive at an important conclusion (though one somewhat contrary to the positions commonly held on the subject), namely, that if anything looks unnatural, there can be no imagination in it (at least not associative). We frequently hear works that have no truth in them justified or elevated on the score of being imaginative. Let it be understood once for all, that imagination never deigns to touch anything but truth; and though it does not follow that where there is the appearance of truth, there has been imaginative operation, of this we may be assured, that where there is appearance of falsehood, the imagination has had no hand.

The final tests, therefore, of the work of associative imagination are, its   248 intense simplicity, its perfect harmony, and its absolute truth. It may be a harmony, majestic or humble, abrupt or prolonged, but it is always a governed and perfect whole; evidencing in all its relations the weight, prevalence, and universal dominion of an awful inexplicable Power; a chastising, animating, and disposing Mind.

CHAPTER III
Of Imagination Penetrative

249 WE must now examine the dealing of the Imagination with its separate conceptions, and endeavour to understand, not only its principles of selection, but its modes of apprehension with respect to what it selects.

When Milton's Satan first "rears from off the pool his mighty stature," the image of leviathan before suggested not being yet abandoned, the effect on the fire-wave is described as of the upheaved monster on the ocean-stream.

> "On each hand the flames
> Driven backward, slope their pointed spires, and, rolled
> In billows, leave i' the midst a horrid vale."[49]

And then follows a fiercely restless piece of volcanic imagery:

> "As when the force
> Of subterranean wind transports a hill
> Torn from Pelorus, or the shattered side
> Of thundering Ætna, whose combustible
> And fuelled entrails, thence conceiving fire,
> Sublimed with mineral fury, aid the winds,
> And leave a singèd bottom all involved
> With stench and smoke: such resting found the sole
> Of unblest feet."

250 Yet I think all this is too far detailed, and deals too much with externals: we feel rather the form of the fire-waves than their fury; we walk upon them too securely; and the fuel, sublimation, smoke, and singeing seem to me images only of partial combustion; they vary and extend the conception, but they lower the thermometer. Look back, if you will, and add to the description the glimmering of the livid flames; the sulphurous hail and red lightning; yet all together, however they overwhelm us with horror, fail of making us thoroughly, unendurably *hot*. The essence of intense flame has not been given. Now hear Dante:

> "Feriami 'l Sole in su l' omero destro,
> Che già raggiando tutto l' Occidente
> *Mutava in bianco aspetto di cilestro.*
> Ed io facea *con l'ombra più rovente*
> *Parer la fiamma.*"[50]

That is a slight touch; he has not gone to Ætna or Pelorus for fuel; but we shall not soon recover from it, he has taken our breath away, and leaves us gasping. No smoke nor cinders there. Pure white, hurtling, formless flame; very fire-crystal, we cannot make spires nor waves of it, nor divide it, nor walk on it; there is no question about singeing soles of feet. It is lambent annihilation.

Such is always the mode in which the highest imaginative faculty seizes its materials. It never stops at crusts or ashes, or outward images of any kind; it ploughs them all aside, and plunges into the very central fiery heart; nothing else will content its spirituality; whatever semblances and various outward shows and phases its subject may possess go for nothing; it gets within all fence, cuts down to the root, and drinks the very vital sap 251 of that it deals with: once therein, it is at liberty to throw up what new shoots it will, so always that the true juice and sap be in them, and to prune and twist them at its pleasure, and bring them to fairer fruit than grew on the old tree; but all this pruning and twisting is work that it likes not, and often does ill; its function and gift are the getting at the root, its nature and dignity depend on its holding things always by the heart. Take its hand from off the beating of that, and it will prophesy no longer; it looks not in the eyes, it judges not by the voice, it describes not by outward features; all that it affirms, judges, or describes, it affirms, from within.

It may seem to the reader that I am incorrect in calling this penetrating possession-taking faculty Imagination. Be it so; the name is of little consequence; the faculty itself, called by what name we will, I insist upon as the highest intellectual power of man. There is no reasoning in it; it works not by algebra, nor by integral calculus; it is a piercing pholas-like[51] mind's tongue, that works and tastes into the very rock heart; no matter what be the subject submitted to it, substance or spirit; all is alike divided asunder, joint and marrow, whatever utmost truth, life, principle it has, laid bare, and that which has no truth, life, nor principle, dissipated into its original smoke at a touch. The whispers at men's ears it lifts into visible angels. Vials that have lain sealed in the deep sea a thousand years it unseals, and brings out of them Genii.

Every great conception of poet or painter is held and treated by this faculty. Every character that is so much as touched by men like Æschylus, 252 Homer, Dante, or Shakspeare, is by them held by the heart; and every circumstance or sentence of their being, speaking, or seeming, is seized by process from within, and is referred to that inner secret spring of which the hold is never lost for an instant; so that every sentence, as it has been thought out from the heart, opens for us a way down to the heart, leads us to the centre, and then leaves us to gather what more we may.

Hence there is in every word set down by the imaginative mind an awful under-current of meaning, and evidence and shadow upon it of the deep places out of which it has come. It is often obscure, often half-told; for he who wrote it, in his clear seeing of the things beneath, may have been impatient of detailed interpretation: but, if we choose to dwell upon it and trace it, it will lead us always securely back to that metropolis of the soul's dominion from which we may follow out all the ways and tracks to its farthest coasts.

The unimaginative writer, on the other hand, as he has never pierced to the heart, so he can never touch it. If he has to paint a passion, he remembers the external signs of it, he collects expressions of it from other writers, he searches for similes, he composes, exaggerates, heaps term on term, figure on figure, till we groan beneath the cold disjointed heap: but 253   it is all faggot and no fire; the life breath is not in it; his passion has the form of the leviathan, but it never makes the deep boil; he fastens us all at anchor in the scaly rind of it; our sympathies remain as idle as a painted ship upon a painted ocean.[52]

And that virtue of originality that men so strain after is not *newness*, as they vainly think (there is nothing new), it is only *genuineness*; it all depends on this single glorious faculty of getting to the spring of things and working out from that; it is the coolness, and clearness, and deliciousness of the water fresh from the fountain head, opposed to the thick, hot, unrefreshing drainage from other men's meadows.[53]

260   Now it is necessary very carefully to distinguish between that character of the work which depends on the imagination of the beholder, and that which results from the imagination of the artist; for a work is often called imaginative when it merely leaves room for the action of the imagination; whereas though nearly all imaginative works do this, yet it may be done also by works that have in them no imagination at all. A few shapeless scratches or accidental stains on a wall, or the forms of clouds, or any other complicated accidents, will set the imagination to work to coin something out of them; and all paintings in which there is much gloom or mystery, possess therein a certain sublimity owing to the play given to the beholder's imagination, without, necessarily, being in the slightest degree imaginative themselves. The vacancy of a truly imaginative work results not from absence of ideas, or incapability of grasping and detailing them, but from the painter having told the whole pith and power of his subject and disdaining to tell more; and the sign of this being the case is, that the mind of the beholder is forced to act in a certain mode, and feels itself

fig.31   J.M.W. Turner, *Jason*, from *Liber Studiorum*

overpowered and borne away by that of the painter, and not able to defend
itself, nor go which way it will: and the value of the work depends on the
truth, authority, and inevitability of this suggestiveness. Now observe in
this work [fig.31] of Turner that the whole value of it depends on the   261
character of curve assumed by the serpent's body; for had it been a mere
semicircle, or gone down in a series of smaller coils, it would have been in
the first case, ridiculous, as unlike a serpent, or in the second, disgusting,
nothing more than an exaggerated viper; but it is that *coming straight* at the
right hand which suggests the drawing forth of an enormous weight, and
gives the bent part its springing look, that frightens us. Again, remove the
light trunk on the left, and observe how useless all the gloom of the picture
would have been, if this trunk had not given it depth and *hollowness*.
Finally and chiefly, observe that the painter is not satisfied even with all
the suggestiveness thus obtained, but to make sure of us, and force us,
whether we will or not, to walk his way, and not ours, the trunks of the
trees on the right are all cloven into yawning and writhing heads and
bodies, and alive with dragon energy all about us; note especially the
nearest with its gaping jaws and claw-like branch at the seeming shoulder;
a kind of suggestion which in itself is not imaginative, but merely fanciful
(using the term fancy in that third sense not yet explained, corresponding
to the third office of imagination); but it is imaginative in its present use
and application, for the painter addresses thereby that morbid and fearful

condition of mind which he has endeavoured to excite in the spectator, and which in reality would have seen in every trunk and bough, as it penetrated into the deeper thicket, the object of its terror.

It is nevertheless evident, that however suggestive the work or picture may be, it cannot have effect unless we are ourselves both watchful of its every hint, and capable of understanding and carrying it out; and although I think that this power of continuing or accepting the direction of feeling given is less a peculiar gift, like that of the original seizing, than a faculty
262 dependent on attention and improvable by cultivation; yet, to a certain extent, the imaginative work will not, I think, be rightly esteemed except by a mind of some corresponding power: not but that there is an intense enjoyment in minds of feeble yet right conception in the help and food they get from those of stronger thought; but a certain imaginative susceptibility is at any rate necessary, and above all things earnestness and feeling; so that assuredly a work of high conceptive dignity will be always incomprehensible and valueless except to those who go to it in earnest and give it time; and this is peculiarly the case when the imagination acts not merely on the immediate subject, nor in giving a fanciful and peculiar character to prominent objects, as we have just seen, but busies itself throughout in expressing occult and far-sought sympathies in every minor detail; of which action the most sublime instances are found in the works of Tintoret, whose intensity of imagination is such that there is not the commonest subject to which he will not attach a range of suggestiveness almost limitless; nor a stone, leaf, or shadow, nor anything so small, but he will give it meaning and oracular voice.

263   No subject has been more frequently or exquisitely treated by the religious painters than that of the Annunciation; though, as usual, the most perfect type of its pure ideal has been given by Angelico, and by him with the most radiant consummation (so far as I know) in a small reliquary in the sacristy of St̲ᵃ. Maria Novella [fig.60]. The background there,
264 however, is altogether decorative; but, in the fresco of the corridor of St. Mark's, the concomitant circumstances are of exceeding loveliness [fig.32]. The Virgin sits in an open loggia, resembling that of the Florentine church of L'Annunziata. Before her is a meadow of rich herbage, covered with daisies. Behind her is seen, through the door at the end of the loggia, a chamber with a single grated window, through which a starlike beam of light falls into the silence. All is exquisite in feeling, but not inventive nor imaginative. Severe would be the shock and painful the contrast, if we could pass in an instant from that pure vision to the wild thought of Tintoret [fig.33]. For not in meek reception of the adoring messenger, but startled by the rush of his horizontal and rattling wings, the Virgin sits, not in the quiet loggia, not by the green pasture of the restored soul, but houseless, under the shelter of a palace vestibule ruined and

fig.32   Fra Angelico, *The Annunciation*,
fresco from the Museo San Marco, Florence

abandoned, with the noise of the axe and the hammer in her ears, and the
tumult of a city round about her desolation. The spectator turns away at
first, revolted, from the central object of the picture forced painfully and
coarsely forward, a mass of shattered brickwork, with the plaster mildewed
away from it, and the mortar mouldering from its seams; and if he look
again, either at this or at the carpenter's tools beneath it, will perhaps see,
in the one and the other, nothing more than such a study of scene as
Tintoret could but too easily obtain among the ruins of his own Venice,
chosen to give a coarse explanation of the calling and the condition of the
husband of Mary. But there is more meant than this. When he looks at the
composition of the picture, he will find the whole symmetry of it   265
depending on a narrow line of light, the edge of a carpenter's square,
which connects these unused tools with an object at the top of the brickwork, a white stone, four square, the corner-stone of the old edifice, the
base of its supporting column. This, I think, sufficiently explains the
typical character of the whole. The ruined house is the Jewish dispensation; that obscurely arising in the dawning of the sky is the Christian;
but the corner-stone of the old building remains, though the builders'
tools lie idle beside it, and the stone which the builders refused is become
the Headstone of the Corner.

fig.33 Tintoretto, *The Annunciation*, from the
Scuola di San Rocco, Venice

270　　But the most exquisite instance of this imaginative power occurs in an
incident in the background of the Crucifixion [plate 14]. I will not insult
this marvellous picture by an effort at a verbal account of it. I would not
whitewash it with praise, and I refer to it only for the sake of two thoughts
peculiarly illustrative of the intellectual faculty immediately under
discussion. In the common and most Catholic treatment of the subject,
the mind is either painfully directed to the bodily agony, coarsely
expressed by outward anatomical signs, or else it is permitted to rest on
that countenance inconceivable by man at any time, but chiefly so in this
its consummated humiliation. In the first case, the representation is
revolting; in the second, inefficient, false, and sometimes blasphemous.
None even of the greatest religious painters have ever, so far as I know,
succeeded here: Giotto and Angelico were cramped by the traditional
treatment, and the latter especially, as before observed, is but too apt to
indulge in those points of vitiated feeling which attained their worst

development among the Byzantines; Perugino fails in his Christ in almost
every instance: of other men than these, after them, we need not speak.
But Tintoret here, as in all other cases, penetrating into the root and deep
places of his subject, despising all outward and bodily appearances of pain,
and seeking for some means of expressing, not the rack of nerve or sinew,
but the fainting of the deserted Son of God before His Eloi cry, and yet
feeling himself utterly unequal to the expression of this by the countenance, has, on the one hand, filled his picture with such various and
impetuous muscular exertion, that the body of the Crucified is, by com-   271
parison, in perfect repose, and, on the other, has cast the countenance
altogether into shade. But the Agony is told by this, and by this only; that,
though there yet remains a chasm of light on the mountain horizon where
the earthquake darkness closes upon the day, the broad and sunlike glory
about the head of the Redeemer has become wan, *and of the colour of ashes.*

But the great painter felt he had something more to do yet. Not only
that Agony of the Crucified, but the tumult of the people, that rage which
invoked His blood upon them and their children. Not only the brutality
of the soldier, the apathy of the Centurion, or any other merely
instrumental cause of the Divine suffering, but the fury of His own people,
the noise against Him of those for whom He died, were to be set before the
eye of the understanding, if the power of the picture was to be complete.
This rage, be it remembered, was one of disappointed pride; and the
disappointment dated essentially from the time when, but five days
before, the King of Zion came, and was received with hosannahs, riding
upon an ass, and a colt the foal of an ass. To this time, then, it was
necessary to direct the thoughts, for therein are found both the cause and
the character, the excitement of, and the witness against, this madness of
the people. In the shadow behind the cross, a man, riding on an ass colt,
looks back to the multitude, while he points with a rod to the Christ
crucified. The ass is feeding on the *remnants* of *withered palm-leaves.*

With this master-stroke, I believe, I may terminate all illustration of the
peculiar power of the imagination over the feelings of the spectator, by the
elevation into dignity and meaning of the smallest accessory circum-   272
stances. But I have not yet sufficiently dwelt on the fact from which this
power arises, the absolute truth of statement of the central fact as it was,
or must have been. Without this truth, this awful first moving principle,
all direction of the feelings is useless. That which we cannot excite, it is
of no use to know how to govern.

I have before alluded[54] to the painfulness of Raffaelle's treatment of the
Massacre of the Innocents. Fuseli affirms of it, that, "in dramatic
gradation he disclosed all the mother through every image of pity and of
terror."[55] If this be so, I think the philosophical spirit has prevailed over
the imaginative. The imagination never errs; it sees all that is, and all the

relations and bearings of it; but it would not have confused the mortal frenzy of maternal terror with various development of maternal character. Fear, rage, and agony, at their utmost pitch, sweep away all character: humanity itself would be lost in maternity, the woman would become the mere personification of animal fury or fear. For this reason all the ordinary representations of this subject are, I think, false and cold: the artist has not heard the shrieks, nor mingled with the fugitives; he has sat down in his study to convulse features methodically, and philosophize over insanity. Not so Tintoret [fig.34]. Knowing, or feeling, that the expression of the human face was, in such circumstances, not to be rendered, and that the effort could only end in an ugly falsehood, he denies himself all aid from the features, he feels that if he is to place himself or us in the midst of that maddened multitude, there can be no time allowed for watching expression. Still less does he depend on details of murder and ghastliness of death; there is no blood, no stabbing or cutting, but there is an awful 273   substitute for these in the chiaroscuro. The scene is the outer vestibule of

fig.34   Tintoretto, *The Massacre of the Innocents,* from the
Scuola di San Rocco, Venice

a palace, the slippery marble floor is fearfully barred across by sanguine shadows, so that our eyes seem to become bloodshot and strained with strange horror and deadly vision; a lake of life before them, like the burning seen of the doomed Moabite on the water that came by the way of Edom; a huge flight of stairs, without parapet, descends on the left; down this rush a crowd of women mixed with the murderers; the child in the arms of one has been seized by the limbs, *she hurls herself over the edge, and falls head downmost, dragging the child out of the grasp by her weight;*—she will be dashed dead in a second;—close to us is the great struggle; a heap of the mothers entangled in one mortal writhe with each other and the swords, one of the murderers dashed down and crushed beneath them, the sword of another caught by the blade and dragged at by a woman's naked hand; the youngest and fairest of the women, her child just torn away from a death grasp, and clasped to her breast with the grip of a steel vice, falls backwards, helplessly over the heap, right on the sword points; all knit together and hurled down in one hopeless, frenzied, furious abandonment of body and soul in the effort to save. Far back, at the bottom of the stairs, there is something in the shadow like a heap of clothes. It is a woman, sitting quiet,—quite quiet,—still as any stone; she looks down steadfastly on her dead child, laid along on the floor before her, and her hand is pressed softly upon her brow.

This, to my mind, is the only Imaginative, that is, the only true, real, heartfelt representation of the being and actuality of the subject, in existence. I should exhaust the patience of the reader, if I were to dwell at length on the various stupendous developments of the imagination of Tintoret in the Scuola di San Rocco alone. I shall at present terminate our series of illustrations by reference to a work of less touching, but more tremendous appeal; the Last Judgment in the Church of Santa Maria dell' Orto [fig.35]. In this subject, almost all realizing or local statement had been carefully avoided by the most powerful painters, they judging it better to represent its chief circumstances as generic thoughts, and present them to the mind in a typical or abstract form.

By Tintoret only has this unimaginable event been grappled with in its Verity; not typically nor symbolically, but as they may see it who shall not sleep, but be changed. Only one traditional circumstance he has received with Dante and Michael Angelo, the Boat of the Condemned; but the impetuosity of his mind bursts out even in the adoption of this image; he has not stopped at the scowling ferryman of the one, nor at the sweeping blow and demon dragging of the other, but seized Hylas-like by the limbs,[56] and tearing up the earth in his agony, the victim is dashed into his destruction: nor is it the sluggish Lethe, nor the fiery lake that bears the cursed vessel, but the oceans of the earth and the waters of the firmament gathered into one white, ghastly cataract; the river of the

fig.35   Tintoretto, *The Last Judgement*, from the
Madonna dell'Orto, Venice (detail)

wrath of God, roaring down into the gulf where the world has melted with
its fervent heat, choked with the ruin of nations, and the limbs of its
corpses tossed out of its whirling, like water-wheels. Bat-like, out of the
holes and caverns and shadows of the earth, the bones gather and the clay

heaps heave, rattling and adhering into half-kneaded anatomies, that crawl, and startle, and struggle up among the putrid weeds, with the clay clinging to their clotted hair, and their heavy eyes sealed by the earth darkness yet, like his of old who went his way unseeing to the Siloam Pool;[57] shaking off one by one the dreams of the prison-house, hardly hearing the clangour of the trumpets of the armies of God, blinded yet more, as they awake, by the white light of the new Heaven, until the great vortex of the four winds bears up their bodies to the judgment-seat: the Firmament is all full of them, a very dust of human souls, that drifts, and floats, and falls in the interminable, inevitable light; the bright clouds are darkened with them as with thick snow, currents of atom life in the arteries of heaven, now soaring up slowly, and higher and higher still, till the eye and the thought can follow no farther, borne up, wingless, by their inward faith and by the angel powers invisible, now hurled in countless drifts of horror before the breath of their condemnation.

Now, I wish the reader particularly to observe throughout all these   278
works of Tintoret, the distinction of the Imaginative Verity from falsehood on the one hand, and from realism on the other. The power of every picture depends on the penetration of the imagination into the TRUE nature of the thing represented, and on the utter scorn of the imagination for all shackles and fetters of mere external fact that stand in the way of its suggestiveness.

In the Massacre it covers the marble floor with visionary light, that it may strike terror into the spectator without condescending to butchery; it defies the bare fact, but creates in him the fearful feeling; in the Crucifixion it annihilates locality, and brings the palm leaves to Calvary, so only that it may bear the mind to the Mount of Olives; and all this it does in the daring consciousness of its higher and spiritual verity, and in the entire knowledge of the fact and substance of all that it touches. The imaginary boat of the demon angel expands the rush of the visible river into the descent of irresistible condemnation; but to make that rush and roar felt by the eye and heard by the ear, the rending of the pine branches above the cataract is taken directly from nature; it is an abstract of Alpine storm. Hence, while we are always placed face to face with whatever is to be told, there is in and beyond its reality a voice supernatural; and that which is doubtful in the vision has strength, sinew, and assuredness, built up in it by fact.

Now, in all these instances, let it be observed that the virtue of the   284
Imagination is its reaching, by intuition and intensity of gaze (not by reasoning, but by its authoritative opening and revealing power), a more essential truth than is seen at the surface of things. It matters not whether the reader is willing to call this faculty Imagination or not; I do not care about the name; but I would be understood when I speak of imagination

285 hereafter, to mean this, the base of whose authority and being is its perpetual thirst for truth and purpose to be true. It has no food, no delight, no care, no perception, except of truth; it is forever looking under masks, and burning up mists; no fairness of form, no majesty of seeming will satisfy it; the first condition of its existence is incapability of being deceived; and though it sometimes dwells upon and substantiates the fictions of fancy, yet its own operation is to trace to their farthest limit the true laws and likelihoods even of the fictitious creation.

286 I hear modern works constantly praised as being imaginative, in which I can trace no virtue of any kind; but simple, slavish, unpalliated falsehood

287 and exaggeration. I see not what merit there can be in pure, ugly, resolute fiction; it is surely easy enough to be wrong; there are many ways of being unlike nature. I understand not what virtue that is which entitles one of these ways to be called imaginative, rather than another; and I am still further embarrassed by hearing the portions of those works called especially imaginative in which there is the most effort at minute and mechanical statement of contemptible details, and in which the artist would have been as actual and absolute in imitation as an echo, if he had known how. Against convictions which I do not understand I cannot argue; but I may warn the artist that imagination of this strange kind is not capable of bearing the time test; nothing of its doing has continued its influence over men; and if he desires to take place among the great men of older time, there is but one way for it; and one kind of imagination that will stand the immortal light: I know not how far it is by effort cultivable; but we have evidence enough before us to show in what direction that effort must be made.

We have seen that the Imagination is in no small degree dependent on acuteness of moral emotion; in fact, all moral truth can only thus be apprehended—and it is observable, generally, that all true and deep emotion is imaginative, both in conception and expression; and that the mental sight becomes sharper with every full beat of the heart: and, therefore, all egotism, and selfish care, or regard are, in proportion to their constancy, destructive of imagination; whose play and power depend altogether on our being able to forget ourselves and enter, like possessing spirits, into the bodies of things about us.

Again, as the Life of Imagination is in the discovering of truth, it is clear it can have no respect for sayings or opinions: knowing in itself when it has invented truly, restless and tormented except when it has this

288 knowledge, its sense of success or failure is too acute to be affected by praise or blame. Sympathy it desires—but can do without; of opinions it is regardless, not in pride but because it is conscious of a rule of action and object of aim in which it cannot be mistaken; partly, also, in pure energy of desire, and longing to do and to invent more and more, which suffer it

not to suck the sweetness of praise—unless a little with the end of the rod in its hand, and without pausing in its march. It goes straight forward up the hill; no voices nor mutterings can turn it back, nor petrify it from its purpose.

Finally, it is evident that, like the theoretic faculty, the imagination must be fed constantly by external nature—after the illustrations we have given this may seem mere truism, for it is clear that to the exercise of the penetrative faculty a subject of penetration is necessary; but I note it because many painters of powerful mind have been lost to the world by their suffering the restless writhing of their imagination in its cage to take place of its healthy and exulting activity in the fields of nature. The most imaginative men always study the hardest, and are the most thirsty for new knowledge. Fancy plays like a squirrel in its circular prison, and is happy: but Imagination is a pilgrim on the earth—and her home is in heaven. Shut her from the fields of the celestial mountains—bar her from breathing their lofty, sun-warmed air; and we may as well turn upon her the last bolt of the Tower of Famine, and give the keys to the keeping of the wildest surge that washes Capraja and Gorgona.[58]

CHAPTER IV
Of Imagination Contemplative

289   WE have, in the two preceding chapters, arrived at definite conclusions respecting the power and essence of the imaginative faculty. It remains for us only to observe a certain habit or mode of operation in which it frequently delights, and by which it addresses itself to our perceptions more forcibly, and asserts its presence more distinctly than in those mighty but more secret workings wherein its life consists.

In our examination of the combining imagination, we chose to assume the first or simple conception to be as clear in the absence as in the presence of the object of it. This, I suppose, is, in point of fact, never the case, nor is an approximation to such distinctness of conception always a characteristic of the imaginative mind.

The form in which Conception actually occurs to ordinary minds appears to derive value and preciousness from that indefiniteness which we alluded to in the second chapter; for there is an unfailing charm in the memory and anticipation of things beautiful, more sunny and spiritual than attaches to their presence; for with their presence it is possible to be sated, and even wearied, but with the imagination of them never; in so far that it needs some self discipline to prevent the mind from falling into a morbid condition of dissatisfaction with all that it immediately possesses,

291   and continual longing for things absent. But it is evident that this agreeableness, whatever it be, is not by art attainable, for all art is, in some sort, realization; it may be the realization of obscurity or indefiniteness, but still it must differ from the mere *conception* of obscurity and indefiniteness; so that whatever emotions depend absolutely on imperfectness of conception, as the horror of Milton's Death, [59] cannot be rendered by art; for art can only lay hold of things which have shape, and destroys by its touch the fearfulness or pleasurableness of those which "shape have none."

But on this indistinctness of conception, itself comparatively valueless and unaffecting, is based the operation of the Imaginative faculty with which we are at present concerned, and in which its glory is consummated; whereby, depriving the subject of material and bodily shape, and regarding such of its qualities only as it chooses for particular purpose, it forges these qualities together in such groups and forms as it desires, and

269

gives to their abstract being consistency and reality, by striking them as it were with the die of an image belonging to other matter, which stroke having once received, they pass current at once in the peculiar conjunction and for the peculiar value desired.

Thus, in the description of Satan quoted in the first chapter, "And like a comet burned," the bodily shape of the angel is destroyed, the inflaming of the formless spirit is alone regarded; and this, and his power of evil, associated in one fearful and abstract conception, are stamped to give them distinctness and permanence with the image of the comet, "That   292 fires the length of Ophiuchus huge." Yet this could not be done, but that the image of the comet itself is in a measure indistinct, capable of awful expansion, and full of threatening and fear. Again, in that yet more noble passage at the close of the fourth book, where almost every operation of the contemplative imagination is concentrated; the angelic squadron first gathered into one burning mass by the single expression "sharpening in mooned horns," then told out in their unity and multitude and stooped hostility, by the image of the wind upon the corn; Satan endowed with godlike strength and endurance in that mighty line, "Like Teneriff or Atlas, unremoved," with infinitude of size the next instant, and with all the vagueness and terribleness of spiritual power, by the "Horrour plumed," and the "*what seemed* both spear and shield."[60]

Now, it is evident that the bold action of either the fancy or the   299 imagination, dependent on a bodiless and spiritual image of the object, is not to be by lines or colours represented.[61] Yet certain powers there are, within due limits, of marking the thing represented with an ideal character; and it was to these powers that I alluded in defining the meaning of the term Ideal.[62] For it is by this operation that the productions of high art are separated from those of the Realist.

And, first, there is evidently capability of separating colour and form,   300 and considering either separately. Form we find abstractedly considered by the sculptor; how far it would be possible to advantage a statue by the addition of colour, I venture not to affirm; the question is too extensive to be here discussed. High authorities, and ancient practice, are in favour of colour; but I have never seen colour on any solid forms, that did not, to my mind, neutralize all other power.

Colour, without form, is less frequently obtainable; and it may be   301 doubted whether it be desirable; yet I think that to the full enjoyment of it a certain sacrifice of form is necessary; sometimes by reducing it to the shapeless glitter of the gem, as often Tintoret and Bassano; sometimes by loss of outline and blending of parts, as Turner; sometimes by flatness of mass, as often Giorgione and Titian. My impression is, that there is no true abstract mode of considering colour; and that all the loss of form in the works of Titian or Turner is not ideal, but the representation of the natural conditions under which bright colour is seen; for form is always in a measure lost by Nature herself when colour is very vivid.

302 Again, there is capability of representing the essential character, form, and colour of an object, without external texture. Compare a dog of Edwin Landseer with a dog of Paul Veronese [fig.57]. In the first, the outward texture is wrought out with exquisite dexterity of handling, and minute attention to all the accidents of curl and gloss which can give appearance of reality; while the hue and power of the sunshine, and the truth of the shadow, on all these forms are neglected, and the large relations of the animal, as a mass of colour, to the sky or ground, or other parts of the picture, utterly lost. This is realism at the expense of ideality; it is treatment essentially unimaginative. With Veronese, there is no curling nor crisping, nor glossiness nor sparkle, hardly even hair; a mere type of hide, laid on with a few scene-painter's touches; but the essence of dog is there; the entire, magnificent, generic animal type, muscular and living, and with broad, pure, sunny daylight upon him, and bearing his

303 true and harmonious relation of colour to all colour about him. This is ideal treatment.

The same treatment is found in the works of all the greatest men; they all paint the lion more than his mane, and the horse rather than his hide; and I think also they are often more careful to obtain the right expression of large and universal light and colour, than accuracy of features; for the warmth of sunshine, and the force of sunlighted hue, are always sublime on whatever subject they may be exhibited; and so also are light and shade, if grandly arranged, as may be well seen in an etching of Rembrandt's of a spotted shell, which he has made altogether sublime by broad truth and large ideality of light and shade.[63]

Again, it is possible to represent objects capable of various accidents in a generic or symbolical form.

How far this may be done with things having necessary form, as animals, I am not prepared to say. The Lions of the Egyptian room in the British Museum, and the Fish beside Michael Angelo's Jonah,[64] are instances; and there is imaginative power about both which we find not in the more

304 perfectly realized Florentine boar, nor in Raffaelle's fish of the Draught.[65] And yet the propriety and nobility of these types depend on the architectural use and character of the one, and on the typical meaning of the other; we should be grieved to see the forms of the Egyptian lion substituted for those of Raffaelle's in its struggle with Samson, nor would the whale of Michael Angelo be tolerated in the nets of Gennesaret. So that I think it is only when the figure of the creature stands, not for any representation of vitality, but merely for a letter or type of certain symbolical meaning, or else is adopted as a form of decoration or support in architecture, that such generalization is allowable; and in such

circumstances it is perhaps necessary to adopt a typical form. Other   307
abstractions there are which are necessarily consequent on the
imperfection of materials, as of the hair in sculpture, which is necessarily
treated in masses that are in no sort imitative, but only stand for hair, and
have the grace, flow, and feeling of it without the texture or division; and
other abstractions there are in which the form of one thing is fancifully
indicated in the matter of another; as in phantoms and cloud shapes, the   308
use of which, in mighty hands, is often most impressive; only such
operations of the imagination are to be held of lower kind, and dangerous
consequence if frequently trusted in; for those painters only have the right
imaginative power who can set the supernatural form before us, fleshed
and boned like ourselves. Other abstractions occur, frequently, of things
which have much accidental variety of form; as of waves, on Greek
sculptures in successive volutes, and of clouds often in supporting volumes
in the sacred pictures: but these I do not look upon as results of
imagination at all, but mere signs and letters; and whenever a very highly
imaginative mind touches them, it always realizes as far as may be.
Nevertheless, when the realization is impossible, bold symbolism is of the   309
highest value, and in religious art, as we shall presently see, even
necessary; and sometimes the attention is directed by some strange form
to the meaning of the image, which may be missed if it remains in its
natural purity.

The last mode we have here to note in which the Imagination regardant
may be expressed in art is Exaggeration, of which, as it is the vice of all bad
artists, and may be constantly resorted to without any warrant of imagination, it is necessary to note strictly the admissible limits.

In the first place a colossal statue is not necessarily any more an   310
exaggeration of what it represents, than a miniature is a diminution; it
need not be a representation of a giant, but a representation, on a large
scale, of a man: only it is to be observed, that as any plane intersecting the
cone of rays between us and the object must receive an image smaller than
the object, a small image is rationally and completely expressive of a larger
one; but not a large of a small one. Hence I think that all statues above
the Elgin standard, or that of Michael Angelo's Night and Morning, are,
in a measure, taken by the eye for representations of giants, and I think
them always disagreeable. The amount of exaggeration admitted by
Michael Angelo is valuable, because it separates the emblematic from the
human form, and gives greater freedom to the grand lines of the frame.

Another kind of Exaggeration is of things whose size is variable to a size   311
or degree greater than that usual with them, as in waves and mountains;
and there are hardly any limits to this exaggeration, so long as the laws
which Nature observes in her increase be observed. Thus, for instance, the
form and polished surface of a breaking ripple three inches high, are not

representative of either the form or the surface of the surf of a storm, nodding ten feet above the beach; neither would the cutting ripple of a breeze upon a lake, if simply exaggerated, represent the forms of Atlantic surges: but as Nature increases her bulk, she diminishes the angles of ascent, and increases her divisions; and if we would represent surges of size greater than ever existed, which it is lawful to do, we must carry out these operations to still greater extent. Thus Turner, in his picture of the Slave Ship [plate 6], divides the whole sea into two masses of enormous swell, and conceals the horizon by a gradual slope of only two or three degrees. This is intellectual exaggeration. Again, in mountains, we have repeatedly observed the necessary building up and multitudinous division of the higher peaks, and the smallness of the slopes by which they usually rise.

312 We may, therefore, build up the mountain as high as we please, but we must do it in nature's way, and not in impossible peaks and precipices: not but that a daring feature is admissible here and there, as the Matterhorn is admitted by nature; but we must not compose a picture out of such exceptions; we may use them, but they must be as exceptions exhibited.

Another kind of Exaggeration is necessary to retain the characteristic impressions of nature on reduced scale. It is not possible, for instance, to give the leafage of trees in its proper proportion, on a small scale, without entirely losing their grace of form and curvature. In order to retain, therefore, their character of flexibility, the painter is often compelled to increase the proportionate size of the leaves, and to arrange them in

313 generic masses. In all these cases exaggeration is only lawful as the sole means of arriving at truth of impression when strict fidelity is out of the question.

CHAPTER V
Of the Superhuman Ideal

THERE are four ways in which Beings supernatural may be conceived   314
as manifesting themselves to human sense. The first, by external
types, signs, or influences; as God to Moses in the flames of the bush, and
to Elijah in the voice of Horeb.

The second, by the assuming of a form not properly belonging to them;
as the Holy Spirit of that of a Dove; the second person of the Trinity of
that of a Lamb; and so such manifestations, under Angelic or other form,
of the first person of the Trinity, as seem to have been made to Abraham,   315
Moses, and Ezekiel.

The third, by the manifestation of a form properly belonging to them,
but not necessarily seen; as of the Risen Christ to His disciples when the
doors were shut. And the fourth, by their operation on the human form
which they influence or inspire; as in the shining of the face of Moses.

It is evident that in all these cases, wherever there is form at all, it is the
form of some creature to us known. It is no new form peculiar to spirit, nor
can it be. We can conceive of none. Our inquiry is simply therefore, by
what modifications those creature forms to us known, as of a lamb, a bird,
or a human creature, may be explained as signs or habitations of Divinity,
or of angelic essence, and not creatures such as they seem.

This may be done in two ways. First, by effecting some change in the
appearance of the creature inconsistent with its actual nature; as by giving
it colossal size, or unnatural colour or material, as of gold, or silver, or
flame, instead of flesh; or taking away its property of matter altogether,
and forming it of light or shade, or in an intermediate step, of cloud or
vapour; or explaining it by terrible concomitant circumstances, as of
wounds in the body, or strange lights and seemings round about it; or
joining of two bodies together, as in angels' wings.

But the second means of obtaining supernatural character is that with
which we are now concerned, namely, retaining the actual form in its full
and material presence, and, without aid from any external interpretation
whatsoever, to raise that form by mere inherent dignity to such pitch of   316
power and impressiveness as cannot but assert and stamp it for
superhuman.

274

On the north side of the Campo Santo at Pisa, are a series of paintings from the Old Testament history by Benozzo Gozzoli.[66] In the earlier of these, angelic presences, mingled with human, occur frequently, illustrated by no awfulness of light, nor incorporeal tracing. Clear revealed they move, in human forms, in the broad daylight and on the open earth, side by side, and hand in hand with men. But they never miss of the angel.

He who can do this, has reached the last pinnacle and utmost power of ideal, or any other art. He stands in no need, thenceforward, of cloud, or lightning, or tempest, or terror of mystery. His sublime is independent of the elements. It is of that which shall stand when they shall melt with fervent heat, and light the firmament when the sun is as sackcloth of hair.

Let us consider by what means this has been effected, so far as they are by analysis traceable; and that is not far, for here, as always, we find that the greater part of what has been rightly accomplished has been done by faith and intense feeling, and cannot, by aid of any rules or teaching, be either tried, estimated, or imitated.

317 I have affirmed, in the conclusion of the first Section, that "of that which is more than Creature no Creature ever conceived."[67] I think this almost self-evident, for it is clear that the illimitableness of Divine attributes cannot be by matter represented (though it may be typified); and I believe that all who are acquainted with the range of sacred art will admit, not only that no representation of Christ has ever been even partially successful, but that the greatest painters fall therein below their accustomed level; Perugino and Fra Angelico especially: Leonardo has, I think, done best; but perhaps the beauty of the fragment left at Milan (for in spite of all that is said of repainting and destruction, that Cenacolo is

318 still the finest in existence[68]) is as much dependent on the very untraceableness resulting from injury as on its original perfection. Of more daring attempts at representation of Divinity we need not speak, but may limit ourselves to considering the purest modes of giving a conception of superhuman but still creature form, as of angels; in equal rank with whom, perhaps, we may without offence place the mother of Christ; at least we must so regard the type of the Madonna in receiving it from Romanist painters.

319 And first, much is to be done by right modification of accessary circumstances, so as to express miraculous power exercised over them by the Spiritual creature. There is a beautiful instance of this in John Bellini's picture of St. Jerome at Venice [fig. 7]. The Saint sits upon a rock, his grand form defined against clear green open sky; he is reading; a noble tree springs out of a cleft in the rock, bends itself suddenly back to form a rest for the volume, then shoots up into the sky. There is something very beautiful in this obedient ministry of the lower creature; but be it observed that the sweet feeling of the whole depends upon the service being such

as is consistent with its nature. It is not animated, it does not *listen* to the saint, nor bend itself towards him as if in affection; this would have been mere fancy, illegitimate and effectless. But the simple bend of the trunk to receive the book is miraculous subjection of the true nature of the tree; it is therefore imaginative, and very touching.

It is not often, however, that the religious painters even go this length: 320 they content themselves usually with impressing on the landscape perfect symmetry and order, such as may seem consistent with, or induced by, the spiritual nature they would represent. All signs of decay, disturbance, and imperfection are also banished; and in doing this it is evident that some unnaturalness and singularity must result, inasmuch as there are no veritable forms of landscape but express or imply a state of progression or of imperfection. All mountain forms are seen to be produced by convulsion and modelled by decay; the finer forms of cloud have threatenings in them of storm; all forest grouping is wrought out with varieties of strength and growth among its several members, and bears evidences of struggle with unkind influences. All such appearances are banished in the supernatural landscape; the trees grow straight, equally branched on each side, and of such slight and feathery frame as shows them never to have encountered blight, or frost, or tempest. The mountains stand up in fantastic pinnacles; there is on them no trace of torrent, no scathe of lightning; no fallen fragments encumber their foundations, no worn ravines divide their flanks; the seas are always waveless, the skies always calm, crossed only by fair, horizontal, lightly wreathed, white clouds.

In some cases these conditions result partly from feeling, partly from ignorance of the facts of nature, or incapability of representing them, as in the first type of the treatment found in Giotto and his school; in others they are observed on principle, as by Benozzo Gozzoli, Perugino, and Raffaelle. There is a beautiful instance by the former in the frescoes of the Ricardi Palace,[69] where, behind the adoring angel groups, the landscape is governed by the most absolute symmetry; roses, and pomegranates, their leaves drawn to the last rib and vein, twine themselves in fair and perfect order about delicate trellises; broad stone pines and tall cypresses overshadow them, bright birds hover here and there in the serene sky, and groups of angels, hand joined with hand, and wing with wing, glide and   321 float through the glades of the unentangled forest. But behind the human figures, behind the pomp and turbulence of the kingly procession descending from the distant hills, the spirit of the landscape is changed. Severer mountains rise in the distance, ruder prominences and less flowery vary the nearer ground, and gloomy shadows remain unbroken beneath the forest branches.

The landscape of Perugino, for grace, purity, and as much of nature as is consistent with the above-named conditions, is unrivalled; and the more interesting because in him, certainly, whatever limits are set to the rendering of nature proceed not from incapability. The sea is in the distance almost always, then some blue promontories and undulating dewy park ground, studded with glittering trees. In the landscape of the fresco in St^a. Maria Maddalena at Florence there is more variety than is usual with him: a gentle river winds round the bases of rocky hills, a river

322 like our own Wye or Tees in their loveliest reaches; level meadows stretch away on its opposite side; mounds set with slender-stemmed foliage occupy the nearer ground, and a small village with its simple spire peeps from the forest at the bend of the valley.

323   In all these cases, while I would uphold the landscape thus employed and treated, as worthy of all admiration, I should be sorry to advance it for imitation. What is right in its mannerism arose from keen feeling in the painter: imitated without the same feeling it would be painful; the only safe mode of following in such steps is to attain perfect knowledge of Nature herself, and then to suffer our own feelings to guide us in the selection of what is fitting for any particular purpose. Every painter ought to paint what he himself loves, not what others have loved; if his mind be pure and sweetly toned, what he loves will be lovely; if otherwise, no example can guide his selection, no precept govern his hand; and farther, let it be distinctly observed, that all this mannered landscape is only right under the supposition of its being a background to some supernatural presence; behind mortal beings it would be wrong, and by itself, as landscape, ridiculous; and farther, the chief virtue of it results from the exquisite refinement of those natural details consistent with its character; from the botanical drawing of the flowers, and the clearness and brightness of the sky.

    Another mode of attaining supernatural character is by purity of colour almost shadowless, no more darkness being allowed than is absolutely necessary for the explanation of the forms and the vividness of the effect, enhanced, as far as may be, by use of gilding, enamel, and other jewellery.

324 I think the smaller works of Angelico are perfect models in this respect; the glories about the heads being of beaten rays of gold, on which the light plays and changes as the spectator moves (and which therefore throw the purest flesh colour out in dark relief); and such colour and light being obtained by the enamelling of the angel wings as, of course, is utterly unattainable by any other expedient of art; the colours of the draperies always pure and pale, blue, rose, or tender green, or brown, but never dark or gloomy; the faces of the most celestial fairness, brightly flushed.

    I cannot think it necessary, while I insist on the value of all these seemingly childish means when in the hands of a noble painter, to assert also their futility, and even absurdity, if employed by no exalted power. I think the error has commonly been on the side of scorn, and that we reject much in our foolish vanity, which, if wiser and more earnest, we should delight in. But two points it is very necessary to note in the use of such accessaries.

The first, that the ornaments used by Angelico, Giotto, and Perugino, but especially by Angelico, are always of a *generic* and *abstract* character. They are not diamonds, nor brocades, nor velvets, nor gold embroideries; they are mere spots of gold or of colour, simple patterns upon *textureless* draperies; the angel wings burn with transparent crimson and purple and amber, but they are not set forth with peacocks' plumes; the golden circlets gleam with changeful light, but they are not beaded with pearls, nor set with sapphires.

In the works of Filippino Lippi, Mantegna, and many other painters following, interesting examples may be found of the opposite treatment; and as in Lippi the heads are usually very sweet, and the composition severe, the degrading effect of the realized decorations and imitated dress 325 may be seen in him simply, and without any addition of painfulness from other deficiencies of feeling.

The second point to be observed is that brightness of colour is altogether inadmissible without purity and harmony; and that the sacred painters must not be followed in their frankness of unshadowed colour, unless we can also follow them in its clearness. I hesitate not to affirm that in such art, more than in any other, clearness, luminousness, and intensity of hue are essential to right impression; and from the walls of the Arena chapel in their rainbow play of brilliant harmonies, to the solemn purple tones of Perugino's fresco in the Albizzi Palace,[70] I know not any great 326 work of sacred art which is not as precious in colour as in all other qualities.

But leaving these accessary circumstances, and touching the treatment of the bodily form, it is evident, in the first place, that whatever typical beauty the human body is capable of possessing must be bestowed upon it when it is to be understood as spiritual. And therefore those general proportions and types which are deducible from comparison of the nobler 327 individuals of the race, must be adopted and adhered to; admitting among them not, as in the human ideal, such varieties as result from past suffering, or contest with sin, but such only as are consistent with sinless nature, or are the signs of instantly or continually operative affections; for though it is conceivable that spirit should suffer, it is inconceivable that spiritual frame should retain, like the stamped inelastic human clay, the brand of sorrow past, unless fallen:

> "His face
> Deep scars of thunder had intrenched, and care
> Sat on his faded cheek."[71]

Yet so far forth the Angelic idea is diminished, nor could this be suffered in pictorial representation.

Again, such muscular development as is necessary to the perfect beauty of the body is to be rendered. But that which is necessary to strength, or which appears to have been the result of laborious exercise, is inadmissible. No herculean form is spiritual, for it is degrading the spiritual creature to suppose it operative through impulse of bone and sinew; its power is immaterial and constant, neither dependent on, nor developed by, exertion. How far it is possible to subdue or generalize the naked form I venture not to affirm; but I believe that it is best to conceal it, as far as may be, not with light and undulating draperies, that fall in with and exhibit its principal lines, but with severe and linear draperies, such as were constantly employed before the time of Raffaelle. I recollect no single instance of a naked angel that does not look boylike or childlike, and unspiritualized; even Fra Bartolomeo's might with advantage be spared from the pictures at Lucca: and, afterwards, the sky is merely 328 encumbered with sprawling infants; those of Domenichino are peculiarly offensive, studies of bare-legged children howling and kicking in volumes of smoke. Confusion seems to exist in the minds of subsequent painters between angels and Cupids.

Farther, the qualities of symmetry and repose are of peculiar value in spiritual form. We find the former most earnestly sought by all the great painters in the arrangement of the hair, wherein no loosely flowing nor varied form is admitted, but all restrained in undisturbed and equal ringlets.

Of repose, and its exalting power, I have already said enough for our present purpose, though I have not insisted on the peculiar manifestation of it in the Christian ideal as opposed to the Pagan. But this, as well as all other questions relating to the particular development of the Greek mind, is foreign to the immediate inquiry, which therefore I shall here conclude; always, however, holding this for certain, that of whatever kind or degree the shortcoming may be, it is not possible but that shortcoming should be visible in every Pagan conception, when set beside Christian: and believing, for my own part, that there is not only deficiency, but such 329 difference in kind as must make all Greek conception full of danger to the student in proportion to his admiration of it.

331 It is vain to attempt to pursue the comparison; the two orders of art have in them nothing common, and the field of sacred history, the intent and scope of Christian feeling, are too wide and exalted to admit of the juxtaposition of any other sphere or order of conception; they embrace all other fields like the dome of heaven. With what comparison shall we compare the types of the martyr saints; the St. Stephen of Fra Bartolomeo, with his calm forehead crowned by the stony diadem, or

the St. Catherine of Raffaelle [72] looking up to heaven in the dawn of the eternal day, with her lips parted in the resting from her pain; or with what the Madonnas of Francia and Pinturicchio, in whom the hues of the morning and the solemnity of eve, the gladness in accomplished promise, and sorrow of the sword-pierced heart, are gathered into one human Lamp of ineffable love? or with what the angel choirs of Angelico, [73] with the   332 flames on their white foreheads waving brighter as they move, and the sparkles streaming from their purple wings like the glitter of many suns upon a sounding sea, listening in the pauses of alternate song, for the prolonging of the trumpet blast, and the answering of psaltery and cymbal, throughout the endless deep, and from all the star shores of heaven?

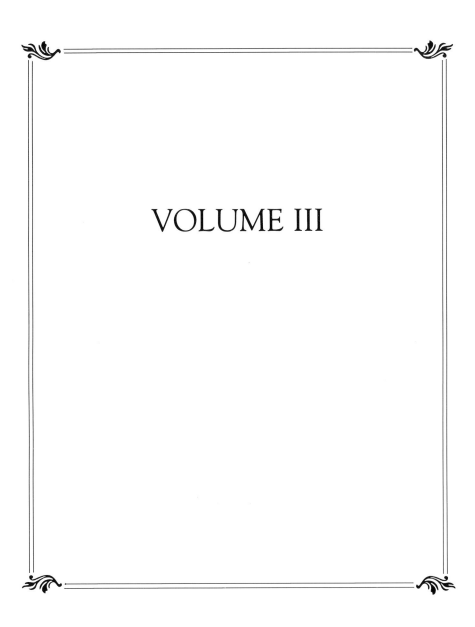

VOLUME III

PART IV
Of Many Things

CHAPTER I
Of the Received Opinions
Touching the "Grand Style"

18   IT remains for us to examine the various success of artists, especially of the great landscape-painter whose works have been throughout our principal subject, in addressing these faculties of the human mind, and to consider who among them has conveyed the noblest ideas of beauty, and touched the deepest sources of thought.

   I do not intend, however, now to pursue the inquiry in a method so laboriously systematic; for the subject may, it seems to me, be more usefully treated by pursuing the different questions which arise out of it just as they occur to us, without too great scrupulousness in marking connections, or insisting on sequences. I purpose, therefore, henceforward to arrange my chapters with a view to convenient reference, rather than to any careful division of subjects, and to follow out, in any by-ways that may open, on right hand or left, whatever question it seems useful at any moment to settle.

   And, in the outset, I find myself met by one which I ought to have
19 touched upon before—one of especial interest in the present state of the Arts. I have said that the art is greatest which includes the greatest ideas;[1] but I have not endeavoured to define the nature of this greatness in the ideas themselves. We speak of great truths, of great beauties, great thoughts. What is it which makes one truth greater than another, one thought greater than another? This question is, I repeat, of peculiar importance at the present time; for, during a period now of some hundred and fifty years, all writers on Art who have pretended to eminence, have insisted much on a supposed distinction between what they call the Great and the Low Schools; using the terms "High Art," "Great or Ideal Style," and other such, as descriptive of a certain noble manner of painting, which it was desirable that all students of Art should be early led to reverence and adopt; and characterising as "vulgar," or "low," or "realist," another manner of painting and conceiving, which it was equally necessary that all students should be taught to avoid.

20   And first, let us get, as quickly as may be, at the exact meaning with

which the advocates of "High Art" use that somewhat obscure and figurative term.

I do not know that the principles in question are anywhere more distinctly expressed than in two papers in the *Idler*, written by Sir Joshua Reynolds, of course under the immediate sanction of Johnson; and which may thus be considered as the utterance of the views then held upon the subject by the artists of chief skill, and critics of most sense, arranged in a form so brief and clear, as to admit of their being brought before the public for a morning's entertainment. I cannot, therefore, it seems to me, do better than quote these two letters, or at least the important parts of them, examining the exact meaning of each passage as it occurs.

No. 79 (Saturday, Oct. 20th, 1759)[2] begins, after a short preamble, with the following passage:—

"Amongst the Painters, and the writers on Painting, there is one maxim universally admitted and continually inculcated. *Imitate nature* is the invariable rule; but I know none who have explained in what manner this rule is to be understood; the consequence of which is, that every one takes it in the most obvious sense—that objects are represented naturally, when they have such relief that they seem real. It may appear strange, perhaps, to hear this sense of the rule disputed; but it must be considered, that, if   21 the excellency of a Painter consisted only in this kind of imitation, Painting must lose its rank, and be no longer considered as a liberal art, and sister to Poetry: this imitation being merely mechanical, in which the slowest intellect is always sure to succeed best; for the Painter of genius cannot stoop to drudgery, in which the understanding has no part; and what pretence has the Art to claim kindred with Poetry, but by its power over the imagination? To this power the Painter of genius directs him; in this sense he studies Nature, and often arrives at his end, even by being unnatural in the confined sense of the word.

"The grand style of Painting requires this minute attention to be carefully avoided, and must be kept as separate from it as the style of Poetry from that of History. (Poetical ornaments destroy that air of truth and plainness which ought to characterise History; but the very being of Poetry consists in departing from this plain narrative, and adopting every ornament that will warm the imagination.*) To desire to see the excellences of each style united—to mingle the Dutch with the Italian

---

* I have put this sentence in a parenthesis, because it is inconsistent with the rest of the statement, and with the general teaching of the paper; since that which "attends only to the invariable," cannot certainly adopt "every ornament that will warm the imagination."

school, is to join contrarieties which cannot subsist together, and which destroy the efficacy of each other."

22 We find, first, from this interesting passage, that the writer considers the Dutch and Italian masters as severally representative of the low and high schools; next, that he considers the Dutch painters as excelling in a mechanical imitation, "in which the slowest intellect is always sure to succeed best;" and, thirdly, that he considers the Italian painters as excelling in a style which corresponds to that of imaginative poetry in literature, and which has an exclusive right to be called the grand style.

I wish that it were in my power entirely to concur with the writer, and to enforce this opinion thus distinctly stated. I have never been a zealous partisan of the Dutch school, and should rejoice in claiming Reynolds's authority for the assertion, that their manner was one "in which the slowest intellect is always sure to succeed best." But first we must observe Reynolds's exact meaning, for (though the assertion may at first appear singular) a man who uses accurate language is always more liable to misinterpretation than one who is careless in his expressions.

23 Now, in the instance before us, a person not accustomed to good writing might very rashly conclude that when Reynolds spoke of the Dutch School as one "in which the slowest intellect was sure to succeed best," he meant to say that every successful Dutch painter was a fool. We have no right to take his assertion in that sense. He says, the *slowest* intellect. We have no right to assume that he meant the *weakest*. For it is true, that in order to succeed in the Dutch style, a man has need of qualities of mind eminently deliberate and sustained. But it by no means follows that they are necessarily those of weak or foolish men.

We observe, however, farther, that the imitation which Reynolds supposes to be characteristic of the Dutch School is that which gives to objects such relief that they seem real, and that he then speaks of this art of realistic imitation as corresponding to *history* in literature.

Reynolds, therefore, seems to class these dull works of the Dutch School under a general head, to which they are not commonly referred—that of *Historical* painting; while he speaks of the works of the Italian School not as historical, but as *poetical* painting. His next sentence will farther manifest his meaning.

24 "The Italian attends only to the invariable, the great and general ideas which are fixed and inherent in universal Nature; the Dutch, on the contrary, to literal truth, and a minute exactness in the detail, as I may say, of Nature modified by accident. The attention to these petty peculiarities is the very cause of this naturalness so much admired in the Dutch pictures, which, if we suppose it to be a beauty, is certainly of a

lower order, which ought to give place to a beauty of a superior kind, since one cannot be obtained but by departing from the other.

"If my opinion were asked concerning the works of Michael Angelo, whether they would receive any advantage from possessing this mechanical merit, I should not scruple to say, they would not only receive no advantage, but would lose, in a great measure, the effect which they now have on every mind susceptible of great and noble ideas. His works may be said to be all genius and soul; and why should they be loaded with heavy matter, which can only counteract his purpose by retarding the progress of the imagination?"

Examining carefully this and the preceding passage, we find the author's unmistakable meaning to be, that Dutch painting is *history*; attending to literal truth and "minute exactness in the details of nature modified by accident." That Italian painting is *poetry*, attending only to the invariable; and that works which attend only to the invariable are full of genius and soul; but that literal truth and exact detail are "heavy matter which retards the progress of the imagination."

This being then indisputably what Reynolds means to tell us, let us think a little whether he is in all respects right. And first, as he compares his two kinds of painting to history and poetry, let us see how poetry and history themselves differ, in their use of *variable* and *invariable* details. I am writing at a window which commands a view of the head of the Lake of Geneva; and as I look up from my paper, to consider this point, I see, beyond it, a blue breadth of softly moving water, and the outline of the mountains above Chillon, bathed in morning mist. The first verses which   25 naturally come into my mind are—

> "A thousand feet in depth below
> The massy waters meet and flow;
> So far the fathom line was sent
> From Chillon's snow-white battlement."[3]

Let us see in what manner this poetical statement is distinguished from a historical one.

It is distinguished from a truly historical statement, first, in being simply false. The water under the Castle of Chillon is not a thousand feet deep, nor anything like it. Herein, certainly, these lines fulfil Reynolds's first requirement in poetry, "that it should be inattentive to literal truth and minute exactness in detail." In order, however, to make our comparison more closely in other points, let us assume that what is stated is indeed a fact, and that it was to be recorded, first historically, and then poetically.

Historically stating it, then, we should say: "The lake was sounded from the walls of the Castle of Chillon, and found to be a thousand feet deep."

Now, if Reynolds be right in his idea of the difference between history and poetry, we shall find that Byron leaves out of this statement certain unnecessary details, and retains only the invariable,—that is to say, the points which the Lake of Geneva and Castle of Chillon have in common with all other lakes and castles.

Let us hear, therefore.

"A thousand feet in depth below."

26   "Below?" Here is, at all events, a word added (instead of anything being taken away); invariable, certainly in the case of lakes, but not absolutely necessary.

"The massy waters meet and flow."

"Massy!" why massy? Because deep water is heavy. The word is a good word, but it is assuredly an added detail, and expresses a character, not which the Lake of Geneva has in common with all other lakes, but which it has in distinction from those which are narrow, or shallow.

"Meet and flow." Why meet and flow? Partly to make up a rhyme; partly to tell us that the waters are forceful as well as massy, and changeful as well as deep. Observe, a farther addition of details, and of details more or less peculiar to the spot, or, according to Reynolds's definition, of "heavy matter, retarding the progress of the imagination."

"So far the fathom line was sent."

Why fathom line? All lines for sounding are not fathom lines. If the lake was ever sounded from Chillon, it was probably sounded in mètres, not fathoms. This is an addition of another particular detail, in which the only compliance with Reynolds's requirement is, that there is some chance of its being an inaccurate one.

"From Chillon's snow-white battlement."

Why snow-white? Because castle battlements are not usually snow-white. This is another added detail, and a detail quite peculiar to Chillon, and therefore exactly the most striking word in the whole passage.

"Battlement!" Why battlement? Because all walls have not battlements, and the addition of the term marks the castle to be not merely a prison, but a fortress.

This is a curious result. Instead of finding, as we expected, the poetry distinguished from the history by the omission of details, we find it consist entirely in the *addition* of details; and instead of being characterised by 27 regard only of the invariable, we find its whole power to consist in the clear expression of what is singular and particular!

The reader may pursue the investigation for himself in other instances. He will find in every case that a poetical is distinguished from a merely historical statement, not by being more vague, but more specific; and it might, therefore, at first appear that our author's comparison should be simply reversed, and that the Dutch School should be called poetical, and the Italian historical. But the term poetical does not appear very applicable to the generality of Dutch painting; and a little reflection will show us, that if the Italians represent only the invariable, they cannot be properly compared even to historians. For that which is incapable of change has no history, and records which state only the invariable need not be written, and could not be read.

It is evident, therefore, that our author has entangled himself in some grave fallacy, by introducing this idea of invariableness as forming a distinction between poetical and historical art. What the fallacy is, we shall discover as we proceed; but as an invading army should not leave an untaken fortress in its rear, we must not go on with our inquiry into the views of Reynolds until we have settled satisfactorily the question already suggested to us, in what the essence of poetical treatment really consists. For though, as we have seen, it certainly involves the addition of specific details, it cannot be simply that addition which turns the history into poetry. For it is perfectly possible to add any number of details to a historical statement, and to make it more prosaic with every added word. As, for instance, "The lake was sounded out of a flat-bottomed boat, near the crab-tree at the corner of the kitchen-garden, and was found to be a thousand feet nine inches deep, with a muddy bottom." It thus appears that it is not the multiplication of details which constitutes poetry; nor their subtraction which constitutes history, but that there must be something either in the nature of the details themselves, or the method   28 of using them, which invests them with poetical power or historical propriety.

It seems to me, and may seem to the reader, strange that we should need to ask the question, "What is poetry?" Here is a word we have been using all our lives, and, I suppose, with a very distinct idea attached to it; and when I am now called upon to give a definition of this idea, I find myself at a pause. What is more singular, I do not at present recollect hearing the question often asked, though surely it is a very natural one; and I never recollect hearing it answered, or even attempted to be answered.

I come, after some embarrassment, to the conclusion that poetry is "the suggestion, by the imagination, of noble grounds for the noble emotions." I mean, by the noble emotions, those four principal sacred passions— Love, Veneration, Admiration, and Joy (this latter especially, if unselfish); and their opposites—Hatred, Indignation (or Scorn), Horror, and Grief,—this last, when unselfish, becoming Compassion. These passions

in their various combinations constitute what is called "poetical feeling," when they are felt on noble grounds, that is, on great and true grounds. Indignation, for instance, is a poetical feeling, if excited by serious injury; but it is not a poetical feeling if entertained on being cheated out of a small sum of money. It is very possible the manner of the cheat may
29 have been such as to justify considerable indignation; but the feeling is nevertheless not poetical unless the grounds of it be large as well as just.

Farther, it is necessary to the existence of poetry that the grounds of these feelings should be *furnished by the imagination*. Poetical feeling, that is to say, mere noble emotion, is not poetry. It is happily inherent in all human nature deserving the name, and is found often to be purest in the least sophisticated. But the power of assembling, by *the help of the imagination*, such images as will excite these feelings, is the power of the poet or literally of the "Maker."

30 Now this power of exciting the emotions depends of course on the richness of the imagination, and on its choice of those images which, in combination, will be most effective, or, for the particular work to be done, most fit. And it is altogether impossible for a writer not endowed with invention to conceive what tools a true poet will make use of, or in what way he will apply them, or what unexpected results he will bring out by them; so that it is vain to say that the details of poetry ought to possess, or ever do possess, any *definite* character.

31 In like manner, in painting, it is altogether impossible to say beforehand what details a great painter may make poetical by his use of them to excite noble emotions: and we shall, therefore, find presently that a painting is to be classed in the great or inferior schools, not according to the kind of details which it represents, but according to the uses for which it employs them.

This question being thus far determined, we may proceed with our paper in the *Idler*.

"It is very difficult to determine the exact degree of enthusiasm that the arts of Painting and Poetry may admit. There may, perhaps, be too great an indulgence as well as too great a restraint of imagination; if the one produces incoherent monsters, the other produces what is full as bad, lifeless insipidity. An intimate knowledge of the passions, and good sense, but not common sense, must at last determine its limits. It has been thought, and I believe with reason, that Michael Angelo sometimes transgressed those limits; and, I think, I have seen figures of him of which it was very difficult to determine whether they were in the highest degree sublime or extremely ridiculous. Such faults may be said to be the ebullitions of genius; but at least he had this merit, that he never was insipid;

and whatever passion his works may excite, they will always escape contempt.

"What I have had under consideration is the sublimest style, particularly that of Michael Angelo, the Homer of painting. Other kinds may admit of this naturalness, which of the lowest kind is the chief merit; but in painting, as in poetry, the highest style has the least of common nature."   32

From this passage we gather three important indications of the supposed nature of the Great Style. That it is the work of men in a state of enthusiasm. That it is like the writing of Homer; and that it has as little as possible of "common nature" in it.

First, it is produced by men in a state of enthusiasm. That is, by men who feel *strongly* and *nobly*; for we do not call a strong feeling of envy, jealousy, or ambition, enthusiasm. That is, therefore, by men who feel poetically. This much we may admit, I think, with perfect safety. Great art is produced by men who feel acutely and nobly; and it is in some sort an expression of this personal feeling.

Secondly, Great Art is like the writing of Homer, and this chiefly because it has little of "common nature" in it. We are not clearly informed what is meant by common nature in this passage. Homer seems to describe a great deal of what is common:—cookery, for instance, very carefully in all its processes. I suppose the passage in the *Iliad* which, on the whole, has excited most admiration, is that which describes a wife's sorrow at parting from her husband, and a child's fright at its father's helmet:[4] and I hope, at least, the former feeling may be considered "common nature." But the true greatness of Homer's style is, doubtless, held by our author to consist in his imaginations of things not only uncommon but impossible (such as spirits in brazen armour, or monsters with heads of men and bodies of beasts), and in his occasional delineations of the human character and form in their utmost, or heroic, strength and   33 beauty. We gather then on the whole, that a painter in the Great Style must be enthusiastic, or full of emotion, and must paint the human form in its utmost strength and beauty, and perhaps certain impossible forms besides, liable by persons not in an equally enthusiastic state of mind to be looked upon as in some degree absurd. This I presume to be Reynolds's meaning, and to be all that he intends us to gather from his comparison of the Great Style with the writings of Homer.

Let us, however, proceed with our paper.

"One may very safely recommend a little more enthusiasm to the modern Painters; too much is certainly not the vice of the present age. The Italians seem to have been continually declining in this respect from the time of Michael Angelo to that of Carlo Maratti,[5] and from thence to the very bathos of insipidity to which they are now sunk; so that there is no need of remarking, that where I mentioned the Italian painters in opposition to the Dutch, I mean not the moderns, but the heads of the old Roman and Bolognian Schools; nor did I mean to include, in my idea of an Italian painter, the Venetian school, *which may be said to be the Dutch part of the Italian genius.*

34   I have only to add a word of advice to the Painters,—that, however excellent they may be in painting naturally, they would not flatter themselves very much upon it; and to the Connoisseurs, that when they see a cat or a fiddle painted so finely, that, as the phrase is, it looks as if you could take it up, they would not for that reason immediately compare the Painter to Raffaelle and Michael Angelo."

In this passage there are four points chiefly to be remarked. The first, that in the year 1759 the Italian painters were, in our author's opinion, sunk in the very bathos of insipidity. The second, that the Venetian painters, i.e. Titian, Tintoret, and Veronese, are, in our author's opinion, to be classed with the Dutch; that is to say, are painters in a style "in which the slowest intellect is always sure to succeed best." Thirdly, that painting naturally is not a difficult thing, nor one on which a painter should pride himself. And, finally, that connoisseurs, seeing a cat or a fiddle successfully painted, ought not therefore immediately to compare the painter to Raphael or Michael Angelo.

Yet Raphael painted fiddles very carefully in the foreground of his St. Cecilia,—so carefully, that they quite look as if they might be taken up. So carefully, that I never yet looked at the picture without wishing that somebody *would* take them up, and out of the way. And I am under a very strong persuasion that Raphael did not think painting "naturally" an easy thing. It will be well to examine into this point a little; and for the present, with the reader's permission, we will pass over the first two statements in this passage, and immediately examine some of the evidence existing as to the real dignity of "natural" painting—that is to say, of painting carried to the point at which it reaches a deceptive appearance of reality.

CHAPTER II
Of Realization

Iᴺ the outset of this inquiry, the reader must thoroughly understand　35
that we are not now considering *what* is to be painted, but *how far* it
is to be painted. Not whether Raphael does right in representing angels
playing upon violins, or whether Veronese does right in allowing cats and
monkeys to join the company of kings: but whether, supposing the
subjects rightly chosen, they ought on the canvas to look like real angels
with real violins, and substantial cats looking at veritable kings; or only
like imaginary angels with soundless violins, ideal cats, and unsubstantial
kings.

Now, from the first moment when painting began to be a subject of
literary inquiry and general criticism, I cannot remember any writer, not
professedly artistical, who has not, more or less, in one part of his book or
another, countenanced the idea that the great end of art is to produce a
deceptive resemblance of reality.

In a large number of instances, a person is attracted to a picture by the　36
beauty of its colour, interested by the liveliness of its story, and touched
by certain countenances or details which remind him of friends whom he
loved, or scenes in which he delighted. But he is ashamed to confess, or
perhaps does not know, that he is so much a child as to be fond of bright
colours and amusing incidents; and he is quite unconscious of the
associations which have so secret and inevitable a power over his heart.
He casts about for the cause of his delight, and can discover no other than
that he thought the picture like reality.

In another, perhaps, a still larger number of cases, such language will be
found to be that of simple ignorance—the ignorance of persons whose
position in life compels them to speak of art, without having any real
enjoyment of it. It is inexcusably required from people of the world that
they should see merit in Claudes and Titians; and the only merit which
many persons can either see or conceive in them is, that they must be
"like nature."

In other cases, the deceptive power of the art is really felt to be a source
of interest and amusement. This is the case with a large number of the
collectors of Dutch pictures. They enjoy seeing what is flat made to look

round, exactly as a child enjoys a trick of legerdemain: they rejoice in flies which the spectator vainly attempts to brush away, and in dew which he
37   endeavours to dry by putting the picture in the sun. They take it for the greatest compliment to their treasures that they should be mistaken for windows; and think the parting of Abraham and Hagar adequately represented if Hagar seems to be really crying.

It is against critics and connoisseurs of this latter stamp that the essay of Reynolds, which we have been examining, was justly directed. But very different men from these have held precisely the same language; and one, amongst the rest, whose authority is absolutely, and in all points, overwhelming.

There was probably never a period in which the influence of art over the minds of men seemed to depend less on its merely *imitative* power, than the close of the thirteenth century. No painting or sculpture at that time reached more than a rude resemblance of reality. Its despised perspective, imperfect chiaroscuro, and unrestrained flights of fantastic imagination, separated the artist's work from nature by an interval which there was no attempt to disguise, and little to diminish. And yet, at this very period, the greatest poet of that, or perhaps of any other age, and the attached
38   friend of its greatest painter,[6] who must over and over again have held full and free conversation with him respecting the objects of his art, speaks in the following terms of painting and sculpture, supposed to be carried to its highest perfection:—

> "Qual di pennel fu maestro, e di stile,
>   Che ritraesse l' ombre e i tratti, ch' ivi
>   Mirar farieno uno ingegno sottile?
> Morti li morti, e i vivi parean vivi:
>   Non vide me' di me, chi vide il vero,
>   Quant' io calcai, fin che chinato givi."
>   —DANTE, *Purgatorio*, canto xii. l.64.

> "What master of the pencil, or the style,
> Had traced the shades and lines that might have made
> The subtlest workman wonder? *Dead, the dead,*
> *The living seemed alive; with clearer view,*
> *His eye beheld not, who beheld the truth,*
> Than mine what I did tread on, while I went
> Low bending."   —CARY.

Dante has here clearly no other idea of the highest art than that it should bring back, as a mirror or vision, the aspect of things passed or absent. Nor do I think that Dante's authority is absolutely necessary to compel us to admit that such art as this *might*, indeed, be the highest possible. Whatever delight we may have been in the habit of taking in pictures, if it were but truly offered to us, to remove at our will the canvas

from the frame, and in lieu of it to behold, fixed for ever, the image of
some of those mighty scenes which it has been our way to make mere
themes for the artist's fancy; and this, not feebly nor fancifully, but as if   39
some silver mirror that had leaned against the wall of the chamber, had
been miraculously commanded to retain for ever the colours that had
flashed upon it for an instant,—would we not part with our picture—
Titian's or Veronese's though it might be?

   Yes, the reader answers, in the instance of such scenes as these, but not
if the scene represented were uninteresting. Not, indeed, if it were utterly
vulgar or painful; but we are not yet certain that the art which represents
what is vulgar or painful is itself of much value; and with respect to the art
whose aim is beauty, even of an inferior order, it seems that Dante's idea
of its perfection has still much evidence in its favour. For among persons
of native good sense, and courage enough to speak their minds, we shall
often find a considerable degree of doubt as to the use of art, in consequence of their habitual comparison of it with reality. "Nay," but the
reader interrupts (if he is of the Idealist school), "I deny that more beau-   40
tiful things are to be seen in nature than in art; on the contrary, everything in nature is faulty, and art represents nature as perfected." Be it so.
Must, therefore, this perfected nature be imperfectly represented? Is it
absolutely required of the painter, who has conceived perfection, that he
should so paint it as to look only like a picture? Or is not Dante's view of
the matter right even here, and would it not be well that the perfect
conception of Pallas should be so given as to look like Pallas herself, rather
then merely like a picture of Pallas?

   It is not easy for us to answer this question rightly, owing to the difficulty
of imagining any art which should reach the perfection supposed. Our
actual powers of imitation are so feeble that wherever deception is
attempted, a subject of a comparatively low or confined order must be
chosen. But let the reader make the effort, and consider seriously what he
would give at any moment to have the power of arresting the fairest
scenes, those which so often rise before him only to vanish; to stay the
cloud in its fading, the leaf in its trembling, and the shadows in their
changing; to bid the fitful foam be fixed upon the river, and the ripples be
everlasting upon the lake; and then to bear away with him no darkened
or feeble sunstain (though even that is beautiful), but a counterfeit which
should seem no counterfeit—the true and perfect image of life indeed. Or
rather (for the full majesty of such a power is not thus sufficiently
expressed) let him consider that it would be in effect nothing else than a   41
capacity of transporting himself at any moment into any scene—a gift as
great as can be possessed by a disembodied spirit: and suppose, also, this
necromancy embracing not only the present but the past, and enabling us
seemingly to enter into the very bodily presence of men long since

gathered to the dust; to behold them in act as they lived, but—with greater privilege than ever was granted to the companions of those transient acts of life—to see them fastened at our will in the gesture and expression of an instant, and stayed, on the eve of some great deed, in immortality of burning purpose. Conceive, so far as it is possible, such power as this, and then say whether the art which conferred it is to be spoken lightly of, or whether we should not rather reverence, as half divine, a gift which would go so far as to raise us into the rank, and invest us with the felicities, of angels?

Yet such would imitative art be in its perfection. Not by any means an easy thing, as Reynolds supposes it. Far from being easy, it is so utterly beyond all human power that we have difficulty even in conceiving its nature or results—the best art we as yet possess comes so far short of it.

But we must not rashly come to the conclusion that such art would, indeed, be the highest possible. There is much to be considered hereafter on the other side; the only conclusion we are as yet warranted in forming is, that Reynolds had no right to speak lightly or contemptuously of imitative art. There is an instinctive consciousness in his own mind of the difference between high and low art; but he is utterly incapable of explaining it, and every effort which he makes to do so involves him in unexpected fallacy and absurdity. It is *not* true that Poetry does not concern herself with minute details. It is *not* true that high art seeks only the Invariable. It is *not* true that imitative art is an easy thing. It is *not* true that the faithful rendering of nature is an employment in which "the slowest intellect is likely to succeed best." All these successive assertions are utterly false and untenable, while the plain truth, a truth lying at the very door, has all the while escaped him,—that which was incidentally stated in the preceding chapter,—namely, that the difference between great and mean art lies, not in definable methods of handling, or styles of representation, or choices of subjects, but wholly in the nobleness of the end to which the effort of the painter is addressed. We cannot say that a painter is great because he paints boldly, or paints delicately; because he generalizes or particularizes; because he loves detail, or because he disdains it. He is great if, by any of these means, he has laid open noble truths, or aroused noble emotions. It does not matter whether he paint the petal of a rose, or the chasms of a precipice, so that Love and Admiration attend him as he labours, and wait for ever upon his work. It does not matter whether he toil for months upon a few inches of his canvas, or cover a palace front with colour in a day, so only that it be with a solemn purpose that he has filled his heart with patience, or urged his hand to haste. And it does not matter whether he seek for his subjects among peasants or nobles, among the heroic or the simple, in courts or in fields, so only

that he behold all things with a thirst for beauty, and a hatred of mean-   43
ness and vice. So that true criticism of art never can consist in the mere
application of rules; it can be just only when it is founded on quick sympathy with the innumerable instincts and changeful efforts of human
nature, chastened and guided by unchanging love of all things that God
has created to be beautiful, and pronounced to be good.

CHAPTER III

Of the Real Nature of Greatness of Style

47　WE have at all times some instinctive sense that the function of one painter is greater than that of another, even supposing each equally successful in his own way; and we feel that, if it were possible to conquer prejudice, and do away with the iniquities of personal feeling, and the insufficiencies of limited knowledge, we should all agree in this estimate, and be able to place each painter in his right rank, measuring them by a true scale of nobleness. We feel that the men in the higher classes of the scale would be, in the full sense of the word, Great,—men whom one would give much to see the faces of but for an instant; and that those in the lower classes of the scale (though none were admitted but who had true merit of some kind) would be very small men, not greatly exciting either reverence or curiosity. And with this fixed instinct in our minds, we permit our teachers daily to exhort their pupils to the cultivation of "great art,"—neither they nor we having any clear notion as to what the greatness consists in.

48　Let us therefore look into the facts of the thing, not with any metaphysical, or otherwise vain and troublesome effort at acuteness, but in a plain way; for the facts themselves are plain enough, and may be plainly stated, only the difficulty is, that out of these facts, right and left, the different forms of misapprehension branch into grievous complexity, and branch so far and wide, that if once we try to follow them, they will lead us quite from our mark into other separate, though not less interesting discussions. The best way will be, therefore, I think, to sketch out at once in this chapter, the different characters which really constitute "greatness" of style, and to indicate the principal directions of the outbranching misapprehensions of them: then, in the succeeding chapters, to take up in succession those which need more talk about them, and follow out at leisure whatever inquiries they may suggest.

I. CHOICE OF NOBLE SUBJECT.—Greatness of style consists, then: first, in the habitual choice of subjects of thought which involve wide interests
49　and profound passions as opposed to those which involve narrow interests and slight passions. The style is greater or less in exact proportion to the nobleness of the interests and passions involved in the subject. The

habitual choice of sacred subjects, such as the Nativity, Transfiguration, Crucifixion (if the choice be sincere), implies that the painter has a natural disposition to dwell on the highest thoughts of which humanity is capable; it constitutes him so far forth a painter of the highest order, as, for instance, Leonardo, in his painting of the Last Supper: he who delights in representing the acts or meditations of great men, as, for instance, Raphael painting the School of Athens, is, so far forth, a painter of the second order: he who represents the passions and events of ordinary life, of the third. And in this ordinary life, he who represents deep thoughts and sorrows, as, for instance, Hunt, in his Claudio and Isabella, and such other works, is of the highest rank in his sphere; and he who represents the slight malignities and passions of the drawing-room, as, for instance, Leslie,[7] of the second rank; he who represents the sports of boys, or simplicities of clowns, as Webster[8] or Teniers, of the third rank; and he who represents brutalities and vices (for delight in them, and not for rebuke of them), of no rank at all, or rather of a negative rank, holding a certain order in the abyss.

The reader will, I hope, understand how much importance is to be attached to the sentence in the first parenthesis, "if the choice be sincere;" for choice of subject is, of course, only available as a criterion of the rank of the painter, when it is made from the heart. Indeed, in the lower orders of painting, the choice is always made from such a heart as the painter has; for his selection of the brawls of peasants or sports of children can, of course, proceed only from the fact that he has more   50 sympathy with such brawls or pastimes than with nobler subjects. But the choice of the higher kind of subjects is often insincere; and may, therefore, afford no real criterion of the painter's rank. The greater number of men who have lately painted religious or heroic subjects have done so in mere ambition, because they had been taught that it was a good thing to be a "high art" painter; and the fact is that in nine cases out of ten, the so-called historical or "high art" painter is a person infinitely inferior to the painter of flowers or still life. He is, in modern times, nearly always a man who has great vanity without pictorial capacity, and differs from the landscape or fruit painter merely in misunderstanding and over-estimating his own powers. He mistakes his vanity for inspiration, his ambition for greatness of soul, and takes pleasure in what he calls "the ideal," merely because he has neither humility nor capacity enough to comprehend the real.

The choice which characterizes the school of high art is seen as much   51 in the treatment of a subject as in its selection, and the expression of the thoughts of the persons represented will always be the first thing considered by the painter who worthily enters that highest school. For the   52 artist who sincerely chooses the noblest subject will also choose chiefly to represent what makes that subject noble, namely, the various heroism or other noble emotions of the persons represented. If, instead of this, the artist seeks only to make his picture agreeable by the composition of its masses and colours, or by any other merely pictorial merit, as fine drawing of limbs, it is evident, not only that any other subject would have answered his purpose as well, but that he is unfit to approach the subject he has chosen, because he cannot enter into its deepest meaning, and therefore cannot in reality have chosen it for that meaning. Nevertheless, while the expression is always to be the first thing considered, all other merits must be added to the utmost of the painter's power; for until he can both colour and draw beautifully he has no business to consider himself a painter at all, far less to attempt the noblest subjects of painting; and, when he has once possessed himself of these powers, he will naturally and fitly employ them to deepen and perfect the impression made by the sentiment of his subject.

The perfect unison of expression, as the painter's main purpose, with the full and natural exertion of his pictorial power in the details of the work, is found only in the old Pre-Raphaelite periods, and in the modern Pre-Raphaelite school. In the works of Giotto, Angelico, Orcagna, John Bellini, and one or two more, these two conditions of high art are entirely fulfilled, so far as the knowledge of those days enabled them to be fulfilled; and in the modern Pre-Raphaelite school they are fulfilled nearly to the uttermost. Hunt's Light of the World [plate 15], is, I believe, the most perfect instance of expressional purpose with technical power, which the world has yet produced.

53   Now in the Post-Raphaelite period of ancient art, and in the spurious high art of modern times, two broad forms of error divide the schools; the one consisting in (A) the superseding of expression by technical excellence, and the other in (B) the superseding of technical excellence by expression.

55   LOVE OF BEAUTY.—The second characteristic of the great school of art is, that it introduces in the conception of its subject as much beauty as is possible, consistently with truth.

56   For instance, in any subject consisting of a number of figures, it will make as many of those figures beautiful as the faithful representation of humanity will admit. It will not deny the facts of ugliness or decrepitude, or relative inferiority and superiority of feature as necessarily manifested in a crowd, but it will, so far as it is in its power, seek for and dwell upon the fairest forms, and in all things insist on the beauty that is in them, not on the ugliness. In this respect, schools of art become higher in exact proportion to the degree in which they apprehend and love the beautiful. Thus, Angelico, intensely loving all spiritual beauty, will be of the highest rank; and Paul Veronese and Correggio, intensely loving physical and

corporeal beauty, of the second rank; and Albert Dürer, Rubens, and in general the Northern artists, apparently insensible to beauty, and caring only for truth, whether shapely or not, of the third rank; and Teniers and Salvator, Caravaggio, and other such worshippers of the depraved, of no rank, or as we said before, of a certain order in the abyss.

The corruption of the schools of high art, so far as this particular quality   57
is concerned, consists in the sacrifice of truth to beauty. Great art dwells on all that is beautiful; but false art omits or changes all that is ugly. Great art accepts Nature as she is, but directs the eyes and thoughts to what is most perfect in her; false art saves itself the trouble of direction by removing or altering whatever it thinks objectionable. The evil results of which proceeding are twofold.

First. That beauty deprived of its proper foils and adjuncts ceases to be enjoyed as beauty, just as light deprived of all shadow ceases to be enjoyed as light. A white canvas cannot produce an effect of sunshine; the painter must darken it in some places before he can make it look luminous in others; nor can an uninterrupted succession of beauty produce the true effect of beauty; it must be foiled by inferiority before its own power can be developed. Nature has for the most part mingled her inferior and noble elements as she mingles sunshine with shade, giving due use and influence to both, and the painter who chooses to remove the shadow, perishes in the burning desert he has created. The truly high and beautiful art of Angelico is continually refreshed and strengthened by his frank portraiture of the most ordinary features of his brother monks and of the recorded peculiarities of ungainly sanctity; but the modern German and Raphaelesque schools lose all honour and nobleness in barber-like admiration of handsome faces, and have, in fact, no real faith except in straight noses, and curled hair. Paul Veronese opposes the dwarf to the soldier, and the negress to the queen [plate 16]; Shakspeare places Caliban beside Miranda, and Autolycus beside Perdita; but the vulgar idealist withdraws his beauty to the safety of the saloon, and his innocence to the seclusion of the cloister; he pretends that he does this in delicacy of choice and purity of sentiment, while in truth he has neither courage   58
to front the monster, nor wit enough to furnish the knave.

It is only by the habit of representing faithfully all things, that we can truly learn what is beautiful, and what is not. The ugliest objects contain some element of beauty; and in all it is an element peculiar to themselves, which cannot be separated from their ugliness, but must either be enjoyed together with it or not at all. The more a painter accepts nature as he finds it, the more unexpected beauty he discovers in what he at first despised; but once let him arrogate the right of rejection, and he will gradually contract his circle of enjoyment, until what he supposed to be nobleness of selection ends in narrowness of perception. Dwelling perpetually upon one class of ideas, his art becomes at once monstrous and morbid; until at last he cannot faithfully represent even what he chooses to retain; his discrimination contracts into darkness, and his fastidiousness fades into fatuity.

High art, therefore, consists neither in altering, nor in improving nature; but in seeking throughout nature for "whatsoever things are lovely, and whatsoever things are pure";[9] in loving these, in displaying to the utmost of the painter's power such loveliness as is in them, and directing the thoughts of others to them by winning art or gentle emphasis. Of the degree in which this can be done, and in which it may be permitted to gather together, without falsifying, the finest forms or thoughts, so as to create a sort of perfect vision, we shall have to speak hereafter.

59   III. SINCERITY.—The next characteristic of great art is that it includes the largest possible quantity of Truth in the most perfect possible harmony. If it were possible for art to give all the truths of nature it ought to do it. But this is not possible. Choice must always be made of some facts which *can* be represented, from among others which must be passed by in silence, or even, in some respects, misrepresented. The inferior artist chooses unimportant and scattered truths; the great artist chooses the most necessary first, and afterwards the most consistent with these, so as to obtain the greatest possible and most harmonious *sum*. For instance, Rembrandt always chooses to represent the exact force with which light on the most illumined part of an object is opposed to its obscurer portions. In order to obtain this, in most cases, not very important truth, he sacrifices the light and colour of five-sixths of his picture, and the expression of every character of objects which depends on tenderness of shape or tint. But he obtains his single truth, and what picturesque and forcible expression is dependent upon it, with magnificent skill and subtlety. Veronese, on the contrary, chooses to represent the great relations of visible things to each other, to the heaven above, and to the earth beneath them. He holds it more important to show how a figure stands relieved from delicate air, or marble wall; how as a red, or purple, or white figure, it separates itself, in clear discernibility, from things not red, nor purple, nor white; how infinite daylight shines round it; how innumerable veils of faint shadow invest it; how its blackness and darkness are, in the excess of their nature, just as limited and local as its intensity of light; all this, I say, he feels to be more important than showing merely the exact *measure* of the spark of sunshine that gleams on a dagger-hilt, or glows on a jewel. All this, moreover, he feels to be harmonious,—capable of being joined in one great system of spacious truth. And with inevitable watchfulness, inestimable subtlety, he unites all this in tenderest balance,

60   noting in each hair's-breadth of colour, not merely what its rightness or

wrongness is in itself, but what its relation is to every other on his canvas; restraining, for truth's sake, his exhaustless energy, reining back, for truth's sake, his fiery strength; veiling, before truth, the vanity of brightness; penetrating, for truth, the discouragement of gloom; ruling his restless invention with a rod of iron; pardoning no error, no thoughtlessness, no forgetfulness; and subduing all his powers, impulses, and imaginations, to the arbitrament of a merciless justice, and the obedience of an incorruptible verity.

It follows from this principle, that in general all *great* drawing is *distinct* drawing; for truths which are rendered indistinctly might, for the most part, as well not be rendered at all. There are, indeed, certain facts of mystery, and facts of indistinctness, in all objects, which must have their proper place in the general harmony. We may, however, understand this apparent contradiction, by reflecting that the highest knowledge always involves a more advanced perception of the fields of the unknown; and, therefore, it may most truly be said, that to know anything well involves a profound sensation of ignorance, while yet it is equally true that good and noble knowledge is distinguished from vain and useless knowledge chiefly by its clearness and distinctness, and by the vigorous consciousness of what is known and what is not.

So in art. The best drawing involves a wonderful perception and expression of indistinctness; and yet all noble drawing is separated from the ignoble by its distinctness, by its fine expression and firm assertion of   61 *Something*; whereas the bad drawing, without either firmness or fineness, expresses and asserts *Nothing*. The first thing, therefore, to be looked for as a sign of noble art, is a clear consciousness of what is drawn and what is not; the bold statement, and frank confession—"*This* I know," "*that* I know not"; and, generally speaking, all haste, slurring, obscurity, indecision, are signs of low art, and all calmness, distinctness, luminousness, and positiveness, of high art.

It follows, secondly, from this principle, that as the great painter is always attending to the sum and harmony of his truths rather than to one or the other of any group, a quality of Grasp is visible in his work, like the power of a great reasoner over his subject, or a great poet over his conception, manifesting itself very often in missing out certain details or less truths (which, though good in themselves, he finds are in the way of others), and in a sweeping manner of getting the beginnings and ends of things shown at once, and the squares and depths rather than the surfaces; hence, on the whole, a habit of looking at large masses rather than small ones; and even a physical largeness of handling, and love of working, if possible, on a large scale; and various other qualities, more or less imperfectly expressed by such technical terms as breadth, massing, unity, boldness, etc., all of which are, indeed, great qualities, when they mean breadth of truth, weight of truth, unity of truth, and courageous assertion of truth; but which have all their correlative errors and mockeries, almost universally mistaken for them,—the breadth which has no contents, the weight which has no value, the unity which plots deception, and the boldness which faces out fallacy.

And it is to be noted especially respecting largeness of scale, that though for the most part it is characteristic of the more powerful masters, they having both more invention wherewith to fill space (as Ghirlandajo wished that he might paint all the walls of Florence),[10] and, often, an impetuosity of mind which makes them like free play for hand and arm (besides that they usually desire to paint everything in the foreground of their picture of the natural size), yet, as this largeness of scale involves the placing of the picture at a considerable distance from the eye, and this distance involves the loss of many delicate details, and especially of the subtle lines of expression in features, it follows that the masters of refined detail and human expression are apt to prefer a small scale to work upon; so that the chief masterpieces of expression which the world possesses are small pictures by Angelico, in which the figures are rarely more than six or seven inches high; in the best works of Raphael and Leonardo the figures are almost always less than life, and the best works of Turner do not exceed the size of 18 inches by 12.

As its greatness depends on the sum of truth, and this sum of truth can always be increased by delicacy of handling, it follows that all great art must have this delicacy to the utmost possible degree. This rule is infallible and inflexible. All coarse work is the sign of low art. Only, it is to be remembered, that coarseness must be estimated by the distance from the eye; it being necessary to consult this distance, when great, by laying on touches which appear coarse when seen near; but which, so far from being coarse, are, in reality, more delicate in a master's work than the finest close handling, for they involve a calculation of result, and are laid on with a subtlety of sense precisely correspondent to that with which a good archer draws his bow; the spectator seeing in the action nothing but the strain of the strong arm, while there is in reality, in the finger and eye, an ineffably delicate estimate of distance, and touch on the arrow plume. And, indeed, this delicacy is generally quite perceptible to those who know what the truth is, for strokes by Tintoret or Paul Veronese, which were done in an instant, and look to an ignorant spectator merely like a violent dash of loaded colour (and are, as such, imitated by blundering artists), are, in fact, modulated by the brush and finger to that degree of delicacy that no single grain of the colour could be taken from the touch without injury; and little golden particles of it, not the size of a gnat's head, have important share and function in the balances of light in a picture perhaps fifty feet long. Nearly *every* other rule applicable to art has some exception but this. This has absolutely none. All great art is delicate art, and all coarse art is bad art. Nay, even, to a certain extent, all *bold* art is bad art; for boldness is not the proper word to apply to the courage and swiftness of a great master, based on knowledge, and coupled with fear and love. There is as much difference between the boldness of the true and the false masters, as there is between the courage of a sure woman and the shamelessness of a lost one.

IV. INVENTION.—The last characteristic of great art is that it must be inventive, that is, be produced by the imagination. In this respect, it must precisely fulfil the definition already given of poetry; and not only present grounds for noble emotion, but furnish these grounds by *imaginative power*. Hence there is at once a great bar fixed between the two schools of Lower and Higher art. The lower merely copies what is set before it, whether in portrait, landscape, or still-life; the higher either entirely imagines its subject, or arranges the materials presented to it, so as to manifest the imaginative power in all the three phases which have been already explained in the second volume.

And this was the truth which was confusedly present in Reynolds's 64 mind when he spoke, as above quoted, of the difference between Historical and Poetical Painting. *Every relation of the plain facts which the painter saw* is proper *historical* painting. If those facts are unimportant (as that he saw a gambler quarrel with another gambler, or a sot enjoying himself with another sot), then the history is trivial; if the facts are important (as that he saw such and such a great man look thus, or act thus, at such a time), then the history is noble: in each case perfect truth of narrative being supposed, otherwise the whole thing is worthless, being neither history nor poetry, but plain falsehood.

And now, finally, if we glance back to the other qualities required in 65 great art, and put all together, we find that the sum of them is simply the sum of all the powers of man. For as (1) the choice of the high subject involves all conditions of right moral choice, and as (2) the love of beauty involves all conditions of right admiration, and as (3) the grasp of truth 66 involves all strength of sense, evenness of judgment, and honesty of purpose, and as (4) the poetical power involves all swiftness of invention, and accuracy of historical memory, the sum of all these powers is the sum of the human soul. Hence we see why the word "Great" is used of this art. It is literally great. It compasses and calls forth the entire human spirit, whereas any other kind of art, being more or less small or narrow, compasses and calls forth only *part* of the human spirit. Hence the idea of its magnitude is a literal and just one, the art being simply less or greater in proportion to the number of faculties it exercises and addresses. And this is the ultimate meaning of the definition I gave of it long ago, as containing the "greatest number of the greatest ideas."[11]

Such, then, being the characters required in order to constitute high art, if the reader will think over them a little, and over the various ways in which they may be falsely assumed, he will easily perceive how spacious and dangerous a field of discussion they open to the ambitious critic, and of error to the ambitious artist; he will see how difficult it must be, either to distinguish what is truly great art from the mockeries of it, or to rank the real artists in anything like a progressive system of greater and less. For it will have been observed that the various qualities which form greatness are partly inconsistent with each other (as some virtues are, docility and firmness for instance), and partly independent of each other: and the fact is, that artists differ not more by mere capacity, than by the component *elements* of their capacity, each possessing in very different proportions the several attributes of greatness; so that, classed by one kind of merit, as, for instance, purity of expression, Angelico will
67 stand highest; classed by another, sincerity of manner, Veronese will stand highest; classed by another, love of beauty, Leonardo will stand highest; and so on: hence arise continual disputes and misunderstandings among those who think that high art must always be one and the same, and that great artists ought to unite all great attributes in an equal degree.

68   And from these considerations one most important practical corollary is to be deduced, namely, that the greatness or smallness of a man is, in the most conclusive sense, determined for him at his birth, as strictly as it is determined for a fruit whether it is to be a currant or an apricot. Education, favourable circumstances, resolution, and industry can do much; in a certain sense they do *everything*; that is to say, they determine whether the poor apricot shall fall in the form of a green bead, blighted by the east wind, and be trodden under foot, or whether it shall expand into tender pride, and sweet brightness of golden velvet. But apricot out of currant,—great man out of small,—did never yet art or effort make; and, in a general way, men have their excellence nearly fixed for them when they are born; a little cramped and frost-bitten on one side, a little sunburnt and fortune-spotted on the other, they reach, between good and evil chances, such size and taste as generally belong to the men of their calibre, and, the small in their serviceable bunches, the great in their golden isolation, have, these no cause for regret, nor those for disdain.

Therefore it is, that every system of teaching is false which holds forth "great art" as in any wise to be taught to students, or even to be aimed at
69 by them. Great art is precisely that which never was, nor will be taught, it is pre-eminently and finally the expression of the spirits of great men; so that the only wholesome teaching is that which simply endeavours to fix those characters of nobleness in the pupil's mind, of which it seems easily susceptible; and without holding out to him, as a possible or even probable

result, that he should ever paint like Titian, or carve like Michael Angelo, enforces upon him the manifest possibility, and assured duty, of endeavouring to draw in a manner at least honest and intelligible; and cultivates in him those general charities of heart, sincerities of thought, and graces of habit which are likely to lead him, throughout life, to prefer openness to affectation, realities to shadows, and beauty to corruption.

CHAPTER IV
Of the False Ideal:—First, Religious

70   THE pursuit, by the imagination, of beautiful and strange thoughts or subjects, to the exclusion of painful or common ones, is called among us, in these modern days, the pursuit of "*the ideal*"; nor does any subject deserve more attentive examination than the manner in which this pursuit is entered upon by the modern mind. The reader must pardon me for making in the outset one or two statements which may appear to him somewhat wide of the matter, but which, (if he admits their truth,) he will, I think, presently perceive to reach to the root of it. Namely,

That men's proper business in this world falls mainly into three divisions:

71   First, to know themselves, and the existing state of the things they have to do with.

Secondly, to be happy in themselves, and in the existing state of things.

Thirdly, to mend themselves, and the existing state of things, as far as either are marred and mendable.

These, I say, are the three plain divisions of proper human business on this earth. For these three, the following are usually substituted and adopted by human creatures:

First, to be totally ignorant of themselves, and the existing state of things.

Secondly, to be miserable in themselves, and in the existing state of things.

Thirdly, to let themselves, and the existing state of things, alone (at least, in the way of correction).

The dispositions which induce us to manage, thus wisely, the affairs of this life seem to be:

First, a fear of disagreeable facts, and conscious shrinking from clearness of light, which keep us from examining ourselves, and increase gradually into a species of instinctive terror at all truth, and love of glosses, veils, and decorative lies of every sort.

Secondly, a general readiness to take delight in anything past, future, far off, or somewhere else, rather than in things now, near, and here; leading us gradually to place our pleasure principally in the exercise of the imagination, and to build all our satisfaction on things as they are *not*. Which power being one not accorded to the lower animals, and having indeed, when disciplined, a very noble use, we pride ourselves upon it, whether disciplined or not, and pass our lives complacently, in substantial discontent, and visionary satisfaction.

Now *nearly* all artistical and poetical seeking after the ideal is only one branch of this base habit—the abuse of the imagination in allowing it to find its whole delight in the impossible and untrue; while the faithful pursuit of the ideal is an honest use of the imagination, giving full power   72 and presence to the possible and true.

It is the difference between these two uses of it which we have to examine.

And, first, consider what are the legitimate uses of the imagination, that is to say, of the power of perceiving, or conceiving with the mind, things which cannot be perceived by the senses.

Its first and noblest use is, to enable us to bring sensibly to our sight the things which are recorded as belonging to our future state, or as invisibly surrounding us in this. Its second and ordinary use is to empower us to traverse the scenes of all other history, and force the facts to become again visible, so as to make upon us the same impression which they would have made if we had witnessed them; and in the minor necessities of life, to enable us, out of any present good, to gather the utmost measure of enjoyment by investing it with happy associations, and, in any present evil, to lighten it, by summoning back the images of other hours; and,   73 also, to give to all mental truths some visible type in allegory, simile, or personification, which shall more deeply enforce them; and finally, when the mind is utterly outwearied, to refresh it with such innocent play as shall be most in harmony with the suggestive voices of natural things, permitting it to possess living companionship instead of silent beauty, and create for itself fairies in the grass and naiads in the wave.

These being the uses of imagination, its abuses are either in creating, for mere pleasure, false images, where it is its *duty* to create true ones; or in turning what was intended for the mere refreshment of the heart into its daily food, and changing the innocent pastime of an hour into the guilty occupation of a life.

Let us examine the principal forms of this misuse, one by one.

First, then, the imagination is chiefly warped and dishonoured by being allowed to create false images, where it is its duty to create true ones. And this most dangerously in matters of religion. For a long time when art was in its infancy, it remained unexposed to this danger, because it could not, with any power, realize or create *any* thing. Such art excited the imagination, while it pleased the eye. But it *asserted* nothing, for it could realize nothing. The reader glanced at it as a glittering symbol, and went on to form truer images for himself.

74 But as soon as art obtained the power of realization, it obtained also that of *assertion*. As fast as the painter advanced in skill he gained also in credibility, and that which he perfectly represented was perfectly believed, or could be disbelieved only by an actual effort of the beholder to escape from the fascinating deception. What had been faintly declared, might be painlessly denied; but it was difficult to discredit things forcibly alleged; and representations, which had been innocent in discrepancy, became guilty in consistency.

For instance, when in the thirteenth century, the Nativity was habitually represented by such a symbol as that on this page, [fig.36], there was not the smallest possibility that such a picture could disturb, in the mind of the reader of the New Testament, the simple meaning of the words[12] "wrapped Him in swaddling clothes, and laid Him in a manger." That this manger was typified by a trefoil arch would no more prevent his distinct understanding of the narrative, than the grotesque heads introduced above it would interfere with his firm comprehension of the words "ox" or "ass"; while if there were anything in the action of the principal figures suggestive of

fig.36

75 real feeling, that suggestion he would accept, together with the general pleasantness of the lines and colours in the decorative letter; but without having his faith in the unrepresented and actual scene obscured for a moment. But it was far otherwise when Francia or Perugino, with exquisite power of representing the human form, and high knowledge of the mysteries of art, devoted all their skill to the delineation of an impossible scene; and painted, for their subjects of the Nativity, a beautiful and queenly lady, her dress

embroidered with gold, and with a crown of jewels upon her hair, kneeling, on a floor of inlaid and precious marble, before a crowned child, laid under a portico of Lombardic* architecture; with a sweet, verdurous, and vivid landscape in the distance, full of winding rivers, village spires, and baronial towers. It is quite true that the frank absurdity of the thought prevented its being received as a deliberate contradiction of the truths of Scripture; but it is no less certain, that the continual presentment to the mind of this beautiful and fully realized imagery more and more chilled its power of apprehending the real truth; and that when pictures of this description met the eye in every corner of every chapel, it was physically impossible to dwell distinctly upon facts the direct reverse of those represented. The word "Virgin" or "Madonna," instead of calling up the vision of a simple Jewish girl, bearing the calamities of poverty, and the dishonours of inferior station, summoned instantly the idea of a graceful princess, crowned with gems, and surrounded by obsequious ministry of kings and saints. The fallacy which was presented to the imagination was indeed discredited, but also the fact which was *not* presented to the imagination was forgotten; all true grounds of faith were gradually undermined, and the beholder was either enticed into mere luxury of fanciful enjoyment, believing nothing; or left, in his confusion of mind, the prey of vain tales and traditions; while in his best feelings he was unconsciously subject to the power of the fallacious picture, and, with no sense of the real cause of his error, bowed himself, in prayer or adoration, to the lovely lady on her golden throne, when he would never have dreamed of doing so to the Jewish girl in her outcast poverty, or, in her simple household, to the carpenter's wife.

76

But a shadow of increasing darkness fell upon the human mind as art proceeded to still more perfect realization. These fantasies of the earlier painters, though they darkened faith, never hardened *feeling*; on the contrary, the frankness of their unlikelihood proceeded mainly from the endeavour on the part of the painter to express, not the actual fact, but the enthusiastic state of his own feelings about the fact; he covers the Virgin's dress with gold, not with any idea of representing the Virgin as she ever was, or ever will be seen, but with a burning desire to show what his love and reverence would think fittest for her. He erects for the stable a Lombardic portico, not because he supposes the Lombardi to have built stables in Palestine in the days of Tiberius, but to show that the manger in which Christ was laid is, in his eyes, nobler than the greatest

---

*Lombardic, i.e. in the style of Pietro and Tullio Lombardo, in the fifteenth century (not *Lombard*).

architecture in the world. He fills his landscape with church spires and silver streams, not because he supposes that either were in sight at Bethlehem, but to remind the beholder of the peaceful course and succeeding power of Christianity. And, regarded with due sympathy and clear understanding of these thoughts of the artist, such pictures remain most impressive and touching, even to this day. I shall refer to them in future, in general terms, as the pictures of the "Angelican Ideal"—Angelico being the central master of the school.

It was far otherwise in the next step of the Realistic progress. The greater his powers became, the more the mind of the painter was absorbed in their attainment, and complacent in their display. The early arts of laying on bright colours smoothly, of burnishing golden ornaments, or tracing, leaf by leaf, the outlines of flowers, were not so difficult as that they should materially occupy the thoughts of the artist, or furnish foundation for his conceit; he learned these rudiments of his work without pain, and employed them without pride, his spirit being left free to express, so far as it was capable of them, the reaches of higher thought. But when accurate shade, and subtle colour, and perfect anatomy, and complicated perspective, became necessary to the work, the artist's whole energy was employed in learning the laws of these, and his whole pleasure consisted in exhibiting them. His life was devoted, not to the objects of art, but to the cunning of it; and the sciences of composition and light and shade were pursued as if there were abstract good in them:—as if, like astronomy or mathematics, they were ends in themselves, irrespective of anything to be effected by them. And without perception, on the part of any one, of the abyss to which all were hastening, a fatal change of aim took place throughout the whole world of art. In early times *art was employed for the display of religious facts*; now, *religious facts were employed for the display of art*. The transition, though imperceptible, was consummate; it involved the entire destiny of painting. It was passing from the paths of life to the paths of death.

And this change was all the more fatal, because at first veiled by an appearance of greater dignity and sincerity than were possessed by the older art. One of the earliest results of the new knowledge was the putting away the greater part of the *unlikelihoods* and fineries of the ancient pictures, and an apparently closer following of nature and probability. All the fantasy which I have just been blaming as disturbant of the simplicity of faith, was first subdued—then despised and cast aside.

Was not this, then, a healthy change? No. It *would* have been healthy if it had been effected with a pure motive, and the new truths would have been precious if they had been sought for truth's sake. But they were not sought for truth's sake, but for pride's; and truth which is sought for display may be just as harmful as truth which is spoken in malice. The glittering childishness of the old art was rejected, not because it was false, but because it was easy; and, still more, because the painter had no longer any religious passion to express. He could think of the Madonna now very calmly, with no desire to pour out the treasures of earth at her feet, or crown her brows with the golden shafts of heaven. He could think of her as an available subject for the display of transparent shadows, skilful tints, and scientific foreshortenings,—as a fair woman, forming, if well painted, a pleasant piece of furniture for the corner of a boudoir, and best imagined by combination of the beauties of the prettiest contadinas. He could think of her, in her last maternal agony, with academical discrimination; sketch in first her skeleton, invest her, in serene science, with the muscles of misery and the fibres of sorrow; then cast the grace of antique drapery over the nakedness of her desolation, and fulfil, with studious lustre of tears and delicately painted pallor, the perfect type of the "Mater Dolorosa."

It was thus that Raphael thought of the Madonna.

Now observe, when the subject was thus scientifically completed, it   79
became necessary, as we have just said, to the full display of all the power of the artist, that it should in many respects be more faithfully imagined than it had been hitherto. "Keeping,"[13] "Expression," "Historical Unity," and such other requirements, were enforced on the painter, in the same tone, and with the same purpose, as the purity of his oil and the accuracy of his perspective. He was told that the figure of Christ should be "dignified," those of the Apostles "expressive," that of the Virgin "modest," and those of children "innocent." All this was perfectly true; and in obedience to such directions, the painter proceeded to manufacture certain arrangements of apostolic sublimity, virginal mildness, and infantine innocence, which, being free from the quaint imperfection and contradictoriness of the early art, were looked upon by the European public as true things, and trustworthy representations of the events of religious history. The pictures of Francia and Bellini had been received as pleasant visions. But the cartoons of Raphael were received as representations of historical fact.

Now, neither they, nor any other work of the period, were representations either of historical or of possible fact. They were, in the strictest sense of the word, "compositions,"—cold arrangements of propriety and agreeableness, according to academical formulas, the painter never in any case making the slightest effort to conceive the thing as it really must have happened, but only to gather together graceful lines and beautiful faces, in such compliance with commonplace ideas of the subject as might obtain for the whole an "epic unity," or some such other form of scholastic perfectness.

Take a very important instance.

I suppose there is no event in the whole life of Christ, to which, in hours   80 of doubt or fear, men turn with more anxious thirst to know the close facts of it, or with more earnest and passionate dwelling upon every syllable of its recorded narrative, than Christ's showing Himself to His disciples at the lake of Galilee. There is something pre-eminently open, natural, full fronting our disbelief, in this manifestation. The others, recorded after the resurrection, were sudden, phantom-like, occurring to men in profound sorrow and wearied agitation of heart; not, it might seem, safe judges of what they saw. But the agitation was now over. They had gone back to their daily work, thinking still their business lay net-wards, unmeshed from the literal rope and drag. "Simon Peter saith unto them, 'I go a fishing.' They say unto him, 'We also go with thee.'" True words enough, and having far echo beyond those Galilean hills. That night they caught nothing; but when the morning came, in the clear light of it, behold, a figure stood on the shore. They were not thinking of anything but their fruitless hauls. They had no guess who it was. It asked them simply if they had caught anything. They said No; and it tells them to cast yet again. And John shades his eyes from the morning sun with his hand, to look who it is; and though the glinting of the sea, too, dazzles, him, he makes out who it is, at last; and poor Simon, not to be outrun this time, tightens his fisher's coat about him, and dashes in, over the nets. One would have liked to see him swim those hundred yards, and stagger to his knees on the beach.

Well, the others get to the beach, too, in time, in such slow way as men in general do get, in this world, to its true shore, much impeded by that wonderful "dragging the net with fishes"; but they get there—seven of them in all;—first the Denier, and then the slowest believer, and then the quickest believer, and then the two throne-seekers, and two more, we know not who.

81   They sit down on the shore face to face with Him, and eat their broiled fish as He bids. And then, to Peter, all dripping still, shivering and amazed, staring at Christ in the sun, on the other side of the coal fire,— thinking a little, perhaps, of what happened by another coal fire, when it was colder, and having had no word once changed with him by his Master since that look of His,—to him, so amazed, comes the question, "Simon, lovest thou Me?" Try to feel that a little, and think of it till it is true to you: and then, take up that infinite monstrosity and hypocrisy—Raphael's cartoon of the Charge to Peter [fig.37]. Note, first, the bold fallacy—the putting *all* the Apostles there, a mere lie to serve the Papal heresy of the Petric supremacy, by putting them all in the background while Peter receives the charge, and making them all witnesses to it. Note the handsomely curled hair and neatly tied sandals of the men who had been out all night in the sea-mists and on the slimy decks. Note their convenient dresses for going a-fishing, with trains that lie a yard along the ground,

fig.37   Raphael, *The Charge to Peter*

and goodly fringes,—all made to match, an apostolic fishing costume. Note how Peter especially (whose chief glory was in his wet coat *girt* about him, and naked limbs) is enveloped in folds and fringes, so as to kneel and hold his keys with grace. No fire of coals at all, nor lonely mountain shore, but a pleasant Italian landscape, full of villas and churches, and a flock of sheep to be pointed at; and the whole group of Apostles, not round Christ, as they would have been naturally, but straggling away in a line, that they may all be shown.

The simple truth is, that the moment we look at the picture we feel our belief of the whole thing taken away. There is, visibly, no possibility of that group ever having existed, in any place, or on any occasion. It is all a mere mythic absurdity, and faded concoction of fringes, muscular arms, and curly heads of Greek philosophers. 82

Now, the evil consequences of the acceptance of this kind of religious idealism for true, were instant and manifold. So far as it was received and trusted in by thoughtful persons, it only served to chill all the conceptions of sacred history which they might otherwise have obtained. Whatever they could have fancied for themselves about the wild, strange, infinitely stern, infinitely tender, infinitely varied veracities of the life of Christ, was blotted out by the vapid fineries of Raphael: the rough Galilean pilot, the orderly custom receiver, and all the questioning wonder and fire of uneducated apostleship, were obscured under an antique mask of philosophical faces and long robes.

Now, no vigorously minded religious person could possibly receive pleasure or help from such art as this; and the necessary result was the instant rejection of it by the healthy religion of the world. Raphael ministered, with applause, to the impious luxury of the Vatican, but was trampled under foot at once by every believing and advancing Christian of his own and subsequent times; and thenceforward pure Christianity and "high art" took separate roads, and fared on, as best they might, independently of each other.

Has there, then (the reader asks emphatically), been *no* true religious ideal? Has religious art never been of any service to mankind? I fear, on the whole, not. Of true religious ideal, representing events historically recorded, with solemn effort at a sincere and unartificial conception, there exist, as yet, hardly any examples. Nearly all good religious pictures fall into one or other branch of the false ideal already examined, either into the Angelican (passionate ideal) or the Raphaelesque (philosophical ideal). But there is one true form of religious art, nevertheless, in the pictures of the passionate ideal which represent imaginary beings of another world. All the paradises imagined by the religious painters—the choirs of glorified saints, angels, and spiritual powers, when painted with full belief in this possibility of their existence, are true ideals; and so far from our having dwelt on these too much, I believe, rather, we have not trusted them enough, nor accepted them enough, as possible statements of most precious truth.

For the rest, there is a reality of conception in some of the works of Benozzo Gozzoli, Ghirlandajo, and Giotto, which approaches to a true ideal, even of recorded facts. But my impression is, up to the present moment, that the best religious art has been *hitherto* rather a fruit, and attendant sign, of sincere Christianity than a promoter of or help to it. More, I think, has always been done for God by few words than many pictures, and more by few acts than many words.

I must not, however, quit the subject without insisting on the chief practical consequence of what we have observed, namely, that sacred art, so far from being exhausted, has yet to attain the development of its highest branches; and the task, or privilege, yet remains for mankind, to produce an art which shall be at once entirely skilful and entirely *sincere*. All the histories of the Bible are, in my judgment, yet waiting to be painted. Moses has never been painted; Elijah never; David never (except as a mere ruddy stripling); Deborah never; Gideon never; Isaiah never. What single example does the reader remember of painting which suggested so much as the faintest shadow of these people, or of their deeds? Let him meditate over the matter, and he will find ultimately that what I say is true, and that religious art, at once complete and sincere, never yet has existed.

It will exist; nay, I believe the era of its birth has come, and that those bright Turnerian imageries, which the European public declared to be "dotage," and those calm Pre-Raphaelite studies which, in like manner, it pronounced "puerility," form the first foundation that has been ever laid for true sacred art. But, be it as it may, if we would cherish the hope that sacred art may, indeed, arise for *us*, two separate cautions are to be addressed to the two opposed classes of religionists whose influence will   88 chiefly retard that hope's accomplishment. The group calling themselves Evangelical ought no longer to render their religion an offence to men of the world by associating it only with the most vulgar forms of art.

The opposite class of men, whose natural instincts lead them to mingle the refinements of art with all the offices and practices of religion, are to be warned, on the contrary, how they mistake their enjoyments for their duties, or confound poetry with faith. And for us all there is in this matter   89 even a deeper danger than that of indulgence. There is the danger of Artistical Pharisaism. Of all the forms of pride and vanity, as there are none more subtle, so I believe there are none more sinful, than those which are manifested by the Pharisees of art. To be proud of birth, of place, of wit, of bodily beauty, is comparatively innocent, just because such pride is more natural, and more easily detected. But to be proud of our sanctities; to pour contempt upon our fellows, because, forsooth, we like to look at Madonnas in bowers of roses, better than at plain pictures of plain things; and to make this religious art of ours the expression of our own perpetual self-complacency,—congratulating ourselves, day by day, on our purities, proprieties, elevations, and inspirations, as above the reach of common mortals,—this I believe to be one of the wickedest and foolishest forms of human egotism; and, truly, I had rather, with great, thoughtless, humble Paul Veronese, make the Supper at Emmaus a background for two children playing with a dog[14] (as, God knows, men do   90 usually put it in the background to everything, if not out of sight altogether), than join that school of modern Germanism[15] which wears its pieties for decoration as women wear their diamonds, and spreads the dry fleeces of its sanctities between its dust and the dew of heaven.

CHAPTER V
Of the False Ideal:—Secondly, Profane

91   I SAID just now that we might be tempted to consider how this pursuit of the ideal *affected* profane art. Strictly speaking, it brought that art into existence. As long as men sought for truth first, and beauty secondarily, they cared chiefly, of course, for the *chief* truth, and all art was instinctively religious. But as soon as they sought for beauty first, and truth secondarily, they were punished by losing sight of spiritual truth altogether, and the profane (properly so called) schools of art were instantly developed.

92   Little thinking this, they gave themselves up fearlessly to the chase of the new delight, and exhausted themselves in the pursuit of an ideal now doubly false. Formerly, though they attempted to reach an unnatural beauty, it was yet in representing historical facts and real persons; *now* they sought for the same unnatural beauty in representing tales which they knew to be fictitious, and personages who, they knew, had never existed. Such a state of things had never before been found in any nation. Every people till then had painted the acts of their kings, the triumphs of their armies, the beauty of their race, or the glory of their gods. They showed the things they had seen or done; the beings they truly loved or faithfully adored. But the ideal art of modern Europe was the shadow of a shadow; and, with mechanism substituted for perception, and bodily beauty for spiritual life, it set itself to represent men it had never seen,

93   customs it had never practised, and gods in whom it had never believed.

We find, then, at the close of the sixteenth century, the arts of painting and sculpture wholly devoted to entertain the indolent and satiate the luxurious.

94   Meanwhile, the art of sculpture, less capable of ministering to mere amusement, was more or less reserved for the affectations of taste. It is a matter of extreme difficulty to explain the exact character of this modern sculpturesque ideal; but its relation to the true ideal may be best understood by considering it as in exact parallelism with the relation of the word "taste" to the word "love." Wherever the word "taste" is used with respect to matters of art, it indicates either that the thing spoken of

belongs to some inferior class of objects, or that the person speaking has
a false conception of its nature. For, consider the exact sense in which a
work of art is said to be "in good or bad taste." It does not mean that it
is true or false; that it is beautiful or ugly: but that it does or does not
comply either with the laws of choice, which are enforced by certain
modes of life, or the habits of mind produced by a particular sort of
education. It does not mean merely fashionable, that is, complying with
a momentary caprice of the upper classes; but it means agreeing with the
habitual sense which the most refined education, common to those upper
classes at the period, gives to their whole mind. Now, therefore, so far as
that education does indeed tend to make the senses delicate, and the
perceptions accurate, and thus enables people to be pleased with quiet   95
instead of gaudy colour, and with graceful instead of coarse form; and, by
long acquaintance with the best things, to discern quickly what is fine
from what is common;—so far, acquired taste is an honourable faculty, and
it is true praise of anything to say it is "in good taste." But so far as this
higher education has a tendency to narrow the sympathies and harden the
heart, diminishing the interest of all beautiful things by familiarity, until
even what is best can hardly please, and what is brightest hardly
entertain;—so far as it fosters pride, and leads men to found the pleasure
they take in anything, not on the worthiness of the thing, but on the
degree in which it indicates some greatness of their own;—so far as it leads
people to prefer gracefulness of dress, manner, and aspect, to value of
substance and heart, liking a well *said* thing better than a true thing, and
a well-trained manner better than a sincere one, and a delicately formed
face better than a good-natured one, and in all other ways and things
setting custom and semblance above everlasting truth;—so far, finally, as
it induces a sense of inherent distinction between class and class, and
causes everything to be more or less despised which has no social rank, so
that the affection, pleasure, and grief of a clown are looked upon as of no
interest compared with the affection and grief of a well-bred man;—just so   96
far, in all these several ways, the feeling induced by what is called a
"liberal education" is utterly adverse to the understanding of noble art;
and the name which is given to the feeling,—Taste, Goût, Gusto,—in all
languages indicates the baseness of it, for it implies that art gives only a
kind of pleasure analogous to that derived from eating by the palate.

Modern education, not in art only, but in all other things referable to
the same standard, has invariably given taste in this bad sense; it has given
fastidiousness of choice without judgment, superciliousness of manner
without dignity, refinement of habit without purity, grace of expression
without sincerity, and desire of loveliness without love; and the modern
"ideal" of high art is a curious mingling of the gracefulness and reserve of
the drawing-room with a certain measure of classical sensuality. It seems   97

to me a subject of the very deepest interest to determine what has been the effect upon the European nations of the great change by which art became again capable of ministering delicately to the lower passions, as it had in the worst days of Rome; how far, indeed, in all ages, the fall of nations may be attributed to art's arriving at this particular stage among them.

98   I cannot, however, pursue this inquiry here. For our present purpose it is enough to note that the feeling, in itself so debased, branches upwards into that of which, while no one has cause to be ashamed, no one, on the other hand, has cause to be proud, namely, the admiration of physical beauty in the human form as distinguished from expression of character.

99   But even this vulgar pursuit of physical beauty (vulgar in the profoundest sense, for there is no vulgarity like the vulgarity of education) would be less contemptible if it really succeeded in its object; but, like all pursuits carried to inordinate lengths, it defeats itself. Physical beauty *is* a noble thing when it is seen in perfectness; but the manner in which the moderns pursue their ideal prevents their ever really seeing what they are always seeking; for, requiring that all forms should be regular and faultless, they permit, or even compel, their painters and sculptors to work chiefly by rule, altering their models to fit their preconceived notions of what is right. When such artists look at a face, they do not give it the attention necessary to discern what beauty is already in its peculiar features; but only to see how best it may be altered into something for which they have themselves laid down the laws. Nature never unveils her beauty to such a gaze. She keeps whatever she has done best, close sealed, until it is regarded with reverence. To the painter who honours her, she will open a revelation in the face of a street mendicant; but in the work of a painter who alters her, she will make Portia become ignoble, and Perdita graceless.

CHAPTER VI
Of the True Ideal:—First, Purist

HITHERTO we have spoken as if every change wilfully wrought by the 102 imagination was an error; apparently implying that its only proper work was to summon up the memories of past events, and the anticipations of future ones, under aspects which would bear the sternest tests of historical investigation, or abstract reasoning. And in general this is, indeed, its noblest work. Nevertheless, it has also permissible functions peculiarly its own, and certain rights of feigning, adorning, and fancifully arranging, inalienable from its nature.

(A.) It was noted in speaking above of the Angelican or passionate ideal, that there was a certain virtue in it dependent on the expression of its loving enthusiasm.

(B.) In speaking of the pursuit of beauty as one of the characteristics of the highest art, it was also said that there were certain ways of showing this beauty by gathering together, without altering, the finest forms, and marking them by gentle emphasis.

(C.) And in speaking of the true uses of imagination, it was said, that we 103 might be allowed to create for ourselves, in innocent play, fairies and naiads, and other such fictitious creatures.

Now this loving enthusiasm, which seeks for a beauty fit to be the object of eternal love; this inventive skill, which kindly displays what exists around us in the world; and this playful energy of thought which delights in various conditions of the impossible, are three forms of idealism more or less connected with the three tendencies of the artistical mind which I had occasion to explain in the chapter on the Nature of Gothic, in the *Stones of Venice*. It was there pointed out, that, the things around us containing mixed good and evil, certain men chose the good and left the evil (thence properly called Purists); others received both good and evil together (thence properly called Naturalists); and others had a tendency to choose the evil and leave the good, whom, for convenience' sake, I termed Sensualists. I do not mean to say that painters of fairies and naiads must belong to this last and lowest class, or habitually choose the evil and leave the good; but there is, nevertheless a strange connection between the reinless play of the imagination, and a sense of the presence of evil, which is usually more or less developed in those creations of the imagination to which we properly attach the word *Grotesque*.

For this reason, we shall find it convenient to arrange what we have to note respecting true idealism under the three heads—

    A. Purist Idealism.
    B. Naturalist Idealism.
    C. Grotesque Idealism.

    A. Purist Idealism.—It results from the unwillingness of men whose dispositions are more than ordinarily tender and holy, to contemplate the

104   various forms of definite evil which necessarily occur in the daily aspects of the world around them. They shrink from them as from pollution, and endeavour to create for themselves an imaginary state, in which pain and imperfection either do not exist, or exist in some edgeless and enfeebled condition.

As, however, pain and imperfection are, by eternal laws, bound up with existence, so far as it is visible to us, the endeavour to cast them away invariably indicates a comparative childishness of mind, and produces a childish form of art. In general, the effort is more successful when it is most naïve, and when the ignorance of the draughtsman is in some frank proportion to his innocence. It is, however, evident, at the first thought, that all representations of nature without evil must either be ideals of a future world, or be false ideals, if they are understood to be representations of facts. They can only be classed among the branches of the true ideal, in so far as they are understood to be nothing more than expressions of the painter's personal affections or hopes.

Let us take one or two instances in order clearly to explain our meaning.

The life of Angelico was almost entirely spent in the endeavour to imagine the beings belonging to another world. By purity of life, habitual elevation of thought, and natural sweetness of disposition, he was enabled to express the sacred affections upon the human countenance as no one ever did before or since. In order to effect clearer distinction between heavenly beings and those of this world, he represents the former as

105   clothed in draperies of the purest colour, crowned with glories of burnished gold, and entirely shadowless. With exquisite choice of gesture, and disposition of folds of drapery, this mode of treatment gives, perhaps, the best idea of spiritual beings which the human mind is capable of forming. It is, therefore, a true ideal; but the mode in which it is arrived at (being so far mechanical and contradictory of the appearances of nature) necessarily precludes those who practise it from being complete masters of their art. It is always childish, but beautiful in its childishness.

But the perfect truth will at last vindicate itself against the partial truth; the help which we can gain from the unsubstantial vision will be only like that which we may sometimes receive, in weariness, from the scent of a flower or the passing of a breeze. For all firm aid, and steady use, we must look to harder realities; and as far as the painter himself is regarded, we can 106 only receive such work as the sign of an amiable imbecility. It is indeed ideal; but ideal as a fair dream is in the dawn of morning, before the faculties are astir.

But, on the other hand, it is to be noted that entire scorn of this purist 108 ideal is the sign of a far greater weakness. Multitudes of petty artists, incapable of any noble sensation whatever, but acquainted, in a dim way, with the technicalities of the schools, mock at the art whose depths they cannot fathom, and whose motives they cannot comprehend, but of which they can easily detect the imperfections, and deride the simplicities. And a large portion of the resistance to the noble Pre-Raphaelite movement of our own days has been offered by men who suppose the entire function of the artist in this world to consist in laying 109 on colour with a large brush, and surrounding dashes of flake white with bituminous brown; men whose entire capacities of brain, soul, and sympathy, applied industriously to the end of their lives, would not enable them, at last, to paint so much as one of the leaves of the nettles at the bottom of Hunt's picture of the Light of the World.

It is finally to be remembered, therefore, that Purism is always noble when it is *instinctive*. It is not the greatest thing that can be done, but it is probably the greatest thing that the man who does it can do, provided it comes from his heart. True, it is a sign of weakness, but it is not in our choice whether we will be weak or strong; and there is a certain strength which can only be made perfect in weakness. If he is working in humility, fear of evil, desire of beauty, and sincere purity of purpose and thought, he will produce good and helpful things; but he must be much on his guard against supposing himself to be greater than his fellows, because he has shut himself into this calm and cloistered sphere. His only safety lies in knowing himself to be, on the contrary, *less* than his fellows, and in always striving, so far as he can find it in his heart, to extend his delicate narrowness towards the great naturalist ideal.

CHAPTER VII

Of the True Ideal:—Secondly, Naturalist

111   WE now enter on the consideration of that central and highest branch of ideal art which concerns itself simply with things as they ARE, and accepts, in all of them, alike the evil and the good. The question is, therefore, how the art which represents things simply as they are, can be called ideal at all. How does it meet that requirement stated in Chap. III. as imperative on all great art, that it shall be inventive, and a product of the imagination? It meets it pre-eminently by that power of arrangement which I have endeavoured, at great length and with great pains, to define accurately in the chapter on Imagination associative in the second volume.[16] That is to say, accepting the weaknesses, faults, and wrongnesses in all things that it sees, it so places and harmonizes them that they form a noble whole, in which the imperfection of each several part is not only harmless, but absolutely essential, and yet in which whatever is good in each several part shall be completely displayed.

This operation of true idealism holds, from the least things to the greatest. For instance, in the arrangement of the smallest masses of colour, the false idealist, or even the purist, depends upon perfecting each separate hue, and raises them all, as far as he can, into costly brilliancy; but the naturalist takes the coarsest and feeblest colours of the things around him, and so interweaves and opposes them that they become more lovely than if they had all been bright. So in the treatment of the human form. The naturalist will take it as he finds it; but, with such examples as

112   his picture may rationally admit of more or less exalted beauty, he will associate inferior forms, so as not only to set off those which are most beautiful, but to bring out clearly what good there is in the inferior forms themselves; finally using such measure of absolute evil as there is commonly in nature, both for teaching and for contrast.

In Tintoret's Adoration of the Magi,[17] the Madonna is not an enthroned queen, but a fair girl, full of simplicity and almost childish sweetness. To her are opposed (as Magi) two of the noblest and most thoughtful of the Venetian senators in extreme old age,—the utmost manly dignity, in its decline, being set beside the utmost feminine simplicity, in its dawn.

The steep foreheads and refined features of the nobles are, again, opposed to the head of a negro servant, and of an Indian; both, however, noble of their kind. On the other side of the picture, the delicacy of the Madonna is farther enhanced by contrast with a largely made farm-servant, leaning on a basket. All these figures are in repose; outside, the troop of the attendants of the Magi is seen coming up at the gallop.

I bring forward this picture, observe, not as an example of the ideal in conception of religious subject, but of the general ideal treatment of the human form; in which the peculiarity is, that the beauty of each figure is displayed to the utmost, while yet, taken separately, the Madonna is an unaltered portrait of a Venetian girl, the Magi are unaltered Venetian senators, and the figure with the basket, an unaltered market-woman of Mestre.

It is evident that *within* this faithful idealism, and as one branch of it 113 only, will arrange itself the representation of the human form and mind in perfection, when this perfection is rationally to be supposed or introduced,—that is to say, in the highest personages of the story. The careless habit of confining the term "ideal" to such representations, and not understanding the imperfect ones to be *equally* ideal in their place, has greatly added to the embarrassment and multiplied the errors of artists.

Now, therefore, observe the main conclusions which follow from these two conditions, attached always to art of this kind. First, it is to be taken 114 straight from nature: it is to be the plain narration of something the painter or writer saw. Herein is the chief practical difference between the higher and lower artists; a difference which I feel more and more every day that I give to the study of art. All the great men *see* what they paint before they paint it,—see it in a perfectly passive manner,—cannot help seeing it if they would; whether in their mind's eye, or in bodily fact, does not matter; very often the mental vision is, I believe, in men of imagination, clearer than the bodily one; but vision it is, of one kind or another,—the whole scene, character, or incident passing before them as in second sight, whether they will or no, and requiring them to paint it as they see it; they not daring, under the might of its presence, to alter one jot or tittle of it as they write it down or paint it down; it being to them in its own kind and degree always a true vision or Apocalypse, and invariably accompanied in their hearts by a feeling correspondent to the words,—"Write the things *which thou hast seen,* and the things which *are.*"[18]

And the whole power, whether of painter or poet, to describe rightly what we call an ideal thing, depends upon its being thus, to him, not an ideal, but a *real* thing. No man ever did or ever will work well, but either from actual sight or sight of faith; and all that we call ideal in Greek or any other art, because to us it is false and visionary, was, to the makers of it, true and existent.

115 And just because it is always something that it sees or believes in, there is the peculiar character above noted, almost unmistakable, in all high and true ideals, of having been as it were studied from the life, and involving pieces of sudden familiarity, and close *specific* painting which never would have been admitted or even thought of, had not the painter drawn either from the bodily life or from the life of faith. For instance, Dante's centaur, Chiron, dividing his beard with his arrow before he can speak,[19] is a thing that no mortal would ever have thought of, if he had not actually seen the centaur do it. They might have composed handsome bodies of men and horses in all possible ways, through a whole life of pseudo-idealism, and yet never dreamed of any such thing. But the real living centaur actually trotted across Dante's brain, and he saw him do it.

  And on account of this reality it is, that the great idealists venture into all kinds of what, to the pseudo-idealists, are "vulgarities." Nay, *venturing* is the wrong word; the great men have no choice in the matter; they do not know or care whether the things they describe are vulgarities or not. They *saw* them; they are the facts of the case. If they had merely composed what they describe, they would have had it at their will to refuse this circumstance or add that. But they did not compose it. It came to them ready fashioned; they were too much impressed by it to think what was vulgar or not vulgar in it. It might be a very wrong thing in a centaur to have so much beard; but so it was. And, therefore, among the various ready tests of true greatness there is not any more certain than this daring reference to, or use of, mean and little things—mean and little, that is, to mean and little minds; but, when used by the great men, evidently part of the noble whole which is authoritatively present before them.

118 We may dismiss this matter of vulgarity in plain and few words, at least as far as regards art. There is never vulgarity in a *whole* truth, however commonplace. It may be unimportant or painful. It cannot be vulgar. Vulgarity is only in concealment of truth, or in affectation.

  "Well, but," (at this point the reader asks doubtfully,) "if then your great central idealist is to show all truth, low as well as lovely, receiving it in this passive way, what becomes of all your principles of selection, and of setting in the right place, which you were talking about up to the end of your fourth paragraph? How is Homer to enforce upon Achilles the cutting of the pork chops 'only at such time as Homer chooses,'[20] if Homer is to have *no* choice, but merely to see the thing done, and sing it as he sees it?" Why, the choice, as well as the vision, is *manifested* to Homer. The vision comes to him in its chosen order. Chosen *for* him, not *by* him, but yet full of visible and exquisite choice, just as a sweet and perfect dream will come to a sweet and perfect person, so that, in some sense, they may be said to have chosen their dream, or composed it; and yet they could not help dreaming it so, and in no otherwise. Thus, exactly thus, in all results of true inventive power, the whole harmony of the thing done seems as if it had been wrought by the most exquisite rules. But to him who did it, it presented itself so, and his will, and knowledge, and personality, for the moment went for nothing; he became simply a scribe, and wrote what he heard and saw.

And all efforts to do things of a similar kind by rule or by thought, and all efforts to mend or rearrange the first order of the vision, are not inventive; on the contrary, they ignore and deny invention. Thus the knowing of rules and the exertion of judgment have a tendency to check and confuse the fancy in its flow; so that it will follow, that, in exact proportion as a master knows anything about rules of right and wrong, he is likely to be uninventive; and, in exact proportion as he holds higher rank and has nobler inventive power, he will know less of rules; not despising them, but simply feeling that between him and them there is nothing in common,—that dreams cannot be ruled—that as they come, so they must be caught, and they cannot be caught in any other shape than that they come in; and that he might as well attempt to rule a rainbow into rectitude, or cut notches in a moth's wing to hold it by, as in any wise attempt to modify, by rule, the forms of the involuntary vision. 119

And this, which by reason we have thus anticipated, is in reality universally so. There is no exception. The great men never know how or why they do things. They have no rules; cannot comprehend the nature of rules;—do not, usually, even know, in what they do, what is best or what is worst: to them it is all the same; something they cannot help saying or doing,—one piece of it as good as another, and none of it (it seems to *them*) worth much. The moment any man begins to talk about rules, in whatsoever art, you may know him for a second-rate man; and, if he talks about them *much*, he is a third-rate, or not an artist at all. To *this* rule there is no exception in any art.

It is, of course, only with caution that such a broad statement should be made; but I have seen much of different kinds of artists, and I have always found the knowledge of, and attention to, rules so *accurately* in the inverse ratio to the power of the painter, that I have myself no doubt that the law is constant, and that men's smallness may be trigonometrically estimated by the attention which, in their work, they pay to principles, especially principles of composition. The general way in which the great men speak is of "*trying* to do" this or that, just as a child would tell of something he had seen and could not utter. Thus, in speaking of the drawing of which I have given an etching farther on (a scene on the St. Gothard) [plate 17], Turner asked if I had been to see "that litter of stones which I *endeavoured* to represent;" and William Hunt, when I asked him one day as he was painting, why he put on such and such a colour, answered, "I don't know; I am just *aiming* at it;" and Turner, and he, and all the other men I have 122

123   known who could paint, always spoke and speak in the same way; not in any selfish restraint of their knowledge, but in pure simplicity. While all the men whom I know, who *cannot* paint, are ready with admirable reasons for everything they have done; and can show, in the most conclusive way, that Turner is wrong, and how he might be improved.

And this is the reason for the somewhat singular, but very palpable truth that the Chinese, and Indians, and other semi-civilized nations, can colour better than we do, and that an Indian shawl and China vase are still, in invention of colour, inimitable by us. It is their glorious ignorance of all rules that does it; the pure and true instincts have play, and do their work,—instincts so subtle, that the least warping or compression breaks or blunts them; and the moment we begin teaching people any rules about colour, and make them do this or that, we crush the instinct, generally for ever. Hence, hitherto, it has been an actual necessity, in order to obtain power of colouring, that a nation should be half savage: everybody could colour in the twelfth and thirteenth centuries; but we were ruled and legalized into grey in the fifteenth;—only a little salt simplicity of their sea natures at Venice still keeping their precious, shell-fishy purpleness and power; and now that is gone; and nobody can colour anywhere, except the Hindoos and Chinese; but that need not be so, and will not be so long; for, in a little while, people will find out their mistake, and give up talking about rules of colour, and then everybody will colour again, as easily as they now talk.

Such, then, being the generally passive or instinctive character of right invention, it may be asked how these unmanageable instincts are to be rendered practically serviceable in historical or poetical painting,—especially historical, in which given facts are to be represented. Simply by

124   the sense and self-control of the whole man; not by control of the particular fancy or vision. He who habituates himself, in his daily life, to seek for the stern facts in whatever he hears or sees, will have these facts again brought before him by the involuntary imaginative power in their noblest associations; and he who seeks for frivolities and fallacies, will have frivolities and fallacies again presented to him in his dreams.

125   It follows from all this, evidently, that a great idealist never can be egotistic. The whole of his power depends upon his losing sight and feeling of his own existence, and becoming a mere witness and mirror of truth, and a scribe of visions,—always passive in sight, passive in utterance,—lamenting continually that he cannot completely reflect nor clearly utter all he has seen—not by any means a proud state for a man to be in. But the man who has no invention is always setting things in order, and putting the world to rights, and mending, and beautifying, and pluming himself on his doings as supreme in all ways.

CHAPTER VIII
Of the True Ideal:—Thirdly, Grotesque

I HAVE already, in the *Stones of Venice*, had occasion to analyze, as far as 130
I was able, the noble nature and power of grotesque conception.

The Grotesque is in that chapter* divided principally into three kinds:

(A.) Art arising from healthful but irrational play of the imagination in times of rest.

(B.) Art arising from irregular and accidental contemplation of terrible things; or evil in general.

(C.) Art arising from the confusion of the imagination by the presence of truths which it cannot wholly grasp.

It is the central form of this art, arising from contemplation of evil, 131
which forms the link of connection between it and the sensualist ideals,
as pointed out above in the second paragraph of the sixth chapter, the fact
being that the imagination, when at play, is curiously like bad children,
and likes to play with fire: in its entirely serious moods it dwells by
preference on beautiful and sacred images, but in its mocking or playful
moods it is apt to jest, sometimes bitterly, with under-current of sternest
pathos, sometimes waywardly, sometimes slightly and wickedly, with
death and sin; hence an enormous mass of grotesque art, some most noble
and useful, as Holbein's Dance of Death, and Albert Dürer's Knight and
Death [fig.55], going down gradually through various conditions of less
and less seriousness into an art whose only end is that of mere excitement,
or amusement by terror, like a child making mouths at another, more or
less redeemed by the degree of wit or fancy in the grimace it makes, as in
the demons of Teniers and such others; and, lower still, in the demon-
ology of the stage.

The form arising from an entirely healthful and open play of the
imagination, as in Shakspere's Ariel and Titania, and in Scott's White
Lady,[21] is comparatively rare. It hardly ever is free from some slight taint
of the inclination to evil; still more rarely is it, when so free, natural to the

---

* On the Grotesque Renaissance, vol. iii.

mind; for the moment we begin to contemplate sinless beauty we are apt to get serious; and moral fairy tales, and such other innocent work, are hardly ever truly, that is to say, naturally, imaginative; but for the most part laborious inductions and compositions. The moment any real vitality enters them, they are nearly sure to become satirical, or slightly gloomy, and so connect themselves with the evil-enjoying branch.

The third form of the Grotesque is a thoroughly noble one. It is that which arises out of the use or fancy of tangible signs to set forth an otherwise less expressible truth; including nearly the whole range of symbolical and allegorical art and poetry.

A fine grotesque is the expression, in a moment, by a series of symbols thrown together in bold and fearless connection, of truths which it would have taken a long time to express in any verbal way, and of which the connection is left for the beholder to work out for himself; the gaps, left or overleaped by the haste of the imagination, forming the grotesque character.

For instance, Spenser desires to tell us, (1) that envy is the most untamable and unappeasable of the passions, not to be soothed by any kindness; (2) that with continual labour it invents evil thoughts out of its own heart; (3) that even in this, its power of doing harm is partly hindered by the decaying and corrupting nature of the evil it lives in; (4) that it looks every way, and that whatever it sees is altered and discoloured by its own nature; (5) which discolouring, however, is to it a veil, or disgraceful dress, in the sight of others; (6) and that it never is free from the most bitter suffering, (7) which cramps all its acts and movements, enfolding and crushing it while it torments. All this it has required a somewhat long and languid sentence for me to say in unsymbolical terms,—not, by the way, that they *are* unsymbolical altogether, for I have been forced, whether I would or not, to use *some* figurative words; but even with this help the sentence is long and tiresome, and does not with any vigour represent the truth. It would take some prolonged enforcement of each sentence to make it felt, in ordinary ways of talking. But Spenser puts it all into a grotesque, and it is done shortly and at once, so that we feel it fully, and see it, and never forget it. I have numbered above the statements which had to be made. I now number them with the same numbers, as they occur in the several pieces of the grotesque:—

> "And next to him malicious Envy rode
> (1)   Upon a ravenous wolfe, and (2, 3) still did chaw
>   Between his cankred* teeth a venemous tode,
>   That all the poison ran about his jaw.

* Cankred—because he cannot then bite hard.

132

133

    (4, 5)   All in a kirtle of discolourd say
             He clothed was, y-paynted full of eies;
    (6)   And in his bosome secretly there lay
             An hateful snake, the which his taile uptyes
    (7)   In many folds, and mortall sting implyes."[22]

There is the whole thing in nine lines; or, rather in one image, which
will hardly occupy any room at all on the mind's shelves, but can be lifted
out, whole, whenever we want it. All noble grotesques are concentrations
of this kind, and the noblest convey truths which nothing else could
convey; and not only so, but convey them, in minor cases with a
delightfulness,—in the higher instances with an awfulness,—which no
mere utterance of the symbolised truth would have possessed, but which
belongs to the effort of the mind to unweave the riddle, or to the sense it
has of there being an infinite power and meaning in the thing seen,
beyond all that is apparent therein, giving the highest sublimity even to
the most trivial object so presented and so contemplated.

And thus in all ages and among all nations, grotesque idealism has been   134
the element through which the most appalling and eventful truth has
been wisely conveyed, from the most sublime words of true Revelation, to
the "ἀλλ' ὅτ' ἂν ἡμίονος βασιλεύς,"[23] etc., of the oracles, and the more or
less doubtful teaching of dreams; and so down to ordinary poetry. No
element of imagination has a wider range, a more magnificent use, or so
colossal a grasp of sacred truth.

How, then, is this noble power best to be employed in the art of
painting?

We hear it not unfrequently asserted that symbolism or personification
should not be introduced in painting at all. Such assertions are in their
grounds unintelligible, and in their substance absurd. Whatever is in
words described as visible, may with all logical fitness be rendered so by
colours, and not only is this a legitimate branch of ideal art, but I believe
there is hardly any other so widely useful and instructive. And as far as
authority bears on the question, the simple fact is that allegorical painting
has been the delight of the greatest men and of the wisest multitudes, from
the beginning of art, and will be till art expires. The greater and more   135
thoughtful the artists, the more they delight in symbolism, and the more
fearlessly they employ it. Dead symbolism, second-hand symbolism,
pointless symbolism, are indeed objectionable enough; but so are most
other things that are dead, second-hand, and pointless. It is also true that
both symbolism and personification are somewhat more apt than most
things to have their edges taken off by too much handling; and what with
our modern Fames, Justices, and various metaphorical ideals largely used
for signs and other such purposes, there is some excuse for our not well
knowing what the real power of personification is. But that power is

gigantic and inexhaustible, and ever to be grasped with peculiar joy by the painter, because it permits him to introduce picturesque elements and flights of fancy into his work, which otherwise would be utterly inadmissible;—to bring the wild beasts of the desert into the room of state, fill the air with inhabitants as well as the earth, and render the least (visibly) interesting incidents themes for the most thrilling drama.

136 For observe, not only does the introduction of these imaginary beings permit greater fantasticism of *incident*, but also infinite fantasticism of *treatment*; and, I believe, so far from the pursuit of the false ideal having in any wise exhausted the realms of fantastic imagination, those realms have hardly yet been entered, and that a universe of noble dream-land lies before us, yet to be conquered.

137 There is, however, unquestionably, a severe limit, in the case of all inferior masters, to the degree in which they may venture to realize grotesque conception, and partly, also, a limit in the nature of the thing itself; there being many grotesque ideas which may be with safety suggested dimly by words or slight lines, but which will hardly bear being painted into perfect definiteness. Unless in the hands of the very greatest men, the grotesque seems better to be expressed merely in line, or light and shade, or mere abstract colour, so as to mark it for a thought rather than a substantial fact. Even if Albert Dürer had perfectly painted his Knight and Death [fig.55], I question if we should feel it so great a thought as we do in the dark engraving. Blake, perfectly powerful in the etched

138 grotesque of the book of Job, fails always more or less as soon as he adds colour; not merely for want of power (his eye for colour being naturally good), but because his subjects seem, in a sort, insusceptible of completion.

For these several reasons, it seems not only permissible, but even desirable, that the art by which the grotesque is expressed should be more or less imperfect, and this seems a most beneficial ordinance, as respects the human race in general. Hence it is an infinite good to mankind when there is full acceptance of the grotesque, slightly sketched or expressed, and, if field for such expression be frankly granted, an enormous mass of

139 intellectual power is turned to everlasting use, which, in this present century of ours, evaporates in street gibing or vain revelling; all the good wit and satire expiring in daily talk, (like foam on wine,) which in the thirteenth and fourteenth centuries had a permitted and useful expression in the arts of sculpture and illumination, like foam fixed into chalcedony. It is with a view (not the least important among many others bearing upon art) to the reopening of this great field of human intelligence, long entirely closed, that I am striving to introduce Gothic architecture into daily domestic use; and to revive the art of illumination, properly so called; not the art of miniature-painting in books, or on vellum, which has

ridiculously been confused with it; but of making *writing*, simple writing, beautiful to the eye, by investing it with the great chord of perfect colour, blue, purple, scarlet, white, and gold, and in that chord of colour, permitting the continual play of the fancy of the writer in every species of grotesque imagination, carefully excluding shadow; the distinctive difference between illumination and painting proper, being, that illumination admits *no* shadows, but only gradations of pure colour.

Such being the manifold and precious uses of the true grotesque, it only   140
remains for us to note carefully how it is to be distinguished from the false and vicious grotesque which results from idleness, instead of noble rest; from malice, instead of the solemn contemplation of necessary evil; and from general degradation of the human spirit, instead of its subjection, or confusion, by thoughts too high for it. It is easy to understand what a difference there must indeed be between these; and yet how difficult it may be always to define it, or lay down laws for the discovery of it, except by the just instinct of minds set habitually in all things to discern right from wrong.

Nevertheless, one good and characteristic instance may be of service in marking the leading directions in which the contrast is discernible. On the opposite page, I have put, beside each other, a piece of true grotesque, from the Lombard-Gothic, and of false grotesque from classical (Roman) architecture [fig.38]. They are both griffins: the one on the left carries on his back one of the main pillars of the porch of the cathedral of Verona;   141
the one on the right is on the frieze of the temple of Antoninus and Faustina at Rome, much celebrated by Renaissance and bad modern architects.

In some respects, however, this classical griffin deserves its reputation. It is exceedingly fine in lines of composition, and, I believe, very exquisite in execution. For these reasons, it is all the better for our purpose. I do not want to compare the worst false grotesque with the best true, but rather, on the contrary, the best false with the simplest true, in order to see how the delicately wrought lie fails in the presence of the rough truth; for rough truth in the present case it is, the Lombard sculpture being altogether untoward and imperfect in execution.

"Well, but," the reader says, "what do you mean by calling *either* of them true? There never were such beasts in the world as either of these?"

No, never: but the difference is, that the Lombard workman did really see a griffin in his imagination, and carved it from the life, meaning to declare to all ages that he had verily seen with his immortal eyes such a griffin as that; but the classical workman never saw a griffin at all, nor anything else; but put the whole thing together by line and rule.

"How do you know that?"

Very easily. Look at the two, and think over them. You know a griffin

fig.38 *True and False Griffins*

Mediaeval (John Ruskin)   Classical (from lithograph)

is a beast composed of lion and eagle. The classical workman set himself to fit these together in the most ornamental way possible. He accordingly carves a sufficiently satisfactory lion's body, then attaches very gracefully cut wings to the sides: then, because he cannot get the eagle's head on the broad lion's shoulders, fits the two together by something like a horse's neck (some griffins being wholly composed of horse and eagle), then, finding the horse's neck look weak and unformidable, he strengthens it by a series of bosses, like vertebræ, in front, and by a series of spiny cusps, instead of a mane, on the ridge; next, not to lose the whole leonine character about the neck, he gives a remnant of the lion's beard, turned into a sort of griffin's whisker, and nicely curled and pointed; then an eye, probably meant to look grand and abstracted, and therefore neither lion's nor eagle's; and, finally, an eagle's beak, very sufficiently studied from a real one. The whole head being, it seems to him, still somewhat wanting in weight and power, he brings forward the right wing behind it, so as to enclose it with a broad line. This is the finest thing in the composition, and very masterly, both in thought, and in choice of the exactly right point where the lines of wing and beak should intersect (and it may be noticed in passing, that all men, who can compose at all, have this habit of encompassing or governing broken lines with broad ones, wherever it is possible, of which we shall see many instances hereafter). The whole griffin, thus gracefully composed, being, nevertheless, when all is done, a very composed griffin, is set to very quiet work, and raising his left foot,

142

to balance his right wing, sets it on the tendril of a flower so lightly as not even to bend it down, though, in order to reach it, his left leg is made half as long again as his right.

We may be pretty sure, if the carver had ever seen a griffin, he would have reported of him as doing something else than *that* with his feet. Let us see what the Lombardic workman saw him doing.

Remember, first, the griffin, though part lion and part eagle, has the united *power of both*. He is not merely a bit of lion and a bit of eagle, but whole lion incorporate with whole eagle. So when we really see one, we may be quite sure we shall not find him wanting in anything necessary to the might either of beast or bird.

Well, among things essential to the might of a lion, perhaps, on the   143 whole, the most essential are his *teeth*. He could get on pretty well even without his claws, usually striking his prey down with a blow, woundless; but he could by no means get on without his teeth. Accordingly, we see that the real or Lombardic griffin has the carnivorous teeth bare to the root, and the peculiar hanging of the jaw at the back, which marks the flexible and gaping mouth of the devouring tribes.

Again; among things essential to the might of an eagle, next to his wings (which are of course prominent in both examples), are his *claws*. It is no use his being able to tear anything with his beak, if he cannot first hold it in his claws; he has comparatively no leonine power of striking with his feet, but a magnificent power of grip with them. Accordingly, we see that the real griffin, while his feet are heavy enough to strike like a lion's, has them also extended far enough to give them the eagle's grip with the back claw; and has, moreover, some of the bird-like wrinkled skin over the whole foot, marking this binding power the more: and that he has besides verily got something to hold with his feet, other than a flower; of which more presently.

Now, observe, the Lombardic workman did not do all this because he had thought it out, as you and I are doing together; he never thought a bit about it. He simply saw the beast; saw it as plainly as you see the writing on this page, and of course could not be wrong in anything he told us of it.

Well, what more does he tell us? Another thing, remember, essential to an eagle is that it should fly *fast*. It is no use its having wings at all if it is to be impeded in the use of them. Now it would be difficult to impede him more thoroughly than by giving him two cocked ears to catch the wind.

Look, again, at the two beasts. You see the false griffin *has* them so set, and, consequently, as he flew, there would be a continual humming of the wind on each side of his head, and he would have an infallible ear-ache   144 when he got home. But the real griffin has his ears flat to his head, and all the hair of them blown back, even to a point, by his fast flying, and the aperture is downwards, that he may hear anything going on upon the earth, where his prey is. In the false griffin the aperture is upwards.

Well, what more? As he is made up of the natures of lion and eagle, we may be very certain that a real griffin is, on the whole, fond of eating, and that his throat will look as if he occasionally took rather large pieces, besides being flexible enough to let him bend and stretch his head in every direction as he flies.

Look again at the two beasts. You see the false one has got those bosses upon his neck like vertebræ, which must be infinitely in his way when he is swallowing, and which are evidently inseparable, so that he cannot *stretch* his neck any more than a horse. But the real griffin is all loose about the neck, evidently being able to make it almost as much longer as he likes; to stretch and bend it anywhere, and swallow anything, besides having some of the grand strength of the bull's dewlap in it when at rest.

What more? Having both lion and eagle in him, it is probable that the real griffin will have an infinite look of repose as well as power of activity. One of the notablest things about a lion is his magnificent *indolence*, his look of utter disdain of trouble when there is no occasion for it; as, also, one of the notablest things about an eagle is his look of inevitable vigilance, even when quietest. Look again at the two beasts. You see the false griffin is quite sleepy and dead in the eye, thus contradicting his eagle's nature, but is putting himself to a great deal of unnecessary trouble with his paws, holding one in a most painful position merely to touch a flower, and bearing the whole weight of his body on the other, thus contradicting his lion's nature.

But the real griffin is primarily, with his eagle's nature, wide awake; evidently quite ready for whatever may happen; and with his lion's nature, laid all his length on his belly, prone and ponderous; his two paws as simply put out before him as a drowsy puppy's on a drawing-room hearthrug; not but that he has got something to do with them, worthy of such paws; but he takes not one whit more trouble about it than is absolutely necessary. He has merely got a poisonous winged dragon to hold, and for such a little matter as that, he may as well do it lying down and at his ease, looking out at the same time for any other piece of work in his way. He takes the dragon by the middle, one paw under the wing, another above, gathers him up into a knot, puts two or three of his claws well into his back, crashing through the scales of it and wrinkling all the flesh up from the wound, flattens him down against the ground, and so lets him do what he likes. The dragon tries to bite him, but can only bring his head round far enough to get hold of his own wing, which he bites in agony instead; flapping the griffin's dewlap with it, and wriggling his tail up against the griffin's throat; the griffin being, as to these minor proceedings, entirely indifferent, sure that the dragon's body cannot drag itself one hair's breadth off those ghastly claws, and that its head can do no harm but to itself.

Now observe how in all this, through every separate part and action of the creature, the imagination is *always* right. It evidently *cannot* err; it meets every one of our requirements respecting the griffin as simply as if it were gathering up the bones of the real creature out of some ancient rock. It does not itself know or care, any more than the peasant labouring with his spade and axe, what is wanted to meet our theories or fancies. It knows simply what is there, and brings out the positive creature, errorless, unquestionable. So it is throughout art, and in all that the imagination does; if anything be wrong it is not the imagination's fault, but some inferior faculty's, which would have its foolish say in the matter, and meddled with the imagination, and said, the bones ought to be put together tail first, or upside down.

This, however, we need not be amazed at, because the very essence of the imagination is already defined to be the seeing to the heart; and it is not therefore wonderful that it should never err; but it is wonderful, on the other hand, how the composing legalism does *nothing else* than err. One would have thought that, by mere chance, in this or the other element of griffin, the griffin-composer might have struck out a truth; that he might have had the luck to set the ears back, or to give some grasp to the claw. But no; from beginning to end it is evidently impossible for him to be anything but wrong; his whole soul is instinct with lies; no veracity can come within hail of him; to him all regions of right and life are for ever closed.   146

And another notable point is, that while the imagination receives truth in this simple way, it is all the while receiving statutes of composition also, far more noble than those for the sake of which the truth was lost by the legalist. The ornamental lines in the classical griffin appear at first finer than in the other; but they only appear so because they are more commonplace and more palpable. The subtlety of the sweeping and rolling curves in the real griffin, the way they waver and change and fold, down the neck, and along the wing, and in and out among the serpent coils, is incomparably grander, merely as grouping of ornamental line, than anything in the other; nor is it fine as ornamental only, but as massively useful, giving weight of stone enough to answer the entire purpose of pedestal sculpture. Note, especially, the insertion of the three plumes of the dragon's broken wing in the outer angle, just under the large coil of his body; this filling of the gap being one of the necessities, not of the pedestal block merely, but a means of getting mass and breadth, which all composers desire more or less, but which they seldom so perfectly accomplish.

So that, taking the truth first, the honest imagination gains everything; it has its griffinism, and grace, and usefulness, all at once: but the false

147 composer, caring for nothing but himself and his rules, loses everything, —griffinism, grace, and all.

I believe the reader will now sufficiently see how the terms "true" and "false" are in the most accurate sense attachable to the opposite branches of what might appear at first, in both cases, the merest wildness of inconsistent reverie. But they are even to be attached, in a deeper sense than that in which we have hitherto used them, to these two compositions. For the imagination hardly ever works in this intense way, unencumbered by the inferior faculties, unless it be under the influence of some solemn purpose or sentiment. And to all the falseness and all the verity of these two ideal creatures this farther falsehood and verity have yet to be added, that the classical griffin has, at least in this place, no other intent than that of covering a level surface with entertaining form; but the Lombardic griffin is a profound expression of the most passionate symbolism. Under its eagle's wings are two wheels,[24] which mark it as connected, in the mind of him who wrought it, with the living creatures of the vision of Ezekiel: "When they went, the wheels went by them," and "whithersoever the spirit was to go, they went; and the wheels were lifted up over against them, for the spirit of the living creatures was in the wheels."[25] Thus signed, the winged shade becomes at once one of the acknowledged symbols of the divine power; and, in its unity of lion and eagle, the workmen of the Middle Ages always meant to set forth the unity of the human and divine natures. In this unity it bears up the pillars of the

148 Church, set for ever as the corner-stone. And the faithful and true imagination beholds it, in this unity, with everlasting vigilance and calm omnipotence, restrain the seed of the serpent crushed upon the earth; leaving the head of it free, only for a time, that it may inflict in its fury profounder destruction upon itself,—in this also full of deep meaning. The divine power does not slay the evil creature. It wounds and restrains it only. Its final and *deadly* wound is inflicted by itself.

CHAPTER IX
Of Finish

W E have, in the preceding chapters, glanced through the various   150
operations of the imaginative power of man; with this almost painfully monotonous result, that its greatness and honour were always simply
in proportion to the quantity of truth it grasped. And now the question,
left undetermined some hundred pages back, recurs to us in a simpler form
than it could before. How far is this true imagination to be truly represented? How far should the perfect conception of Pallas be so given as
to look like Pallas herself, rather than like the picture of Pallas?

I purpose, therefore, in the present chapter, to examine, as thoroughly
as I can, the real signification of this word, Finish, as applied to art, and
to see if in this, as in other matters, our almost tiresome test is not the only
right one; whether there be not a *fallacious* finish and a *faithful* finish, and
whether the dispute, which seems to be only about completion and
incompletion, has not therefore, at the bottom of it, the old and deep
grounds of fallacy and fidelity.

Observe, first, there are two great and separate senses in which we call   151
a thing finished, or well-finished. One, which refers to the mere neatness
and completeness of the actual work, as we speak of a well-finished knife-
handle or ivory toy (as opposed to ill-cut ones); and secondly, a sense
which refers to the effect produced by the thing done, as we call a picture
well-finished if it is so full in its details, as to produce the effect of reality
on the spectator. And, in England, we seem at present to value highly the
first sort of finish which belongs to work*manship*, in our manufactures and
general doings of any kind, but to despise totally the impressive finish
which belongs to the *work*; and therefore we like smooth ivories better
than rough ones,—but careless scrawls or daubs better than the most
complete paintings. Now, I believe that we exactly reverse the fitness of
judgment in this matter, and that we ought, on the contrary, to despise
the finish of work*manship*, which is done for vanity's sake, and to love the
finish of *work*, which is done for truth's sake,—that we ought, in a word,
to finish our ivory toys more roughly, and our pictures more delicately.

Let us think over this matter.

338

Perhaps one of the most remarkable points of difference between the English and Continental nations is in the degree of finish given to their ordinary work. It is enough to cross from Dover to Calais to feel this difference: and to travel farther only increases the sense of it. English windows for the most part fit their sashes, and their woodwork is neatly planed and smoothed: French windows are larger, heavier, and framed with wood that looks as if it had been cut to its shape with a hatchet; they have curious and cumbrous fastenings, and can only be forced asunder or together by some ingenuity and effort, and even then not properly. So with everything else—French, Italian, and German, and as far as I know, Continental; and we commonly plume ourselves much upon this, believing that generally the English people do their work better and more thoroughly, or as they say, "turn it out of their hands in better style," than foreigners. I do not know how far this is really the case. Still, I think that there is really in the English mind, for the most part, a stronger desire to do things as well as they can be done, and less inclination to put up with inferiorities or insufficiencies, than in general characterize the temper of foreigners. But the feeling with which this perfection is insisted upon (however desirable as a sign of energy of purpose) is not in itself a peculiarly amiable or noble feeling; there are many little things which to do admirably is to waste both time and cost; and the real question is not so much whether we have done a given thing as well as possible, as whether we have turned a given quantity of labour to the best account.

Now, so far from the labour's being turned to good account which is given to our English "finishing," I believe it to be usually destructive of the best powers of our workmen's minds. For it is evident, in the first place, that there is almost always a useful and a useless finish; the hammering and welding which are necessary to produce a sword blade of the best quality, are useful finishing; the polish of its surface, useless. In nearly all work this distinction will, more or less, take place between substantial finish and apparent finish, or what may be briefly characterized as "Make" and "Polish." And so far as finish is bestowed for purposes of "make," I have nothing to say against it. Even the vanity which displays itself in giving strength to our work is rather a virtue than a vice. But so far as finish is bestowed for purposes of "polish," there is much to be said against it; this first, and very strongly, that the qualities aimed at in common finishing, namely, smoothness, delicacy, or fineness, *cannot* in reality *exist*, in a degree worth admiring, in anything done by human hands. Our best finishing is but coarse and blundering work after all. God alone can finish; and the more intelligent the human mind becomes, the more the infiniteness of interval is felt between human and divine work in this respect. So then it is not a little absurd to weary ourselves in struggling towards a point which we never can reach, and to exhaust our strength in vain endeavours to produce qualities which exist inimitably and inexhaustibly in the commonest things around us.

But more than this: the fact is, that in multitudes of instances, instead of gaining greater fineness of finish by our work, we are only destroying the fine finish of nature, and substituting coarseness and imperfection. For instance, when a rock of any kind has lain for some time exposed to the weather, Nature finishes it in her own way; first, she takes wonderful pains about its forms, sculpturing it into exquisite variety of dint and dimple, and rounding or hollowing it into contours, which for fineness no human hand can follow; then she colours it; and every one of her touches of colour, instead of being a powder mixed with oil, is a minute forest of living trees, glorious in strength and beauty, and concealing wonders of structure which in all probability are mysteries even to the eyes of angels. Man comes, and digs up this finished and marvellous piece of work, which in his ignorance he calls a "rough stone." He proceeds to finish it in *his* fashion, that is, to split it in two, rend it into ragged blocks, and, finally, to chisel its surface into a large number of lumps and knobs, all equally shapeless, colourless, deathful, and frightful. And the block thus dis-   155 figured he calls "finished," and proceeds to build therewith, and thinks himself great, forsooth, and an intelligent animal. Whereas, all that he has really done is, to destroy with utter ravage a piece of divine art, which, under the laws appointed by the Deity to regulate His work in this world, it must take good twenty years to produce the like of again. I do not say that stone must not be cut; it needs to be cut for certain uses; only I say that the cutting is not "finishing," but *un*finishing, it; and that so far as the mere fact of chiselling goes, the stone is ruined by the human touch. In like manner, a tree is a finished thing. But a plank, though ever so polished, is not. We need stones and planks, as we need food; but we no more bestow an additional admirableness upon stone in hewing it, or upon a tree in sawing it, than upon an animal in killing it.

Well, but it will be said, there is certainly a kind of finish in stone-cutting, and in every other art, which *is* meritorious, and which consists in smoothing and refining as much as possible. Yes, assuredly there is a meritorious finish. First, as it has just been said, that which fits a thing for its uses,—as a stone to lie well in its place, or a cog of an engine-wheel to play well on another; and, secondly, a finish belonging properly to the arts; but *that* finish does not consist in smoothing or polishing, but in the *completeness of the expression of ideas.* For in painting there is precisely the   156 same difference between the ends proposed in finishing that there is in manufacture. Some artists finish for the finish' sake; dot their pictures all over, as in some kinds of miniature painting (when a wash of colour would have produced as good an effect); or polish their pictures all over, making the execution so delicate that the touch of the brush cannot be seen, for the sake of the smoothness merely, and of the credit they may thus get for great labour; which kind of execution, seen in great perfection in many works of the Dutch school, and in those of Carlo Dolci,[26] is that polished "language" against which I have spoken at length in various portions of the first volume; nor is it possible to speak of it with too great severity or contempt, where it has been made an ultimate end.

But other artists finish for the impression's sake, not to show their skill, nor to produce a smooth piece of work, but that they may, with each stroke, render clearer the expression of knowledge. And this sort of finish is not, properly speaking, so much *completing* the picture as *adding* to it. It is not that what is painted is more delicately done, but that infinitely *more* is painted. This finish is always noble, and, like all other noblest things, hardly ever understood or appreciated.

164   All true finish is *added fact*; and Turner's word for finishing a picture was always this significant one, "carry forward." But labour without added knowledge can only blacken or stain a picture, it cannot finish it.

Some degree of ignorance may be hidden, in completing what is far away; but there is no concealment possible in close work. It has always been a wonderful thing to me to hear people talk of making foregrounds "vigorous," "marked," "forcible," and so on. If you will lie down on your breast on the next bank you come to (which is bringing it *close* enough, I should think, to give it all the force it is capable of), you will see, in the cluster of leaves and grass close to your face, a mystery of soft shadow in the depths of the grass, with indefinite forms of leaves, which you cannot

165   trace nor count, within it, and out of that, the nearer leaves coming in every subtle gradation of tender light and flickering form, quite beyond all delicacy of pencilling to follow; and yet you will rise up from that bank (certainly not making it appear coarser by drawing a little back from it), and profess to represent it by a few blots of "forcible" foreground colour. "Well, but I cannot draw every leaf that I see on the bank." No, for as we saw, at the beginning of this chapter, that no human work could be finished so as to express the *delicacy* of nature, so neither can it be finished so as to express the *redundance* of nature. Accept that necessity; but do not deny it; do not call your work finished, when you have, in engraving, substituted a confusion of coarse black scratches, or in water-colour a few edgy blots, for ineffable organic beauty. Follow that beauty as far as you can, remembering that just as far as you see, know, and represent it, just so far your work is finished; as far as you fall short of it, your work is *un*finished, and as far as you substitute any other thing for it, your work is spoiled.

How far Turner followed it, is not easily shown; for his finish is so

166   delicate as to be nearly uncopiable. In his painting of Ivy Bridge, the veins are drawn on the wings of a butterfly, not above three lines in diameter; and in one of his smaller drawings of Scarborough, in my own possession,

the mussel-shells on the beach are rounded, and some shown as shut, some as open, though none are as large as one of the letters of this type; and yet this is the man who was thought to belong to the "dashing" school, literally because most people had not patience or delicacy of sight enough to trace his endless detail.

"Suppose it was so," perhaps the reader replies; "still I do not like detail so delicate that it can hardly be seen." Then you like nothing in Nature (for you will find she always carries her detail too far to be traced). This point, however, we shall examine hereafter; it is not the question now whether we *like* finish or not; our only inquiry here is, what finish *means*; and I trust the reader is beginning to be satisfied that it does indeed mean nothing but consummate and accumulated truth, and that our old monotonous test must still serve us here as elsewhere. And it will become us to consider seriously why (if indeed it be so) we dislike this kind of finish—dislike an accumulation of truth. For assuredly all authority is against us, and—*no truly great name can be named in the arts—but it is that of one who finished to his utmost.* Take Leonardo, Michael Angelo, and Raphael for a triad, to begin with. *They* all completed their detail with such subtlety of touch and gradation, that, in a careful drawing by any of the three, you cannot see where the pencil ceased to touch the paper; the stroke of it is so tender, that, when you look close to the drawing you can see nothing; you only see the effect of it a little way back! Thus tender in execution, and so complete in detail, that Leonardo must needs draw *every several vein in the little agates* and pebbles of the gravel under the feet of the St. Anne in the Louvre. Take a quartett after a triad—Titian, Tintoret, Bellini, and Veronese. Examine the vine-leaves of the Bacchus and Ariadne (Titian's), in the National Gallery [fig.39]; examine the borage blossoms, painted petal by petal, though lying loose on the table, in Titian's Supper at Emmaus, in the Louvre, or the snail-shells on the ground in his Entombment; examine the separately designed patterns on every drapery of Veronese, in his Marriage in Cana; go to Venice and see how Tintoret paints the strips of black bark on the birch trunk that sustains the platform in his Adoration of the Magi;[27] how Bellini fills the rents of his ruined walls with the most exquisite clusters of the Erba della Madonna. You will find them all in a tale. Take a quintett after the quartett—Francia, Angelico, Dürer, Memling, Perugino,—and still the witness is one, still the same striving in all to such utmost perfection as their knowledge and hand could reach.

Who shall gainsay these men? Above all, who shall gainsay them when they and Nature say precisely the same thing? for where does Nature pause in *her* finishing—that finishing which consists not in the smoothing of surface, but the filling of space, and the multiplication of life and thought?

Who shall gainsay them? I, for one, dare not; but accept their teaching, with Nature's, in all humbleness.

167

168

fig.39 Titian, *Bacchus and Ariadne* (detail)

CHAPTER X
Of the Use of Pictures

I DOUBT not that one objection has struck the reader very forcibly. He will wonder how it was that Turner, finishing in this exquisite way, and giving truths by the thousand, where other painters gave only one or two, yet, of all painters, seemed to obtain least acknowledgeable resemblance to nature, so that the world cried out upon him for a madman, at the moment when he was giving exactly the highest and most consummate truth that had ever been seen in landscape. 169

And he will wonder why still there seems reason for this outcry. Still, after what analysis and proof of his being right have as yet been given, the reader may perhaps be saying to himself: "All this reasoning is of no use to me. Turner does *not* give me the idea of nature; I do not feel before one of his pictures as I should in a real scene. Constable takes me out into the shower, and Claude into the sun; and De Wint makes me feel as if I were walking in the fields; but Turner keeps me in the house, and I know always that I am looking at a picture." 170

I might answer to this: Well, what else *should* he do? If you want to feel as if you were in a shower, cannot you go and get wet without help from Constable? If you want to feel as if you were walking in the fields, cannot you go and walk in them without help from De Wint? But if you want to sit in your room and look at a beautiful picture, why should you blame the artist for giving you one? This *was* the answer actually made to me by various journalists, when first I showed that Turner was truer than other painters: "Nay," said they, "we do not want truth, we want something else than truth; we would not have nature, but something better than nature."

I do not mean to accept that answer, although it seems at this moment to make for me: I have never accepted it. As I raise my eyes from the paper, to think over the curious mingling in it, of direct error, and faraway truth, I see upon the room-walls, first, Turner's drawing of the chain of the Alps from the Superga above Turin; then a study of a block of gneiss at Chamouni, with the purple Aiguilles Rouges behind it; another of the towers of the Swiss Fribourg [fig.40], with a cluster of pine forest behind

344

fig.40   John Ruskin, *The Towers of Fribourg*

171   them; then another Turner, Isola Bella, with the blue opening to the St.
      Gothard in the distance; and then a fair bit of thirteenth-century
      illumination, depicting, at the top of the page, the Salutation; and
      beneath, the painter who painted it, sitting in his little convent cell, with
      a legend above him to this effect:—

               " ɽɡo joħɾ̄s s̄ɾpsi hunɾ librum."
               I, John, wrote this book.

      None of these things are bad pieces of art; and yet,—if it were offered me
      to have, instead of them, so many windows, out of which I should see,
      first, the real chain of the Alps from the Superga; then the real block of

gneiss, and Aiguilles Rouges; then the real towers of Fribourg, and pine forest; the real Isola Bella; and, finally, the true Mary and Elizabeth; and beneath them, the actual old monk at work in his cell,—I would very unhesitatingly change my five pictures for the five windows; and so, I apprehend, would most people, not, it seems to me, unwisely.

"Well, then," the reader goes on to question me, "the more closely the picture resembles such a window, the better it must be?"

Yes.

"Then, if Turner does not give me the impression of such a window, that is, of Nature, there must be something wrong in Turner?"

Yes.

"And if Constable and De Wint give me the impression of such a window, there must be something right in Constable and De Wint?"

Yes.

"And something more right than in Turner?"

No.

"Will you explain yourself?"

I *have* explained myself, long ago, and that fully; perhaps too fully for the simple sum of the explanation to be remembered. If the reader will glance back to, and in the present state of our inquiry, reconsider in the first volume, Part I. Sec. I. Chap. v., and Part II. Sec. I. Chap. vii.,[28] he will   172 find our present difficulties anticipated. There are some truths, easily obtained, which give a deceptive resemblance to Nature; others only to be obtained with difficulty, which cause no deception, but give inner and deeper resemblance. These two classes of truths cannot be obtained together; choice must be made between them. The bad painter gives the cheap deceptive resemblance. The good painter gives the precious non-deceptive resemblance. Constable perceives in a landscape that the grass is wet, the meadows flat, and the boughs shady; that is to say, about as much as, I suppose, might in general be apprehended, between them, by an intelligent fawn, and a skylark. Turner perceives at a glance the whole sum of visible truth open to human intelligence. So Berghem perceives nothing in a figure, beyond the flashes of light on the folds of its dress; but Michael Angelo perceives every flash of thought that is passing through its spirit: and Constable and Berghem may imitate windows; Turner and Michael Angelo can by no means imitate windows. But Turner and Michael Angelo are nevertheless the best.

"Well but," the reader persists, "you admitted just now that because Turner did not get his work to look like a window there was something wrong in him."

I did so; if he were quite right he would have *all* truth, low as well as high; that is, he would be Nature and not Turner, but that is impossible to man. There is much that is wrong in him; much that is infinitely wrong in all human effort. But, nevertheless, in some an infinity of Betterness above other human effort.

"Well, but you said you would change your Turners for windows; why not, therefore, for Constables?"

Nay, I did not say that I would change them for windows *merely*, but for windows which commanded the chain of the Alps and Isola Bella. That is to say, for all the truth that there is in Turner, and all the truth besides which is not in him; but I would not change them for Constables, to have a small piece of truth which is not in Turner, and none of the mighty truth which there is.

Thus far, then, though the subject is one requiring somewhat lengthy explanation, it involves no real difficulty. There is not the slightest inconsistency in the mode in which, throughout this work, I have desired the relative merits of painters to be judged. I have always said, he who is closest to Nature is best. All rules are useless, all genius is useless, all labour is useless, if you do not give facts; the more facts you give, the greater you are; and there is no fact so unimportant as to be prudently despised, if it be possible to represent it. Nor, but that I have long known the truth of Herbert's lines,

"Some men are
Full of themselves, and answer their own notion,"[29]

would it have been without intense surprise that I heard querulous readers asking, "how it was possible" that I could praise Pre-Raphaelitism and Turner also. For, from the beginning of this book to this page of it, I have never praised Turner highly for any other cause than that he *gave facts* more *delicately*, more Pre-Raphaelitically, than other men. Careless readers, who dashed at the descriptions and missed the arguments, took up their own conceptions of the cause of my liking Turner, and said to themselves: "Turner cannot draw, Turner is generalizing, vague, visionary; and the Pre-Raphaelites are hard and distinct. How can any one like both?" But I never said that Turner could not draw. I never said that he was vague or visionary. What I said was, that nobody had ever drawn so well: that nobody was so certain, so *un*-visionary; that nobody had ever given so many hard and downright facts.

Thus far, then, all I have been saying is absolutely consistent, and tending to one simple end. Turner is praised for his truth and finish; that truth of which I am beginning to give examples. Pre-Raphaelitism is praised for its truth and finish; and the whole duty inculcated upon the artist is that of being in all respects as like Nature as possible.

And yet this is not all I have to do. There is more than this to be inculcated upon the student, more than this to be admitted or established, before the foundations of just judgment can be laid.

For, observe, although I believe any sensible person would exchange his pictures, however good, for windows, he would not feel, and ought not to feel, that the arrangement was *entirely* gainful to him. He would feel it was an exchange of a less good of one kind, for a greater of another kind, but that it was definitely *exchange*, not pure gain, not merely getting more truth instead of less. The picture would be a serious loss; something gone which the actual landscape could never restore, though it might give something better in its place, as age may give to the heart something better than its youthful delusion, but cannot give again the sweetness of that delusion.

What is this in the picture which is precious to us, and yet is not natural?   176
Hitherto our arguments have tended, on the whole, somewhat to the depreciation of art; and the reader may every now and then, so far as he has been convinced by them, have been inclined to say, "Why not give up this whole science of Mockery at once, since its only virtue is in representing facts, and it cannot, at best, represent them completely, besides being liable to all manner of shortcomings and dishonesties,—why not keep to the facts, to real fields, and hills and men, and let this dangerous painting alone?"

No, it would not be well to do this. Painting has its peculiar virtues, not only consistent with, but even resulting from, its shortcomings and weaknesses. Let us see what these virtues are.

Not long ago, as I was leaving one of the towns of Switzerland, early in the morning, I saw in the clouds behind the houses an Alp which I did not know, a grander Alp than any I knew, nobler than the Schreckhorn or the Mönch; terminated, as it seemed, on one side by a precipice of almost unimaginable height; on the other, sloping away for leagues in one field of lustrous ice, clear and fair and blue, flashing here and there into silver under the morning sun. For a moment I received a sensation of as much sublimity as any natural object could possibly excite; the next moment, I saw that my unknown Alp was the glass roof of one of the work-shops of the town rising above its nearer houses and rendered aerial and indistinct by some pure blue wood smoke which rose from intervening chimneys.

It is evident, that so far as the mere delight of the eye was concerned, the glass roof was here equal, or at least equal for a moment, to the Alp. Whether the power of the object over the heart was to be small or great, depended altogether upon what it was understood for, upon its being   177
taken possession of and apprehended in its full nature, either as a granite mountain or a group of panes of glass; and thus, always, the real majesty of the appearance of the thing to us, depends upon the degree in which we ourselves possess the power of understanding it,—that penetrating, possession-taking power of the imagination, which has been long ago defined[30] as the very life of the man, considered as a *seeing* creature. For

though the casement had indeed been an Alp, there are many persons on whose minds it would have produced no more effect than the glass roof. It would have been to them a glittering object of a certain apparent length and breadth, and whether of glass or ice, whether twenty feet in length, or twenty leagues, would have made no difference to them; or, rather, would not have been in any wise conceived or considered by them. Examine the nature of your own emotion (if you feel it) at the sight of the Alp, and you find all the brightness of that emotion hanging, like dew on gossamer, on a curious web of subtle fancy and imperfect knowledge. First, you have a vague idea of its size, coupled with wonder at the work of the great Builder of its walls and foundations, then an apprehension of its eternity, a pathetic sense of its perpetualness, and your own transientness, as of the grass upon its sides; then, and in this very sadness, a sense of strange companionship with past generations in seeing what they saw. They did not see the clouds that are floating over your head: nor the cottage wall on the other side of the field; nor the road by which you are travelling. But they saw *that*. The wall of granite in the heavens was the same to them as to you. They have ceased to look upon it; you will soon cease to look also, and the granite wall will be for others. Then, mingled with these more solemn imaginations, come the understandings of the gifts and glories of the Alps, the fancying forth of all the fountains that 178 well from its rocky walls, and strong rivers that are born out of its ice, and of all the pleasant valleys that wind between its cliffs, and all the châlets that gleam among its clouds, and happy farmsteads couched upon its pastures; while together with the thoughts of these, rise strange sympathies with all the unknown of human life, and happiness, and death, signified by that narrow white flame of the everlasting snow, seen so far in the morning sky.

These images, and far more than these, lie at the root of the emotion which you feel at the sight of the Alp. You may not trace them in your heart, for there is a great deal more in your heart, of evil and good, than you ever can trace; but they stir you and quicken you for all that. Assuredly, so far as you feel more at beholding the snowy mountain than any other object of the same sweet silvery grey, these are the kind of images which cause you to do so; and, observe, these are nothing more than a greater apprehension of the *facts* of the thing. We call the power "Imagination," because it imagines or conceives; but it is only noble imagination if it imagines or conceives *the truth*. And, according to the degree of knowledge possessed, and of sensibility to the pathetic or impressive character of the things known, will be the degree of this imaginative delight.

But the main point to be noted at present is, that if the imagination can be excited to this its peculiar work, it matters comparatively little what it is excited by. If the smoke had not cleared partially away, the glass roof might have pleased me as well as an Alp, until I had quite lost sight of it; and if, in a picture, the imagination can be once caught, and, without absolute affront from some glaring fallacy, set to work in its own field, the imperfection of the historical details themselves is, to the spectator's enjoyment, of small consequence.

Hence it is, that poets, and men of strong feeling in general, are apt to be among the very worst judges of painting. The slightest hint is enough for them. Tell them that a white stroke means a ship, and a black stain, 179 a thunderstorm, and they will be perfectly satisfied with both, and immediately proceed to remember all that they ever felt about ships and thunderstorms, attributing the whole current and fulness of their own feelings to the painter's work; while probably, if the picture be really good, and full of stern fact, the poet, or man of feeling, will find some of its fact *in his way*, out of the particular course of his own thoughts,—be offended at it, take to criticizing and wondering at it, detect, at last, some imperfection in it, such as must be inherent in all human work,—and so finally quarrel with, and reject the whole thing.

Hence, also, the error into which many superficial artists fall, in speaking of "addressing the imagination" as the only end of art. It is quite true that the imagination must be addressed; but it may be very sufficiently addressed by the stain left by an ink-bottle thrown at the wall. The thrower has little credit, though an imaginative observer may find, perhaps, more to amuse him in the erratic nigrescence than in many a laboured picture. And thus, in a slovenly or ill-finished picture, it is no credit to the artist that he has "addressed the imagination;" nor is the success of such an appeal any criterion whatever of the merit of the work. The duty of an artist is not only to address and awaken, but to *guide* the imagination; and there is no safe guidance but that of simple concurrence with fact.

Hence it is also that so much grievous difficulty stands in the way of obtaining *real opinion* about pictures at all. Tell any man, of the slightest 180 imaginative power, that such and such a picture is good, and means this or that: tell him, for instance, that a Claude is good, and that it means trees, and grass, and water; and forthwith, whatever faith, virtue, humility, and imagination there are in the man, rise up to help Claude, and to declare that indeed it is all "excellent good, i'faith;"[31] and whatever in the course of his life he has felt of pleasure in trees and grass, he will begin to reflect upon and enjoy anew, supposing all the while it is the picture he is enjoying. Hence, when once a painter's reputation is accredited, it must be a stubborn kind of person indeed whom he will not please, or seem to please; for all the vain and weak people pretend to be pleased with him, for their own credit's sake, and all the humble and imaginative people seriously and honestly fancy they *are* pleased with him, deriving indeed, very certainly, delight from his work, but a delight which, if they were kept in the same temper, they would equally derive (and, indeed, constantly do derive) from the grossest daub that can be manufactured in imitation by the pawnbroker. Is, therefore, the pawnbroker's imitation as good as the original? Not so. There is the certain test of goodness and badness, which I am always striving to get people to use. As long as they are satisfied if they find their feelings pleasantly stirred and their fancy gaily occupied, so long there is for them no good, no bad. Anything may please, or anything displease, them; and their entire manner of thought and talking about art is mockery, and all their judgments are laborious injustices. But let them, in the teeth of their pleasure or displeasure, simply put the calm question,—Is it so? Is that the way a stone is shaped, the way a cloud is wreathed, the way a leaf is veined? and they are safe. They will do no more injustice to themselves nor to other men; they will learn to whose guidance they may trust their imagination, and from whom they must for ever withold its reins.

181   "Well, but why have you dragged in this poor spectator's imagination at all, if you have nothing more to say for it than this; if you are merely going to abuse it, and go back to your tiresome facts?"

Nay; I am not going to abuse it. On the contrary, I have to assert, in a temper profoundly venerant of it, that though we must not suppose everything is right when this is aroused, we may be sure that something is wrong when this is *not* aroused. The something wrong may be in the spectator or in the picture; and if the picture be demonstrably in accordance with truth, the odds are, that it is in the spectator; but there is wrong somewhere; for the work of the picture is indeed eminently to get at this imaginative power in the beholder, and all its facts are of no use whatever if it does not. No matter how much truth it tells if the hearer be asleep. Its first work is to wake him, then to teach him.

Now, observe, while, as it penetrates into the nature of things, the imagination is pre-eminently a beholder of things, *as they are*, it is, in its creative function, an eminent beholder of things *when* and *where* they are NOT; a seer, that is, in the prophetic sense, calling "the things that are not as though they were,"[32] and for ever delighting to dwell on that which is not tangibly present. And its great function being the calling forth, or back, that which is not visible to bodily sense, it has of course been made to take delight in the fulfilment of its proper function, and pre-eminently to enjoy, and spend its energy on, things past and future, or out of sight, rather than things present, or in sight. So that if the imagination is to be called to take delight in any object, it will not be always well, if we can help it, to put the *real* object there, before it. The imagination would on the whole rather have it *not* there;—the reality and substance are rather in the imagination's way; it would think a good deal more of the thing if it could not see it. Hence, that strange and sometimes fatal charm,   182 which there is in all things as long as we wait for them, and the moment we have lost them; but which fades while we possess them;—that sweet bloom of all that is far away, which perishes under our touch. Yet the feeling of this is not a weakness; it is one of the most glorious gifts of the human mind, making the whole infinite future, and imperishable past, a richer inheritance, if faithfully inherited, than the changeful, frail, fleeting present: it is also one of the many witnesses in us to the truth that these present and tangible things are not meant to satisfy us.

Another character of the imagination is equally constant, and, to our present inquiry, of yet greater importance. It is eminently a *weariable* faculty, eminently delicate, and incapable of bearing fatigue; so that if we give it too many objects at a time to employ itself upon, or very grand ones for a long time together, it fails under the effort, becomes jaded, exactly as the limbs do by bodily fatigue, and incapable of answering any farther appeal till it has had rest. And this is the real nature of the weariness which is so often felt in travelling, from seeing too much. It is not that the monotony and number of the beautiful things seen have made them valueless, but that the imaginative power has been overtaxed; and, instead of letting it rest, the traveller, wondering to find himself dull, and   183 incapable of admiration, seeks for something more admirable, excites and torments, and drags the poor fainting imagination up by the shoulders: "Look at this, and look at that, and this more wonderful still!"—until the imaginative faculty faints utterly away, beyond all further torment, or pleasure, dead for many a day to come; and the despairing prodigal takes to horse-racing in the Campagna, good now for nothing else than that; whereas, if the imagination had only been laid down on the grass, among simple things, and left quiet for a little while, it would have come to itself gradually, recovered its strength and colour, and soon been fit for work again. So that, whenever the imagination is tired, it is necessary to find for it something, not *more* admirable but *less* admirable; such as in that weak state it can deal with; then give it peace and it will recover.

I well recollect the walk on which I first found out this; it was on the winding road from Sallenches, sloping up the hills towards St. Gervais, one cloudless Sunday afternoon. The road circles softly between bits of rocky bank and mounded pasture; little cottages and chapels gleaming out from among the trees at every turn. Behind me, some leagues in length, rose the jagged range of the mountains of the Réposoir; on the other side of the valley, the mass of the Aiguille de Varens, heaving its seven thousand feet of cliff into the air at a single effort, its gentle gift of waterfall, the Nant d'Arpenaz, like a pillar of cloud at its feet; Mont Blanc and all its aiguilles, one silver flame, in front of me; marvellous blocks of mossy granite and dark glades of pine around me; but I could enjoy nothing, and could not for a long while make out what was the matter with me, until at last I discovered that if I confined myself to one thing,— and that a little thing,—a tuft of moss or a single crag at the top of the Varens, or a wreath or two of foam at the bottom of the Nant d'Arpenaz, I began to enjoy it directly, because then I had mind enough to put into the thing, and the enjoyment arose from the quantity of the imaginative energy I could bring to bear upon it; but when I looked at or thought of all together, moss, stones, Varens, Nant d'Arpenaz, and Mont Blanc, I had not mind enough to give to all, and none were of any value. The conclusion which would have been formed, upon this, by a German philosopher, would have been that the Mont Blanc *was* of no value; that he and his imagination only were of value; that the Mont Blanc, in fact, except so far as he was able to look at it, could not be considered as having any existence. But the only conclusion which occurred to me as reasonable under the circumstances (I have seen no ground for altering it since) was, that I was an exceedingly small creature, much tired, and, at the moment, not a little stupid; for whom a blade of grass, or a wreath of foam, was quite food enough and to spare, and that if I tried to take any more, I should make myself ill. Whereupon, associating myself fraternally with some ants, who were deeply interested in the conveyance of some small sticks over the road, and rather, as I think they generally are, in too great a hurry about it, I returned home in a little while with great con-tentment; thinking how well it was ordered that, as Mont Blanc and his pine forests could not be everywhere, nor all the world come to see them, the human mind, on the whole, should enjoy itself most surely, in an ant-like manner, and be happy and busy with the bits of sticks and grains of crystal that fall in its way to be handled, in daily duty.

It follows evidently from the first of these characters of the imagination, its dislike of substance and presence, that a picture has in some measure even an advantage with us in not being real. The imagination rejoices in having something to do, springs up with all its willing power, flattered and happy; and ready with its fairest colours and most tender pencilling, to prove itself worthy of the trust, and exalt into sweet supremacy the shadow that has been confided to its fondness. And thus, so far from its being at all an object to the painter to make his work look real, he ought to dread such a consummation as the loss of one of its most precious claims upon the heart. So far from striving to convince the beholder that what he sees is substance, his mind should be to what he paints as the fire to the body on the pile, burning away the ashes, leaving the unconquerable shade—an immortal dream. So certain is this, that the slightest local success in giving the deceptive appearance of reality—the imitation, for instance, of the texture of a bit of wood, with its grain in relief—will instantly destroy the charm of a whole picture; the imagination feels itself insulted and injured, and passes by with cold contempt; nay, however beautiful the whole scene may be, the mere fact of its being deceptively real is enough to make us tire of it; we may be surprised and pleased for a moment, but the imagination will not on those terms be persuaded to give any of its help, and, in a quarter of an hour we wish the scene would change.

"Well, but then, what becomes of all these long dogmatic chapters of yours about giving nothing but the truth, and as much truth as possible?"

The chapters are all quite right. "Nothing but the Truth," I say still. "As much Truth as possible," I say still. But truth so presented that it will need the help of the imagination to make it real. Between the painter and beholder, each doing his proper part, the reality should be sustained; and after the beholding imagination has come forward and done its best, then, with its help and in the full action of it, the beholder should be able to say, I feel as if I were at the real place, or seeing the real incident. But not without that help.

Farther, in consequence of that other character of the imagination,   186 fatiguableness, it is a great advantage to the picture that it need not present too much at once, and that what it does present may be so chosen and ordered as not only to be more easily seized, but to give the imagination rest, and, as it were, places to lie down and stretch its limbs in; kindly vacancies, beguiling it back into action, with pleasant and cautious sequence of incident; all jarring thoughts being excluded, all vain redundance denied, and all just and sweet transition permitted.

And thus it is, that, for the most part, imperfect sketches, engravings, outlines, rude sculptures, and other forms of abstraction, possess a charm which the most finished picture frequently wants. For not only does the finished picture excite the imagination less, but, like nature itself, it *taxes* it more. None of it can be enjoyed till the imagination is brought to bear upon it; and the details of the completed picture are so numerous, that it needs greater strength and willingness in the beholder to follow them all out; the redundance, perhaps, being not too great for the mind of a careful observer, but too great for a casual or careless observer. So that, although the perfection of art will always consist in the utmost *acceptable* completion, yet, as every added idea will increase the difficulty of apprehension, and every added touch advance the dangerous realism which makes the imagination languid, the difference between a noble and ignoble painter is in nothing more sharply defined than in this,—that he first wishes to put into his work as much truth as possible, and yet to keep it looking *un*-real; the second wishes to get through his work lazily, with as little truth as possible, and yet to make it look real; and, so far as they add colour to their abstract sketch, the first realizes for the sake of the colour, and the second colours for the sake of the realization.

187 And then, lastly, it is another infinite advantage possessed by the picture, that in these various differences from reality it becomes the expression of the power and intelligence of a companionable human soul. In all this choice, arrangement, penetrative sight, and kindly guidance, we recognize a supernatural operation, and perceive, not merely the landscape or incident as in a mirror; but, besides, the presence of what, after all, may perhaps be the most wonderful piece of divine work in the whole matter—the great human spirit through which it is manifested to us. So that, although with respect to many important scenes, it might, as we saw above, be one of the most precious gifts that could be given us to see them with *our own eyes*, yet also in many things it is more desirable to be permitted to see them with the eyes of others; and although, to the small, conceited, and affected painter displaying his narrow knowledge and tiny dexterities, our only word may be, "Stand aside from between that nature and me:" yet to the great imaginative painter—greater a million times in every faculty of soul than we—our word may wisely be, "Come between this nature and me—this nature which is too great and too wonderful for me; temper it for me, interpret it to me; let me see with your eyes, and hear with your ears, and have help and strength from your great spirit."

All the noblest pictures have this character. They are true or inspired ideals, seen in a moment to *be* ideal; that is to say, the result of all the highest powers of the imagination, engaged in the discovery and apprehension of the purest truths, and having so arranged them as best to show their preciousness and exalt their clearness. They are always orderly, always one, ruled by one great purpose throughout, in the fulfilment of which every atom of the detail is called to help, and would be missed if removed; this peculiar oneness being the result, not of obedience to any teachable law, but of the magnificence of tone in the perfect mind, which accepts only what is good for its great purposes, rejects whatever is foreign

188 or redundant, and instinctively and instantaneously ranges whatever it accepts, in sublime subordination and helpful brotherhood.

Then, this being the greatest art, the lowest art is the mimicry of it,—the subordination of nothing to nothing; the elaborate arrangement of sightlessness and emptiness: the order which has no object; the unity which has no life, and the law which has no love; the light which has nothing to illumine, and shadow which has nothing to relieve.

And then, between these two, comes the wholesome, happy, and noble—though not noblest—art of simple transcript from nature; into which, so far as our modern Pre-Raphaelitism falls, it will indeed do sacred service in ridding us of the old fallacies and componencies, but cannot itself rise above the level of simple and happy usefulness. So far as it is to be great, it must add,—and so far as it *is* great, has already added,—the great imaginative element to all its faithfulness in transcript.

Greatness in art is not a teachable nor gainable thing, but *the expression   189 of a mind of a God-made great man*; teach, or preach, or labour as you will, everlasting difference is set between one man's capacity and another's; and this God-given supremacy is the priceless thing, always just as rare in the world at one time as another. What you can manufacture or communicate, you can lower the price of, but this mental supremacy is incommunicable; you will never multiply its quantity, nor lower its price; and nearly the best thing that men can generally do is to set themselves,   190 not to the attainment, but the discovery of this; learning to know gold, when we see it, from iron-glance, and diamonds from flint-sand, being for most of us a more profitable employment than trying to make diamonds out of our own charcoal. And for this God-made supremacy, I generally have used, and shall continue to use, the word Inspiration, not carelessly nor lightly, but in all logical calmness and perfect reverence. We English have many false ideas about reverence; we should be shocked, for instance, to see a market-woman come into church with a basket of eggs on her arm: we think it more reverent to lock her out till Sunday; and to surround the church with respectability of iron railings, and defend it with pacing inhabitation of beadles. I believe this to be *ir*reverence; and that it is more truly reverent, when the market-woman, hot and hurried, at six in the morning, her head much confused with calculations of the probable price of eggs, can nevertheless get within church porch, and church aisle, and church chancel, lay the basket down on the very steps of the altar, and receive thereat so much of help and hope as may serve her for the day's work. In like manner we are solemnly, but I think not wisely, shocked at any one who comes hurriedly into church, in any figurative way, with his basket on his arm; and perhaps so long as we feel it so, it is better to keep the basket out. But, as for this one commodity of high mental supremacy, it cannot be kept out, for the very fountain of it is in the church wall, and there is no other right word for it but this of Inspiration; a word, indeed, often ridiculously perverted, and irreverently used of fledgling poets and pompous orators—no one being offended then: and yet cavilled at when quietly used of the spirit that is in a truly great man; cavilled at, chiefly, it seems to me, because we expect to know inspiration by the look of it. Let a man have shaggy hair, dark eyes, a rolling voice, plenty of animal energy, and a facility of rhyming or sentencing, and—improvisatore or   191 sentimentalist—we call him "inspired" willingly enough; but let him be a rough, quiet worker, not proclaiming himself melodiously in anywise, but familiar with us, unpretending, and letting all his littleness and feebleness be seen, unhindered,—wearing an ill-cut coat withal; and, though he be such a man as is only sent upon the earth once in five hundred years, for some special human teaching, it is irreverent to call him "inspired." But, be it irreverent or not, this word I must always use; and the rest of what work I have here before me, is simply to prove the truth of it, with respect to the one among these mighty spirits whom we have just lost; who divided his hearers, as many an inspired speaker has done before now, into two great sects—a large and a narrow; these searching the Nature-scripture calmly, "whether those things were so," and those standing haughtily on their Mars' hill, asking, "What will this babbler say?" [33]

CHAPTER XI
Of the Novelty of Landscape

I F the reader has never suspected that landscape-painting was anything   192
but good, right, and healthy work, I should be sorry to put any doubt of
its being so into his mind; but if, as seems to me more likely, he, living in
this busy and perhaps somewhat calamitous age, has some suspicion that
landscape-painting is but an idle and empty business, not worth all our
long talk about it, then, perhaps, he will be pleased to have such suspicion
done away, before troubling himself farther with these disquisitions.

And to this end I would ask him now to imagine himself entering, for   193
the first time in his life, the room of the Old Water-Colour Society: and
to suppose that he has entered it, not for the sake of a quiet examination
of the paintings one by one, but in order to seize such ideas as it may generally suggest respecting the state and meaning of modern, as compared
with elder, art. I suppose him, of course, that he may be capable of such
a comparison, to be in some degree familiar with the different forms in
which art has developed itself within the periods historically known to us;
but never, till that moment, to have seen any completely modern work.
So prepared, and so unprepared, he would, as his ideas began to arrange
themselves, be first struck by the number of paintings representing blue
mountains, clear lakes, and ruined castles or cathedrals, and he would say
to himself: "There is something strange in the mind of these modern
people! Nobody ever cared about blue mountains before, or tried to paint
the broken stones of old walls." And the more he considered the subject,
the more he would feel the peculiarity, observing, with an increasing   194
astonishment, that the human interest had, in many cases, altogether disappeared. That mountains, instead of being used only as a blue ground for
the relief of the heads of saints, were themselves the exclusive subjects of
reverent contemplation; that their ravines, and peaks, and forests, were
all painted with an appearance of as much enthusiasm as had formerly
been devoted to the dimples of beauty, or the frowns of asceticism; and
that all the living interest which was still supposed necessary to the scene,
might be supplied by a traveller in a slouched hat, a beggar in a scarlet
cloak, or, in default of these, even by a heron or a wild duck.

And if he could entirely divest himself of his own modern habits of thought, and regard the subjects in question with the feelings of a knight or monk of the Middle Ages, it might be a question whether those feelings would not rapidly verge towards contempt.

195   There can be no question that this would have been somewhat the tone of thought with which either a Lacedæmonian, a soldier of Rome in her strength, or a knight of the thirteenth century, would have been apt to regard these particular forms of our present art. And the feelings of all the three would have agreed in this,—that their main ground of offence must have been the want of *seriousness* and *purpose* in what they saw.

And exactly so far forth their judgment would be just, as the landscape-painting could indeed be shown, for others as well as for them, to be art of this nugatory kind; and so far forth unjust, as that painting could be shown to depend upon, or cultivate, certain sensibilities which neither
196   the Greek nor mediæval knight possessed, and which have resulted from some extraordinary change in human nature since their time. We have no right to assume, without very accurate examination of it, that this change has been an ennobling one. The simple fact, that we are, in some strange way, different from all the great races that have existed before us, cannot at once be received as the proof of our own greatness; nor can it be granted, without any question, that we have a legitimate subject of complacency in being under the influence of feelings, with which neither Miltiades nor the Black Prince, neither Homer nor Dante, neither Socrates nor St. Francis, could for an instant have sympathized.

Whether, however, this fact be one to excite our pride or not, it is assuredly one to excite our deepest interest. The fact itself is certain. For nearly six thousand years the energies of man have pursued certain beaten paths, manifesting some constancy of feeling throughout all that period, and involving some fellowship at heart, among the various nations who by turns succeeded or surpassed each other in the several aims of art or policy. So that, for these thousands of years, the whole human race might be to some extent described in general terms. Man was a creature separated from all others by his instinctive sense of an Existence superior to his own, invariably manifesting this sense of the being of a God more strongly in proportion to his own perfectness of mind and body; and making enormous and self-denying efforts, in order to obtain some persuasion of the immediate presence or approval of the Divinity. So that, on the whole, the best things he did were done as in the presence, or for the honour, of his gods; and, whether in statues, to help him to imagine them, or temples raised to their honour, or acts of self-sacrifice done in the hope of their love, he brought whatever was best and skilfullest in him into their service, and lived in a perpetual subjection to their unseen power. Also, he was always anxious to know something definite about them; and his

chief books, songs, and pictures were filled with legends about them, 197
or specially devoted to illustration of their lives and nature.

Next to these gods he was always anxious to know something about his
human ancestors; fond of exalting the memory, and telling or painting the
history of old rulers and benefactors; yet full of an enthusiastic confidence
in himself, as having in many ways advanced beyond the best efforts of
past time; and eager to record his own doings for future fame. He was a
creature eminently warlike, placing his principal pride in dominion;
eminently beautiful, and having great delight in his own beauty; setting
forth this beauty by every species of invention in dress, and rendering his
arms and accoutrements superbly decorative of his form. He took, however, very little interest in anything but what belonged to humanity;
caring in no wise for the external world, except as it influenced his own
destiny; honouring the lightning because it could strike him, the sea
because it could drown him, the fountains because they gave him drink,
and the grass because it yielded him seed; but utterly incapable of feeling
any special happiness in the love of such things, or any earnest emotion
about them, considered as separate from man; therefore giving no time to
the study of them;—knowing little of herbs, except only which were
hurtful and which healing; of stones, only which would glitter brightest in
a crown, or last the longest in a wall: of the wild beasts, which were best
for food, and which the stoutest quarry for the hunter;—thus spending
only on the lower creatures and inanimate things his waste energy, his
dullest thoughts, his most languid emotions, and reserving all his acuter
intellect for researches into his own nature and that of the gods; all his
strength of will for the acquirement of political or moral power; all his
sense of beauty for things immediately connected with his own person and
life; and all his deep affections for domestic or divine companionship.

Such, in broad light and brief terms, was man for five thousand years.
Such he is no longer. Let us consider what he is now, comparing the 198
descriptions clause by clause.

I. He *was* invariably sensible of the existence of gods, and went about all
his speculations or works holding this as an acknowledged fact, making his
best efforts in their service. *Now* he is capable of going through life with
hardly any positive idea on this subject,—doubting, fearing, suspecting,
analyzing,—doing everything, in fact, *but* believing; hardly ever getting
quite up to that point which hitherto was wont to be the starting-point for
all generations. And human work has accordingly hardly any reference to
spiritual beings, but is done either from a patriotic or personal interest,—
either to benefit mankind, or reach some selfish end, not (I speak of
human work in the broad sense) to please the gods.

II. He *was* a beautiful creature, setting forth this beauty by all means in
his power, and depending upon it for much of his authority over his

fellows. So that the ruddy cheek of David, and the ivory skin of Atrides, and the towering presence of Saul, and the blue eyes of Cœur de Lion, were among chief reasons why they should be kings; and it was one of the aims of all education, and of all dress, to make the presence of the human form stately and lovely. *Now* it has become the task of grave philosophy partly to depreciate or conceal this bodily beauty; and even by those who esteem it in their hearts, it is not made one of the great ends of education; man has become, upon the whole, an ugly animal, and is not ashamed of his ugliness.

III. He *was* eminently warlike. He is *now* gradually becoming more and more ashamed of all the arts and aims of battle. So that the desire of dominion, which was once frankly confessed or boasted of as a heroic passion, is now sternly reprobated or cunningly disclaimed.

IV. He *used* to take no interest in anything but what immediately concerned himself. *Now*, he has deep interest in the abstract nature of things, inquires as eagerly into the laws which regulate the economy of the material world, as into those of his own being, and manifests a passionate admiration of inanimate objects, closely resembling, in its elevation and tenderness, the affection which he bears to those living souls with which he is brought into the nearest fellowship.

It is this last change only which is to be the subject of our present inquiry; but it cannot be doubted that it is closely connected with all the others, and that we can only thoroughly understand its nature by considering it in this connection.

Of course a complete analysis, or anything like it, would involve a treatise on the whole history of the world. I shall merely endeavour to note some of the leading and more interesting circumstances bearing on the subject, and to show sufficient practical ground for the conclusion, that landscape-painting is indeed a noble and useful art, though one not long known by man.

199

200

CHAPTER XII
Of the Pathetic Fallacy

GERMAN dulness, and English affectation, have of late much multi- 201
plied among us the use of two of the most objectionable words that
were ever coined by the troublesomeness of metaphysicians,—namely,
"Objective," and "Subjective."

No words can be more exquisitely, and in all points, useless; and I
merely speak of them that I may, at once and for ever, get them out of my
way, and out of my reader's. But to get that done, they must be explained.

The word "Blue," say certain philosophers, means the sensation of
colour which the human eye receives in looking at the open sky, or at a
bell gentian.

Now, say they farther, as this sensation can only be felt when the eye is
turned to the object, and as, therefore, no such sensation is produced by
the object when nobody looks at it, therefore the thing, when it is not
looked at, is not blue; and thus (say they) there are many qualities of things
which depend as much on something else as on themselves.

And then they agree that the qualities of things which thus depend
upon our perception of them, and upon our human nature as affected by 202
them, shall be called Subjective; and the qualities of things which they
always have, irrespective of any other nature, as roundness or squareness,
shall be called Objective.

From these ingenious views the step is very easy to a farther opinion,
that it does not much matter what things are in themselves, but only what
they are to us; and that the only real truth of them is their appearance to,
or effect upon, us. From which position, with a hearty desire for mystifi-
cation, and much egotism, selfishness, shallowness, and impertinence, a
philosopher may easily go so far as to believe, and say, that everything in
the world depends upon his seeing or thinking of it, and that nothing,
therefore, exists, but what he sees or thinks of.

Now, to get rid of all these ambiguities and troublesome words at once,
be it observed that the word "Blue" does *not* mean the *sensation* caused by
a gentian on the human eye; but it means the *power* of producing that
sensation: and this power is always there, in the thing, whether we are

362

there to experience it or not, and would remain there though there were not left a man on the face of the earth.

203   Hence I would say to these philosophers: If, instead of using the sonorous phrase, "It is objectively so," you will use the plain old phrase, "It *is* so," and if instead of the sonorous phrase, "It is subjectively so," you will say, in plain old English, "It does so," or "It seems so to me," you will, on the whole, be more intelligible to your fellow-creatures; and besides, if you find that a thing which generally "does so" to other people (as a gentian looks blue to most men), does *not* so to you, on any particular occasion, you will not fall into the impertinence of saying, that the thing is not so, or did not so, but you will say simply (what you will be all the better for speedily finding out), that something is the matter with you.

204   Now, therefore, putting these tiresome and absurd words quite out of our way, we may go on at our ease to examine the point in question,—namely, the difference between the ordinary, proper, and true appearances of things to us; and the extraordinary, or false appearances, when we are under the influence of emotion, or contemplative fancy; false appearances, I say, as being entirely unconnected with any real power or character in the object, and only imputed to it by us.

For instance—

> "The spendthrift crocus, bursting through the mould
> Naked and shivering, with his cup of gold."[34]

This is very beautiful, and yet very untrue. The crocus is not a spendthrift, but a hardy plant; its yellow is not gold, but saffron. How is it that we enjoy so much the having it put into our heads that it is anything else than a plain crocus?

It is an important question. For, throughout our past reasonings about art, we have always found that nothing could be good or useful, or ultimately pleasurable, which was untrue. But here is something pleasurable in written poetry, which is nevertheless *un*true. And what is 205   more, if we think over our favourite poetry, we shall find it full of this kind of fallacy, and that we like it all the more for being so.

It will appear also, on consideration of the matter, that this fallacy is of two principal kinds. Either, as in this case of the crocus, it is the fallacy of wilful fancy, which involves no real expectation that it will be believed; or else it is a fallacy caused by an excited state of the feelings, making us, for the time, more or less irrational. Of the cheating of the fancy we shall have to speak presently; but in this chapter, I want to examine the nature of the other error, that which the mind admits when affected strongly by emotion. Thus, for instance, in *Alton Locke*,—

> "They rowed her in across the rolling foam—
> The cruel, crawling foam."[35]

The foam is not cruel, neither does it crawl. The state of mind which attributes to it these characters of a living creature is one in which the reason is unhinged by grief. All violent feelings have the same effect. They produce in us a falseness in all our impressions of external things, which I would generally characterize as the "pathetic fallacy."

Now we are in the habit of considering this fallacy as eminently a character of poetical description, and the temper of mind in which we allow it, as one eminently poetical, because passionate. But I believe, if we look well into the matter, that we shall find the greatest poets do not often admit this kind of falseness,—that it is only the second order of poets who much delight in it.

Thus, when Dante describes the spirits falling from the bank of Acheron   206 "as dead leaves flutter from a bough,"[36] he gives the most perfect image possible of their utter lightness, feebleness, passiveness, and scattering agony of despair, without, however, for an instant losing his own clear perception that *these* are souls, and *those* are leaves; he makes no confusion of one with the other. But when Coleridge speaks of

> "The one red leaf, the last of its clan,
> That dances as often as dance it can,"[37]

he has a morbid, that is to say, a so far false, idea about the leaf; he fancies a life in it, and will, which there are not; confuses its powerlessness with   207 choice, its fading death with merriment, and the wind that shakes it with music. Here, however, there is some beauty, even in the morbid passage; but take an instance in Homer and Pope. Without the knowledge of Ulysses, Elpenor, his youngest follower, has fallen from an upper chamber in the Circean palace, and has been left dead, unmissed by his leader or companions, in the haste of their departure. They cross the sea to the Cimmerian land; and Ulysses summons the shades from Tartarus. The first which appears is that of the lost Elpenor. Ulysses, amazed, and in exactly the spirit of bitter and terrified lightness which is seen in Hamlet,* addresses the spirit with the simple, startled words:—

"Elpenor! How camest thou under the shadowy darkness? Hast thou come faster on foot than I in my black ship?"[38]

Which Pope renders thus:—

> "O, say, what angry power Elpenor led
> To glide in shades, and wander with the dead?
> How could thy soul, by realms and seas disjoined,
> Outfly the nimble sail, and leave the lagging wind?"

---

*"Well said, old mole! canst work i' the ground so fast?"[39]

I sincerely hope the reader finds no pleasure here, either in the nimbleness of the sail, or the laziness of the wind! And yet how is it that these conceits are so painful now, when they have been pleasant to us in the other instances?

For a very simple reason. They are not a *pathetic* fallacy at all, for they are put into the mouth of the wrong passion—a passion which never could possibly have spoken them—agonized curiosity. Ulysses wants to know the facts of the matter; and the very last thing his mind could do at the moment would be to pause, or suggest in any wise what was *not* a fact. The delay in the first three lines, and conceit in the last, jar upon us instantly like the most frightful discord in music. No poet of true imaginative power could possibly have written the passage.

Therefore we see that the spirit of truth must guide us in some sort, even in our enjoyment of fallacy. Coleridge's fallacy has no discord in it, but Pope's has set our teeth on edge. Without farther questioning, I will endeavour to state the main bearings of this matter.

The temperament which admits the pathetic fallacy, is, as I said above, that of a mind and body in some sort too weak to deal fully with what is before them or upon them; borne away, or over-clouded, or over-dazzled by emotion; and it is a more or less noble state, according to the force of the emotion which has induced it. For it is no credit to a man that he is not morbid or inaccurate in his perceptions, when he has no strength of feeling to warp them; and it is in general a sign of higher capacity and stand in the ranks of being, that the emotions should be strong enough to vanquish, partly, the intellect, and make it believe what they choose. But it is still a grander condition when the intellect also rises, till it is strong enough to assert its rule against, or together with, the utmost efforts of the passions; and the whole man stands in an iron glow, white hot, perhaps, but still strong, and in no wise evaporating; even if he melts, losing none of his weight.

So, then, we have the three ranks: the man who perceives rightly, because he does not feel, and to whom the primrose is very accurately the primrose, because he does not love it. Then, secondly, the man who perceives wrongly, because he feels, and to whom the primrose is anything else than a primrose: a star, or a sun, or a fairy's shield, or a forsaken maiden. And then, lastly, there is the man who perceives rightly in spite of his feelings, and to whom the primrose is for ever nothing else than itself—a little flower apprehended in the very plain and leafy fact of it, whatever and how many soever the associations and passions may be that crowd around it. And, in general, these three classes may be rated in comparative order, as the men who are not poets at all, and the poets of the second order, and the poets of the first; only however great a man may be, there are always some subjects which *ought* to throw him off his balance; some, by which his poor human capacity of thought should be conquered, and brought into the inaccurate and vague state of perception, so that the language of the highest inspiration becomes broken, obscure, and wild in metaphor, resembling that of the weaker man, overborne by weaker things.

And thus, in full, there are four classes: the men who feel nothing, and therefore see truly; the men who feel strongly, think weakly, and see untruly (second order of poets); the men who feel strongly, think strongly, and see truly (first order of poets); and the men who, strong as human creatures can be, are yet submitted to influences stronger than they, and see in a sort untruly, because what they see is inconceivably above them. This last is the usual condition of prophetic inspiration.

I separate these classes, in order that their character may be clearly understood; but of course they are united each to the other by imperceptible transitions, and the same mind, according to the influences to which it is subjected, passes at different times into the various states. Still, the difference between the great and less man is, on the whole, chiefly 210 in this point of *alterability*. That is to say, the one knows too much, and perceives and feels too much of the past and future, and of all things beside and around that which immediately affects him, to be in any wise shaken by it. His mind is made up; his thoughts have an accustomed current; his ways are steadfast; it is not this or that new sight which will at once unbalance him. He is tender to impression at the surface, like a rock with deep moss upon it; but there is too much mass of him to be moved. The smaller man, with the same degree of sensibility, is at once carried off his feet; he wants to do something he did not want to do before; he views all the universe in a new light through his tears; he is gay or enthusiastic, melancholy or passionate, as things come and go to him. Therefore the high creative poet might even be thought, to a great extent, impassive (as shallow people think Dante stern), receiving indeed all feelings to the full, but having a great centre of reflection and knowledge in which he stands serene, and watches the feeling, as it were, from afar off.

Dante, in his most intense moods, has entire command of himself, and can look around calmly, at all moments, for the image or the word that will best tell what he sees to the upper or lower world. But Keats and Tennyson, and the poets of the second order, are generally themselves subdued by the feelings under which they write, or, at least, write as choosing to be so; and therefore admit certain expressions and modes of thought which are in some sort diseased or false.

Now so long as we see that the *feeling* is true, we pardon, or are even pleased by, the confessed fallacy of sight which it induces: we are pleased, for instance, with those lines of Kingsley's above quoted, not because they fallaciously describe foam, but because they faithfully describe sorrow. But

the moment the mind of the speaker becomes cold, that moment every
211 such expression becomes untrue, as being for ever untrue in the external
facts. And there is no greater baseness in literature than the habit of using
these metaphorical expressions in cool blood. An inspired writer, in full
impetuosity of passion, may speak wisely and truly of "raging waves of the
sea foaming out their own shame";[40] but it is only the basest writer who
cannot speak of the sea without talking of "raging waves," "remorseless
floods," "ravenous billows," etc.; and it is one of the signs of the highest
power in a writer to check all such habits of thought, and to keep his eyes
fixed firmly on the *pure fact*, out of which if any feeling comes to him or
his reader, he knows it must be a true one.

215   The greatness of a poet depends upon the two faculties, acuteness of
feeling, and command of it. A poet is great, first in proportion to the
strength of his passion, and then, that strength being granted, in
proportion to his government of it; there being, however, always a point
beyond which it would be inhuman and monstrous if he pushed this
government, and, therefore, a point at which all feverish and wild fancy
becomes just and true.

216   But by how much this feeling is noble when it is justified by the strength
of its cause, by so much it is ignoble when there is not cause enough for
it; and beyond all other ignobleness is the mere affectation of it, in hardness of heart. Simply bad writing may almost always, as above noticed, be
known by its adoption of these fanciful metaphorical expressions as a sort
of current coin; yet there is even a worse, at least a more harmful condition of writing than this, in which such expressions are not ignorantly
and feelinglessly caught up, but, by some master, skilful in handling, yet
insincere, deliberately wrought out with chill and studied fancy; as if we
should try to make an old lava-stream look red hot again, by covering it
with dead leaves, or white-hot, with hoar-frost.
      Hear the cold-hearted Pope say to a shepherd girl—

> "Where'er you walk, cool gales shall fan the glade;
> Trees, where you sit, shall crowd into a shade;
> Your praise the birds shall chant in every grove,
> And winds shall waft it to the powers above.

217
> But would you sing, and rival Orpheus' strain,
> The wondering forests soon should dance again;
> The moving mountains hear the powerful call,
> And headlong streams hang, listening, in their fall."[41]

      This is not, nor could it for a moment be mistaken for, the language of
passion. It is simple falsehood, uttered by hypocrisy; definite absurdity,
rooted in affectation, and coldly asserted in the teeth of nature and fact.
Passion will indeed go far in deceiving itself; but it must be a strong

passion, not the simple wish of a lover to tempt his mistress to sing. Compare a very closely parallel passage in Wordsworth, in which the lover has lost his mistress:

> "Three years had Barbara in her grave been laid,
>   When thus his moan he made:—
>
> 'Oh, move, thou cottage, from behind yon oak,
>   Or let the ancient tree uprooted lie,
> That in some other way yon smoke
>   May mount into the sky.
> If still behind yon pine-tree's ragged bough,
>   Headlong, the waterfall must come,
>   Oh, let it, then, be dumb—
> Be anything, sweet stream, but that which thou art now."[42]

Here is a cottage to be moved, if not a mountain, and a waterfall to be silent, if it is not to hang listening: but with what different relation to the mind that contemplates them! Here, in the extremity of its agony, the soul cries out wildly for relief, which at the same moment it partly knows to be impossible, but partly believes possible, in a vague impression that a miracle *might* be wrought to give relief even to a less sore distress,—that nature is kind, and God is kind, and that grief is strong: it knows not well what *is* possible to such grief. To silence a stream, to move a cottage wall,—one might think it could do as much as that!

I believe these instances are enough to illustrate the main point I insist 218 upon respecting the pathetic fallacy,—that so far as it *is* a fallacy, it is always the sign of a morbid state of mind, and comparatively of a weak one. Even in the most inspired prophet it is a sign of the incapacity of his human sight or thought to bear what has been revealed to it. In ordinary poetry, if it is found in the thoughts of the poet himself, it is at once a sign of his belonging to the inferior school; if in the thoughts of the characters imagined by him, it is right or wrong according to the genuineness of the emotion from which it springs; always, however, implying necessarily *some* degree of weakness in the character.

CHAPTER XIII
Of Classical Landscape

221   MY reason for asking the reader to give so much of his time to the examination of the pathetic fallacy was, that, whether in literature or in art, he will find it eminently characteristic of the modern mind; and in the landscape, whether of literature or art, he will also find the modern painter endeavouring to express something which he, as a living creature, imagines in the lifeless object, while the classical and mediæval painters were content with expressing the unimaginary and actual qualities of the object itself.

It is surely a very notable circumstance that this pathetic fallacy is eminently characteristic of modern painting. For instance, Keats, describing a wave breaking out at sea, says of it—

> "Down whose green back the short-lived foam, all hoar,
> Bursts gradual, with a wayward indolence."[43]

That is quite perfect, as an example of the modern manner. The idea of the peculiar action with which foam rolls down a long, large wave could not have been given by any other words so well as by this "wayward
222   indolence." But Homer would never have written, never thought of, such words. He could not by any possibility have lost sight of the great fact that the wave, from the beginning to the end of it, do what it might, was still nothing else than salt water; and that salt water could not be either wayward or indolent. He will call the waves "over-roofed," "full-charged," "monstrous," "compact-black," "dark-clear," "violet-coloured," "wine-coloured," and so on. But every one of these epithets is descriptive of pure physical nature; they are as accurate and intense in truth as words can be, but they never show the slightest feeling of anything animated in the ocean. Black or clear, monstrous or violet-coloured, cold salt water it is always, and nothing but that.

"Well, but the modern writer, by his admission of the tinge of fallacy, has given an idea of something in the action of the wave which Homer could not, and surely, therefore, has made a step in advance? Also there appears to be a degree of sympathy and feeling in the one writer, which there is not in the other; and as it has been received for a first principle that writers are great in proportion to the intensity of their feelings, and Homer seems to have no feelings about the sea but that it is black and deep, surely in this respect also the modern writer is the greater?''

Stay a moment. Homer *had* some feeling about the sea; a faith in the animation of it much stronger than Keats's. But all this sense of something living in it, he separates in his mind into a great abstract image of a Sea Power. He never says the waves rage, or the waves are idle. But he says there is somewhat in, and greater than, the waves, which rages, and is idle, and *that* he calls a god.

223

I do not think we ever enough endeavour to enter into what a Greek's real notion of a god was. We are so accustomed to the modern mockeries of the classical religion, so accustomed to hear and see the Greek gods introduced as living personages, or invoked for help, by men who believe neither in them nor in any other gods, that we seem to have infected the Greek ages themselves with the breath, and dimmed them with the shade, of our hypocrisy; and are apt to think that Homer, as we know that Pope, was merely an ingenious fabulist; nay, more than this, that all the nations of past time were ingenious fabulists also, to whom the universe was a lyrical drama, and by whom whatsoever was said about it was merely a witty allegory, or a graceful lie, of which the entire upshot and con-summation was a pretty statue in the middle of the court, or at the end of the garden.

This, at least, is one of our forms of opinion about Greek faith; not, indeed, possible altogether to any man of honesty or ordinary powers of thought; but still so venomously inherent in the modern philosophy that all the pure lightning of Carlyle cannot as yet quite burn it out of any of us. And then, side by side with this mere infidel folly, stands the bitter short-sightedness of Puritanism, holding the classical god to be either simply an idol,—a block of stone ignorantly, though sincerely, worshipped—or else an actual diabolic or betraying power, usurping the place of God.

Both these Puritanical estimates of Greek deity are of course to some extent true. The corruption of classical worship is barren idolatry; and that corruption was deepened, and variously directed to their own purposes, by the evil angels. But this was neither the whole, nor the principal part, of Pagan worship.

What, then, was actually the Greek god? In what way were the two ideas of human form, and divine power, credibly associated in the ancient heart, so as to become a subject of true faith irrespective equally of fable, allegory, superstitious trust in stone, and demoniacal influence?

224

It seems to me that the Greek had exactly the same instinctive feeling about the elements that we have ourselves; that to Homer, as much as to

Keats, the sea-wave appeared wayward or idle, or whatever else it may be to the poetical passion. But then the Greek reasoned upon this sensation, saying to himself: "I can dry this water up, or drink it. It cannot be the water that is wayward. But it must be something *in* the water, which I cannot destroy any more than I destroy myself by cutting off my finger; *I* was *in* my finger,—something of me at least was; I had a power over it and felt pain in it, though I am still as much myself when it is gone. So there may be a power in the water which is not water, but to which the water is as a body;—which can strike with it, move in it, suffer in it, yet not be destroyed with it. This something, this Great Water Spirit, I must not confuse with the waves, which are only its body. *They* may flow hither and thither, increase or diminish. *That* must be indivisible—imperishable—a god.

225   It was easy to conceive, farther, that such spirits should be able to assume at will a human form, in order to hold intercourse with men, or to perform any act for which their proper body, whether of fire, earth, or air, was unfitted. And it would have been to place them beneath, instead of above, humanity, if, assuming the form of man, they could not also have tasted his pleasures. Hence the easy step to the more or less material ideas of deities, which are apt at first to shock us, but which are indeed only dishonourable so far as they represent the gods as false and unholy. It is not the materialism, but the vice, which degrades the conception; for the materialism itself is never positive, or complete. There is always some sense of exaltation in the spiritual and immortal body; and of a power proceeding from the visible form through all the infinity of the element ruled by the particular god. The precise nature of the idea is well seen in the passage of the *Iliad* which describes the river Scamander defending the Trojans against Achilles.[44] In order to remonstrate with the hero, the god assumes a human form, which nevertheless is in some way or other instantly recognized by Achilles as that of the river-god: it is addressed at once as a river, not as a man; and its voice is the voice of a river "out of the deep whirlpools." Achilles refuses to obey its commands; and from the human form it returns instantly into its natural or divine one, and

226 endeavours to overwhelm him with waves. Vulcan defends Achilles, and sends fire against the river, which suffers in its water-body, till it is able to bear no more. At last even the "nerve of the river," or "strength of the river" (note the expression), feels the fire, and this "strength of the river" addresses Vulcan in supplications for respite. There is in this precisely the idea of a vital part of the river-body, which acted and felt, to which, if the fire reached, it was death, just as would be the case if it touched a vital part of the human body. But I do not believe that the idea ever weakens itself down to mere allegory. When Pallas is said to attack and strike down Mars, it does not mean merely that Wisdom at that moment prevailed

against Wrath. It means that there are, indeed, two great spirits, one
entrusted to guide the human soul to wisdom and chastity, the other to
kindle wrath and prompt to battle. It means that these two spirits, on the
spot where, and at the moment when, a great contest was to be decided
between all that they each governed in man, then and there (assumed)
human form, and human weapons, and did verily and materially strike at
each other, until the Spirit of Wrath was crushed.

There is not the smallest inconsistency or unspirituality in this   227
conception. If there were, it would attach equally to the appearance of the
angels to Jacob, Abraham, Joshua, or Manoah.[45] In all those instances the
highest authority which governs our own faith requires us to conceive
divine power clothed with a human form (a form so real that it is recognized for superhuman only by its "doing wondrously"), and retaining,
nevertheless, sovereignty and omnipresence in all the world. This is
precisely, as I understand it, the heathen idea of a God; and it is impossible
to comprehend any single part of the Greek mind until we grasp this faithfully, not endeavouring to explain it away in any wise, but accepting, with
frank decision and definition, the tangible existence of its deities;—blue-
eyed—white-fleshed—human-hearted,—capable   at   their   choice   of
meeting man absolutely in his own nature—feasting with him—talking
with him—fighting with him, eye to eye, or breast to breast, as Mars with
Diomed; or else, dealing with him in a more retired spirituality, as Apollo
sending the plague upon the Greeks,[46] when his quiver rattles at his
shoulders as he moves, and yet the darts sent forth of it strike not as
arrows, but as plague; or, finally, retiring completely into the material
universe which they properly inhabit, and dealing with man through that,
as Scamander with Achilles, through his waves.

Nor is there anything whatever in the various actions recorded of the
gods, however apparently ignoble, to indicate weakness of belief in them.
Very frequently things which appear to us ignoble are merely the sim-   228
plicities of a pure and truthful age. When Juno beats Diana about the ears
with her own quiver,[47] for instance, we start at first, as if Homer could not
have believed that they were both real goddesses. But what should Juno
have done? Killed Diana with a look? Nay, she neither wished to do so,
nor could she have done so, by the very faith of Diana's goddess-ship.
Diana is as immortal as herself. Frowned Diana into submission? But
Diana has come expressly to try conclusions with her, and will by no
means be frowned into submission. Wounded her with a celestial lance?
That sounds more poetical, but it is in reality partly more savage and
partly more absurd, than Homer. More savage, for it makes Juno more
cruel, therefore less divine; and more absurd, for it only seems elevated in
tone, because we use the word "celestial," which means nothing. What
sort of a thing is a "celestial" lance? Not a wooden one. Of what then? Of

moonbeams, or clouds, or mist. Well, therefore, Diana's arrows were of mist too; and her quiver, and herself, and Juno, with her lance, and all, vanish into mist. Why not have said at once, if that is all you mean, that two mists met, and one drove the other back? That would have been rational and intelligible, but not to talk of celestial lances. Homer had no such misty fancy; he believed the two goddesses were there in true bodies, with true weapons, on the true earth; and still I ask, what should Juno have done? Not beaten Diana? No; for it is unlady-like. Un-English-lady-like, yes; but by no means un-Greek-lady-like, nor even un-natural-lady-like. If a modern lady does *not* beat her servant or her rival about the ears, it is oftener because she is too weak, or too proud, than because she is of purer mind than Homer's Juno. She will not strike them; but she will overwork the one or slander the other without pity; and Homer would not have thought that one whit more goddess-like than striking them with her open hand.

229   It is only farther to be noted, that the Greek conception of Godhead, as it was much more real than we usually suppose, so it was much more bold and familiar than to a modern mind would be possible. Thus Atrides, enraged at his sword's breaking in his hand upon the helmet of Paris, after

230   he had expressly invoked the assistance of Jupiter, exclaims aloud as he would to a king who had betrayed him, "Jove, Father, there is not another god more evil-minded than thou!"[48]

The modern mind is naturally, but vulgarly and unjustly, shocked by this kind of familiarity. Rightly understood, it is not so much a sign of misunderstanding of the divine nature as of good understanding of the human. The Greek lived, in all things, a healthy, and, in a certain degree, a perfect, life. He had no morbid or sickly feeling of any kind. He was accustomed to face death without the slightest shrinking, to undergo all kinds of bodily hardship without complaint, and to do what he supposed right and honourable, in most cases, as a matter of course. Confident of his own immortality, and of the power of abstract justice, he expected to be dealt with in the next world as was right, and left the matter much in his god's hands; but being thus immortal, and finding in his own soul something which it seemed quite as difficult to master, as to rule the elements, he did not feel that it was an appalling superiority in those gods to have bodies of water, or fire, instead of flesh, and to have various work to do among the clouds and waves, out of his human way; or sometimes, even in a sort of service to himself. Was not the nourishment of herbs and flowers a kind of ministering to his wants; were not the gods in some sort his husbandmen, and spirit-servants? Their mere strength or omnipresence did not seem to him a distinction

231   absolutely terrific. In a general way, they were wiser, stronger, and better than he; and to ask counsel of them, to obey them, to sacrifice to them,

to thank them for all good, this was well: but to be utterly downcast before them, or not to tell them his mind in plain Greek if they seemed to him to be conducting themselves in an ungodly manner—this would not be well.

Such being their general idea of the gods, we can now easily understand the habitual tone of their feelings towards what was beautiful in nature. With us, observe, the idea of the Divinity is apt to get separated from the life of nature; and imagining our God upon a cloudy throne, far above the earth, and not in the flowers or waters, we approach those visible things with a theory that they are dead; governed by physical laws, and so forth. But coming to them, we find the theory fail; that they are not dead; that, say what we choose about them, the instinctive sense of their being alive is too strong for us; and in scorn of all physical law, the wilful fountain sings, and the kindly flowers rejoice. And then, puzzled, and yet happy; pleased, and yet ashamed of being so; accepting sympathy from nature, which we do not believe it gives, and giving sympathy to nature, which we do not believe it receives,—mixing, besides, all manner of purposeful play and conceit with these involuntary fellowships,—we fall necessarily into the curious web of hesitating sentiment, pathetic fallacy, and wandering fancy, which form a great part of our modern view of nature. But the Greek never removed his god out of nature at all; never attempted for a moment to contradict his instinctive sense that God was everywhere. "The tree *is* glad," said he, "I know it is; I can cut it down: no matter, there was a nymph in it. The water *does* sing," said   232 he; "I can dry it up; but no matter, there was a naiad in it." But in thus clearly defining his belief, observe, he threw it entirely into a human form, and gave his faith to nothing but the image of his own humanity. What sympathy and fellowship he had, were always for the spirit *in* the stream, not for the stream; always for the dryad *in* the wood, not for the wood. Content with this human sympathy, he approached the actual waves and woody fibres with no sympathy at all.

Then, observe farther, the Greeks lived in the midst of the most beautiful nature, and were as familiar with blue sea, clear air, and sweet outlines of mountain, as we are with brick walls, black smoke, and level fields. This perfect familiarity rendered all such scenes of natural beauty unexciting, if not indifferent to them, by lulling and over-wearying the imagination as far as it was concerned with such things; but there was another kind of beauty which they found it required effort to obtain, and which, when thoroughly obtained, seemed more glorious than any of this wild loveliness—the beauty of the human countenance and form. This, they perceived, could only be reached by continual exercise of virtue; and it was in Heaven's sight, and theirs, all the more beautiful because it needed this self-denial to obtain it. So they set themselves to reach

this, and having gained it, gave it their principal thoughts, and set it off
233   with beautiful dress as best they might. But making this their object, they
were obliged to pass their lives in simple exercise and disciplined
employments. Living wholesomely, giving themselves no fever fits, either
by fasting or over-eating, constantly in the open air, and full of animal
spirit and physical power, they became incapable of every morbid condition of mental emotion. They had indeed their sorrows, true and deep,
but still, more like children's sorrows than ours, whether bursting into
open cry of pain, or hid with shuddering under the veil, still passing over
the soul as clouds do over heaven, not sullying it, not mingling with it;—
darkening it perhaps long or utterly, but still not becoming one with it,
and for the most part passing away in dashing rain of tears, and leaving
the man unchanged: in nowise affecting, as our sorrow does, the whole
tone of his thought and imagination thenceforward.

Farther, the human beauty, which, whether in its bodily being or in
imagined divinity, had become, for the reasons we have seen, the
principal object of culture and sympathy to these Greeks, was, in its perfection, eminently orderly, symmetrical, and tender. Hence, contem-
234   plating it constantly in this state, they could not but feel a proportionate
fear of all that was disorderly, unbalanced, and rugged. Having trained
their stoutest soldiers into a strength so delicate and lovely, that their
white flesh, with their blood upon it, should look like ivory stained with
purple;[49] and having always around them, in the motion and majesty of
this beauty, enough for the full employment of their imagination, they
shrank with dread or hatred from all the ruggedness of lower nature,—from
the wrinkled forest bark, the jagged hill-crest, and irregular, inorganic
storm of sky; looking to these for the most part as adverse powers, and
taking pleasure only in such portions of the lower world as were at once
conducive to the rest and health of the human frame, and in harmony
with the laws of its gentler beauty.

Thus, as far as I recollect, without a single exception, every Homeric
landscape, intended to be beautiful, is composed of a fountain, a meadow,
and a shady grove. This ideal is very interestingly marked, as intended for
a perfect one, in the fifth book of the *Odyssey*; when Mercury himself stops
for a moment, though on a message, to look at a landscape "which even
an immortal might be gladdened to behold."[50] This landscape consists of
a cave covered with a running vine, all blooming into grapes, and
surrounded by a grove of alder, poplar, and sweet-smelling cypress. Four
fountains of white (foaming) water, springing *in succession* (mark the
orderliness), and close to one another, flow away in different directions,
through a meadow full of violets and parsley; the air is perfumed not only
by these violets, and by the sweet cypress, but by Calypso's fire of finely
chopped cedar-wood, which sends a smoke, as of incense, through the

island; Calypso herself is singing; and finally, upon the trees are resting,   235
or roosting, owls, hawks, and "long-tongued sea-crows."

Now the notable things in this description are, first, the evident
subservience of the whole landscape to human comfort, to the foot, the
taste, or the smell; and, secondly, that throughout the passage there is not
a single figurative word expressive of the things being in any wise other
than plain grass, fruit, or flower.

If we glance through the references to pleasant landscape which occur
in other parts of the *Odyssey*, we shall always be struck by this quiet
subjection of their every feature to human service, and by the excessive
similarity in the scenes.

Now, exactly this same contemplation of subservience to human use   241
makes the Greek take some pleasure in *rocks*, when they assume one
particular form, but one only—that of a *cave*. They are evidently quite
frightful things to him under any other condition, and most of all if they
are rough and jagged; but if smooth, looking "sculptured,"[51] like the   242
sides of a ship, and forming a cave or shelter for him, he begins to think
them endurable. Hence, associating the ideas of rich and sheltering wood,
sea, becalmed and made useful as a port by projecting promontories of
rock, and smoothed caves or grottoes in the rocks themselves, we get the
pleasantest idea which the Greek could form of a landscape, next to a
marsh with poplars in it; not, indeed, if possible, ever to be without these
last; thus, in commending the Cyclops' country as one possessed of every
perfection, Homer first says: "They have soft *marshy* meadows near the
sea, and good, rich, crumbling, ploughing-land, giving fine deep crops,
and vines always giving fruit;" then, "a port so quiet, that they have no
need of cables in it; and at the head of the port, a beautiful clear spring just
under a cave, and *aspen poplars all round it*."[52]

In all this I cannot too strongly mark the utter absence of any trace   243
of the feeling for what we call the picturesque, and the constant dwelling
of the writer's mind on what was available, pleasant, or useful; his ideas
respecting all landscape being not uncharacteristically summed, finally,
by Pallas herself; when, meeting Ulysses, who after his long wandering
does not recognize his own country, and meaning to describe it as politely
and soothingly as possible, she says:[53]—"This Ithaca of ours is, indeed, a
rough country enough, and not good for driving in; but, still, things might
be worse: it has plenty of corn, and good wine, and *always rain*, and soft
nourishing dew, and it has good feeding for goats and oxen, and all   244
manner of wood, and springs fit to drink at all the year round."

We shall see presently how the blundering, pseudo-picturesque, pseudo-
classical minds of Claude and the Renaissance landscape-painters, wholly
missing Homer's practical common sense, and equally incapable of feeling

the quiet natural grace and sweetness of his asphodel meadows, tender aspen poplars, or running vines,—fastened on his *ports* and *caves*, as the only available features of his scenery; and appointed the type of "classical landscape" thenceforward to consist in a bay of insipid sea, and a rock with a hole through it.

CHAPTER XIV

Of Mediæval Landscape:—First, the Fields

I N our examination of the spirit of classical landscape, we were obliged   248
to confine ourselves to what is left to us in written description. In the
Middle Ages, however, the case is widely different. We have written
landscape, sculptured landscape, and painted landscape, all bearing
united testimony to the tone of the national mind in almost every
remarkable locality of Europe.

That testimony, taken in its breadth, is very curiously conclusive. It
marks the mediæval mind as agreeing altogether with the ancients, in
holding that flat land, brooks, and groves of aspens, compose the pleasant
places of the earth, and that rocks and mountains are, for inhabitation,
altogether to be reprobated and detested; but as disagreeing with the
classical mind totally in this other most important respect, that the
pleasant flat land is never a ploughed field, nor a rich lotus meadow good
for pasture, but *garden* ground covered with flowers, and divided by
fragrant hedges, with a castle in the middle of it.

Finally, mountain scenery, though considered as disagreeable for   249
general inhabitation, is always introduced as being proper to meditate in,
or to encourage communion with higher beings; and in the ideal landscape of daily life, mountains are considered agreeable things enough, so
that they be far enough away.

In this great change there are three vital points to be noticed.

The first, the disdain of agricultural pursuits by the nobility; a fatal
change, and one gradually bringing about the ruin of that nobility. It is
expressed in the mediæval landscape by the eminently pleasurable and
horticultural character of everything; by the fences, hedges, castle walls,
and masses of useless, but lovely flowers, especially roses. The knights and
ladies are represented always as singing, or making love, in these pleasant
places.

The second vital point is the evidence of a more sentimental enjoyment   250
of external nature. A Greek, wishing really to enjoy himself, shut himself
into a beautiful atrium, with an excellent dinner, and a society of philosophical or musical friends. But a mediæval knight went into his

pleasance, to gather roses and hear the birds sing; or rode out hunting or hawking.

This change is evidently a healthy, and a very interesting one.

The third vital point is the marked sense that this hawking and apple-eating are not altogether right; that there is something else to be done in the world than that; and that the mountains, as opposed to the pleasant garden-ground, are places where that other something may best be learned; which is evidently a piece of infinite and new respect for the mountains, and another healthy change in the tone of the human heart.

Let us glance at the signs and various results of these changes one by one.

The two first named, evil and good as they are, are very closely connected. The more poetical delight in external nature proceeds just from the fact that it is no longer looked upon with the eye of the farmer; and in proportion as the herbs and flowers cease to be regarded as useful, they are felt to be charming. Leeks are not now the most important objects in the garden, but lilies and roses: the herbage which a Greek would have looked at only with a view to the number of horses it would feed, is regarded by the mediæval knight as a green carpet for fair feet to dance upon, and the beauty of its softness and colour is proportionally felt by him; while the brook, which the Greek rejoiced to dismiss into a reservoir under the palace threshold, would be, by the mediæval, distributed into pleasant pools, or forced into fountains; and regarded alternately as a mirror for fair faces, and a witchery to ensnare the sunbeams and the rainbow.

And this change of feeling involves two others, very important. When the flowers and grass were regarded as means of life, and therefore (as the thoughtful labourer of the soil must always regard them) with the reverence due to those gifts of God which were most necessary to his existence; although their own beauty was less felt, their proceeding from the Divine hand was more seriously acknowledged, and the herb yielding seed, the fruit-tree yielding fruit, though in themselves less admired, were yet solemnly connected in the heart with the reverence of Ceres, Pomona, or Pan. But when the sense of these necessary uses was more or less lost, among the upper classes, by the delegation of the art of husbandry to the hands of the peasant, the flower and fruit, whose bloom or richness thus became a mere source of pleasure, were regarded with less solemn sense of the Divine gift in them; and were converted rather into toys than treasures, chance gifts for gaiety, rather than promised rewards of labour; so that while the Greek could hardly have trodden the formal furrow, or plucked the clusters from the trellised vine, without reverent thoughts of the deities of field and leaf, who gave the seed to fructify, and the bloom to darken, the mediæval knight plucked the violet to wreathe in his lady's hair, or strewed the idle rose on the turf at her feet, with little sense of anything in the nature that gave them, but a frail, accidental, involuntary exuberance; while the peasant, reduced to serf level, was incapable of   252 imaginative thought, owing to his want of general cultivation. But on the other hand, exactly in proportion as the idea of definite spiritual presence in material nature was lost, the mysterious sense of *unaccountable* life in the things themselves would be increased, and the mind would instantly be laid open to all those currents of fallacious, but pensive and pathetic sympathy, which we have seen to be characteristic of modern times.

Farther: a singular difference would necessarily result from the far greater loneliness of baronial life, deprived as it was of all interest in agricultural pursuits. The palace of a Greek leader in early times might have gardens, fields, and farms around it, but was sure to be near some busy city or sea-port: in later times, the city itself became the principal dwelling-place, and the country was visited only to see how the farm went on, or traversed in a line of march. Far other was the life of the mediæval baron, nested on his solitary jut of crag; entering into cities only occasionally for some grave political or warrior's purpose, and, for the most part, passing the years of his life in lion-like isolation; the village inhabited by his retainers straggling indeed about the slopes of the rocks at his feet, but his own dwelling standing gloomily apart, between them and the uncompanionable clouds, commanding, from sunset to sunrise, the flowing flame of some calm unvoyaged river, and the endless undulation of the untraversable hills.

Nor was it without similar effect on the minds of men that their   253 journeyings and pilgrimages became more frequent than those of the Greek, the extent of ground traversed in the course of them larger, and the mode of travel more companionless. To the Greek, a voyage to Egypt, or the Hellespont, was the subject of lasting fame and fable, and the forests of the Danube and the rocks of Sicily closed for him the gates of the intelligible world. But to the mediæval knight, from Scottish moor to Syrian sand, the world was one great exercise ground, or field of adventure; the staunch pacing of his charger penetrated the pathlessness of outmost forest, and sustained the sultriness of the most secret desert. Frequently alone,—or, if accompanied, for the most part only by retainers of lower rank, incapable of entering into complete sympathy with any of his thoughts, he must have been compelled often to enter into dim companionship with the silent nature around him, and must assuredly sometimes have talked to the wayside flowers of his love, and to the fading clouds of his ambition.

But, on the other hand, the idea of retirement from the world for the sake of self-mortification, of combat with demons, or communion with angels, and with their King,—authoritatively commended as it was to all

men by the continual practice of Christ Himself,—gave to all mountain
254 solitude at once a sanctity and a terror, in the mediæval mind, which
were altogether different from anything that it had possessed in the un-
Christian periods. On the one side, there was an idea of sanctity attached
to rocky wilderness, because it had always been among hills that the Deity
had manifested Himself most intimately to men, and to the hills that His
saints had nearly always retired for meditation, for especial communion
with Him, and to prepare for death. But with this impression of their
greater sanctity was involved also that of a peculiar terror. In all this,—
their haunting by the memories of prophets, the presences of angels, and
the everlasting thoughts and words of the Redeemer,—the mountain
ranges seemed separated from the active world, and only to be fitly
approached by hearts which were condemnatory of it. Just in so much as
it appeared necessary for the noblest men to retire to the hill-recesses
before their missions could be accomplished, or their spirits perfected, in
so far did the daily world seem by comparison to be pronounced profane
255 and dangerous; and to those who loved that world, and its work, the
mountains were thus voiceful with perpetual rebuke, and necessarily
contemplated with a kind of pain and fear, such as a man engrossed by
vanity feels at being by some accident forced to hear a startling sermon,
or to assist at a funeral service.

In all these modifications of temper and principle there appears much
which tends to a passionate, affectionate, or awe-struck observance of the
features of natural scenery, closely resembling, in all but this superstitious
dread of mountains, our feelings at the present day. But *one* character
which the mediævals had in common with the ancients, and that exactly
the most eminent character in both, opposed itself steadily to all the
feelings we have hitherto been examining,—the admiration, namely, and
constant watchfulness of human beauty. Exercised in nearly the same
manner as the Greeks, from their youth upwards, their countenances were
cast even in a higher mould; for, although somewhat less regular in
feature, and affected by minglings of Northern bluntness and stolidity of
general expression, together with greater thinness of lip and shaggy
256 formlessness of brow, these less sculpturesque features were, nevertheless,
touched with a seriousness and refinement proceeding first from the
modes of thought inculcated by the Christian religion, and secondly from
their more romantic and various life. Hence a degree of personal beauty,
both male and female, was attained in the Middle Ages, with which
classical periods could show nothing for a moment comparable; and this
beauty was set forth by the most perfect splendour, united with grace, in
dress, which the human race have hitherto invented. The strength of
their art-genius was directed in great part to this object; and their best
workmen and most brilliant fanciers were employed in wreathing the mail

or embroidering the robe. The exquisite arts of enamelling and chasing metal enabled them to make the armour as radiant and delicate as the plumage of a tropical bird; and the most various and vivid imaginations were displayed in the alternations of colour, and fiery freaks of form, on shield and crest: so that of all the beautiful things which the eyes of men could fall upon, in the world about them, the most beautiful must have been a young knight riding out in morning sunshine, and in faithful hope.

Now, the effect of this superb presence of human beauty on men in general was, exactly as it had been in Greek times, first to turn their thoughts and glances in great part away from all other beauty but that, and to make the grass of the field take to them always more or less the aspect   257 of a carpet to dance upon, a lawn to tilt upon, or a serviceable crop of hay; and, secondly, in what attention they paid to this lower nature, to make them dwell exclusively on what was graceful, symmetrical, and bright in colour. All that was rugged, rough, dark, wild, unterminated, they rejected at once, as the domain of "salvage men" and monstrous giants: all that they admired was tender, bright, balanced, enclosed, sym-metrical—only symmetrical in the noble and free sense: for what we moderns call "symmetry," or "balance," differs as much from mediæval symmetry as the poise of a grocer's scales, or the balance of an Egyptian mummy with its hands tied to its sides, does from the balance of a knight on his horse, striking with the battle-axe, at the gallop; the mummy's balance looking wonderfully perfect, and yet sure to be one-sided if you weigh the dust of it,—the knight's balance swaying and changing like the wind, and yet as true and accurate as the laws of life.

And this love of symmetry was still further enhanced by the peculiar duties required of art at the time; for, in order to fit a flower or leaf for inlaying in armour, or showing clearly in glass, it was absolutely necessary to take away its complexity, and reduce it to the condition of a disciplined and orderly pattern; and this the more, because, for all military purposes, the device, whatever it was, had to be distinctly intelligible at extreme distance. That it should be a good imitation of nature, when seen near, was of no moment; but it was of highest moment that when first the knight's banner flashed in the sun at the turn of the mountain road, or rose, torn and bloody, through the drift of the battle dust, it should still be discernible what the bearing was.

Farther, it was necessary to the brilliant harmony of colour, and clear   258 setting forth of everything, that all confusing shadows, all dim and doubtful lines should be rejected: hence at once an utter denial of natural appearances by the great body of workmen; and a calm rest in a practice of representation which would make either boar or lion blue, scarlet, or golden, according to the device of the knight, or the need of such and such

259 a colour in that place of the pattern; and which wholly denied that any substance ever cast a shadow, or was affected by any kind of obscurity.

All this was in its way, and for its end, absolutely right, admirable, and delightful; and those who despise it, laugh at it, or derive no pleasure from it, are utterly ignorant of the highest principles of art, and are mere tyros and beginners in the practice of colour. But, admirable though it might be, one necessary result of it was a farther withdrawal of the observation of men from the refined and subtle beauty of nature; so that the workman who first was led to think *lightly* of natural beauty, as being subservient to human, was next led to think *inaccurately* of natural beauty, because he had continually to alter and simplify it for his practical purposes.

260 Under these lights, let us examine the facts.

The landscape of the Middle Ages is represented in a central manner by the illuminations of the MSS. of Romances, executed about the middle of the fifteenth century. On one side of these stands the earlier landscape work, more or less treated as simple decoration; on the other, the later landscape work, becoming more or less affected with modern ideas and modes of imitation.

These central fifteenth century landscapes are almost invariably composed of a grove or two tall trees, a winding river, and a castle, or a garden: the peculiar feature of both these last being *trimness*; the artist always dwelling especially on the fences; wreathing the espaliers indeed prettily with sweetbriar, and putting pots of orange-trees on the tops of the walls, but taking great care that there shall be no loose bricks in the one, nor broken stake in the other,—the trouble and ceaseless warfare of the times having rendered security one of the first elements of pleasantness, and making it impossible for any artist to conceive Paradise but as surrounded by a moat, or to distinguish the road to it better than by its narrow wicket gate, and watchful porter.

261
262 Together with this peculiar formality, we find an infinite delight in drawing pleasant flowers, always articulating and outlining them completely; the sky is always blue, having only a few delicate white clouds in it, and in the distance are blue mountains, very far away, if the landscape is to be simply delightful; but brought near, and divided into quaint overhanging rocks, if it is intended to be meditative, or a place of saintly seclusion. But the whole of it always,—flowers, castles, brooks, clouds, and rocks, — subordinate to the human figures in the foreground, and painted for no other end than that of explaining their adventures and occupations.

Before the idea of landscape had been thus far developed, the representations of it had been purely typical, the objects which had to be shown in order to explain the scene of the event, being firmly outlined, usually on a pure golden or chequered colour background, not on sky. The change from the golden background (characteristic of the finest thirteenth century work) and the coloured chequer (which in like manner belongs to the finest fourteenth) to the blue sky, gradated to the horizon, takes place early in the fifteenth century, and is the *crisis* of change in the spirit of mediæval art. Strictly speaking, we might divide the art of Christian times into two great masses—Symbolic and Imitative;—the symbolic, reaching from the earliest periods down to the close of the fourteenth century, and the imitative from that close, to the present time; and then the most important circumstance indicative of the culminating point, or turn of tide, would be this of the change from chequered background to sky background.

The moment the sky is introduced (and it is curious how perfectly   263
it is done *at once*, many manuscripts presenting in alternate pages, chequered backgrounds, and deep blue skies exquisitely gradated to the horizon)—the moment, I say, the sky is introduced, the spirit of art becomes for evermore changed, and thenceforward it gradually proposes imitation more and more as an end, until it reaches the Turnerian landscape. But it is only in the earlier or symbolic mediæval art, reaching up to the close of the fourteenth century, that the peculiar modification of natural forms for decorative purposes is seen in its perfection, with all its beauty, and all its necessary shortcomings; the minds of men being accurately balanced between that honour for the superior human form which they shared with the Greek ages, and the sentimental love of nature which was peculiar to their own. The expression of the two feelings will be found to vary according to the material and place of the art; in painting, the conventional forms are more adopted, in order to obtain definition, and brilliancy of colour, while in sculpture the life of nature is   264
often rendered with a love and faithfulness which put modern art to shame.

Nevertheless, in all this perfect and loving decorative art, we have   268
hardly any careful references to other landscape features than herbs and flowers; mountains, water, and clouds are introduced so rudely, that the representations of them can never be received for anything else than letters or signs. We see that the thing carved or painted is not intended in   269
anywise to imitate the truth, or convey to us the feelings which the workman had in contemplating the truth. He has got a way of talking about it so definite and cold, and tells us with his chisel so calmly that the knight had a castle to attack, or the saint a river to cross dryshod, without making the smallest effort to describe pictorially either castle or river, that we are left wholly at fault as to the nature of the emotion with which he contemplated the real objects. But that emotion, as the intermediate step between the feelings of the Grecian and the modern, it must be our aim to ascertain as clearly as possible; and, therefore, finding it not at this period completely expressed in visible art, we must, as we did with the

Greeks, take up the written landscape instead, and examine this mediæval sentiment as we find it embodied in the poem of Dante.

The thing that must first strike us in this respect, as we turn our thoughts to the poem, is, unquestionably, the *formality* of its landscape.

270   Milton's effort, in all that he tells us of his Inferno, is to make it indefinite; Dante's, to make it *definite*. Both, indeed, describe it as entered through gates; but, within the gate, all is wild and fenceless with Milton, having indeed its four rivers,—the last vestige of the mediæval tradition,—but rivers which flow through a waste of mountain and moorland, and by "many a frozen, many a fiery Alp."[54] But Dante's Inferno is accurately separated into circles drawn with well-pointed compasses; mapped and properly surveyed in every direction, trenched in a thoroughly good style of engineering from depth to depth, and divided in the "*accurate* middle" (dritto mezzo)[55] of its deepest abyss into a concentric series of ten moats and embankments, like those about a castle, with bridges from each embankment to the next. These larger fosses are of rock, and the bridges also; but as he goes farther into detail, Dante tells us of various minor fosses and embankments, in which he anxiously points out to us not only the formality, but the neatness and perfectness, of the stonework.

271   When we pass with Dante from the Inferno to Purgatory, we have indeed more light and air, but no more liberty; being now confined on various ledges cut into a mountain side, with a precipice on one hand and a vertical wall on the other; and, lest here also we should make any mistake about magnitudes, we are told that the ledges were eighteen feet wide, and that the ascent from one to the other was by steps, made like those which go up from Florence to the Church of San Miniato.[56]

Lastly, though in the Paradise there is perfect freedom and infinity of space, though for trenches we have planets, and for cornices constel-
272   lations, yet there is more cadence, procession, and order among the redeemed souls than any other; they fly, so as to describe letters and sentences in the air, and rest in circles, like rainbows, or determinate figures, as of a cross and an eagle; in which certain of the more glorified natures are so arranged as to form the eye of the bird, while those most highly blessed are arranged with their white crowds in leaflets, so as to form the image of a white rose in the midst of heaven.[57]

Thus, throughout the poem, I conceive that the first striking character of its scenery is intense definition; precisely the reflection of that definiteness which we have already traced in pictorial art. But the second point which seems noteworthy is, that the flat ground and embanked trenches are reserved for the Inferno: and that the entire territory of the Purgatory is a mountain, thus marking the sense of that purifying and perfecting influence in mountains which we saw the mediæval mind was

so ready to suggest. The same general idea is indicated at the very commencement of the poem, in which Dante is overwhelmed by fear and
sorrow in passing through a dark forest, but revives on seeing the sun
touch the top of a hill, afterwards called by Virgil "the pleasant mount—
the cause and source of all delight." [58]

While, however, we find this greater honour paid to mountains, I think
we may perceive a much greater dread and dislike of woods. To Dante the   273
idea of a forest is exceedingly repulsive, so that, as just noticed, in the
opening of his poem, he cannot express a general despair about life more
strongly than by saying he was lost in a wood so savage and terrible, that
"even to think or speak of it is distress,—it was so bitter,—it was
something next door to death;" [59] and one of the saddest scenes in all the
Inferno is in a forest, of which the trees are haunted by lost souls: while
(with only one exception), whenever the country is to be beautiful, we
find ourselves coming out into open air and open meadows.

As Homer gave us an ideal landscape, which even a god might have   274
been pleased to behold, so Dante gives us, fortunately, an ideal landscape,
which is specially intended for the terrestrial paradise. And it will doubtless be with some surprise, after our reflections above on the general   275
tone of Dante's feelings, that we find ourselves here first entering a *forest*,
and that even a *thick* forest. But there is a peculiar meaning in this. With
any other poet than Dante, it might have been regarded as a wanton
inconsistency. Not so with him: by glancing back to the two lines which
explain the nature of Paradise, we shall see what he means by it. Virgil
tells him, as he enters it, "Henceforward, take thine own pleasure for
guide; thou art beyond the steep ways, and beyond all Art;" [60]—meaning,
that the perfectly purified and noble human creature, having no pleasure
but in right, is past all effort, and past all *rule*. Art has no existence for such
a being. Hence, the first aim of Dante, in his landscape imagery, is to show
evidence of this perfect liberty, and of the purity and sinlessness of the
new nature, converting pathless ways into happy ones.

This forest, then, is very like that of Colonos [61] in several respects—in
its peace and sweetness, and number of birds; it differs from it only in
letting a light breeze through it, being therefore somewhat thinner than
the Greek wood; the tender lines which tell of the voices of the birds
mingling with the wind, and of the leaves all turning one way before it,
have been more or less copied by every poet since Dante's time. They are,
so far as I know, the sweetest passage of wood description which exists in   276
literature. [62]

Before, however, Dante has gone far in this wood,—that is to say, only
so far as to have lost sight of the place where he entered it, or rather, I
suppose, of the light under the boughs of the outside trees, and it must
have been a very thin wood indeed if he did not do this in some quarter

of a mile's walk,—he comes to a little river, three paces over, which bends
the blades of grass to the left, with a meadow on the other side of it; and
in this meadow

"A lady, graced with solitude, who went
    Singing, and setting flower by flower apart,
By which the path she walked on was besprent.
'Ah, lady beautiful, that basking art
    In beams of love, if I may trust thy face,
Which useth to bear witness of the heart,
Let liking come on thee,' said I, 'to trace
    Thy path a little closer to the shore,
Where I may reap the hearing of thy lays.
Thou mindest me, how Proserpine of yore
    Appeared in such a place, what time her mother
Lost her, and she the spring, for evermore.'
As, pointing downwards and to one another
    Her feet, a lady bendeth in the dance,
And barely setteth one before the other,
Thus, on the scarlet and the saffron glance
    Of flowers, with motion maidenlike she bent
(Her modest eyelids drooping and askance);
And there she gave my wishes their content,
    Approaching, so that her sweet melodies
Arrived upon mine ear with what they meant.
When first she came amongst the blades, that rise,
    Already wetted, from the goodly river,
She graced me by the lifting of her eyes."—CAYLEY.[63]

    I have given this passage at length, because, for our purposes, it is by
much the most important, not only in Dante, but in the whole circle of
poetry. This lady, observe, stands on the opposite side of the little stream
which, presently, she explains to Dante is Lethe, having power to cause
forgetfulness of all evil, and she stands just among the bent blades of grass
at its edge. She is first seen gathering flower from flower, then "passing
continually the multitudinous flowers through her hands," smiling at the
same time so brightly, that her first address to Dante is to prevent him
from wondering at her, saying, "if he will remember the verse of the
ninety-second Psalm, beginning 'Delectasti,' he will know why she is so
happy."[64]

    And turning to the verse of this Psalm we find it written, "Thou, Lord,
hast made me glad *through Thy works. I will triumph in the works of Thy
hands*;" or in the very words in which Dante would read it,—

"Quia delectasti me, Domine, in factura Tua,
    Et in operibus manuum Tuarum exultabo."

277

Now we could not for an instant have had any difficulty in understanding this, but that, some way farther on in the poem, this lady is called Matilda, and is with reason supposed by the commentators to be the great Countess Matilda of the eleventh century; notable equally for her ceaseless activity, her brilliant political genius, her perfect piety, and her deep reverence for the see of Rome.[65] This Countess Matilda is therefore Dante's guide in the terrestrial paradise, as Beatrice is afterwards in the celestial; each of them having a spiritual and symbolic character in their glorified state, yet retaining their definite personality.

The question is, then, what is the symbolic character of the Countess Matilda, as the guiding spirit of the terrestrial paradise? Before Dante had entered this paradise he had rested on a step of shelving rock, and as he watched the stars he slept, and dreamed, and thus tells us what he saw:—

> "A lady, young and beautiful, I dreamed,
> Was passing o'er a lea; and, as she came,
> Methought I saw her ever and anon
> Bending to cull the flowers; and thus she sang:
> 'Know ye, whoever of my name would ask,
> That I am Leah; for my brow to weave
> A garland, these fair hands unwearied ply;
> To please me at the crystal mirror, here
> I decked me. But my sister Rachel, she
> Before her glass abides the livelong day,
> Her radiant eyes beholding, charmed no less
> Than I with this delightful task. Her joy
> In contemplation, as in labour mine."[66]

278

This vision of Rachel and Leah has been always, and with unquestionable truth, received as a type of the Active and Contemplative life, and as an introduction to the two divisions of the paradise which Dante is about to enter. Therefore the unwearied spirit of the Countess Matilda is understood to represent the Active life, which forms the felicity of Earth; and the spirit of Beatrice the Contemplative life, which forms the felicity of Heaven. This interpretation appears at first straightforward and certain; but it has missed count of exactly the most important fact in the two passages which we have to explain. Observe: Leah gathers the flowers to decorate *herself*, and delights in *Her Own* Labour. Rachel sits silent, contemplating herself, and delights in *Her Own* Image. These are the types of the Unglorified Active and Contemplative powers of Man. But Beatrice and Matilda are the same powers, Glorified. And how are they Glorified? Leah took delight in her own labour; but Matilda—"in operibus manuum Tuarum"—in God's labour: Rachel in the sight of her own face; Beatrice in the sight of *God's face*.

And thus, when afterwards Dante sees Beatrice on her throne, and prays

plate 13 J.M.W. Turner, *Marly sur Seine*

plate 14 Tintoretto, *The Crucifixion*, from the Scuola di San Rocco, Venice

plate 15   Holman Hunt, *The Light of the World*

plate 16   Veronese, *The Family of Darius before Alexander*

plate 17   J.M.W. Turner, *The Pass of Faido*

plate 18   J.M.W. Turner, *The Falls of the Rhine, Schaffhausen*

her that, when he himself shall die, she would receive him with kindness, Beatrice merely looks down for an instant, and answers with a single smile, then "towards the eternal fountain turns."[67]

Therefore it is evident that Dante distinguishes in both cases, not between earth and heaven, but between perfect and imperfect happiness, whether in earth or heaven. The active life which has only the service of man for its end, and therefore gathers flowers, with Leah, for its own decoration, is indeed happy, but not perfectly so; it has only the happiness of the dream, belonging essentially to the dream of human life, and passing away with it. But the active life which labours for the more and more discovery of God's work, is perfectly happy, and is the life of the terrestrial paradise, being a true foretaste of heaven, and beginning in earth, as heaven's vestibule. So also the contemplative life which is concerned with human feeling and thought and beauty—the life which is in earthly poetry and imagery of noble earthly emotion—is happy, but it is the happiness of the dream; the contemplative life which has God's person and love in Christ for its object, has the happiness of eternity. But because this higher happiness is also begun here on earth, Beatrice descends to earth; and when revealed to Dante first, he sees the image of the twofold personality of Christ reflected in her *eyes*;[68] as the flowers, which are, to the mediæval heart, the chief work of God, are for ever passing through Matilda's *hands*.

Now, therefore, we see that Dante, as the great prophetic exponent of the heart of the Middle Ages, has, by the lips of the spirit of Matilda, declared the mediæval faith,—that all perfect active life was "the expression of man's delight *in God's work*;"[69] and that all their political and warlike energy, as fully shown in the mortal life of Matilda, was yet inferior and impure,—the energy of the dream,—compared with that which on the opposite bank of Lethe stood "choosing flower from flower."[70] And what joy and peace there were in this work is marked by Matilda's being the person who draws Dante through the stream of Lethe, so as to make him forget all sin, and all sorrow; throwing her arms around him, she plunges his head under the waves of it; then draws him through, crying to him, "*hold me, hold me*" (tiemmi, tiemmi),[71] and so presents him thus bathed, free from all painful memory, at the feet of the spirit of the more heavenly contemplation.

The reader will, I think, now see, with sufficient distinctness, why I called this passage the most important, for our present purposes, in the whole circle of poetry. For it contains the first great confession of the discovery by the human race (I mean as a matter of experience, not of revelation), that their happiness was not in themselves, and that their labour was not to have their own service as its chief end. It embodies in a few syllables the *sealing* difference between the Greek and the mediæval, in that the former sought the flower and herb for his own uses, the latter for God's honour; the former, primarily and on principle, contemplated his own beauty and the workings of his own mind, and the latter, primarily and on principle, contemplated Christ's beauty and the workings of the mind of Christ.[72]

Having thus received from Dante this great lesson, as to the spirit in   281
which mediæval landscape is to be understood, what else we have to note respecting it, as seen in his poem, will be comparatively straightforward and easy. And first, we have to observe the place occupied in his mind by *colour*. It has already been shown, in the *Stones of Venice*, vol. ii. chap. v. §§ 30–34, that colour is the most *sacred* element of all visible things.[73] Hence, as the mediæval mind contemplated them first for their sacredness, we should, beforehand, expect that the first thing it would seize would be the colour; and that we should find its expressions and renderings of colour infinitely more loving and accurate than among the Greeks.

We have seen how fond the Greek was of composing his paradises of   284
rather damp grass;[74] but that in this fondness for grass there was always an undercurrent of consideration for his horses; and the characters in it which pleased him most were its depth and freshness; not its colour. Now, if we remember carefully the general expressions, respecting grass, used in modern literature, I think nearly the commonest that occurs to us will be that of "enamelled" turf or sward. This phrase is usually employed by our pseudo-poets, like all their other phrases, without knowing what it means, because it has been used by other writers before them, and because they do not know what else to say of grass. If we were to ask them what enamel was, they could not tell us; and if we asked why grass was like enamel, they could not tell us. The expression *has* a meaning, however, and one peculiarly characteristic of mediæval and modern temper.

The first instance I know of its right use, though very probably it had been so employed before, is in Dante. The righteous spirits of the pre-Christian ages are seen by him, though in the Inferno, yet in a place open, luminous, and high, walking upon the "green enamel."[75]

I am very sure that Dante did not use this phrase as we use it. He knew   285
well what enamel was; and his readers, in order to understand him thoroughly, must remember what it is,—a vitreous paste, dissolved in water, mixed with metallic oxides, to give it the opacity and the colour required, spread in a moist state on metal, and afterwards hardened by fire, so as never to change. And Dante means, in using this metaphor of the grass of the Inferno, to mark, that it is laid as a tempering and cooling substance over the dark, metallic, gloomy ground; but yet so hardened by the fire, that it is not any more fresh or living grass, but a smooth, silent, lifeless bed of eternal green. And we know how *hard* Dante's idea of it was;

because afterwards, in what is perhaps the most awful passage of the whole Inferno, when the three furies rise at the top of the burning tower, and catching sight of Dante, and not being able to get at him, shriek wildly for the Gorgon to come up too, that they may turn him into stone,—the word *stone* is not hard enough for them. Stone might crumble away after it was made, or something with life might grow upon it; no, it shall not be stone; they will make enamel of him; nothing can grow out of that; it is dead forever.

"Venga Medusa, sì lo farem di Smalto."[76]

Now, almost in the opening of the Purgatory, as there at the entrance of the Inferno, we find a company of great ones resting in a grassy place. But the idea of the grass now is very different. The word now used is not "enamel," but "herb," and instead of being merely green, it is covered with flowers of many colours. With the usual mediæval accuracy, Dante insists on telling us precisely what these colours were, and how bright;

286 which he does by naming the actual pigments used in illumination,— "Gold, and fine silver, and cochineal, and white lead, and Indian wood, serene and lucid, and fresh emerald, just broken, would have been excelled, as less is by greater, by the flowers and grass of the place."[77] It is evident that the "emerald" here means the emerald green of the illuminators; for a fresh emerald is no brighter than one which is not fresh, and Dante was not one to throw away his words thus. Observe then, we have here the idea of the growth, life, and variegation of the "green herb," as opposed to the "smalto" of the Inferno; but the colours of the variegation are illustrated and defined by the reference to actual pigments: and, observe, because the other colours are rather bright, the blue ground (Indian wood, indigo?) is sober; lucid, but serene: and presently two angels enter, who are dressed in green drapery, but of a paler green than the grass, which Dante marks, by telling us that it was "the green of leaves, just budded."[78]

In all this, I wish the reader to observe two things: first, the general carefulness of the poet in defining colour, distinguishing it precisely as a painter would (opposed to the Greek carelessness about it); and, secondly, his regarding the grass for its greenness and variegation, rather than, as a Greek would have done, for its depth and freshness.

287 There are, it seems to me, several important deductions to be made from these facts. The Greek, we have seen, delighted in the grass for its usefulness; the mediæval, as also we moderns, for its colour and beauty. But both dwell on it as the *first* element of the lovely landscape; we saw its use in Homer,[79] we see also that Dante thinks the righteous spirits of the heathen enough comforted in Hades by having even the *image* of green grass put beneath their feet;[80] the happy resting-place in Purgatory has no

other delight than its grass and flowers; and, finally, in the terrestrial paradise, the feet of Matilda pause where the Lethe stream first bends the blades of grass. Consider a little what a depth there is in this great instinct of the human race. Gather a single blade of grass, and examine for a minute, quietly, its narrow sword-shaped strip of fluted green. Nothing, as it seems there, of notable goodness or beauty. A very little strength, and a very little tallness, and a few delicate long lines meeting in a point,—not a perfect point neither, but blunt and unfinished, by no means a creditable or apparently much cared-for example of Nature's workmanship; made, as it seems, only to be trodden on to-day, and to-morrow to be cast into the oven; and a little pale and hollow stalk, feeble and flaccid, leading down to the dull brown fibres of roots. And yet, think of it well, and judge whether of all the gorgeous flowers that beam in summer air, and of all strong and goodly trees, pleasant to the eyes or good for food,—stately palm and pine, strong ash and oak, scented citron, burdened vine,—there be any by man so deeply loved, by God so highly graced, as that narrow point of feeble green. It seems to me not to have been without a peculiar significance, that our Lord, when about to work the miracle which, of all that He showed, appears to have been felt by the multitude as the most impressive,—the miracle of the loaves,—commanded the people to sit down by companies "upon the green grass."[81] He was about to feed them with the principal produce of earth and the sea, the simplest representations of the food of mankind. He gave them the *seed* of the herb; He bade them sit down upon the herb itself, which was as great a gift, in its fitness for their joy and rest, as its perfect fruit, for their sustenance; thus, in this single order and act, when rightly understood, indicating for evermore how the Creator had entrusted the comfort, consolation, and sustenance of man, to the simplest and most despised of all the leafy families of the earth. And well does it fulfil its mission. Consider what we owe merely to the meadow grass, to the covering of the dark ground by that glorious enamel, by the companies of those soft, and countless, and peaceful spears. The fields! Follow but forth for a little time the thoughts of all that we ought to recognize in those words. All spring and summer is in them,—the walks by silent, scented paths,—the rests in noonday heat,—the joy of herds and flocks,—the power of all shepherd life and meditation,—the life of sunlight upon the world, falling in emerald streaks, and failing in soft blue shadows, where else it would have struck upon the dark mould, or scorching dust,—pastures beside the pacing brooks,—soft banks and knolls of lowly hills,—thymy slopes of down overlooked by the blue line of lifted sea,—crisp lawns all dim with early dew, or smooth in evening warmth of barred sunshine, dinted by happy feet, and softening in their fall the sound of loving voices; all these are summed in those simple words; and these are

288

not all. We may not measure to the full the depth of this heavenly gift in
our own land; though still, as we think of it longer, the infinite of that
meadow sweetness, Shakspere's peculiar joy,[82] would open on us more
and more, yet we have it but in part. Go out, in the spring-time, among
the meadows that slope from the shores of the Swiss lakes to the roots of
their lower mountains. There, mingled with the taller gentians and the
white narcissus, the grass grows deep and free; and as you follow the
winding mountain paths, beneath arching boughs all veiled and dim with
blossom,—paths that for ever droop and rise over the green banks and
mounds sweeping down in scented undulation, steep to the blue water,
studded here and there with new-mown heaps, filling all the air with
fainter sweetness,—look up towards the higher hills, where the waves of
everlasting green roll silently into their long inlets among the shadows
of the pines; and we may, perhaps, at last know the meaning of those
quiet words of the 147th Psalm, "He maketh grass to grow upon the
mountains."

There are also several lessons symbolically connected with this subject,
which we must not allow to escape us. Observe, the peculiar characters of
the grass, which adapt it especially for the service of man, are its apparent
humility, and *cheerfulness*. Its humility, in that it seems created only for
lowest service,—appointed to be trodden on, and fed upon. Its cheerfulness, in that it seems to exult under all kinds of violence and suffering.
You roll it, and it is stronger the next day; you mow it, and it multiplies
its shoots, as if it were grateful; you tread upon it, and it only sends up
richer perfume. Spring comes, and it rejoices with all the earth,—glowing
with variegated flame of flowers,—waving in soft depth of fruitful
strength. Winter comes, and though it will not mock its fellow plants by
growing then, it will not pine and mourn, and turn colourless and leafless
as they. It is always green; and is only the brighter and gayer for the
hoar-frost.

Now, these two characters—of humility, and joy under trial—are
exactly those which most definitely distinguish the Christian from the
Pagan spirit. Whatever virtue the pagan possessed was rooted in pride, and
fruited with sorrow. It began in the elevation of his own nature, it ended
but in the "verde smalto"—the hopeless green—of the Elysian fields. But
the Christian virtue is rooted in self-debasement, and strengthened under
suffering by gladness of hope. And remembering this, it is curious to
observe how utterly without gladness the Greek heart appears to be in
watching the flowering grass, and what strange discords of expression arise
sometimes in consequence. There is one, recurring once or twice in
Homer, which has always pained me. He says, "The Greek army was on
the fields, as thick as flowers in the spring."[83] It might be so; but flowers
in spring-time are not the image by which Dante would have numbered

soldiers on their path of battle. Dante could not have thought of the
flowering of the grass but as associated with happiness. There is a still
deeper significance in the passage from Homer,[84] describing Ulysses
casting himself down on the *rushes* and the corn-giving land at the river
shore,—the rushes and corn being to him only good for rest and sustenance,—when we compare it with that in which Dante tells us he was
ordered to descend to the shore of the lake as he entered Purgatory, to
gather a *rush*, and gird himself with it, it being to him the emblem not only
of rest, but of humility under chastisement, the rush (or reed) being the
only plant which can grow there;—"no plant which bears leaves, or   291
hardens its bark, can live on that shore, because it does not yield to the
chastisement of its waves."[85] It cannot but strike the reader singularly
how deep and harmonious a significance runs through all these words of
Dante—how every syllable of them, the more we penetrate it, becomes a
seed of farther thought! For, follow up this image of the girding with the
reed, under trial, and see to whose feet it will lead us. As the grass of the
earth, thought of as the herb yielding seed, leads us to the place where our
Lord commanded the multitude to sit down by companies upon the green
grass; so the grass of the waters, thought of as sustaining itself among the
waters of affliction, leads us to the place where a stem of it was put into
our Lord's hand for His sceptre; and in the crown of thorns, and the rod
of reed, was foreshown the everlasting truth of the Christian ages—that all
glory was to be begun in suffering, and all power in humility.
     Assembling the images we have traced, and adding the simplest of all,
from Isaiah xl. 6,[86] we find, the grass and flowers are types, in their
passing, of the passing of human life, and, in their excellence, of the
excellence of human life; and this in twofold way; first, by their
Beneficence, and then, by their Endurance;—the grass of the earth, in
giving the seed of corn, and in its beauty under tread of foot and stroke of
scythe; and the grass of the waters, in giving its freshness to our rest, and
in its bending before the wave.* But understood in the broad human and
Divine sense, the "*herb* yielding seed" (as opposed to the fruit-tree
yielding fruit) includes a third family of plants, and fulfils a third office to
the human race. It includes the great family of the lints and flaxes, and   292
fulfils thus the *three* offices of giving food, raiment, and rest. Follow out
this fulfilment; consider the association of the linen garment and the
linen embroidery, with the priestly office, and the furniture of the

---

* So also in Isa. xxxv. 7, the prevalence of righteousness and peace over all evil
is thus foretold:
     "In the habitation of dragons, where each lay, shall be *grass*, with *reeds* and
rushes."

Tabernacle; and consider how the rush has been, in all time, the first natural carpet thrown under the human foot. Then next observe the three virtues definitely set forth by the three families of plants; not arbitrarily or fancifully associated with them, but in all the three cases marked for us by Scriptural words:

1st. Cheerfulness, or joyful serenity; in the grass for food and beauty.—"Consider the lilies of the field, how they grow; they toil not, neither do they spin."

2nd. Humility; in the grass for rest.—"A bruised reed shall He not break."

3rd. Love; in the grass for clothing (because of its swift kindling).— "The smoking flax shall He not quench."

And then, finally, observe the confirmation of these last two images in, I suppose, the most important prophecy, relating to the future state of the Christian Church, which occurs in the Old Testament, namely, that contained in the closing chapters of Ezekiel. The measures of the Temple of God are to be taken; and because it is only by charity and humility that those measures ever can be taken, the angel has "a line of *flax* in his hand, and a measuring *reed*."[87] The use of the line was to measure the land, and of the reed to take the dimensions of the buildings; so the buildings of the church, or its labours, are to be measured by *humility*, and its territory or land, by *love*.

293 The limits of the Church have, indeed, in later days, been measured, to the world's sorrow, by another kind of flaxen line, burning with the fire of unholy zeal, not with that of Christian charity; and perhaps the best lesson which we can finally take to ourselves, in leaving these sweet fields of the mediæval landscape, is the memory that, in spite of all the fettered habits of thought of his age, this great Dante, this inspired exponent of what lay deepest at the heart of the early Church, placed his terrestrial paradise where there had ceased to be fence or division, and where the grass of the earth was bowed down, in unity of direction, only by the soft waves that bore with them the forgetfulness of evil.

CHAPTER XVI[88]
Of Modern Landscape

WE turn our eyes from these serene fields and skies of mediæval art,   317
to the most characteristic examples of modern landscape. And, I
believe, the first thing that will strike us, or that ought to strike us, is their
cloudiness.

Out of perfect light and motionless air, we find ourselves on a sudden
brought under sombre skies, and into drifting wind; and, with fickle
sunbeams flashing in our face, or utterly drenched with sweep of rain, we
are reduced to track the changes of the shadows on the grass, or watch the
rents of twilight through angry cloud. And we find that whereas all the
pleasure of the mediæval was in *stability, definiteness,* and *luminousness,*
we are expected to rejoice in darkness, and triumph in mutability; to lay
the foundation of happiness in things which momentarily change or fade;
and to expect the utmost satisfaction and instruction from what it is
impossible to arrest, and difficult to comprehend.

We find, however, together with this general delight in breeze and
darkness, much attention to the real form of clouds, and careful drawing
of effects of mist; so that the appearance of objects, as seen through it,
becomes a subject of science with us; and the faithful representation of
that appearance is made of primal importance, under the name of aerial
perspective. The aspects of sunset and sunrise, with all their attendant
phenomena of cloud and mist, are watchfully delineated; and in ordinary
daylight landscape, the sky is considered of so much importance, that a
principal mass of foliage, or a whole foreground, is unhesitatingly thrown
into shade merely to bring out the form of a white cloud. So that, if a   318
general and characteristic name were needed for modern landscape art,
none better could be invented than "the service of clouds."

And this name would, unfortunately, be characteristic of our art in more
ways than one. All the Greeks spoke kindly about the clouds, except
Aristophanes; and he, I am sorry to say (since his report is so unfavourable), is the only Greek who had studied them attentively. He tells us,
first, that they are "great goddesses to idle men"; then, that they are
"mistresses of disputings, and logic, and monstrosities, and noisy chattering"; declares that whoso believes in their divinity must first disbelieve

in Jupiter, and place supreme power in the hands of an unknown god "Whirlwind"; and, finally, he displays their influence over the mind of one of their disciples, in his sudden desire "to speak ingeniously concerning smoke." [89]

There is, I fear, an infinite truth in this Aristophanic judgment applied to our modern cloud-worship. Assuredly, much of the love of mystery in our romances, our poetry, our art, and, above all, in our metaphysics, must come under that definition so long ago given by the great Greek "speaking ingeniously concerning smoke." And much of the instinct, which, partially developed in painting, may be now seen throughout every mode of exertion of mind,—the easily encouraged doubt, easily excited curiosity, habitual agitation, and delight in the changing and the marvellous, as opposed to the old quiet serenity of social custom and religious faith,—is again deeply defined in those few words, the "dethroning of Jupiter," the "coronation of the whirlwind."

Nor of whirlwind merely, but also of darkness or ignorance respecting all stable facts. That darkening of the foreground to bring out the white cloud, is, in one aspect of it, a type of the subjection of all plain and

319   positive fact, to what is uncertain and unintelligible. And, as we examine farther into the matter, we shall be struck by another great difference between the old and modern landscape, namely, that in the old no one ever thought of drawing anything but as well *as he could.* That might not be *well*, as we have seen in the case of rocks; but it was as well as he *could*, and always distinctly. But now our ingenuity is all "concerning smoke." Nothing is truly drawn but that; all else is vague, slight, imperfect; got with as little pains as possible.

The next thing that will strike us, after this love of clouds, is the love of liberty. Whereas the mediæval was always shutting himself into castles, and behind fosses, and drawing brickwork neatly, and beds of flowers primly, our painters delight in getting to the open fields and moors, abhor all hedges and moats; never paint anything but free-growing trees, and rivers gliding "at their own sweet will"; [90] eschew formality down to the smallest detail; break and displace the brickwork which the mediæval would have carefully cemented; leave unpruned the thickets he would have delicately trimmed; and, carrying the love of liberty even to license, and the love of wildness even to ruin, take pleasure at last in every aspect

320   of age and desolation which emancipates the objects of nature from the government of men;—on the castle wall displacing its tapestry with ivy, and spreading, through the garden, the bramble for the rose.

Connected with this love of liberty we find a singular manifestation of love of mountains, and see our painters traversing the wildest places of the globe in order to obtain subjects with craggy foregrounds and purple distances. Some few of them remain content with pollards and flat land;

but these are always men of third-rate order; and the leading masters, while they do not reject the beauty of the low grounds, reserve their highest powers to paint Alpine peaks or Italian promontories. And it is eminently noticeable, also, that this pleasure in the mountains is never mingled with fear, or tempered by a spirit of meditation, as with the mediæval; but is always free and fearless, brightly exhilarating, and wholly unreflective; so that the painter feels that his mountain foreground may be more consistently animated by a sportsman than a hermit; and our modern society in general goes to the mountains, not to fast, but to feast, and leaves their glaciers covered with chicken-bones and egg-shells.

Connected with this want of any sense of solemnity in mountain scenery, is a general profanity of temper in regarding all the rest of nature; that is to say, a total absence of faith in the presence of any deity therein. Whereas the mediæval never painted a cloud, but with the purpose of placing an angel in it; and a Greek never entered a wood without expecting to meet a god in it; *we* should think the appearance of an angel in the cloud wholly unnatural, and should be seriously surprised by meeting a god anywhere. Our chief ideas about the wood are connected with poaching. We have no belief that the clouds contain more than so many inches of rain or hail, and from our ponds and ditches expect nothing more divine than ducks and watercresses.

Finally: connected with this profanity of temper is a strong tendency to deny the sacred element of colour, and make our boast in blackness. For though occasionally glaring or violent, modern colour is on the whole eminently sombre, tending continually to grey or brown, and by many of our best painters consistently falsified, with a confessed pride in what they call chaste or subdued tints; so that, whereas a mediæval paints his sky bright blue and his foreground bright green, gilds the towers of his castles, and clothes his figures with purple and white, we paint our sky grey, our foreground black, and our foliage brown, and think that enough is sacrificed to the sun in admitting the dangerous brightness of a scarlet cloak or a blue jacket.

These, I believe, are the principal points which would strike us instantly, if we were to be brought suddenly into an exhibition of modern landscapes out of a room filled with mediæval work. It is evident that there are both evil and good in this change; but how much evil, or how much good, we can only estimate by considering, as in the former divisions of our inquiry, what are the real roots of the habits of mind which have caused them.

At first, it is evident that the title "Dark Ages," given to the mediæval centuries, is, respecting art, wholly inapplicable. They were, on the contrary, the bright ages; ours are the dark ones. I do not mean metaphysically, but literally. They were the ages of gold; ours are the ages of umber.

This is partly mere mistake in us; we build brown brick walls, and wear brown coats, because we have been blunderingly taught to do so, and go on doing so mechanically. There is, however, also some cause for the change in our own tempers. On the whole, these are much *sadder* ages than the early ones; not sadder in a noble and deep way, but in a dim wearied way,—the way of ennui, and jaded intellect, and uncomfortableness of soul and body. The Middle Ages had their wars and agonies, but also intense delights. Their gold was dashed with blood; but ours is sprinkled with dust. Their life was inwoven with white and purple: ours is one seamless stuff of brown. Not that we are without apparent festivity, but festivity more or less forced, mistaken, embittered, incomplete—not of the heart. How wonderfully, since Shakspere's time, have we lost the power of laughing at bad jests! The very finish of our wit belies our gaiety.

The profoundest reason of this darkness of heart is, I believe, our want of faith. There never yet was a generation of men (savage or civilized) who, taken as a body, so wofully fulfilled the words "having no hope, and without God in the world,"[91] as the present civilized European race. A Red Indian or Otaheitan savage has more sense of a divine existence round him, or government over him, than the plurality of refined Londoners and Parisians: and those among us who may in some sense be said to believe, are divided almost without exception into two broad classes, Romanist and Puritan; who, but for the interference of the unbelieving portions of society, would, either of them, reduce the other sect as speedily as possible to ashes; the Romanist having always done so whenever he could, from the beginning of their separation, and the Puritan at this time holding himself in complacent expectation of the destruction of Rome by volcanic fire. Such division as this between persons nominally of one religion, that is to say, believing in the same God, and the same Revelation, cannot but become a stumbling-block of the gravest kind to all thoughtful and far-sighted men,—a stumbling-block which they can only surmount under the most favourable circumstances of early education. Hence, nearly all our powerful men in this age of the world are unbelievers; the best of them in doubt and misery; the worst in reckless defiance; the plurality, in plodding hesitation, doing, as well as they can, what practical work lies ready to their hands. Most of our scientific men are in this last class: our popular authors either set themselves definitely against all religious form, pleading for simple truth and benevolence, (Thackeray, Dickens,) or give themselves up to bitter and fruitless statement of facts, (De Balzac,) or surface-painting, (Scott,) or careless blasphemy, sad or smiling, (Byron, Beranger). Our earnest poets and deepest thinkers are doubtful and indignant, (Tennyson, Carlyle); one or two, anchored, indeed, but anxious or weeping, (Wordsworth, Mrs. Browning); and of these two, the first is not so sure of his anchor, but that now and then it drags with him, even to make him cry out,—

> "Great God, I had rather be
> A Pagan suckled in some creed outworn;
> So might I, standing on this pleasant lea,
> Have glimpses that would make me less forlorn."[92]

In politics, religion is now a name; in art, a hypocrisy or affectation. Over German religious pictures the inscription, "See how Pious I am," can be read at a glance by any clear-sighted person. Over French and English religious pictures the inscription, "See how Impious I am," is equally legible. All sincere and modest art is, among us, profane.*

This faithlessness operates among us according to our tempers, producing either sadness or levity, and being the ultimate root alike of our discontents and of our wantonnesses. It is marvellous how full of contradiction it makes us; we are first dull, and seek for wild and lonely places because we have no heart for the garden; presently we recover our spirits, and build an assembly-room among the mountains, because we have no reverence for the desert. I do not know if there be game on Sinai, but I am always expecting to hear of some one's shooting over it.   324

There is, however, another, and a more innocent root of our delight in wild scenery.

All the Renaissance principles of art tended, as I have before often explained, to the setting Beauty above Truth, and seeking for it always at the expense of truth. And the proper punishment of such pursuit—the punishment which all the laws of the universe rendered inevitable—was, that those who thus pursued beauty should wholly lose sight of beauty. All the thinkers of the age, as we saw previously, declared that it did not exist. The age seconded their efforts, and banished beauty, so far as human effort could succeed in doing so, from the face of the earth, and the form of man. To powder the hair, to patch the cheek, to hoop the body, to buckle the foot, were all part and parcel of the same system which reduced streets to brick walls, and pictures to brown stains. One desert of Ugliness was extended before the eyes of mankind; and their pursuit of the beautiful, so recklessly continued, received unexpected consummation in high-heeled shoes and periwigs—Gower Street and Gaspar Poussin.

Reaction from this state was inevitable, if any true life was left in the races of mankind; and, accordingly, though still forced, by rule and fashion, to the producing and wearing all that is ugly, men steal out, half-ashamed of themselves for doing so, to the fields and mountains; and,

---

* Pre-Raphaelitism, of course, excepted, which is a new phase of art, in no wise considered in this chapter. Blake was sincere, but full of wild creeds, and somewhat diseased in brain.

finding among these the colour, and liberty, and variety, and power, which are for ever grateful to them, delight in these to an extent never before known; rejoice in all the wildest shattering of the mountain side,
325 as an opposition to Gower Street, gaze in a rapt manner at sunsets and sunrises, to see there the blue, and gold, and purple, which glow for them no longer on knight's armour or temple porch; and gather with care out of the fields, into their blotted herbaria, the flowers which the five orders or architecture have banished from their doors and casements.

326 With this romantic love of beauty, forced to seek in history, and in external nature, the satisfaction it cannot find in ordinary life, we mingle a more rational passion, the due and just result of newly awakened powers of attention. Whatever may first lead us to the scrutiny of natural objects, that scrutiny never fails of its reward. Unquestionably they are intended to be regarded by us with both reverence and delight; and every hour we give to them renders their beauty more apparent, and their interest more engrossing. Natural science—which can hardly be considered to have existed before modern times—rendering our knowledge fruitful in accumulation, and exquisite in accuracy, has acted for good or evil, according to the temper of the mind which received it; and though it has hardened the faithlessness of the dull and proud, has shown new grounds for reverence to hearts which were thoughtful and humble. The neglect of
327 the art of war, while it has somewhat weakened and deformed the body, has given us leisure and opportunity for studies to which, before, time and space were equally wanting; lives which once were early wasted on the battlefield are now passed usefully in the study; nations which exhausted themselves in annual warfare now dispute with each other the discovery of new planets; and the serene philosopher dissects the plants, and analyses the dust, of lands which were of old only traversed by the knight in hasty march, or by the borderer in heedless rapine.

The elements of progress and decline being thus strangely mingled in the modern mind, we might beforehand anticipate that one of the notable characters of our art would be its inconsistency; that efforts would be made in every direction, and arrested by every conceivable cause and manner of failure; that in all we did, it would become next to impossible to distinguish accurately the grounds for praise or for regret; that all previous canons of practice and methods of thought would be gradually over-thrown, and criticism continually defied by successes which no one had expected, and sentiments which no one could define.

Accordingly, while, in our inquiries into Greek and mediæval art, I was able to describe, in general terms, what all men did or felt, I find now many characters in many men; some, it seems to me, founded on the inferior and evanescent principles of modernism, on its recklessness, impatience, or faithlessness; others founded on its science, its new affection for nature, its love of openness and liberty. And among all these characters, good or evil, I see that some, remaining to us from old or transitional periods, do not properly belong to us, and will soon fade away, and others, though not yet distinctly developed, are yet properly our own, 328 and likely to grow forward into greater strength.

For instance: our reprobation of bright colour is, I think, for the most part, mere affectation, and must soon be done away with. Vulgarity, dulness, or impiety, will indeed always express themselves through art in brown and grey, as in Rembrandt, Caravaggio, and Salvator; but we are not wholly vulgar, dull, or impious; nor, as moderns, are we necessarily obliged to continue so in anywise. Our greatest men, whether sad or gay, still delight, like the great men of all ages, in brilliant hues. The colouring of Scott and Byron is full and pure; that of Keats and Tennyson rich even to excess. Our practical failures in colouring are merely the necessary consequences of our prolonged want of practice during the periods of Renaissance affectation and ignorance; and the only durable difference between old and modern colouring, is the acceptance of certain hues, by the modern, which please him by expressing that melancholy peculiar to his more reflective or sentimental character, and the greater variety of them necessary to express his greater science.

We need not, therefore, expect to find any single poet or painter 329 representing the entire group of powers, weaknesses, and inconsistent instincts which govern or confuse our modern life. But we may expect that in the man who seems to be given by Providence as the type of the age (as Homer and Dante were given, as the types of classical and mediæval mind), we shall find whatever is fruitful and substantial to be completely present, together with those of our weaknesses, which are indeed nationally characteristic, and compatible with general greatness of mind, just as the weak love of fences, and dislike of mountains, were found compatible with Dante's greatness in other respects.

Farther: as the admiration of mankind is found, in our times, to have in great part passed from men to mountains, and from human emotion to natural phenomena, we may anticipate that the great strength of art will also be warped in this direction; with this notable result for us, that 330 whereas the greatest painters or painter of classical and mediæval periods, being wholly devoted to the representation of humanity, furnished us with but little to examine in landscape, the greatest painters or painter of modern times will in all probability be devoted to landscape principally; and farther, because in representing human emotion words surpass painting, but in representing natural scenery painting surpasses words, we may anticipate also that the painter and poet (for convenience' sake I here use the words in opposition) will somewhat change their relations of rank in illustrating the mind of the age; that the painter will become of more importance, the poet of less; and that the relations between the men who are the types and first-fruits of the age in word and work,—namely, Scott and Turner,—will be, in many curious respects, different from those between Homer and Phidias, or Dante and Giotto.

It is this relation which we have now to examine.

And, first, I think it probable that many readers may be surprised at my calling Scott the great representative of the mind of the age in literature.

331 So also in painting, those who are acquainted with the sentimental efforts made at present by the German religious and historical schools, and with the disciplined power and learning of the French, will think it beyond all explanation absurd to call a painter of light water-colour landscapes, eighteen inches by twelve, the first representative of the arts of the age. I can only crave the reader's patience, and his due consideration of the following reasons for my doing so, together with those advanced in the farther course of the work.

I believe the first test of a truly great man is his humility. I do not mean, by humility, doubt of his own power, or hesitation in speaking his opinions; but a right understanding of the relation between what *he* can do and say, and the rest of the world's sayings and doings. All great men not only know their business, but usually know that they know it; and are not only right in their main opinions, but they usually know that they are right in them; only, they do not think much of themselves on that account. Arnolfo knows he can build a good dome at Florence; Albert Dürer writes calmly to one who had found fault with his work, "It cannot be better done;" Sir Isaac Newton knows that he has worked out a problem or two that would have puzzled anybody else,—only they do not expect their fellow-men therefore to fall down and worship them; they have a curious under-sense of powerlessness, feeling that the greatness is not *in* them, but *through* them; that they could not do or be anything else than God made them. And they see something Divine and God-made in every other man they meet, and are endlessly, foolishly, incredibly merciful.

Now, I find among the men of the present age, as far as I know them,
332 this character in Scott and Turner pre-eminently; I am not sure if it is not in them alone. I do not find Scott talking about the dignity of literature, nor Turner about the dignity of painting. They do their work, feeling that they cannot well help it; the story must be told, and the effect put down; and if people like it, well and good; and if not, the world will not be much the worse.

Connected with this general humility, is the total absence of affectation in these men,—that is to say, of any assumption of manner or behaviour in their work, in order to attract attention. Not but that they are mannerists both. Scott's verse is strongly mannered, and Turner's oil painting; but the manner of it necessitated by the feelings of the men, entirely natural to both, never exaggerated for the sake of show. I hardly know any other literary or pictorial work of the day which is not in some degree affected.

Again: another very important, though not infallible, test of greatness   333
is, as we have often said, the appearance of Ease with which the thing is done. It may be that, as with Dante and Leonardo, the finish given to the work effaces the evidence of ease; but where the ease is manifest, as in Scott, Turner, and Tintoret, and the thing done is very noble, it is a strong reason for placing the men above those who confessedly work with great pains. Scott writing his chapter or two before breakfast—not retouching; Turner finishing a whole drawing in a forenoon before he goes out to shoot (providing always the chapter and drawing be good), are instantly to be set above men who confessedly have spent a day over the work, and think the hours well spent if it has been a little mended between sunrise and sunset. Indeed, it is no use for men to think to appear great by working fast, dashing, and scrawling; the thing they do must be good and great, cost what time it may; but if it *be* so, and they have honestly and unaffectedly done it with *no effort*, it is probably a greater and better thing than the result of the hardest efforts of others.

Then, as touching the kind of work done by these two men, the more I think of it I find this conclusion more impressed upon me,—that the greatest thing a human soul ever does in this world is to *see* something, and tell what it *saw* in a plain way. Hundreds of people can talk for one who can think, but thousands can think for one who can see. To see clearly is poetry, prophecy, and religion,—all in one.

Therefore, finding the world of Literature more or less divided into Thinkers and Seers, I believe we shall find also that the Seers are wholly the greater race of the two. A true Thinker who has practical purpose in his thinking, and is sincere, as Plato, or Carlyle, or Helps,[93] becomes in   334
some sort a seer, and must be always of infinite use in his generation; but an affected Thinker, who supposes his thinking of any other importance than as it tends to work, is about the vainest kind of person that can be found in the occupied classes. Nay, I believe that metaphysicians and philosophers are, on the whole, the greatest troubles the world has got to deal with; and that while a tyrant or bad man is of some use in teaching people submission or indignation, and a thoroughly idle man is only harmful in setting an idle example, and communicating to other lazy people his own lazy misunderstandings, busy metaphysicians are always entangling *good* and *active* people, and weaving cobwebs among the finest wheels of the world's business; and are as much as possible, by all prudent persons, to be brushed out of their way, like spiders, and the meshed weed that has got into the Cambridgeshire canals, and other such impediments

to barges and business. And if we thus clear the metaphysical element out of modern literature, we shall find its bulk amazingly diminished, and the claims of the remaining writers, or of those whom we have thinned by this abstraction of their straw stuffing, much more easily adjusted.*

Again: the mass of sentimental literature, concerned with the analysis and description of emotion, headed by the poetry of Byron, is altogether of lower rank than the literature which merely describes what it saw. The true Seer always feels as intensely as any one else; but he does not much describe his feelings. He tells you whom he met, and what they said; leaves you to make out, from that, what they feel, and what he feels, but goes into little detail. And, generally speaking, pathetic writing and careful explanation of passion are quite easy, compared with this plain recording of what people said and did, or with the right invention of what they are likely to say and do; for this reason, that to invent a story, or admirably and thoroughly tell any part of a story, it is necessary to grasp the entire mind of every personage concerned in it, and know precisely how they would be affected by what happens; which to do requires a colossal intellect: but to describe a separate emotion delicately, it is only needed that one should feel it oneself; and thousands of people are capable of feeling this or that noble emotion, for one who is able to enter into all the feelings of somebody sitting on the other side of the table.

Having, therefore, cast metaphysical writers out of our way, and sentimental writers into the second rank, I do not think Scott's supremacy among those who remain will any more be doubtful; nor would it, perhaps, have been doubtful before, had it not been encumbered by innumerable faults and weaknesses. But it is pre-eminently in these faults and weaknesses that Scott is the representative of the mind of his age; and because he is the greatest man born amongst us, and intended for the enduring type of us, all our principal faults must be laid on his shoulders, and he must bear down the dark marks to the latest ages.

Thus, the most startling fault of the age being its faithlessness, it is necessary that its greatest man should be faithless. Nothing is more notable or sorrowful in Scott's mind than its incapacity of steady belief in anything. He cannot even resolve hardily to believe in a ghost, or a water-spirit; always explains them away in an apologetic manner, not believing, all the while, even in his own explanation. He never can clearly ascertain

---

* Observe, I do not speak thus of metaphysics because I have no pleasure in them. When I speak contemptuously of philology, it may be answered me, that I am a bad scholar; but I cannot be so answered touching metaphysics, for every one conversant with such subjects may see that I have strong inclination that way, which would, indeed, have led me far astray long ago, if I had not learned also some use of my hands, eyes, and feet.

whether there is anything behind the arras but rats; never draws sword, and thrusts at it for life or death; but goes on looking at it timidly, and saying, "It must be the wind." He is educated a Presbyterian, and remains one, because it is the most sensible thing he can do if he is to live in Edinburgh; but he thinks Romanism more picturesque, and profaneness more gentlemanly; does not see that anything affects human life but love, courage, and destiny; which are, indeed, not matters of faith at all, but of sight.

He is in all this the epitome of his epoch.

Again: as another notable weakness of the age is its habit of looking back, in a romantic and passionate idleness, to the past ages, not understanding them all the while, nor really desiring to understand them, so Scott gives up nearly the half of his intellectual power to a fond, yet purposeless, dreaming over the past, and spends half his literary labours in   337 endeavours to revive it, not in reality, but on the stage of fiction; endeavours which were the best of the kind that modernism made, but still successful only so far as Scott put, under the old armour, the everlasting human nature which he knew; and totally unsuccessful, so far as concerned the painting of the armour itself, which he knew *not*. The excellence of Scott's work is precisely in proportion to the degree in which it is sketched from present nature.

Again: more than any age that had preceded it, ours had been ignorant of the meaning of the word "Art." It had not a single fixed principle, and what unfixed principles it worked upon were all wrong. It was necessary that Scott should know nothing of art. He neither cared for painting nor sculpture, and was totally incapable of forming a judgment about them.

Again: as in reverence and irreverence, so in levity and melancholy,   338 we saw that the spirit of the age was strangely interwoven. Therefore, also, it is necessary that Scott should be light, careless, unearnest, and yet eminently sorrowful. Throughout all his work there is no evidence of any purpose but to while away the hour. His life had no other object than the pleasure of the instant, and the establishing of a family name. All his thoughts were, in their outcome and end, less than nothing, and vanity. And yet, of all poetry that I know, none is so sorrowful as Scott's. Other great masters are pathetic in a resolute and predetermined way, when they choose; but, in their own minds, are evidently stern or hopeful, or serene; never really melancholy. Even Byron is rather sulky and desperate than melancholy; Keats is sad because he is sickly; Shelley because he is impious; but Scott is inherently and consistently sad.

Such, then, being the weaknesses which it was necessary that Scott   339 should share with his age, in order that he might sufficiently represent it, and such the grounds for supposing him, in spite of all these weaknesses, the greatest literary man whom that age produced, let us glance at the principal points in which his view of landscape differs from that of the mediævals.

340   And, first, observe Scott's habit of looking at nature neither as dead, or merely material, in the way that Homer regards it, not as altered by his own feelings, in the way that Keats and Tennyson regard it, but as having an animation and pathos of *its own*, wholly irrespective of human presence or passion,—an animation which Scott loves and sympathises with, as he would with a fellow-creature, forgetting himself altogether, and subduing his own humanity before what seems to him the power of the landscape.

> "Yon lonely Thorn,—would he could tell
> The changes of his parent dell,
> Since he, so grey and stubborn now,
> Waved in each breeze a sapling bough:
> Would he could tell, how deep the shade
> A thousand mingled branches made,
> How broad the shadows of the oak,
> How clung the rowan to the rock,
> And through the foliage show'd his head,
> With narrow leaves and berries red!"[94]

Scott does not dwell on the grey stubbornness of the thorn, because he himself is at that moment disposed to be dull or stubborn; neither on the cheerful peeping forth of the rowan, because he himself is at that moment cheerful or curious: but he perceives them both with the kind of interest that he would take in an old man or a climbing boy; forgetting himself, in sympathy with either age or youth.

341   Observe, therefore, this is not *pathetic* fallacy; for there is no passion in *Scott* which alters nature. It is an inherent and continual habit of thought, which Scott shares with the moderns in general, being, in fact, nothing else than the instinctive sense which men must have of the Divine presence, not formed into distinct belief. In the Greek it created, as we saw, the faithfully believed gods of the elements; in Dante and the mediævals, it formed the faithfully believed angelic presence: in the modern, it creates no perfect form, does not apprehend distinctly any Divine being or operation; but only a dim, slightly credited animation in the natural object, accompanied with great interest and affection for it. This feeling is quite universal with us, only varying in depth according to the greatness of the heart that holds it; and in Scott, being more than usually intense, and accompanied with infinite affection and quickness of sympathy, it enables him to conquer all tendencies to the pathetic fallacy, and, instead of making Nature anywise subordinate to himself, he makes himself subordinate to *her*—follows her lead simply—does not

342   venture to bring his own cares and thoughts into her pure and quiet presence—paints her in her simple and universal truth, adding no result of

momentary passion or fancy, and appears, therefore, at first shallower than other poets, being in reality wider and healthier. And thus, as Nature is bright, serene, or gloomy, Scott takes her temper, and paints her as she is; nothing of himself being ever intruded, except that far-away Æolian tone, of which he is unconscious; and sometimes a stray syllable or two, distinctly stating personal feeling, but all the more modestly for that distinctness.

And in consequence of this unselfishness and humility, Scott's enjoyment of Nature is incomparably greater than that of any other poet   343
I know. All the rest carry their cares to her, and begin maundering in her ears about their own affairs. Tennyson goes out on a furzy common, and sees it is calm autumn sunshine, but it gives him no pleasure. He only remembers that it is

> "Dead calm in that noble breast
> Which heaves but with the heaving deep." [95]

He sees a thundercloud in the evening, and *would* have "doted and pored" on it, [96] but cannot, for fear it should bring the ship bad weather. Keats drinks the beauty of nature violently; but has no more real sympathy with her than he has with a bottle of claret. His palate is fine; but he "bursts joy's grape against it," [97] gets nothing but misery, and a bitter taste of dregs, out of his desperate draught.

Byron and Shelley are nearly the same, only with less truth of perception, and even more troublesome selfishness. Wordsworth is more like Scott, and understands how to be happy, but yet cannot altogether rid himself of the sense that he is a philosopher, and ought always to be saying something wise. He has also a vague notion that nature would not be able to get on well without Wordsworth; and finds a considerable part of his pleasure in looking at himself as well as at her. But with Scott the love is entirely humble and unselfish. "I, Scott, am nothing, and less than nothing; but these crags, and heaths, and clouds, how great they are, how lovely, how for ever to be beloved, only for their own silent, thoughtless sake!"

Nature becomes dear to Scott in a three-fold way; dear to him, first, as   345
containing those remains or memories of the past, which he cannot find in cities, and giving hope of Prætorian mound or knight's grave, in every green slope and shade of its desolate places;—dear, secondly, in its moorland liberty, which has for him just as high a charm as the fenced garden had for the mediæval;—and dear to him, finally, in that perfect beauty, denied alike in cities and in men, for which every modern heart had begun at last to thirst, and Scott's, in its freshness and power, of all men's, most earnestly.

We began our investigation, it will be remembered, in order to   353 determine whether landscape-painting was worth studying or not. We have now reviewed the three principal phases of temper in the civilized human race, and we find that landscape has been mostly disregarded by great men, or cast into a second place, until now; and that now it seems dear to us, partly in consequence of our faults, and partly owing to accidental circumstances, soon, in all likelihood, to pass away: and there seems great room for question still, whether our love of it is a permanent and healthy feeling, or only a healthy crisis in a generally diseased state of mind. If the former, society will for ever hereafter be affected by its results; and Turner, the first great landscape-painter, must take a place in the history of nations corresponding in art accurately to that of Bacon in philosophy;—Bacon having first opened the study of the laws of material nature, when, formerly, men had thought only of the laws of human mind; and Turner having first opened the study of the aspect of material nature, when, before, men had thought only of the aspect of the human form. Whether, therefore, the love of landscape be trivial and transient, or important and permanent, it now becomes necessary to consider. We have, I think, data enough before us for the solution of the question, and we will enter upon it, accordingly, in the following chapter.

CHAPTER XVII
The Moral of Landscape

Supposing then the preceding conclusions correct, respecting the grounds and component *elements* of the pleasure which the moderns take in landscape, we have here to consider what are the probable or usual *effects* of this pleasure. Is it a safe or a seductive one? May we wisely boast of it, and unhesitatingly indulge it? or is it rather a sentiment to be despised when it is slight, and condemned when it is intense; a feeling which disinclines us to labour, and confuses us in thought; a joy only to the inactive and the visionary, incompatible with the duties of life, and the accuracies of reflection?

It seems to me that, as matters stand at present, there is considerable ground for the latter opinion. We saw, in the preceding chapter, that our love of nature had been partly forced upon us by mistakes in our social economy, and led to no distinct issues of action or thought. And when we look to Scott—the man who feels it most deeply—for some explanation of its effect upon him, we find a curious tone of apology (as if for an involuntary folly) running through his confessions of such sentiment and a still more curious inability to define, beyond a certain point, the character of this emotion. Wordsworth definitely and positively affirms that *thought* has nothing whatever to do with the matter, and that though, in his youth, the cataract and wood "haunted him like a passion," it was without the help of any "remoter charm, by thought supplied."[98]

There is not, however, any question but that both Scott and Wordsworth are here mistaken in their analysis of their feelings. Their delight, so far from being without thought, is more than half made up of thought, but of thought in so curiously languid and neutralized a condition that they cannot trace it. The thoughts are beaten to a powder so small that they know not what they are; they know only that in such a state they are not good for much, and disdain to call them thoughts. But the way in which thought, even thus broken, acts in producing the delight will be understood by glancing back to the tenth chapter,[99] in which we observed the power of the imagination in exalting any visible object, by gathering round it, in farther vision, all the facts properly connected with it; this being, as it were, a spiritual or second sight, multiplying the power of enjoyment according to the fulness of the vision.

356   And observe, farther, that this comparative Dimness and Untraceableness of the thoughts which are the sources of our admiration, is not a *fault* in the thoughts, at such a time. It is, on the contrary, a necessary condition of their subordination to the pleasure of Sight. If the thoughts were more distinct we should not *see* so well; and beginning definitely to think, we must comparatively cease to see.

357   It is thus evident that a curiously balanced condition of the powers of mind is necessary to induce full admiration of any natural scene. Let those powers be themselves inert, and the mind vacant of knowledge, and destitute of sensibility; and the external object becomes little more to us than it is to birds or insects; we fall into the temper of the clown. On the other hand, let the reasoning powers be shrewd in excess, the knowledge vast, or sensibility intense, and it will go hard but that the visible object will suggest so much that it shall be soon itself forgotten, or become, at the utmost, merely a kind of keynote to the course of purposeful thought. Newton, probably, did not perceive whether the apple which suggested his meditations on gravity was withered or rosy; nor could Howard[100] be affected by the picturesqueness of the architecture which held the sufferers it was his occupation to relieve.

    This wandering away in thought from the thing seen to the business of life, is not, however, peculiar to men of the highest reasoning powers, or most active benevolence. It takes place more or less in nearly all persons

358 of average mental endowment. They see and love what is beautiful, but forget their admiration of it in following some train of thought which it suggested, and which is of more personal interest to them. Suppose that three or four persons come in sight of a group of pine-trees, not having seen pines for some time. One, perhaps an engineer, is struck by the manner in which their roots hold the ground, and sets himself to examine their fibres, in a few minutes retaining little more consciousness of the beauty of the trees than if he were a rope-maker untwisting the strands of a cable: to another, the sight of the trees calls up some happy association, and presently he forgets them, and pursues the memories they summoned: a third is struck by certain groupings of their colours, useful to him as an artist, which he proceeds immediately to note mechanically for future use, with as little feeling as a cook setting down the constituents of a newly discovered dish; and a fourth, impressed by the wild coiling of boughs and roots, will begin to change them in his fancy into dragons and monsters, and lose his grasp of the scene in fantastic metamorphosis; while, in the mind of the man who has most the power of contemplating the thing itself, all these perceptions and trains of idea are partially present, not distinctly, but in a mingled and perfect harmony. He will not see the colours of the tree so well as the artist, nor its fibres so well as the

engineer; he will not altogether share the emotion of the sentimentalist, nor the trance of the idealist; but fancy, and feeling, and perception, and imagination, will all obscurely meet and balance themselves in him, and he will see the pine-trees somewhat in this manner:

> "Worthier still of note
> Are those fraternal Four of Borrowdale,
> Joined in one solemn and capacious grove;
> Huge trunks! and each particular trunk a growth
> Of intertwisted fibres serpentine
> Up-coiling, and inveterately convolved;
> Nor uninformed with Phantasy, and looks
> That threaten the profane; a pillared shade,
> Upon whose grassless floor of red-brown hue,   359
> By sheddings from the pining umbrage tinged
> Perennially,—beneath whose sable roof
> Of boughs, as if for festal purpose decked
> With unrejoicing berries, ghostly Shapes
> May meet at noontide; Fear and trembling Hope,
> Silence and Foresight; Death the Skeleton,
> And Time the Shadow; there to celebrate,
> As in a natural temple scattered o'er
> With altars undisturbed of mossy stone,
> United worship."[101]

The power, therefore, of thus fully *perceiving* any natural object depends on our being able to group and fasten all our fancies about it as a centre, making a garland of thoughts for it, in which each separate thought is subdued and shortened of its own strength, in order to fit it for harmony with others; the intensity of our enjoyment of the object depending, first, on its own beauty, and then on the richness of the garland. And men who have this habit of clustering and harmonizing their thoughts are a little too apt to look scornfully upon the harder workers who tear the bouquet to pieces to examine the stems. This was the chief narrowness of Wordsworth's mind; he could not understand that to break a rock with a hammer in search of crystal may sometimes be an act not disgraceful to human nature, and that to dissect a flower may sometimes be as proper as to dream over it; whereas all experience goes to teach us, that among men of average intellect the most useful members of society are the dissectors, not the dreamers.

But while these feelings of delight in natural objects cannot be   361 construed into signs of the highest mental powers, or purest moral principles, we see that they are assuredly indicative of minds above the usual standard of power, and endowed with sensibilities of great preciousness to humanity; so that those who find themselves entirely destitute of them, must make this want a subject of humiliation, not of pride. The apathy which cannot perceive beauty is very different from the stern energy which disdains it; and the coldness of heart which receives no emotion from external nature, is not to be confounded with the wisdom of purpose which represses emotion in action. In the case of most men, it is neither acuteness of the reason, nor breadth of humanity, which shields them from the impressions of natural scenery, but rather low anxieties, vain discontents, and mean pleasures: and for one who is blinded to the works of God by profound abstraction or lofty purpose, tens of thousands have their eyes sealed by vulgar selfishness, and their intelligence crushed by impious care.

Observe, then: we have, among mankind in general, the three orders of being;—the lowest, sordid and selfish, which neither sees nor feels; the second, noble and sympathetic, but which sees and feels without concluding or acting; the third and highest, which loses sight in resolution, and feeling in work.

362   "If this be so, it is not well to encourage the observance of landscape, any more than other ways of dreamily and ineffectually spending time?"

363   Stay a moment. We have hitherto observed this love of natural beauty only as it distinguishes one man from another, not as it acts for good or evil on those minds to which it necessarily belongs. It may, on the whole, distinguish weaker men from stronger men, and yet in those weaker men may be of some notable use. And this will become more manifest if we examine somewhat farther into the nature of this instinct, as characteristic especially of youth.

We saw above that Wordsworth described the feeling as independent of thought, and, in the particular place then quoted, he *therefore* speaks of it depreciatingly. But in other places he does not speak of it depreciatingly, but seems to think the absence of thought involves a certain nobleness:

> "In such high hour
> Of visitation from the living God
> *Thought* was not."[102]

And he refers to the intense delight which he himself felt, and which he
364 supposes other men feel, in nature, during their thoughtless youth, as an intimation of their immortality, and a joy which indicates their having come fresh from the hand of God.

Now, if Wordsworth be right in supposing this feeling to be in some degree common to all men, and most vivid in youth, we may question if it can be *entirely* explained as I have now tried to explain it. For if it entirely depended on multitudes of ideas, clustering about a beautiful object, it might seem that the youth could not feel it so strongly as the man, because the man knows more, and must have more ideas to make the garland of. If Wordsworth is at all right in this matter, therefore, there must surely be some other element in the feeling not yet detected.

Now, in a question of this subtle kind, relating to a period of life when self-examination is rare, and expression imperfect, it becomes exceedingly difficult to trace, with any certainty, the movements of the minds of others, nor always easy to remember those of our own. I cannot, from observation, form any decided opinion as to the extent in which this strange delight in nature influences the hearts of young persons in general; and, in stating what has passed in my own mind, I do not mean to draw any positive conclusion as to the nature of the feeling in other children; but the inquiry is clearly one in which personal experience is the only safe ground to go upon, though a narrow one; and I will make no excuse for talking about myself with reference to this subject, because, though there is much egotism in the world, it is often the last thing a man thinks of doing,—and, though there is much work to be done in the world, it is often the best thing a man can do,—to tell the exact truth about the movements of his own mind; and there is this farther reason, that whatever other faculties I may or may not possess, this gift of taking pleasure in landscape I assuredly possess in a greater degree than most men; it having been the ruling passion of my life, and the reason for the choice of its field of labour.   365

The first thing which I remember, as an event in life, was being taken by my nurse to the brow of Friar's Crag on Derwent Water; the intense joy, mingled with awe, that I had in looking through the hollows in the mossy roots, over the crag, into the dark lake, has associated itself more or less with all the twining roots of trees ever since. Two other things I remember as, in a sort, beginnings of life;—crossing Shapfells (being let out of the chaise to run up the hills), and going through Glenfarg, near Kinross, in a winter's morning, when the rocks were hung with icicles; these being culminating points in an early life of more travelling than is usually indulged to a child. In such journeyings, whenever they brought me near hills, and in all mountain ground and scenery, I had a pleasure, as early as I can remember, and continuing till I was eighteen or twenty, infinitely greater than any which has been since possible to me in anything; comparable for intensity only to the joy of a lover in being near a noble and kind mistress, but no more explicable or definable than that feeling of love itself. Only thus much I can remember, respecting it, which is important to our present subject.

First: it was never independent of associated thought. Almost as soon as I could see or hear, I had got reading enough to give me associations   366
with all kinds of scenery; and mountains, in particular, were always partly confused with those of my favourite book, Scott's *Monastery*: so that Glenfarg and all other glens were more or less enchanted to me, filled with forms of hesitating creed about Christie of the Clint Hill, and the

monk Eustace; and with a general presence of White Lady everywhere.[103] I also generally knew, or was told by my father and mother, such simple facts of history as were necessary to give more definite and justifiable association to other scenes which chiefly interested me, such as the ruins of Lochleven and Kenilworth; and thus my pleasure in mountains or ruins was never, even in earliest childhood, free from a certain awe and melancholy, and general sense of the meaning of death, though, in its principal influence, entirely exhilarating and gladdening.

Secondly, it was partly dependent on contrast with a very simple and unamused mode of general life; I was born in London, and accustomed, for two or three years, to no other prospect than that of the brick walls over the way; had no brothers nor sisters, nor companions; and though I could always make myself happy in a quiet way, the beauty of the mountains had an additional charm of change and adventure which a country-bred child would not have felt.

Thirdly: there was no definite religious feeling mingled with it. I partly believed in ghosts and fairies; but supposed that angels belonged entirely to the Mosaic dispensation, and cannot remember any single thought or feeling connected with them. I believed that God was in heaven, and could hear me and see me; but this gave me neither pleasure nor pain, and I seldom thought of it at all. I never thought of nature as God's work, but as a separate fact or existence.

367   Fourthly: it was entirely unaccompanied by powers of reflection or invention. Every fancy that I had about nature was put into my head by some book; and I never reflected about anything till I grew older; and then, the more I reflected, the less nature was precious to me: I could then make myself happy, by thinking, in the dark, or in the dullest scenery; and the beautiful scenery became less essential to my pleasure.

Fifthly: it was, according to its strength, inconsistent with every evil feeling, with spite, anger, covetousness, discontent, and every other hateful passion; but would associate itself deeply with every just and noble sorrow, joy, or affection. It had not, however, always the power to repress what was inconsistent with it; and, though only after stout contention, might at last be crushed by what it had partly repressed. And as it only acted by setting one impulse against another, though it had much power in moulding the character, it had hardly any in strengthening it; it formed temperament but never instilled principle; it kept me generally good-humoured and kindly, but could not teach me perseverance or self-denial: what firmness or principle I had was quite independent of it; and it came itself nearly as often in the form of a temptation as of a safeguard, leading me to ramble over hills when I should have been learning lessons, and lose days in reveries which I might have spent in doing kindnesses.

Lastly: although there was no definite religious sentiment mingled with it, there was a continual perception of Sanctity in the whole of nature, from the slightest thing to the vastest;—an instinctive awe, mixed with delight; an indefinable thrill, such as we sometimes imagine to indicate the presence of a disembodied spirit. I could only feel this perfectly when I was alone; and then it would often make me shiver from head to foot with the joy and fear of it, when after being some time away from hills, I first got to the shore of a mountain river, where the brown water circled   368 among the pebbles, or when I first saw the swell of distant land against the sunset, or the first low broken wall, covered with mountain moss. I cannot in the least *describe* the feeling; but I do not think this is my fault, nor that of the English language, for I am afraid, no feeling *is* describable. If we had to explain even the sense of bodily hunger to a person who had never felt it, we should be hard put to it for words; and the joy in nature seemed to me to come of a sort of heart-hunger, satisfied with the presence of a Great and Holy Spirit. These feelings remained in their full intensity till I was eighteen or twenty, and then, as the reflective and practical power increased, and the "cares of this world"[104] gained upon me, faded gradually away, in the manner described by Wordsworth in his *Intimations of Immortality*.

I cannot, of course, tell how far I am justified in supposing that these sensations may be reasoned upon as common to children in general. But I believe the feelings I have endeavoured to describe are the pure landscape-instinct; and the likelihoods of good or evil resulting from them may be reasoned upon as generally indicating the usefulness or danger of the modern love and study of landscape.

And, first, observe that the charm of romantic association can be felt   369 only by the modern European child. It rises eminently out of the contrast of the beautiful past with the frightful and monotonous present; and it depends for its force on the existence of ruins and traditions, on the remains of architecture, the traces of battlefields, and the precursorship of eventful history.

Again: the influence of surprise in producing the delight, is to be noted, as a suspicious or evanescent element in it. Observe, my pleasure was chiefly when I *first* got into beautiful scenery out of London. The enormous influence of novelty—the way in which it quickens obser-vation, sharpens sensation, and exalts sentiment—is not half enough taken note of by us, and is to me a very sorrowful matter. I think that what Wordsworth speaks of as a glory in the child, because it has come fresh from God's hands, is in reality nothing more than the freshness of all things to its newly opened sight. I find that by keeping long away from hills, I can in great part still restore the old childish feeling about them; and the more I live and work among them, the more it vanishes.

The two points of practical wisdom in this matter are, first, to be   370 content with as little novelty as possible at a time; and, secondly, to preserve, as much as possible in the world, the sources of novelty.

I say, first, to be content with as little change as possible. If the attention is awake, and the feelings in proper train, a turn of a country road, with a cottage beside it, which we have not seen before, is as much as we need for refreshment; if we hurry past it, and take two cottages at a time, it is already too much: hence, in any person who has all his senses about him, a quiet walk along not more than ten or twelve miles of road a day, is the most amusing of all travelling; and all travelling becomes dull in exact proportion to its rapidity. Going by railroad I do not consider as travelling at all; it is merely "being sent" to a place, and very little different from becoming a parcel; the next step to it would of course be telegraphic transport, of which, however, I suppose it has been truly said by Octave Feuillet,

> *"Il y aurait des gens assez bêtes* pour trouver ça amusant."*

If we walk more than ten or twelve miles, it breaks up the day too much; leaving no time for stopping at the stream sides or shady banks, or for any
371 work at the end of the day; besides that the last few miles are apt to be done in a hurry, and may then be considered as lost ground. But if, advancing thus slowly, after some days we approach any more interesting scenery, every yard of the changeful ground becomes precious and piquant; and the continual increase of hope, and of surrounding beauty, affords one of the most exquisite enjoyments possible to the healthy mind; besides that real knowledge is acquired of whatever it is the object of travelling to learn, and a certain sublimity given to all places, so attained, by the true sense of the spaces of earth that separate them. A man who really loves travelling would as soon consent to pack a day of such happiness into an hour of railroad, as one who loved eating would agree, if it were possible, to concentrate his dinner into a pill.

And, secondly, I say that it is wisdom to preserve as much as possible the innocent *sources* of novelty;—not definite inferiorities of one place to another, if such can be done away; but differences of manners and customs, of language and architecture.

The next character we have to note in the landscape-instinct (and on
372 this much stress is to be laid), is its total inconsistency with all evil passions; its absolute contrariety (whether in the contest it were crushed or not), to all care, hatred, envy, anxiety, and moroseness. A feeling of this kind is assuredly not one to be lightly repressed, or treated with contempt.

---

* *Scènes et Proverbes.* La Crise; (Scène en calèche, hors Paris).

But how, if it be so, the reader asks, can it be characteristic of passionate and unprincipled men, like Byron, Shelley, and such others, and not characteristic of the noblest and most highly principled men?

First, because it is itself a passion, and therefore likely to be characteristic of passionate men. Secondly, because it is wholly a separate thing from moral principle, and may or may not be joined to strength of will, or rectitude of purpose; only, this much is always observable in the men whom it characterizes, that, whatever their faults or failings, they always understand and love noble qualities of character: they can conceive (if not certain phases of piety), at all events, self-devotion of the highest kind; they delight in all that is good, gracious, and noble; and, though warped often to take delight also in what is dark or degraded, that delight is mixed with bitter self-reproach; or else is wanton, careless, or affected, while their delight in noble things is constant and sincere.

I think we cannot doubt of our main conclusion, that, though the   376
absence of the love of nature is not an assured condemnation, its presence is an invariable sign of goodness of heart and justness of moral *perception*, though by no means of moral *practice*; that in proportion to the degree in which it is felt, will *probably* be the degree in which all nobleness and beauty of character will also be felt; that when it is originally absent from any mind, that mind is in many other respects hard, worldly, and degraded; that where, having been originally present, it is repressed by art or education, that repression appears to have been detrimental to the person suffering it; and that wherever the feeling exists, it acts for good on the character to which it belongs, though, as it may often belong to characters weak in other respects, it may carelessly be mistaken for a source of evil in them.

One more argument remains, and that, I believe, an unanswerable one.   377
As, by the accident of education, the love of nature has been, among us, associated with *wilfulness*, so, by the accident of time, it has been associated with *faithlessness*. I traced, above, the peculiar mode in which this faithlessness was indicated; but I never intended to imply, therefore, that it was an invariable concomitant of the love. Because it happens that, by various concurrent operations of evil, we have been led according to those words of the Greek poet already quoted, to "dethrone the gods, and crown the whirlwind,"[105] it is no reason that we should forget there was once a time when "the Lord answered Job *out* of the whirlwind."[106] And if we now take final and full view of the matter, we shall find that the love   378
of nature, wherever it has existed, has been a faithful and sacred element of human feeling; that is to say, supposing all circumstances otherwise the same with respect to two individuals, the one who loves nature most will be *always* found to have more *faith in God* than the other. It is intensely difficult, owing to the confusion and counter influences which always

mingle in the data of the problem, to make this abstraction fairly; but so far as we can do it, so far, I boldly assert, the result is constantly the same: the nature-worship will be found to bring with it such a sense of the presence and power of a Great Spirit as no mere reasoning can either induce or controvert; and where that nature-worship is innocently pursued,—*i.e.* with due respect to other claims on time, feeling, and exertion, and associated with the higher principles of religion,—it becomes the channel of certain sacred truths, which by no other means can be conveyed.

This is not a statement which any investigation is needed to prove. It comes to us at once from the highest of all authority. The greater number of the words which are recorded in Scripture, as directly spoken to men by the lips of the Deity, are either simple revelations of His law, or special threatenings, commands, and promises relating to special events. But two passages of God's speaking, one in the Old and one in the New Testament, possess, it seems to me, a different character from any of the rest, having been uttered, the one to effect the last necessary change in the mind of a man whose piety was in other respects perfect; and the other, as the first statement to all men of the principles of Christianity by Christ Himself—I mean the 38th to 41st chapters of the book of Job, and the Sermon on the Mount. Now the first of these passages is, from beginning to end, nothing else than a direction of the mind which was to be perfected to humble observance of the works of God in nature. And the other consists only in the inculcation of *three* things: 1st, right conduct; 2nd, looking for eternal life; 3rd, trusting God, through watchfulness of His dealings with His creation; and the entire contents of the book of Job, and of the Sermon on the Mount, will be found resolvable simply into these three requirements from all men,—that they should act rightly, hope for heaven, and watch God's wonders and work in the earth; the right conduct being always summed up under the three heads of *justice*, *mercy*, and *truth*, and no mention of any doctrinal point whatsoever occurring in either piece of divine teaching.

379

As far as I can judge of the ways of men, it seems to me that the simplest and most necessary truths are always the last believed; and I suppose that well-meaning people in general would rather regulate their conduct and creed by almost any other portion of Scripture whatsoever, than by that Sermon on the Mount which contains the things that Christ thought it first necessary for all men to understand. Nevertheless, I believe the time will soon come for the full force of these two passages of Scripture to be accepted. Instead of supposing the love of nature necessarily connected with the faithlessness of the age, I believe it is connected properly with the benevolence and liberty of the age; that it is precisely the most healthy element which distinctively belongs to us; and that out of it, cultivated no longer in levity or ignorance, but in earnestness, and as a duty, results will spring of an importance at present inconceivable; and lights arise, which, for the first time in man's history, will reveal to him the true nature of his   380 life, the true field for his energies, and the true relations between him and his Maker.

The great mechanical impulses of the age, of which most of us are so proud, are a mere passing fever, half-speculative, half-childish. People will discover at last that royal roads to anything can no more be laid in iron than they can in dust; that there are, in fact, no royal roads to anywhere worth going to; that if there were, it would that instant cease to be worth going to,—I mean, so far as the things to be obtained are in any way estimable in terms of *price*. For there are two classes of precious things in the world: those that God gives us for nothing—sun, air, and life (both mortal life and immortal); and the secondarily precious things which He gives us for a price: these secondarily precious things, worldly wine and milk, can only be bought for definite money; they never can be cheapened. No cheating nor bargaining will ever get a single thing out of nature's "establishment" at half-price. Do we want to be strong?—we must work. To be hungry?—we must starve. To be happy?—we must be kind. To be wise?—we must look and think. No changing of place at a hundred miles an hour, nor making of stuffs a thousand yards a minute, will make us one whit stronger, happier, or wiser. There was always more in the world than men could see, walked they ever so slowly; they will see   381 it no better for going fast. And they will at last, and soon too, find out that their grand inventions for conquering (as they think) space and time, do, in reality, conquer nothing; for space and time are, in their own essence, unconquerable, and besides did not want any sort of conquering; they wanted *using*. A fool always wants to shorten space and time: a wise man wants to lengthen both. A fool wants to kill space and kill time: a wise man, first to gain them, then to animate them. Your railroad, when you come to understand it, is only a device for making the world smaller: and as for being able to talk from place to place, that is, indeed, well and convenient; but suppose you have, originally, nothing to say. We shall be obliged at last to confess, what we should long ago have known, that the really precious things are thought and sight, not pace. It does a bullet no good to go fast; and a man, if he be truly a man, no harm to go slow; for his glory is not at all in going, but in being.

"Well; but railroads and telegraphs are so useful for communicating knowledge to savage nations." Yes, if you have any to give them. If you know nothing *but* railroads, and can communicate nothing but aqueous vapour and gunpowder,—what then? But if you have any other thing than those to give, then the railroad is of use only because it communicates that other thing; and the question is—what that other thing may be. Is it religion? I believe if we had really wanted to communicate that, we could have done it in less than 1800 years, without steam. Most of the good religious communication that I remember, has been done on foot; and it cannot be easily done faster than at foot pace. Is it science? But what science—of motion, meat, and medicine? Well; when you have moved your savage, and dressed your savage, fed him with white bread, and shown him how to set a limb,—what next? Follow out that question. Suppose every obstacle overcome; give your savage every advantage of civilization to the full; suppose that you have put the Red Indian in tight shoes; taught the Chinese how to make Wedgwood's ware, and to paint it with colours that will rub off; and persuaded all Hindoo women that it is more pious to torment their husbands into graves than to burn themselves at the burial,—what next? Gradually, thinking on from point to point, we shall come to perceive that all true happiness and nobleness are near us, and yet neglected by us; and that till we have learned how to be happy and noble we have not much to tell, even to Red Indians. The delights of horse-racing and hunting, of assemblies in the night instead of the day, of costly and wearisome music, of costly and burdensome dress, of chagrined contention for place or power, or wealth, or the eyes of the multitude; and all the endless occupation without purpose, and idleness without rest, of our vulgar world, are not, it seems to me, enjoyments we need be ambitious to communicate. And all real and wholesome enjoyments possible to man have been just as possible to him, since first he was made of the earth, as they are now; and they are possible to him chiefly in peace. To watch the corn grow, and the blossoms set; to draw hard breath over ploughshare or spade; to read, to think, to love, to hope, to pray,— these are the things that make men happy; they have always had the power of doing these, they never *will* have power to do more. The world's prosperity or adversity depends upon our knowing and teaching these few things: but upon iron, or glass, or electricity, or steam, in no wise.

383   And I am Utopian and enthusiastic enough to believe, that the time will come when the world will discover this. It has now made its experiments in every possible direction but the right one: and it seems that it must, at last, try the right one, in a mathematical necessity. It has tried fighting, and preaching, and fasting, buying and selling, pomp and parsimony, pride and humiliation,—every possible manner of existence in which it could conjecture there was any happiness or dignity: and all the while, as it bought, sold, and fought, and fasted, and wearied itself with policies, and ambitions, and self-denials, God had placed its real happiness in the keeping of the little mosses of the wayside, and of the clouds of the firmament. Now and then a wearied king, or a tormented slave, found out where the true kingdoms of the world were, and possessed

himself, in a furrow or two of garden ground, of a truly infinite dominion. But the world would not believe their report, and went on trampling down the mosses, and forgetting the clouds, and seeking happiness in its own way, until, at last, blundering and late, came natural science; and in natural science not only the observation of things, but the finding out of new uses for them. Of course the world, having a choice left to it, went wrong as usual, and thought that these mere material uses were to be the sources of its happiness. It got the clouds packed into iron cylinders, and made them carry its wise self at their own cloud pace. It got weavable fibres out of the mosses, and made clothes for itself, cheap and fine,—here was happiness at last. To go as fast as the clouds, and manufacture everything out of anything,—here was paradise, indeed!

And now, when, in a little while, it is unparadised again, if there were   384 any other mistake that the world could make, it would of course make it. But I see not that there is any other; and, standing fairly at its wits' end, having found that going fast, when it is used to it, is no more paradisiacal than going slow; and that all the prints and cottons in Manchester cannot make it comfortable in its mind, I do verily believe it will come, finally, to understand that God paints the clouds and shapes the moss-fibres, that men may be happy in seeing Him at His work, and that in resting quietly beside Him, and watching His working, and—according to the power He has communicated to ourselves, and the guidance he grants,—in carrying out His purposes of peace and charity among all His creatures, are the only real happinesses that ever were, or will be, possible to mankind.

How far art is capable of helping us in such happiness we hardly yet know; but I hope to be able, in the subsequent parts of this work, to give some data for arriving at a conclusion in the matter.[107] Enough has been advanced to relieve the reader from any lurking suspicion of unworthiness in our subject, and to induce him to take interest in the mind and work of the great painter who has headed the landscape school among us. Therefore I have only one point more to notice here, namely, the exact relation between landscape-painting and natural science, properly so called.

For it may be thought that I have rashly assumed that the Scriptural authorities above quoted apply to that partly superficial view of nature which is taken by the landscape-painter, instead of to the accurate view taken by the man of science. So far from there being rashness in such an   385 assumption, the whole language, both of the book of Job and the Sermon on the Mount, gives precisely the view of nature which is taken by the uninvestigating affection of a humble, but powerful mind. There is no dissection of muscles or counting of elements, but the boldest and broadest glance at the apparent facts, and the most magnificent metaphor in expressing them. "His eyes are like the eyelids of the morning. In his neck remaineth strength, and sorrow is turned into joy before him."[108] And in the often repeated, never obeyed, command, "Consider the lilies of the field," observe there is precisely the delicate attribution of life which we have seen to be the characteristic of the modern view of landscape,—"They toil not." There is no science, or hint of science; no counting of petals, nor display of provisions for sustenance; nothing but the expression of sympathy, at once the most childish, and the most profound,—"They toil not."[109]

And we see in this, therefore, that the instinct which leads us thus to attribute life to the lowest forms of organic nature, does not necessarily spring from faithlessness, nor the deducing a moral out of them from an irregular and languid conscientiousness. In this, as in almost all things connected with moral discipline, the same results may follow from contrary causes; and as there are a good and evil contentment, a good and evil discontent, a good and evil care, fear, ambition, and so on, there are also good and evil forms of this sympathy with nature, and disposition to moralize over it. In general, active men, of strong sense and stern 386 principle, do not care to see anything in a leaf, but vegetable tissue, and are so well convinced of useful moral truth, that it does not strike them as a new or notable thing when they find it in any way symbolized by material nature; hence there is a strong presumption, when first we perceive a tendency in any one to regard trees as living, and enunciate moral aphorisms over every pebble they stumble against, that such tendency proceeds from a morbid temperament, like Shelley's, or an inconsistent one, like Jaques's. But when the active life is nobly fulfilled, and the mind is then raised beyond it into clear and calm beholding of the world around us, the same tendency again manifests itself in the most sacred way: the simplest forms of nature are strangely animated by the sense of the Divine presence; the trees and flowers seem all, in a sort, children of God; and we ourselves, their fellows, made out of the same dust, and greater than they only in having a greater portion of the Divine power exerted on our frame, and all the common uses and palpably visible forms of things, become subordinate in our minds to their inner glory,—to the mysterious voices in which they talk to us about God, and the changeful and typical aspects by which they witness to us of holy truth, and fill us with obedient, joyful, and thankful emotion.

It is in raising us from the first state of inactive reverie to the second of useful thought, that scientific pursuits are to be chiefly praised. But in restraining us at this second stage, and checking the impulses towards higher contemplation, they are to be feared or blamed. They may in certain minds be consistent with such contemplation; but only by an effort: in their nature they are always adverse to it, having a tendency to chill and subdue the feelings, and to resolve all things into atoms and numbers. For most men, an ignorant enjoyment is better than an informed one; it is better to conceive the sky as a blue dome than a dark cavity, and   387 the cloud as a golden throne than a sleety mist. I much question whether any one who knows optics, however religious he may be, can feel in equal degree the pleasure or reverence which an unlettered peasant may feel at the sight of a rainbow. And it is mercifully thus ordained, since the law of life, for a finite being, with respect to the works of an infinite one, must be always an infinite ignorance. We cannot fathom the mystery of a single flower, nor is it intended that we should; but that the pursuit of science should constantly be stayed by the love of beauty, and accuracy of knowledge by tenderness of emotion.

Nor is it even just to speak of the love of beauty as in all respects unscientific; for there is a science of the aspects of things, as well as of their nature; and it is as much a fact to be noted in their constitution, that they produce such and such an effect upon the eye or heart (as, for instance, that minor scales of sound cause melancholy), as that they are made up of certain atoms or vibrations of matter.

It is as the master of this science of *Aspects*, that I said, some time ago,[110] Turner must eventually be named always with Bacon, the master of the science of *Essence*. As the first poet who has, in all their range, understood the grounds of noble emotion which exist in landscape, his future influence will be of a still more subtle and important character.

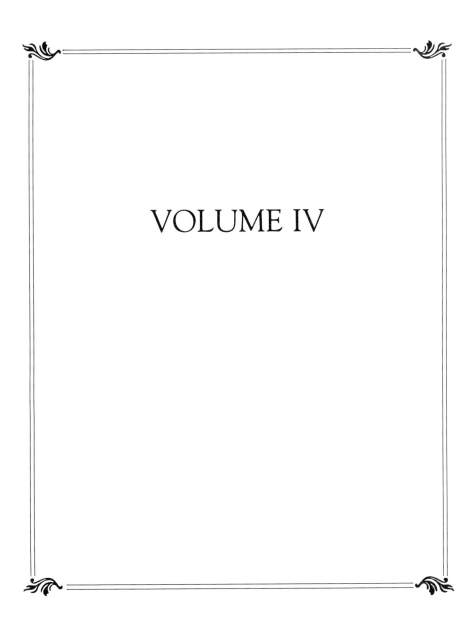

VOLUME IV

PART V
Of Mountain Beauty

CHAPTER I
Of the Turnerian Picturesque

9   THE work which we proposed to ourselves, towards the close of the last
     volume,[1] as first to be undertaken in this, was the examination of
those peculiarities of system in which Turner either stood alone, even in
the modern school, or was a distinguished representative of modern, as
opposed to ancient, practice.

And the most interesting of these subjects of inquiry, with which,
therefore, it may be best to begin, is the precise form under which he has
admitted into his work the modern feeling of the picturesque, which, so
far as it consists in a delight in ruin, is perhaps the most suspicious and
questionable of all the characters distinctively belonging to our temper,
and art.

It is especially so, because it never appears, even in the slightest
measure, until the days of the decline of art in the seventeenth century.
The love of neatness and precision, as opposed to all disorder, maintains
itself down to Raphael's childhood without the slightest interference of
any other feeling; and it is not until Claude's time, and owing in great part
to his influence, that the new feeling distinctly establishes itself.

10   The essence of picturesque character has been already defined[2] to be a
sublimity not inherent in the nature of the thing, but caused by something
external to it; as the ruggedness of a cottage roof possesses something of a
mountain aspect, not belonging to the cottage as such. And this sublimity
may be either in mere external ruggedness, and other visible character, or
it may lie deeper, in an expression of sorrow and old age, attributes which

11   are both sublime; not a dominant expression, but one mingled with such
familiar and common characters as prevent the object from becoming
perfectly pathetic in its sorrow, or perfectly venerable in its age.

For instance, I cannot find words to express the intense pleasure I have
always in first finding myself, after some prolonged stay in England, at the
foot of the old tower of Calais church. The large neglect, the noble
unsightliness of it; the record of its years written so visibly, yet without
sign of weakness or decay; its stern wasteness and gloom, eaten away by
the Channel winds, and overgrown with the bitter sea grasses; its slates

427

and tiles all shaken and rent, and yet not falling; its desert of brickwork
full of bolts, and holes, and ugly fissures, and yet strong, like a bare brown
rock; its carelessness of what any one thinks or feels about it, putting forth
no claim, having no beauty or desirableness, pride, nor grace; yet neither
asking for pity; not, as ruins are, useless and piteous, feebly or fondly gar-
rulous of better days; but useful still, going through its own daily work,—as
some old fisherman beaten grey by storm, yet drawing his daily nets: so it
stands, with no complaint about its past youth, in blanched and meagre
massiveness and serviceableness, gathering human souls together underneath it; the sound of its bells for prayer still rolling through its rents; and
the grey peak of it seen far across the sea, principal of the three that rise
above the waste of surfy sand and hillocked shore,—the lighthouse for life,
and the belfry for labour, and this for patience and praise.

I cannot tell the half of the strange pleasures and thoughts that come
about me at the sight of that old tower; for, in some sort, it is the epitome
of all that makes the Continent of Europe interesting, as opposed to new
countries; and, above all, it completely expresses that agedness in the
midst of active life which binds the old and the new into harmony. We,
in England, have our new street, our new inn, our green shaven lawn, and   12
our piece of ruin emergent from it,—a mere *specimen* of the Middle Ages
put on a bit of velvet carpet to be shown, which, but for its size, might as
well be on a museum shelf at once, under cover. But, on the Continent,
the links are unbroken between the past and present, and, in such use as
they can serve for, the grey-headed wrecks are suffered to stay with men;
while, in unbroken line, the generations of spared buildings are seen
succeeding each in its place. And thus in its largeness, in its permitted
evidence of slow decline, in its poverty, in its absence of all pretence, of
all show and care for outside aspect, that Calais tower has an infinite of
symbolism in it, all the more striking because usually seen in contrast with
English scenes expressive of feelings the exact reverse of these.

And I am sorry to say that the opposition is most distinct in that noble
carelessness as to what people think of it. Once, on coming from the
Continent, almost the first inscription I saw in my native English was this:

> "To Let, a Genteel House, up this road."

And it struck me forcibly, for I had not come across the idea of gentility,
among the upper limestones of the Alps, for seven months; nor do I think
that the Continental nations in general *have* the idea. They would have
advertised a "pretty" house, or a "large" one, or a "convenient" one; but
they could not, by any use of the terms afforded by their several languages,
have got at the English "genteel." Consider, a little, all the meanness that
there is in that epithet, and then see, when next you cross the Channel,
how scornful of it that Calais spire will look.

13   Of which spire the largeness and age are also opposed exactly to the chief appearances of modern England, as one feels them on first returning to it; that marvellous smallness both of houses and scenery, so that a ploughman in the valley has his head on a level with the tops of all the hills in the neighbourhood; and a house is organized into complete establishment,—parlour, kitchen, and all, with a knocker to its door, and a garret window to its roof, and a bow to its second story,* on a scale of 12 feet wide by 15 high, so that three such at least would go into the granary of an ordinary Swiss cottage: and also our serenity of perfection, our peace of conceit, everything being done that vulgar minds can conceive as wanting to be done; the spirit of well-principled housemaids everywhere, exerting itself for perpetual propriety and renovation, so that nothing is old, but only "old-fashioned," and contemporary, as it were, in date and impressiveness only with last year's bonnets. Abroad, a building of the eighth or tenth century stands ruinous in the open street; the children play round it, the peasants heap their corn in it, the buildings of yesterday nestle about it, and fit their new stones into its rents, and tremble in sympathy as it trembles. No one wonders at it, or thinks of it as separate, and of another time; we feel the ancient world to be a real thing, and one with the new: antiquity is no dream; it is rather the children playing about the old stones that are the dream. But all is continuous; and the words, "from generation to generation," understandable there. Whereas here we have a living present, consisting merely of what is "fashionable" and "old-fashioned"; and a past, of which there are no vestiges; a past which peasant or citizen can no more conceive; all equally far away; Queen Elizabeth as old as Queen Boadicea, and both incredible. At Verona we look out of Can Grande's window to his tomb;

14   and if he does not stand beside us, we feel only that he is in the grave instead of the chamber,—not that he is *old*, but that he might have been beside us last night. But in England the dead are dead to purpose. One cannot believe they ever were alive, or anything else than what they are now—names in school-books.

Then that spirit of trimness. The smooth paving stones; the scraped, hard, even, rutless roads; the neat gates and plates, and essence of border and order, and spikiness and spruceness. Abroad, a country-house has some confession of human weakness and human fates about it. There are the old grand gates still, which the mob pressed sore against at the Revolution, and the strained hinges have never gone so well since; and the broken greyhound on the pillar—still broken—better so: but the long avenue is gracefully pale with fresh green, and the courtyard bright with

*The principal street of Canterbury has some curious examples of this *tininess*.

orange-trees; the garden is a little run to waste—since Mademoiselle was married nobody cares much about it; and one range of apartments is shut up—nobody goes into them since Madame died. But with us, let who will be married or die, we neglect nothing. All is polished and precise again next morning; and whether people are happy or miserable, poor or prosperous, still we sweep the stairs of a Saturday.*

Now, I have insisted long on this English character, because I want the reader to understand thoroughly the opposite element of the noble picturesque: its expression, namely, of *suffering*, of *poverty*, or *decay*, nobly endured by unpretending strength of heart. Nor only unpretending, but unconscious. If there be visible pensiveness in the building, as in a ruined abbey, it becomes, or claims to become, beautiful; but the picturesqueness   15 is in the unconscious suffering,—the look that an old labourer has, not knowing that there is anything pathetic in his grey hair, and withered arms, and sunburnt breast; and thus there are the two extremes, the consciousness of pathos in the confessed ruin, which may or may not be beautiful, according to the kind of it; and the entire denial of all human calamity and care, in the swept proprieties and neatnesses of English modernism: and, between these, there is the unconscious confession of the facts of distress and decay, in by-words; the world's hard work being gone through all the while, and no pity asked for, nor contempt feared. And this is the expression of that Calais spire, and of all picturesque things, in so far as they have mental or human expression at all.

I say, in so far as they have mental expression, because their merely outward delightfulness—that which makes them pleasant in painting, or, in the literal sense, picturesque—is their actual variety of colour and form. A broken stone has necessarily more various forms in it than a whole one; a bent roof has more various curves in it than a straight one; every excrescence or cleft involves some additional complexity of light and shade, and every stain of moss on eaves or wall adds to the delightfulness of colour. Hence, in a completely picturesque object, as an old cottage or mill, there are introduced, by various circumstances not essential to it, but, on the whole, generally somewhat detrimental to it as cottage or mill, such elements of sublimity—complex light and shade, varied colour, undulatory form, and so on—as can generally be found only in noble natural objects, woods, rocks, or mountains. This sublimity, belonging in a parasitical manner to the building, renders it, in the usual sense of the word, "picturesque."

---

*This, however, is of course true only of insignificant duties, necessary, for appearance' sake. Serious duties, necessary for kindness' sake, must be permitted in any domestic affliction, under pain of shocking the English public.

Now, if this outward sublimity be sought for by the painter, without any regard for the real nature of the thing, and without any comprehension of the pathos of character hidden beneath, it forms the low school of the surface-picturesque; that which fills ordinary drawing-books and scrap-books, and employs, perhaps, the most popular living landscape painters of France, England, and Germany. But if these same outward characters be sought for in subordination to the inner character of the object, every source of pleasurableness being refused which is incompatible with that, while perfect sympathy is felt at the same time with the object as to all that it tells of itself in those sorrowful by-words, we have the school of true or noble picturesque; still distinguished from the school of pure beauty and sublimity, because, in its subjects, the pathos and sublimity are all *by the way*, as in Calais old spire,—not inherent, as in a lovely tree or mountain; while it is distinguished still more from the schools of the lower picturesque by its tender sympathy, and its refusal of all sources of pleasure inconsistent with the perfect nature of the thing to be studied.

The reader will only be convinced of the broad scope of this law by careful thought, and comparison of picture with picture; but a single example will make the principle of it clear to him.

On the whole, the first master of the lower picturesque, among our living artists, is Clarkson Stanfield; his range of art being, indeed, limited by his pursuit of this character. I take, therefore, a windmill, forming the principal subject in his drawing of Brittany near Dol (engraved in the Coast Scenery),[3] and beside it I place a windmill, which forms also the principal subject in Turner's study of the Lock [fig.41], in the Liber Studiorum. At first sight I dare say the reader may like Stanfield's best; and there is, indeed, a great deal more in it to attract liking. Its roof is nearly as interesting in its ruggedness as a piece of the stony peak of a mountain, with a châlet built on its side; and it is exquisitely varied in swell and curve. Turner's roof, on the contrary, is a plain, ugly gable,—a windmill roof, and nothing more. Stanfield's sails are twisted into most effective wrecks, as beautiful as pine bridges over Alpine streams; only they do not look as if they had ever been serviceable windmill sails; they are bent about in cross and awkward ways, as if they were warped or cramped; and their timbers look heavier than necessary. Turner's sails have no beauty about them like that of Alpine bridges; but they have the exact switchy sway of the sail that is always straining against the wind; and the timbers form clearly the lightest possible framework for the canvas,— thus showing the essence of windmill sail. Then the clay wall of Stanfield's mill is as beautiful as a piece of chalk cliff, all worn into furrows by the rain, coated with mosses, and rooted to the ground by a heap of crumbled stone, embroidered with grass and creeping plants. But this is not a serviceable state for a windmill to be in. The essence of a windmill,

fig.41   The Picturesque of Windmills
Stanfield   Turner
1. Pure Modern   2. Turnerian

as distinguished from all other mills, is, that it should turn round, and be a spinning thing, ready always to face the wind; as light, therefore, as possible, and as vibratory; so that it is in no wise good for it to approximate itself to the nature of chalk cliffs.

Now observe how completely Turner has chosen his mill so as to mark this great fact of windmill nature; how high he has set it; how slenderly he has supported it; how he has built it all of wood; how he has bent the lower planks so as to give the idea of the building lapping over the pivot on which it rests inside; and how, finally, he has insisted on the great leverage of the beam behind it, while Stanfield's lever looks more like a prop than a thing to turn the roof with. And he has done all this fearlessly, though none of these elements of form are pleasant ones in themselves, but tend, on the whole, to give a somewhat mean and spider-like look to the principal feature in his picture; and then, finally, because he could not get the windmill dissected, and show us the real heart and centre of the whole, behold, he has put a pair of old millstones, *lying outside*, at the bottom of it. These—the first cause and motive of all the fabric—laid at its foundation; and beside them the cart which is to fulfil the end of the fabric's being, and take home the sacks of flour.

So far of what each painter chooses to draw. But do not fail also to consider the spirit in which it is drawn. Observe, that though all this ruin has befallen Stanfield's mill, Stanfield is not in the least sorry for it. On the contrary, he is delighted, and evidently thinks it the most fortunate thing possible. The owner is ruined, doubtless, or dead; but his mill forms

18

an admirable object in our view of Brittany. So far from being grieved about it, we will make it our principal light;—if it were a fruit-tree in spring-blossom, instead of a desolate mill, we could not make it whiter or brighter; we illumine our whole picture with it, and exult over its every rent as a special treasure and possession.

Not so Turner. *His* mill is still serviceable; but, for all that, he feels somewhat pensive about it. It is a poor property, and evidently the owner of it has enough to do to get his own bread out from between its stones. Moreover, there is a dim type of all melancholy human labour in it,— catching the free winds, and setting them to turn grindstones. It is poor work for the winds; better, indeed, than drowning sailors or tearing down forests, but not their proper work of marshalling the clouds, and bearing the wholesome rains to the place where they are ordered to fall, and fanning the flowers and leaves when they are faint with heat. Turning round a couple of stones, for the mere pulverization of human food, is not noble work for the winds. So, also, of all low labour to which one sets human souls. It is better than no labour; and, in a still higher degree, better than destructive wandering of imagination; but yet that grinding in the darkness, for mere food's sake, must be melancholy work enough for many a living creature. All men have felt it so; and this grinding at the mill, whether it be breeze or soul that is set to it, we cannot much rejoice in. Turner has no joy of his mill. It shall be dark against the sky, yet proud, and on the hill-top; not ashamed of its labour, and brightened from beyond, the golden clouds stooping over it, and the calm summer sun going down behind, far away, to his rest.

Now in all this observe how the higher condition of art (for I suppose the reader will feel, with me, that Turner *is* the highest) depends upon largeness of sympathy. It is mainly because the one painter has communion of heart with his subject, and the other only casts his eyes upon it feelinglessly, that the work of the one is greater than that of the other. And, as we think farther over the matter, we shall see that this is indeed the eminent cause of the difference between the lower picturesque and the higher. For, in a certain sense, the lower picturesque ideal is eminently a *heartless* one; the lover of it seems to go forth into the world in a temper as merciless as its rocks. All other men feel some regret at the sight of disorder and ruin. He alone delights in both; it matters not of what. Fallen cottage—desolate villa—deserted village—blasted heath—mouldering castle—to him, so that they do but show jagged angles of stone and timber, all are sights equally joyful. Poverty, and darkness, and guilt, bring in their several contributions to his treasury of pleasant thoughts. The shattered window, opening into black and ghastly rents of wall, the foul rag or straw wisp stopping them, the dangerous roof, decrepit floor and stair, ragged misery, or wasting age of the inhabitants,—all these conduce, each in due measure, to the fulness of his satisfaction. What is it to him that the old man has passed his seventy years in helpless darkness and untaught waste of soul? The old man has at last accomplished his destiny, and filled the corner of a sketch, where something of an unshapely nature was wanting. What is it to him that the people fester in that feverish misery in the low quarter of the town, by the river? Nay, it is much to him. What else were they made for? what could they have done better? The black timbers, and the green water, and the soaking wrecks of boats, and the torn remnants of clothes hung out to dry in the sun;—truly the fever-struck creatures, whose lives have been given for the production of these materials of effect, have not died in vain.

Yet, for all this, I do not say the lover of the lower picturesque is a monster in human form. He is by no means this, though truly we might at first think so, if we came across him unawares, and had not met with any such sort of person before. Generally speaking, he is kind-hearted, innocent of evil, but not broad in thought; somewhat selfish, and incapable of acute sympathy with others; gifted at the same time with strong artistic instincts and capacities for the enjoyment of varied form, and light, and shade, in pursuit of which enjoyment his life is passed, as the lives of other men are for the most part, in the pursuit of what *they* also like,—be it honour, or money, or indolent pleasure,—very irrespective of the poor people living by the stagnant canal. And, in some sort, the hunter of the picturesque is better than many of these; inasmuch as he is simple-minded and capable of unostentatious and economical delights, which, if not very helpful to other people, are at all events not utterly injurious, even to the victims or subjects of his picturesque fancies; while to many others his work is entertaining and useful. And, more than all this, even that delight which he *seems* to take in misery is not altogether unvirtuous. Through all his enjoyment there runs a certain undercurrent of tragical passion,—a real vein of human sympathy;—it lies at the root of all those strange morbid hauntings of his; a sad excitement, such as other people feel at a tragedy, only less in degree, just enough, indeed, to give a deeper tone to his pleasure, and to make him choose for his subject the broken stones of a cottage wall rather than of a roadside bank, the picturesque beauty of form in each being supposed precisely the same: and, together with this slight tragical feeling, there is also a humble and romantic sympathy; a vague desire, in his own mind, to live in cottages rather than in palaces; a joy in humble things, a contentment and delight in makeshifts, a secret persuasion (in many respects a true one) that there is in these ruined cottages a happiness often quite as great as in kings' palaces, and a virtue and nearness to God infinitely greater and holier than can commonly be found in any other kind of place; so that the misery in which he exults is not, as he sees it, misery, but nobleness,—"poor and sick in body, and beloved by the Gods.''* And thus, being nowise sure that these things can be mended at all, and very sure that he knows not how to mend them, and also that the strange pleasure he feels in them *must* have some good reason in the nature of things, he yields to his destiny, enjoys his dark canal without scruple, and mourns over every improvement in the town, and every movement made by its sanitary commissioners, as a miser would over a planned robbery of his chest; in all this being not only innocent, but even respectable and admirable, compared with the kind of person who has *no* pleasure in sights of this kind, but only in fair façades, trim gardens, and park palings, and who would thrust all poverty and misery out of his way, collecting it into back alleys, or sweeping it finally out of the world, so that the street might give wider play for his chariot-wheels, and the breeze less offence to his nobility.

Therefore, even the love for the lower picturesque ought to be cultivated with care, wherever it exists: not with any special view to artistic, but to merely humane, education. It will never really or seriously interfere with practical benevolence; on the contrary, it will constantly lead, if associated with other benevolent principles, to a truer sympathy with the poor, and better understanding of the right ways of helping them; and, in the present stage of civilization, it is the most important element of character, not directly moral, which can be cultivated in youth; since it is mainly for the want of this feeling that we destroy so many ancient monuments, in order to erect "handsome" streets and shops instead, which might just as well have been erected elsewhere, and whose effect on our minds, so far as they have any, is to increase every disposition to frivolity, expense, and display.

23

It is evident, from what has been advanced, that there is no definite bar of separation between the two; but that the dignity of the picturesque increases from lower to higher, in exact proportion to the sympathy of the artist with his subject. And in like manner, his own greatness depends (other things being equal) on the extent of this sympathy. If he rest content with narrow enjoyment of outward forms, and light sensation of luxurious tragedy, and so goes on multiplying his sketches of mere picturesque material, he necessarily settles down into the ordinary "clever" artist, very good and respectable, maintaining himself by his sketching and painting in an honourable way, as by any other daily business, and in due time passing away from the world without having, on the whole, done much for it. Such has been the necessary, not very lamentable, destiny of a large number of men in these days, whose gifts urged them to the

---

*Epitaph on Epictetus.

practice of art, but who possessing no breadth of mind, nor having met with masters capable of concentrating what gifts they had towards nobler use, almost perforce remained in their small picturesque circle; getting more and more narrowed in range of sympathy as they fell more and more into the habit of contemplating the one particular class of subjects that pleased them, and recomposing them by rules of art.

CHAPTER II
Of Turnerian Topography

27   WE saw, in the course of the last chapter, with what kind of feeling an artist ought to regard the character of every object he undertakes to paint. The next question is, what objects he *ought* to undertake to paint; how far he should be influenced by his feelings in the choice of subjects; and how far he should permit himself to alter, or in the usual art language, improve, nature. For it has already been stated[4] that all great art must be inventive; that is to say, its subject must be produced by the imagination. If so, then great landscape art cannot be a mere copy of any given scene; and we have now to inquire what else than this it may be.

    If the reader will glance over that same chapter, he will see that we there divided art generally into "historical" and "poetical," or the art of relating facts simply, and facts imaginatively. Now with respect to landscape, the historical art is simply topography, and the imaginative art is what I have in the heading of the present chapter called Turnerian topography, and must in the course of it endeavour to explain.

    Observe, however, at the outset, that, touching the duty or fitness of altering nature at all, the quarrels which have so wofully divided the world of art are caused only by want of understanding this simplest of all canons,—"It is always wrong to draw what you don't see." This law is 28 inviolable. But then, some people see only things that exist, and others see things that do not exist, or do not exist apparently. And if they really *see* these non-apparent things, they are quite right to draw them; the only harm is when people try to draw non-apparent things, who *don't* see them, but think they can calculate or compose into existence what is to them for evermore invisible. If some people really see angels where others see only empty space, let them paint the angels; only let not anybody else think *he* can paint an angel too, on any calculated principles of the angelic.

    If, therefore, when we go to a place, we see nothing else than is there, we are to paint nothing else, and to remain pure topographical or historical landscape painters. If, going to the place, we see something quite different from what is there, then we are to paint that—nay, we *must* paint that, whether we will or not; it being, for us, the only reality we can

437

get at. But let us beware of pretending to see this unreality if we do not.

The simple observance of this rule would put an end to nearly all disputes, and keep a large number of men in healthy work who now totally waste their lives; so that the most important question that an artist can possibly have to determine for himself, is whether he has invention or not. And this he can ascertain with ease. If visions of unreal things present themselves to him with or without his own will, praying to be painted, quite ungovernable in their coming or going,—neither to be summoned if they do not choose to come, nor banished if they do,—he has invention. If, on the contrary, he only sees the commonly visible facts; and, should he not like them, and want to alter them, finds that he must think of a *rule* whereby to do so, he has no invention. All the rules in the world will do him no good; and if he tries to draw anything else than those materially visible facts, he will pass his whole life in uselessness, and produce nothing but scientific absurdities.

Let him take his part at once, boldly, and be content. Pure history and   29 pure topography are most precious things; in many cases more useful to the human race than high imaginative work; and assuredly it is intended that a large majority of all who are employed in art should never aim at anything higher. It is *only* vanity, never love, nor any other noble feeling, which prompts men to desert their allegiance to the simple truth, in vain pursuit of the imaginative truth which has been appointed to be for evermore sealed to them.

Nor let it be supposed that artists who possess minor degrees of imaginative gift need be embarrassed by the doubtful sense of their own powers. In general, when the imagination is at all noble, it is irresistible, and therefore those who can at all resist it *ought* to resist it. Be a plain topographer if you possibly can; if Nature meant you to be anything else, she will force you to it; but never try to be a prophet; go on quietly with your hard camp-work, and the spirit will come to you in the camp, as it did to Eldad and Medad,[5] if you are appointed to have it; but try above all things to be quickly perceptive of the noble spirit in others, and to discern in an instant between its true utterance and the diseased mimicries of it. In a general way, remember it is a far better thing to find out other great men, than to become one yourself: for you can but become *one* at best, but you may bring others to light in numbers.

We have, therefore, to inquire what kind of changes these are, which must be wrought by the imaginative painter on landscape, and by whom they have been thus nobly wrought. First, for the better comfort of the non-imaginative painter, be it observed, that it is not possible to find a landscape, which if painted precisely as it is, will not make an impressive picture. No one knows, till he has tried, what strange beauty and subtle composition is prepared to his hand by Nature, wherever she is left to   30 herself; and what deep feeling may be found in many of the most homely scenes, even where man has interfered with those wild ways of hers. But, beyond this, let him note that though historical topography forbids *alteration*, it neither forbids sentiment nor choice.

31   Generally speaking, therefore, the duty of every painter at present, who has not much invention, is to take subjects of which the portraiture will be precious in after times: views of our abbeys and cathedrals; distant views of cities, if possible chosen from some spot in itself notable by association; perfect studies of the battle-fields of Europe, of all houses of celebrated men, and places they loved, and, of course, of the most lovely natural scenery. And, in doing all this, it should be understood, primarily, whether the picture is topographical or not: if topographical, then not a line is to be altered, not a stick nor stone removed, not a colour deepened, not a form improved; the picture is to be, as far as possible, the reflection of the place in a mirror; and the artist to consider himself only as a sensitive and skilful reflector, taking care that no false impression is conveyed by any error on his part which he might have avoided.

32   But if a painter has inventive power he is to treat his subject in a totally different way; giving not the actual facts of it, but the impression it made on his mind.

33   First, he receives a true impression from the place itself, and takes care to keep hold of that as his chief good; indeed, he needs no care in the matter, for the distinction of his mind from that of others consists in his instantly receiving such sensations strongly, and being unable to lose them; and then he sets himself as far as possible to reproduce that impression on the mind of the spectator of his picture.

Now, observe, this impression on the mind never results from the mere piece of scenery which can be included within the limits of the picture. It depends on the temper into which the mind has been brought, both by all the landscape round, and by what has been seen previously in the course of the day; so that no particular spot upon which the painter's glance may at any moment fall, is then to him what, if seen by itself, it will be to the spectator far away; nor is it what it would be, even to that spectator, if he had come to the reality through the steps which Nature has appointed to be the preparation for it, instead of seeing it isolated on an exhibition wall. For instance, on the descent of the St. Gothard, towards Italy, just

34   after passing through the narrow gorge above Faido, the road emerges into a little breadth of valley, which is entirely filled by fallen stones and débris, partly disgorged by the Ticino as it leaps out of the narrower chasm, and partly brought down by winter avalanches from a loose and decomposing mass of mountain on the left. Beyond this first promontory is seen a considerably higher range, but not an imposing one, which rises above the village of Faido. The etching [fig.42] is a topographical outline

fig.42 John Ruskin, Simple Topography of Pass of Faido
(engraving after J.M.W. Turner)

of the scene, with the actual blocks of rock which happened to be lying in the bed of the Ticino at the spot from which I chose to draw it. The masses of loose débris (which, for any permanent purpose, I had no need to draw, as their arrangement changes at every flood) I have not drawn, but only those features of the landscape which happen to be of some continual importance. Of which note, first, that the little three-windowed building on the left is the remnant of a gallery built to protect the road which once went on that side, from the avalanches and stones that come down the "couloir" in the rock above. It is only a ruin, the greater part having been by said avalanches swept away, and the old road, of which a remnant is also seen on the extreme left, abandoned and carried now along the hill side on the right, partly sustained on rough stone arches, and winding down, as seen in the sketch, to a weak wooden bridge, which enables it to recover its old track past the gallery. It seems formerly (but since the destruction of the gallery) to have gone about a mile farther down the river on the right bank, and then to have been carried across by a longer wooden bridge, of which only the two butments are seen in the sketch, the rest having been swept away by the Ticino, and the new bridge erected near the spectator.

There is nothing in this scene, taken by itself, particularly interesting or impressive. The mountains are not elevated, nor particularly fine in form, and the heaps of stones which encumber the Ticino present nothing

35

notable to the ordinary eye. But, in reality, the place is approached through one of the narrowest and most sublime ravines in the Alps, and after the traveller during the early part of the day has been familiarized with the aspect of the highest peaks of the Mont St. Gothard. Hence it speaks quite another language to him from that in which it would address itself to an unprepared spectator: the confused stones, which by themselves would be almost without any claim upon his thoughts, become exponents of the fury of the river by which he has journeyed all day long; the defile beyond, not in itself narrow or terrible, is regarded nevertheless with awe, because it is imagined to resemble the gorge that had just been traversed above; and, although no very elevated mountains immediately overhang it, the scene is felt to belong to, and arise in its essential characters out of, the strength of those mightier mountains in the unseen north.

Any topographical delineation of the facts, therefore, must be wholly incapable of arousing in the mind of the beholder those sensations which would be caused by the facts themselves, seen in their natural relations to others. And the aim of the great inventive landscape painter must be to give the far higher and deeper truth of mental vision, rather than that of the physical facts, and to reach a representation which, though it may be totally useless to engineers or geographers, and, when tried by rule and measure, totally unlike the place, shall yet be capable of producing on the far-away beholder's mind precisely the impression which the reality would have produced, and putting his heart into the same state in which it would have been, had he verily descended into the valley from the gorges of Airolo.

Now observe; if in his attempt to do this the artist does not understand the sacredness of the truth of *Impression*, and supposes that, once quitting hold of his first thought, he may by Philosophy compose something prettier than he saw and mightier than he felt, it is all over with him. Every such attempt at composition will be utterly abortive, and end in something that is neither true nor fanciful; something geographically useless, and intellectually absurd.

But if, holding fast his first thought, he finds other ideas insensibly gathering to it, and, whether he will or not, modifying it into something which is not so much the image of the place itself, as the spirit of the place, let him yield to such fancies, and follow them wherever they lead. For, though error on this side is very rare among us in these days, it *is* possible to check these finer thoughts by mathematical accuracies, so as materially to impair the imaginative faculty. I shall be able to explain this better after we have traced the actual operation of Turner's mind on the scene under discussion.

Turner was always from his youth fond of stones. Whether large or

small, loose or embedded, hewn into cubes or worn into boulders, he
loved them as much as William Hunt loves pineapples and plums. So that
this great litter of fallen stones, which to any one else would have been
simply disagreeable, was to Turner much the same as if the whole valley
had been filled with plums and pineapples, and delighted him
exceedingly, much more than even the gorge of Dazio Grande just above.
But that gorge had its effect upon him also, and was still not well out of
his head when the diligence stopped at the bottom of the hill, just at that
turn of the road on the right of the bridge; which favourable opportunity   37
Turner seized to make what he called a "memorandum" of the place,
composed of a few pencil scratches on a bit of thin paper, that would roll
up with others of the sort and go into his pocket afterwards. These pencil
scratches he put a few blots of colour upon (I suppose at Bellinzona the
same evening, certainly *not* upon the spot), and showed me this blotted
sketch when he came home. I asked him to make me a drawing of it,
which he did, and casually told me afterwards (a rare thing for him to do)
that he liked the drawing he had made [plate 17 & fig.43].

fig.43 John Ruskin, *The Pass of Faido* – Turnerian Topography
(engraving after J.M.W. Turner)

In which, primarily, observe that the whole place is altered in scale, and
brought up to the general majesty of the higher forms of the Alps. It will
be seen that, in my topographical sketch, there are a few trees rooted in
the rock on this side of the gallery, showing, by comparison, that it is not
above four or five hundred feet high. These trees Turner cuts away, and

gives the rock a height of about a thousand feet, so as to imply more power and danger in the avalanche coming down the couloir.

Next, he raises, in a still greater degree, all the mountains beyond, putting three or four ranges instead of one, but uniting them into a single massy bank at their base, which he makes overhang the valley, and thus reduces it nearly to such a chasm as that which he had just passed through above, so as to unite the expression of this ravine with that of the stony valley. The few trees, in the hollow of the glen, he feels to be contrary in spirit to the stones, and fells them, as he did the others; so also he feels the bridge in the foreground, by its slenderness, to contradict the aspect of violence in the torrent; he thinks the torrent and avalanches should have it all their own way hereabouts; so he strikes down the nearer bridge, and restores the one farther off, where the force of the stream may be supposed less. Next, the bit of road on the right, above the bank, is not built on a wall, nor on arches high enough to give the idea of an Alpine road in general; so he makes the arches taller, and the bank steeper, introducing, as we shall see presently, a reminiscence from the upper part of the pass.

I say, he "*thinks*" this, and "introduces" that. But, strictly speaking, he does not think at all. If he thought, he would instantly go wrong; it is only the clumsy and uninventive artist who thinks. All these changes come into his head involuntarily; an entirely imperative dream, crying, "Thus it must be," has taken possession of him; he can see, and do, no otherwise than as the dream directs.

This is especially to be remembered with respect to the next incident— the introduction of figures. Most persons to whom I have shown the drawing, and who feel its general character, regret that there is any living thing in it; they say it destroys the majesty of its desolation. But the dream said not so to Turner. The dream insisted particularly upon the great fact of its having come by the road. The torrent was wild, the storms were wonderful; but the most wonderful thing of all was how we ourselves, the dream and I, ever got here. By our feet we could not—by the clouds we could not—by any ivory gates* we could not—in no other wise could we have come than by the coach road. One of the great elements of sensation, all the day long, has been that extraordinary road, and its goings on, and gettings about; here, under avalanches of stones, and among insanities of torrents, and overhangings of precipices, much tormented and driven to all manner of makeshifts and coils to this side and the other, still the marvellous road persists in going on, and that so smoothly and safely, that it is not merely great diligences, going in a caravannish manner, with whole teams of horses, that can traverse it, but

---

* [Through which come false visions: see Homer, *Od.* xix. 562.]

little postchaises with small postboys, and a pair of ponies. And the dream declared that the full essence and soul of the scene, and consummation of all the wonderfulness of the torrents and Alps, lay in a postchaise with small ponies and post-boy, which accordingly it insisted upon Turner's inserting, whether he liked it or not, at the turn of the road.

Now, it will be observed by any one familiar with ordinary principles of arrangement of form (on which principles I shall insist at length in another place), that while the dream introduces these changes bearing on the expression of the scene, it is also introducing other changes, which appear to be made more or less in compliance with received rules of composition, rendering the masses broader, the lines more continuous,   40 and the curves more graceful. But the curious part of the business is, that these changes seem not so much to be wrought by imagining an entirely new condition of any feature, as by *remembering* something which will fit better in that place. For instance, Turner felt the bank on the right ought to be made more solid and rocky, in order to suggest firmer resistance to the stream, and he turns it, as will be seen by comparing the etchings, into a kind of rock buttress to the wall, instead of a mere bank. Now the buttress into which he turns it is very nearly a facsimile of one which he had drawn on that very St. Gothard road, far above, at the Devil's Bridge, at least thirty years before, and which he had himself etched and engraved for the Liber Studiorum, although the plate was never published. Fig. 44 is a copy of the bit of the etching in question. Note how the wall winds over it, and observe especially the peculiar depression in the middle of its surface, and compare it in those parts generally with the features introduced in the later composition. Of course, this might be set down as a mere chance

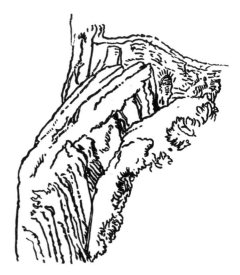

fig.44   Rock buttress from an
engraving by J.M.W. Turner

coincidence, but for the frequency of the cases in which Turner can be shown to have done the same thing, and to have introduced, after a   41 lapse of many years, memories of something which, however apparently small or unimportant, had struck him in his earlier studies. I think they are numerous enough to induce a doubt whether Turner's composition was not universally an arrangement of remembrances, summoned just as they were wanted, and set each in its fittest place. It is this very character which appears to me to mark it as so distinctly an act of dream-vision; for in a dream there is just this kind of confused remembrance of the forms of things which we have seen long ago, associated by new and strange laws. That common dreams are grotesque and disorderly, and Turner's dream natural and orderly, does not, to my thinking, involve any necessary difference in the real species of act of mind.

The kind of mental chemistry by which the dream summons and associates its materials, I have already endeavoured, not to explain, for it is utterly inexplicable, but to illustrate, by a well-ascertained though equally inexplicable fact in common chemistry. That illustration[6] I see more and more ground to think correct. How far I could show that it held with all great inventors, I know not, but with all those whom I have carefully studied (Dante, Scott, Turner, and Tintoret) it seems to me to hold absolutely; their imagination consisting, not in a voluntary production of new images, but an involuntary remembrance, exactly at the right moment, of something they had actually seen.

Imagine all that any of these men had seen or heard in the whole course of their lives, laid up accurately in their memories as in vast storehouses, extending, with the poets, even to the slightest intonations of syllables heard in the beginning of their lives, and with the painters, down to minute folds of drapery, and shapes of leaves or stones; and over all this unindexed and immeasurable mass of treasure, the imagination brooding and wandering, but dream-gifted, so as to summon at any moment exactly such groups of ideas as shall justly fit each other: this I conceive to be the real nature of the imaginative mind, and this, I believe, it would be oftener explained to us as being, by the men themselves who possess it, but that they have no idea what the state of other persons' minds is in comparison; they suppose every one remembers all that he has seen in the same way, and do not understand how it happens that they alone can produce good drawings or great thoughts.

Whether this be the case with all inventors or not, it was assuredly the case with Turner, to such an extent that he seems never either to have lost, or cared to disturb, the impression made upon him by any scene,— even in his earliest youth. He never seems to have gone back to a place to look at it again, but, as he gained power, to have painted and repainted it as first seen, associating with it certain new thoughts or new knowledge, but never shaking the central pillar of the old image.

How far this manly power itself acted merely in the accumulation of memories, remains, as I said, a question undetermined; but at all events, Turner's mind is not more, in my estimation, distinguished above others by its demonstrably arranging and ruling faculties, than by its demonstrably retentive and submissive faculties; and the longer I investigate it, the more this tenderness of perception and grasp of memory seem to me the root of its greatness. So that I am more and more convinced of what I had to state[7] respecting the imagination, now many years ago, viz., that its true force lies in its marvellous insight and foresight,—that it is, instead of a false and deceptive faculty, exactly the most accurate and truth-telling faculty which the human mind possesses; and all the more truth-telling, because in *its* work, the vanity and individualism of the man himself are crushed, and he becomes a mere instrument or mirror, used by a higher power for the reflection to others of a truth which no effort of his could ever have ascertained; so that all mathematical, and arithmetical, and generally scientific truth, is, in comparison, truth of the husk and surface, hard and shallow; and only the imaginative truth is precious. Hence, whenever we want to know what are the chief facts of any case, it is better not to go to political economists, nor to mathematicians, but to the great poets; for I find they always see more of the matter than any one else; and in like manner those who want to know the real facts of the world's outside aspect, will find that they cannot trust maps, nor charts, nor any manner of mensuration; the most important facts being always quite immeasurable, and that, (with only some occasional and trifling inconvenience, if they form too definite anticipations as to the position of a bridge here, or a road there) the Turnerian topography is the only one to be trusted.

45

CHAPTER III

Of Turnerian Light

48   Having in the preceding chapter seen the grounds on which to explain and justify Turner's *choice* of facts, we proceed to examine finally those modes of *representing* them introduced by him; modes so utterly at variance with the received doctrines on the subject of art, as to cause his works to be regarded with contempt, or severe blame, by all reputed judges, at the period of their first appearance. And, chiefly, I must confirm and farther illustrate the general statements made respecting light and shade in the chapters on Truth of Tone, and on Infinity,[8] deduced from the great fact that "nature surpasses us in power of obtaining light as much as the sun surpasses white paper." In order to know this practically, let the reader take a piece of pure white drawing-paper, and place it in the position in which a drawing is usually seen. This is, properly, upright, as a picture is seen on a room wall. Also, the usual place in which paintings or drawings are seen is at some distance from a window, with a gentle side light falling upon them, front lights being unfavourable to nearly all

49   drawing. Therefore the highest light an artist can ordinarily command for his work is that of white paint, or paper, under a gentle side light. But if we wished to get as much light as possible, and to place the artist under the most favourable circumstances, we should take the drawing near the window. You will notice that as you come nearer the window the light gradually *increases* on the paper. If, however, the sun actually falls upon it, the experiment is unfair, for the picture is not meant to be seen in sunshine, and your object is to compare pure white paper, as ordinarily used, *with* sunshine.

   Now, leaning a little over the window sill, bring the edge of the paper against the sky, rather low down on the horizon (I suppose you choose a

50   fine day for the experiment, that the sun is high, and the sky clear blue, down to the horizon). The moment you bring your white paper against the sky you will be startled to find this bright white paper suddenly appear in shade. You will draw it back, thinking you have changed its position. But no; the paper is not in shade. It is as bright as ever it was; brighter than under ordinary circumstances it ever can be. But, behold, the blue sky of the horizon is far brighter. The one is indeed blue, and the other white,

447

but the *white* is *darkest*, and by a great deal. And you will, though perhaps not for the first time in your life, perceive that though black is not easily proved to be white, white may, under certain circumstances, be very nearly proved black, or at all events brown.

When this fact is first shown to them, the general feeling with most people is, that, by being brought against the sky, the white paper is somehow or other brought into "shade." But this is not so; the paper remains exactly as it was; it is only compared with an actually brighter hue, and looks darker by comparison. The hue of the paper, and that of the sky, are just as fixed as temperatures are; and the sky is actually a brighter thing than white paper, by a certain number of degrees of light, scientifically determinable. In the same way, every other colour, or force of colour, is a fixed thing, not dependent on sensation, but numerically representable   51 with as much exactitude as a degree of heat by a thermometer. And of these hues, that of open sky is one not producible by human art. The sky is not blue *colour* merely,—it is blue *fire*, and cannot be painted.

Next, observe, this blue fire has in it *white* fire; that is, it has white clouds, as much brighter than itself as *it* is brighter than the white paper. So, then, above this azure light, we have another equally exalted step of white light. Supposing the value of the light of the pure white paper represented by the number 10, then that of the blue sky will be (approximately) about 20, and of the white clouds 30.

But look at the white clouds carefully, and it will be seen they are not all of the same white; parts of them are quite grey compared with other parts, and they are as full of passages of light and shade as if they were of solid earth. Nevertheless, their most deeply shaded part is that already so much lighter than the blue sky, which has brought us up to our number 30, and all these high lights of white are some ten degrees above that, or, to white paper, as 40 to 10. And now if you look from the blue sky and white clouds towards the sun, you will find that this cloud white, which is four times as white as white paper, is quite dark and lightless compared with those silver clouds that burn nearer the sun itself, which you cannot gaze upon,—an infinite of brightness. How will you estimate that?

And yet to express all this, we have but our poor white paper after all. We must not talk too proudly of our "truths" of art: I am afraid we shall have to let a good deal of black fallacy into it, at the best.

Well, of the sun, and of the silver clouds, we will not talk for the present. But this principal fact we have learned by our experiment with the white paper, that, taken all in all, the calm sky, with such light and   52 shade as are in it, is brighter than the earth; brighter than the whitest thing on earth which has not, at the moment of comparison, heaven's own direct light on it. Which fact it is generally one of the first objects of noble painters to render.

But this may be done either nobly or basely, as any other solemn truth may be asserted. It may be spoken with true feeling of all that it means; or it may be declared, as a Turk declares that "God is great," when he means only that he himself is lazy. The "heaven is bright," of many vulgar painters, has precisely the same amount of signification; it means that they know nothing,—will do nothing, are without thought—without care—without passion. They will not walk the earth, nor watch the ways of it, nor gather the flowers of it. They will sit in the shade, and only assert that very perceptible, long-ascertained fact, "heaven is bright." And as it may be *asserted* basely, so it may be *accepted* basely. Many of our capacities for receiving noblest emotion are abused, in mere idleness, for pleasure's sake, and people take the excitement of a solemn sensation as they do that

53 of a strong drink. Thus when, by spotting and splashing, such a painter as Constable reminds them somewhat of wet grass and green leaves, forthwith they fancy themselves in all the happiness of a meadow walk; and when Gaspar Poussin throws out his yellow horizon with black hills, forthwith they are touched as by the solemnity of a real Italian twilight, altogether forgetting that wet grass and twilight do not constitute the universe; and prevented by their joy at being pleasantly cool, or gravely warm, from seeking any of those more precious truths which cannot be caught by momentary sensation, but must be thoughtfully pursued.

I say "more precious," for the simple fact that the sky is brighter than the earth is *not* a precious truth unless the earth itself be first understood. Despise the earth, or slander it; fix your eyes on its gloom, and forget its loveliness; and we do not thank you for your languid or despairing perception of brightness in heaven. But rise up actively on the earth,—learn what there is in it, know its colour and form, and the full measure and make of it, and if *after that* you can say "heaven is bright," it will be a precious truth, but not till then.

54 Let us next ascertain what are the colours of the earth itself.

A mountain five or six miles off, in a sunny summer morning in Switzerland, will commonly present itself in some such pitch of dark force, as related to the sky, as that shown in fig. 45, while the sky itself will still, if there are white clouds in it, tell as a clear dark, throwing out those white clouds in vigorous relief of light; yet, conduct the experiment of the white paper as already described, and you will, in all probability, find that the darkest part of the mountain—its most vigorous nook of almost black-looking shadow—is *whiter than the paper.*

55 And it will thus generally be found impossible to represent, in any of its *true* colours, scenery distant more than two or three miles, in full daylight. The deepest shadows are whiter than white paper.

As, however, we pass to nearer objects, true representation gradually becomes possible;—to what degree is always of course ascertainable

fig.45   John Ruskin, *Distant Mountain*

accurately by the same mode of experiment. Bring the edge of the paper against the thing to be drawn, and on that edge—as precisely as a lady would match the colours of two pieces of a dress—match the colour of the landscape (with a little opaque white mixed in the tints you use, so as to render it easy to lighten or darken them). Take care not to imitate the tint as you believe it to be, but accurately as it is; so that the coloured edge of the paper shall not be discernible from the colour of the landscape. You will then find (if before inexperienced) that shadows of trees, which you thought were dark green or black, are pale violets and purples; that lights, which you thought were green, are intensely yellow, brown, or golden, and most of them far too bright to be matched at all. When you have got all the imitable hues truly matched, sketch the masses of the landscape out completely in those true and ascertained colours; and you will find, to your amazement, that you have painted it in the colours of Turner,—in those very colours which perhaps you have been laughing at all your life,—the fact being that he, and he alone, of all men, *ever painted Nature in her own colours.*

"Well, but," you will answer, impatiently, "how is it, if they are the true colours, that they look so unnatural?"

Because they are not shown in true contrast to the sky, and to other high lights. Nature paints her shadows in pale purple, and then raises her lights of heaven and sunshine to such heights that the pale purple becomes, by   56
comparison, a vigorous dark. But poor Turner has no sun at his command to oppose his pale colours. He follows Nature submissively as far as he can; puts pale purple where she does, bright gold where she does; and then when, on the summit of the slope of light, she opens her wings and quits

the earth altogether, burning into ineffable sunshine, what can he do but sit helpless, stretching his hands towards her in calm consent, as she leaves him and mocks at him!

"Well," but you will farther ask, "is this right or wise? ought not the contrast between the masses to be given, rather than the actual hues of a few parts of them, when the others are inimitable?"

Yes, if this *were* possible, it ought to be done; but the true contrasts can NEVER be given. The whole question is simply whether you will be false at one side of the scale or at the other,—that is, whether you will lose yourself in light or in darkness. This necessity is easily expressible in numbers. Suppose the utmost light you wish to imitate is that of serene, feebly lighted clouds in ordinary sky (not sun or stars, which it is, of course, impossible deceptively to imitate in painting by any artifice). Then, suppose the degrees of shadow between those clouds and Nature's utmost darkness accurately measured, and divided into a hundred degrees (darkness being zero). Next we measure our own scale, calling our utmost possible black, zero;* and we shall be able to keep parallel with Nature, perhaps up to as far as her 40 degrees; all above that being whiter than our white paper. Well, with our power of contrast between zero and 40, we have to imitate her contrasts between zero and 100. Now, if we want true contrasts, we can first set our 40 to represent her 100, our 20 for her 80, and our zero for her 60; everything below her 60 being lost in blackness. This is, with certain modifications, Rembrandt's system. Or, secondly, we can put zero for her zero, 20 for her 20, and 40 for her 40; everything above 40 being lost in *white*ness. This is, with certain modifications, Paul Veronese's system. Or, finally, we can put our zero for her zero, and our 40 for her 100; our 20 for her 50, our 30 for her 75, and our 10 for her 25, proportioning the intermediate contrasts accordingly. This is, with certain modifications, Turner's system;† the modifications, in each case, being the adoption, to a certain extent, of either of the other systems. Thus, Turner inclines to Paul Veronese; liking, as far as possible, to get his hues perfectly true up to a certain point,—that is to say, to let his zero stand for Nature's zero, and his 10 for her 10, and his 20 for her 20, and then to expand towards the light by quick but cunning steps, putting 27 for 50, 30 for 70, and reserving some force still for the last 90 to 100. So Rembrandt modifies his system on the other side, putting his 40 for 100, his 30 for 90, his 20 for 80; then going subtly downwards, 10 for 50, 5 for

57

* Even here we shall be defeated by Nature, her utmost darkness being deeper than ours.

† When the clouds are brilliantly lighted, it may rather be, as stated above, in the proportion of 160 to 40. I take the number 100 as more calculable.

30; nearly everything between 30 and zero being lost in gloom, yet so as still to reserve his zero for zero. The systems expressed in tabular form will stand thus:—

NATURE.		REMBRANDT.		TURNER.		VERONESE.
0	. . .	0	. . .	0	. . .	0
10	. . .	1	. . .	10	. . .	10
20	. . .	3	. . .	20	. . .	20
30	. . .	5	. . .	24	. . .	30
40	. . .	7	. . .	26	. . .	32
50	. . .	10	. . .	27	. . .	34
60	. . .	13	. . .	28	. . .	36
70	. . .	17	. . .	30	. . .	37
80	. . .	20	. . .	32	. . .	38
90	. . .	30	. . .	36	. . .	39
100	. . .	40	. . .	40	. . .	40

Now it is evident that in Rembrandt's system, while the *contrasts* are not more right than with Veronese, the *colours* are all wrong, from beginning to end. With Turner and Veronese, Nature's 10 is their 10, and Nature's 20 their 20; enabling them to give pure truth up to a certain point. But with Rembrandt, *not one colour* is absolutely true, from one side of the scale to the other; only the contrasts are true at the top of the scale. Of course, this supposes Rembrandt's system applied to a subject which shall try it to the utmost, such as landscape. Rembrandt generally chose subjects in which the real colours were very nearly imitable,—as single heads with dark backgrounds, in which Nature's highest light was little above his own; her 40 being then truly representable by his 40, his picture became nearly an absolute truth. But his system is only right when applied to such subjects: clearly, when we have the full scale of natural light to deal with, Turner's and Veronese's convey the greatest sum of truth. But not the most complete deception, for people are so much more easily and instinctively impressed by force of light than truth of colour, that they instantly miss the relative power of the sky, and the upper tones; and all the true local colouring looks strange to them, separated from its adjuncts of high light; whereas, give them the true contrast of light, and they will not observe the false local colour. Thus all Gaspar Poussin's and Salvator's pictures, and all effects obtained by leaving high lights in the midst of exaggerated darkness, catch the eye and are received for true, while the pure truth of Veronese and Turner is rejected as unnatural; only not so much in Veronese's case as in Turner's, because Veronese confines himself to more imitable things, as draperies, figures, and architecture, in which his exquisite truth at the bottom of the scale tells on the eye at once; but Turner works a good deal also (see the table) at the *top* of the

58

natural scale, dealing with effects of sunlight and other phases of the upper colours, more or less inimitable, and betraying, therefore, more or less, the 59 artifices used to express them. It will be observed, also, that in order to reserve some force for the top of his scale, Turner is obliged to miss his gradations chiefly in middle tints (see the table), where the feebleness is sure to be felt. His principal point for missing the midmost gradations is almost always between the earth and sky; he draws the earth truly as far as he can, to the horizon; then the sky as far as he can, with his 30 to 40 part of the scale. They run together at the horizon; and the spectator complains that there is no distinction between earth and sky, or that the earth does not *look solid enough.*

62 Now, from all the preceding inquiry, the reader must perceive more and more distinctly the great truth, that all forms of right art consist in a certain *choice* made between various classes of truths, a few only being represented, and others necessarily excluded; and that the excellence of each style depends first on its consistency with itself,—the perfect fidelity, 63 as far as possible, to the truths it has chosen; and secondly, on the breadth of its harmony, or number of truths it has been able to reconcile, and the consciousness with which the truths refused are acknowledged, even though they may not be represented. A great artist is just like a wise and hospitable man with a small house: the large companies of truths, like guests, are waiting his invitation; he wisely chooses from among this crowd the guests who will be happiest with each other, making those whom he receives thoroughly comfortable, and kindly remembering even those whom he excludes; while the foolish host, trying to receive all, leaves a large part of his company on the staircase, without even knowing who is there, and destroys, by inconsistent fellowship, the pleasure of those who gain entrance.

But even those hosts who choose well will be farther distinguished from each other by their choice of nobler or inferior companies; and we find the greatest artists mainly divided into two groups,—those who paint principally with respect to local colour, headed by Paul Veronese, Titian, and Turner; and those who paint principally with reference to light and shade irrespective of colour, headed by Leonardo da Vinci, Rembrandt, and Raphael. The noblest members of each of these classes introduce the element proper to the other class, in a subordinate way. Paul Veronese introduces a subordinate light and shade, and Leonardo introduces a subordinate local colour. The main difference is, that with Leonardo, Rembrandt, and Raphael, vast masses of the picture are lost in comparatively colourless (dark grey or brown) shadow; these painters *beginning* with the *lights* and going *down* to blackness; but with Veronese, Titian, and Turner, the whole picture is like the rose,—glowing with colour in the shadows, and rising into paler and more delicate hues, or masses of whiteness, in the lights; they having *begun* with the *shadows*, and gone up *to* whiteness.

The colourists have in this respect one disadvantage, and three advantages. The disadvantage is, that between their less violent hues, it is not possible to draw all the forms which can be represented by the exaggerated shadows of the chiaroscurists, and therefore a slight tendency to flatness is always characteristic of the greater colourists, as opposed to Leonardo or Rembrandt. When the form of some single object is to be given, and its subtleties are to be rendered to the utmost, the Leonardesque manner of drawing is often very noble. It is generally adopted by Albert Dürer, in his engravings, and is very useful, when employed by a thorough master, in many kinds of engravings; but it is an utterly false method of *study*, as we shall see presently. 64

Of the three advantages possessed by the colourists over the chiaroscurists, the first is, that they have in the greater portions of their pictures *absolute* truth, as shown above, while the chiaroscurists have no absolute truth anywhere. With the colourists the shadows are right; the lights untrue: but with the chiaroscurists lights and shadows are both untrue. The second advantage is, that also the *relations* of colour are broader and vaster with the colourists than the chiaroscurists. All painters who endeavour in their studies of objects to get rid of the idea of colour, and give the abstract shade, exaggerate the shadows, not with respect to the thing itself, but with respect to all around it; and they exaggerate the lights also, by leaving pure white for the high light of what in reality is grey, rose-coloured, or, in some way, not white. 65

This method of study, being peculiarly characteristic of the Roman and Florentine schools, and associated with very accurate knowledge of form and expression, has gradually got to be thought by a large body of artists the *grand* way of study; an idea which has been fostered all the more because it was an unnatural way, and therefore thought to be a philosophical one. Almost the first idea of a child, or of a simple person looking at any thing, is, that it is a red, or a black, or a green, or a white thing. Nay, say the artists; that is an unphilosophical and barbarous view of the matter. Red and white are mere vulgar appearances; look farther into the matter, and you will see such and such wonderful other appearances. Abstract those, *they* are the heroic, epic, historic, and generally eligible appearances. And acting on this grand principle, they draw flesh white, leaves white, ground white, everything white in the light, and everything black in the shade—and think themselves wise. But, the longer I live, the more ground I see to hold in high honour a certain sort of childishness or innocent susceptibility. Generally speaking, I find that when we first look at a subject, we get a glimpse of some of the greatest truths about it: as we look longer, our vanity, and false reasoning, and half-knowledge, lead us 66 into various wrong opinions; but as we look longer still, we gradually return to our first impressions, only with a full understanding of their mystical and innermost reasons; and of much beyond and beside them, not then known to us, now added (partly as a foundation, partly as a corollary) to what at first we felt or saw. It is thus eminently in this matter of colour.

67   Half the degradation of art in modern times has been owing to endeavours, much fostered by the metaphysical Germans, to see things without colour, as if colour were a vulgar thing, the result being, in most students, that they end by not being able to see anything at all; whereas the true and perfect way of studying any object is simply to look what its colour is in high light, and put that safely down, if possible; or, if you are making a chiaroscuro study, to take the grey answering to that colour, and cover the *whole* object at once with that grey, firmly resolving that no part of it shall be brighter than that; then look for the darkest part of it, and if, as is probable, its darkest part be still a great deal lighter than black, or than other things about it, assume a given shade, as dark as, with due reference to other things, you can have it, but no darker. Mark that for your extreme dark on the object, and between those limits get as much drawing as you can, by subtlety of gradation. That will tax your powers of drawing indeed; and you will find this, which seems a childish and simple way of going to work, requires verily a thousandfold more power to carry out than all the pseudo-scientific abstractions that ever were invented.

Nor can it long be doubted that it is also the most impressive way to others; for the third great advantage possessed by the colourists is, that the delightfulness of their picture, its sacredness, and general nobleness, are increased exactly in proportion to the quantity of light and of lovely colour they can introduce in *the shadows*, as opposed to the black and grey of the chiaroscurists. I have already, in the *Stones of Venice*, Vol. II. Chap.
68   v. §§ 30–36, insisted upon the fact of the sacredness of colour, and its necessary connection with all pure and noble feeling. What we have seen of the use of colour by the poets will help to confirm this truth; but perhaps I have not yet enough insisted on the simplest and readiest to hand of all proofs,—the way, namely, in which God has employed colour in His creation as the unvarying accompaniment of all that is purest, most innocent, and most precious; while for things precious only in material uses, or dangerous, common colours are reserved. Consider for a little while what sort of a world it would be if all flowers were grey, all leaves black, and the sky *brown*. Imagine that, as completely as may be, then observe how constantly innocent things are bright in colour; look at a dove's neck, and compare it with the grey back of a viper; I have often heard talk of brilliantly coloured serpents; and I suppose there are such,— as there are gay poisons, like the foxglove and kalmia—types of deceit: but

all the venomous serpents I have really *seen* are grey, brick-red, or brown, variously mottled; and the most awful serpent I have seen, the Egyptian asp, is precisely of the colour of gravel, or only a little greyer. So, again, the crocodile and alligator are grey, but the innocent lizard green and beautiful. I do not mean that the rule is invariable, otherwise it would be more convincing than the lessons of the natural universe are intended ever to be; there are beautiful colours on the leopard and tiger, and in the berries of the nightshade; and there is nothing very notable in brilliancy of colour either in sheep or cattle (though, by the way, the velvet of a brown bull's hide in the sun, or the tawny white of the Italian oxen, is, to   69 my mind, lovelier than any leopard's or tiger's skin): but take a wider view of nature, and compare generally rainbows, sunrises, roses, violets, butterflies, birds, goldfish, rubies, opals, and corals, with alligators, hippopotami, lions, wolves, bears, swine, sharks, slugs, bones, fungi, fogs, and corrupting, stinging, destroying things in general, and you will feel then how the question stands between the colourists and chiaroscurists,—which of them have nature and life on their side, and which have sin and death.

Finally: the ascertainment of the sanctity of colour is not left to human sagacity. It is distinctly stated in Scripture. I have before alluded to the sacred chord of colour (blue, purple, and scarlet, with white and gold) as appointed in the tabernacle; this chord is the fixed base of all colouring with the workmen of every great age; the purple and scarlet will be found constantly employed by noble painters, in various unison, to the exclusion in general of pure crimson. In this chord the scarlet is the powerful colour, and is on the whole the most perfect representation of abstract colour which exists; blue being in a certain degree associated with shade, yellow with light, and scarlet, as absolute *colour*, standing alone. All men,   71 completely organised and justly tempered, enjoy colour; it is meant for the perpetual comfort and delight of the human heart; it is richly bestowed on the highest works of creation, and the eminent sign and seal of perfection in them; being associated with *life* in the human body, with *light* in the sky, with *purity* and hardness in the earth,—death, night, and pollution of all kinds being colourless. And although if form and colour be brought into complete opposition, so that it should be put to us as a matter of stern choice whether we should have a work of art all of form, without colour (as an Albert Dürer's engraving), or all of colour, without form (as an imitation of mother-of-pearl), form is beyond all comparison the more   72 precious of the two; and in explaining the essence of objects, form is essential, and colour more or less accidental; yet if colour be introduced at all, it is necessary that, whatever else may be wrong, *that* should be right: just as, though the music of a song may not be so essential to its influence as the meaning of the words, yet if the music be given at all, *it* must be right, or its discord will spoil the words; and it would be better, of the two, that the words should be indistinct, than the notes false. Hence, as I have said elsewhere,[9] the business of a painter is to paint. If he can colour, he is a painter, though he can do nothing else; if he cannot colour, he is no painter, though he may do everything else. But it is, in fact, impossible, if he can colour, but that he should be able to do more; for a faithful study of colour will always give power over form, though the most intense study of form will give no power over colour. The man who can see all the greys, and reds, and purples in a peach, will paint the peach rightly round, and rightly altogether; but the man who has only studied its roundness, may not see its purples and greys, and if he does not, will never get it to look like a peach; so that great power over colour is always a sign of large general art-intellect. Expression of the most subtle kind can be often reached by the slight studies of caricaturists; sometimes elaborated by the toil of the dull, and sometimes by the sentiment of the feeble; but to colour well requires real talent and earnest study, and to colour perfectly is the rarest and most precious power an artist can possess. Every other gift may be erroneously cultivated, but this will guide to all healthy, natural, and forcible truth; the student may be led into folly by philosophers, and into falsehood by purists; but he is always safe, if he holds the hand of a colourist.

CHAPTER XIX

The Mountain Gloom

WE have now cursorily glanced[10] over those conditions of mountain 385
structure which appear constant in duration, and universal in
extent; and we have found them, invariably, calculated for the delight,
the advantage, or the teaching of men; prepared, it seems, so as to
contain, alike in fortitude or feebleness, in kindliness or in terror, some
beneficence of gift, or profoundness of counsel. We have found that where
at first all seemed disturbed and accidental, the most tender laws were
appointed to produce forms of perpetual beauty; and that where to the
careless or cold observer all seemed severe or purposeless, the well-being
of man has been chiefly consulted, and his rightly directed powers, and
sincerely awakened intelligence, may find wealth in every falling rock,
and wisdom in every talking wave.

It remains for us to consider what actual effect upon the human race has
been produced by the generosity, or the instruction of the hills; how far, in
past ages, they have been thanked, or listened to; how far, in coming ages,
it may be well for us to accept them for tutors, or seek them for friends.

What they have already taught us may, one would think, be best
discerned in the midst of them,—in some place where they have had their
own way with the human soul; where no veil has been drawn between it
and them, no contradicting voice has confused their ministries of sound,
or broken their pathos of silence: where war has never streaked their
streams with bloody foam, nor ambition sought for other throne than their
cloud-courtiered pinnacles, nor avarice for other treasure than, year by 386
year, is given to their unlaborious rocks, in budded jewels and mossy gold.

I do not know any district possessing a more pure or uninterrupted
fulness of mountain character (and that of the highest order), or which
appears to have been less disturbed by foreign agencies, than that which
borders the course of the Trient between Valorcine and Martigny. The
paths which lead to it out of the valley of the Rhone, rising at first in steep
circles among the walnut trees, like winding stairs among the pillars of a
Gothic tower, retire over the shoulders of the hills into a valley almost
unknown, but thickly inhabited by an industrious and patient population.

458

Along the ridges of the rocks, smoothed by old glaciers into long, dark, billowy swellings, like the backs of plunging dolphins, the peasant watches the slow colouring of the tufts of moss and roots of herb which, little by little, gather a feeble soil over the iron substance; then, supporting the narrow strip of clinging ground with a few stones, he subdues it to the spade; and in a year or two a little crest of corn is seen waving upon the rocky casque. The irregular meadows run in and out like inlets of lake among these harvested rocks, sweet with perpetual streamlets, that seem always to have chosen the steepest places to come down, for the sake of the leaps, scattering their handfuls of crystal this way and that, as the wind takes them, with all the grace, but with none of the formalism of fountains.

387   Green field, and glowing rock, and glancing streamlet, all slope together in the sunshine towards the brows of ravines, where the pines take up their own dominion of saddened shade; and with everlasting roar in the twilight, the stronger torrents thunder down, pale from the glaciers, filling all their chasms with enchanted cold, beating themselves to pieces against the great rocks that they have themselves cast down, and forcing fierce way beneath their ghastly poise.

The mountain paths stoop to these glens in forky zig-zags, leading to some grey and narrow arch, all fringed under its shuddering curve with the ferns that fear the light; a cross of rough-hewn pine, iron-bound to its parapet, standing dark against the lurid fury of the foam. Far up the glen, as we pause beside the cross, the sky is seen through the openings in the pines, thin with excess of light; and, in its clear, consuming flame of white space, the summits of the rocky mountains are gathered into solemn crowns and circlets, all flushed in that strange, faint silence of possession by the sunshine which has in it so deep a melancholy; full of power, yet as frail as shadows; lifeless, like the walls of a sepulchre, yet beautiful in tender fall of crimson folds, like the veil of some sea spirit, that lives and dies as the foam flashes; fixed on a perpetual throne, stern against all strength, lifted above all sorrow, and yet effaced and melted utterly into the air by that last sunbeam that has crossed to them from between the two golden clouds.

388   High above all sorrow: yes; but not unwitnessing to it. The traveller on his happy journey, as his foot springs from the deep turf and strikes the pebbles gaily over the edge of the mountain road, sees with a glance of delight the clusters of nutbrown cottages that nestle among those sloping orchards, and glow beneath the boughs of the pines. Here it may well seem to him, if there be sometimes hardship, there must be at least innocence and peace, and fellowship of the human soul with nature. It is not so. The wild goats that leap along those rocks have as much passion of joy in all that fair work of God as the men that toil among them. Perhaps more.

Enter the street of one of those villages, and you will find it foul with that gloomy foulness that is suffered only by torpor, or by anguish of soul. Here, it is torpor—not absolute suffering—not starvation or disease, but darkness of calm enduring; the spring known only as the time of the scythe, and the autumn as the time of the sickle, and the sun only as a warmth, the wind as a chill, and the mountains as a danger. They do not understand so much as the name of beauty, or of knowledge. They understand dimly that of virtue. Love, patience, hospitality, faith,—these things they know. To glean their meadows side by side, so happier; to bear the burden up the breathless mountain flank, unmurmuringly; to bid the stranger drink from their vessel of milk; to see at the foot of their low deathbeds a pale figure upon a cross, dying, also patiently;—in this they are different from the cattle and from the stones, but in all this unrewarded as far as concerns the present life. For them, there is neither hope nor passion of spirit; for them neither advance nor exultation. Black bread, rude roof, dark night, laborious day, weary arm at sunset, and life ebbs away. No books, no thoughts, no attainments, no rest; except only sometimes a little sitting in the sun under the church wall, as the bell tolls thin and far in the mountain 389 air; a pattering of a few prayers, not understood, by the altar rails of the dimly gilded chapel, and so back to the sombre home, with the cloud upon them still unbroken—that cloud of rocky gloom, born out of the wild torrents and ruinous stones, and unlightened, even in their religion, except by the vague promise of some better thing unknown, mingled with threatening, and obscured by an unspeakable horror,—a smoke, as it were, of martyrdom, coiling up with the incense, and, amidst the images of tortured bodies and lamenting spirits in hurtling flames, the very cross, for them, dashed more deeply than for others, with gouts of blood.

Do not let this be thought a darkened picture of the life of these mountaineers. It is literal fact. No contrast can be more painful than that between the dwelling of any well-conducted English cottager, and that of the equally honest Savoyard. The one, set in the midst of its dull flat fields and uninteresting hedgerows, shows in itself the love of brightness and beauty; its daisy-studded garden-beds, its smoothly swept brick path to the threshold, its freshly sanded floor and orderly shelves of household furniture, all testify to energy of heart, and happiness in the simple course and simple possessions of daily life. The other cottage, in the midst of an inconceivable, inexpressible beauty, set on some sloping bank of golden sward, with clear fountains flowing beside it, and wild flowers, and noble trees, and goodly rocks gathered round into a perfection as of Paradise, is itself a dark and plague-like stain in the midst of the gentle landscape. Within a certain distance of its threshold the ground is foul and cattle-trampled; its timbers are black with smoke, its garden choked with weeds and nameless refuse, its chambers empty and joyless, the light and wind

gleaming and filtering through the crannies of their stones. All testifies
390   that to its inhabitant the world is labour and vanity; that for him neither
flowers bloom, nor birds sing, nor fountains glisten; and that his soul
hardly differs from the grey cloud that coils and dies upon his hills, except
in having no fold of it touched by the sunbeams.

Is it not strange to reflect, that hardly an evening passes in London or
Paris, but one of those cottages is painted for the better amusement of the
fair and idle, and shaded with pasteboard pines by the scene-shifter; and
that good and kind people, poetically-minded, delight themselves in
imagining the happy life led by peasants who dwell by Alpine fountains,
and kneel to crosses upon peaks of rock?—that nightly we give our gold,
to fashion forth simulacra of peasants, in gay ribands and white bodices,
singing sweet songs, and bowing gracefully to the picturesque crosses: and
all the while the veritable peasants are kneeling, songlessly, to veritable
crosses, in another temper than the kind and fair audiences deem of, and
assuredly with another kind of answer than is got out of the opera
catastrophe; an answer having reference, it may be in dim futurity, to
those very audiences themselves? If all the gold that has gone to paint the
simulacra of the cottages, and to put new songs in the mouths of the
simulacra of the peasants, had gone to brighten the existent cottages, and
to put new songs in the mouths of the existent peasants, it might in the
end, perhaps, have turned out better so, not only for the peasant, but for
even the audience. For that form of the False Ideal has also its correspondent True Ideal,—consisting not in the naked beauty of statues, nor in the
gauze flowers and crackling tinsel of theatres, but in the clothed and fed
beauty of living men, and in the lights and laughs of happy homes. Night
after night, the desire of such an ideal springs up in every idle human
heart; and night after night, as far as idleness can, we work out this desire
in costly lies. We paint the faded actress, build the lath landscape, feed our
benevolence with fallacies of felicity, and satisfy our righteousness with
391   poetry of justice. The time will come when, as the heavy-folded curtain
falls upon our own stage of life, we shall begin to comprehend that the
justice we loved was intended to have been done in fact, and not in
poetry, and the felicity we sympathized in, to have been bestowed and not
feigned. We talk much of money's worth, yet perhaps may one day be
surprised to find that what the wise and charitable European public gave
to one night's rehearsal of hypocrisy,—to one hour's pleasant warbling of
Linda or Lucia,—would have filled a whole Alpine valley with happiness,
and poured the waves of harvest over the famine of many a Lammermoor.
392   "Nay," perhaps the reader answers, "it is vain to hope that this could
ever be. The perfect beauty of the ideal must always be fictitious. It is
rational to amuse ourselves with the fair imagination; but it would be
madness to endeavour to put it into practice, in the face of the ordinances

of Nature. Real shepherdesses must always be rude, and real peasants
miserable; suffer us to turn away our gentle eyes from their coarseness and   393
their pain, and to seek comfort in cultivated voices and purchased smiles.
We cannot hew down the rocks nor turn the sands of the torrent into
gold."

This is no answer. Be assured of the great truth—that what is impossible
in reality, is ridiculous in fancy. If it is not in the nature of things that
peasants should be gentle and happy, then the imagination of such
peasantry is ridiculous, and to delight in such imagination, wrong; as
delight in any kind of falsehood is always. But if in the nature of things it
be possible among the wildness of hills the human heart should be refined,
and if the comfort of dress, and the gentleness of language, and the joy of
progress in knowledge, and of variety in thought, are possible to the
mountaineer in his true existence, let us strive to write this true poetry
upon the rocks before we indulge it in our visions, and try whether, among
all the fine arts, one of the finest be not that of painting cheeks with
health rather than rouge.

"But is such refinement possible? Do not the conditions of the
mountain peasant's life, in the plurality of instances, necessarily forbid
it?"

As bearing sternly on this question, it is necessary to examine one
peculiarity of feeling which manifests itself among the European nations,
so far as I have noticed, irregularly. I mean the capability of enduring, or
even delighting in, the contemplation of objects of terror—a sentiment
which especially influences the temper of some groups of mountaineers,
and of which it is necessary to examine the causes, before we can form   394
any conjecture whatever as to the real effect of mountains on human
character.

We are walking, perhaps, in a summer afternoon, up the valley of   395
Zermatt (a German valley), the sun shining brightly on grassy knolls and
through fringes of pines, the goat leaping happily, and the cattle bells
ringing sweetly, and the snowy mountains shining like heavenly castles far
above. We see, a little way off, a small white chapel, sheltered behind one
of the flowery hillocks of mountain turf; and we approach its little
window, thinking to look through it into some quiet home of prayer; but
the window is grated with iron, and open to the winds, and when we look
through it, behold—a heap of white human bones mouldering into whiter
dust!

So also in that same sweet valley, of which I have just been speaking,
between Chamouni and the Valais, at every turn of the pleasant pathway,
where the scent of the thyme lies richest upon its rock, we shall see a little
cross and shrine set under one of them; and go up to it, hoping to receive
some happy thought of the Redeemer, by whom all these lovely things

were made, and still consist. But when we come near—behold, beneath the cross, a rude picture of souls tormented in red tongues of hell fire, and pierced by demons.

As we pass towards Italy the appearance of this gloom deepens; and when we descend the southern slope of the Alps we shall find this bringing forward of the image of Death associated with an endurance of the most painful aspects of disease; so that conditions of human suffering, which in any other country would be confined in hospitals, are permitted to be openly exhibited by the wayside; and with this exposure of the degraded human form is farther connected an insensibility to ugliness and imperfection in other things; so that the ruined wall, neglected garden, and uncleansed chamber, seem to unite in expressing a gloom of spirit possessing the inhabitants of the whole land. It does not appear to arise from poverty, nor careless contentment with little: there is here nothing of Irish recklessness or humour; but there seems a settled obscurity in the soul,—a chill and plague, as if risen out of a sepulchre, which partly deadens, partly darkens, the eyes and hearts of men, and breathes a leprosy of decay through every breeze, and every stone. "Instead of well-set hair, baldness, and burning instead of beauty."[11]

Nor are definite proofs wanting that the feeling is independent of mere poverty or indolence. In the most gorgeous and costly palace garden the statues will be found green with moss, the terraces defaced or broken; the palace itself, partly coated with marble, is left in other places rough with cementless and jagged brick, its iron balconies bent and rusted, its pavements overgrown with grass. The more energetic the effort has been to recover from this state, and to shake off all appearance of poverty, the more assuredly the curse seems to fasten on the scene, and the unslaked mortar, and unfinished wall, and ghastly desolation of incompleteness entangled in decay, strike a deeper despondency into the beholder.

The feeling would be also more easily accounted for if it appeared inconsistent in its regardlessness of beauty,—if what was *done* were altogether as inefficient as what was deserted. But the balcony, though rusty and broken, is delicate in design, and supported on a nobly carved slab of marble; the window, though a mere black rent in ragged plaster, is encircled by a garland of vine and fronted by a thicket of the sharp leaves and aurora-coloured flowers of the oleander; the courtyard, overgrown by mournful grass, is terminated by a bright fresco of gardens, and fountains; the corpse, borne with the bare face to heaven, is strewn with flowers; beauty is continually mingled with the shadow of death.

So also is a kind of merriment,—not true cheerfulness, neither careless or idle jesting, but a determined effort at gaiety, a resolute laughter, mixed with much satire, grossness, and practical buffoonery, and, it always seemed to me, void of all comfort or hope,—with this eminent character

397

in it also, that it is capable of touching with its bitterness even the most
fearful subjects, so that as the love of beauty retains its tenderness in the
presence of death, this love of jest also retains its boldness, and the
skeleton becomes one of the standard masques of the Italian comedy.

It might appear, to a traveller crossing and recrossing the Alps between   404
Switzerland and Italy, that the main strength of the evil lay on the south
of the chain, and was attributable to the peculiar circumstances and
character of the Italian nation at this period. But as he examined the
matter farther he would note that in the districts of Italy generally
supposed to be *healthy*, the evidence of it was less, and that it seemed to
gain ground in places exposed to malaria, centralizing itself in the Val
d'Aosta. He would then, perhaps, think it inconsistent with justice to lay
the blame on the mountains, and transfer his accusation to the marshes,
yet would be compelled to admit that the evil manifested itself most where
these marshes were surrounded by hills. He would next, probably, suppose
it produced by the united effect of hardship, solitude, and unhealthy air;
and be disposed to find fault with the mountains, at least so far as they
required painful climbing and laborious agriculture:—but would again be
thrown into doubt by remembering that one main branch of the
feeling,—the love of ugliness, seemed to belong in a peculiar manner to
Northern Germany. If at all familiar with the art of the North and South,
he would perceive that the *endurance* of ugliness, which in Italy resulted
from languor or depression (while the mind yet retained some apprehension of the difference between fairness and deformity), was not to be
confounded with that absence of perception of the Beautiful, which
introduced a general hard-featuredness of figure into all German and
Flemish early art, even when Germany and Flanders were in their
brightest national health and power. And as he followed out in detail   405
the comparison of all the purest ideals north and south of the Alps, and
perceived the perpetual contrast existing between the angular and bony
sanctities of the one latitude, and the drooping graces and pensive pieties
of the other, he would no longer attribute to the ruggedness, or miasma,
of the mountains the origin of a feeling which showed itself so strongly in
the comfortable streets of Antwerp and Nuremberg, and in the
unweakened and active intellects of Van Eyck and Albert Dürer.

Sion, the capital of the [Valais], presents one of the most remarkable   412
scenes for the study of the particular condition of human feeling at present
under consideration that I know among mountains. It consists of little
more than one main street, winding round the roots of two ridges of crag,
and branching, on the side towards the rocks, into a few narrow lanes, on
the other, into spaces of waste ground, of which part serve for military
exercises, part are enclosed in an uncertain and vague way; a ditch half-
filled up, or wall half-broken down, seeming to indicate their belonging,

or having been intended to belong, to some of the unfinished houses which are springing up amidst their weeds. But it is difficult to say, in any part of the town, what is garden ground and what is waste; still more, what is new building and what old. The houses have been for the most part built roughly of the coarse limestone of the neighbouring hills, then coated with plaster, and painted, in imitation of Palladian palaces, with grey architraves and pilasters, having draperies from capital to capital. With this false decoration is curiously contrasted a great deal of graceful, honest, and original ironwork, in bulging balconies, and floreted gratings of huge windows, and branching sprays, for any and every purpose of support or guard. The plaster, with its fresco, has in most instances dropped away, leaving the houses peeled and scarred; daubed into uncertain restoration with new mortar, and in the best cases thus left; but commonly fallen also, more or less, into ruin, and either roofed over at the first story when the second has fallen, or hopelessly abandoned;—not pulled down, but left in white and ghastly shells to crumble into heaps of limestone and dust, a pauper or two still inhabiting where inhabitation is possible. The lanes wind among these ruins; the blue sky and mountain grass are seen through the windows of their rooms and over their partitions, on which old gaudy papers flaunt in rags: the weeds gather, and the dogs scratch about their foundations; yet there are no luxuriant weeds, for their ragged leaves are blanched with lime, crushed under perpetually falling fragments, and worn away by listless standing of idle feet. There is always mason's work doing, always some fresh patching and whitening; a dull smell of mortar, mixed with that of stale foulness of every kind, rises with the dust, and defiles every current of air; the corners are filled with accumulations of stones, partly broken, with crusts of cement sticking to them, and blotches of nitre oozing out of their pores. The lichenous rocks and sunburnt slopes of grass stretch themselves hither and thither among the wreck, curiously traversed by stairs and walls and half-cut paths that disappear below starkly black arches, and cannot be followed, or rise in windings round the angles, and in unfenced slopes along the fronts, of the two masses of rock which bear, one the dark castle, the other the old church and convent of Sion; beneath, in a rudely inclosed square at the outskirts of the town, a still more ancient Lombardic church raises its grey tower, a kind of esplanade extending between it and the Episcopal palace, and laid out as a plot of grass, intersected by gravel walks; but the grass, in strange sympathy with the inhabitants, will not grow *as* grass, but chokes itself with a network of grey weeds, quite wonderful in their various expression of thorny discontent and savageness; the blue flower of the borage, which mingles with them in quantities, hardly interrupting their character, for the violent black spot in the centre of its blue takes away the tenderness of the flower, and it seems to have grown there in some supernatural

mockery of its old renown of being good against melancholy. The rest of
the herbage is chiefly composed of the dwarf mallow, the wild succory, the
wall-rocket, goose-foot, and milfoil; plants, nearly all of them, jagged in   414
the leaf, broken and dimly clustered in flower, haunters of waste ground
and places of outcast refuse.

Beyond this plot of ground the Episcopal palace, a half-deserted,
barrack-like building, overlooks a *neglected vineyard*, of which the clusters,
black on the under side, snow-white on the other with lime-dust, gather
around them a melancholy hum of flies. Through the arches of this trellis-
work the avenue of the great valley is seen in descending distance,
enlarged with line beyond line of tufted foliage, languid and rich, degen-
erating at last into leagues of grey Maremma, wild with the thorn and the
willow; on each side of it, sustaining themselves in mighty slopes and
unbroken reaches of colossal promontory, the great mountains secede into
supremacy through rosy depths of burning air, and the crescents of snow
gleam over their dim summits, as—if there could be Mourning, as once
there was War, in heaven—a line of waning moons might be set for lamps
along the sides of some sepulchral chamber in the Infinite.

I know not how far this universal grasp of the sorrowful spirit might be
relaxed if sincere energy were directed to amend the ways of life of the
Valaisan. But it has always appeared to me that there was, even in more
healthy mountain districts, a certain degree of inevitable melancholy; nor
could I ever escape from the feeling that here, where chiefly the beauty of
God's working was manifested to men, warning was also given, and that
to the full, of the enduring of His indignation against sin.

It seems one of the most cunning and frequent of self-deceptions to turn
the heart away from this warning, and refuse to acknowledge anything in
the fair scenes of the natural creation but beneficence. Men in general
lean towards the light, so far as they contemplate such things at all, most
of them passing "by on the other side,"[12] either in mere plodding pursuit
of their own work, irrespective of what good or evil is around them, or else   415
in selfish gloom, or selfish delight, resulting from their own circumstances
at the moment. Of those who give themselves to any true contemplation,
the plurality, being humble, gentle, and kindly hearted, look only in
nature for what is lovely and kind; partly, also, God gives the disposition
to every healthy human mind in some degree to pass over or even harden
itself against evil things, else the suffering would be too great to be borne;
and humble people, with a quiet trust that everything is for the best, do
not fairly represent the facts to themselves, thinking them none of their
business. So, what between hard-hearted people, thoughtless people,
busy people, humble people, and cheerfully-minded people,—giddiness of
youth, and preoccupations of age,—philosophies of faith, and cruelties of
folly,—priest and Levite, masquer and merchantman, all agreeing to

keep their own side of the way,—the evil that God sends to warn us gets to be forgotten, and the evil that He sends to be mended by us gets left unmended. And then, because people shut their eyes to the dark indisputableness of the facts in front of them, their Faith, such as it is, is shaken or uprooted by every darkness in what is revealed to them. In the present day it is not easy to find a well-meaning man among our more earnest thinkers, who will not take upon himself to dispute the whole system of redemption, because he cannot unravel the mystery of the punishment of sin. But can he unravel the mystery of the punishment of NO sin? Can he entirely account for all that happens to a cab-horse? Has he ever looked fairly at the fate of one of those beasts as it is dying,—measured the work it has done, and the reward it has got,—put his hand upon the bloody wounds through which its bones are piercing, and so looked up to Heaven with an entire understanding of Heaven's ways

416   about the horse? Yet the horse is a fact—no dream—no revelation among the myrtle trees by night; and the dust it dies upon, and the dogs that eat it, are facts; and yonder happy person,—whose the horse was till its knees were broken over the hurdles, who had an immortal soul to begin with, and wealth and peace to help forward his immortality; who has also devoted the powers of his soul, and body, and wealth, and peace, to the spoiling of houses, the corruption of the innocent, and the oppression of the poor; and has, at this actual moment of his prosperous life, as many curses waiting round about him in calm shadow, with their death's eyes fixed upon him, abiding their time, as ever the poor cab-horse had launched at him in meaningless blasphemies, when his failing feet stumbled at the stones,—this happy person shall have no stripes,—shall have only the horse's fate of annihilation: or, if other things are indeed reserved for him, Heaven's kindness or omnipotence is to be doubted therefore.

We cannot reason of these things. But this I know—and this may by all men be known—that no good or lovely thing exists in this world without its correspondent darkness; and that the universe presents itself continually to mankind under the stern aspect of warning, or of choice, the good and the evil set on the right hand and the left.

And in this mountain gloom, which weighs so strongly upon the human heart that in all time hitherto, as we have seen, the hill defiles have been either avoided in terror or inhabited in penance, there is but the fulfilment of the universal law, that where the beauty and wisdom of the Divine working are most manifested, there also are manifested most clearly the terror of God's wrath, and inevitableness of His power.

Nor is this gloom less wonderful so far as it bears witness to the error of human choice, even when the nature of good and evil is most definitely set before it. The trees of Paradise were fair; but our first parents hid

themselves from God "in medio ligni Paradisi,"—in the midst of the trees
of the garden.[13] The hills were ordained for the help of man; but instead   417
of raising his eyes to the hills, from whence cometh his help, he does his
idol sacrifice "upon every high hill and under every green tree."[14] The
mountain of the Lord's house is established above the hills; but Nadab and
Abihu shall see under His feet the body of heaven in his clearness, yet go
down to kindle the censer against their own souls. And so to the end of
time it will be; to the end, that cry will still be heard along the Alpine
winds, "Hear, oh ye mountains, the Lord's controversy!"[15] Still, their
gulfs of thawless ice, and unretarded roar of tormented waves, and deathful falls of fruitless waste, and unredeemed decay, must be the image of the
souls of those who have chosen the darkness, and whose cry shall be to the
mountains to fall on them, and to the hills to cover them; and still, to the
end of time, the clear waters of the unfailing springs, and the white
pasture-lilies in their clothed multitude, and the abiding of the burning
peaks in their nearness to the opened heaven, shall be the types, and the
blessings, of those who have chosen light, and of whom it is written, "The
mountains shall bring peace to the people, and the little hills,
righteousness."[16]

CHAPTER XX
The Mountain Glory

418   I HAVE dwelt, in the foregoing chapter, on the sadness of the hills with the greater insistence that I feared my own excessive love for them might lead me into too favourable interpretation of their influences over the human heart; or, at least, that the reader might accuse me of fond prejudice, in the conclusions to which, finally, I desire to lead him concerning them. For, to myself, mountains are the beginning and the end of all natural scenery; in them, and in the forms of inferior landscape that lead to them, my affections are wholly bound up; and though I can look with happy admiration at the lowland flowers, and woods, and open skies, the happiness is tranquil and cold, like that of examining detached flowers in a conservatory, or reading a pleasant book; and if the scenery be resolutely level, insisting upon the declaration of its own flatness in all the detail of it, as in Holland, or Lincolnshire, or Central Lombardy, it appears to me like a prison, and I cannot long endure it. But the slightest rise and fall in the road,—a mossy bank at the side of a crag of chalk, with brambles at its brow, overhanging it,—a ripple over three or four stones in the stream by the bridge,—above all, a wild bit of ferny ground under a fir or two, looking as if, possibly, one might see a hill if one got to the other side of the trees, will instantly give me intense delight, because the shadow, or the hope, of the hills, is in them.

419   And thus, although there are few districts of Northern Europe, however apparently dull or tame, in which I cannot find pleasure, though the whole of Northern France (except Champagne), dull as it seems to most travellers, is to me a perpetual Paradise; and, putting Lincolnshire, Leicestershire, and one or two such other perfectly flat districts aside, there is not an English county which I should not find entertainment in exploring the cross-roads of, foot by foot; yet all my best enjoyment would be owing to the imagination of the hills, colouring, with their far-away memories, every lowland stone and herb. The pleasant French coteau, green in the sunshine, delights me, either by what real mountain character it has in itself, or by its broken ground and rugged steps among the vines, and rise of the leafage above, against the blue sky, as it might rise

469

at Vevay or Como. There is not a wave of the Seine but is associated in my mind with the first rise of the sandstones and forest pines of Fontainebleau; and with the hope of the Alps, as one leaves Paris with the horses' heads to the south-west, the morning sun flashing on the bright waves at Charenton. If there be *no* hope or association of this kind, and if I cannot deceive myself into fancying that perhaps at the next rise of the road there may be seen the film of a blue hill in the gleam of sky at the horizon, the landscape, however beautiful, produces in me even a kind of sickness and pain; and the whole view from Richmond Hill or Windsor Terrace,—nay, the gardens of Alcinous, [17] with their perpetual summer,—or of the Hesperides (if they were flat, and not close to Atlas), golden apples and all,—I would give away in an instant, for one mossy granite   420 stone a foot broad, and two leaves of lady-fern.

I know that this is in great part idiosyncrasy; and that I must not trust to my own feelings, in this respect, as representative of the modern landscape instinct: yet I know it is not idiosyncrasy, in so far as there may be proved to be indeed an increase of the absolute beauty of all scenery in exact proportion to its mountainous character, providing that character be *healthily* mountainous. I do not mean to take the Col de Bonhomme as representative of hills, any more than I would take Romney Marsh as representative of plains; but putting Leicestershire or Staffordshire fairly beside Westmoreland, and Lombardy or Champagne fairly beside the Pays de Vaud or the Canton Berne, I find the increase in the calculable sum of elements of beauty to be steadily in proportion to the increase of mountainous character; and that the best image which the world can give of Paradise is in the slope of the meadows, orchards, and corn-fields on the sides of a great Alp, with its purple rocks and eternal snows above; this excellence not being in any wise a matter referable to feeling, or individual preferences, but demonstrable by calm enumeration of the number of lovely colours on the rocks, the varied grouping of the trees, and quantity of noble incidents in stream, crag, or cloud, presented to the eye at any given moment.

For consider, first, the difference produced in the whole tone of   421 landscape colour by the introductions of purple, violet, and deep ultramarine blue, which we owe to mountains. In an ordinary lowland landscape we have the blue of the sky; the green of grass, which I will suppose (and this is an unnecessary concession to the lowlands) entirely fresh and bright; the green of trees; and certain elements of purple, far more rich and beautiful than we generally should think, in their bark and shadows (bare hedges and thickets, or tops of trees, in subdued afternoon sunshine, are nearly perfect purple, and of an exquisite tone), as well as in ploughed fields, and dark ground in general. But among mountains, in *addition* to all this, large unbroken spaces of pure violet and purple are introduced in their distances; and even near, by films of cloud passing over the darkness of ravines or forests, blues are produced of the most subtle tenderness; these azures and purples passing into rose-colour of otherwise wholly unattainable delicacy among the upper summits, the blue of the sky being at the same time purer and deeper than in the plains. Nay, in some sense, a person who has never seen the rose colour of the rays of dawn crossing a blue mountain twelve or fifteen miles away, can hardly be said to know what *tenderness* in colour means at all; *bright* tenderness he may, indeed, see in the sky or in a flower, but this grave tenderness of the far-away hill-purples he cannot conceive.

422　　Together with this great source of pre-eminence in *mass* of colour, we have to estimate the influence of the finished inlaying and enamel-work of the colour-jewellery on every stone; and that of the continual variety in species of flower; most of the mountain flowers being, besides, separately lovelier than the lowland ones. The wood hyacinth and wild rose are, indeed, the only *supreme* flowers that the lowlands can generally show; and the wild rose is also a mountaineer, and more fragrant in the hills, while the wood hyacinth, or grape hyacinth, at its best, cannot match even the dark bell-gentian, leaving the light-blue star-gentian in its uncontested queenliness, and the Alpine rose and Highland heather wholly without similitude. The violet, lily of the valley, crocus, and wood anemone are, I suppose, claimable partly by the plains as well as the hills; but the large orange lily and narcissus I have never seen but on hill pastures, and the exquisite oxalis is pre-eminently a mountaineer.

　　To this supremacy in mosses and flowers we have next to add an inestimable gain in the continual presence and power of water. Neither in its clearness, its colour, its fantasy of motion, its calmness of space, depth, and reflection, or its wrath, can water be conceived by a lowlander, out of sight of sea. A sea wave is far grander than any torrent—but of the sea and its influences we are not now speaking; and the sea itself, though it *can* be clear, is never calm, among our shores, in the sense that a mountain lake

423　　can be calm. The sea seems only to pause; the mountain lake to sleep, and to dream. Out of sight of the ocean a lowlander cannot be considered ever to have seen water at all. The mantling of the pools in the rock shadows, with the golden flakes of light sinking down through them like falling leaves, the ringing of the thin currents among the shallows, the flash and the cloud of the cascade, the earthquake and foam-fire of the cataract, the long lines of alternate mirror and mist that lull the imagery of the hills reversed in the blue of morning,—all these things belong to those hills as their undivided inheritance.

　　To this supremacy in wave and stream is joined a no less manifest pre-eminence in the character of trees. It is possible among plains, in the species of trees which properly belong to them, the poplars of Amiens, for

instance, to obtain a serene simplicity of grace, which is a better help to
the study of gracefulness, as such, than any of the wilder groupings of the
hills; so, also, there are certain conditions of symmetrical luxuriance
developed in the park and avenue, rarely rivalled in their way among
mountains; and yet the mountain superiority in foliage is, on the whole,
nearly as complete as it is in water: for exactly as there are some
expressions in the broad reaches of a navigable lowland river, such as the
Loire or Thames, not, in their way, to be matched among the rock rivers,
and yet for all that a lowlander cannot be said to have truly seen the
element of water at all; so even in the richest parks and avenues he cannot
be said to have truly seen trees. For the resources of trees are not developed
until they have difficulty to contend with; neither their tenderness of
brotherly love and harmony, till they are forced to choose their ways
of various life where there is contracted room for them, talking to each
other with their restrained branches. The various action of trees rooting
themselves in inhospitable rocks, stooping to look into ravines, hiding
from the search of glacier winds, reaching forth to the rays of rare sun-   424
shine, crowding down together to drink at sweetest streams, climbing
hand in hand among the difficult slopes, opening in sudden dances round
the mossy knolls, gathering into companies at rest among the fragrant
fields, gliding in grave procession over the heavenward ridges—nothing of
this can be conceived among the unvexed and unvaried felicities of the
lowland forest: while to all these direct sources of greater beauty are
added, first the power of redundance,—the mere quantity of foliage visible
in the folds and on the promontories of a single Alp being greater than
that of an entire lowland landscape (unless a view from some cathedral
tower); and to this charm of redundance, that of clearer *visibility*,—tree
after tree being constantly shown in successive height, one behind
another, instead of the mere tops and flanks of masses, as in the plains; and
the forms of multitudes of them continually defined against the clear sky,
near and above, or against white clouds entangled among their branches,
instead of being confused in dimness of distance.

Finally, to this supremacy in foliage we have to add the still less
questionable supremacy in clouds. There is no effect of sky possible in the
lowlands which may not in equal perfection be seen among the hills; but
there are effects by tens of thousands, for ever invisible and inconceivable
to the inhabitant of the plains, manifested among the hills in the course
of one day. The mere power of familiarity with the clouds, of walking with
them and above them, alters and renders clear our whole conception of
the baseless architecture of the sky; and for the beauty of it, there is more
in a single wreath of early cloud, pacing its way up an avenue of pines, or
pausing among the points of their fringes, than in all the white heaps that
filled the arched sky of the plains from one horizon to the other. And of

the nobler cloud manifestations,—the breaking of their troublous seas against the crags, their black spray sparkling with lightning; or the going forth of the morning along their pavements of moving marble, level-laid between dome and dome of snow;—of these things there can be as little imagination or understanding in an inhabitant of the plains as of the scenery of another planet than his own.

And, observe, all these superiorities are matters plainly measurable and calculable, not in any wise to be referred to estimate of *sensation*. Of the grandeur or expression of the hills I have not spoken; how far they are great, or strong, or terrible, I do not for the moment consider, because vastness, and strength, and terror, are not to all minds subjects of desired contemplation. It may make no difference to some men whether a natural object be large or small, whether it be strong or feeble. But loveliness of colour, perfectness of form, endlessness of change, wonderfulness of structure, are precious to all undiseased human minds; and the superiority of the mountains in all these things to the lowland is, I repeat, as measurable as the richness of a painted window matched with a white one, or the wealth of a museum compared with that of a simply furnished chamber. They seem to have been built for the human race, as at once their schools and cathedrals; full of treasures of illuminated manuscript for the scholar, kindly in simple lessons to the worker, quiet in pale cloisters for the thinker, glorious in holiness for the worshipper. And of these great cathedrals of the earth, with their gates of rock, pavements of cloud, choirs of stream and stone, altars of snow, and vaults of purple traversed by the continual stars,—of these, as we have seen, it was written, nor long ago, by one of the best of the poor human race for whom they were built, wondering in himself for whom their Creator *could* have made them, and thinking to have entirely discerned the Divine intent in them—"They are inhabited by the Beasts."[18]

Was it then indeed thus with us, and so lately? Had mankind offered no worship in their mountain churches? Was all that granite sculpture and floral painting done by the angels in vain?

Not so. It will need no prolonged thought to convince us that in the hills the purposes of their Maker have indeed been accomplished in such measure as, through the sin or folly of men, He ever permits them to be accomplished. It may not seem, from the general language held concerning them, or from any directly traceable results, that mountains have had serious influence on human intellect; but it will not, I think, be difficult to show that their occult influence has been both constant and essential to the progress of the race.

Consider, first, whether we can justly refuse to attribute to their mountain scenery some share in giving the Greeks and Italians their intellectual lead among the nations of Europe.

The vague expression which I have just used—"intellectual lead," may   427
be expanded into four great heads; lead in Religion, Art and Literature,
War, and Social Economy.

It will be right to examine our subject eventually under these four heads;
but I shall limit myself, for the present, to some consideration of the first
two.

I. We have before had occasion to note the peculiar awe with which
mountains were regarded in the Middle Ages, as bearing continual witness
against the frivolity or luxury of the world. Though the sense of this
influence of theirs is perhaps more clearly expressed by the mediæval
Christians than by any other sect of religionists, the influence itself has
been constant in all time. Mountains have always possessed the power,
first, of exciting religious enthusiasm; secondly, of purifying religious
faith. These two operations are partly contrary to one another: for the
faith of enthusiasm is apt to be *impure*, and the mountains, by exciting
morbid conditions of the imagination, have caused in great part the
legendary and romantic forms of belief; on the other hand, by fostering
simplicity of life and dignity of mortals, they have purified by action what
they falsified by imagination. But, even in their first and most dangerous
influence, it is not the mountains that are to blame, but the human heart.
While we mourn over the fictitious shape given to the religious visions of
the anchorite, we may envy the sincerity and the depth of the emotion
from which they spring: in the deep feeling, we have to acknowledge the
solemn influences of the hills; but for the erring modes or forms of
thought, it is human wilfulness, sin, and false teaching, that are
answerable.

And, in fact, much of the apparently harmful influence of hills on the   428
religion of the world is nothing else than their general gift of exciting, in
peculiarly solemn tones, the poetical and inventive faculties. Their terror
leads into devotional casts of thought; their beauty and wildness prompt
the invention at the same time; and where the mind is not gifted with
stern reasoning powers, or protected by purity of teaching, it is sure to
mingle the invention with its creed, and the vision with its prayer. Strictly
speaking, we ought to consider the superstitions of the hills, universally,
as a form of poetry; regretting only that men have not yet learned how to
distinguish poetry from well-founded faith. And if we do this, and enable
ourselves thus to review, without carping or sneering, the shapes of
solemn imagination which have arisen among the inhabitants of Europe,
we shall find, on the one hand, the mountains of Greece and Italy forming
all the loveliest dreams, first of the Pagan, then of the Christian myth-
ology; on the other, those of Scandinavia to be the first sources of
whatever mental (as well as military) power was brought by the Normans
into Southern Europe. We have thus one branch of the Northern religious   429

imagination rising among the Scandinavian fiords, tempered in France by various encounters with elements of Arabian, Italian, Provençal, or other Southern poetry, and then reacting upon Southern England; while other forms of the same rude religious imagination, resting like clouds upon the mountains of Scotland and Wales, met and mingled with the Norman Christianity, retaining even to the latest times some dark colour of superstition, but giving all its poetical and military pathos to Scottish poetry, and a peculiar sternness and wildness of tone to the Reformed faith, in its manifestations among the Scottish hills.

It is on less disputable ground that I may claim the reader's gratitude to the mountains, as having been the centres not only of imaginative energy, but of purity both in doctrine and practice. The enthusiasm of the persecuted Covenanter, and his variously modified claims to miraculous protection or prophetic inspiration, hold exactly the same relation to the smooth proprieties of lowland Protestantism that the demon combats, fastings, visions, and miracles of the mountain monk or anchorite hold to the wealth and worldliness of the Vatican. It might indeed happen, whether at Canterbury, Rheims, or Rome, that a good bishop should occasionally grasp the crozier; and a vast amount of prudent, educated, and admirable piety is to be found among the ranks of the lowland clergy. But still the large aspect of the matter is always, among Protestants, that formalism, respectability, orthodoxy, caution, and propriety, live by the slow stream that encircles the lowland abbey or cathedral; and that enthusiasm, poverty, vital faith, and audacity of conduct, characterize the

430   pastor dwelling by the torrent side. In like manner, taking the large aspects of Romanism, we see that its worst corruption, its cunning, its worldliness, and its permission of crime, are traceable for the most part to lowland prelacy; but its self-denials, its obediences, humilities, sincere claims to miraculous power, and faithful discharges of pastoral duty, are traceable chiefly to its anchorites and mountain clergy.

Of course the inquiry into this branch of the hill influence is partly complicated with that into its operation on domestic habits and personal character, of which hereafter: but there is one curious witness borne to the general truth of the foregone conclusions, by an apparently slight, yet very

431   significant circumstance in art. Nearly all the genuine religious painters use *steep mountain distances*. All the merely artistical ones, or those of intermediate temper, in proportion as they lose the religious element, use flat or simply architectural distances. Of course the law is liable to many exceptions, chiefly dependent on the place of birth and early associations of painters; but its force is, I think, strongly shown in this;—that, though the Flemish painters never showed any disposition to paint, *for its own sake*, other scenery than of their own land, the sincerely religious ones continually used Alpine distances, bright with snow. In like manner

Giotto, Perugino, Angelico, the young Raphael, and John Bellini, always, if, with any fitness to their subject, they can introduce them, use craggy or blue mountain distances, and this with definite expression of love towards them; Leonardo, conventionally, as feeling they were necessary for his sacred subjects, while yet his science and idealism had destroyed his mountain sincerity; Michael Angelo, wholly an artist, and Raphael in later years, show no love of mountains whatever, while the relative depths of feeling in Tintoret, Titian, and Veronese, are precisely measurable by their affection to mountains. Tintoret, though born in Venice, yet, because capable of the greatest reaches of feeling, is the first of the old painters who ever drew mountain detail rightly: Titian, though born in   432 Cadore, and recurring to it constantly, yet being more worldly-minded, uses his hills somewhat more conventionally, though still in his most deeply felt pictures, such as the St. Jerome in the Brera, giving to the rocks and forests a consummate nobleness; and Veronese, in his gay grasp of the outside aspects of the world, contentedly includes his philosophy within porticoes and pillars, or at the best overshadows it with a few sprays of laurel.

The test fails, however, utterly when applied to the later or transitional landscape schools, mountains being there introduced in mere wanton savageness by Salvator, or vague conventionalism by Claude, Berghem, and hundreds more. This need not, however, in the least invalidate our general conclusions: we surely know already that it is possible to misuse the best gifts, and pervert the purest feelings; nor need we doubt the real purpose, or, on honest hearts, the real effect, of mountains, because various institutions have been founded among them by the banditti of Calabria, as well as by St. Bruno.

I cannot leave this part of my subject without recording a slight incident, which happened to myself, singularly illustrative of the religious character of the Alpine peasant when under favourable circumstances of teaching. I was coming down one evening from the Rochers de Naye, above Montreux, having been at work among the limestone rocks, where I could get no water, and both weary and thirsty. Coming to a spring at a turn of the path, conducted, as usual, by the herdsmen into a hollowed pine-trunk, I stooped to it, and drank deeply: as I raised my head, drawing breath heavily, some one behind me said, "Celui qui boira de cette eau-ci,   433 aura encore soif." I turned, not understanding for the moment what was meant; and saw one of the hill-peasants, probably returning to his châlet from the market-place at Vevay or Villeneuve. As I looked at him with an uncomprehending expression, he went on with the verse:—"Mais celui qui boira de l'eau que je lui donnerai, n'aura jamais soif."

I doubt if this would have been thought of, or said, by even the most intelligent lowland peasant. The thought might have occurred to him, but the frankness of address, and expectation of being at once understood without a word of preparative explanation, as if the language of the Bible were familiar in all men, mark, I think, the mountaineer.

II. We were next to examine the influence of hills on the artistical power of the human race. Which power, so far as it depends on the imagination, must evidently be fostered by the same influences which give vitality to religious vision. But so far as artistical productiveness and skill are concerned, it is evident that the mountaineer is at a radical and insurmountable disadvantage. The strength of his character depends upon the absence of luxury; but it is eminently by luxury that art is supported. We are not, therefore, to deny the mountain influence, because we do not find finished frescoes on the timbers of châlets, or delicate bas-reliefs on the bastion which protects the mountain church from the avalanche; but to consider how far the tone of mind shown by the artists labouring in the lowland is dependent for its intensity on the distant influences of the hills, whether during the childhood of those born among them, or under the casual contemplation of men advanced in life.

Glancing broadly over the strength of the mediæval—that is to say, of the peculiar and energetic—art of Europe, so as to discern through the clear flowing of its waves over France, Italy, and England, the places in the pool where the fountain heads are, and where the sand dances, I should first point to Normandy and Tuscany. From the cathedral of Pisa, and the sculpture of the Pisans, the course is straight to Giotto, Angelico and Raphael,—to Orcagna and Michael Angelo;—the Venetian school, in many respects mightier, being nevertheless, subsequent and derivative. From the cathedrals of Caen and Coutances the course is straight to the Gothic of Chartres and Notre Dame of Paris, and thence forward to all French and English noble art, whether ecclesiastical or domestic. Now the mountain scenery above Pisa is precisely the most beautiful that surrounds any great Italian city, owing to the wonderful outlines of the peaks of Carrara. Milan and Verona have indeed finer ranges in sight, but rising farther in the distance, and therefore not so directly affecting the popular mind. The Norman imagination, as already noticed, is Scandinavian in origin, and fostered by the lovely granite scenery of Normandy itself. But there is, nevertheless, this great difference between French art and Italian, that the French paused strangely at a certain point, as the Norman hills are truncated at the summits, while the Italian rose steadily to a vertex, as the Carrara hills to their crests. Let us observe this a little more in detail.

The sculpture of the Pisans was taken up and carried into various per-fection by the Lucchese, Pistojans, Sienese, and Florentines. All these are inhabitants of truly mountain cities, Florence being as completely among the hills as Innspruck is, only the hills have softer outlines. Those around Pistoja and Lucca are in a high degree majestic. Giotto was born and bred among these hills. Angelico lived upon their slope. The mountain towns of Perugia and Urbino furnish the only important branches of correlative art; for Leonardo, however individually great, originated no new school;   435 he only carried the *executive* delicacy of landscape detail so far beyond other painters as to necessitate my naming the fifteenth-century manner of landscape after him, though he did not invent it; and although the school of Milan is distinguished by several peculiarities, and definitely enough separable from the other schools of Italy, all its peculiarities are mannerisms, not inventions.

Correggio, indeed, created a new school, though he himself is almost its only master. But the only entirely great group of painters after the Tuscans are the Venetians, and they are headed by Titian and Tintoret, on whom we have noticed the influence of hills already; and although we cannot trace it in Paul Veronese, I will not quit the mountain claim upon him; for I believe all that gay and gladdening strength of his was fed by the breezes of the hills of Garda, and brightened by the swift glancing of the waves of the Adige.

Observe, however, before going farther, of all the painters we have named, the one who obtains most executive perfection is Leonardo, who on the whole lived at the greatest distance from the hills. The two who have most feeling are Giotto and Angelico, both hill-bred. And generally, I believe, we shall find that the hill country gives its inventive depth of feeling to art, as in the work of Orcagna, Perugino, and Angelico, and the plain country executive neatness. The executive precision is joined with feeling in Leonardo, who saw the Alps in the distance; it is totally unaccompanied by feeling in the pure Dutch schools, or schools of the dead flats.

I do not know if any writer on art, or on the development of national   436 mind, has given his attention to what seems to me one of the most singular phenomena in the history of Europe,—the pause of the English and French in pictorial art after the fourteenth century. From the days of Henry III. to those of Elizabeth, and of Louis IX. to those of Louis XIV., the general intellect of the two nations was steadily on the increase. But their art intellect was as steadily retrograde. The only art work that France and England have done nobly is that which is centralized by the Cathedral of Lincoln, and the Sainte Chapelle. We had at that time (*we*—French and English—but the French first) the incontestable lead among European nations; no thirteenth-century work in Italy is comparable for majesty of conception, or wealth of imaginative detail, to the Cathedrals of Chartres, Rheims, Rouen, Amiens, Lincoln, Peterborough, Wells, or Lichfield. But every hour of the fourteenth century saw French and English art in precipitate decline, Italian in steady ascent; and by the time that painting and sculpture had developed themselves in an approximated perfection, in the work of Ghirlandajo and Mino of Fésole, we had in France and England no workman, in any art, deserving a workman's name: nothing but skilful masons, with more or less love of the picturesque, and redundance of undisciplined imagination, flaming itself away in wild and rich traceries, and crowded bosses of grotesque figure sculpture, and expiring at last in barbarous imitation of the perfected skill and erring choice of Renaissance Italy. Painting could not decline, for it had not reached any eminence; the exquisite arts of illumination and glass design had led to no effective results in other materials; they themselves, incapable of any higher perfection than they had reached in the 437 thirteenth century, perished in the vain endeavour to emulate pictorial excellence, bad *drawing* being substituted, in books, for lovely *writing*, and opaque precision, in glass, for transparent power; nor in any single department of exertion did artists arise of such calibre or class as any of the great Italians; and yet all the while, in literature, *we* were gradually and steadily advancing in power up to the time of Shakespere; the Italians, on the contrary, not advancing after the time of Dante.

Of course I have no space here to pursue a question such as this: but I may state my belief that *one* of the conditions involved in it was the mountain influence of Italian scenery, inducing a disposition to such indolent or enthusiastic reverie, as could only express itself in the visions of art; while the comparatively flat scenery, and severer climate, of England and France, fostering less enthusiasm, and urging to more exertion, brought about a practical and rational temperament, progressive in policy, science, and literature, but wholly retrograde in art; that is to say (for great art may be properly so defined), in the Art of *Dreaming*.

III. In admitting this, we seem to involve the supposition that mountain influence is either unfavourable or inessential to literary power; but for this also the mountain influence is still necessary, only in a subordinate degree. It is true, indeed, that the Avon is no mountain torrent, and that the hills round the vale of Stratford are not sublime; true, moreover, that the cantons Berne and Uri have never yet, so far as I know, produced a great poet; but neither, on the other hand, has Antwerp or Amsterdam. And, I believe, the natural scenery which will be found, on the whole, productive of most literary intellect is that mingled of hill and plain, as all available light is of flame and darkness; the flame being the active element, and the darkness the tempering one.

454 It will be remembered, we first entered on this subject[19] in order to obtain some data as to the possibility of a Practical Ideal in Swiss life, correspondent, in some measure, to the poetical ideal of the same, which so largely entertains the European public. Of which possibility, I do not think, after what we have even already seen of the true effect of mountains on the human mind, there is any reason to doubt, even if that ideal had

not been presented to us already in some measure, in the older life of the Swiss republics. But of its possibility, *under present circumstances*, there is, I grieve to say, the deepest reason to doubt; and that the more, because the question is not whether the mountaineer can be raised into a happier life by the help of the active nations of the plains; but whether he can yet be protected from the infection of the folly and vanity of those nations. I urged, in the preceding chapter, some consideration of what might be accomplished, if we chose to devote to the help, what we now devote to the mockery, of the Swiss. But I would that the enlightened population of Paris and London were content with doing nothing;—that they were satisfied with expenditure upon their idle pleasures, in their idle way; and would leave the Swiss to their own mountain gloom of unadvancing independence. I believe that every franc now spent by travellers among   455 the Alps tends more or less to the undermining of whatever special greatness there is in the Swiss character; and the persons I met in Switzerland, whose position and modes of life rendered them best able to give me true information respecting the present state of their country, among many causes of national deterioration, spoke with chief fear of the influx of English wealth, gradually connecting all industry with the wants and ways of strangers, and inviting all idleness to depend upon their casual help; thus gradually resolving the ancient consistency and pastoral simplicity of the mountain life into the two irregular trades of innkeeper and mendicant.

I could say much on this subject if I had any hope of doing good by saying anything. But I have none. The influx of foreigners into Switzerland must necessarily be greater every year, and the greater it is, the larger in the crowd will be the majority of persons whose objects in travelling will be, first, to get as fast as possible from place to place, and, secondly, at every place where they arrive, to obtain the kind of accommodation and amusement to which they are accustomed in Paris, London, Brighton, or Baden. Railroads are already projected round the head of the Lake of Geneva, and through the town of Fribourg; the head of the Lake of Geneva being precisely and accurately the one spot of Europe whose character, and influence on human mind, are special; and unreplaceable if destroyed, no other spot resembling, or being in any wise comparable to it, in its peculiar way: while the town of Fribourg is in like   456 manner the only mediæval mountain town of importance left to us; Innspruck and such others being wholly modern, while Fribourg yet retains much of the aspect it had in the fourteenth and fifteenth centuries. The valley of Chamouni, another spot also unique in its way, is rapidly being turned into a kind of Cremorne Gardens; and I can foresee, within the perspective of but few years, the town of Lucerne consisting of a row of symmetrical hotels round the foot of the lake, its old bridges destroyed, an iron one built over the Reuss, and an acacia promenade carried along the lake-shore, with a German band playing under a Chinese temple at the end of it, and the enlightened travellers, representatives of European civilization, performing before the Alps, in each afternoon summer sunlight, in their modern manner, the Dance of Death.

All this is inevitable; and it has its good as well as its evil side. I can imagine the zealous modernist replying to me that when all this is happily accomplished, my melancholy peasants of the valley of Trient will be turned into thriving shopkeepers, the desolate streets of Sion into glittering thoroughfares, and the marshes of the Valais into prosperous market-gardens. I hope so; and indeed am striving every day to conceive more accurately, and regulate all my efforts by the expectation of, the state of society, not now, I suppose, much more than twenty years in advance of us, when Europe, having satisfactorily effaced all memorials of the past, and reduced itself to the likeness of America, or of any other new country (only with less room for exertion), shall begin to consider what is next to be done, and to what newness of arts and interests may best be devoted the wealth of its marts, and the strength of its multitudes. Which anticipations and estimates, however, I have never been able, as yet, to carry out with any clearness, being always arrested by the confused notion of a necessity for solitude, disdain of buying and selling, and other elements of that old mediæval and mountain gloom, as in some way connected with the efforts of nearly all men who have either seen far into the destiny, or been much helpful to the souls, of their race. And the grounds of this feeling, whether right or wrong, I hope to analyze more fully in the next volume; only noting, finally, in this, one or two points for the consideration of those among us with whom it may sometimes become a question, whether they will help forward, or not, the turning of a sweet mountain valley into an abyss of factory-stench and toil, or the carrying of a line of traffic through some green place of shepherd solitude.

For, if there be any truth in the impression which I have always felt, and just now endeavoured to enforce, that the mountains of the earth are its natural cathedrals, or natural altars, overlaid with gold, and bright with broidered work of flowers, and with their clouds resting on them as the smoke of a continual sacrifice, it may surely be a question with some of us, whether the tables of the moneychanger, however fit and commendable they may be as furniture in other places, are precisely the things which it is the whole duty of man to get well set up in the mountain temple.

And perhaps it may help to the better determination of this question, if we endeavour, for a few patient moments, to bear with that weakness of our forefathers in feeling an *awe* for the hills; and, divesting ourselves, as far as may be, of our modern experimental or exploring activity, and habit of regarding mountains chiefly as places for gymnastic exercise, try to understand the temper, not indeed altogether exemplary, but yet having certain truths and dignities in it, to which we owe the founding of the Benedictine and Carthusian cloisters in the thin Alpine air. And this monkish temper we may, I suppose, best understand by considering the aspect under which mountains are represented in the Monk's book. I found that in my late lectures, at Edinburgh,[20] I gave great offence by supposing, or implying, that scriptural expressions could have any force as bearing upon modern practical questions; so that I do not now, nor shall I any more, allude to such expressions as in any wise necessarily bearing on the worldly business of the practical Protestant, but only as necessary to be glanced at in order to understand the temper of those old monks, who had the awkward habit of understanding the Bible literally; and to get any little good which momentary sympathy with the hearts of a large and earnest class of men may surely bring to us.

The monkish view of mountains, then, was derived wholly from that Latin Vulgate of theirs; and, speaking as a monk, it may perhaps be permitted me to mark the significance of the earliest mention of mountains in the Mosaic books; at least, of those in which some Divine appointment or command is stated respecting them. They are first brought before us as refuges for God's people from the two judgments, of   459
water and fire. The ark *rests* upon "the mountains of Ararat"; and man, having passed through that great baptism unto death, kneels upon the earth first where it is nearest heaven, and mingles with the mountain clouds the smoke of his sacrifice of thanksgiving. Again: from the midst of the first judgment by fire, the command of the Deity to His servant is, "Escape to the mountain"; and the morbid fear of the hills, which fills any human mind after long stay in places of luxury and sin, is strangely marked in Lot's complaining reply: "I cannot escape to the mountain, lest some evil take me." The third mention, in way of ordinance, is a far more solemn one: "Abraham lifted up his eyes, and saw the place afar off." "The Place," the Mountain of Myrrh, or of bitterness, chosen to fulfil to all the seed of Abraham, far off and near, the inner meaning of promise regarded in that vow: "I will lift up mine eyes unto the hills, from whence cometh mine help."[21]

And the fourth is the delivery of the law on Sinai.

It seemed, then, to the monks, that the mountains were appointed by their Maker to be to man, refuges from Judgment, signs of Redemption, and altars of Sanctification and Obedience; and they saw them afterwards connected, in the manner the most touching and gracious, with the death, after his task had been accomplished, of the first anointed Priest; the death, in like manner, of the first inspired Lawgiver; and, lastly, with the assumption of his office by the Eternal Priest, Lawgiver, and Saviour.

Observe the connection of these three events. Although the *time* of the deaths of Aaron and Moses was hastened by God's displeasure, we have not, it seems to me, the slightest warrant for concluding that the *manner* of their deaths was intended to be grievous or dishonourable to them. Far from this: it cannot, I think, be doubted that in the denial of the permission to enter the Promised Land, the whole punishment of their sin was included; and that as far as regarded the manner of their deaths, it must have been appointed for them by their Master in all tenderness and love; and with full purpose of ennobling the close of their service upon the earth. It might have seemed to *us* more honourable that both should have been permitted to die beneath the shadow of the Tabernacle, the congregation of Israel watching by their side; and all whom they loved gathered together to receive the last message from the lips of the meek lawgiver, and the last blessing from the prayer of the anointed priest. But it was not thus they were permitted to die. Try to realize that going forth of Aaron from the midst of the congregation. He who had so often done sacrifice for their sin, going forth now to offer up his own spirit. He who had stood, among them, between the dead and the living, and had seen the eyes of all that great multitude turned to him, that by his intercession their breath might yet be drawn a moment more, going forth now to meet the Angel of Death face to face, and deliver himself into his hand. Try if you cannot walk, in thought, with those two brothers, and the son, as they passed the outmost tents of Israel, and turned, while yet the dew lay round about the camp, towards the slopes of Mount Hor; talking together for the last time, as, step by step, they felt the steeper rising of the rocks, and hour after hour, beneath the ascending sun, the horizon grew broader as they climbed, and all the folded hills of Idumea, one by one subdued, showed amidst their hollows in the haze of noon, the windings of that long desert journey, now at last to close. But who shall enter into the thoughts of the High Priest, as his eye followed those paths of ancient pilgrimage; and, through the silence of the arid and endless hills, stretching even to the dim peak of Sinai, the whole history of those forty years was unfolded before him, and the mystery of his own ministries revealed to him; and that other Holy of Holies, of which the mountain peaks were the altars, and the mountain clouds the veil, the firmament of his Father's dwelling, opened to him still more brightly and infinitely as he drew nearer his death; until at last, on the shadeless summit,—from him on whom sin was to be laid no more—from him, on whose heart the names of sinful nations were to press their graven fire no longer,—the brother and the son took breastplate and ephod, and left him to his rest.

There is indeed a secretness in this calm faith and deep restraint of sorrow, into which it is difficult for us to enter; but the death of Moses himself is more easily to be conceived, and had in it circumstances still more touching, as far as regards the influence of the external scene. For forty years Moses had not been alone. The care and burden of all the people, the weight of their woe, and guilt, and death, had been upon him continually. The multitude had been laid upon him as if he had conceived them; their tears had been his meat, night and day, until he had felt as if God had withdrawn His favour from him, and he had prayed that he might be slain, and not see his wretchedness. And now, at last, the command came, "Get thee up into this mountain."[22] The weary hands that had been so long stayed up against the enemies of Israel, might lean again upon the shepherd's staff, and fold themselves for the shepherd's prayer—for the shepherd's slumber. Not strange to his feet, though forty years unknown, the roughness of the bare mountain-path, as he climbed from ledge to ledge of Abarim; not strange to his aged eyes the scattered clusters of the mountain herbage, and the broken shadows of the cliffs, indented far across the silence of uninhabited ravines; scenes such as those among which, with none, as now, beside him but God, he had led his flocks so often; and which he had left, how painfully! taking upon him the appointed power, to make of the fenced city a wilderness, and to fill the desert with songs of deliverance. It was not to embitter the last hours of his life that God restored to him, for a day, the beloved solitudes he had lost; and breathed the peace of the perpetual hills around him, and cast the world in which he had laboured and sinned far beneath his feet, in that mist of dying blue;—all sin, all wandering, soon to be forgotten for ever; the Dead Sea—a type of God's anger understood by him, of all men, most clearly, who had seen the earth open her mouth, and the sea his depth, to overwhelm the companies of those who contended with his Master—laid waveless beneath him; and beyond it, the fair hills of Judah, and the soft plains and banks of Jordan, purple in the evening light as with the blood of redemption, and fading in their distant fulness into mysteries of promise and of love. There, with his unabated strength, his undimmed glance, lying down upon the utmost rocks, with angels waiting near to contend for the spoils of his spirit, he put off his earthly armour. We do deep reverence to his companion prophet, for whom the chariot of fire came down from heaven; but was his death less noble, whom his Lord Himself buried in the vales of Moab, keeping, in the secrets of the eternal counsels, the knowledge of a sepulchre, from which he was to be called, in the fulness of time, to talk with that Lord, upon Hermon, of the death that He should accomplish at Jerusalem?

And lastly, let us turn our thoughts for a few moments to the cause of the resurrection of these two prophets. We are all of us too much in the habit of passing it by, as a thing mystical and inconceivable, taking place in the life of Christ for some purpose not by us to be understood, or, at the best, merely as a manifestation of His divinity by brightness of heavenly

462

plate 19   J.M.W. Turner, *The Goddess of Discord choosing the Apple of Contention in the Garden of the Hesperides*

plate 20 J.M.W. Turner, *Apollo and Python*

plate 21 J.M.W. Turner, *Ulysses Deriding Polyphemus*

plate 22 J.M.W. Turner, *The Bay of Baiae*

plate 23 J.M.W. Turner, *Childe Harold's Pilgrimage, Italy*

plate 24 Holman Hunt, *The Finding of the Saviour in the Temple*

light, and the ministering of the spirits of the dead, intended to strengthen
the faith of His three chosen apostles. And in this, as in many other events
recorded by the Evangelists, we lose half the meaning, and evade the
practical power upon ourselves, by never accepting in its fulness the idea
that our Lord was "perfect man," "tempted in all things like as we are." [23]
Our preachers are continually trying, in all manner of subtle ways, to
explain the union of the Divinity with the Manhood, an explanation
which certainly involves first their being able to describe the nature of
Deity itself, or, in plain words, to comprehend God. They never can
explain, in any one particular, the union of the natures; they only succeed
in weakening the faith of their hearers as to the entireness of either. The
thing they have to do is precisely the contrary of this—to insist upon the
entireness of both. We never think of Christ enough as God, never enough
as Man; the instinctive habit of our minds being always to miss of the
Divinity, and the reasoning and enforced habit to miss of the Humanity.
We are afraid to harbour in our own hearts, or to utter in the hearing of
others, any thought of our Lord, as hungering, tired, sorrowful, having a
human soul, a human will, and affected by events of human life as a finite
creature is; and yet one half of the efficiency of His atonement, and the
whole of the efficiency of His example, depend on His having been this
to the full.

Consider, therefore, the Transfiguration as it relates to the human
feelings of our Lord. It was the first definite preparation for His death. He
had foretold it to His disciples six days before; then takes with Him the
three chosen ones into "an high mountain apart." [24] From an exceeding
high mountain, at the first taking on Him the ministry of life, He had
beheld, and rejected the kingdoms of the earth, and their glory; now, on
a high mountain, He takes upon Him the ministry of death. Peter and
they that were with Him, as in Gethsemane, were heavy with sleep.
Christ's work had to be done alone.

The tradition is, that the Mount of Transfiguration was the summit of
Tabor; but Tabor is neither a high mountain, nor was it in any sense a
mountain "*apart*"; being in those years both inhabited and fortified. All
the immediately preceding ministries of Christ had been at Cesarea
Philippi. There is no mention of travel southward in the six days that
intervened between the warning given to His disciples, and the going up
into the hill. What other hill could it be than the southward slope of that
goodly mountain, Hermon, which is indeed the centre of all the Promised
Land, from the entering in of Hamath unto the river of Egypt; the mount
of fruitfulness, from which the springs of Jordan descended to the valleys
of Israel? Along its mighty forest avenues, until the grass grew fair with the
mountain lilies, His feet dashed in the dew of Hermon, He must have
gone to pray His first recorded prayer about death; and from the steep of

it, before He knelt, could see to the south all the dwelling-place of the people that had sat in darkness, and seen the great light, the land of Zabulon and of Naphtali, Galilee of the nations;—could see, even with His human sight, the gleam of that lake by Capernaum and Chorazin, and many a place loved by Him, and vainly ministered to, whose house was now left unto them desolate; and, chief of all, far in the utmost blue, the hills above Nazareth, sloping down to His old home: hills on which yet the stones lay loose, that had been taken up to cast at Him, when He left them for ever.

"And as He prayed, two men stood by Him."[25] Among the many ways in which we miss the help and hold of Scripture, none is more subtle than our habit of supposing that, even as man, Christ was free from the Fear of Death. How could He then have been tempted as we are? since among·all the trials of the earth, none spring from the dust more terrible than that   465
Fear. It had to be borne by Him, indeed, in a unity, which we can never comprehend, with the foreknowledge of victory,—as His sorrow for Lazarus, with the consciousness of the power to restore him; but it *had* to be borne, and that in its full earthly terror; and the presence of it is surely marked for us enough by the rising of those two at His side. When, in the desert, He was girding Himself for the work of life, angels of life came and ministered unto Him: now, in the fair world, when He is girding Himself for the work of death, the ministrants come to Him from the grave.

But from the grave conquered. One, from that tomb under Abarim, which His own hand had sealed so long ago; the other, from the rest into which He had entered, without seeing corruption. There stood by Him Moses and Elias, and spake of His decease.

Then, when the prayer is ended, the task accepted, first, since the star paused over Him at Bethlehem, the full glory falls upon Him from heaven, and the testimony is borne to His everlasting Sonship and power. "Hear ye Him."[26]

If, in their remembrance of these things, and in their endeavour to follow in the footsteps of their Master, religious men of bygone days, closing themselves in the hill solitudes, forgot sometimes, and sometimes feared, the duties they owed to the active world, we may perhaps pardon them more easily than we ought to pardon ourselves, if we neither seek any influence for good nor submit to it unsought, in scenes to which thus all the men whose writings we receive as inspired, together with their Lord, retired whenever they had any task or trial laid upon them needing more than their usual strength of spirit. Nor, perhaps, should we have unprofitably entered into the mind of the earlier ages, if among our other thoughts, as we watch the chains of the snowy mountains rise on the horizon, we should sometimes admit the memory of the hour in which   466
their Creator, among their solitudes, entered on His travail for the

salvation of our race; and indulge the dream, that as the flaming and trembling mountains of the earth seem to be the monuments of the manifesting of His terror on Sinai,—these pure and white hills, near to the heaven, and sources of all good to the earth, are the appointed memorials of that Light of His Mercy, that fell, snow-like, on the Mount of Transfiguration.

VOLUME V

PART VIII[1]

Of Ideas of Relation:—First, of Invention Formal

CHAPTER I
The Law of Help

203   WE have now reached the last and the most important part of our subject. We have seen in the first division of this book, how far art may be, and has been, consistent with physical or material facts. In its second division, we examined how far it may be and has been obedient to the laws of physical beauty. In this last division we have to consider the relations of art to God and man: its work in the help of human beings, and service of their Creator.

We have to inquire into the various Powers, Conditions, and Aims of mind involved in the conception or creation of pictures; in the choice of subject, and the mode and order of its history;—the choice of forms, and the modes of their arrangement.

And these phases of mind being concerned, partly with choice and arrangement of incidents, partly with choice and arrangement of forms and colours, the whole subject will fall into two main divisions, namely, expressional or spiritual invention; and material or formal invention.

They are of course connected;—all good formal invention being expressional also; but as a matter of convenience it is best to say what may be ascertained of the nature of formal invention, before attempting to illustrate the faculty in its higher field.

204   First, then, of INVENTION FORMAL, otherwise and most commonly called technical composition; that is to say, the arrangement of lines, forms, or colours, so as to produce the best possible effect.

I have often been accused of slighting this quality in pictures; the fact being that I have avoided it only because I considered it too great and wonderful for me to deal with. The longer I thought, the more wonderful it always seemed: and it is, to myself personally, the quality, above all others, which gives me delight in pictures. Many others I admire, or respect; but this one I rejoice in. Expression, sentiment, truth to nature, are essential: but all these are not enough. I never care to look at a picture again, if it be ill composed; and if well composed I can hardly leave off looking at it.

"Well composed." Does that mean according to rule?

No. Precisely the contrary. Composed as only the man who did it could have done it; composed as no other picture is, or was, or ever can be again. Every great work stands alone.

Yet there are certain elementary laws of arrangement traceable a little way; a few of these only I shall note, not caring to pursue the subject far in this work, so intricate it becomes even in its first elements: nor could it be treated with any approach to completeness, unless I were to give many and elaborate outlines of large pictures.

Composition may be best defined as the help of everything in the   205 picture by everything else.

I wish the reader to dwell a little on this word "Help." It is a grave one.

In substance which we call "inanimate," as of clouds, or stones, their atoms may cohere to each other, or consist with each other, but they do not help each other. The removal of one part does not injure the rest.

But in a plant, the taking away of any one part does injure the rest. Hurt or remove any portion of the sap, bark, or pith, the rest is injured. If any part enters into a state in which it no more assists the rest, and has thus become "helpless," we call it also "dead."

The power which causes the several portions of the plant to help each other, we call life. Much more is this so in an animal. We may take away the branch of a tree without much harm to it; but not the animal's limb. Thus, intensity of life is also intensity of helpfulness—completeness of depending of each part on all the rest. The ceasing of this help is what we call corruption; and in proportion to the perfectness of the help, is the dreadfulness of the loss. The more intense the life has been, the more terrible is its corruption.

The decomposition of a crystal is not necessarily impure at all. The   206 fermentation of a wholesome liquid begins to admit the idea slightly; the decay of leaves yet more; of flowers, more; of animals, with greater painfulness and terribleness in exact proportion to their original vitality; and the foulest of all corruption is that of the body of man; and, in his body, that which is occasioned by disease, more than that of natural death.

I said just now, that though atoms of inanimate substance could not help each other, they could "consist" with each other. "Consistence" is their virtue. Thus the parts of a crystal are consistent, but of dust, inconsistent. Orderly adherence, the best help its atoms can give, con-stitutes the nobleness of such substance.

When matter is either consistent, or living, we call it pure, or clean; when inconsistent or corrupting (unhelpful), we call it impure, or unclean. The greatest uncleanliness being that which is essentially most opposite to life.

Life and consistency, then, both expressing one character (namely, helpfulness of a higher or lower order), the Maker of all creatures and things, "by whom all creatures live, and all things consist,"[2] is essentially and for ever the Helpful One, or in softer Saxon, the "Holy" One.[3]

The word has no other ultimate meaning: Helpful, harmless, undefiled: "living" or "Lord of life."

The idea is clear and mighty in the cherubim's cry: "Helpful, helpful, helpful, Lord God of Hosts";[4] *i.e.* of all the hosts, armies, and creatures of the earth.

207   A pure or holy state of anything, therefore, is that in which all its parts are helpful or consistent. They may or may not be homogeneous. The highest or organic purities are composed of many elements in an entirely helpful state. The highest and first law of the universe—and the other name of life is, therefore, "help." The other name of death is "separation." Government and co-operation are in all things and eternally the laws of life. Anarchy and competition, eternally, and in all things, the laws of death.[5]

Perhaps the best, though the most familiar example we could take of the nature and power of consistence, will be that of the possible changes in the dust we tread on.

Exclusive of animal decay, we can hardly arrive at a more absolute type of impurity than the mud or slime of a damp, over-trodden path, in the outskirts of a manufacturing town. I do not say mud of the road, because that is mixed with animal refuse; but take merely an ounce or two of the blackest slime of a beaten footpath on a rainy day, near a large manufacturing town.

That slime we shall find in most cases composed of clay (or brickdust, which is burnt clay) mixed with soot, a little sand, and water. All these elements are at helpless war with each other, and destroy reciprocally each other's nature and power, competing and fighting for place at every tread of your foot;—sand squeezing out clay, and clay squeezing out water, and soot meddling everywhere and defiling the whole. Let us suppose that this ounce of mud is left in perfect rest, and that its elements gather together, like to like, so that their atoms may get into the closest relations possible.

Let the clay begin. Ridding itself of all foreign substance, it gradually

208   becomes a white earth, already very beautiful; and fit, with help of congealing fire, to be made into finest porcelain, and painted on, and be kept in kings' palaces. But such artificial consistence is not its best. Leave it still quiet to follow its own instinct of unity, and it becomes not only white, but clear; not only clear, but hard; nor only clear and hard, but so set that it can deal with light in a wonderful way, and gather out of it the loveliest blue rays only, refusing the rest. We call it then a sapphire.

Such being the consummation of the clay, we give similar permission of quiet to the sand. It also becomes, first, a white earth, then proceeds to grow clear and hard, and at last arranges itself in mysterious, infinitely fine, parallel lines, which have the power of reflecting not merely the blue rays, but the blue, green, purple, and red rays in the greatest beauty in which they can be seen through any hard material whatsoever. We call it then an opal.

In next order the soot sets to work; it cannot make itself white at first, but instead of being discouraged, tries harder and harder, and comes out clear at last, and the hardest thing in the world; and for the blackness that it had, obtains in exchange the power of reflecting all the rays of the sun at once in the vividest blaze that any solid thing can shoot. We call it then a diamond.

Last of all the water purifies or unites itself, contented enough if it only reach the form of a dew-drop; but if we insist on its proceeding to a more perfect consistence, it crystallizes into the shape of a star.

And for the ounce of slime which we had by political economy of competition, we have by political economy of co-operation, a sapphire, an opal, and a diamond, set in the midst of a star of snow.

Now invention in art signifies an arrangement, in which everything in the work is thus consistent with all things else, and helpful to all else. 209

It is the greatest and rarest of all the qualities of art. The power by which it is effected is absolutely inexplicable and incommunicable; but exercised with entire facility by those who possess it, in many cases even unconsciously.

In work which is not composed, there may be many beautiful things, but they do not help each other. They at the best only stand beside, and more usually compete with and destroy, each other. They may be connected artificially in many ways, but the test of there being no invention is, that if one of them be taken away, the others are no worse than before. But in true composition, if one be taken away, all the rest are helpless and valueless. Generally, in falsely composed work, if anything be taken away, the rest will look better; because the attention is less distracted. Hence the pleasure of inferior artists in sketching, and their inability to finish: all that they add destroys.

Also in true composition, everything not only helps everything else a *little*, but helps with its utmost power. Every atom is in full energy; and *all* that energy is kind. Not a line, nor spark of colour, but is doing its very best, and that best is aid. The extent to which this law is carried in truly right and noble work is wholly inconceivable to the ordinary observer, and no true account of it would be believed.

True composition being entirely easy to the man who can compose, he 210 is seldom proud of it, though he clearly recognizes it. Also, true composition is inexplicable. No one can explain how the notes of a Mozart melody, of the folds of a piece of Titian's drapery, produce their essential effects on each other. If you do not feel it, no one can by reasoning make you feel it. And the highest composition is so subtle, that it is apt to become unpopular, and sometimes seem insipid.

The reader may be surprised at my giving so high a place to invention. But if he ever come to know true invention from false, he will find that it is not only the highest quality of art, but is simply the most wonderful act or power of humanity. It is pre-eminently the deed of human creation; ποίησις, otherwise, poetry.

Men in their several professed employments, looked at broadly, may be properly arranged under five classes:—

1. Persons who see. These in modern language are sometimes called sight-seers, that being an occupation coming more and more into vogue every day. Anciently they used to be called, simply, seers.

2. Persons who talk. These, in modern language, are usually called talkers, or speakers, as in the House of Commons, and elsewhere. They used to be called prophets.

3. Persons who make. These, in modern language, are usually called manufacturers. Anciently they were called poets.

211 4. Persons who think. There seems to be no very distinct modern title for this kind of person, anciently called philosophers, nevertheless we have a few of them among us.

5. Persons who do: in modern language, called practical persons; anciently, believers.

Of the first two classes I have only this to note—that we ought neither to say that a person sees, if he sees falsely, nor speaks, if he speaks falsely. For seeing falsely is worse than blindness, and speaking falsely, than silence. A man who is too dim-sighted to discern the road from the ditch, may feel which is which;—but if the ditch appears manifestly to him to be the road, and the road to be the ditch, what shall become of him? False seeing is unseeing, on the negative side of blindness; and false speaking, unspeaking,—on the negative side of silence.

To the persons who think, also, the same test applies very shrewdly. Theirs is a dangerous profession; and from the time of the Aristophanes thought-shop[6] to the great German establishment, or thought-manufactory, whose productions have, unhappily, taken in part the place of the older and more serviceable commodities of Nuremberg toys and Berlin wool, it has been often harmful enough to mankind. It should not be so, for a false thought is more distinctly and visibly no thought, than a false saying is no saying. But it is touching the two great productive classes of the doers and makers, that we have one or two important points to note here.

Has the reader ever considered, carefully, what is the meaning of "doing" a thing?

Suppose a rock falls from a hill-side, crushes a group of cottages, and kills

a number of people. The stone has produced a great effect in the world. If any one asks, respecting the broken roofs, "What did it?" you say the stone did it. Yet you don't talk of the deed of the stone. If you enquire farther, and find that a goat had been feeding beside the rock, and had loosened it by gnawing the roots of the grasses beneath, you find the goat   212
to be the active cause of the calamity, and you say the goat did it. Yet you don't call the goat the doer, nor talk of its evil deed. But if you find any one went up to the rock, in the night, and with deliberate purpose loosened it, that it might fall on the cottages, you say in quite a different sense, "It is his deed; he is the doer of it."

It appears, then, that deliberate purpose and resolve are needed to constitute a deed or doing, in the true sense of the word; and that when, accidentally or mechanically, events take place without such purpose, we have indeed effects or results, and agents or causes, but neither deeds nor doers.

Now it so happens, as we all know, that by far the largest part of things happening in practical life *are* brought about with no deliberate purpose. There are always a number of people who have the nature of stones; they fall on other persons and crush them. Some again have the nature of weeds, and twist about other people's feet and entangle them. More have the nature of logs, and lie in the way, so that every one falls over them. And most of all have the nature of thorns, and set themselves by waysides, so that every passer-by must be torn, and all good seed choked; or perhaps make wonderful crackling under various pots, even to the extent of practically boiling water and working pistons. All these people produce immense and sorrowful effect in the world. Yet none of them are doers; it is their nature to crush, impede, and prick; but deed is not in them.

And farther, observe, that even when some effect is finally intended, you cannot call it the person's deed, unless it is *what* he intended.

If an ignorant person, purposing evil, accidentally does good, (as if a thief's disturbing a family should lead them to discover in time that their   213
house was on fire); or, *vice versâ*, if an ignorant person intending good accidentally does evil (as if a child should give hemlock to his companions for celery), in neither case do you call them the doers of what may result. So that in order to a true deed, it is necessary that the effect of it should be foreseen. Which, ultimately, it cannot be, but by a person who knows, and in his deed obeys, the laws of the universe, and of its Maker. And this knowledge is in its highest form, respecting the will of the Ruling Spirit, called Trust. For it is not the knowledge that a thing is, but that, according to the promise and nature of the Ruling Spirit, a thing will be. Also obedience in its highest form is not obedience to a constant and compulsory law, but a persuaded or voluntarily yielded obedience to an issued command.

214   Thus far then of practical persons, once called believers, as set forth in the last word of the noblest group of words ever, so far as I know, uttered by simple man concerning his practice, being the final testimony of the leaders of a great practical nation, whose deed thenceforward became an example of deed to mankind:

Ὦ ξεῖν᾽, ἀγγέλλειν Λακεδαιμονίοις, ὅτι τῇδε
κείμεθα, τοῖς κείνων ῥήμασι πειθόμενοι.

"O stranger! (we pray thee), tell the Lacedæmonians that we are lying here, having *obeyed* their words."[7]

What, let us ask next, is the ruling character of the person who produces—the creator or maker, anciently called the poet?

We have seen what a deed is. What then is a "creation"? Nay, it may be replied, to "create" cannot be said of man's labour.

On the contrary, it not only can be said, but is and must be said continually. You certainly do not talk of creating a watch, or creating a shoe; nevertheless you *do* talk of creating a feeling. Why is this?

Look back to the greatest of all creations, that of the world. Suppose the trees had been ever so well or so ingeniously put together, stem and leaf, yet if they had not been able to grow, would they have been well created? Or suppose the fish had been cut and stitched finely out of skin and whalebone; yet, cast upon the waters, had not been able to swim? Or suppose Adam and Eve had been made in the softest clay, ever so neatly, and set

215   at the foot of the tree of knowledge, fastened up to it, quite unable to fall, or do anything else, would they have been well created, or in any true sense created at all?

It will, perhaps, appear to you, after a little farther thought, that to create anything in reality is to put life into it.

A poet, or creator, is therefore a person who puts things together, not as a watchmaker steel, or a shoemaker leather, but who puts life into them.

His work is essentially this: it is the gathering and arranging of material by imagination, so as to have in it at last the harmony or helpfulness of life, and the passion or emotion of life. Mere fitting and adjustment of material is nothing; that is watchmaking. But helpful and passionate harmony, essentially choral harmony, is the harmony of Apollo and the Muses. For which reason I could not bear to use any baser word than this of invention. And if the reader will think over these things, and follow them out, he will not any more think it wrong in me to place invention

216   so high among the powers of man. Nor any more think it strange that the last act of the life of Socrates should have been to purify himself from the sin of having negligently listened to the voice within him, which, through all his past life, had bid him "labour, and make harmony."[8]

CHAPTER II
The Task of the Least

T HE reader has probably been surprised at my assertions made often   217
before now,[9] and reiterated here, that the *minutest* portion of a great
composition is helpful to the whole. It certainly does not seem easily
conceivable that this should be so. I will go farther, and say that it is
inconceivable. But it is the fact.

We shall discern it to be so by taking one or two compositions to pieces,
and examining the fragments. In doing which, we must remember that a
great composition always has a leading emotional purpose, technically
called its motive, to which all its lines and forms have some relation.
Undulating lines, for instance, are expressive of action; and would be false
in effect if the motive of the picture was one of repose. Horizontal and
angular lines are expressive of rest and strength; and would destroy a
design whose purpose was to express disquiet and feebleness. It is therefore
necessary to ascertain the motive before descending to the detail.

One of the simplest subjects, in the series of the Rivers of France, is
"Rietz, near Saumur" [fig.46]. My rough etching, fig.47, sufficiently
shows the arrangement of its lines. What is their motive?

To get at it completely, we must know something of the Loire.

The district through which it here flows is, for the most part, a low   218
place, yet not altogether at the level of the stream, but cut into steep
banks of chalk or gravel, thirty or forty feet high, running for miles at
about an equal height above the water.

These banks are excavated by the peasantry, partly for houses, partly for
cellars, so economizing vineyard space above; and thus a kind of continuous village runs along the river-side, composed half of caves, half of
rude buildings, backed by the cliff, propped against it, therefore always
leaning away from the river; mingled with overlappings of vineyard trellis
from above, and little towers or summer-houses for outlook, when the
grapes are ripe, or for gossip over the garden wall.

It is an autumnal evening, then, by this Loire side. The day has been
hot, and the air is heavy and misty still; the sunlight warm, but dim; the
brown vine-leaves motionless: all else quiet. Not a sail in sight on the

fig.46   J. M. W. Turner, *Rietz near Saumur*

fig.47   John Ruskin, *Loire-side* (engraving after J. M. W. Turner)

river, its strong noiseless current lengthening the stream of low sunlight.

The motive of the picture, therefore, is the expression of rude but perfect peace, slightly mingled with an indolent languor and despondency; the space between intervals of enforced labour; happy, but listless, and having little care or hope about the future; cutting its home out of this gravel bank, and letting the vine and the river twine and undermine as they will; careless to mend or build, so long as the walls hold together, and the black fruit swells in the sunshine.

To get this repose, together with rude stability, we have therefore horizontal lines and bold angles. The grand horizontal space and sweep of Turner's distant river depend wholly for value on the piece of near wall. It is the vertical line of its dark side which drives the eye up into the   219 distance, right against the horizontal, and so makes it felt, while the flatness of the stone prepares the eye to understand the flatness of the river. Farther: hide with your finger the little ring on that stone, and you will find the river has stopped flowing. That ring is to repeat the curved lines of the river bank, which express its line of current, and to bring the feeling of them down near us. On the other side of the road the horizontal lines are taken up again by the dark pieces of wood, without which we should still lose half our space.

Next: The repose is to be not only perfect, but indolent: the repose of out-wearied people; not caring much what becomes of them.

You see the road is covered with litter. Even the crockery is left outside the cottage to dry in the sun, after being washed up. The steps of the cottage door have been too high for comfort originally, only it was less trouble to cut three large stones than four or five small. They are now all aslope and broken, not repaired for years. Their weighty forms increase the sense of languor throughout the scene, and of stability also, because we feel how difficult it would be to stir them. The crockery has its work to do also;—the arched door on the left being necessary to show the great thickness of walls and the strength they require to prevent falling in of the cliff above;—as the horizontal lines must be diffused on the right, so this arch must be diffused on the left; and the large round plate on one side of the steps, with the two small ones on the other, are to carry down the element of circular curvature. Hide them, and see the result.

As they carry the arched group of forms down, the arched window-shutter diffuses it upwards, where all the lines of the distant buildings suggest one and the same idea of disorderly and careless strength, mingling masonry with rock.

So far of the horizontal and curved lines. How of the radiating ones?   220 What has the black vine trellis got to do?

Lay a pencil or ruler parallel with its lines. You will find that they point to the massive building in the distance. To which, as nearly as is possible without at once showing the artifice, every other radiating line points also; almost ludicrously when it is once pointed out; even the curved line of the top of the terrace runs into it, and the last sweep of the river evidently leads to its base. And so nearly is it in the exact centre of the picture, that one diagonal from corner to corner passes through it, and the other only misses the base by the twentieth of an inch.

If you are accustomed to France, you will know in a moment by its outline that this massive building is an old church.

Without it, the repose would not have been essentially the labourer's rest—rest as of the Sabbath. Among all the groups of lines that point to it, two are principal: the first, those of the vine trellis: the second, those of the handles of the saw left in the beam: the blessing of human life, and its labour.

Whenever Turner wishes to express profound repose, he puts in the foreground some instrument of labour cast aside. See, in Rogers's *Poems*, the last vignette, "Datur hora quieti," [fig.48] with the plough in the furrow: and in the first vignette of the same book, the scythe on the shoulder of the peasant going home. (There is nothing about the scythe in the passage of the poem which this vignette illustrates.)

Observe, farther, the outline of the church itself. As our habitations are, so is our church, evidently a heap of old, but massive walls, patched, and

fig.48 engraving after J.M.W.Turner, *Datur hora quieti*, from *Poems*
by Samuel Rogers

repaired, and roofed in, and over and over, until its original shape is hardly recognizable. I know the kind of church well—can tell even here, two   221 miles off, that I shall find some Norman arches in the apse, and a flam-boyant porch, rich and dark, with every statue broken out of it; and a rude wooden belfry above all; and a quantity of miserable shops built in among the buttresses; and that I may walk in and out as much as I please, but that how often soever, I shall always find some one praying at the Holy Sepulchre, in the darkest aisle, and my going in and out will not disturb them. For they *are* praying, which in many a handsomer and highlier-furbished edifice might, perhaps, not be so assuredly the case.

Lastly: What kind of people have we on this winding road? Three indolent ones, leaning on the wall to look over into the gliding water; and a matron with her market panniers; by her figure, not a fast rider. The road, besides, is bad, and seems unsafe for trotting, and she has passed without disturbing the cat, who sits comfortably on the block of wood in the middle of it.

Next to this piece of quietness, let us glance at a composition in which the motive is one of tumult: that of the Fall of Schaffhausen [plate 18]. I have etched in fig.49 at the top, the chief lines of its composition, in which the first great purpose is to give swing enough to the water. The line of fall is straight and monotonous in reality. Turner wants to get the great concave sweep and rush of the river well felt, in spite of the unbroken form. The column of spray, rocks, mills, and bank, all radiate like a plume,   222 sweeping round together in grand curves to the left, where the group of figures, hurried about the ferry boat, rises like a dash of spray; they also radiating: so as to form one perfectly connected cluster, with the two gens-d'armes and the millstones; the millstones at the bottom being the root of it; the two soldiers laid right and left to sustain the branch of figures beyond, balanced just as a tree bough would be.

One of the gens-d'armes is flirting with a young lady in a round cap and full sleeves, under pretence of wanting her to show him what she has in her bandbox. The motive of which flirtation is, so far as Turner is concerned in it, primarily the bandbox: this and the millstones below, give him a series of concave lines, which, concentrated by the recumbent soldiers, intensify the hollow sweep of the fall, precisely as the ring on the stone does the Loire eddies. These curves are carried out on the right by the small plate of eggs, laid to be washed at the spring; and, all these concave lines being a little too quiet and recumbent, the staggering casks are set on the left, and the ill-balanced milk-pail on the right, to give a general feeling of things being rolled over and over. The things which are to give this sense of rolling are dark, in order to hint at the way in which the cataract rolls boulders of rock; while the forms which are to give the sense of its sweeping force are white. The little spring, splashing out of its

fig.49   John Ruskin, *The Falls of Schaffhausen* (engraving after J.M.W. Turner)

pine-trough, is to give contrast with the power of the fall,—while it carries out the general sense of splashing water.

This spring exists on the spot, and so does everything else in the picture; but the combinations are wholly arbitrary; it being Turner's fixed principle to collect out of any scene, whatever was characteristic, and put it together just as he liked. The changes made in this instance are highly curious. The mills have no resemblance whatever to the real group as seen from this spot; for there is a vulgar and formal dwelling-house in front of them. But if you climb the rock behind them, you find they form on that side a towering cluster, which Turner has put with little modification into the drawing. What he has done to the mills, he has done with still greater audacity to the central rock. Seen from this spot, it shows, in reality, its greatest breadth, and is heavy and uninteresting; but on the Lauffen side, exposes its consumed base, worn away by the rush of water, which Turner resolving to show, serenely draws the rock as it appears from the other side of the Rhine, and brings that view of it over to this side.

Finally, the castle of Lauffen itself, being, when seen from this spot, too much foreshortened to show its extent, Turner walks a quarter of a mile lower down the river, draws the castle accurately there, brings it back with him, and puts it in all its extent, where he chooses to have it, beyond the rocks.

These two examples may sufficiently serve to show the mode in which

minor details, both in form and spirit, are used by Turner to aid his main motives; of course I cannot, in the space of this volume, go on examining subjects at this length, even if I had time to etch them; but every design of Turner's would be equally instructive, examined in a similar manner.   224
All that I can do is to indicate the vast field open to the student's analysis   228
if he cares to pursue the subject; and to mark for the general reader these two strong conclusions:—that nothing in great work is ever either fortuitous or contentious.

It is not fortuitous; that is to say, not left to fortune. The "must do it by a kind of felicity" of Bacon[10] is true; it is true also that an accident is often suggestive to an inventor. Turner himself said, "I never lose an accident." But it is this not *losing* it, this taking things out of the hands of Fortune, and putting them into those of force and foresight, which attest the   229
master. Chance may sometimes help, and sometimes provoke, a success; but must never rule, and rarely allure.

And, lastly, nothing must be contentious. Art has many uses and many pleasantnesses; but of all its services, none are higher than its setting forth, by a visible and enduring image, the nature of all true authority and freedom;—Authority which defines and directs the action of benevolent law; and Freedom which consists in deep and soft consent of individual helpfulness.

CHAPTER III
The Rule of the Greatest

230   I N the entire range of art principles, none perhaps present a difficulty so great to the student, or require from the teacher expression so cautious, and yet so strong, as those which concern the nature and influence of magnitude.

In one sense, and that deep, there is no such thing as magnitude. The least thing is as the greatest, and one day as a thousand years, in the eyes of the Maker of great and small things. In another sense, and that close to us and necessary, there exist both magnitude and value. Though not a sparrow falls to the ground unnoted, there are yet creatures who are of more value than many; and the same Spirit which weighs the dust of the earth in a balance, counts the isles as a little thing.

The just temper of human mind in this matter may, nevertheless, be told shortly. Greatness can only be rightly estimated when minuteness is justly reverenced. Greatness is the aggregation of minuteness; nor can its sublimity be felt truthfully by any mind unaccustomed to the affectionate watching of what is least.

But if this affection for the least be unaccompanied by the powers of comparison and reflection; if it be intemperate in its thirst, restless in curiosity, and incapable of the patient and self-commandant pause which is wise to arrange, and submissive to refuse, it will close the paths of noble art to the student as effectually, and hopelessly, as even the blindness of pride, or impatience of ambition.

231   I say the paths of noble art, not of useful art. All accurate investigation will have its reward; the morbid curiosity will at least slake the thirst of others, if not its own; and the diffused and petty affections will distribute, in serviceable measure, their minute delights and narrow discoveries. The opposite error, the desire of greatness as such, or rather of what appears great to indolence and vanity;—the instinct which I have described in the *Seven Lamps*,[11] noting it, among the Renaissance builders, to be an especial and unfailing sign of baseness of mind, is as fruitless as it is vile; no way profitable—every way harmful; the widest and most corrupting expression of vulgarity. The microscopic drawing of an insect may be

precious; but nothing except disgrace and misguidance will ever be gathered from such work as that of Haydon or Barry.[12]

The work I have mostly had to do, since this essay was begun, has been that of contention against such debased issues of swollen insolence and windy conceit; but I have noticed lately, that some lightly-budding philosophers have depreciated true greatness; confusing the relations of scale, as they bear upon human instinct and morality; reasoning as if a mountain were no nobler than a grain of sand, or as if many souls were not of mightier interest than one. To whom it must be shortly answered that the Lord of power and life knew which were His noblest works, when He bade His servant watch the play of the Leviathan, rather than dissect the spawn of the minnow; and that when it comes to practical question whether a single soul is to be jeoparded for many, such question is to be   232 solved by the simple human instinct respecting number and magnitude, not by reasoning on infinity:—

"Le navigateur, qui, la nuit, voit l'océan étinceler de lumière, danser en guirlande de feu, s'égaye d'abord de ce spectacle. Il fait dix lieues; la guirlande s'allonge indéfiniment, elle s'agite, se tord, se noue, aux mouvements de la lame; c'est un serpent monstrueux qui va toujours s'allongeant, jusqu'à trente lieues, quarante lieues. Et tout cela n'est qu'une danse d'animalcules imperceptibles. En quel nombre? À cette question l'imagination s'effraye; elle sent là une autre nature, de puissance immense, de richesse épouvantable. ... Que sont ces petits des petits? Rien moins que les constructeurs du globe où nous sommes. De leurs corps, de leurs débris, ils ont préparé le sol qui est sous nos pas. ... Et ce sont les plus petits qui ont fait les plus grandes choses. L'imperceptible rhizopode s'est bâti un monument bien autre que les Pyramides, pas moins que l'Italie centrale, une notable partie de la chaîne des Apennins. Mais c'était trop peu encore; les masses énormes du Chili, les prodigieuses Cordillières qui regardent le monde à leurs pieds, sont le monument funéraire où cet être insaisissable, et pour ainsi dire, invisible, a enseveli les débris de son espèce disparue."—(Michelet: *L'Insecte.*)

In these passages, and those connected with them in the chapter from which they are taken,[13] itself so vast in scope, and therefore so sublime, we may perhaps find the true relations of minuteness, multitude, and magnitude. We shall not feel that there is no such thing as littleness, or no such thing as magnitude. Nor shall we be disposed to confuse a Volvox with the Cordilleras; but we may learn that they both are bound together by links of eternal life and toil; we shall see the vastest thing noble, chiefly for what it includes; and the meanest for what it accomplishes. Thence we might gather—and the conclusion will be found in experience true—that the sense of largeness would be most grateful to minds capable of comprehending, balancing, and comparing; but capable also of great patience and expectation; while the sense of minute wonderfulness would

233　be attractive to minds acted upon by sharp, small, penetrative sympathies, and apt to be impatient, irregular, and partial. This fact is curiously shown in the relations between the temper of the great composers and the modern pathetic school.[14] I was surprised at the first rise of that school, now some years ago, by observing how they restrained themselves to subjects which in other hands would have been wholly uninteresting: and in their succeeding efforts, I saw with increasing wonder, that they were almost destitute of the power of feeling vastness, or enjoying the forms which expressed it. A mountain or great building only appeared to them as a piece of colour of a certain shape. The powers it represented, or included, were invisible to them. In general they avoided subjects expressing space or mass, and fastened on confined, broken, and sharp forms; liking furze, fern, reeds, straw, stubble, dead leaves, and such like, better than strong stones, broad-flowing leaves, or rounded hills; in all such greater things, when forced to paint them, they missed the main and mighty lines; and this no less in what they loved than in what they disliked; for though fond of foliage, their trees always had a tendency to congeal into little acicular[15] thorn-hedges, and never tossed free. Which modes of choice proceed naturally from a petulant sympathy with local and immediately visible interests or sorrows, not regarding their large consequences, nor capable of understanding more massive view or more deeply deliberate mercifulness;—but peevish and horror-struck, and often incapable of self-control, though not of self-sacrifice. There are more people who can forget themselves than govern themselves.

This narrowly pungent and bitter virtue has, however, its beautiful uses, and is of special value in the present day, when surface-work, shallow generalization, and cold arithmetical estimates of things, are among the chief dangers and causes of misery, which men have to deal with.

234　On the other hand, and in clear distinction from all such workers, it is to be remembered that the great composers, not less deep in feeling, are in the fixed habit of regarding as much the relations and positions, as the separate nature, of things; that they reap and thresh in the sheaf, never pluck ears to rub in the hand; fish with net, not line, and sweep their prey together within great cords of errorless curve;—that nothing ever bears to them a separate or isolated aspect, but leads or links a chain of aspects— that to them it is not merely the surface, nor the substance, or anything that is of import; but its circumference and continence; that they are pre-eminently patient and reserved; observant, not curious;—comprehensive, not conjectural; calm exceedingly; unerring, constant, terrible in stedfastness of intent; unconquerable; incomprehensible; always suggesting, implying, including, more than can be told.

And this may be seen down to their treatment of the smallest things.

For there is nothing so small but we may, as we choose, see it in the whole, or in part, and in subdued connection with other things, or in individual and petty prominence. The greatest treatment is always that which gives conception the widest range, and most harmonious guidance;—it being permitted us to employ a certain quantity of time, and certain number of touches of pencil—he who with these embraces the largest sphere of thought, and suggests within that sphere the most perfect order of thought, has wrought the most wisely, and therefore most nobly.

I do not, however, purpose here to examine or illustrate the nature of great treatment—to do so effectually would need many examples from the figure composers. Here I will only state in conclusion what it is 235 chiefly important for all students to be convinced of, that all the technical qualities by which greatness of treatment is known, such as reserve in colour, tranquillity and largeness of line, and refusal of unnecessary objects of interest are, when they are real, the exponents of an habitually noble temper of mind, never the observances of a precept supposed to be useful. The refusal or reserve of a mighty painter cannot be imitated; it is only by reaching the same intellectual strength that you will be able to give an equal dignity to your self-denial. No one can tell you beforehand what to accept, or what to ignore; only remember always, in painting as in eloquence, the greater your strength, the quieter will be your manner, and the fewer your words; and in painting, as in all the arts and acts of life, the secret of high success will be found, not in a fretful and various excellence, but in a quiet singleness of justly chosen aim.

CHAPTER IV
The Law of Perfectness

236   A MONG the several characteristics of great treatment which in the last chapter were alluded to without being enlarged upon, one will be found several times named;—reserve.

It is necessary for our present purpose that we should understand this quality more distinctly. I mean by it the power which a great painter exercises over himself in fixing certain limits, either of force, of colour, or of quantity of work;—limits which he will not transgress in any part of his picture, even though here and there a painful sense of incompletion may exist, under the fixed conditions, and might tempt an inferior workman to infringe them. The nature of this reserve we must understand in order that we may also determine the nature of true completion or perfectness, which is the end of composition.

For perfectness, properly so called, means harmony. The word signifies literally the doing our work *thoroughly*. It does not mean carrying it up to any constant and established degree of finish, but carrying the whole of it up to a degree determined upon. In a chalk or pencil sketch by a great master, it will often be found that the deepest shades are feeble tints of pale gray; the outlines nearly invisible, and the forms brought out by a ghostly delicacy of touch, which, on looking close to the paper, will be indistinguishable from its general texture. A single line of ink, occurring

237   anywhere in such a drawing, would of course destroy it; placed in the darkness of a mouth or nostril, it would turn the expression into a caricature; on a cheek or brow it would be simply a blot. Yet let the blot remain, and let the master work up to it with lines of similar force; and the drawing which was before perfect, in terms of pencil, will become, under his hand, perfect in terms of ink; and what was before a scratch on the cheek will become a necessary and beautiful part of its gradation.

All great work is thus reduced under certain conditions, and its right to be called complete depends on its fulfilment of them, not on the nature of the conditions chosen. Habitually, indeed, we call a coloured work which is satisfactory to us, finished, and a chalk drawing unfinished; but in the mind of the master, all his work is, according to the sense in which you use the word, equally perfect or imperfect. Perfect, if you regard its purpose and limitation; imperfect, if you compare it with the natural standard. In what appears to you consummate, the master has assigned to himself terms of shortcoming, and marked with a sad severity the point up to which he will permit himself to contend with nature. Were it not for his acceptance of such restraint, he could neither quit his work, nor endure it. He could not quit it, for he would always perceive more that might be done; he could not endure it, because all doing ended only in more elaborate deficiency.

But we are apt to forget in modern days, that the reserve of a man who is not putting forth half his strength is different in manner and dignity from the effort of one who can do no more. Charmed, and justly charmed, by the harmonious sketches of great painters, and by the grandeur of their acquiescence in the point of pause, we have put ourselves to produce sketches as an end instead of a means, and thought to imitate the painter's scornful restraint of his own power, by a scornful rejection of the things beyond ours. For many reasons, therefore, it becomes desirable to understand precisely and finally what a good painter means by completion.

The sketches of true painters may be classed under the following   238
heads:—

I. *Experimental.*—In which they are assisting an imperfect conception of a subject by trying the look of it on paper in different ways.

By the greatest men this kind of sketch is hardly ever made; they conceive their subjects distinctly at once, and their sketch is not to try them, but to fasten them down. Raphael's form the only important exception—and the numerous examples of experimental work by him are evidence of his composition being technical rather than imaginative. I have never seen a drawing of the kind by any great Venetian. Among the nineteen thousand sketches[16] by Turner—which I arranged in the National Gallery—there was, to the best of my recollection, *not one.*

II. *Determinant.*—The fastening down of an idea in the simplest terms, in order that it may not be disturbed or confused by after work. Nearly all the great composers do this, methodically, before beginning a painting. Such sketches are usually in a high degree resolute and compressive; the best of them outlined or marked calmly with the pen, and deliberately washed with colour, indicating the places of the principal lights.

Fine drawings of this class never show any hurry or confusion. They are the expression of concluded operations of mind, are drawn slowly, and are not so much sketches, as maps.

III. *Commemorative.*—Containing records of facts which the master required. These in their most elaborate form are "studies," or drawings from Nature, of parts needed in the composition, often highly finished in

239 the part which is to be introduced. In this form, however, they never occur by the greatest imaginative masters. For by a truly great inventor everything is invented; no atom of the work is unmodified by his mind; and no study from Nature, however beautiful, could be introduced by him into his design without change; it would not fit with the rest. Finished studies for introduction are therefore chiefly by Leonardo and Raphael, both technical designers rather than imaginative ones.

Commemorative sketches by great masters are generally hasty, merely to put them in mind of motives of invention, or they are shorthand memoranda of things with which they do not care to trouble their memory; or, finally, accurate notes of things which they must *not* modify by invention, as local detail, costume, and such like. You may find perfectly accurate drawings of coats of arms, portions of dresses, pieces of architecture, and so on, by all the great men; but you will not find elaborate studies of bits of their pictures.

When the sketch is made merely as a memorandum, it is impossible to say how little, or what kind of drawing, may be sufficient for the purpose. It is of course likely to be hasty from its very nature, and unless the exact purpose be understood, it may be as unintelligible as a piece of shorthand writing.

241 Fig. 50 is a facsimile of one of Turner's "memoranda," of a complete subject, Lausanne, from the road to Fribourg.

This example is entirely characteristic of his usual drawings from nature, which unite two characters, being *both* commemorative and determinant:—Commemorative, in so far as they note certain facts about

fig.50 John Ruskin, *Lausanne from the Road to Fribourg*
(engraving after J.M.W. Turner)

the place: determinant, in that they record an impression received from the place there and then, together with the principal arrangement of the composition in which it was afterwards to be recorded. In this mode of sketching, Turner differs from all other men whose work I have studied. He never draws accurately on the spot, with the intention of modifying or composing afterwards from the materials; but instantly modifies as he draws, placing his memoranda where they are to be ultimately used, and taking exactly what he wants, not a fragment or line more.

This sketch has been made in the afternoon. He had been impressed, as   242
he walked up the hill, by the vanishing of the lake in the golden horizon, without end of waters, and by the opposition of the pinnacled castle and cathedral to its level breadth. That must be drawn! and from this spot, where all the buildings are set well together. But it lucklessly happens that, though the buildings come just where he wants them in situation, they don't in height. For the castle (the square mass on the right) is in reality higher than the cathedral, and would block out the end of the lake. Down it goes instantly a hundred feet, that we may see the lake over it; without the smallest regard for the military position of Lausanne.

Next: The last low spire on the left is in truth concealed behind the nearer bank, the town running far down the hill (and climbing another hill) in that direction. But the group of spires, without it, would not be rich enough to give a proper impression of Lausanne, as a spiry place. Turner quietly sends to fetch the church from round the corner, places it where he likes, and indicates its distance only by aerial perspective (much greater in the pencil drawing than in the woodcut).

But again: Not only the spire of the lower church, but the peak of the Rochers d'Enfer (that highest in the distance) would in reality be out of sight; it is much farther round to the left. This would never do either; for without it, we should have no idea that Lausanne was opposite the mountains, nor should we have a nice sloping line to lead us into the distance.

With the same unblushing tranquillity of mind in which he had ordered up the church, Turner sends also to fetch the Rochers d'Enfer; and puts *them* also where he chooses, to crown the slope of distant hill, which, as every traveller knows, in its decline to the west, is one of the most notable features of the view from Lausanne.

These modifications, easily traceable in the large features of the design, are carried out with equal audacity and precision in every part of it. Every   243
one of those confused lines on the right indicates something that is really there, only everything is shifted and sorted into the exact places that Turner chose. The group of dark objects near us at the foot of the bank is a cluster of mills, which, when the picture was completed, were to be the blackest things in it, and to throw back the castle, and the golden horizon;

while the rounded touches at the bottom, under the castle, indicate a row of trees, which follow a brook coming out of the ravine behind us; and were going to be made very round indeed in the picture (to oppose the spiky and angular masses of castle), and very consecutive, in order to form another conducting line into the distance.

These motives, or motives like them, might perhaps be guessed on looking at the sketch. But no one without going to the spot would understand the meaning of the vertical lines in the left-hand lowest corner.

They are a "memorandum" of the artificial verticalness of a low sandstone cliff, which has been cut down there to give space for a bit of garden belonging to a public-house beneath, from which garden a path leads along the ravine to the Lausanne rifle-ground. The value of these vertical lines in repeating those of the cathedral, is very great; it would be greater still in the completed picture, increasing the sense of looking down from a height, and giving grasp of, and power over, the whole scene.

Throughout the sketch, as in all that Turner made, the observing and combining intellect acts in the same manner. Not a line is lost, nor a moment of time; and though the pencil flies, and the whole thing is literally done as fast as a piece of shorthand writing, it is to the full as purposeful and compressed, so that while there are indeed dashes of the pencil which are unintentional, they are only unintentional as the form of a letter is, in fast writing, not from want of intention, but from the accident of haste.

244   I know not if the reader can understand,—I myself cannot, though I see it to be demonstrable,—the simultaneous occurrence of idea which produces such a drawing as this: the grasp of the whole, from the laying of the first line, which induces continual modifications of all that is done, out of respect to parts not done yet. No line is ever changed or effaced: no experiment made; but every touch is placed with reference to all that are to succeed, as to all that have gone before; every addition takes its part, as the stones in an arch of a bridge; the last touch locks the arch. Remove that keystone, or remove any other of the stones of the vault, and the whole will fall.

I repeat—the power of mind which accomplishes this, is yet wholly inexplicable to me, as it was when first I defined it in the chapter on imagination associative, in the second volume.[17] But the grandeur of the power impresses me daily more and more; and, in quitting the subject of invention, let me assert finally, in clearest and strongest terms, that no painting is of any true imaginative perfectness at all, unless it has been thus conceived.

One sign of its being thus conceived may be always found in the straightforwardness of its work. There are continual disputes among artists as to the best way of doing things, which may nearly all be resolved into confessions of indetermination. If you know precisely what you want, you will not feel much hesitation in setting about it; and a picture may be painted almost any way, so only that it be a straight way. Give a true painter a ground of black, white, scarlet, or grèen, and out of it he will bring what you choose. From the black, brightness; from the white, sadness; from the scarlet, coolness; from the green, glow; he will make anything out of anything, but in each case his method will be pure, direct, perfect, the shortest and simplest possible. You will find him, moreover, indifferent as to succession of process. Ask him to begin at the bottom of the picture instead of the top,—to finish two square inches of it without touching the rest, or to lay a separate ground for every part before finishing any;—it is all the same to him! What he will do, if left to himself, depends on mechanical convenience, and on the time at his disposal. But the absolutely best, or centrally, and entirely *right* way of painting is as follows:—   245

A light ground, white, red, yellow, or gray, not brown, or black. On that an entirely accurate, and firm black outline of the whole picture, in its principal masses. The outline to be exquisitely correct as far as it reaches, but not to include small details; the use of it being to limit the masses of first colour. The ground-colours then to be laid firmly, each on its own proper part of the picture, as inlaid work in a mosaic table, meeting each other truly at the edges: as much of each being laid as will get itself into the state which the artist requires it to be in for his second painting, by the time he comes to it. On this first colour, the second colours and subordinate masses laid in due order, now, of course, necessarily without previous outline, and all small detail reserved to the last, the bracelet being not touched, nor indicated in the least, till the arm is finished.

This is, as far as it can be expressed in a few words, the right, or Venetian   246
way of painting; but it is incapable of absolute definition, for it depends on the scale, the material, and the nature of the object represented, *how much* a great painter will do with his first colour; or how many after processes he will use. Very often the first colour, richly blended and worked into, is also the last; sometimes it wants a glaze only to modify it; sometimes an entirely different colour above it. Turner's storm-blues, for instance, were produced by a black ground with opaque blue, mixed with white, struck over it. The amount of detail given in the first colour will also depend on convenience. For instance, if a jewel *fastens* a fold of dress, a Venetian will lay probably a piece of the jewel colour in its place at the time he draws the fold; but if the jewel *falls upon* the dress, he will paint the folds only in the ground colour, and the jewel afterwards. For in the first case his hand must pause, at any rate, where the fold is fastened; so that he may as well mark the colour of the gem: but he would have to check his hand in

the sweep with which he drew the drapery, if he painted a jewel that fell upon it with the first colour. So far, however, as he can possibly use the under colour, he will, in whatever he has to superimpose. There is a pretty little instance of such economical work in the painting of the pearls on the breast of the elder princess, in our best Paul Veronese (Family of Darius) [plate 16 & fig.51]. The lowest is about the size of a small hazel-nut, and

247 falls on her rose-red dress. Any other but a Venetian would have put a complete piece of white paint over the dress, for the whole pearl, and painted into that the colours of the stone. But Veronese knows beforehand that all the dark side of the pearl will reflect the red of the dress. He will not put white over the red, only to put red over the white again. He leaves the actual dress for the dark side of the pearl, and with two small separate touches, one white, another brown, places its high light and shadow. This he does with perfect care and calm; but in two decisive seconds. There is no dash, nor display, nor hurry, nor error. The exactly right thing is done in the exactly right place, and not one atom of colour, nor moment of time spent vainly. Look close at the two touches,—you wonder what they mean. Retire six feet from the picture—the pearl is there!

The degree in which the ground colours are extended over his picture, as he works, is to a great painter absolutely indifferent. It is all the same to him whether he grounds a head, and finishes it at once to the shoulders, leaving all round it white; or whether he grounds the whole picture. His harmony, paint as he will, never can be complete till the last touch is given; so long as it remains incomplete, he does not care how little of it is suggested, or how many notes are missing. All is wrong, till all is right; and he must be able to bear the all wrongness till his work is done, or he cannot paint at all. His mode of treatment will, therefore, depend on the nature of his subject, as is beautifully shown in the water-colour sketches by Turner in the National Gallery.[18] His general system was to complete inch by inch; leaving the paper quite white all round, especially if the work was to be delicate. The most exquisite drawings left unfinished in the collection—those at Rome and Naples—are thus outlined accurately on pure white paper, begun in the middle of the sheet, and worked out to

248 the side, finishing as he proceeds. If, however, any united effect of light or colour is to embrace a large part of the subject, he will lay it in with a broad wash over the whole paper at once; then paint into it, using it as a ground, and modifying it in the pure Venetian manner. His oil pictures were laid roughly with ground colours, and painted into with such rapid skill, that the artists who used to see him finishing at the Academy sometimes suspected him of having the picture finished underneath the colours he showed, and removing, instead of adding, as they watched.

But, whatever the means used may be, the certainty and directness of

fig.51 Paul Veronese, *The Family of Darius before Alexander* (detail)

them imply absolute grasp of the whole subject, and without this grasp there is no good painting. This, finally, let me declare, without qualification—that partial conception is no conception. The whole picture must be imagined, or none of it is. And this grasp of the whole implies very strange and sublime qualities of mind. It is not possible, unless the feelings are completely under control; the least excitement or passion will disturb the measured equity of power; a painter needs to be as cool as a general; and as little moved or subdued by his sense of pleasure, as a soldier by the sense of pain. Nothing good can be done without intense feeling; but it must be feeling so crushed, that the work is set about with mechanical steadiness, absolutely untroubled, as a surgeon—not without pity, but conquering it and putting it aside—begins an operation. Until the feelings can give strength enough to the will to enable it to conquer them, they are not strong enough. If you cannot leave your picture at any moment;—cannot turn from it, and go on with another, while the colour is drying;—cannot work at any part of it you choose with equal contentment—you have not firm enough grasp of it.

It follows, also, that no vain or selfish person can possibly paint, in the noble sense of the word. Vanity and selfishness are troublous, eager, anxious, petulant:—painting can only be done in calm of mind. Resolution is not enough to secure this; it must be secured by disposition as well. You may resolve to think of your picture only; but, if you have been fretted before beginning, no manly or clear grasp of it will be possible for you. No forced calm is calm enough. Only honest calm,—natural calm. You might as well try by external pressure to smooth a lake till it could reflect the sky, as by violence of effort to secure the peace through which only you can reach imagination. That peace must come in its own time; as the waters settle themselves into clearness as well as quietness; you can no more filter your mind into purity than you can compress it into calmness; you must keep it pure, if you would have it pure; and throw no stones into it, if you would have it quiet. Great courage and self-command may, to a certain extent, give power of painting without the true calmness underneath; but never of doing first-rate work. There is sufficient evidence of this, in even what we know of great men, though of the greatest, we nearly always know the least (and that necessarily; they being very silent, and not much given to setting themselves forth to questioners; apt to be contemptuously reserved, no less than unselfishly). But in such writings and sayings as we possess of theirs, we may trace a quite curious gentleness and serene courtesy. Rubens' letters are almost ludicrous in their unhurried politeness. Reynolds, swiftest of painters, was gentlest of companions; so also Velasquez, Titian, and Veronese.

It is gratuitous to add that no shallow or petty person can paint. Mere cleverness or special gift never made an artist. It is only perfectness of mind, unity, depth, decision,—the highest qualities, in fine, of the intellect, which will form the imagination.

And, lastly, no false person can paint. A person false at heart may, when it suits his purposes, seize a stray truth here or there; but the relations of truth,—its perfectness,—that which makes it wholesome truth, he can never perceive. As wholeness and wholesomeness go together, so also sight with sincerity; it is only the constant desire of and submissiveness to truth, which can measure its strange angles and mark its infinite aspects; and fit them and knit them into the strength of sacred invention.

Sacred, I call it deliberately; for it is thus, in the most accurate senses, humble as well as helpful; meek in its receiving, as magnificent in its disposing; the name it bears being rightly given even to invention formal, not because it forms, but because it finds. For you cannot find a lie; you must make it for yourself. False things may be imagined, and false things composed; but only truth can be invented.

PART IX

Of Ideas of Relation:—Second, of Invention Spiritual

CHAPTER I
The Dark Mirror

I N the course of our inquiry into the moral of landscape,[19] we promised   253
at the close of our work to seek for some better, or at least clearer, conclusions than were then possible to us. We confined ourselves in that
chapter to the vindication of the probable utility of the *love* of natural
scenery. We made no assertion of the usefulness of *painting* such scenery.
It might be well to delight in the real country, or admire the real flowers
and true mountains. But it did not follow that it was advisable to paint
them.

Far from it. Many reasons might be given why we should not paint
them. All the purposes of good which we saw that the beauty of Nature
could accomplish, may be better fulfilled by the meanest of her realities,
than by the brightest of imitations. For prolonged entertainment, no picture can be compared with the wealth of interest which may be found in
the herbage of the poorest field, or blossoms of the narrowest copse. As
suggestive of supernatural power, the passing away of a fitful raincloud, or
opening of dawn, are in their change and mystery more pregnant than any
pictures. A child would, I suppose, receive a religious lesson from a flower
more willingly than from a print of one; and might be taught to understand the nineteenth Psalm, on a starry night, better than by diagrams of
the constellations.

Whence it might seem a waste of time to draw landscape at all.   254

I believe it is;—to draw landscape mere and solitary, however beautiful
(unless it be for the sake of geographical or other science, or of historical
record). But there *is* a kind of landscape which it is not inexpedient to
draw.

All true landscape, whether simple or exalted, depends primarily for its   255
interest on connection with humanity, or with spiritual powers. Banish
your heroes and nymphs from the classical landscape—its laurel shades
will move you no more. Show that the dark clefts of the most romantic
mountain are uninhabited and untraversed; it will cease to be romantic.
Fields without shepherds and without fairies will have no gaiety in their
green, nor will the noblest masses of ground or colours of cloud arrest or
raise your thoughts, if the earth has no life to sustain, and the heaven none   256
to refresh.

It might perhaps be thought that, since from scenes in which the figure was principal, and landscape symbolical and subordinate (as in the art of Egypt), the process of ages had led us to scenes in which landscape was principal and the figure subordinate,—a continuance in the same current of feeling might bring forth at last an art from which humanity and its interests should wholly vanish, leaving us to the passionless admiration of herbage and stone. But this will not, and cannot, be. Fragrant tissue of flowers, golden circlets of clouds, are only fair when they meet the fondness of human thoughts, and glorify human visions of heaven.

257

It is the leaning on this truth which, more than any other, has been the distinctive character of all my own past work. And in closing a series of Art-studies, prolonged during so many years, it may be perhaps permitted me to point out this speciality—the rather that it has been, of all their characters, the one most denied. I constantly see that the same thing takes place in the estimation formed by the modern public of the work of almost any true person, living or dead. It is not needful to state here the causes of such error; but the fact is indeed so, that precisely the distinctive root and leading force of any true man's work and way are the things denied concerning him.

And in these books of mine, their distinctive character, as essays on art, is their bringing everything to a root in human passion or human hope. Arising first not in any desire to explain the principles of art, but in the endeavour to defend an individual painter from injustice, they have been coloured throughout,—nay, continually altered in shape, and even warped and broken, by digressions respecting social questions, which had for me an interest tenfold greater than the work I had been forced into undertaking. Every principle of painting which I have stated is traced to some vital or spiritual fact; and in my works on architecture the preference accorded finally to one school over another, is founded on a comparison of their influences on the life of the workman—a question by all other writers on the subject of architecture wholly forgotten or despised.

258

The essential connection of the power of landscape with human emotion is not less certain, because in many impressive pictures the link is slight or local. That the connection should exist at a single point is all that we need. The comparison with the dress of the body may be carried out into the extremest parallelism. It may often happen that no part of the figure wearing the dress is discernible, nevertheless, the perceivable fact that the drapery is worn by a figure makes all the difference. In one of the most sublime figures in the world this is actually so: one of the fainting Maries in Tintoret's Crucifixion [plate 14] has cast her mantle over her head, and her face is lost in its shade, and her whole figure veiled in folds of gray. But what the difference is between that gray woof, that gathers round her as she falls, and the same folds cast in a heap upon the ground, that difference, and more, exists between the power of Nature through which humanity is seen, and her power in the desert. Desert—whether of leaf or sand—true desertness is not in the want of leaves, but of life. Where humanity is not, and was not, the best natural beauty is more than vain. It is even terrible; not as the dress cast aside from the body; but as an embroidered shroud hiding a skeleton.

And on each side of a right feeling in this matter there lie, as usual, two opposite errors.

The first, that of caring for man only; and for the rest of the universe, little, or not at all, which, in a measure, was the error of the Greeks and Florentines; the other, that of caring for the universe only;—for man, not at all—which, in a measure, is the error of modern science, and of the Art connecting itself with such science.

The degree of power which any man may ultimately possess in landscape-painting will depend finally on his perception of this influence. If he has to paint the desert, its awfulness—if the garden, its gladsomeness—will arise simply and only from his sensibility to the story of life. Without this he is nothing but a scientific mechanist; this, though it cannot make him yet a painter, raises him to the sphere in which he may become one. Nay, the mere shadow and semblance of this have given dangerous power to works in all other respects unnoticeable; and the least degree of its true presence has given value to work in all other respects vain. 259

The true presence, observe, of sympathy with the spirit of man. Where this is not, sympathy with any higher spirit is impossible.

For the directest manifestation of Deity to man is in His own image, that is, in man.

"In His own image. After His likeness." *Ad imaginem et Similitudinem Suam.*[20] I do not know what people in general understand by those words. I suppose they ought to be understood. The truth they contain seems to lie at the foundation of our knowledge both of God and man; yet do we not usually pass the sentence by, in dull reverence, attaching no definite sense to it at all? For all practical purpose, might it not as well be out of the text?

I have no time, nor much desire, to examine the vague expressions of belief with which the verse has been encumbered. Let us try to find its only possible plain significance.

It cannot be supposed that the bodily shape of man resembles, or resembled, any bodily shape in Deity. The likeness must therefore be, or have been, in the soul. Had it wholly passed away, and the divine soul been altered into a soul brutal or diabolic, I suppose we should have been told of the change. But we are told nothing of the kind. The verse still stands as if for our use and trust. It was only death which was to be our

260 punishment. Not *change*. So far as we live, the image is still there; defiled, if you will; broken, if you will; all but effaced, if you will, by death and the shadow of it. But not changed. We are not made now in any other image than God's. There are, indeed, the two states of this image—the earthly and heavenly, but both Adamite, both human, both the same likeness; only one defiled, and one pure. So that the soul of man is still a mirror, wherein may be seen, darkly, the image of the mind of God.

These may seem daring words. I am sorry that they do; but I am helpless to soften them. Discover any other meaning of the text if you are able;—but be sure that it *is* a meaning—a meaning in your head and heart;—not a subtle gloss, nor a shifting of one verbal expression into another, both idealess. I repeat that, to me, the verse has, and can have, no other signification than this—that the soul of man is a mirror of the mind of God. A mirror, dark, distorted, broken, use what blameful words you please of its state; yet in the main, a true mirror, out of which alone, and by which alone, we can know anything of God at all.

"How?" the reader, perhaps, answers indignantly. "I know the nature of God by revelation, not by looking into myself."

Revelation to what? To a nature incapable of receiving truth? That cannot be; for only to a nature capable of truth, desirous of it, distinguishing it, feeding upon it, revelation is possible. To a being undesirous of it, and hating it, revelation is impossible. There can be none to a brute, or fiend. In so far, therefore, as you love truth, and live therein, in so far revelation can exist for you;—and in so far, your mind is the image of God's.

But consider, farther, not only *to* what, but *by* what, is the revelation. By sight? or word? If by sight, then to eyes which see justly. Otherwise, no sight would be revelation. So far, then, as your sight is just, it is the image of God's sight.

261 If by words,—how do you know their meanings? Here is a short piece of precious word revelation, for instance. "God is love." [21]

Love! yes. But what is *that*? The revelation does not tell you that, I think. Look into the mirror, and you will see. Out of your own heart, you may know what love is. In no other possible way,—by no other help or sign. All the words and sounds ever uttered, all the revelations of cloud, or flame, or crystal, are utterly powerless. They cannot tell you, in the smallest point, what love means. Only the broken mirror can.

Here is more revelation. "God is just!" [22] Just! What is that? The revelation cannot help you to discover. You say it is dealing equitably or equally. But how do you discern the equality? Not by inequality of mind; not by a mind incapable of weighing, judging, or distributing. If the lengths seem unequal in the broken mirror, for you they are unequal; but if they seem equal, then the mirror is true. So far as you recognize equality, and your conscience tells you what is just, so far your mind is the image of God's; and so far as you do *not* discern this nature of justice or equality, the words "God is just" bring no revelation to you.

"But His thoughts are not as our thoughts."[23] No; the sea is not as the standing pool by the wayside. Yet when the breeze crisps the pool, you may see the image of the breakers, and a likeness of the foam. Nay, in some sort, the same foam. If the sea is for ever invisible to you, something you may learn of it from the pool. Nothing, assuredly, any otherwise.

"But this poor miserable Me! Is *this*, then, all the book I have got to read about God in?" Yes, truly so. No other book, nor fragment of book, than that, will you ever find; no velvet-bound missal, nor frankincensed manuscript;—nothing hieroglyphic nor cuneiform; papyrus and pyramid   262
are alike silent on this matter;—nothing in the clouds above, nor in the earth beneath. That flesh-bound volume is the only revelation that is, that was, or that can be. In that is the image of God painted; in that is the law of God written; in that is the promise of God revealed. Know thyself; for through thyself only thou canst know God.

Through the glass, darkly.[24] But, except through the glass, in nowise.

A tremulous crystal, waved as water, poured out upon the ground;—you may defile it, despise it, pollute it, at your pleasure and at your peril; for on the peace of those weak waves must all the heaven you shall ever gain be first seen; and through such purity as you can win for those dark waves, must all the light of the risen Sun of Righteousness be bent down, by faint refraction. Cleanse them, and calm them, as you love your life.

Therefore it is that all the power of nature depends on subjection to the human soul. Man is the sun of the world; more than the real sun. The fire of his wonderful heart is the only light and heat worth gauge or measure. Where he is, are the tropics; where he is not, the ice-world.

CHAPTER II

The Lance of Pallas

263 I T might be thought that the tenor of the preceding chapter was in some sort adverse to my repeated statement that all great art is the expression of man's delight in God's work, not in *his own*. But observe, he is not himself his own work: he is himself precisely the most wonderful piece of God's workmanship extant. In this best piece not only he is bound to take delight, but cannot, in a right state of thought, take delight in anything else, otherwise than through himself. Through himself, however, as the sun of creation, not as *the* creation. In himself, as the light of the world. Not as being the world. Let him stand in his due relation to other creatures, and to inanimate things—know them all and love them, as made for him, and he for them;—and he becomes himself the greatest and holiest of them. But let him cast off this relation, despise and forget the less creation round him, and instead of being the light of the world, he is a sun in space—a fiery ball, spotted with storm.

All the diseases of mind leading to fatalest ruin consist primarily in this isolation. They are the concentration of man upon himself, whether his heavenly interests or his worldly interests, matters not; it is the being *his own* interests which makes the regard of them so mortal. Every form of asceticism on one side, of sensualism on the other, is an isolation of his

264 soul or of his body; the fixing his thoughts upon them alone; while every healthy state of nations and of individual minds consists in the unselfish presence of the human spirit everywhere, energizing over all things; speaking and living through all things.

Man being thus the crowning and ruling work of God, it will follow that all his best art must have something to tell about himself, as the soul of things, and ruler of creatures. It must also make this reference to himself under a true conception of his own nature. Therefore all art which involves no reference to man is inferior or nugatory. And all art which involves misconception of man, or base thought of him, is in that degree false and base.

Now the basest thought possible concerning him is, that he has no spiritual nature; and the foolishest misunderstanding of him possible is, that he has or should have, no animal nature. For his nature is nobly animal, nobly spiritual—coherently and irrevocably so; neither part of it may, but at its peril, expel, despise, or defy the other. All great art confesses and worships both.

The art which, since the writings of Rio and Lord Lindsay,[25] is specially known as "Christian," erred by pride in its denial of the animal nature of man;—and, in connection with all monkish and fanatical forms of religion, by looking always to another world instead of this. It wasted its strength in visions, and was therefore swept away, notwithstanding all its good and glory, by the strong truth of the naturalist art of the sixteenth century. But that naturalist art erred on the other side; denied at last the spiritual nature of man, and perished in corruption.

Perhaps an accurate analysis of the schools of art of all time might show   265
us that when the immortality of the soul was practically and completely believed, the elements of decay, danger, and grief in visible things were always disregarded. However this may be, it is assuredly so in the early Christian schools. The ideas of danger or decay seem not merely repugnant, but inconceivable to them; the expression of immortality and perpetuity is alone possible. I do not mean that they take no note of the absolute fact of corruption. This fact the early painters often compel themselves to look fuller in the front than any other men: as in the way they usually paint the Deluge (the raven feeding on the bodies), and in all the various triumphs and processions of the power of Death, which formed one great chapter of religious teaching and painting, from Orcagna's time   266
to the close of the Purist epoch. But I mean that this external fact of corruption is separated in their minds from the main conditions of their work; and its horror enters no more into their general treatment of landscape than the fear of murder or martyrdom, both of which they had nevertheless continually to represent. None of these things appeared to them as affecting the general dealings of the Deity with His world. Death, pain, and decay were simply momentary accidents in the course of immortality, which never ought to exercise any depressing influence over the hearts of men, or in the life of Nature. God, in intense life, peace, and helping power, was always and everywhere. Human bodies, at one time or another, had indeed to be made dust of, and raised from it; and this becoming dust was hurtful and humiliating, but not in the least melancholy, nor, in any very high degree, important; except to thoughtless persons who needed sometimes to be reminded of it, and whom, not at all fearing the things much himself, the painter accordingly did remind of it, somewhat sharply.

A similar condition of mind seems to have been attained, not unfrequently, in modern times, by persons whom either narrowness of circumstance or education, or vigorous moral efforts, have guarded from the troubling of the world, so as to give them firm and childlike trust in the power and presence of God, together with peace of conscience, and a belief in the passing of all evil into some form of good. It is impossible that a person thus disciplined should feel, in any of its more acute phases, the sorrow for any of the phenomena of nature, or terror in any material danger which would occur to another. The absence of personal fear, the consciousness of security as great in the midst of pestilence and storm, as amidst beds of flowers on a summer's morning, and the certainty that whatever appeared evil, or was assuredly painful, must eventually issue in a far greater and enduring good—this general feeling and conviction, I say, would gradually lull, and at last put to entire rest, the physical sensations of grief and fear; so that the man would look upon danger without dread,—expect pain without lamentation.

It may perhaps be thought that this is a very high and right state of mind.

Unfortunately, it appears that the attainment of it is never possible without inducing some form of intellectual weakness.

No painter belonging to the purist religious schools ever mastered his art. Perugino nearly did so; but it was because he was more rational—more a man of the world—than the rest. No literature exists of a high class produced by minds in the pure religious temper. On the contrary, a great deal of literature exists, produced by persons in that temper, which is markedly, and very far, below average literary work.

The reason of this I believe to be, that the right faith of man is not intended to give him repose, but to enable him to do his work. It is not intended that he should look away from the place he lives in now, and cheer himself with thoughts of the place he is to live in next, but that he should look stoutly into this world, in faith that if he does his work thoroughly here, some good to others or himself, with which however he is not at present concerned, will come of it hereafter. And this kind of brave, but not very hopeful or cheerful faith, I perceive to be always rewarded by clear practical success and splendid intellectual power; while the faith which dwells on the future fades away into rosy mist, and emptiness of musical air. That result indeed follows naturally enough on its habit of assuming that things must be right, or must come right, when, probably, the fact is, that so far as we are concerned, they are entirely wrong; and going wrong: and also on its weak and false way of looking on what these religious persons call "the bright side of things," that is to say, on one side of them only, when God has given them two sides, and intended us to see both.

I was reading but the other day, in a book by a zealous, useful, and able Scotch clergyman, one of these rhapsodies, in which he described a scene in the Highlands to show (he said) the goodness of God. In this Highland scene there was nothing but sunshine, and fresh breezes, and bleating lambs, and clean tartans, and all manner of pleasantness. Now a Highland scene is, beyond dispute, pleasant enough in its own way; but, looked close at, has its shadows. Here, for instance, is the very fact of one, as pretty as I can remember—having seen many. It is a little valley of soft turf, enclosed in its narrow oval by jutting rocks and broad flakes of nodding fern. From one side of it to the other winds, serpentine, a clear brown stream, drooping into quicker ripple as it reaches the end of the oval field, and then, first islanding a purple and white rock with an amber pool, it dashes away into a narrow fall of foam under a thicket of mountain-ash and alder. The autumn sun, low but clear, shines on the scarlet ash-berries and on the golden birch-leaves, which, fallen here and there, when the breeze has not caught them, rest quiet in the crannies of the purple rock. Beside the rock, in the hollow under the thicket, the carcase of a ewe, drowned in the last flood, lies nearly bare to the bone, its white ribs protruding through the skin, raven-torn; and the rags of its wool still flickering from the branches that first stayed it as the stream swept it down. A little lower, the current plunges, roaring, into a circular chasm like a well, surrounded on three sides by a chimney-like hollowness of polished rock, down which the foam slips in detached snow-flakes.   269 Round the edges of the pool beneath, the water circles slowly, like black oil; a little butterfly lies on its back, its wings glued to one of the eddies, its limbs feebly quivering; a fish rises, and it is gone. Lower down the stream, I can just see over a knoll, the green and damp turf roofs of four or five hovels, built at the edge of a morass, which is trodden by the cattle into a black Slough of Despond at their doors, and traversed by a few ill-set stepping-stones, with here and there a flat slab on the tops, where they have sunk out of sight, and at the turn of the brook I see a man fishing, with a boy and a dog—a picturesque and pretty group enough certainly, if they had not been there all day starving. I know them, and I know the dog's ribs also, which are nearly as bare as the dead ewe's; and the child's wasted shoulders, cutting his old tartan jacket through, so sharp are they. We will go down and talk with the man.

Or, that I may not piece pure truth with fancy, for I have none of his words set down, let us hear a word or two from another such, a Scotchman also, and as true-hearted, and in just as fair a scene. I write out the passage, in which I have kept his few sentences, word for word, as it stands in my private diary:—"22nd April (1851). Yesterday I had a long walk up the Via Gellia, at Matlock, coming down upon it from the hills above, all sown with anemones and violets, and murmuring with sweet springs. Above all the mills in the valley, the brook, in its first purity, forms a small shallow pool, with a sandy bottom covered with cresses and other water plants. A man was wading in it for cresses as I passed up the valley, and bade me good-day. I did not go much farther; he was there when I returned. I passed him again, about one hundred yards, when it struck me I might as well learn all I could about watercresses: so I turned back. I asked the man, among other questions, what he called the common weed, something like watercress, but with a serrated leaf, which grows at the edge of nearly all such pools. 'We calls that brooklime, hereabouts,' said a voice behind me. I turned, and saw three men, miners or manufacturers—two evidently Derbyshire men, and respectable-looking in their way; the third, thin, poor, old, and harder-featured, and utterly in rags. 'Brooklime?' I said. 'What do you call it lime for?' The man said he did not know; it was called that. 'You'll find that in the British 'Erba,' said the weak, calm voice of the old man. I turned to him in much surprise; but he went on saying something drily (I hardly understood what) to the cress-gatherer; who contradicting him, the old man said he 'didn't know fresh water,' he 'knew enough of sa't.' 'Have you been a sailor?' I asked. 'I was a sailor for eleven years and ten months of my life,' he said, in the same strangely quiet manner. 'And what are you now?' 'I lived for ten years after my wife's death by picking up rags and bones; I hadn't much occasion afore.' 'And now how do you live?' 'Why, I lives hard and honest, and haven't got to live long,' or something to that effect. He then went on, in a kind of maundering way, about his wife. 'She had rheumatism and fever very bad; and her second rib growed over her hench-bone. A' was a clever woman, but a' grow'd to be a very little one' (this, with an expression of deep melancholy). 'Eighteen years after her first lad she was in the family-way again, and they had doctors up from Lunnon about it. They wanted to rip her open, and take the child out of her side. But I never would give my consent.' (Then, after a pause:) 'She died twenty-six hours and ten minutes after it. I never cared much what come of me since; but I know that I shall soon reach her; that's a knowledge I would na gie for the king's crown.' 'You are a Scotchman, are not you?' I asked. 'I'm from the Isle of Skye, sir; I'm a McGregor.' I said something about his religious faith. 'Ye'll know I was bred in the Church of Scotland, sir,' he said, 'and I love it as I love my own soul: but I think thae Wesleyan Methodists ha' got salvation among them too.' "

271 Truly, this Highland and English hill-scenery is fair enough; but has its shadows; and deeper colouring, here and there, than that of heath and rose.

Now, as far as I have watched the main powers of human mind, they have risen first from the resolution to see fearlessly, pitifully, and to its very worst, what these deep colours mean, wheresoever they fall; not by any means to pass on the other side, looking pleasantly up to the sky, but to stoop to the horror, and let the sky, for the present, take care of its own clouds. However this may be in moral matters, with which I have nothing here to do, in my own field of inquiry the fact is so; and all great and beautiful work has come of first gazing without shrinking into the darkness. If, having done so, the human spirit can, by its courage and faith, conquer the evil, it rises into conceptions of victorious and consummated beauty. It is then the spirit of the highest Greek and Venetian Art. If unable to conquer the evil, but remaining in strong though melancholy war with it, not rising into supreme beauty, it is the spirit of the best northern art, typically represented by that of Holbein and Dürer. If, itself conquered by the evil, infected by the dragon breath of it, and at last brought into captivity, so as to take delight in evil for ever, it becomes the spirit of the dark, but still powerful sensualistic art, represented typically by that of Salvator. We must trace this fact briefly through Greek, Venetian, and Düreresque art; we shall then see how the art of decline came of avoiding the evil, and seeking pleasure only; and thus obtain, at last, some power of judging whether the tendency of our own contemplative art be right or ignoble.

The ruling purpose of Greek poetry is the assertion of victory, by heroism, over fate, sin, and death. The terror of these great enemies is dwelt upon chiefly by the tragedians. The victory over them, by Homer.

Now observe that in their dealing with these subjects the Greeks never   274 shrink from horror; down to its uttermost depth, to its most appalling physical detail, they strive to sound the secrets of sorrow. For them there is no passing by on the other side, no turning away the eyes to vanity from pain. Literally, they have not "lifted up their souls unto vanity."[26]   275 Whether there be consolation for them or not, neither apathy nor blindness shall be their saviour; if, for them, thus knowing the facts of the grief of earth, any hope, relief, or triumph may hereafter seem possible,— well; but if not, still hopeless, reliefless, eternal, the sorrow shall be met face to face. This Hector, so righteous, so merciful, so brave, has, nevertheless, to look upon his dearest brother in miserablest death. His own soul passes away in hopeless sobs through the throat-wound of the Grecian spear. That is one aspect of things in this world, a fair world truly, but having, among its other aspects, this one, highly ambiguous.

Meeting it boldly as they may, gazing right into the skeleton face of it, the ambiguity remains; nay, in some sort gains upon them. We trusted in the gods;—we thought that wisdom and courage would save us. Our wisdom and courage themselves deceive us to our death. Athena had the aspect of Deiphobus—terror of the enemy. She has not terrified him, but left us, in our mortal need.

And beyond that mortality, what hope have we? Nothing is clear to us on that horizon, nor comforting. Funeral honours; perhaps also rest; perhaps a shadowy life—artless, joyless, loveless. No devices in that darkness of the grave, nor daring, nor delight. Neither marrying nor giving in marriage, nor casting of spears, nor rolling of chariots, nor voice of fame. Lapped in pale Elysian mist, chilling the forgetful heart and feeble frame, shall we waste on for ever? Can the dust of earth claim more of immortality than this? Or shall we have even so much as rest? May we, indeed, lie down again in the dust: or have not our sins hidden from us even the things that belong to that peace? May not chance and the whirl of passion govern us there: when there shall be no thought, nor work, nor wisdom, nor breathing of the soul?[27]

Be it so. With no better reward, no brighter hope, we will be men while we may: men, just, and strong, and fearless, and up to our power, perfect. Athena herself, our wisdom and our strength, may betray us:—Phœbus, our sun, smite us with plague, or hide his face from us helpless;—Jove and all the powers of fate oppress us, or give us up to destruction. While we live, we will hold fast our integrity; no weak tears shall blind us, no untimely tremors abate our strength of arm nor swiftness of limb. The gods have given us at least this glorious body and this righteous conscience; these will we keep bright and pure to the end. So may we fall to misery, but not to baseness; so may we sink to sleep, but not to shame.

And herein was conquest. So defied, the betraying and accusing shadows shrank back; the mysterious horror subdued itself to majestic sorrow. Death was swallowed up in victory. Their blood, which seemed to be poured out upon the ground, rose into hyacinthine flowers. All the beauty of earth opened to them; they had ploughed into its darkness, and they reaped its gold; the gods, in whom they had trusted through all semblance of oppression, came down to love them and be their helpmates. All nature round them became divine,—one harmony of power and peace. The sun hurt them not by day, nor the moon by night; the earth opened no more her jaws into the pit: the sea whitened no more against them the teeth of his devouring waves. Sun, and moon, and earth, and sea,—all melted into grace and love; the fatal arrows rang not now at the shoulders of Apollo, the healer; lord of life, and of the three great spirits of life— Care, Memory, and Melody. Great Artemis guarded their flocks by night; Selene kissed in love the eyes of those who slept. And from all came the help of heaven to body and soul; a strange spirit lifting the lovely limbs; strange light glowing on the golden hair; and strangest comfort filling the trustful heart, so that they could put off their armour, and lie down to sleep,—their work well done, whether at the gates of their temples or of their mountains; accepting the death they once thought terrible, as the gift of Him who knew and granted what was best.

CHAPTER III
The Wings of the Lion

SUCH being the heroic spirit of Greek religion and art, we may now   279
with ease trace the relations between it and that which animated the
Italian, and chiefly the Venetian, schools.

Observe, all the nobleness, as well as the faults, of the Greek art were
dependent on its making the most of this present life. It might do so in the
Anacreontic temper— $T i\ \Pi\lambda\epsilon\iota\acute{a}\delta\epsilon\sigma\sigma\iota,\ \kappa\mathring{a}\mu o\acute{\iota}\,;$ "What have I to do with
the Pleiads?"[28] or in the defiant or the trustful endurance of fate;—but its
dominion was in this world.

Florentine art was essentially Christian, ascetic, expectant of a better
world, and antagonistic, therefore, to the Greek temper. So that the
Greek element, once forced upon it, destroyed it. There was absolute
incompatibility between them. Florentine art, also, could not produce
landscape. It despised the rock, the tree, the vital air itself, aspiring to
breathe empyreal air.

Venetian art began with the same aim and under the same restrictions.
Both are healthy in the youth of art. Heavenly aim and severe law for
boyhood; earthly work and fair freedom for manhood.

The Venetians began, I repeat, with asceticism; always, however,   280
delighting in more massive and deep colour than other religious painters.
They are especially fond of saints who have been cardinals, because of
their red hats, and they sunburn all their hermits into splendid russet
brown.

They differed from the Pisans in having no Maremma between them
and the sea; from the Romans in continually quarrelling with the Pope;
and from the Florentines in having no gardens.

They had another kind of garden, deep furrowed, with blossom in white
wreaths—fruitless. Perpetual May therein, and singing of wild, nestless
birds. And they had no Maremma to separate them from this garden of
theirs. The destiny of Pisa was changed, in all probability, by the ten miles
of marsh-land and poisonous air between it and the beach. The Genoese
energy was feverish; too much heat reflected from their torrid Apennine.
But the Venetian had his free horizon, his salt breeze, and sandy Lido-

shore; sloped far and flat,—ridged sometimes under the Tramontane winds with half a mile's breadth of rollers;—sea and sand shrivelled up together in one yellow careering field of fall and roar.

They were, also, we said, always quarrelling with the Pope. Their religious liberty came, like their bodily health, from that wave training; for it is one notable effect of a life passed on ship-board to destroy weak beliefs in appointed forms of religion. A sailor may be grossly superstitious, but his superstitions will be connected with amulets and omens, not cast in systems. He must accustom himself, if he prays at all, to pray anywhere and anyhow. Candlesticks and incense not being portable into the maintop, he perceives those decorations to be, on the whole, inessential to a maintop mass. Sails must be set and cables bent, be it never so strict a saint's day, and it is found that no harm comes of it. Absolution on a lee-shore must be had of the breakers, it appears, if at all, and they give it plenary and brief, without listening to confession.

Whereupon our religious opinions become vague, but our religious confidences strong; and the end of it all is that we perceive the Pope to be on the other side of the Apennines, and able, indeed, to sell indulgences, but not winds, for any money. Whereas, God and the sea are with us, and we must even trust them both, and take what they shall send.

Then, farther. This ocean-work is wholly adverse to any morbid conditions of sentiment. Reverie, above all things, is forbidden by Scylla and Charybdis. By the dogs and the depths, no dreaming! The first thing required of us is presence of mind. Neither love, nor poetry, nor piety, must ever so take up our thoughts as to make us slow or unready. In sweet Val d'Arno it is permissible enough to dream among the orange blossoms, and forget the day in twilight of ilex. But along the avenues of the Adrian waves there can be no careless walking. Vigilance, night and day, required of us, besides learning of many practical lessons in severe and humble dexterities. It is enough for the Florentine to know how to use his sword and to ride. We Venetians, also, must be able to use our swords, and on ground which is none of the steadiest; but, besides, we must be able to do nearly everything that hands can turn to—rudders, and yards, and cables, all needing workmanly handling and workmanly knowledge, from captain as well as from men. To drive a nail, lash a spar, reef a sail—rude work this for noble hands; but to be done sometimes, and done well on pain of death. All which not only takes mean pride out of us, and puts nobler pride of power in its stead; but it tends partly to soothe, partly to chasten, partly to employ and direct, the hot Italian temper, and make us every way greater, calmer, and happier.

Moreover, it tends to induce in us great respect for the whole human body; for its limbs, as much as for its tongue or its wit. Policy and eloquence are well; and, indeed, we Venetians can be politic enough, and can speak melodiously when we choose; but to put the helm up at the right moment is the beginning of all cunning—and for that we need arm and eye;—not tongue. And with this respect for the body as such, comes also the sailor's preference of massive beauty in bodily form. The landsmen, among their roses and orange-blossoms, and chequered shadows of twisted vine, may well please themselves with pale faces, and finely drawn eyebrows, and fantastic braiding of hair. But from the sweeping glory of the sea we learn to love another kind of beauty; broad-breasted, level-browed, like the horizon;—thighed and shouldered like the billows; footed like their stealing foam;—bathed in cloud of golden hair like their sunsets.

Such were the physical influences constantly in operation on the Venetians; their painters, however, were partly prepared for their work by others in their infancy. Associations connected with early life among mountains softened and deepened the teaching of the sea; and the wildness of form of the Tyrolese Alps gave greater strength and grotesqueness to their imaginations than the Greek painters could have found among the cliffs of the Ægean. Thus far, however, the influences on both are nearly similar. The Greek Sea was indeed less bleak, and the Greek hills were less grand; but the difference was in degree rather than in the nature of their power. The moral influences at work on the two races were far more sharply opposed.

Evil, as we saw, had been fronted by the Greek, and thrust out of his path. Once conquered, if he thought of it more, it was involuntarily, as we remember a painful dream, yet with a secret dread that the dream might return and continue for ever. But the teaching of the Church in the Middle Ages had made the contemplation of evil one of the duties of men. As sin, it was to be duly thought upon, that it might be confessed. As suffering, endured joyfully, in hope of future reward. 283

Therefore the Christian painters differed from the Greek in two main points. They had been taught a faith which put an end to restless questioning and discouragement. All was at last to be well—and their best genius might be peacefully given to imagining the glories of heaven and the happiness of its redeemed. But on the other hand, though suffering was to cease in heaven, it was to be not only endured, but honoured upon earth. And from the Crucifixion, down to a beggar's lameness, all the tortures and maladies of men were to be made, at least in part, the subjects of art. The Venetian was, therefore, in his inner mind, less serious than the Greek: in his superficial temper, sadder. In his heart there was none of the deep horror which vexed the soul of Æschylus or Homer. His Pallas-shield was the shield of Faith, not the shield of the Gorgon. All was at last to issue happily; in sweetest harpings and seven-fold circles of light. But for the present he had to dwell with the maimed and the blind, and 284 to revere Lazarus more than Achilles.

This reference to a future world has a morbid influence on all their conclusions. For the earth and all its natural elements are despised. They are to pass away like a scroll. Man, the immortal, is alone revered; his work and presence are all that can be noble or desirable. Men, and fair architecture, temples and courts such as may be in a celestial city, or the clouds and angels of Paradise; these are what we must paint when we want beautiful things. But the sea, the mountains, the forests, are all adverse to us,—a desolation. The ground that was cursed for our sake;—the sea that executed judgment on all our race, and rages against us still, though bridled; storm-demons churning it into foam in nightly glare on Lido, and hissing from it against our palaces. Nature is but a terror, or a temptation. She is for hermits, martyrs, murderers,—for St. Jerome, and St. Mary of Egypt, and the Magdalen in the desert, and monk Peter, falling before the sword.

But the worst point we have to note respecting the spirit of Venetian landscape is its pride.

It was observed in the course of the third volume how the mediæval temper had rejected agricultural pursuits, and whatever pleasures could come of them.

At Venice this negation had reached its extreme. Though the Florentines and Romans had no delight in farming, they had in gardening. The Venetian possessed, and cared for, neither fields nor pastures. Being delivered, to his loss, from all the wholesome labours of tillage, he was also shut out from the sweet wonders and charities of the earth, and from the pleasant natural history of the year.

No simple joy was possible to him. Only stateliness and power; high intercourse with kingly and beautiful humanity, proud thoughts, or splendid pleasures; throned sensualities, and ennobled appetites. But of innocent, childish, helpful, holy pleasures, he had none. As in the classical landscape, nearly all rural labour is banished from the Titianesque. The mountains are dark blue; the clouds glowing or soft gray, always massive; the light, deep, clear, melancholy; the foliage, neither intricate nor graceful, but compact and sweeping (with undulated trunks), dividing much into horizontal flakes, like the clouds; the ground rocky and broken somewhat monotonously, but richly green with wild herbage; here and there a flower, by preference white or blue, rarely yellow, still more rarely red.

This heroic landscape of theirs was peopled by spiritual beings of the highest order. And in this rested the dominion of the Venetians over all later schools. They were the *last believing* school of Italy. Although, as I said above, always quarrelling with the Pope, there is all the more evidence of an earnest faith in their religion. People who trusted the Madonna less, flattered the Pope more. But down to Tintoret's time, the

Roman Catholic religion was still real and sincere at Venice; and though faith in it was compatible with much which to us appears criminal or   287 absurd, the religion itself was entirely sincere.

Perhaps when you see one of Titian's splendidly passionate subjects, or find Veronese making the Marriage in Cana one blaze of worldly pomp, you imagine that Titian must have been a sensualist, and Veronese an unbeliever.

Put the idea from you at once, and be assured of this for ever; it will guide you through many a labyrinth of life, as well as of painting,—that of an evil tree, men never gather good fruit—good of any sort or kind; even good sensualism.

Let us look to this calmly. We have seen what physical advantage the Venetian had, in his sea and sky: also what moral disadvantage he had, in scorn of the poor; now finally, let us see with what power he was invested, which men since his time have never recovered more.

"Neither of a bramble bush gather they grapes." [29]

The great saying has twofold help for us. Be assured, first, that if it were bramble from which you gathered them, these are not grapes in your hand, though they look like grapes. Or if these are indeed grapes, it was no bramble you gathered them from, though it looked like one.

It is difficult for persons, accustomed to receive, without questioning, the modern English idea of religion, to understand the temper of the Venetian Catholics. I do not enter into examination of our own feelings; but I have to note this one significant point of difference between us.

An English gentleman, desiring his portrait, gives probably to the painter a choice of several actions, in any of which he is willing to be represented. As for instance, riding his best horse, shooting with his favourite pointer, manifesting himself in his robes of state on some great   288 public occasion, meditating in his study, playing with his children, or visiting his tenants; in any of these or other such circumstances, he will give the artist free leave to paint him. But in one important action he would shrink even from the suggestion of being drawn. He will assuredly not let himself be painted praying.

Strangely, this is the action which, of all others, a Venetian desires to be painted in. If they want a noble and complete portrait, they nearly all choose to be painted on their knees.

For one profane picture by great Venetians, you will find ten of sacred   289 subjects; and those, also, including their grandest, most laboured, and most beloved works. Tintoret's power culminates in two great religious pictures: the Crucifixion [plate 14], and the Paradise. Titian's in the Assumption, the Peter Martyr, and Presentation of the Virgin. Veronese's in the Marriage in Cana. [30] John Bellini and Basaiti never, so far as I remember, painted any other than sacred subjects. By the Palmas,

Vincenzo Catena, and Bonifazio, I remember no profane subject of importance.

There is, moreover, one distinction of the very highest import between the treatment of sacred subjects by Venetian painters and by all others.

Throughout the rest of Italy, piety had become abstract, and opposed theoretically to worldly life; hence the Florentine and Umbrian painters generally separated their saints from living men. They delighted in imagining scenes of spiritual perfectness;—Paradises, and companies of the redeemed at the judgment;—glorified meetings of martyrs;— madonnas surrounded by circles of angels. If, which was rare, definite

290 portraitures of living men were introduced, these real characters formed a kind of chorus or attendant company, taking no part in the action. At Venice all this was reversed, and so boldly as at first to shock, with its seeming irreverence, a spectator accustomed to the formalities and abstractions of the so-called sacred schools. The madonnas are no more seated apart on their thrones, the saints no more breathe celestial air. They are on our own plain ground—nay, here in our houses with us. All kind of worldly business going on in their presence, fearlessly; our own friends and respected acquaintances, with all their mortal faults, and in their mortal flesh, looking at them face to face unalarmed: nay, our dearest children playing with their pet dogs at Christ's very feet.

I once myself thought this irreverent. How foolishly! As if children whom He loved *could* play anywhere else.

The picture most illustrative of this feeling is perhaps that at Dresden, of Veronese's family, painted by himself.

He wishes to represent them as happy and honoured. The best happiness and highest honour he can imagine for them is that they should be presented to the Madonna, to whom, therefore, they are being brought by the three virtues—Faith, Hope, and Charity.

The Virgin stands in a recess behind two marble shafts, such as may be seen in any house belonging to an old family in Venice. She places the boy Christ on the edge of a balustrade before her. At her side are St. John the Baptist, and St. Jerome. This group occupies the left side of the picture.

291 The pillars, seen sideways, divide it from the group formed by the Virtues, with the wife and children of Veronese. He himself stands a little behind, his hands clasped in prayer.

His wife kneels full in front, a strong Venetian woman, well advanced in years. She has brought up her children in fear of God, and is not afraid to meet the Virgin's eyes. She gazes steadfastly on them; her proud head and gentle, self-possessed face are relieved in one broad mass of shadow against a space of light, formed by the white robes of Faith, who stands beside her—guardian, and companion. Perhaps a somewhat disappointing Faith at the first sight, for her face is not in any special way exalted or refined. Veronese knew that Faith had to companion simple and slow-hearted people, perhaps oftener than able or refined people—does not therefore insist on her being severely intellectual, or looking as if she were always in the best company. So she is only distinguished by her pure white (not bright white) dress, her delicate hand, her golden hair drifted in light ripples across her breast, from which the white robes fall nearly in the shape of a shield—the shield of Faith. A little behind her stands Hope; she also, at first, not to most people a recognizable Hope. We usually paint Hope as young, and joyous. Veronese knows better. The young hope is vain hope—passing away in rain of tears; but the Hope of Veronese is aged, assured, remaining when all else has been taken away. "For tribulation worketh patience, and patience experience, and experience hope"; and *that* hope maketh not ashamed.[31]

She has a black veil on her head.

Then again, in the front, is Charity, red-robed; stout in the arms,—a servant of all work, she; but small-headed, not being specially given to thinking; soft-eyed, her hair braided brightly; her lips rich red, sweet-blossoming. She has got some work to do even now, for a nephew of Veronese's is doubtful about coming forward, and looks very humbly and penitently towards the Virgin—his life perhaps not having been quite so   292
exemplary as might at present be wished. Faith reaches her small white hand lightly back to him, lays the tips of her fingers on his; but Charity takes firm hold of him by the wrist from behind, and will push him on presently, if he still hangs back.

In front of the mother kneel her two eldest children, a girl of about sixteen, and a boy a year or two younger. They are both rapt in adoration—the boy's being the deepest. Nearer us, at their left side, is a younger boy, about nine years old—a black-eyed fellow, full of life—and evidently his father's darling (for Veronese has put him full in light in the front; and given him a beautiful white silken jacket, barred with black, that nobody may ever miss seeing him to the end of time). He is a little shy about being presented to the Madonna, and for the present has got behind the pillar, blushing, but opening his black eyes wide; he is just summoning courage to peep round and see if she looks kind. A still younger child, about six years old, is really frightened, and has run back to his mother, catching hold of her dress at the waist. She throws her right arm round him and over him, with exquisite instinctive action, not moving her eyes from the Madonna's face. Last of all, the youngest child, perhaps about three years old, is neither frightened nor interested, but finds the ceremony tedious, and is trying to coax the dog to play with him; but the dog, which is one of the little curly, short-nosed, fringy-pawed things, which all Venetian ladies petted, will not now be coaxed. For the dog is the last link in the chain of lowering feeling, and takes his doggish views of the matter. He cannot understand, first, how the Madonna got into the house; nor, secondly, why she is allowed to stay, disturbing the family, and taking all their attention from his dogship. And he is walking away, much offended.

The dog is thus constantly introduced by the Venetians in order to give the fullest contrast to the highest tones of human thought and feeling. I shall examine this point presently farther, in speaking of pastoral land-scape and animal painting; but at present we will merely compare the use of the same mode of expression in Veronese's Presentation of the Queen of Sheba.

This picture is at Turin [fig.52], and is of quite inestimable value. It is hung high; and the really principal figure the Solomon, being in the shade, can hardly be seen, but is painted with Veronese's utmost tenderness, in the bloom of perfect youth, his hair golden, short, crisply curled. He is seated high on his lion throne: two elders on each side beneath him, the whole group forming a tower of solemn shade. I have alluded, elsewhere, to the principle on which all the best composers act, of supporting these lofty groups by some vigorous mass of foundation. This column of noble shade is curiously sustained. A falconer leans forward from the left-hand side, bearing on his wrist a snow-white falcon, its wings spread, and brilliantly relieved against the purple robe of one of the elders. It touches with its wings one of the golden lions of the throne, on which the light also flashes strongly; thus forming, together with it, the lion and eagle symbol, which is the type of Christ throughout mediæval work. In order to show the meaning of this symbol, and that Solomon is typically invested with the Christian royalty, one of the elders, by a bold anachronism, holds a jewel in his hand in the shape of a cross, with which he (by accident of gesture) points to Solomon; his other hand is laid on an open book.

The group opposite, of which the Queen forms the centre, is also painted with Veronese's highest skill; but contains no point of interest bearing on our present subject, except its connection by a chain of descending emotion. The Queen is wholly oppressed and subdued; kneeling, and nearly fainting, she looks up to Solomon with tears in her eyes; he, startled by fear for her, stoops forward from the throne, opening his right hand, as if to support her, so as almost to drop the sceptre. At her side her first maid of honour is kneeling also, but does not care about Solomon; and is gathering up her dress that it may not be crushed; and looking back to encourage a negro-girl, who, carrying two toy-birds, made of enamel and jewels, for presentation to the King, is frightened at seeing her Queen fainting, and does not know what she ought to do; while, lastly, the Queen's dog, another of the little fringy-paws, is wholly unabashed by Solomon's presence, or anybody else's; and stands with his forelegs well apart, right in front of his mistress, thinking everybody has

293

294

fig.52   Paul Veronese, *The Presentation of the Queen of Sheba*

lost their wits; and barking violently at one of the attendants, who has set down a golden vase disrespectfully near him.

Throughout these designs I want the reader to notice the purpose of representing things as they were likely to have occurred, down to trivial, or even ludicrous detail—the nobleness of all that was intended to be noble being so great that nothing could detract from it.

A more touching instance of this realization occurs in the treatment of the Saint Veronica (in the Ascent to Calvary), at Dresden. Most painters merely represent her as one of the gentle, weeping, attendant women; and show her giving the handkerchief as though these women had been allowed to approach Christ without any difficulty. But in Veronese's conception, she has to break through the executioners to Him. She is not weeping; and the expression of pity, though intense, is overborne by that of resolution. She is determined to reach Christ; has set her teeth close, and thrusts aside one of the executioners, who strikes fiercely at her with a heavy doubled cord.

These instances are enough to explain the general character of the mind of Veronese, capable of tragic power to the utmost, if he chooses to exert it in that direction, but, by habitual preference, exquisitely graceful and playful; religious, without severity, and winningly noble; delighting in

295

slight, sweet, every-day incident, but hiding deep meanings underneath it; rarely painting a gloomy subject, and never a base one.

I have, in other places, entered enough into the examination of the great religious mind of Tintoret;[32] supposing then, that he was distinguished from Titian chiefly by this character. But in this I was mistaken;—the religion of Titian is like that of Shakspere—occult behind his magnificent equity. It is not possible, however, within the limits of this work, to give any just account of the mind of Titian: nor shall I attempt it; but will only explain some of those more strange and apparently inconsistent attributes of it, which might otherwise prevent the reader from getting clue to its real tone. The first of these is its occasional coarseness in choice of type of feature.

In the second volume I had to speak of Titian's Magdalen, in the Pitti Palace, as treated basely, and that in strong terms, "the disgusting Magdalen of the Pitti."[33]

296   Truly she is so, as compared with the received types of the Magdalen. A stout, red-faced woman, dull, and coarse of feature, with much of the animal in even her expression of repentance—her eyes strained, and inflamed with weeping. I ought, however, to have remembered another picture of the Magdalen by Titian (Mr. Rogers's, now in the National Gallery), in which she is just as refined, as in the Pitti Palace she is gross; and had I done so, I should have seen Titian's meaning. It had been the fashion before his time to make the Magdalen always young and beautiful; her, if no one else, even the rudest painters flattered; her repentance was not thought perfect unless she had lustrous hair and lovely lips. Titian first dared to doubt the romantic fable, and reject the narrowness of sentimental faith. He saw that it was possible for plain women to love no less vividly than beautiful ones; and for stout persons to repent, as well as those more delicately made. It seemed to him that the Magdalen would have received her pardon not the less quickly because her wit was none of the readiest; and would not have been regarded with less compassion by her Master because her eyes were swollen, or her dress disordered. It is just because he has set himself sternly to enforce this lesson that the picture is so painful: the only instance, so far as I remember, of Titian's painting a woman markedly and entirely belonging to the lowest class.

It may perhaps appear more difficult to account for the alternation of Titian's great religious pictures with others devoted wholly to the expression of sensual qualities, or to exulting and bright representation of heathen deities.

The Venetian mind, we have said, and Titian's especially, as the central type of it, was wholly realist, universal, and manly.

In this breadth and realism, the painter saw that sensual passion in man was, not only a fact, but a Divine fact; the human creature, though the

highest of the animals, was, nevertheless, a perfect animal, and his 297
happiness, health, and nobleness, depended on the due power of every
animal passion, as well as the cultivation of every spiritual tendency.

He thought that every feeling of the mind and heart, as well as every
form of the body, deserved painting. Also to a painter's true and highly
trained instinct, the human body is the loveliest of all objects. I do not
stay to trace the reasons why, at Venice, the female body could be found
in more perfect beauty than the male; but so it was, and it becomes the
principal subject, therefore, both with Giorgione and Titian. They
painted it fearlessly, with all right and natural qualities; never, however,
representing it as exercising any overpowering attractive influence on
man; but only on the Faun or Satyr.

Yet they did this so majestically that I am perfectly certain no
untouched Venetian picture ever yet excited one base thought (otherwise
than in base persons anything may do so); while in the greatest studies of
the female body by the Venetians, all other characters are overborne by
majesty, and the form becomes as pure as that of a Greek statue.

There is no need, I should think, to point out how this contemplation
of the entire personal nature was reconcilable with the severest conceptions of religious duty and faith.

But the fond introduction of heathen gods may appear less explicable.

On examination, however, it will be found, that these deities are never 298
painted with any heart-reverence or affection. They are introduced for the
most part symbolically (Bacchus and Venus oftenest, as incarnations of
the spirit of revelry and beauty), of course always conceived with deep
imaginative truth, much resembling the mode of Keats's conception; but
never so as to withdraw any of the deep devotion rendered to the objects
of Christian faith.

In all its roots of power, and modes of work;—in its belief, its breadth,
and its judgment, I find the Venetian mind perfect.

How, then, did its art so swiftly pass away? How become, what it became
unquestionably, one of the chief causes of the corruption of the mind of
Italy, and of her subsequent decline in moral and political power?

By reason of one great, one fatal fault;—recklessness in aim. Wholly
noble in its sources, it was wholly unworthy in its purposes.

Separate and strong, like Samson, chosen from its youth, and with the
spirit of God visibly resting on it,—like him, it warred in careless strength,
and wantoned in untimely pleasure. No Venetian painter ever worked
with any aim beyond that of delighting the eye, or expressing fancies
agreeable to himself or flattering to his nation. They could not be either,
unless they were religious. But he did not desire the religion. He desired
the delight.

The Assumption is a noble picture, because Titian believed in the

Madonna. But he did not paint it to make any one else believe in her. He painted it, because he enjoyed rich masses of red and blue, and faces flushed with sunlight.

Tintoret's Paradise is a noble picture, because he believed in Paradise. But he did not paint it to make any one think of heaven; but to form a beautiful termination for the hall of the Greater Council.

299   Other men used their effete faiths and mean faculties with a high moral purpose. The Venetian gave the most earnest faith, and the lordliest faculty, to gild the shadows of an antechamber, or heighten the splendours of a holiday.

Strange and lamentable as this carelessness may appear, I find it to be almost the law with the great workers. Weak and vain men have acute consciences, and labour under a profound sense of responsibility. The strong men, sternly disdainful of themselves, do what they can, too often merely as it pleases them at the moment, reckless what comes of it.

I know not how far in humility, or how far in bitter and hopeless levity, the great Venetians gave their art to be blasted by the sea-winds or wasted by the worm. I know not whether in sorrowful obedience, or in wanton compliance, they fostered the folly, and enriched the luxury of their age. This only I know, that in proportion to the greatness of their power was the shame of its desecration and the suddenness of its fall. The en-chanter's spell, woven by centuries of toil, was broken in the weakness of a moment; and swiftly, and utterly, as a rainbow vanishes, the radiance and the strength faded from the wings of the Lion.

CHAPTER IV
Dürer and Salvator
"Emigravit"

WE have next to examine the art which cannot conquer the evil, but   300
remains at war with, or in captivity to it.

Up to the time of the Reformation, it was possible for men even of the
highest powers of intellect, to obtain a tranquillity of faith, in the highest
degree favourable to the pursuit of any particular art. Possible, at least, we
see it to have been; there is no need—nor, so far as I see, any ground for
argument about it. I am myself unable to understand how it was so, but the
fact is unquestionable. It is not that I wonder at men's trust in the Pope's
infallibility, or in his virtue; nor at their surrendering their private
judgment; nor at their being easily cheated by imitations of miracles; nor
at their thinking indulgences could be purchased with money. But I
wonder at this one thing only; the acceptance of the doctrine of eternal
punishment as dependent on accident of birth, or momentary excitement
of devotional feeling. I marvel at the acceptance of the system which   301
condemned guiltless persons to the loss of heaven because they had lived
before Christ, and which made the obtaining of Paradise turn frequently
on a passing thought or a momentary invocation. How this came to pass,
it is no part of our work here to determine. That in this faith, it was
possible to attain entire peace of mind, to live calmly, and die hopefully,
is indisputable.

But this possibility ceased at the Reformation. Thenceforward human
life became a school of debate, troubled and fearful. Fifteen hundred years
of spiritual teaching were called into fearful question, whether indeed it
had been teaching by angels or devils? Whatever it had been, there was no
longer any way of trusting it peacefully.

A dark time for all men. We cannot now conceive it. The great horror
of it lay in this:—that, as in the trial-hour of the Greek, the heavens
themselves seemed to have deceived those who had trusted in them.

Then came the Resurrection of Death. Never since man first saw him
face to face, had his terror been so great. "Swallowed up in victory":[34]
alas! no; but king over all the earth. All faith, hope, and fond belief were   302
betrayed. Nothing of futurity was now sure but the grave.

For the Pan-Athenaic Triumph, and the Feast of Jubilee, there came up, through fields of spring, the Dance of Death.

The brood of weak men fled from the face of him. A new Bacchus and his crew this, with worm for snake and gall for wine. They recoiled to such pleasure as yet remained possible to them—feeble infidelities, and luxurious sciences, and so went their way.

At least, of the men with whom we are concerned—the artists—this was almost the universal fate. They gave themselves to the following of pleasure only; and, as a religious school, after a few pale rays of fading sanctity from Guido, and brown gleams of gipsy Madonnahood from Murillo, came utterly to an end.

Three men only stood firm, facing the new Dionysiac revel, to see what would come of it.

Two in the north, Holbein and Dürer; and, later, one in the south, Salvator.

But the ground on which they stood differed strangely; Dürer and Holbein, amidst the formal delights, the tender religions, and practical science, of domestic life and honest commerce. Salvator, amidst the pride of lascivious wealth, and the outlawed distress of impious poverty.

It would be impossible to imagine any two phases of scenery or society more contrary in character, more opposite in teaching, than those surrounding Nuremberg and Naples, in the sixteenth and seventeenth centuries. What they were then, both districts still to all general intents remain. The cities have in each case lost their splendour and power, but not their character. The surrounding scenery remains wholly unchanged. It is still in our power, from the actual aspect of the places, to conceive their effect on the youth of the two painters.

303   Nuremberg is gathered at the base of a sandstone rock, rising in the midst of a dry but fertile plain. The rock forms a prolonged and curved ridge, of which the concave side, at the highest point, is precipitous; the other slopes gradually to the plain. Fortified with wall and tower along its whole crest, and crowned with a stately castle, it defends the city—not with its precipitous side—but with its slope. The precipice is turned to the town. It wears no aspect of hostility towards the surrounding fields; the roads lead down into them by gentle descents from the gates. To the south and east the walls are on the level of the plain; within them, the city itself stands on two swells of hill, divided by a winding river.

304   Though not comparable for an instant to any great Italian or French city, Nuremberg possesses one character peculiar to itself, that of a self-restrained, contented, quaint domesticity. It would have been vain to expect any first-rate painting, sculpture, or poetry, from the well-regulated community of merchants of small ware. But it is evident they were affectionate and trustworthy—that they had playful fancy and honourable

pride. There is no exalted grandeur in their city, not any deep beauty; but an imaginative homeliness, mingled with some elements of melancholy and power, and a few even of grace.

In Dürer's own engraving, "The Cannon," [fig.53] the distance is an   305 actual portrait of part of the landscape seen from [the] castle ramparts, looking towards Franconian Switzerland.

fig.53   Albrecht Dürer, *The Cannon*

If the reader will be at the pains to turn to it, he will see at a glance the elements of the Nuremberg country, as they still exist. Wooden cottages, thickly grouped, enormously high in the roofs; the sharp church spire, small and slightly grotesque, surmounting them; beyond, a richly culti-vated, healthy plain, bounded by woody hills. By a strange coincidence the very plant which constitutes the staple produce of those fields, is in almost ludicrous harmony with the grotesqueness and neatness of the architecture around; and one may almost fancy that the builders of the little knotted spires and turrets of the town, and workers of its dark iron flowers, are in spiritual presence, watching and guiding the produce of the field,—when one finds the footpaths bordered, everywhere, by the bossy spires and lustrous jetty flowers of the black hollyhock.

When Dürer penetrated among those hills of Franconia he would find himself in a pastoral country, much resembling the Gruyère districts of

Switzerland, but less thickly inhabited, and giving in its steep, though not
306   lofty, rocks,—its scattered pines,—and its fortresses and chapels, the
motives of all the wilder landscape introduced by the painter in such
pieces as his St. Jerome, or St. Hubert.

Among this pastoral simplicity and formal sweetness of domestic peace,
Dürer had to work out his question concernng the grave. It haunted him
long; he learnt to engrave death's-heads well before he had done with it;
looked deeper than any other man into those strange rings, their jewels
lost; and gave answer at last conclusively in his great Knight and
Death—of which more presently. But while the Nuremberg landscape is
still fresh in our minds, we had better turn south quickly, and compare
the elements of education which formed, and of creation which com-
panioned, Salvator.

Born with a wild and coarse nature (how coarse I will show you soon),
but nevertheless an honest one, he set himself in youth hotly to the war,
and cast himself carelessly on the current, of life. No rectitude of ledger-
lines stood in his way; no tender precision of household customs; no calm
successions of rural labour. But past his half-starved lips rolled profusion of
pitiless wealth; before him glared and swept the troops of shameless
pleasure. Above him muttered Vesuvius; beneath his feet shook the
Solfatara.[35]

In heart disdainful, in temper adventurous; conscious of power,
307   impatient of labour, and yet more of the pride of the patrons of his youth,
he fled to the Calabrian hills, seeking, not knowledge, but freedom.[36] If
he was to be surrounded by cruelty and deceit, let them at least be those
of brave men or savage beasts, not of the timorous and the contemptible.
Better the wrath of the robber, than enmity of the priest; and the cunning
of the wolf than of the hypocrite.

We are accustomed to hear the south of Italy spoken of as a beautiful
country. Its mountain forms are graceful above others, its sea bays
exquisite in outline and hue; but it is only beautiful in superficial aspect.
In closer detail it is wild and melancholy. Its forests are sombre-leaved,
labyrinth-stemmed; the carubbe, the olive, laurel, and ilex, are alike in
that strange feverish twisting of their branches, as if in spasms of half
human pain:—Avernus forests; one fears to break their boughs, lest they
should cry to us from the rents; the rocks they shade are of ashes, or thrice-
molten lava; iron sponge whose every pore has been filled with fire.
Silent villages, earthquake shaken, without commerce, without industry,
without knowledge, without hope, gleam in white ruin from hillside to
hillside; far-winding wrecks of immemorial walls surround the dust of
cities long forsaken: the mountain streams moan through the cold arches
of their foundations, green with weed, and rage over the heaps of their
fallen towers. Far above, in thunder-blue serration, stand the eternal edges

of the angry Apennine, dark with rolling impendence of volcanic cloud.

Yet even among such scenes as these, Salvator might have been calmed and exalted, had he been, indeed, capable of exaltation. But he was not of high temper enough to perceive beauty. He had not the sacred sense—the sense of colour; all the loveliest hues of the Calabrian air were invisible to him; the sorrowful desolation of the Calabrian villages unfelt.   308 He saw only what was gross and terrible,—the jagged peak, the splintered tree, the flowerless bank of grass, and wandering weed, prickly and pale. His temper confirmed itself in evil, and became more and more fierce and morose; though not, I believe, cruel, ungenerous, or lascivious. I should not suspect Salvator of wantonly inflicting pain. His constantly painting it does not prove he delighted in it; he felt the horror of it, and in that horror, fascination. Also, he desired fame, and saw that here was an untried field rich enough in morbid excitement to catch the humour of his indolent patrons. But the gloom gained upon him, and grasped him. He could jest, indeed, as men jest in prison-yards (he became afterwards a renowned mime in Florence); his satires are full of good mocking, but his own doom to sadness is never repealed.

Of all men whose work I have ever studied, he gives me most distinctly the idea of a lost spirit. I see in him, notwithstanding all his baseness, the last traces of spiritual life in the art of Europe. He was the last man to whom the thought of a spiritual existence presented itself as a conceivable reality. All succeeding men, however powerful—Rembrandt, Rubens, Vandyck, Reynolds—would have mocked at the idea of a spirit. They were men of the world; they are never in earnest, and they are never appalled. But Salvator was capable of pensiveness, of faith, and of fear. The misery of the earth is a marvel to him; he cannot leave off gazing at it. The religion of the earth is a horror to him. He gnashes his teeth at it, rages at it, mocks and gibes at it. He would have acknowledged religion, had he seen any that was true. Anything rather than that baseness which he did   309 see. "If there is no other religion than this of pope and cardinals, let us to the robber's ambush and the dragon's den." He was capable of fear also. The gray spectre, horse-headed, striding across the sky—(in the Pitti Palace)—its bat wings spread, green bars of the twilight seen between its bones; it was no play to him—the painting of it. [fig.54][37] Helpless Salvator! A little early sympathy, a word of true guidance, perhaps, had saved him. What says he of himself? "Despiser of wealth and of death." Two grand scorns; but, oh, condemned Salvator! the question is not for man what he can scorn, but what he can love.

I do not care to trace the various hold which Hades takes on this fallen soul. It is no part of my work here to analyze his art, nor even that of Dürer; all that we need to note is the opposite answer they gave to the question about death.

fig.54 Salvator Rosa, *The Temptation of St Anthony*

To Salvator it came in narrow terms. Desolation, without hope, throughout the fields of nature he had to explore; hypocrisy and sensuality, triumphant and shameless, in the cities from which he derived his support. His life, so far as any nobility remained in it, could only pass in horror, disdain, or despair. It is difficult to say which of the three

310

prevails most in his common work; but his answer to the great question was of despair only.

On the contrary, in the sight of Dürer, things were for the most part as they ought to be. Men did their work in his city and in the fields round it. The clergy were sincere. Great social questions unagitated; great social evils either non-existent, or seemingly a part of the nature of things, and inevitable. His answer was that of patient hope; and twofold, consisting of one design in praise of Fortitude, and another in praise of Labour. The Fortitude, commonly known as the "Knight and Death," [fig.55] represents a knight riding through a dark valley overhung by leafless trees, and with a great castle on a hill beyond. Beside him, but a little in advance, rides Death on a pale horse. Death is gray-haired and crowned;—serpents wreathed about his crown; (the sting of Death involved in the kingly power). He holds up the hour-glass, and looks earnestly into the knight's face. Behind him follows Sin; but Sin powerless; he has been conquered and passed by, but follows yet, watching if any way of assault remains. On his forehead are two horns—I think of   311 sea-shell—to indicate his insatiableness and instability. He has also the twisted horns of the ram, for stubbornness, the ears of an ass, the snout of a swine, the hoofs of a goat. Torn wings hang useless from his shoulders, and he carries a spear with two hooks, for catching as well as wounding. The knight does not heed him, nor even Death, though he is conscious of the presence of the last.

He rides quietly, his bridle firm in his hand, and his lips set close in a slight sorrowful smile, for he hears what Death is saying; and hears it as the word of a messenger who brings pleasant tidings, thinking to bring evil ones. A little branch of delicate heath is twisted round his helmet. His horse trots proudly and straight; its head high, and with a cluster of oak on the brow where on the fiend's brow is the sea-shell horn. But the horse of Death stoops its head; and its rein catches the little bell which hangs from the knight's horse-bridle, making it toll as a passing-bell.

Dürer's second answer is the plate of "Melencholia," [fig. 56] which is   312 the history of the sorrowful toil of the earth, as the "Knight and Death" is of its sorrowful patience under temptation.

Salvator's answer, remember, is in both respects that of despair. Death, as he reads, lord of temptation, is victor over the spirit of man; and lord of ruin, is victor over the work of man. Dürer declares the sad but unsullied conquest over Death the tempter; and the sad but enduring conquest over Death the destroyer.

Though the general intent of the Melencholia is clear, and to be felt at a glance, I am in some doubt respecting its special symbolism. I do not know how far Dürer intended to show that labour, in many of its most earnest forms, is closely connected with the morbid sadness or "dark   313

fig.55   Albrecht Dürer, *The Knight and Death*

anger,'' of the northern nations. Truly some of the best work ever done for man, has been in that dark anger; but I have not yet been able to determine for myself how far this is necessary, or how far great work may also be done with cheerfulness. If I knew what the truth was, I should be able to interpret Dürer better; meantime the design seems to me his answer to the complaint, ''Yet is his strength labour and sorrow.''[38]

fig.56   Albrecht Dürer, *Melencolia*

"Yes," he replies, "but labour and sorrow are his strength."

The labour indicated is in the daily work of men. Not the inspired or gifted labour of the few (it is labour connected with the sciences, not with the arts), shown in its four chief functions: thoughtful, faithful, calculating, and executing.

Thoughtful, first; all true power coming of that resolved, resistless calm of melancholy thought. This is the first and last message of the whole design. Faithful, the right arm of the spirit resting on the book. Calculating (chiefly in the sense of self-command), the compasses in her right hand. Executive—roughest instruments of labour at her feet: a crucible, and geometrical solids, indicating her work in the sciences. Over her head the hour-glass and the bell, for their continual words, "Whatsoever thy hand findeth to do." [39] Beside her, childish labour (lesson-learning?) sitting on an old millstone, with a tablet on its knees. I do not know what instrument it has in its hand. At her knees a wolf-hound asleep. In the distance a comet (the disorder and threatening of the universe) setting, the rainbow dominant over it. Her strong body is close girded for work; at her waist hang the keys of wealth; but the coin is cast aside contemptuously under her feet. She has eagle's wings, and is crowned with fair leafage of spring.

Yes, Albert of Nuremberg, it was a noble answer, yet an imperfect one. This is indeed the labour which is crowned with laurel and has the wings of the eagle. It was reserved for another country to prove, for another hand to pourtray, the labour which is crowned with fire, and has the wings of the bat. [40]

CHAPTER V

Claude and Poussin

IT was stated in the last chapter that Salvator was the last painter of   315
Italy on whom any fading trace of the old faithful spirit rested. Carrying
some of its passion far into the seventeenth century, he deserved to be
remembered together with the painters whom the questioning of the
Reformation had exercised eighty years before. Not so his contemporaries.
The whole body of painters around him, but chiefly those of landscape,
had cast aside all regard for the faith of their fathers, or for any other; and
founded a school of art properly called "classical," of which the following
are the chief characteristics.

The belief in a supreme benevolent Being having ceased, and the sense
of spiritual destitution fastening on the mind, together with the hopeless
perception of ruin and decay in the existing world, the imagination sought
to quit itself from the oppression of these ideas by realizing a perfect
worldly felicity, in which the inevitable ruin should at least be lovely, and
the necessarily short life entirely happy and refined. Labour must be
banished, since it was to be unrewarded. Humiliation and degradation of
body must be prevented, since there could be no compensation for them
by preparation of the soul for another world. Let us eat and drink
(refinedly), for to-morrow we die, and attain the highest possible dignity
as men in this world, since we shall have none as spirits in the next.

Observe, this is neither the Greek nor the Roman spirit. Neither Claude   316
nor Poussin, nor any other painter or writer, properly termed "classical,"
ever could enter into the Greek or Roman heart, which was as full, in
many cases fuller, of the hope of immortality than our own.

On the absence of belief in a good supreme Being, follows, necessarily,
the habit of looking to ourselves for supreme judgment in all matters, and
for supreme government. Hence, first, the irreverent habit of judgment
instead of admiration. It is generally expressed under the justly degrading
term "good taste."

Hence, in the second place, the habit of restraint or self-government
(instead of impulsive and limitless obedience), based upon pride, and

involving, for the most part, scorn of the helpless and weak, and respect only for the orders of men who have been trained to this habit of self-government. Whence the title classical, from the Latin *classicus*.[41]

The school is, therefore, generally to be characterized as that of taste and restraint. As the school of taste, everything is, in its estimation, beneath it, so as to be tasted or tested; not above it, to be thankfully received. Nothing was to be fed upon as bread; but only palated as a dainty. This spirit has destroyed art since the close of the sixteenth century, and nearly destroyed French literature, our English literature being at the same time severely depressed, and our education (except in bodily strength) rendered nearly nugatory by it, so far as it affects commonplace minds. It is not possible that the classical spirit should ever take possession of a mind of the highest order. Again, as the school of reserve, it refuses to allow itself in any violent or "spasmodic" passion; the schools of literature which have been in modern times called "spasmodic" being reactionary against it. The word, though an ugly one, is quite accurate, the most spasmodic books in the world being Solomon's Song, Job, and Isaiah.

The classical landscape, properly so called, is therefore the representative of perfectly trained and civilized human life, associated with perfect natural scenery and with decorative spiritual powers.

I will expand this definition a little.

(1.) Perfectly civilized human life; that is, life freed from the necessity of humiliating labour, from passions inducing bodily disease, and from abasing misfortune. The personages of the classical landscape, therefore, must be virtuous and amiable; if employed in labour, endowed with strength, such as may make it not oppressive. (Considered as a practical ideal, the classical life necessarily implies slavery, and the command, therefore, of a higher order of men over a lower, occupied in servile work.) Pastoral occupation is allowable as a contrast with city life. War, if undertaken by classical persons, must be a contest for honour, more than for life, not at all for wealth, and free from all fearful or debasing passion. Classical persons must be trained in all the polite arts, and, because their health is to be perfect, chiefly in the open air. Hence, the architecture around them must be of the most finished kind, the rough country and ground being subdued by frequent and happy humanity.

(2.) Such personages and buildings must be associated with natural scenery, uninjured by storms or inclemency of climate (such injury implying interruption of the open-air life); and it must be scenery conducing to pleasure, not to material service; all cornfields, orchards, olive-yards, and such like, being under the management of slaves, and the superior beings having nothing to do with them; but passing their lives under avenues of scented and otherwise delightful trees,—under picturesque rocks, and by clear fountains.

(3.) The spiritual powers in classical scenery must be decorative; ornamental gods, not governing gods; otherwise they could not be subjected to the principles of taste, but would demand reverence. In order, therefore, as far as possible, without taking away their supernatural power, to destroy their dignity, they are made more criminal and capricious than men, and, for the most part, those only are introduced who are the lords of lascivious pleasures. For the appearance of any great god would at once destroy the whole theory of the classical life; therefore, Pan, Bacchus, and the Satyrs, with Venus and the Nymphs, are the principal spiritual powers of the classical landscape. Apollo with the Muses appear as the patrons of the liberal arts. Minerva rarely presents herself (except to be insulted by judgment of Paris); Juno seldom, except for some purpose of tyranny; Jupiter seldom, but for purpose of amour.

Such being the general ideal of the classical landscape, it can hardly be necessary to show the reader how such charm as it possesses must in general be strong only over weak or second-rate orders of mind. It has, however, been often experimentally or playfully aimed at by great men; but I shall only take note of its two leading masters.

Claude. (I.) As I shall have no farther occasion to refer to this painter, I will resume, shortly, what has been said of him throughout the work. He had a fine feeling for beauty of form, and considerable tenderness of perception. His aerial effects are unequalled. Their character appears to me to arise rather from a delicacy of bodily constitution in Claude, than from any mental sensibility: such as they are, they give a kind of feminine charm to his work, which partly accounts for its wide influence. To whatever the character may be traced, it renders him incapable of enjoying or painting anything energetic or terrible. Hence the weakness of his conceptions of rough sea.

(II.) He had sincerity of purpose. But in common with other landscape painters of his day, neither earnestness, humility, nor love, such as would ever cause him to forget himself.

That is to say, so far as he felt the truth, he tried to be true; but he never felt it enough to sacrifice supposed propriety or habitual method to it. Very few of his sketches, and none of his pictures, show evidence of interest in other natural phenomena than the quiet afternoon sunshine which would fall methodically into a composition. One would suppose he had never seen scarlet in a morning cloud, nor a storm burst on the Apennines. But he enjoys a quiet misty afternoon in a ruminant sort of way, yet truly; and strives for the likeness of it, therein differing from Salvator, who never attempts to be truthful, but only to be impressive.

(III.) His seas are the most beautiful in old art. For he studied tame waves, as he did tame skies, with great sincerity, and some affection; and modelled them with more care not only than any other landscape painter

319

of his day, but even than any of the great men; for they, seeing the perfect
320 painting of sea to be impossible, gave up the attempt, and treated it
conventionally. But Claude took so much pains about this, feeling it was
one of his *fortes*, that I suppose no one can model a small wave better than
he.

IV. He first set the pictorial sun in the pictorial heaven. We will give
him the credit of this, with no drawbacks.

V. He had hardly any knowledge of physical science, and shows a
peculiar incapacity of understanding the main point of a matter.
Connected with which incapacity is his want of harmony in expression.

Such were the principal qualities of the leading painter of classical
landscape, his effeminate softness causing him to dislike all evidences of
toil, or distress, or terror, and to delight in the calm formalities which
mark the school.

Although he often introduces romantic incidents and mediæval as well
as Greek or Roman personages, his landscape is always in the true sense
classic—everything being "elegantly" (selectingly or tastefully), not
passionately, treated. The absence of indications of rural labour, of
hedges, ditches, haystacks, ploughed fields, and the like; the frequent
occurrence of ruins of temples, or masses of unruined palaces; and the
graceful wildness of growth in his trees, are the principal sources of the
"elevated" character which so many persons feel in his scenery.

There is no other sentiment traceable in his work than this weak dislike
to entertain the conception of toil or suffering. Ideas of relation, in the
true sense, he has none; nor ever makes an effort to conceive an event
in its probable circumstances, but fills his foregrounds with decorative
figures, using commonest conventionalism to indicate the subject he
intends.

322 The admiration of his works was legitimate, so far as it regarded their
sunlight effects and their graceful details. It was base, in so far as it
involved irreverence both for the deeper powers of nature, and carelessness as to conception of subject. Large admiration of Claude is wholly
impossible in any period of national vigour in art. He may by such
tenderness as he possesses, and by the very fact of his banishing painfulness, exercise considerable influence over certain classes of minds; but this
influence is almost exclusively hurtful to them.

Nevertheless, on account of such small sterling qualities as they possess,
and of their general pleasantness, as well as their importance in the history
of art, genuine Claudes must always possess a considerable value, either as
drawing-room ornaments or museum relics. They may be ranked with fine
pieces of china manufacture, and other agreeable curiosities, of which the
price depends on the rarity rather than the merit, yet always on a merit of
a certain low kind.

The other characteristic master of classical landscape is Nicolo Poussin.

I named Claude first, because the forms of scenery he has represented are richer and more general than Poussin's; but Poussin has a far greater power, and his landscapes, though more limited in material, are incomparably nobler than Claude's. It would take considerable time to enter into accurate analysis of Poussin's strong but degraded mind; and bring us no reward, because whatever he has done has been done better by Titian. His peculiarities are, without exception, weaknesses, induced in a highly intellectual and inventive mind by being fed on medals, books, and bassi-relievi instead of nature, and by the want of any deep sensibility. His best works are his Bacchanalian revels, always brightly wanton and wild, full of frisk and fire; but they are coarser than Titian's, and infinitely less beautiful. In all minglings of the human and brutal character he leans on the bestial, yet with a sternly Greek severity of treatment. This restraint, peculiarly classical, is much too manifest in him; for, owing to his habit of never letting himself be free, he does nothing as well as it ought to be done, rarely even as well as he can himself do it; and his best beauty is poor, incomplete, and characterless, though refined.

His want of sensibility permits him to paint frightful subjects, without feeling any true horror. His battle-pieces are cold and feeble; his religious subjects wholly nugatory, they do not excite him enough to develop even his ordinary powers of invention. Neither does he put much power into his landscape when it becomes principal; the best pieces of it occur in fragments behind his figures. Beautiful vegetation, more or less ornamental in character, occurs in nearly all his mythological subjects, but his pure landscape is notable only for its dignified reserve; the great squareness and horizontality of its masses, with lowness of tone, giving it a deeply meditative character. Whatever power this lowness of tone, light in the distance, etc., give to his landscape, or to Gaspar's, is in both conventional and artificial.

323

324

CHAPTER VI

Rubens and Cuyp

326   THE examination of the causes which led to the final departure of the religious spirit from the hearts of painters, would involve discussion of the whole scope of the Reformation on the minds of persons unconcerned directly in its progress. This is of course impossible.

One or two broad facts only can be stated, which the reader may verify, if he pleases, by his own labour. I do not give them rashly.

The strength of the Reformation lay entirely in its being a movement towards purity of practice.

The Catholic priesthood was hostile to it in proportion to the degree in which they had been false to their own principles of moral action, and had become corrupt or worldly in heart.

The Reformers indeed cast out many absurdities, and demonstrated many fallacies, in the teaching of the Roman Catholic Church. But they themselves introduced errors, which rent the ranks, and finally arrested the march of the Reformation, and which paralyze the Protestant Church to this day. Errors of which the fatality was increased by the controversial bent which lost accuracy of meaning in force of declamation, and turned expressions, which ought to be used only in retired depth of thought, into phrases of custom, or watchwords of attack. Owing to which habits of hot, ingenious, and unguarded controversy, the Reformed Churches themselves soon forgot the meaning of the word which, of all words, was oftenest in their mouths. They forgot that $\pi i \sigma \tau \iota s$ is a derivative of $\pi \epsilon i \theta o \mu a \iota$, not of $\pi \iota \sigma \tau \epsilon \acute{\upsilon} \omega$, and that "fides," closely connected with

327   "fido" [42] on one side, and with "confido" on the other, is but distantly related to "credo."

By whatever means, however, the reader may himself be disposed to admit, the Reformation *was* arrested; and got itself shut up into chancels of cathedrals in England (even those, generally too large for it), and into conventicles everywhere else. Then rising between the infancy of Reformation, and the palsy of Catholicism;—between a new shell of half-built religion on one side, daubed with untempered mortar, and a falling ruin of out-worn religion on the other, lizard-crannied, and ivy-grown;—

rose, on its independent foundation, the faithless and materialized mind of modern Europe—ending in the rationalism of Germany, the polite formalism of England, the careless blasphemy of France, and the helpless sensualities of Italy; in the midst of which, steadily advancing science, and the charities of more and more widely extended peace, are preparing the way for a Christian Church, which shall depend neither on ignorance for its continuance, nor on controversy for its progress, but shall reign at once in light and love.

The whole body of painters (such of them as were left,) necessarily fell into the rationalistic chasm. The Evangelicals despised the arts, while the Roman Catholics were effete or insincere, and could not retain influence over men of strong reasoning power.

The painters could only associate frankly with men of the world, and   328
themselves became men of the world. Men, I mean, having no belief in spiritual existences, no interests or affections beyond the grave.

Not but that they still painted scriptural subjects. Altar-pieces were wanted occasionally, and pious patrons sometimes commissioned a cabinet Madonna. But there is just this difference between the men of this modern period, and the Florentines or Venetians—that whereas the latter never exert themselves fully except on a sacred subject, the Flemish and Dutch masters are always languid unless they are profane. Leonardo is only to be seen in the Cena;[43] Titian only in the Assumption; but Rubens only in the Battle of the Amazons, and Vandyck only at court.

Altar-pieces, when wanted, of course either of them will supply as readily as anything else. Virgins in blue, or St. Johns in red, as many as you please. Martyrdoms also, by all means: Rubens especially delights in these. St. Peter, head downwards, is interesting anatomically; writhings of impenitent thieves, and bishops having their tongues pulled out, display our powers to advantage, also. Theological instruction, if required: "Christ armed with thunder, to destroy the world, spares it at the intercession of St. Francis." Last Judgments even, quite Michael-Angelesque, rich in twistings of limbs, with spiteful biting, and scratching; and fine aerial effects in smoke of the pit.

In all this, however, there is not a vestige of religious feeling or reverence. We have even some visible difficulty in meeting our patron's pious wishes. Daniel in the lion's den is indeed an available subject, but duller than a lion hunt; and Mary of Nazareth must be painted if an order   329
come for her; but (says polite Sir Peter), Mary of Medicis, or Catherine, her bodice being fuller, and better embroidered, would, if we might offer a suggestion, probably give greater satisfaction.

No phenomenon in human mind is more extraordinary than the junction of this cold and worldly temper with great rectitude of principle, and tranquil kindness of heart. Rubens was an honourable and entirely well-intentioned man, earnestly industrious, simple and temperate in habits of life, high-bred, learned and discreet. His affection for his mother was great; his generosity to contemporary artists unfailing. He is a healthy, worthy, kind-hearted, courtly-phrased—Animal—without any clearly perceptible traces of a soul, except when he paints his children.

330   We saw how Veronese painted himself, and his family, as worshipping the Madonna.[44]

Rubens has also painted himself and his family in an equally elaborate piece. But they are not *worshipping* the Madonna. They are *performing* the Madonna, and her saintly entourage. His favourite wife "en Madonne"; his youngest boy "as Christ"; his father-in-law (or father, it matters not which) "as Simeon"; another elderly relation, with a beard, "as St. Jerome"; and he himself "as St. George."

331   Rembrandt has also painted (it is, on the whole, his greatest picture, so far as I have seen) himself and his wife in a state of ideal happiness. He sits at supper with his wife on his knee, flourishing a glass of champagne, with a roast peacock on the table.

The Rubens is in the Church of St. James at Antwerp; the Rembrandt at Dresden—marvellous pictures, both. No more precious works by either painter exist. Their hearts, such as they have, are entirely in them; and the two pictures, not inaptly, represent the Faith and Hope of the seventeenth century. We have to stoop somewhat lower, in order to comprehend the pastoral and rustic scenery of Cuyp and Teniers, which must yet be held as forming one group with the historical art of Rubens, being connected with it by Rubens' pastoral landscape. To these, I say, we must stoop lower; for they are destitute, not of spiritual character only, but of spiritual thought.

Rubens often gives instructive and magnificent allegory; Rembrandt, pathetic or powerful fancies, founded on real scripture reading, and on his interest in the picturesque character of the Jew. And Vandyck, a graceful dramatic rendering of received scriptural legends.

But in the pastoral landscape we lose, not only all faith in religion, but all remembrance of it. Absolutely now at last we find ourselves without sight of God in all the world.

So far as I can hear or read, this is an entirely new and wonderful state of things achieved by the Hollanders. The human being never got wholly quit of the terror of spiritual being before. Persian, Egyptian, Assyrian, Hindoo, Chinese, all kept some dim, appalling record of what they called "gods." Farthest savages had—and still have—their Great Spirit, or, in extremity, their feather-idols, large-eyed; but here in Holland we have at

332   last got utterly done with it all. Our only idol glitters dimly, in tangible shape of a pint pot, and all the incense offered thereto, comes out of a small censer or bowl at the end of a pipe. "Of deities or virtues, angels,

principalities, or powers, in the name of our ditches, no more. Let us have cattle and market vegetables.''

This is the first and essential character of the Holland landscape art. Its second is a worthier one; respect for rural life.

I should attach greater importance to this rural feeling, if there were any true humanity in it, or any feeling for beauty. But there is neither. No incidents of this lower life are painted for the sake of the incidents, but only for the effects of light. You will find that the best Dutch painters do not care about the people, but about the lustres on them. Paul Potter, their best herd and cattle painter, does not care even for sheep, but only for wool; regards not cows, but cowhide. He attains great dexterity in drawing tufts and locks, lingers in the little parallel ravines and furrows of fleece that open across sheep's backs as they turn; is unsurpassed in twisting a horn or pointing a nose; but he cannot paint eyes, nor perceive any condition of an animal's mind, except its desire of grazing. Cuyp can, indeed, paint sunlight, the best that Holland's sun can show; he is a man of large natural gift, and sees broadly, nay, even seriously; finds out—a wonderful thing for men to find out in those days—that there are reflections in water, and that boats require often to be painted upside down. A brewer by trade, he feels the quiet of a summer afternoon, and his work will make you marvellously drowsy. It is good for nothing else that I know of; strong; but unhelpful and unthoughtful. Nothing happens in his pictures, except some indifferent person's asking the way of somebody else, who, by his cast of countenance, seems not likely to know it. For farther entertainment perhaps a red cow and a white one; or puppies at play, not playfully; the man's heart not going even with the puppies. Essentially he sees nothing but the shine on the flaps of their ears.

Observe always, the fault lies not in the thing's being little, or the incident being slight. Titian could have put issues of life and death into the face of a man asking the way; nay, into the back of him, if he had so chosen.

Into the causes of which grandeur we must look a little, with respect not only to these puppies, and gray horses, and cattle of Cuyp, but to the hunting pieces of Rubens and Snyders. For closely connected with the Dutch rejection of motives of spiritual interest, is the increasing importance attached by them to animals, seen either in the chase or in agriculture; and to judge justly of the value of this animal painting, it will be necessary for us to glance at that of earlier times.

And first of the animals which have had more influence over the human soul, in its modern life, than ever Apis or the crocodile had over Egyptian—the dog and horse. I stated, in speaking of Venetian religion, that the Venetians always introduced the dog as a contrast to the high aspects of humanity. They do this, not because they consider him the basest of animals, but the highest—the connecting link between men and animals; in whom the lower forms of really human feeling may be best exemplified, such as conceit, gluttony, indolence, petulance. But they saw the noble qualities of the dog, too;—all his patience, love, and faithfulness; therefore Veronese, hard as he is often on lap-dogs, has painted one great heroic poem on the dog.

Two mighty brindled mastiffs, and beyond them, darkness [fig.57]. You scarcely see them at first, against the gloomy green. No other sky for them—poor things. They are gray themselves, spotted with black all over; their multitudinous doggish vices may not be washed out of them,—are in grain of nature. Strong thewed and sinewed, however,—no blame on them as far as bodily strength may reach; their heads coal-black, with drooping ears and fierce eyes, bloodshot a little. Wildest of beasts perhaps they would have been, by nature. But between them stands the spirit of their human love, dove-winged and beautiful, the resistless Greek boy, golden quivered; his glowing breast and limbs the only light upon the sky,—purple and pure. He has cast his chain about the dogs' necks, and holds it in his strong right hand, leaning proudly a little back from them. They will never break loose.

This is Veronese's highest, or spiritual view of the dog's nature. He can

fig.57   Paul Veronese, *Cupid with Dogs*

only give this when looking at the creature alone. When he sees it in company with men, he subdues it, like an inferior light in presence of the sky; and generally then gives it a merely brutal nature, not insisting even on its affection. It is thus used in the Marriage in Cana to symbolize gluttony.[45] That great picture I have not yet had time to examine in all its bearings of thought; but the chief purpose of it is, I believe, to express the pomp and pleasure of the world, pursued without thought of the presence of Christ; therefore the Fool with the bells is put in the centre, immediately underneath the Christ; and in front are the couple of dogs in leash, one gnawing a bone. A cat lying on her back scratches at one of the vases which hold the wine of the miracle.

336

In the Supper at Emmaus,[46] the dog's affection is, however, fully dwelt upon. Veronese's own two little daughters are playing, on the hither side of the table, with a great wolf-hound, larger than either of them. One with her head down, nearly touching his nose, is talking to him—asking him questions it seems, nearly pushing him over at the same time:—the other raising her eyes, half archly, half dreamily,—some far-away thought coming over her,—leans against him on the other side, propping him with her little hand, laid slightly on his neck. He, all passive, and glad at heart, yielding himself to the pushing or sustaining hand, looks earnestly into the face of the child close to his; would answer her with the gravity of a senator, if so it might be:—can only look at her, and love her.

As we pass from the Venetians and Florentines to the Dutch, the passing away of the soul-power is indicated by every animal becoming savage or foul. The dog is used by Teniers, and many other Hollanders, merely to obtain unclean jest; while by the more powerful men, Rubens, Snyders, Rembrandt, it is painted only in savage chase, or butchered agony. I know no pictures more shameful to humanity than the boar and lion hunts of Rubens and Snyders, signs of disgrace all the deeper, because the powers desecrated are so great. The painter of the village ale-house sign may, not dishonourably, paint the fox-hunt for the village squire; but the occupation of magnificent art-power in giving semblance of perpetuity to those bodily pangs which Nature has mercifully ordained to be transient, and in forcing us, by the fascination of its stormy skill, to dwell on that from which eyes of merciful men should instinctively turn away, and eyes of high-minded men scornfully, is dishonourable, alike in the power which it degrades, and the joy to which it betrays.

337

In our modern treatment of the dog, of which the prevailing tendency is marked by Landseer, the interest taken in him is disproportionate to that taken in man, and leads to a somewhat trivial mingling of senti-ment, or warping by caricature; giving up the true nature of the animal for the sake of a pretty thought or pleasant jest. Neither Titian nor Velasquez ever jests; and though Veronese jests gracefully and tenderly, he never for an instant oversteps the absolute facts of nature.

340   In painting, I find that no real interest is taken in the horse until Vandyck's time, he and Rubens doing more for it than all previous painters put together. Rubens was a good rider, and rode nearly every day, as I doubt not, Vandyck also. The horse has never, I think, been painted worthily again, since he died.[47] Of the influence of its unworthy painting, and unworthy use, I do not at present care to speak, noticing only that it brought about in England the last degradations of feeling and of art. The Dutch, indeed, banished all Deity from the earth; but I think only in England has death-bed consolation been sought in a fox's tail.

341   Lastly, of cattle.

The period when the interest of men began to be transferred from the ploughman to his oxen is very distinctly marked by Bassano. In him the descent is even greater, being, accurately, from the Madonna to the

342   Manger—one of perhaps his best pictures representing an adoration of shepherds with nothing to adore, they and their herds forming the subject, and the Christ "being supposed" at the side.[48] From that time cattle-pieces become frequent, and gradually form a staple art commodity. Cuyp's are the best; nevertheless, neither by him nor any one else have I ever seen an entirely well-painted cow. All the men who have skill enough to paint cattle nobly, disdain them. The real influence of these Dutch cattle-pieces, in subsequent art, is difficult to trace, and is not worth tracing. They contain a certain healthy appreciation of simple pleasure which I cannot look upon wholly without respect. On the other hand, their cheap tricks of composition degraded the entire technical system of landscape; and their clownish and blunt vulgarities too long blinded us, and continue, so far as in them lies, to blind us yet, to all the true refinement and passion of rural life. There have always been truth and depth of pastoral feeling in the works of great poets and novelists; but never, I think, in painting, until lately.

We must not, however, yet pass to the modern school, having still to examine the last phase of Dutch design, in which the vulgarities which might be forgiven to the truth of Cuyp, and forgotten in the power of Rubens, became unpardonable and dominant in the works of men who were at once affected and feeble.

CHAPTER VIII
Wouvermans and Angelico

HAVING determined the general nature of vulgarity,[49] we are now 363
able to close our view of the character of the Dutch school.

It is a strangely mingled one, which I have the more difficulty in investigating, because I have no power of sympathy with it. However inferior in capacity, I can enter measuredly into the feelings of Correggio or of Titian; what they like, I like; what they disdain, I disdain. Going lower down, I can still follow Salvator's passion, or Albano's prettiness;[50] and lower still, I can measure modern German heroics, or French sensualities. I see what the people mean,—know where they are, and what they are. But no effort of fancy will enable me to lay hold of the temper of Teniers, or Wouvermans, any more than I can enter into the feelings of one of the lower animals. I cannot see why they painted,—what they are aiming at,—what they liked or disliked. All their life and work is the same sort of mystery to me as the mind of my dog when he rolls on carrion. He is a well enough conducted dog in other respects, and many of these Dutchmen were doubtless very well-conducted persons: certainly they learned their business well; both Teniers and Wouvermans touch with a workmanly hand, such as we cannot see rivalled now; and they seem 364 never to have painted indolently, but gave the purchaser his thorough money's worth of mechanism, while the burgesses who bargained for their cattle and card parties were probably more respectable men than the princes who gave orders to Titian for nymphs, and to Raphael for nativities. But whatever patient merit or commercial value may be in Dutch labour, this at least is clear, that it is wholly insensitive.

The very mastery these men have of their business proceeds from their never really seeing the whole of anything, but only that part of it which they know how to do. Out of all nature they felt their function was to extract the grayness and shininess. Give them a golden sunset, a rosy dawn, a green waterfall, a scarlet autumn on the hills, and they merely look curiously into it to see if there is anything gray and glittering which can be painted on their common principles.

If this, however, were their only fault, it would not prove absolute insensibility, any more than it could be declared of the makers of Florentine tables, that they were blind or vulgar, because they took out of nature only what could be represented in agate. A Dutch picture is, in fact, merely a Florentine table more finely touched; it has its regular ground of slate, and its mother-of-pearl and tinsel put in with equal precision; and perhaps the fairest view one can take of a Dutch painter, is that he is a respectable tradesman furnishing well-made articles in oil paint; but when we begin to examine the designs of these articles, we may see immediately that it is his inbred vulgarity, and not the chance of fortune, which has made him a tradesman, and kept him one;— which essential character of Dutch work, as distinguished from all other, may be best seen in that hybrid landscape, introduced by Wouvermans and Berghem. Of this landscape Wouvermans' is the most character-

365 istic. We will examine the motives of one of the most elaborate Wouvermans existing—landscape with a hunting party, in the Pinaco- thek of Munich [fig.58].

fig.58 Philips Wouverman, *Stag Hunt*

A large lake in the distance narrows into a river in the foreground; but the river has no current, nor has the lake either reflections or waves. It is a piece of gray slate table, painted with horizontal touches, and only explained to be water by boats upon it. Some of the figures in these are fishing (the corks of a net are drawn in bad perspective); others are bathing, one man pulling his shirt over his ears, others are swimming. On the farther side of the river are some curious buildings, half villa, half ruin; or rather ruin dressed. There are gardens at the top of them, with beautiful and graceful trellised architecture and wandering tendrils of vine. A gentleman is coming down from a door in the ruins to get into his pleasure-boat. His servant catches his dog.

On the nearer side of the river, a bank of broken ground rises from the water's edge up to a group of very graceful and carefully studied trees, with a French-antique statue on a pedestal in the midst of them, at the foot of which are three musicians, and a well-dressed couple dancing; their coach is in waiting behind. In the foreground are hunters. A richly and highly dressed woman with falcon on fist, the principal figure in the picture, is wrought with Wouvermans' best skill. A stouter lady rides into the water after a stag and hind, who gallop across the middle of the river without sinking. Two horsemen attend the two Amazons, of whom one pursues the game cautiously, but the other is thrown headforemost into the river, with a splash which shows it to be deep at the edge, though the hart and hind find bottom in the middle. Running footmen, with other dogs, are coming up, and children are sailing a toy-boat in the immediate fore- 366 ground. The tone of the whole is dark and gray, throwing out the figures in spots of light, on Wouvermans' usual system. The sky is cloudy, and very cold.

You observe that in this picture the painter has assembled all the elements which he supposes pleasurable. We have music, dancing, hunting, boating, fishing, bathing, and child-play, all at once. Water, wide and narrow; architecture, rustic and classical; trees also of the finest; clouds, not ill-shaped. Nothing wanting to our Paradise: not even practical jest; for to keep us always laughing, somebody shall be for ever falling with a splash into the Pison. Things proceed, nevertheless, with an oppressive quietude. The dancers are uninterested in the hunters, the hunters in the dancers; the hirer of the pleasure-boat perceives neither hart nor hind; the children are unconcerned at the hunter's fall; the bathers regard not the draught of fishes; the fishers fish among the bathers, without apparently anticipating any diminution in their haul.

Let the reader ask himself, would it have been possible for the painter in any clearer way to show an absolute, clay-cold, ice-cold incapacity of understanding what a pleasure meant? Had he had as much heart as a minnow, he would have given some interest to the fishing; with the soul of a grasshopper, some spring to the dancing; had he half the will[51] of a dog, he would have made some one turn to look at the hunt, or given a little fire to the dash down to the water's edge. If he had been capable of pensiveness, he would not have put the pleasure-boat under the ruin;— capable of cheerfulness, he would not have put the ruin above the pleasure-boat. Paralyzed in heart and brain, he delivers his inventoried articles of pleasure one by one to his ravenous customers; palateless; gluttonous. "We cannot taste it. Hunting is not enough; let us have dancing. That's dull; now give us a jest, or what is life! The river is too narrow, let us have a lake; and, for mercy's sake, a pleasure-boat, or how can we spend another minute of this languid day! But what pleasure can be in a boat? let us swim; we see people always drest, let us see them naked."

367

Such is the unredeemed, carnal appetite for mere sensual pleasure. I am aware of no other painter who consults it so exclusively, without one gleam of higher hope, thought, beauty, or passion.

As the pleasure of Wouvermans, so also is his war. That, however, is not hybrid, it is of one character only.

The best example I know is the great battle-piece with the bridge, in the gallery of Turin.

There are some twenty figures in the mêlée whose faces can be seen (about sixty in the picture altogether), and of these twenty, there is not one whose face indicates courage or power; or anything but animal rage and cowardice; the latter prevailing always. Every one is fighting for his life, with the expression of a burglar defending himself at extremity against a party of policemen. There is the same terror, fury, and pain which a low thief would show on receiving a pistol-shot through his arm. Most of them appear to be fighting only to get away; the standard-bearer *is* retreating, but whether with the enemy's flag or his own I do not see; he slinks away with it, with reverted eye, as if he were stealing a pocket-handkerchief. The swordsmen cut at each other with clenched teeth and terrified eyes; they are too busy to curse each other; but one sees that the feelings they have could be expressed no otherwise than by low oaths. Far

368

away, to the smallest figures in the smoke, and to one drowning under the distant arch of the bridge, all are wrought with a consummate skill in vulgar touch; there is no good painting, properly so called, anywhere, but of clever, dotty, sparkling, telling execution, as much as the canvas will hold, and much delicate gray and blue colour in the smoke and sky.

Now, in order fully to feel the difference between this view of war, and a gentleman's, go, if possible, into our National Gallery, and look at the young Malatesta riding into the battle of Sant' Egidio (as he is painted by Paul Uccello) [fig.59]. His uncle Carlo, the leader of the army, a grave man of about sixty, has just given orders for the knights to close: two have pushed forward with lowered lances, and the mêlée has begun only a few yards in front; but the young knight, riding at his uncle's side, has not yet put his helmet on, nor intends doing so yet. Erect he sits, and quiet, waiting for his captain's order to charge; calm as if he were at a hawking party, only more grave; his golden hair wreathed about his proud white brow, as about a statue's.

fig.59   Uccello, *The Battle of San Romano* (detail)

"Yes," the thoughtful reader replies, "this may be pictorially very beautiful; but those Dutchmen were good fighters, and generally won the day; whereas, this very battle of Sant' Egidio, so calmly and bravely begun, was lost."

Indeed, it is very singular that unmitigated expressions of cowardice in battle should be given by the painters of so brave a nation as the Dutch. Not but that it is possible enough for a coward to be stubborn, and a brave man weak; the one may win his battle by a blind persistence, and the other lose it by a thoughtful vacillation. Nevertheless, the want of all expression of resoluteness in Dutch battle-pieces remains, for the present, a mystery to me. In those of Wouvermans, it is only a natural development of his perfect vulgarity in all respects.

369   I do not think it necessary to trace farther the evidences of insensitive conception in the Dutch school. I have associated the name of Teniers with that of Wouvermans in the beginning of this chapter, because Teniers is essentially the painter of the pleasures of the ale-house and card-table, as Wouvermans of those of the chase; and the two are leading masters of the peculiar Dutch trick of white touch on gray or brown ground; but Teniers is higher in reach and more honest in manner. Berghem is the real associate of Wouvermans in the hybrid school of landscape. But all three are alike insensitive; that is to say, unspiritual or deathful, and that to the uttermost, in every thought,—producing, therefore, the lowest phase of possible art of a skilful kind. There are deeper elements in De Hooghe and Gerard Terburg; sometimes expressed with superb quiet painting by the former; but the whole school is inherently mortal to all its admirers; having by its influence in England destroyed our perception of all purposes of painting, and throughout the north of the Continent effaced the sense of colour among artists of every rank.

        We have, last, to consider what recovery has taken place from the paralysis to which the influence of this Dutch art had reduced us in England seventy years ago. But, in closing my review of older art, I will endeavour to illustrate, by four simple examples, the main directions of its spiritual power, and the cause of its decline.

        The frontispiece of this volume is engraved from an old sketch of mine, a pencil outline of the little Madonna by Angelico, in the Annunciation preserved in the sacristy of Santa Maria Novella [fig.60]. This Madonna
370   is one of the most characteristic of the Purist school. It is well to turn back to it now, from the wholly carnal work of Wouvermans, in order to feel its purity: so that, if we err, it may be on this side. The opposition is the most accurate which I can set before the student, for the technical disposition of Wouvermans, in his search after delicate form and minute grace, much resembles that of Angelico. But the thoughts of Wouvermans are wholly of this world. For him there is no heroism, awe, or mercy, hope, or faith. Eating and drinking, and slaying; rage and lust; the pleasures and distresses of the debased body—from these, his thoughts, if so we may call them, never for an instant rise or range.

        The soul of Angelico is in all ways the precise reverse of this; habitually as incognizant of any earthly pleasure as Wouvermans of any heavenly one. Both are exclusive with absolute exclusiveness;—neither desiring nor conceiving anything beyond their respective spheres. Wouvermans lives under gray clouds, his lights come out as spots. Angelico lives in an unclouded light: his shadows themselves are colour; his lights are not the spots, but his darks. Wouvermans lives in perpetual tumult—tramp of horse—clash of cup—ring of pistol-shot. Angelico in perpetual peace. Not

fig.60   John Ruskin, *Ancilla Domini* (engraving after Fra Angelico)

seclusion from the world. No shutting out of the world is needful for him. There is nothing to shut out. Envy, lust, contention, discourtesy, are to him as though they were not; and the cloister walk of Fiesole no penitential solitude, barred from the stir and joy of life, but a possessed land of tender blessing, guarded from the entrance of all but holiest sorrow. The little cell was as one of the houses of heaven prepared for him by his Master. What need had it to be elsewhere? Was not the Val d'Arno, with its olive woods in white blossom, paradise enough for a poor monk? or could Christ be indeed in heaven more than here? Was He not always with him? Could he breathe or see, but that Christ breathed beside him, and looked into his eyes? Under every cypress avenue the angels walked; he had seen their white robes, whiter than the dawn, at his bed-side, as he awoke in early summer. They had sung with him, one on each side, when his voice failed for joy at sweet vesper and matin time; his eyes were blinded by their wings in the sunset, when it sank behind the hills of Luni.

371

There may be weakness in this, but there is no baseness; and while I rejoice in all recovery from monasticism which leads to practical and healthy action in the world, I must, in closing this work, severely guard my pupils from the thought that sacred rest may be honourably exchanged for selfish and mindless activity.

In order to mark the temper of Angelico, by a contrast of another kind, I give in fig. 61 a facsimile of one of the heads in Salvator's etching of the Academy of Plato. It is accurately characteristic of Salvator, showing, by quite a central type, his indignant, desolate, and degraded power.

372

Then, in fig. 62 (overleaf), you have also a central type of the mind of Dürer.[52] Complete, yet quaint; severely rational and practical, yet capable of the highest imaginative religious feeling, and as gentle as a child's, it seemed to be well represented by this figure of the old

fig.61

figure of the old bishop, with all the infirmities, and all the victory, of his life, written on his calm, kind, and worldly face. He has been no dreamer, nor persecutor, but a helpful and undeceivable man; and by careful comparison of this conception with the common kinds of episcopal ideal in modern religious art, you will gradually feel how the force of Dürer is joined with an unapproachable refinement, so that he can give the most practical view of whatever he treats, without the slightest taint or shadow of vulgarity. Lastly, the fresco of Giorgione [fig.63], which is as fair a type as I am able to give in any single figure, of the central Venetian art, will complete for us a series, sufficiently symbolical of the several ranks of art, from lowest to highest. In Wouvermans (of whose work I suppose no

example is needed, it being so generally known), we have the entirely
carnal mind,—wholly versed in the material world, and incapable of   373
conceiving any goodness or greatness whatsoever.

In Angelico, you have the entirely spiritual mind, wholly versed in the
heavenly world, and incapable of conceiving any wickedness or vileness
whatsoever.

In Salvator, you have an awakened conscience, and some spiritual power,
contending with evil, but conquered by it, and brought into captivity to it.

In Dürer, you have a far purer conscience and higher spiritual power, yet,
with some defect still in intellect, contending with evil, and nobly
prevailing over it; yet retaining the marks of the contest, and never so
entirely victorious as to conquer sadness.

In Giorgione, you have the same high spiritual power and practical sense;
but now, with entirely perfect intellect, contending with evil; conquering
it utterly, casting it away for ever, and rising beyond it into magnificence of
rest.

fig.62   Albrecht Dürer,
St Arnulf, Bishop of Metz

fig.63   W. Holl, *The Hesperid Aeglé* (engraving after Giorgione)

CHAPTER IX
The Two Boyhoods

Born half-way between the mountains and the sea—that young   374
George of Castelfranco—of the Brave Castle:—Stout George they
called him, George of Georges, so goodly a boy he was—Giorgione.

Have you ever thought what a world his eyes opened on—fair, searching
eyes of youth? What a world of mighty life, from those mountain roots to
the shore;—of loveliest life, when he went down, yet so young, to the
marble city—and became himself as a fiery heart to it?

A city of marble, did I say? nay, rather a golden city, paved with
emerald. For truly, every pinnacle and turret glanced or glowed, overlaid
with gold, or bossed with jasper. Beneath, the unsullied sea drew in deep
breathing, to and fro, its eddies of green wave. Deep-hearted, majestic,
terrible as the sea,—the men of Venice moved in sway of power and war;
pure as her pillars of alabaster, stood her mothers and maidens; from foot
to brow, all noble, walked her knights; the low bronzed gleaming of sea-
rusted armour shot angrily under their blood-red mantle-folds. Fearless,
faithful, patient, impenetrable, implacable,—every word a fate—sate her
senate. In hope and honour, lulled by flowing of wave around their isles
of sacred sand, each with his name written and the cross graved at his side,
lay her dead. A wonderful piece of world. Rather, itself a world. It lay
along the face of the waters, no larger, as its captains saw it from their
masts at evening, than a bar of sunset that could not pass away; but for its   375
power, it must have seemed to them as if they were sailing in the expanse
of heaven, and this a great planet, whose orient edge widened through
ether. A world from which all ignoble care and petty thoughts were
banished, with all the common and poor elements of life. No foulness, nor
tumult, in those tremulous streets, that filled, or fell, beneath the moon;
but rippled music of majestic change, or thrilling silence. No weak walls
could rise above them; no low-roofed cottage, nor straw-built shed. Only
the strength as of rock, and the finished setting of stones most precious.
And around them, far as the eye could reach, still the soft moving of
stainless waters, proudly pure; as not the flower, so neither the thorn nor
the thistle, could grow in the glancing fields. Ethereal strength of Alps,

dreamlike, vanishing in high procession beyond the Torcellan shore; blue islands of Paduan hills, poised in the golden west. Above, free winds and fiery clouds ranging at their will;—brightness out of the north, and balm from the south, and the stars of the evening and morning clear in the limitless light of arched heaven and circling sea.

Such was Giorgione's school—such Titian's home.

Near the south-west corner of Covent Garden, a square brick pit or well is formed by a close-set block of houses, to the back windows of which it admits a few rays of light. Access to the bottom of it is obtained out of Maiden Lane, through a low archway and an iron gate; and if you stand long enough under the archway to accustom your eyes to the darkness you may see on the left hand a narrow door, which formerly gave quiet access to a respectable barber's shop, of which the front window, looking into Maiden Lane,[53] is still extant, filled, in this year (1860), with a row of bottles, connected, in some defunct manner, with a brewer's business. A more fashionable neighbourhood, it is said, eighty years ago than now— never certainly a cheerful one—wherein a boy being born on St. George's day, 1775, began soon after to take interest in the world of Covent Garden, and put to service such spectacles of life as it afforded.

No knights to be seen there, nor, I imagine, many beautiful ladies; their costume at least disadvantageous, depending much on incumbency of hat and feather, and short waists; the majesty of men founded similarly on shoebuckles and wigs;—impressive enough when Reynolds will do his best for it; but not suggestive of much ideal delight to a boy.

"Bello ovile dov' io dormii agnello";[54] of things beautiful, besides men and women, dusty sunbeams up or down the street on summer mornings; deep furrowed cabbage-leaves at the greengrocer's; magnificence of oranges in wheelbarrows round the corner; and Thames' shore within three minutes' race.

None of these things very glorious;. the best, however, that England, it seems, was then able to provide for a boy of gift: who, such as they are, loves them—never, indeed, forgets them. The short waists modify to the last his visions of Greek ideal. His foregrounds had always a succulent cluster or two of greengrocery at the corners. Enchanted oranges gleam in Covent Gardens of the Hesperides; and great ships go to pieces in order to scatter chests of them on the waves.[55] That mist of early sunbeams in the London dawn crosses, many and many a time, the clearness of Italian air; and by Thames' shore, with its stranded barges and glidings of red sail, dearer to us than Lucerne lake or Venetian lagoon—by Thames' shore we will die.

With such circumstance round him in youth, let us note what necessary effects followed upon the boy. I assume him to have had Giorgione's sensibility (and more than Giorgione's, if that be possible) to colour and

376

377

form. I tell you farther, and this fact you may receive trustfully, that his sensibility to human affection and distress was no less keen than even his sense for natural beauty—heartsight deep as eyesight.

Consequently, he attaches himself with the faithfullest child-love to everything that bears an image of the place he was born in. No matter how ugly it is,—has it anything about it like Maiden Lane, or like Thames' shore? If so, it shall be painted for their sake. Hence, to the very close of life, Turner could endure ugliness which no one else, of the same sensibility, would have borne with for an instant. Dead brick walls, blank square windows, old clothes, market-womanly types of humanity—anything fishy and muddy, like Billingsgate or Hungerford Market, had great attraction for him; black barges, patched sails, and every possible condition of fog.

You will find these tolerations and affections guiding or sustaining him to the last hour of his life; the notablest of all such endurances being that of dirt. No Venetian ever draws anything foul; but Turner devoted picture after picture to the illustration of effects of dinginess, smoke, soot, dust, and dusty texture; old sides of boats, weedy roadside vegetation, dung-hills, straw-yards, and all the soilings and stains of every common labour.

And more than this, he not only could endure, but enjoyed and looked for *litter*, like Covent Garden wreck after the market. His pictures are often full of it, from side to side; their foregrounds differ from all others in   378 the natural way that things have of lying about in them. Even his richest vegetation, in ideal work, is confused; and he delights in shingle, débris, and heaps of fallen stones. The last words he ever spoke to me about a picture were in gentle exultation about his St. Gothard: "that *litter* of stones which I endeavoured to represent." [plate 17]

The second great result of this Covent Garden training was, understanding of and regard for the poor, whom the Venetians, we saw, despised; whom, contrarily, Turner loved, and more than loved—understood. He got no romantic sight of them, but an infallible one, as he prowled about the end of his lane, watching night effects in the wintry streets; nor sight of the poor alone, but of the poor in direct relations with the rich. He knew, in good and evil, what both classes thought of, and how they dealt with, each other.

Reynolds and Gainsborough, bred in country villages, learned there the country boy's reverential theory of "the squire," and kept it. They painted the squire and the squire's lady as centres of the movements of the universe, to the end of their lives. But Turner perceived the younger squire in other aspects about his lane, occurring prominently in its night scenery, as a dark figure, or one of two, against the moonlight. He saw also the working of city commerce, from endless warehouse, towering over Thames, to the back shop in the lane, with its stale herrings—highly interesting these last; one of his father's best friends, whom he often afterwards visited affectionately at Bristol, being a fishmonger and glue-boiler;[56] which gives us a friendly turn of mind towards herring-fishing, whaling, Calais poissardes, and many other of our choicest subjects in after-life; all this being connected with that mysterious forest below London Bridge on one side; and, on the other, with these masses of human power and national wealth which weigh upon us, at Covent Garden here, with strange compression, and crush us into narrow Hand Court.

379

"That mysterious forest below London Bridge"—better for the boy than wood of pine, or grove of myrtle. How he must have tormented the watermen, beseeching them to let him crouch anywhere in the bows, quiet as a log, so only that he might get floated down there among the ships, and round and round the ships, and with the ships, and by the ships, and under the ships, staring, and clambering;—these the only quite beautiful things he can see in all the world, except the sky; but these, when the sun is on their sails, filling or falling, endlessly disordered by sway of tide and stress of anchorage, beautiful unspeakably; which ships also are inhabited by glorious creatures—red-faced sailors, with pipes, appearing over the gunwales, true knights, over their castle parapets—the most angelic beings in the whole compass of London world. And Trafalgar happening long before we can draw ships, we, nevertheless, coax all current stories out of the wounded sailors, do our best at present to show Nelson's funeral streaming up the Thames; and vow that Trafalgar shall have its tribute of memory some day. Which, accordingly, is accomplished —once, with all our might, for its death; twice, with all our might, for its victory; thrice, in pensive farewell to the old *Téméraire* [fig.10], and with it, to that order of things.[57]

380

Now this fond companying with sailors must have divided his time, it appears to me, pretty equally between Covent Garden and Wapping (allowing for incidental excursions to Chelsea on one side, and Greenwich on the other), which time he would spend pleasantly, but not magnificently, being limited in pocket-money, and leading a kind of "Poor Jack" life on the river.

In some respects, no life could be better for a lad. But it was not calculated to make his ear fine to the niceties of language, nor form his moralities on an entirely regular standard. Picking up his first scraps of vigorous English chiefly at Deptford and in the markets, and his first ideas of female tenderness and beauty among nymphs of the barge and the barrow,—another boy might, perhaps, have become what people usually term "vulgar." But the original make and frame of Turner's mind being not vulgar, but as nearly as possible a combination of the minds of Keats and Dante, joining capricious waywardness, and intense openness to every fine pleasure of sense, and hot defiance of formal precedent, with a quite infinite tenderness, generosity, and desire of justice and truth—this kind of mind did not become vulgar, but very tolerant of vulgarity, even fond of it in some forms; and on the outside, visibly infected by it, deeply enough; the curious result, in its combination of elements, being to most people wholly incomprehensible. It was as if a cable had been woven of blood-crimson silk, and then tarred on the outside. People handled it, and the tar came off on their hands; red gleams were seen through the black underneath, at the places where it had been strained. Was it ochre?—said the world—or red lead?

Schooled thus in manners, literature, and general moral principles at Chelsea and Wapping, we have finally to inquire concerning the most important point of all. We have seen the principal differences between this boy and Giorgione, as respects sight of the beautiful, understanding of poverty, of commerce, and of order of battle; then follows another cause of difference in our training—not slight,—the aspect of religion, namely, in the neighbourhood of Covent Garden. I say the aspect; for that was all   381 the lad could judge by. Disposed, for the most part, to learn chiefly by his eyes, in this special matter he finds there is really no other way of learning. His father had taught him "to lay one penny upon another." Of mother's teaching, we hear of none; of parish pastoral teaching, the reader may guess how much.

I chose Giorgione rather than Veronese to help me in carrying out this parallel; because I do not find in Giorgione's work any of the early Venetian monarchist element. He seems to me to have belonged more to an abstract contemplative school. I may be wrong in this; it is no matter;—suppose it were so, and that he came down to Venice somewhat recusant or insentient, concerning the usual priestly doctrines of his day, how would the Venetian religion, from an outer intellectual standing-point, have *looked* to him?

He would have seen it to be a religion indisputably powerful in human affairs; often very harmfully so; sometimes devouring widows' houses, and consuming the strongest and fairest from among the young: freezing into merciless bigotry the policy of the old: also, on the other hand, animating national courage, and raising souls, otherwise sordid, into heroism: on the whole, always a real and great power; served with daily sacrifice of gold, time, and thought; putting forth its claims, if hypocritically, at least in bold hypocrisy, not waiving any atom of them in doubt or fear; and, assuredly, in large measure, sincere, believing in itself, and believed: a goodly system, moreover, in aspect; gorgeous, harmonious, mysterious; —a thing which had either to be obeyed or combated, but could not be scorned. A religion towering over all the city—many-buttressed— luminous in marble stateliness, as the dome of our Lady of Safety shines over the sea; many-voiced, also, giving, over all the eastern seas, to the   382

sentinel his watchword, to the soldier his war-cry; and, on the lips of all
who died for Venice, shaping the whisper of death.

I suppose the boy Turner to have regarded the religion of his city also
from an external intellectual standing-point.

What did he see in Maiden Lane?

Let not the reader be offended with me: I am willing to let him describe,
at his own pleasure, what Turner saw there; but to me, it seems to have
been this. A religion maintained occasionally, even the whole length of
the lane, at point of constable's staff; but, at other times, placed under
the custody of the beadle, within certain black and unstately iron railings
of St. Paul's, Covent Garden. Among the wheelbarrows and over the
vegetables, no perceptible dominance of religion; in the narrow, dis-
quieted streets, none; in the tongues, deeds, daily ways of Maiden Lane,
little. Some honesty, indeed, and English industry, and kindness of heart,
and general idea of justice; but faith, of any national kind, shut up from
one Sunday to the next, not artistically beautiful even in those Sabbatical
exhibitions; its paraphernalia being chiefly of high pews, heavy elocution,
and cold grimness of behaviour.

What chiaroscuro belongs to it—(dependent mostly on candlelight),—
we will, however, draw, considerably; no goodliness of escutcheon, nor
other respectability being omitted, and the best of their results confessed,
a meek old woman and a child being let into a pew, for whom the reading
by candlelight will be beneficial.*

For the rest, this religion seems to him discreditable—discredited—not
believing in itself: putting forth its authority in a cowardly way, watching
how far it might be tolerated, continually shrinking, disclaiming, fencing,
finessing; divided against itself, not by stormy rents, but by thin fissures,
and splittings of plaster from the walls. Not to be either obeyed, or
combated, by an ignorant, yet clear-sighted youth! only to be scorned.
And scorned not one whit the less, though also the dome dedicated to *it*
looms high over distant winding of the Thames; as St. Mark's campanile
rose, for goodly landmark, over mirage of lagoon. For St. Mark ruled over
life; the Saint of London over death; St. Mark over St. Mark's Place, but
St. Paul over St. Paul's Churchyard.

Under these influences pass away the first reflective hours of life, with
such conclusion as they can reach. In consequence of a fit of illness, he
was taken—I cannot ascertain in what year[58]—to live with an aunt, at

383

---

*Liber Studiorum. "Interior of a church." It is worthy of remark that Giorgione
and Titian are always delighted to have an opportunity of drawing priests. The
English Church may, perhaps, accept it as matter of congratulation that this is the
only instance in which Turner drew a clergyman.

Brentford; and here, I believe, received some schooling, which he seems
to have snatched vigorously; getting knowledge, at least by translation, of
the more picturesque classical authors, which he turned presently to use,
as we shall see. Hence also, walks about Putney and Twickenham in the
summer time acquainted him with the look of English meadow-ground in
its restricted states of paddock and park; and with some round-headed
appearances of trees, and stately entrances to houses of mark: the avenue
at Bushey, and the iron gates and carved pillars of Hampton, impressing
him apparently with great awe and admiration; so that in after-life his
little country house[59] is,—of all places in the world,—at Twickenham! Of
swans and reedy shores he now learns the soft motion and the green
mystery, in a way not to be forgotten.

And at last fortune wills that the lad's true life shall begin; and one
summer's evening, after various wonderful stage-coach experiences on the
north road, which gave him a love of stage-coaches ever after, he finds   384
himself sitting alone among the Yorkshire hills. For the first time, the
silence of Nature round him, her freedom sealed to him, her glory opened
to him. Peace at last; no roll of cart-wheel, nor mutter of sullen voices in
the back shop; but curlew-cry in space of heaven, and welling of bell-
toned streamlet by its shadowy rock. Freedom at last. Dead-wall, dark
railing, fenced field, gated garden, all passed away like the dream of a
prisoner; and behold, far as foot or eye can race or range, the moor, and
cloud. Loveliness at last. It is here then, among these deserted vales! Not
among men. Those pale, poverty-struck, or cruel faces;—that multitudinous, marred humanity—are not the only things that God has made.
Here is something He has made which no one has marred. Pride of purple
rocks, and river pools of blue, and tender wilderness of glittering trees, and
misty lights of evening on immeasurable hills.

Beauty, and freedom, and peace; and yet another teacher, graver than
these. Sound preaching at last here, in Kirkstall crypt,[60] concerning fate
and life. Here, where the dark pool reflects the chancel pillars, and the
cattle lie in unhindered rest, the soft sunshine on their dappled bodies,
instead of priests' vestments; their white furry hair ruffled a little, fitfully,
by the evening wind deep-scented from the meadow thyme.

Consider deeply the import to him of this, his first sight of ruin, and
compare it with the effect of the architecture that was around Giorgione.   385
There were indeed aged buildings, at Venice, in his time, but none in
decay. All ruin was removed, and its place filled as quickly as in our
London; but filled always by architecture loftier and more wonderful than
that whose place it took, the boy himself happy to work upon the walls of
it; so that the idea of the passing away of the strength of men and beauty
of their works never could occur to him sternly. Brighter and brighter the
cities of Italy had been rising and broadening on hill and plain, for three

hundred years. He saw only strength and immortality, could not but paint both; conceived the form of man as deathless, calm with power, and fiery with life.

Turner saw the exact reverse of this. In the present work of men, meanness, aimlessness, unsightliness: thin-walled, lath-divided, narrow-garreted houses of clay; booths of a darksome Vanity Fair, busily base.

But on Whitby Hill, and by Bolton Brook, remained traces of other handiwork. Men who could build had been there; and who also had wrought, not merely for their own days. But to what purpose? Strong faith, and steady hands, and patient souls—can this, then, be all you have left? this the sum of your doing on the earth;—a nest whence the night-owl may whimper to the brook, and a ribbed skeleton of consumed arches, looming above the bleak banks of mist, from its cliff to the sea?

As the strength of men to Giorgione, to Turner their weakness and vileness, were alone visible. They themselves, unworthy or ephemeral; their work, despicable, or decayed. In the Venetian's eyes, all beauty depended on man's presence and pride; in Turner's, on the solitude he had left, and the humiliation he had suffered.

And thus the fate and issue of all his work were determined at once. He must be a painter of the strength of nature, there was no beauty elsewhere than in that; he must paint also the labour and sorrow and passing away of men: this was the great human truth visible to him.

Their labour, their sorrow, and their death. Mark the three. Labour; by sea and land, in field and city, at forge and furnace, helm and plough. No pastoral indolence nor classic pride shall stand between him and the troubling of the world; still less between him and the toil of his country,—blind, tormented, unwearied, marvellous England.

Also their Sorrow; Ruin of all their glorious work, passing away of their thoughts and their honour, mirage of pleasure, FALLACY OF HOPE;[61] gathering of weed on temple step; gaining of wave on deserted strand; weeping of the mother for the children, desolate by her breathless firstborn in the streets of the city, desolate by her last sons slain, among the beasts of the field [fig.64].[62]

And their Death. That old Greek question again;—yet unanswered. The unconquerable spectre still flitting among the forest trees at twilight; rising ribbed out of the sea-sand;—white, a strange Aphrodite,—out of the sea-foam; stretching its gray, cloven wings among the clouds; turning the light of their sunsets into blood. This has to be looked upon, and in a more terrible shape than ever Salvator or Dürer saw it. The wreck of one guilty country does not infer the ruin of all countries, and need not cause general terror respecting the laws of the universe. Neither did the orderly and narrow succession of domestic joy and sorrow in a small German community bring the question in its breadth, or in any unresolvable shape,

386

fig.64   J.M.W. Turner, *Rispah watching the Bodies of her sons,*
from *Liber Studiorum*

before the mind of Dürer. But the English death—the European death of
the nineteenth century—was of another range and power; more terrible a
thousand-fold in its merely physical grasp and grief; more terrible, incal-   387
culably, in its mystery and shame. What were the robber's casual pang, or
the range of the flying skirmish, compared to the work of the axe, and the
sword, and the famine, which was done during this man's youth on all the
hills and plains of the Christian earth, from Moscow to Gibraltar? He was
eighteen years old when Napoleon came down on Arcola. Look on the map
of Europe and count the blood-stains on it, between Arcola and Waterloo.

   Not alone those blood-stains on the Alpine snow, and the blue of the
Lombard plain. The English death was before his eyes also. No decent,
calculable, consoled dying; no passing to rest like that of the aged burghers
of Nuremberg town. No gentle processions to churchyards among the
fields, the bronze crests bossed deep on the memorial tablets, and the skylark singing above them from among the corn. But the life trampled out
in the slime of the street, crushed to dust amidst the roaring of the wheel,
tossed countlessly away into howling winter wind along five hundred
leagues of rock-fanged shore. Or, worst of all, rotted down to forgotten
graves through years of ignorant patience, and vain seeking for help from
man, for hope in God—infirm, imperfect yearning, as of motherless

infants starving at the dawn; oppressed royalties of captive thought, vague ague-fits of bleak, amazed despair.

A goodly landscape this, for the lad to paint, and under a goodly light. Wide enough the light was, and clear; no more Salvator's lurid chasm on jagged horizon, nor Dürer's spotted rest of sunny gleam on hedgerow and field; but light over all the world. Full shone now its awful globe, one pallid charnel-house,—a ball strewn bright with human ashes, glaring in poised sway beneath the sun, all blinding-white with death from pole to pole,—death, not of myriads of poor bodies only, but of will, and mercy, and conscience; death, not once inflicted on the flesh, but daily fastening on the spirit; death, not silent or patient, waiting his appointed hour, but voiceful, venomous; death with the taunting word, and burning grasp, and infixed sting.

388

"Put ye in the sickle, for the harvest is ripe."[63] The word is spoken in our ears continually to other reapers than the angels,—to the busy skeletons that never tire for stooping. When the measure of iniquity is full, and it seems that another day might bring repentance and redemption,—"Put ye in the sickle." When the young life has been wasted all away, and the eyes are just opening upon the tracks of ruin, and faint resolution rising in the heart for nobler things,—"Put ye in the sickle." When the roughest blows of fortune have been borne long and bravely, and the hand is just stretched to grasp its goal,—"Put ye in the sickle." And when there are but a few in the midst of a nation, to save it, or to teach, or to cherish; and all its life is bound up in those few golden ears,—"Put ye in the sickle, pale reapers, and pour hemlock for your feast of harvest home."

This was the sight which opened on the young eyes, this the watchword sounding within the heart of Turner in his youth.

So taught, and prepared for his life's labour, sate the boy at last alone among his fair English hills; and began to paint, with cautious toil, the rocks, and fields, and trickling brooks, and soft white clouds of heaven.

CHAPTER X

The Nereid's Guard

THE work of Turner, in its first period, is said in my account of his drawings at the National Gallery to be distinguished by "boldness of handling, generally gloomy tendency of mind, subdued colour, and perpetual reference to precedent in composition." I must refer the reader to those two catalogues* for a more special account of his early modes of technical study. Here we are concerned only with the expression of that gloomy tendency of mind, whose causes we are now better able to understand.

It was prevented from overpowering him by his labour. This, continual, and as tranquil in its course as a ploughman's in the field, by demanding an admirable humility and patience, averted the tragic passion of youth. Full of stern sorrow and fixed purpose, the boy set himself to his labour silently and meekly, like a workman's child on its first day at the cotton-mill. Without haste, but without relaxation,—accepting all modes and means of progress, however painful or humiliating, he took the burden on his shoulder and began his march. There was nothing so little, but he noticed it; nothing so great, but he began preparations to cope with it. For some time his work is, apparently, feelingless, so patient and mechanical are the first essays. It gains gradually in power and grasp; there is no perceptible *aim* at freedom, or at fineness, but the force insensibly becomes swifter, and the touch finer. The colour is always dark or subdued.

Of the first forty subjects which he exhibited at the Royal Academy, thirty-one are architectural, and of these, twenty-one are of elaborate Gothic architecture (Peterborough Cathedral, Lincoln Cathedral, Malmesbury Abbey, Tintern Abbey, etc.). I look upon the discipline given to his hand by these formal drawings as of the highest importance. His mind was also gradually led by them into a calmer pensiveness. Education amidst country possessing architectural remains of some noble

---

*"Notes on the Turner Collection at Marlborough House." 1857. "Catalogue of the Sketches of J. M. W. Turner exhibited at Marlborough House." 1858.[64]

kind, I believe to be wholly essential to the progress of a landscape artist. The first verses he ever attached to a picture were in 1798. They are from *Paradise Lost*, and refer to a picture of Morning, on the Coniston Fells:—

> "Ye mists and exhalations, that now rise
> From hill or steaming lake, dusky or gray,
> Till the sun paints your fleecy skirts with gold,
> In honour to the world's great Author rise." [65]

By glancing over the verses, which in following years he quotes from Milton, Thomson, and Mallet, it may be seen at once how his mind was set, so far as natural scenes were concerned, on rendering atmospheric 391 effect;—and so far as emotion was to be expressed, how consistently it was melancholy.

He paints, first of heroic or meditative subjects, the Fifth Plague of Egypt; [66] next, the Tenth Plague of Egypt. His first tribute to the Memory of Nelson is the "Battle of the Nile," 1799. I presume an unimportant picture, as the power was not then availably developed. His first classical subject is Narcissus and Echo, in 1805:— [67]

> "So melts the youth, and languishes away,
> His beauty withers, and his limbs decay."

392 The year following he summons his whole strength, and paints what we might suppose would be a happier subject, the Garden of the Hesperides [plate 19]. This being the most important picture of the first period, I will analyse it completely.

The fable of the Hesperides had, it seems to me, in the Greek mind two distinct meanings; the first referring to natural phenomena, and the second to moral. The natural meaning of it I believe to have been this:—

The Garden of the Hesperides was supposed to exist in the westernmost part of the Cyrenaica; it was generally the expression for the beauty and luxuriant vegetation of the coast of Africa in that district. The centre of the Cyrenaica "is occupied by a moderately elevated table-land, whose edge runs parallel to the coast, to which it sinks down in a succession of terraces, clothed with verdure, intersected by mountain-streams running through ravines filled with the richest vegetation; well watered by frequent rains, exposed to the cool sea-breeze from the north, and sheltered by the mass of the mountain from the sands and hot winds of the Sahara."*

The Greek colony of Cyrene itself was founded ten miles from the sea-shore, "in a spot backed by the mountains on the south, and thus sheltered from the fiery blasts of the desert; while at the height of about

---

* Smith's *Dictionary of Greek and Roman Geography*. Art. "Cyrenaica."

1,800 feet an inexhaustible spring bursts forth amidst luxuriant vegetation, and pours its waters down to the Mediterranean through a most beautiful ravine."

The nymphs of the west, or Hesperides, are, therefore, I believe, as natural types, the representatives of the soft western winds and sunshine, which were in this district most favourable to vegetation. In this sense they are called daughters of Atlas and Hesperis, the western winds being cooled by the snow of Atlas. The dragon, on the contrary, is the representative of the Sahara wind, or Simoom, which blew over the garden from above the hills on the south, and forbade all advance of cultivation beyond their ridge. Whether this was the physical meaning of the tradition in the Greek mind or not, there can be no doubt of its being Turner's first interpretation of it. A glance at the picture may determine this: a clear fountain being made the principal object in the foreground,— a bright and strong torrent in the distance,—while the dragon, wrapped in flame and whirlwind, watches from the top of the cliff.

But, both in the Greek mind and in Turner's, this natural meaning of the legend was a completely subordinate one. The moral significance of it lay far deeper. In the second, but principal sense, the Hesperides were not daughters of Atlas, nor connected with the winds of the west, but with its splendour. They are properly the nymphs of the sunset, and are the daughters of night, having many brothers and sisters, of whom I shall take Hesiod's account.[68]

"And the Night begat Doom, and short-withering Fate, and Death.

"And begat Sleep, and the company of Dreams, and Censure, and Sorrow.

"And the Hesperides, who keep the golden fruit beyond the mighty Sea.

"And the Destinies, and the Spirits of merciless punishment.

"And Jealousy, and Deceit, and Wanton Love; and Old Age, that fades away; and Strife, whose will endures."

We have not, I think, hitherto quite understood the Greek feeling about those nymphs and their golden apples, coming as a light in the midst of a cloud;—between Censure, and Sorrow,—and the Destinies. We must look to the precise meaning of Hesiod's words, in order to get the force of the passage.

"The night begat Doom"; that is to say, the doom of unforeseen accident—doom essentially of darkness.

"And short-withering Fate." Ill translated. I cannot do it better.[69] It means especially the sudden fate which brings untimely end to all purpose, and cuts off youth and its promise: called, therefore (the epithet hardly ever leaving it), "black Fate."

"And Death." This is the universal, inevitable death, opposed to the

393

394

interfering, untimely death. These three are named as the elder children. Hesiod pauses, and repeats the word "begat" before going on to number the others.

"And begat Sleep, and the Company of Dreams."

"And *Censure*." "Momus," the Spirit of Blame—the spirit which desires to blame rather than to praise;—false, base, unhelpful, unholy judgment;—ignorant and blind, child of the Night.

"And Sorrow." Accurately, sorrow of mourning; the sorrow of the night when no man can work: of the night that falls when what was the light of the eyes is taken from us; lamenting, sightless sorrow, without hope,—child of Night.

"And the Hesperides." We will come back to these.

"And the Destinies, and the Spirits of Merciless Punishment." These are the great Fates which have rule over conduct; the first fate spoken of (short-withering) is that which has rule over occurrence. These great Fates are Clotho, Lachesis, Atropos. Their three powers are,—Clotho's over the clue, the thread, or connecting energy,—that is, the conduct of life; Lachesis' over the lot—that is to say, the chance which warps, entangles, or bends the course of life. Atropos, inflexible, cuts the thread for ever.

395   "And Jealousy," especially the jealousy of Fortune, in balancing all good by evil. The Greeks had a peculiar dread of this form of fate.

"And Deceit, and sensual Love. And Old Age that fades, and Strife that endures"; that is to say, old age, which, growing not in wisdom, is marked only by its failing power—by the gradual gaining of darkness on the faculties, and helplessness on the frame. Such age is the forerunner of true death—the child of Night. "And Strife," the last and the mightiest, the nearest to man of the Night-children—blind leader of the blind.

Understanding thus whose sisters they are, let us consider of the Hesperides themselves—spoken of commonly as the "Singing Nymphs."[70] They are four.

Their names are, Ægle,—Brightness; Erytheia,—Blushing; Hestia,—the (spirit of the) Hearth; Arethusa,—the Ministering.

O English reader! hast thou ever heard of these fair and true daughters of Sunset, beyond the mighty sea?

And was it not well to trust to such keepers the guarding of the golden fruit which the earth gave to Juno at her marriage? Not fruit only: fruit on the tree, given by the earth, the great mother, to Juno (female power), at her marriage with Jupiter, or *ruling* manly power (distinguished from the tried and *agonizing* strength of Hercules). I call Juno, briefly, female power. She is, especially, the goddess presiding over marriage, regarding the woman as the mistress of a household. Vesta (the goddess of the

hearth*), with Ceres, and Venus, are variously dominant over marriage,   396
as the fulfilment of love; but Juno is pre-eminently the housewives'
goddess. She therefore represents, in her character, whatever good or evil
may result from female ambition, or desire of power: and, as to a
housewife, the earth presents its golden fruit to her, which she gives to two
kinds of guardians. The wealth of the earth, as the source of household
peace and plenty, is watched by the singing nymphs—the Hesperides. But,
as the source of household sorrow and desolation, it is watched by the
Dragon.

We must, therefore, see who the Dragon was, and what kind of dragon.

We traced in an earlier chapter,[71] the birth of the Gorgons, through
Phorcys and Ceto, from Nereus. The youngest child of Phorcys and Ceto
is the Dragon of the Hesperides;[72] but this latest descent is not, as in
Northern traditions, a sign of fortunateness: on the contrary, the children
of Nereus receive gradually more and more terror and power, as they are
later born, till this last of the Nereids unites horror and power at their
utmost. Observe the gradual change. Nereus himself is said to have been
perfectly *true*, and *gentle*.

This is Hesiod's account of him:—

"And Pontus begat Nereus, simple and true, the oldest of children; but
they call him the aged man, in that he is errorless and kind; neither forgets
he what is right; but knows all just and gentle counsel."[73]

Now the children of Nereus, like the Hesperides themselves, bear a
twofold typical character; one physical, the other moral. In his physical
symbolism, Nereus himself is the calm and gentle sea, from which rise, in
gradual increase of terror, the clouds and storms. In his moral character,   397
Nereus is the type of the deep, pure, rightly-tempered human mind, from
which, in gradual degeneracy, spring the troubling passions.

Keeping this double meaning in view, observe the whole line of descent
to the Hesperides' Dragon. Nereus, by the Earth, begets (1) Thaumas (the
wonderful), physically, the father of the Rainbow; morally, the type of the
enchantments and dangers of imagination. His grandchildren, besides the
Rainbow, are the Harpies. (2) Phorcys (Orcus?), physically, the treachery
or devouring spirit of the sea; morally, covetousness or malignity of heart.
(3) Ceto, physically, the deep places of the sea; morally, secretness of
heart, called "fair-cheeked," because tranquil in outward aspect. (4)

---

*Her name is also that of the Hesperid nymph; but I give the Hesperid her
Greek form of name, to distinguish her from the goddess. The Hesperid Arethusa
has the same subordinate relation to Ceres; and Erytheia, to Venus. Ægle
signifies especially the spirit of brightness or cheerfulness; including even the
subordinate idea of household neatness or cleanliness.

Eurybia (wide strength), physically, the flowing, especially the tidal power of the sea (she, by one of the sons of Heaven, becomes the mother of three great Titans,[74] one of whom, Astræus, and the Dawn, are the parents of the four Winds); morally, the healthy passion of the heart. Thus far the children of Nereus.

Next, Phorcys and Ceto, in their physical characters (the grasping or devouring of the sea, reaching out over the land, and its depth), beget the Clouds and Storms—namely, first, the Graiæ, or soft rain-clouds; then the Gorgons, or storm-clouds; and youngest and last, the Hesperides' Dragon,—Volcanic or earth-storm, associated, in conception, with the Simoom and fiery African winds.

But, in its moral significance, the descent is this. Covetousness, or malignity (Phorcys), and Secretness (Ceto), beget, first, the darkening passions, whose hair is always gray; then the stormy and merciless passions, brazen-winged (the Gorgons), of whom the dominant, Medusa, is ice-cold, turning all who look on her to stone. And, lastly, the consuming (poisonous and volcanic) passions—the "flame-backed dragon,"[75] uniting the powers of poison, and instant destruction. Now the reader may have heard, perhaps, in other books of Genesis than Hesiod's, of a dragon being busy about a tree which bore apples, and of crushing the head of that dragon; but seeing how, in the Greek mind, this serpent was descended from the sea, he may, perhaps, be surprised to remember another verse, bearing also on the matter:—"Thou brakest the heads of the dragons in the waters";[76] and yet more surprised, going on with the Septuagint version, to find where he is being led: "Thou brakest the head of the dragon, and gavest him to be meat to the Ethiopian people. Thou didst tear asunder the strong fountains and the storm-torrents; thou didst dry up the rivers of Etham," πηγὰς καὶ χειμάρρους, the Pegasus fountains—"Etham on the edge of the wilderness."

Returning then to Hesiod, we find he tells us of the Dragon himself:— "He, in the secret places of the desert land, kept the all-golden apples in his great knots" (coils of rope, or extremities of anything).[77] With which compare Euripides' report of him:—"And Hercules came to the Hesperian dome, to the singing maidens, plucking the apple-fruit from the golden petals; slaying the flame-backed dragon, who, twined round and round, kept guard in unapproachable spires"[78] (spirals or whirls, as of a whirlwind-vortex).

Farther, we hear from other scattered syllables of tradition, that this dragon was sleepless, and that he was able to take various tones of human voice.[79]

And we find a later tradition than Hesiod's calling him a child of Typhon and Echidna. Now Typhon is volcanic storm, generally the evil spirit of tumult.

Echidna (the adder) is a descendant of Medusa.[80] She is a daughter of Chrysaor (the lightning), by Callirhoë (the fair flowing), a daughter of Ocean;—that is to say, she joins the intense fatality of the lightning with perfect gentleness. In form she is half-maiden, half-serpent; therefore she is the spirit of all the fatallest evil, veiled in gentleness: or, in one word, treachery;—having dominion over many gentle things;—and chiefly over a kiss, given, indeed, in another garden than that of the Hesperides, yet in relation to keeping of treasure also.[81]

Having got this farther clue, let us look who it is whom Dante makes the typical Spirit of Treachery. The eighth or lowest pit of hell is given to its keeping; at the edge of which pit, Virgil casts a *rope* down for a signal; instantly there rises, as from the sea, "as one returns who hath been down to loose some anchor," "the fell monster with the deadly sting, who passes mountains, breaks through fenced walls, and firm embattled spears; and with his filth taints all the world."[82]

Think for an instant of another place:—"Sharp stones are under him, he laugheth at the shaking of a spear."[83] We must yet keep to Dante, however. Echidna, remember, is half-maiden, half-serpent;—hear what Dante's Fraud is like:—

> "Forthwith that image vile of Fraud appear'd,
> His head and upper part exposed on land,
> But laid not on the shore his bestial train.
> His face the semblance of a just man's wore,
> So kind and gracious was its outward cheer;
> The rest was serpent all: two shaggy claws
> Reach'd to the armpits; and the back and breast,
> And either side, were painted o'er with nodes
> And orbits. Colours variegated more
> Nor Turks nor Tartars e'er on cloth of state
> With interchangeable embroidery wove,
> Nor spread Arachne o'er her curious loom.
> As oft-times a light skiff moor'd to the shore,
> Stands part in water, part upon the land;
> Or, as where dwells the greedy German boor,
> The beaver settles, watching for his prey;
> So on the rim, that fenced the sand with rock,
> Sat perch'd the fiend of evil. In the void
> Glancing, his tail upturn'd, its venomous fork
> With sting like scorpion's arm'd."[84]

400

You observe throughout this description the leaning on the character of the *Sea* Dragon; a little farther on, his way of flying is told us:—

> "As a small vessel, backening out from land,
> Her station quits; so thence the monster loos'd,
> And, when he felt himself at large, turn'd round

There, where the breast had been, his forked tail.
Thus, like an eel, outstretch'd, at length he steer'd,
Gathering the air up with retractile claws.''[85]

And, lastly, his name is told us: Geryon.[86] Whereupon, looking back to Hesiod, we find that Geryon is Echidna's brother.[87] Man-serpent, therefore, in Dante, as Echidna is woman-serpent.

We find next that Geryon lived in the island of Erytheia (blushing), only another kind of blushing than that of the Hesperid Erytheia. But it is on, also, a western island, and Geryon kept red oxen in it (said to be near the red setting sun); and Hercules kills him, as he does the Hesperian dragon: but in order to be able to reach him, a golden boat is given to Hercules by the Sun, to cross the sea in.

We will return to this part of the legend presently, having enough of it now collected to get at the complete idea of the Hesperian dragon, who
401 is, in fine, the "Pluto il gran nemico" of Dante;[88] the demon of all evil passions connected with covetousness; that is to say, essentially of fraud, rage, and gloom. Regarded as the demon of Fraud, he is said to be descended from the viper Echidna, full of deadly cunning, in whirl on whirl; as the demon of consuming Rage from Phorcys; as the demon of Gloom, from Ceto;—in his watching and melancholy, he is sleepless; breathing whirlwind and fire, he is the destroyer, descended from Typhon as well as Phorcys; having, moreover, with all these, the irresistible strength of his ancestral sea.

Now, look at him, as Turner has drawn him [fig.65]. I cannot reduce the creature to this scale without losing half his power; his length, especially, seems to diminish more than it should in proportion to his bulk. In the picture he is far in the distance, cresting the mountain; and may be, perhaps, three-quarters of a mile long. The actual length on the canvas is a foot and eight inches; so that it may be judged how much he loses by the reduction, and of the loss which, however well he might have been engraved, he would still have sustained, in the impossiblity of expressing the lurid colour of his armour, alternate bronze and blue.

Still, the main points of him are discernible enough: and among all the wonderful things that Turner did in his day, I think this nearly the most wonderful. How far he had really found out for himself the collateral
402 bearings of the Hesperid tradition I know not; but that he had got the main clue of it, and knew who the Dragon was, there can be no doubt; the strange thing is, that his conception of it throughout, down to the minutest detail, fits every one of the circumstances of the Greek traditions. There is, first, the Dragon's descent from Medusa and Typhon, indicated in the serpent-clouds floating from his head; then note the grovelling and ponderous body, ending in a serpent, of which we do not see the end. He drags the weight of it forward by his claws, not being able

fig.65 John Ruskin, *Quivi Trovammo* (engraving after J.M.W. Turner)

to lift himself from the ground ("Mammon, the least erected spirit that fell"[89]); then the grip of the claws themselves as if they would clutch (rather than tear) the rock itself into pieces; but chiefly, the designing of the body. Remember, one of the essential characters of the creature, as descended from Medusa, is its coldness and petrifying power; this, in the demon of covetousness, must exist to the utmost; breathing fire, he is yet himself of ice. Now, if I were merely to draw this dragon as white, instead of dark, and take his claws away, his body would become a representation of a great glacier, so nearly perfect, that I know no published engraving of glacier breaking over a rocky brow so like the truth as this dragon's shoulders would be, if they were thrown out in light; there being only this difference, that they have the form, but not the fragility of the ice; they are at once ice and iron. "His bones are like solid pieces of brass; his bones are like bars of iron; by his neesings a light doth shine."[90]

The strange unity of vertebrated action, and of a true bony contour, infinitely varied in every vertebra, with this glacial outline;— together with the adoption of the head of the Ganges crocodile, the fish-eater, to show his sea descent (and this in the year 1806, when hardly a single fossil saurian skeleton existed within Turner's reach), renders the whole conception one of the most curious exertions of the imaginative intellect with which I am acquainted in the arts.

403

Thus far then, of the dragon; next, we have to examine the conception of the Goddess of Discord. We must return, for a moment, to the tradition about Geryon. I cannot yet decipher the meaning of his oxen, said to be fed together with those of Hades; nor of the journey of Hercules, in which, after slaying Geryon, he returns through Europe like a border forager, driving these herds, and led into farther battle in protection or recovery of them.[91] But it seems to me the main drift of the legend cannot be mistaken; viz., that Geryon is the evil spirit of wealth, as arising from commerce; hence, placed as a guardian of isles in the most distant sea, and reached in a golden boat; while the Hesperian dragon is the evil spirit of wealth, as possessed in households; and associated, therefore, with the true household guardians, or singing nymphs. Hercules (manly labour), slaying both Geryon and Ladon, presents oxen and apples to Juno who is their proper mistress; but the Goddess of Discord, contriving that one portion of this household wealth shall be ill bestowed by Paris, he, according to Coleridge's interpretation,[92] choosing pleasure instead of wisdom or power;—there issue from this evil choice the catastrophe of the Trojan war, and the wanderings of Ulysses, which are essentially, both in the *Iliad* and *Odyssey*, the troubling of household peace; terminating with the restoration of this peace by repentance and patience; Helen and Penelope seen at last sitting upon their household thrones, in the Hesperian light of age.

404

We have, therefore, to regard Discord, in the Hesperides garden, eminently as the disturber of households, assuming a different aspect from Homer's wild and fierce discord of war. They are, nevertheless, one and the same power; for she changes her aspect at will. I cannot get at the root of her name, Eris. It seems to me as if it ought to have one in common with Erinnys (Fury); but it means always contention, emulation, or competition, either in mind or in words;—the final work of Eris is essentially "division," and she is herself always double-minded; shouts two ways at once (in *Iliad*, xi. 6), and wears a mantle rent in half (*Æneid*, viii. 702). Homer makes her loud-voiced,[93] and insatiably covetous. This last attribute is, with him, the source of her usual title. She is little when she first is seen, then rises till her head touches heaven.[94] By Virgil she is called mad; and her hair is of serpents, bound with bloody garlands.[95]

This is the conception first adopted by Turner, but combined with another which he found in Spenser; only note that there is some confusion in the minds of English poets between Eris (Discord) and Ate (Error), who is a daughter of Discord, according to Hesiod.[96] She is properly—mischievous error, tender-footed; for she does not walk on the earth, but on heads of men (*Iliad*, xix. 92); *i.e.*, not on the solid ground, but on human vain thoughts; therefore, her hair is glittering (*Iliad*, xix. 126).

405 I think she is mainly the confusion of mind coming of pride, as Eris

comes of covetousness; therefore, Homer makes her a daughter of Jove.[97] Spenser, under the name of Até, describes Eris. But the stanzas from which Turner derived his conception of her are these—

> "Als, as she double spake, so heard she double,
>   With matchless eares deformed and distort,
>   Fild with false rumors and seditious trouble,
>   Bred in assemblies of the vulgar sort,
>   That still are led with every light report:
>   And as her eares, so eke her feet were odde,
>   And much unlike; th' one long, the other short,
>   And both misplast; that, when th' one forward yode,
>   The other backe retired and contrárie trode.

> "Likewise unequall were her handës twaine;
>   That one did reach, the other pusht away;
>   That one did make, the other mard againe,
>   And sought to bring all things unto decay;
>   Whereby great riches, gathered manie a day,
>   She in short space did often bring to nought,
>   And their possessours often did dismay:
>   For all her studie was, and all her thought,
>   How she might overthrow the things that Concord wrought.

> "So much her malice did her might surpas,
>   That even th' Almightie selfe she did maligne,
>   Because to man so merciful He was,
>   And unto all His creatures so benigne,
>   Sith she herself was of His grace indigne:
>   For all this worlds faire workmanship she tride
>   Unto his last confusion to bring,
>   And that great golden chaine quite to divide,
>   With which it blessed Concord hath together tide."[98]

All these circumstances of decrepitude and distortion Turner has followed, through hand and limb, with patient care: he has added one final touch of his own. The nymph who brings the apples to the goddess, offers her one in each hand; and Eris, of the divided mind, cannot choose. 406

One farther circumstance must be noted, in order to complete our understanding of the picture,—the gloom extending, not to the dragon only, but also to the fountain and the tree of golden fruit. The reason of this gloom may be found in two other passages of the authors from which Turner had taken his conception of Eris—Virgil and Spenser. For though the Hesperides in their own character, as the nymphs of domestic joy, are entirely bright (and the garden always bright around them), yet seen or remembered in sorrow, or in the presence of discord, they deepen distress. Their entirely happy character is given by Euripides:—"The fruit-planted shore of the Hesperides,—songstresses,—where the ruler of the purple lake allows not any more to the sailor his way, assigning the boundary of Heaven which Atlas holds; where the ambrosial fountains flow, and the fruitful and divine land increases the happiness of the gods."[99]

But to the thoughts of Dido, in her despair, they recur under another aspect; she remembers their priestess as a great enchantress; who *feeds the dragon* and preserves the boughs of the trees; sprinkling moist honey and drowsy poppy; who also has power over ghosts; "and the earth shakes and the forests stoop from the hills at her bidding."[100]

This passage Turner must have known well, from his continual interest in Carthage: but his diminution of the splendour of the old Greek garden was certainly caused chiefly by Spenser's describing the Hesperides fruit as growing first in the garden of Mammon:—[101]

407

> "There mournfull cypresse grew in greatest store
> And trees of bitter gall; and heben sad;
> Dead sleeping poppy; and black hellebore;
> Cold coloquintida; and tetra mad;
> Mortal samnitis; and cicuta bad,
> With which th' unjust Atheniens made to dy
> Wise Socrates, who, thereof quaffing glad,
> Pourd out his life and last philosophy.

> * * * * *

> "The gardin of Prosérpina this hight:
> And in the midst thereof a silver seat,
> With a thick arber goodly over-dight,
> In which she often usd from open heat
> Herselfe to shroud, and pleasures to entreat:
> Next thereunto did grow a goodly tree,
> With braunches broad dispredd and body great,
> Clothed with leaves, that none the wood mote see,
> And loaden all with fruit as thick as it might bee.

> "Their fruit were golden apples glistring bright,
> That goodly was their glory to behold;
> On earth like never grew, ne living wight
> Like ever saw, but they from hence were sold;
> For those, which Hercules with conquest bold
> Got from great Atlas daughters, hence began.

> * * * * *

> "Here eke that famous golden apple grew,
> The which emongst the gods false Até threw."

There are two collateral evidences in the pictures of Turner's mind having been partly influenced by this passage. The excessive darkness of the stream,—though one of the Cyrene fountains—to remind us of Cocytus;

and the breaking of the bough of the tree by the weight of its apples—not healthily, but as a diseased tree would break.

Such then is our English painter's first great religious picture; and exponent of our English faith. A sad-coloured work, not executed in Angelico's white and gold; nor in Perugino's crimson and azure; but in a sulphurous hue, as relating to a paradise of smoke. That power, it appears, on the hill-top, is our British Madonna: whom, reverently, the English devotional painter must paint, thus enthroned, with nimbus about the gracious head. Our Madonna,—or our Jupiter on Olympus,— or, perhaps, more accurately still, our unknown god, sea-born, with the cliffs, not of Cyrene, but of England, for his altar; and no chance of any Mars' Hill proclamation concerning him, "whom therefore ye ignorantly worship."[102]

This is no irony. The fact is verily so. The greatest man of our England, in the first half of the nineteenth century, in the strength and hope of his youth, perceives this to be the thing he has to tell us of utmost moment, connected with the spiritual world. In each city and country of past time, the master-minds had to declare the chief worship which lay at the nation's heart; to define it; adorn it; show the range and authority of it. Thus in Athens, we have the triumph of Pallas; and in Venice the Assumption of the Virgin; here, in England, is our great spiritual fact for ever interpreted to us—the Assumption of the Dragon. No St. George any more to be heard of; no more dragon-slaying possible: this child, born on St. George's Day, can only make manifest the dragon, not slay him, sea-serpent as he is; whom the English Andromeda, not fearing, takes for her lord. The fairy English Queen once thought to command the waves, but it is the sea-dragon now who commands her valleys; of old the Angel of the Sea ministered to them, but now the Serpent of the Sea; where once flowed their clear springs now spreads the black Cocytus pool; and the fair blooming of the Hesperid meadows fades into ashes beneath the Nereid's Guard.

Yes, Albert of Nuremberg; the time has at last come. Another nation has arisen in the strength of its Black anger; and another hand has pourtrayed the spirit of its toil. Crowned with fire, and with the wings of the bat.

408

CHAPTER XI
The Hesperid Ægle

409   FIVE years after the Hesperides were painted, another great mythologi-cal subject appeared by Turner's hand. Another dragon—this time not triumphant, but in death-pang, the Python slain by Apollo [plate 20].

Not in a garden, this slaying, but in a hollow, among wildest rocks, beside a stagnant pool. Yet, instead of the sombre colouring of the Hesperid hills, strange gleams of blue and gold flit around the mountain peaks, and colour the clouds above them.

The picture is at once the type, and the first expression of a great change which was passing in Turner's mind. A change, which was not clearly manifested in all its results until much later in his life; but in the colouring of this picture are the first signs of it; and in the subject of this picture, its symbol.

410   Had Turner died early, the reputation he would have left, though great and enduring, would have been strangely different from that which ultimately must now attach to his name. He would have been remembered as one of the severest of painters; his iron touch and positive forms would have been continually opposed to the delicacy of Claude and richness of Titian; he would have been spoken of, popularly, as a man who had no eye for colour. Perhaps here and there a watchful critic might have shown this popular idea to be false; but no conception could have been formed by any one of the man's real disposition or capacity.

It was only after the year 1820 that these were determinable, and his peculiar work discerned.

He had begun by faithful declaration of the sorrow there was in the world. It is now permitted him to see also its beauty. He becomes, separately and without rival, the painter of the loveliness and light of the creation.

Of its loveliness: that which may be beloved in it, the tenderest, kindest, most feminine of its aspects. Of its light: light not merely diffused, but interpreted; light seen pre-eminently in colour.

Claude and Cuyp had painted the sun*shine*, Turner alone, the sun *colour*.

Observe this accurately. Those easily understood effects of afternoon light, gracious and sweet so far as they reach, are produced by the softly warm or yellow rays of the sun falling through mist. They are low in tone, even in nature, and disguise the colours of objects. They are imitable even by persons who have little or no gift of colour, if the tones of the picture are kept low and in true harmony, and the reflected lights warm. But they never could be painted by great colourists. The fact of blue and crimson being effaced by yellow and gray, puts such effect at once out of the notice or thought of a colourist, unless he has some special interest in the motive of it. You might as well ask a musician to compose with only three notes, as Titian to paint without crimson and blue. Accordingly the colourists in   411 general, feeling that no other than this yellow sunshine was imitable, refused it, and painted in twilight, when the colour was full.

Turner, however, as a landscape painter, had to represent sunshine of one kind or another. He went steadily through the subdued golden chord, and painted Cuyp's favourite effect, "sun rising through vapour,"[103] for many a weary year. But this was not enough for him. He must paint the sun in his strength, the sun rising *not* through vapour. If you glance at that Apollo slaying the Python, you will see there is rose colour and blue on the clouds, as well as gold; and if then you turn to the Apollo in the Ulysses and Polyphemus [plate 21]—his horses are rising beyond the horizon,—you see he is not "rising through vapour," but above it;—gaining somewhat of a victory over vapour, it appears.

The old Dutch brewer, with his yellow mist, was a great man and a good guide, but he was not Apollo. He and his dray-horses led the way through the flats, cheerily, for a little time; we have other horses now flaming out "beyond the mighty sea."[104]

A victory over vapour of many kinds; Python-slaying in general. Look how the Python's jaws smoke as he falls back between the rocks:—a   412 vaporous serpent! We will see who he was presently.

The public remonstrated loudly in the cause of Python: "He had been so yellow, quiet, and pleasant a creature; what meant these azure-shafted arrows, this sudden glare into darkness, this Iris message;—Thaumantian; —miracle-working; scattering our slumber down in Cocytus?" It meant much, but that was not what they should have first asked about it. They should have asked simply was it a true message? Were these Thaumantian things so in the real universe?

It might have been known easily they were. One fair dawn or sunset, obediently beheld, would have set them right; and shown that Turner was indeed the only true speaker concerning such things that ever yet had appeared in the world. They would neither look nor hear;—only shouted continuously, "Perish Apollo. Bring us back Python."

We must understand the real meaning of this cry, for herein rests not merely the question of the great right or wrong in Turner's life, but the question of the right or wrong of all painting. Nay, on this issue hangs the nobleness of painting as an art altogether, for it is distinctively the art of colouring, not of shaping or relating. Sculptors and poets can do these, the painter's own work is colour.

Thus, then, for the last time, rises the question, what is the true dignity of colour? We left that doubt a little while ago among the clouds, wondering what they had been made so scarlet for.[105] Now Turner brings the doubt back to us, unescapable any more. No man, hitherto, had
413 painted the clouds scarlet. Hesperid Æglé, and Erytheia, throned there in the west, fade into the twilights of four thousand years, unconfessed. Here is at last one who confesses them, but is it well? Men say these Hesperides are sensual goddesses,—traitresses,—that the Graiæ are the only true ones. Nature made the western and the eastern clouds splendid in fallacy. Crimson is impure and vile; let us paint in black if we would be virtuous.

Note, with respect to this matter, that the peculiar innovation of Turner was the perfection of the colour chord by means of *scarlet*. Other painters had rendered the golden tones, and the blue tones, of sky; Titian especially the last, in perfectness. But none had dared to paint, none seem to have seen, the scarlet and purple.

Nor was it only in seeing this colour in vividness when it occurred in full light, that Turner differed from preceding painters. His most distinctive innovation as a colourist was his discovery of the scarlet *shadow*. "True, there is a sunshine whose light is golden, and its shadow gray; but there is another sunshine, and that the purest, whose light is white, and its shadow scarlet." This was the essentially offensive, inconceivable thing, which he could not be believed in. There was some ground for the incredulity, because no colour is vivid enough to express the pitch of light of pure white sunshine, so that the colour given without the true intensity of light *looks* false. Nevertheless, Turner could not but report of the colour truly. "I must indeed be lower in the key, but that is no reason why I should be false in the note. Here is sunshine which glows even when subdued; it has not cool shade, but fiery shade."* This is the glory of sunshine.
414 Now, this scarlet colour,—or pure red, intensified by expression of light,—is, of all the three primitive colours, that which is most distinctive.

---

*Not, accurately speaking, shadow, but dark side. All shadow proper is negative in colour, but, generally, reflected light is warmer than direct light; and when the direct light is warm, pure, and of the highest intensity, its reflection is scarlet. Turner habitually, in his later sketches, used vermilion for his pen outline in effects of sun.

Yellow is of the nature of simple light; blue connected with simple shade; but red is an entirely abstract colour. It is red to which the colour-blind are blind, as if to show us that it was not necessary merely for the service or comfort of man, but that there was a special gift or teaching in this colour. Observe, farther, that it is this colour which the sunbeams take in passing through the *earth's atmosphere*. The rose of dawn and sunset is the hue of the rays passing close over the earth. It is also concentrated in the blood of man.

Unforeseen requirements have compelled me to disperse through various works, undertaken between the first and last portions of this essay, the examination of many points respecting colour, which I had intended to reserve for this place. I can now only refer the reader to these several passages, and sum their import; which is briefly, that colour generally, but chiefly the scarlet, used with the hyssop, in the Levitical law,[106] is the great sanctifying element of visible beauty, inseparably connected with purity and life. 415

I must not enter here into the solemn and far-reaching fields of thought which it would be necessary to traverse, in order to detect the mystical connection between life and love, set forth in that Hebrew system of sacrificial religion to which we may trace most of the received ideas respecting sanctity, consecration, and purification. This only I must hint to the reader—for his own following out—that if he earnestly examines the original sources from which our heedless popular language respecting the washing away of sins has been borrowed, he will find that the fountain, in which sins are indeed to be washed away, is that of love, not of agony. 416 417

But, without approaching the presence of this deeper meaning of the sign, the reader may rest satisfied with the connection given him directly in written words, between the cloud and its bow. The cloud, or firmament, signifies the ministration of the heavens to man. That ministration may be in judgment or mercy—in the lightning, or the dew. But the bow, or colour of the cloud, signifies always mercy, the sparing of life; such ministry of the heaven as shall feed and prolong life. And as the sunlight, undivided, is the type of the wisdom and righteousness of God, so divided, and softened into colour by means of the firmamental ministry, fitted to every need of man, as to every delight, and becoming one chief source of human beauty, by being made part of the flesh of man;—thus divided, the sunlight is the type of the wisdom of God, becoming sanctification and redemption. Various in work—various in beauty—various in power. 418

Colour is, therefore, in brief terms, the type of love. Hence it is especially connected with the blossoming of the earth; and again, with its fruits; also, with the spring and fall of the leaf, and with the morning and evening of the day, in order to show the waiting of love about the birth and death of man. 419

And now, I think, we may understand, even far away in the Greek mind, the meaning of that Contest of Apollo with the Python. It was a far greater contest than that of Hercules with Ladon.[107] Fraud and avarice might be overcome by frankness and force; but this Python was a darker enemy, and could not be subdued but by a greater god. Nor was the conquest slightly esteemed by the victor deity. He took his great name from it thenceforth—his prophetic and sacred name—the Pythian.

420 It could, therefore, be no merely devouring dragon—no mere wild beast with scales and claws. It must possess some more terrible character to make conquest over it so glorious. Consider the meaning of its name, "THE CORRUPTER." That Hesperid dragon was a treasure-guardian. This is the treasure-destroyer,—where moth and rust doth corrupt—the worm of eternal decay.

Apollo's contest with him is the strife of purity with pollution; of life with forgetfulness; of love, with the grave.

I believe this great battle stood, in the Greek mind, for the type of the struggle of youth and manhood with deadly sin—venomous, infectious, irrecoverable sin. In virtue of his victory over this corruption, Apollo becomes thenceforward the guide; the witness; the purifying and helpful God. The other gods help waywardly, whom they choose. But Apollo helps always: he is by name, not only Pythian, the conqueror of death; but Pæan—the healer of the people.

Well did Turner know the meaning of that battle: he has told its tale with fearful distinctness. The Mammon dragon was armed with adamant; but this dragon of decay is a mere colossal worm: wounded, he bursts asunder in the midst, and melts to pieces, rather than dies, vomiting smoke—a smaller serpent-worm rising out of his blood.

Alas, for Turner! This smaller serpent-worm, it seemed, he could not conceive to be slain. In the midst of all the power and beauty of nature, he still saw this death-worm writhing among the weeds. A little thing

421 now, yet enough: you may see it in the foreground of the Bay of Baiæ [plate 22 & fig.66], which has also in it the story of Apollo and the Sibyl; Apollo giving love; but not youth, nor immortality: you may see it again in the foreground of the Lake Avernus—the Hades lake—which Turner surrounds with delicatest beauty, the Fates dancing in circle; but in front, is the serpent beneath the thistle and the wild thorn. The same Sibyl, Deiphobe, holding the golden bough. I cannot get at the meaning of this legend of the bough; but it was, assuredly, still connected, in Turner's mind, with that help from Apollo. He indicated the strength of his feeling at the time when he painted the Python contest, by the drawing exhibited the same year, of the Prayer of Chryses. There the priest is on the beach alone, the sun setting. He prays to it as it descends; flakes of its sheeted

fig.66   J.M.W. Turner, *The Bay of Baiæ* (detail)

light are borne to him by the melancholy waves, and cast away with sighs upon the sand.

How this sadness came to be persistent over Turner, and to conquer him, we shall see in a little while. It is enough for us to know at present that our most wise and Christian England, with all her appurtenances of school-porch and church-spire, had so disposed her teaching as to leave this somewhat notable child of hers without even cruel Pandora's gift.

He was without hope.

True daughter of Night, Hesperid Æglé was to him; coming between Censure, and Sorrow,—and the Destinies.

What, for us, his work yet may be, I know not. But let not the real nature of it be misunderstood any more.

He is distinctively, as he rises into his own peculiar strength, separating himself from all men who had painted forms of the physical world   422 before,—the painter of the loveliness of nature, with the worm at its root: Rose and cankerworm,—both with his utmost strength; the one *never* separate from the other.

In which his work was the true image of his own mind.

I would fain have looked last at the rose; but that is not the way Atropos will have it, and there is no pleading with her.

So, therefore, first of the rose.

That is to say, of this vision of the loveliness and kindness of Nature, as distinguished from all visions of her ever received by other men. By the Greek she had been distrusted. She was to him Calypso, the Concealer, Circe, the Sorceress. By the Venetian, she had been dreaded. Her wildernesses were desolate; her shadows stern. By the Fleming, she had been despised; what mattered the heavenly colours to him? But at last, the time comes for her loveliness and kindness to be declared to men. Had they helped Turner, listened to him, believed in him, he had done it wholly for them. But they cried out for Python, and Python came; came literally as well as spiritually; all the perfectest beauty and conquest which Turner wrought is already withered. The cankerworm stood at his right hand, and of all his richest, most precious work, there remains only the shadow. Yet that shadow is more than other men's sunlight; it is the scarlet shade, shade of the Rose. Wrecked, and faded, and defiled, his work still, in what remains of it, or may remain, is the loveliest ever yet done by man, in imagery of the physical world. Whatsoever is there of fairest, you will find recorded by Turner, and by him alone.

I say *you* will find, not knowing to how few I speak; for in order to find what is fairest, you must delight in what is fair; and I know not how few or how many there may be who take such delight. Once I could speak joyfully about beautiful things, thinking to be understood;—now I cannot any more; for it seems to me that no one regards them. Wherever I look or travel in England or abroad, I see that men, wherever they can reach, destroy all beauty. They seem to have no other desire or hope but to have large houses and to be able to move fast. Every perfect and lovely spot which they can touch, they defile.

Nevertheless, though not joyfully, or with any hope of being at present heard, I would have tried to enter here into some examination of the right and worthy effect of beauty in Art upon human mind, if I had been myself able to come to demonstrable conclusions. But the question is so complicated with that of the enervating influence of all luxury, that I cannot get it put into any tractable compass. Nay, I have many inquiries to make, many difficult passages of history to examine, before I can determine the just limits of the hope in which I may permit myself to continue to labour in any cause of Art.

Nor is the subject connected with the purpose of this book. I have written it to show that Turner is the greatest landscape painter who ever lived; and this it has sufficiently accomplished. What the final use may be to men, of landscape painting, or of any painting, or of natural beauty, I do not yet know. Thus far, however, I *do* know.

424   Three principal forms of asceticism have existed in this weak world.

Religious asceticism, being the refusal of pleasure and knowledge for the sake (as supposed) of religion; seen chiefly in the Middle Ages. Military asceticism, being the refusal of pleasure and knowledge for the sake of power; seen chiefly in the early days of Sparta and Rome. And monetary asceticism, consisting in the refusal of pleasure and knowledge for the sake of money; seen in the present days of London and Manchester.

"We do not come here to look at the mountains," said the Carthusian to me at the Grande Chartreuse. "We do not come here to look at the mountains," the Austrian generals would say, encamping by the shores of Garda. "We do not come here to look at the mountains," so the thriving manufacturers tell me, between Rochdale and Halifax.

All these asceticisms have their bright and their dark sides. I myself like the military asceticism best, because it is not so necessarily a refusal of general knowledge as the two others, but leads to acute and marvellous use of mind, and perfect use of body. Nevertheless, none of the three are a healthy or central state of man. There is much to be respected in each, but they are not what we should wish large numbers of men to become. A monk of La Trappe, a French soldier of the Imperial Guard, and a thriving mill-owner, supposing each a type, and no more than a type, of his class, are all interesting specimens of humanity, but narrow ones,—so narrow that even all the three together would not make up a perfect man. Nor does it appear in any way desirable that either of the three classes should extend itself so as to include a majority of the persons in the world, and turn large cities into mere groups of monastery, barracks, or factory. I do not say that it may not be desirable that one city, or one country, sacrificed for the good of the rest, should become a mass of barracks or   425 factories. Perhaps, it may be well that this England should become the furnace of the world; so that the smoke of the island, rising out of the sea, should be seen from a hundred leagues away, as if it were a field of fierce volcanoes; and every kind of sordid, foul, or venomous work which, in other countries, men dreaded or disdained, it should become England's duty to do,—becoming thus the offscourer of the earth, and taking the hyena instead of the lion upon her shield. I do not, for a moment, deny this; but, looking broadly, not at the destiny of England, nor of any country in particular, but of the world, this is certain—that men exclusively occupied either in spiritual reverie, mechanical destruction, or mechanical productiveness, fall below the proper standard of their race, and enter into a lower form of being; and that the true perfection of the race, and, therefore, its power and happiness, are only to be attained by a life which is neither speculative nor productive; but essentially contemplative and protective, which (A) does not lose itself in the monk's vision or hope, but delights in seeing present and real things as they truly are; which (B) does not mortify itself for the sake of obtaining powers of destruction, but seeks the more easily attainable powers of affection, observance, and protection; which (C), finally, does not mortify itself with a view to productive accumulation, but delights itself in peace, with its appointed portion. So that the things to be desired for man in a healthy state, are that he should not see dreams, but realities; that he should not

426 destroy life, but save it; and that he should be not rich, but content.

Towards which last state of contentment, I do not see that the world is at present approximating. There are, indeed, two forms of discontent: one laborious, the other indolent and complaining. We respect the man of laborious desire, but let us not suppose that his restlessness is peace, or his ambition meekness. It is because of the special connection of meekness with contentment that it is promised that the meek shall "inherit the earth."[108] Neither covetous men, nor the Grave, can *inherit* anything;* they can but consume. Only contentment can possess.

The most helpful and sacred work, therefore, which can at present be done for humanity, is to teach people (chiefly by example, as all best teaching must be done) not how "to better themselves," but how to "satisfy themselves." It is the curse of every evil nation and evil creature to eat, and *not* be satisfied. The words of blessing are, that they shall eat and be satisfied. And as there is only one kind of water which quenches all thirst, so there is only one kind of bread which satisfies all hunger—the bread of justice, or righteousness; which hungering after, men shall always be filled, that being the bread of heaven; but hungering after the bread, or wages, of unrighteousness, shall not be filled, that being the bread of Sodom.

427 And, in order to teach men how to be satisfied, it is necessary fully to understand the art and joy of humble life,—this, at present, of all arts or sciences being the one most needing study. Humble life,—that is to say, proposing to itself no future exaltation, but only a sweet continuance; not excluding the idea of foresight, but wholly of fore-sorrow, and taking no troublous thought for coming days; so, also, not excluding the idea of providence, or provision, but wholly of accumulation;—the life of domestic affection and domestic peace, full of sensitiveness to all elements of costless and kind pleasure;—therefore, chiefly to the loveliness of the natural world.

What length and severity of labour may be ultimately found necessary for the procuring of the due comforts of life, I do not know; neither what degree of refinement it is possible to unite with the so-called servile

---

* "There are three things that are never satisfied, yea, four things say not, It is enough: the grave; and the barren womb; the earth that is not filled with water; and the fire, that saith not, It is enough!" [Proverbs xxx. 15, 16.]

occupations of life: but this I know, that right economy of labour will, as it is understood, assign to each man as much as it will be healthy for him, and no more; and that no refinements are desirable which cannot be connected with toil.

I say, first, that due economy of labour will assign to each man the share which is right. Let no technical labour be wasted on things useless or unpleasurable; and let all physical exertion, so far as possible, be utilised, and it will be found no man need ever work more than is good for him. I believe an immense gain in the bodily health and happiness of the upper classes would follow on their steadily endeavouring, however clumsily, to make the physical exertion they now necessarily take in amusements, definitely serviceable. It would be far better, for instance, that a gentle- man should mow his own fields, than ride over other people's.

Again, respecting degrees of possible refinement, I cannot yet speak positively, because no effort has yet been made to teach refined habits to persons of simple life.

The idea of such refinement has been made to appear absurd, partly by the foolish ambition of vulgar persons in low life, but more by the worse than foolish assumption, acted on so often by modern advocates of improvement, that "education" means teaching Latin, or algebra, or music, or drawing, instead of developing or "drawing out" the human soul.

It may not be the least necessary that a peasant should know algebra, or Greek, or drawing. But it may, perhaps, be both possible and expedient that he should be able to arrange his thoughts clearly, to speak his own language intelligibly, to discern between right and wrong, to govern his passions, and to receive such pleasures of ear or sight as his life may render accessible to him. I would not have him taught the science of music; but most assuredly I would have him taught to sing. I would not teach him the science of drawing; but certainly I would teach him to see; without learning a single term of botany, he should know accurately the habits and uses of every leaf and flower in his fields; and unencumbered by any theories of moral or political philosophy, he should help his neighbour, and disdain a bribe.

All effort in social improvement is paralyzed, because no one has been bold or clear-sighted enough to put and press home this radical question: "What is indeed the noblest tone and reach of life for men; and how can the possibility of it be extended to the greatest numbers?" It is answered, broadly and rashly, that wealth is good; that knowledge is good; that art is good; that luxury is good. Whereas none of them are good in the abstract, but good only if rightly received. Nor have any steps whatever been yet securely taken,—nor, otherwise than in the resultless rhapsody of moralists,—to ascertain what luxuries and what learning it is either kind

428

429

430

to bestow, or wise to desire. This, however, at least we know, shown clearly by the history of all time, that the arts and sciences, ministering to the pride of nations, have invariably hastened their ruin; and this, also, without venturing to say that I know, I nevertheless firmly believe, that the same arts and sciences will tend as distinctly to exalt the strength and quicken the soul of every nation which employs them to increase the comfort of lowly life, and grace with happy intelligence the unambitious courses of honourable toil.

    Thus far, then, of the Rose.

    Last, of the Worm.

    I said that Turner painted the labour of men, their sorrow, and their death. This he did nearly in the same tones of mind which prompted Byron's poem of Childe Harold, and the loveliest result of his art, in the central period of it, was an effort to express on a single canvas the meaning of that poem [plate 23]. It may be now seen, by strange coincidence, associated with two others—Caligula's Bridge[109] and the Apollo and Sibyl [plate 22]; the one illustrative of the vanity of human labour, the other of the vanity of human life. He painted these, as I said, in the same tone of mind which formed the Childe Harold poem, but with different capacity: Turner's sense of beauty was perfect; deeper, therefore, far than Byron's; only that of Keats and Tennyson being comparable with it. And Turner's love of truth was as stern and patient as Dante's; so that when over these great capacities come the shadows of despair, the wreck is infinitely sterner and more sorrowful. With no sweet home for his childhood— friendless in youth, loveless in manhood,—and hopeless in death, Turner was what Dante might have been, without the "bello ovile," without Casella,[110] without Beatrice, and without Him who gave them all, and took them all away.

    I will trace this state of his mind farther, in a little while. Meantime, I want you to note only the result upon his work;—how, through all the remainder of his life, wherever he looked, he saw ruin.

    Ruin and twilight. What was the distinctive effect of light which he introduced, such as no man had painted before? Brightness, indeed, he gave, as we have seen, because it was true and right; but in this he only perfected what others had attempted. His own favourite light is not Ægle, but Hesperid Ægle. Fading of the last rays of sunset. Faint breathing of the sorrow of night.

    And fading of sunset, note also, on ruin. I cannot but wonder that this difference between Turner's work and previous art-conception has not been more observed. None of the great early painters draw ruins, except compulsorily. The shattered buildings introduced by them are shattered artificially, like models. There is no real sense of decay; whereas Turner only momentarily dwells on anything else than ruin. Take up the Liber

Studiorum, and observe how this feeling of decay and humiliation gives solemnity to all its simplest subjects; even to his view of daily labour. I have marked its tendency in examining the design of the Mill and Lock, [fig.67][111] but observe its continuance through the book. There is no exultation in thriving city, or mart, or in happy rural toil, or harvest gathering. Only the grinding at the mill, and patient striving with hard conditions of life.

Such is his view of human labour. Of human pride, see what records.[112]   433
Morpeth tower, roofless and black; gate of old Winchelsea wall, the flock   434
of sheep driven *round* it, not through it; and Rievaulx choir, and Kirkstall crypt; and Dunstanborough, wan above the sea; and Chepstow, with arrowy light through traceried windows; and Lindisfarne, with failing height of wasted shaft and wall; and last and sweetest, Raglan, in utter solitude, amidst the wild wood of its own pleasance; the towers rounded with ivy, and the forest roots choked with undergrowth, and the brook languid amidst lilies and sedges. Legends of gray knights and enchanted ladies keeping the woodman's children away at the sunset.

These are his types of human pride. Of human love: Procris, dying by the arrow [fig.30]; Hesperie, by the viper's fang; and Rizpah, more than dead, beside her children [fig.64].

Such are the lessons of the Liber Studiorum. Silent always with a bitter silence, disdaining to tell his meaning, when he saw there was no ear to receive it, Turner only indicated this purpose by slight words of con-temptuous anger, when he heard of any one's trying to obtain this or the other separate subject as more beautiful than the rest. "What is the use of them," he said, "but together?"* The meaning of the entire book was symbolized in the frontispiece, which he engraved with his own hand: 435
Tyre at sunset, with the Rape of Europa, indicating the symbolism of the decay of Europe by that of Tyre, its beauty passing away into terror and judgment (Europa being the mother of Minos and Rhadamanthus).

---

* Turner appears never to have desired, from any one, care in favour of his separate works. The only thing he would say sometimes was, "Keep them together." He seemed not to mind how much they were injured, if only the record of the thought were left in them, and they were kept in the series which would give the key to their meaning. I never saw him, at my father's house, look for an instant at any of his own drawings: I have watched him sitting at dinner nearly opposite one of his chief pictures—his eyes never turned to it.

But the want of appreciation, nevertheless, touched him sorely; chiefly the not understanding his meaning. He tried hard one day for a quarter of an hour to make me guess what he was doing in the picture of Napoleon,[113] before it had been exhibited, giving me hint after hint in a rough way: but I could not guess, and he would not tell me.

fig.67   J.M.W. Turner, *The Windmill and the Lock,* from *Liber Studiorum*

436   I need not trace the dark clue farther, the reader may follow it unbroken
437   through all his work and life, this thread of Atropos. I will only point, in
conclusion, to the intensity with which his imagination dwelt always on
the three great cities of Carthage, Rome, and Venice—Carthage in
connection especially with the thoughts and study which led to the
painting of the Hesperides' Garden, showing the death which attends the
vain pursuit of wealth; Rome showing the death which attends the vain
pursuit of power; Venice, the death which attends the vain pursuit of
beauty.
438   How strangely significative, thus understood, those last Venetian
dreams of his become, themselves so beautiful and so frail; wrecks of all
that they were once—twilights of twilight!
Vain beauty; yet not all in vain. Unlike in birth, how like in their
labour, and their power over the future, these masters of England and
Venice—Turner and Giorgione. But ten years ago, I saw the last traces of
439   the greatest works of Giorgione yet glowing [fig.63] like a scarlet cloud, on
the Fondaco de' Tedeschi. And though that scarlet cloud may, indeed,
melt away into paleness of night, and Venice herself waste from her
islands as a wreath of wind-driven foam fades from their weedy beach;—
that which she won of faithful light and truth shall never pass away.

Deiphobe of the sea,—the Sun God measures her immortality to her by its   440
sand. Flushed, above the Avernus of the Adrian lake, her spirit is still seen
holding the golden bough; from the lips of the Sea Sibyl men shall learn
for ages yet to come what is most noble and most fair; and, far away, as the
whisper in the coils of the shell, withdrawn through the deep hearts of
nations, shall sound for ever the enchanted voice of Venice.

CHAPTER XII

Peace

441 LOOKING back over what I have written, I find that I have only now the power of ending this work,—it being time that it should end, but not of "concluding" it; for it has led me into fields of infinite inquiry, where it is only possible to break off with such imperfect result as may, at any given moment, have been attained.

Full of far deeper reverence for Turner's art than I felt when this task of his defence was undertaken (which may, perhaps, be evidenced by my having associated no other names with his—but of the dead—in my speaking of him throughout this volume*), I am more in doubt respecting the real use to mankind of that, or any other transcendent art; incomprehensible as it must always be to the mass of men. Full of far deeper love for what I remember of Turner himself, as I become better capable of understanding it, I find myself more and more helpless to explain his errors and his sins.

His errors, I might say, simply. Perhaps, some day, people will again begin to remember the force of the old Greek word for sin; and to learn that all sin is in essence—"Missing the mark"; losing sight or conscious442 ness of heaven; and that this loss may be various in its guilt; it cannot be judged by us. It is this of which the words are spoken so sternly, "Judge not"; which words people always quote, I observe, when they are called upon to "do judgment and justice."[114] For it is truly a pleasant thing to condemn men for their wanderings; but it is a bitter thing to acknowledge a truth, or to take any bold share in working out an equity. So that the

---

* It is proper, however, for the reader to know, that the title which I myself originally intended for this book was "*Turner and the Ancients*"; nor did I purpose to refer in it to any other modern painters than Turner. The title was changed; and the notes on other living painters inserted in the first volume, in deference to the advice of friends, probably wise; for unless the change had been made, the book might never have been read at all. But, as far as I am concerned, I regretted the change then, and regret it still.

habitual modern practical application of the precept "Judge not," is to avoid the trouble of pronouncing verdict by taking, of any matter, the pleasantest malicious view which first comes to hand, and to obtain licence for our own convenient iniquities; by being indulgent to those of others.

These two methods of obedience being just the two which are most directly opposite to the law of mercy and truth.

"Bind them about thy neck."[115] I said, but now, that of an evil tree men never gathered good fruit. And the lesson we have finally to learn from Turner's life is broadly this, that all the power of it came of its mercy and sincerity; all the failure of it, from its want of faith. It has been asked of me, by several of his friends, that I should endeavour to do some justice to his character, mistaken wholly by the world. If my life is spared, I will.[116] But that character is still, in many respects, inexplicable to me; the materials within my reach are imperfect; and my experience in the world not yet large enough to enable me to use them justly. His life is to be written by a biographer, who will, I believe, spare no pains in collecting the few scattered records which exist of a career so uneventful and secluded. I will not anticipate the conclusions of this writer; but if they appear to me just, will endeavour afterwards, so far as may be in my power, to confirm and illustrate them; and, if unjust, to show in what degree. 443

Which, lest death or illness should forbid me, this only I declare now of what I know respecting Turner's character. Much of his mind and heart I do not know;—perhaps never shall know. But this much I do: and if there is anything in the previous course of this work to warrant trust in me of any kind, let me be trusted when I tell you that Turner had a heart as intensely kind, and as nobly true, as ever God gave to one of His creatures. I offer, as yet, no evidence in this matter. When I *do* give it, it shall be sifted and clear. Only this one fact I now record joyfully and solemnly, that, having known Turner for ten years, and that during the period of his life when the brightest qualities of his mind were, in many respects, diminished, and when he was suffering most from the evil-speaking of the world, I never heard him say one depreciating word of living man, or man's work; I never saw him look an unkind or blameful look; I never knew him let pass, without some sorrowful remonstrance, or endeavour at mitigation, a blameful word spoken by another.

Of no man but Turner, whom I have ever known, could I say this. And of this kindness and truth came, I repeat, all his highest power. And all his failure and error, deep and strange, came of his faithlessness. 444

Faithlessness, or despair, the despair which has been shown already[117] to be characteristic of this present century, and most sorrowfully manifested in its greatest men; but existing in an infinitely more fatal form in 445 the lower and general mind, reacting upon those who ought to be its teachers.

The form which the infidelity of England, especially, has taken, is one hitherto unheard of in human history. No nation ever before declared boldly, by print and word of mouth, that its religion was good for show, but

446 "would not work." Over and over again it has happened that nations have denied their gods, but they denied them bravely. The Greeks in their decline jested at their religion, and frittered it away in flatteries and fine arts; the French refused theirs fiercely, tore down their altars and brake

447 their carven images. The question about God with both these nations was still, even in their decline, fairly put, though falsely answered. "Either there is or is not a Supreme Ruler; we consider of it, declare there is not, and proceed accordingly." But we English have put the matter in an

448 entirely new light: "There *is* a Supreme Ruler, no question of it, only He cannot rule. His orders won't work. He will be quite satisfied with euphonious and respectful repetition of them. Execution would be too dangerous under existing circumstances, which He certainly never contemplated."

I had no conception of the absolute darkness which has covered the national mind in this respect, until I began to come into collision with persons engaged in the study of economical and political questions. The entire naïveté and undisturbed imbecility with which I found them declare that the laws of the Devil were the only practicable ones, and that the laws of God were merely a form of poetical language, passed all that I had ever before heard or read of mortal infidelity. I knew the fool had often said in his heart, there was *no* God; but to hear him say clearly out with his lips, "There is a foolish God," was something which my art studies had not prepared me for.

Now this form of unbelief in God is connected with, and necessarily productive of, a precisely equal unbelief in man.

Co-relative with the assertion, "There is a foolish God," is the assertion, "There is a brutish man." "As no laws but those of the Devil are practicable in the world, so no impulses but those of the brute" (says the modern political economist) "are appealable to in the world. Faith, generosity, honesty, zeal, and self-sacrifice are poetical phrases. None of these things can, in reality, be counted upon; there is no truth in man which can be used as a moving or productive power. All motive force in him is essentially brutish, covetous, or contentious. His power is only

449 power of prey: otherwise than the spider, he cannot design; otherwise than the tiger, he cannot feed." This is the modern interpretation of that embarrassing article of the Creed "the communion of saints."

It has always seemed very strange to me, not indeed that this creed should have been adopted, it being the entirely necessary consequence of the previous fundamental article;—but that no one should ever seem to have any misgivings about it;—that, practically, no one had *seen* how strong work *was* done by man; how either for hire, or for hatred, it never had been done; and that no amount of pay had ever made a good soldier, a good teacher, a good artist, or a good workman. You pay your soldiers and sailors so many pence a day, at which rated sum, one will do good fighting for you; another, bad fighting. Pay as you will, the entire goodness of the fighting depends, always, on its being done for nothing; or rather, less than nothing, in the expectation of no pay but death. Examine the work of your spiritual teachers, and you will find the statistical law respecting them is, "The less pay, the better work." Examine also your writers and artists: for ten pounds you shall have a *Paradise Lost*, and for a plate of figs, a Dürer drawing;[118] but for a million of money sterling, neither. Examine your men of science: paid by starvation, Kepler will discover the laws of the orbs of heaven for you;—and, driven out to die in   450 the street, Swammerdam[119] shall discover the laws of life for you:—such hard terms do they make with you, these brutish men, who can only be had for hire.

Neither is good work ever done for hatred, any more than hire;—but for love only. For love of their country, or their leader, or their duty, men fight steadily; but for massacre and plunder, feebly. Your signal, "England expects every man to do his duty," they will answer; your signal of Black flag and death's-head, they will not answer. And verily they will answer it no more in commerce than in battle. The cross-bones will not make a good shop-sign, you will find ultimately, any more than a good battle-standard. Not the cross-bones, but the cross.

Now the practical result of this infidelity in man is the utter ignorance of all the ways of getting his right work out of him. From a given quantity of human power and intellect, to produce the least possible result, is a problem solved, nearly with mathematical precision, by the present methods of the nation's economical procedure. The power and intellect are enormous. With the best soldiers, at present existing, we survive in battle, and but survive, because, by help of Providence, a man whom we have kept all his life in command of a company forces his way at the age of seventy so far up as to obtain permission to save us, and die, unthanked.[120] With the shrewdest thinkers in the world, we have not yet succeeded in arriving at any national conviction respecting the uses of life. And with the best artistical material in the world, we spend millions of money in raising a building for our Houses of Talk,[121] of the delightfulness and utility of which (perhaps roughly classing the Talk and its tabernacle together,) posterity will, I believe, form no very grateful   451 estimate;—while for sheer want of bread, we brought the question to the balance of a hair, whether the most earnest of our young painters should give up his art altogether, and go to Australia,—or fight his way through all neglect and obloquy to the painting of the Christ in the Temple [plate 24].[122]

The marketing was indeed done in this case, as in all others, on the usual terms. For the millions of money, we got a mouldering toy: for the starvation, five years' work of the prime of a noble life. Yet neither that picture, great as it is, nor any other of Hunt's, are the best he could have done. They are the least he could have done. By no expedient could we have repressed him more than he has been repressed; by no abnegation received from him less than we have received.

My dear friend and teacher, Lowell, right as he is in almost everything, is for once wrong in these lines, though with a noble wrongness:—

> "Disappointment's dry and bitter root,
> Envy's harsh berries, and the choking pool
> Of the world's scorn, are the right mother-milk
> To the tough hearts that pioneer their kind."[123]

They are *not* so; love and trust are the only mother-milk of any man's soul. So far as he is hated and mistrusted, his powers are destroyed. Do not think that with impunity you can follow the eyeless fool, and shout with the shouting charlatan; and that the men you thrust aside with gibe and blow, are thus sneered and crushed into the best service they can do you. I have told you they *will* not serve you for pay. They *cannot* serve you for scorn. Even from Balaam, money-lover though he be, no useful prophecy is to be had for silver or gold. From Elisha, saviour of life though he be, no saving of life—even of children's, who "know no better,"—is to be got by the cry, Go up, thou bald-head. No man can serve you either for purse or curse; neither kind of pay will answer. No *pay* is, indeed, receivable by any true man; but *power* is receivable by him, in the love and faith you give him. So far only as you give him these can he serve you; that is the meaning of the question which his Master asks always, "Believest thou that I am able?"[124] And from every one of his servants—to the end of time—if you give them the Capernaum measure of faith, you shall have from them Capernaum measure of works, and no more.

Do you think that I am irreverently comparing great and small things? The system of the world is entirely one; small things and great are alike part of one mighty whole. As the flower is gnawed by frost, so every human heart is gnawed by faithlessness. And as surely,—as irrevocably,— as the fruit-bud falls before the east wind, so fails the power of the kindest human heart, if you meet it with poison.

Now the condition of mind in which Turner did all his great work was simply this: "What I do must be done rightly; but I know also that no man now living in Europe cares to understand it; and the better I do it, the

452

less he will see the meaning of it." There never was yet, so far as I can hear or read, isolation of a great spirit so utterly desolate. Columbus had succeeded in making other hearts share his hope, before he was put to 453 hardest trial; and knew that, by help of Heaven, he could finally show that he was right. Kepler and Galileo could demonstrate their conclusions up to a certain point; so far as they felt they were right, they were sure that after death their work would be acknowledged. But Turner could demonstrate nothing of what he had done;—saw no security that after death he would be understood more than he had been in life. Only another Turner could apprehend Turner. Such praise as he received was poor and superficial: he regarded it far less than censure. My own admiration of him was wild in enthusiasm, but it gave him no ray of pleasure; he could not make me at that time understand his main meanings; he loved me, but cared nothing for what I said, and was always trying to hinder me from writing, because it gave pain to his fellow-artists. To the praise of other persons he gave not even the acknowledgment of this sad affection; it passed by him as murmur of the wind: and most justly, for not one of his own special powers was ever perceived by the world. I have said in another place that all great modern artists will own their obligation to him as a guide. They will; but they are in error in this gratitude, as I was, when I quoted it as a sign of their respect. Close analysis of the portions of modern art founded on Turner has since shown me that in every case his imitators misunderstood him:—that they caught merely at superficial brilliancies, and never saw the real character of his mind or of his work.

And at this day, while I write, the catalogue allowed to be sold at the 454 gates of the National Gallery, for the instruction of the common people, describes Callcott and Claude as the greater artists.

To censure, on the other hand, Turner was acutely sensitive, owing to his own natural kindness; he felt it, for himself, or for others, not as criticism, but as cruelty. He knew that however little his higher power could be seen, he had at least done as much as ought to have saved him from wanton insult; and the attacks upon him in his later years were to him not merely contemptible in their ignorance, but amazing in their ingratitude. "A man may be weak in his age," he said to me once, at the time when he felt he was dying; "but you should not tell him so."

What Turner might have done for us, had he received help and love, instead of disdain, I can hardly trust myself to imagine. Increasing calmly in power and loveliness, his work would have formed one mighty series of poems, each great as that which I have interpreted,—the Hesperides; but 455 becoming brighter and kinder as he advanced to happy age. Soft as Correggio's, solemn as Titian's, the enchanted colour would have glowed, imperishable and pure; and the subtle thoughts risen into loftiest teaching, helpful for centuries to come.

What we have asked from him, instead of this, and what received, we know. But few of us yet know how true an image those darkening wrecks of radiance give to the shadow which gained sway at last over his once pure and noble soul.

Not unresisted, nor touching the heart's core, nor any of the old kindness and truth: yet festering work of the worm—inexplicable and terrible, such as England, by her goodly gardening, leaves to infect her earth-flowers.

So far as in it lay, this century has caused every one of its great men, whose hearts were kindest, and whose spirits most perceptive of the work of God, to die without hope:—Scott, Keats, Byron, Shelley, Turner. Great England, of the Iron-heart now, not of the Lion-heart; for these souls of her children an account may perhaps be one day required of her.

She has not yet read often enough that old story of the Samaritan's mercy. He whom he saved was going down from Jerusalem to Jericho—to the accursed city (so the old Church used to understand it). He should not have left Jerusalem; it was his own fault that he went out into the desert, and fell among the thieves, and was left for dead. Every one of these English children, in their day, took the desert by-path as he did, and fell among fiends—took to making bread out of stones at their bidding, and then died, torn and famished; careful England, in her pure, priestly dress, 456 passing by on the other side. So far as we are concerned, that is the account *we* have to give of them.

So far as *they* are concerned, I do not fear for them;—there being one Priest Who never passes by. The longer I live, the more clearly I see how all souls are in His hand—the mean and the great. Fallen on the earth in their baseness, or fading as the mist of morning in their goodness;—still in the hand of the potter as the clay, and in the temple of their master as the cloud. It was not the mere bodily death that He conquered—that death had no sting. It was this spiritual death which He conquered, so that at last it should be swallowed up—mark the word—not in life; but in victory. As the dead body shall be raised to life, so also the defeated soul to victory, if only it has been fighting on its Master's side, has made no covenant with death; nor itself bowed its forehead for his seal. Blind from the prison-house, maimed from the battle, or mad from the tombs, their souls shall surely yet sit, astonished, at His feet Who giveth peace.

Who *giveth* peace? Many a peace we have made and named for ourselves, but the falsest is in that marvellous thought that we, of all generations of the earth, only know the right; and that to us at last,—to us alone,—all the scheme of God, about the salvation of men, has been 457 shown. "This is the light in which *we* are walking. Those vain Greeks are gone down to their Persephone for ever—Egypt and Assyria, Elam and her multitude,—uncircumcised, their graves are round about them—Pathros and careless Ethiopia—filled with the slain. Rome, with her thirsty sword, and poison wine, how did she walk in her darkness! We only have no idolatries—ours are the seeing eyes; in our pure hands at last, the seven-sealed book is laid; to our true tongues entrusted the preaching of a perfect gospel. Who shall come after us? Is it not Peace? The poor Jew, Zimri, who slew his master, there is no peace for him: [125] but, for us? tiara on head, may we not look out of the windows of heaven?''

Another kind of peace I look for than this, though I hear it said of me that I am hopeless.

I am not hopeless, though my hope may be as Veronese's: the dark-veiled. [126]

Veiled, not because sorrowful, but because blind. I do not know what my England desires, or how long she will choose to do as she is doing now;—with her right hand casting away the souls of men, and with her left the gifts of God.

In the prayers which she dictates to her children, she tells them to fight against the world, the flesh, and the devil. Some day, perhaps, it may also occur to her as desirable to tell those children what she means by this. What is the world which they are to "fight with," and how does it differ from the world which they are to "get on in"? The explanation seems to me the more needful, because I do not, in the book we profess to live by, find anything very distinct about fighting with the world. I find something about fighting with the rulers of its darkness, and something also about overcoming it; but it does not follow that this conquest is to be by   458 hostility, since evil may be overcome with good. But I find it written very distinctly that God loved the world, and that Christ is the light of it. [127]

What the much-used words, therefore, mean, I cannot tell. But this, I believe, they *should* mean. That there is, indeed, one world which is full of care, and desire, and hatred: a world of war, of which Christ is not the light, which indeed is without light, and has never heard the great "Let there be." Which is, therefore, in truth, as yet no world; but chaos, on the face of which, moving, the Spirit of God yet causes men to hope that a world will come. The better one, they call it: perhaps they might, more wisely, call it the real one. Also, I hear them speak continually of going to it, rather than of its coming to them; which, again, is strange, for in that prayer which they had straight from the lips of the Light of the world, and which He apparently thought sufficient prayer for them, there is not anything about going to another world; only something of another government coming into this; or rather, not another, but the only government,—that government which will constitute it a world indeed. New heavens and new earth. Earth, no more without form and void, but sown with fruit of righteousness. Firmament, no more of passing cloud, but of cloud risen out of the crystal sea—cloud in which, as He was once received up, so He shall again come with power, and every eye shall see Him, and all kindreds of the earth shall wail because of Him.

Kindreds of the earth, or tribes of it! the "earth begotten," the Chaos
459 children—children of this present world, with its desolate seas and its Medusa clouds: the Dragon children, merciless: they who dealt as clouds without water: serpent clouds, by whose sight men were turned into stone;—the time must surely come for their wailing.

"Thy kingdom come," we are bid to ask then! But how shall it come? With power and great glory, it is written; and yet not with observation, it is also written. Strange kingdom! Yet its strangeness is renewed to us with every dawn.

When the time comes for us to wake out of the world's sleep, why should it be otherwise than out of the dreams of the night? Singing of birds, first, broken and low, as, not to dying eyes, but eyes that wake to life, "the casement slowly grows a glimmering square";[128] and then the gray, and then the rose of dawn; and last the light, whose going forth is to the ends of heaven.

This kingdom it is not in our power to bring; but it is, to receive. Nay, it is come already, in part; but not received, because men love chaos best; and the Night, with her daughters. That is still the only question for us, as in the old Elias days, "If ye will receive it."[129] With pains it may be shut out still from many a dark place of cruelty; by sloth it may be still unseen for many a glorious hour. But the pain of shutting it out must grow greater and greater:—harder, every day, that struggle of man with man in the abyss, and shorter wages for the fiend's work. But it is still at our choice; the simoom-dragon may still be served if we will, in the fiery desert, or else God walking in the garden, at cool of day. Coolness now, not of Hesperus
460 over Atlas, stooped endurer of toil; but of Heosphorus[130] over Sion, the joy of the earth.* The choice is no vague nor doubtful one. High on the desert mountain, full descried, sits throned the tempter, with his old promise—the kingdoms of this world, and the glory of them. He still calls you to your labour, as Christ to your rest;—labour and sorrow, base desire, and cruel hope. So far as you desire to possess, rather than to give; so far as you look for power to command, instead of to bless; so far as your own prosperity seems to you to issue out of contest or rivalry, of any kind, with other men, or other nations; so long as the hope before you is for supremacy instead of love; and your desire is to be greatest, instead of least;—first, instead of last;—so long you are serving the Lord of all that is

---

*This joy it is to receive and to give, because its officers (governors of its acts) are to be Peace, and its exactors (governors of its dealings), Righteousness (Isaiah 60.17).

last, and least;—the last enemy that shall be destroyed—Death; and you shall have death's crown, with the worm coiled in it; and death's wages, with the worm feeding on them; kindred of the earth shall you yourself become; saying to the grave, "Thou art my father"; and to the worm, "Thou art my mother, and my sister."

I leave you to judge, and to choose, between this labour, and the bequeathed peace; these wages, and the gift of the Morning Star; this obedience, and the doing of the will which shall enable you to claim another kindred than of the earth, and to hear another voice than that of the grave, saying, "My brother, and sister, and mother."[131]

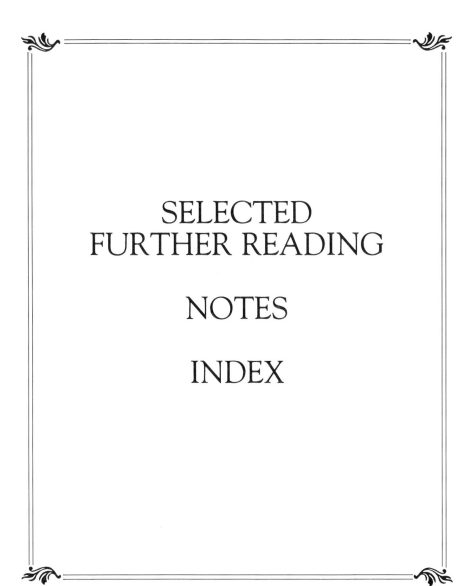

SELECTED
FURTHER READING

NOTES

INDEX

SELECTED FURTHER READING

WORKS

Eds E.T. Cook and Alexander Wedderburn, *The Works of John Ruskin, Library Edition* (39 vols, London, 1903–12)

BIOGRAPHY

Derrick Leon, *Ruskin, The Great Victorian* (London, 1949)

John Dixon Hunt, *The Wider Sea: A Life of John Ruskin* (New York, 1982)

Tim Hilton, *John Ruskin, The Early Years* (London, 1985). The first volume of a two-volume biography, the second part of which had yet to appear at the time of writing. The first volume ends in 1860.

STUDIES

John D. Rosenberg, *The Darkening Glass: A Portrait of Ruskin's Genius* (New York, 1961)

George P. Landow, *The Aesthetic and Critical Theories of John Ruskin* (Princeton, 1971)

Patricia M. Ball, *The Science of Aspects: The Changing Role of Fact in the Work of Coleridge, Ruskin and Hopkins* (London, 1971)

Robert Hewison, *John Ruskin or the Argument of the Eye* (London, 1975)

Elizabeth K. Helsinger, *Ruskin and the Art of the Beholder* (Cambridge, Mass., 1982)

Paul L. Sawyer, *Ruskin's Poetic Argument: The Design of the Major Works* (Ithaca, 1985)

George P. Landow, *Ruskin* (Oxford, 1985)

RUSKIN THE ARTIST

Paul H. Walton, *The Drawings of John Ruskin* (Oxford, 1972)

Readers wishing to find out more about works by Turner referred to in *Modern Painters* are advised to consult Andrew Wilton's *The Life and Work of J.M.W. Turner* (London, 1979) which, apart from providing a critical and biographical study of the artist, also includes exhaustive catalogues of his paintings and drawings.

NOTES

Abbreviations: references to the Library Edition are by volume and page number: 'V.370'. The editors of the Library Edition — Cook and Wedderburn — are abbreviated as 'C & W'.

VOLUME I

1   'Gaspar' is Gaspar Dughet (1615–75), brother-in-law and pupil of Nicolas Poussin. Ruskin also refers to him as 'Gaspar Poussin'.

2   Carlo Dolci (1616–86), a prominent Florentine painter of the late Baroque period whose later works are characterised by their high finish and intricate detail.

3   This definition comes from Locke's *Essay concerning Human Understanding* (1690), Book II, Chap.i.

4   *Merchant of Venice*, IV. i.328.

5   Sir Joshua Reynolds, from *The Idler*, ed. Dr Johnson, no.79, Saturday 20 October 1759.

6   An archaic term for a pretence or disguise.

7   The two preceding chapters, in which Ruskin seeks to demonstrate that 'particular truths' are more important than 'general' ones and that 'rare truths' are more important than 'frequent' ones, have been omitted. It may however be worth quoting a short passage from Chapter IV which neatly summarises Ruskin's views on the duty of the landscape painter: 'The teaching of nature is as varied and infinite as it is constant; and the duty of the painter is to watch for every one of her lessons, and to give (for human life will admit of nothing more) those in which she has manifested each of her principles in the most peculiar and striking way' (III.156). He goes on to liken the painter to the preacher, both being 'commentators on infinity' and concludes that 'All really great pictures...exhibit the general habits of nature, manifested in some peculiar, rare, and beautiful way.' (III.157)

8   Ruskin's uncritical reliance on Locke's questionable distinction between 'primary' and 'secondary' qualities weakens this part of his argument. But in any case his relegation of truths of colour to the 'second rank' does not mean that he regards colour as

insignificant. He later made it clear that he attached the greatest importance to the expressive and symbolic properties of colour. See, for example, Vol.IV, Chap.iii (p.455ff), and Vol.V, Chap.xi (p.601ff).

9   According to C & W, *Memoirs of Marmontel, written by himself*, Book viii.

10 Most of the rest of this chapter first appeared in the third edition of 1846. Its place was taken in the earlier editions by a much shorter and more highly coloured conclusion, which included a passage in which Ruskin described Turner as 'a prophet of God' sent 'to reveal to men the mysteries of His universe, standing, like the great angel of the Apocalypse, clothed with a cloud, and with a rainbow upon his head, and with the sun and stars given into his hand'. This attracted the charge of blasphemy, which may explain its removal from the third edition. It is possible that Turner may have had it in mind in painting *The Angel standing in the Sun* of 1846 (Tate Gallery, London).

11 This work was destroyed in a fire in 1866, according to C & W.

12 *The Church Porch*, stanza 15.

13 See p.276ff.

14 Lines published in 1845. Ruskin later described the following paragraph as 'one of the important passages leading to Pre-Raphaelitism' (III.178).

15 In the Brancacci Chapel, Sta Maria del Carmine, Florence.

16 The passage reads:
    'There may be as much greatness of mind, as much nobility of manner, in a master's treatment of the smallest features, as in his management of the most vast; and this greatness of manner chiefly consists in seizing the specific character of the object, together with all the great qualities of beauty which it has in common with higher orders of existence, while he utterly rejects the meaner beauties which are accidentally peculiar to the object, and yet not specifically characteristic of it'
    (Preface to second edition, III. 32−3).

17 Anthonie Waterlo (1609−76), an engraver of paintings.

18 The passage referred to is in the preface to the second edition (III.44−5): 'the praise which, in this first portion of the work is given to many English artists, would be justifiable on this ground only; that, although frequently with little power or desultory effect, they have yet, in an honest and good heart, received the word of God from clouds, and leaves, and waves, and kept it . . .'. A footnote at this point adds that 'The feelings of Constable with respect to his art might be almost a model for the young student,

were it not that they err a little on the other side, and are perhaps in need of chastening and guiding from the works of his fellow-men.'

19 Leslie, in his *Memoirs of the Life of John Constable RA* (1845), quotes a letter written by Constable in which he records the influential painter Fuseli (1741–1825) as saying 'I *like* de *landscape* of Constable but he makes me call for my great coat and umbrella.' Fuseli was Swiss-born, hence the accent.

20 A lengthy passage has been omitted at this point, in which Ruskin discusses the merits of various well-known contemporary artists, including David Cox (1783–1859), Copley Fielding (1787–1855), David Roberts (1796–1864), Clarkson Stanfield (1793–1867) and Samuel Prout (1783–1852). Discussion of Prout's architectural drawings leads Ruskin into an examination of the architectural paintings of the old masters, including Canaletto whom he cruelly attacks:

> 'The mannerism of Canaletto is the most degraded that I know in the whole range of art. Professing the most servile and mindless imitation, it imitates nothing but the blackness of the shadows; it gives no single architectural ornament, however near, so much form as might enable us even to guess at its actual one...it gives the buildings neither their architectural beauty nor their ancestral dignity, for there is no texture of stone nor character of age in Canaletto's touch; which is invariably a violent, black, sharp, ruled penmanlike line, as far removed from the grace of nature as from her faintness and transparency...'

(III.215).

21 These appeared partly in Dr T.D. Whitaker's *History of Richmondshire* (1819–23) and partly in the *Picturesque Views in England and Wales* (1827–1838).

22 Turner was first able to visit the continent in 1802 during the brief peace following the signature of the Treaty of Amiens in October 1801.

23 The *Liber Studiorum* was a set of seventy-one landscape engravings published between 1807 and 1819, inspired by Claude's *Liber Veritatis*.

24 *Snow Storm: Hannibal and his army crossing the Alps*, Tate Gallery, London.

25 In the Tate Gallery.

26 In a private collection in the USA.

27 In the National Gallery, London. A detail is given in fig.39.

28 Juvenal, *Satires* IV, 116: 'a blind sycophant, only fit to beg alms at the wheel-side on the road to Ariccia and throw coaxing kisses

after the chariot as it goes down hill'. But it is Catullus (L. Valerius Catullus Messalinus – Consul in 73 and 85 AD), and not Veiento, whom Juvenal describes in these terms. Ariccia is on the Via Appia, about twenty miles south of Rome.

29 The *Marriage of Isaac and Rebekah* is one of the two Claudes which, in accordance with a stipulation in Turner's will, hang on either side of his *Sun rising through Vapour* and *Dido building Carthage* (plate 4) in the National Gallery, London. Ruskin launched a sustained attack on it in the preface to the second edition where he described it *inter alia* as 'a fair example of what is commonly called an "ideal" landscape; i.e. a group of the artist's studies from Nature, individually spoiled, selected with such opposition of character as may insure their neutralizing each other's effect, and united with sufficient unnaturalness and violence of association to insure the producing a general sensation of the impossible'. (III.42)

30 'brought up in dense shade and not in the pure sun' (Plato, *Phaedrus*, 239C).

31 Chapter IV has been entirely omitted. In it Ruskin puts forward the rather unconvincing view that objects in the foreground of a painting should not be shown with the same degree of distinctness as objects in the distance, since the eye cannot focus simultaneously on two objects, one of which is much farther off than the other. He goes on to use this theory to justify the 'singular, and to the ignorant in art, the offensive execution' of figures in Turner's works. He later acknowledged that this argument was less than totally convincing (III.319 footnote).

32 *A Roman Road.*

33 Commenting on this passage in 1875 Ruskin wrote: 'At least I thought so, when I was four-and-twenty. At five-and-fifty, I fancy that it is just possible there may be other creatures in the universe to be pleased, or, – it may be, – displeased, by the weather'. (III.343 footnote)

34 Wordsworth, from *Poems of Imagination*, no.viii ('She was a phantom of delight'), ll.17 & 18.

35 An old-fashioned name for nitrogen.

36 This work is entitled *Herdsmen with Cows*. The Hazlitt reference is in the section of *Sketches of the Principal Picture Galleries in England* (1824) which deals with the Dulwich Picture Gallery.

37 Ruskin questioned the adequacy of this account of the mechanism of cloud formation in a passage in Vol.V which has been cut (see VII.165 ff).

38 This work is entitled *Monks Fishing*. It is no longer hung.

39 *Dido and Aeneas* and *Landscape with a Storm.*

40 Engraved by J.T. Willmore in 1826 for *England and Wales*.

41 For Cox see note 20 above. John Frederick Tayler (1802–89).

42 See note 29 above.

43 C & W's identification of this work as the vignette on the title page of *Heath's Picturesque Annual* for 1832 is questionable. The view of Lago Maggiore reproduced in fig.21 is a more likely candidate.

44 *Mountainous Landscape*, now ascribed to the School of Salvator Rosa. It is no longer hung.

45 *Destruction of Niobe's Children*, Dulwich Picture Gallery. It is now ascribed to the School of Gaspar Dughet and is no longer hung.

46 There is no work by Turner with this title, but *Apollo and Daphne* answers the description perfectly.

47 *Snow-storm, Avalanche and inundation — a scene in the upper part of the Val d'Aout, Piedmont*, Art Institute, Chicago.

48 *Landscape with Hagar and the Angel*, National Gallery, London.

49 From this point onwards, the chapter was almost entirely different in the first two editions.

50 Now known as '*Now for the Painter', (Rope.) Passengers going on Board*, City Art Gallery, Manchester.

51 *Cattle Near a River*. This is no longer hung.

52 *Landscape with Cattle*, now attributed to Abraham van Borssom. It is no longer hung.

53 According to C & W, this work is entitled *Winter, or the Great Flood*.

54 The whole of the chapter entitled 'Of Water, as painted by the Moderns' has been omitted. It is however worth quoting Ruskin's famous description of the Falls of Schaffhausen (III.529–30):

'Stand for half an hour beside the Fall of Schaffhausen, on the north side where the rapids are long, and watch how the vault of water first bends, unbroken, in pure polished velocity, over the arching rocks at the brow of the cataract, covering them with a dome of crystal twenty feet thick, so swift that its motion is unseen except when a foam-globe from above darts over it like a falling star; and how the trees are lighted above it under all their leaves, at the instant that it breaks into foam; and how all the hollows of that foam burn with green fire like so much shattering chrysoprase; and how, ever and anon, startling you with its white flash, a jet of spray leaps hissing out of the fall, like a rocket, bursting in the wind and driven away in dust, filling the air with light; and how, through the curdling wreaths of the restless crashing abyss below, the blue of the water, paled by the foam in its body, shows purer than the sky through white rain-cloud; while the shuddering iris stoops in tremulous stillness over all, fading and flushing alternately through the choking spray and shattered sunshine, hiding itself at last among the thick golden leaves which toss to and fro in sympathy with the wild water; their dripping masses lifted at intervals, like sheaves of loaded corn, by some stronger gush from the cataract, and bowed again upon the mossy rocks as its roar dies away; the dew gushing from their thick branches through drooping clusters of emerald herbage, and sparkling in white threads along the dark rocks of the shore, feeding the lichens which chase and chequer them with purple and silver. I believe, when you have stood by this for half an hour, you will have discovered that there is something more in nature than has been given by Ruysdael.'

55   The first ten paragraphs of this chapter, which give detailed examples of Turner's accuracy in depicting reflections in water, have been omitted.

56   Plate 8, *England and Wales.*

57   Engraved by R. Wallis for *Turner's Annual Tour — the Loire* (1833). The original drawing is in the Ashmolean Museum, Oxford.

58   Almost all the identifiable drawings mentioned in this paragraph are in private collections. There is however a view of the Lake of Lucerne from Brunnen (1845) in the Pantzer Collection, Indianapolis.

59   The correct title of this work — *Slavers throwing overboard the dead and dying — Typhon coming on* — contradicts Ruskin's statement that the storm is passed. Ruskin was given the painting by his father as a New Year's present in 1844 in gratitude for Vol.I of *Modern Painters.*

60   This is an echo of *Macbeth*, II.ii.61: '... The multitudinous seas incarnadine...'

61   In the National Gallery, London.

62   The rest of this chapter has been deleted; it is devoted to consideration of the work of various contemporary artists, such as J.D. Harding (1797–1863) and David Cox. It is however worth quoting a passage which appeared in the third and fourth editions (published in 1846 and 1848 respectively) in which Ruskin discusses the work of Samuel Palmer (1805–81):

'A less known artist, S. Palmer, lately admitted a member of the Old Water-Colour Society, is deserving of the very highest place among faithful followers of nature. His studies of foreign foliage especially are beyond all praise for care and fulness. I have never seen a stone-pine or a cypress drawn except by him; and his feeling is as pure and grand as his fidelity is exemplary. He has not, however, yet, I think, discovered what is necessary and unnecessary in a great picture; and his works, sent to the Society's rooms, have been most unfavourable examples of his power, and have been generally, as yet, in places where all that is best in them is out of sight. I look to him, nevertheless, unless he lose himself in over-reverence for certain conventionalisms of the older schools, as one of the probable renovators and correctors of whatever is failing or erroneous in the practice of English art.'

(III.604–5)

63   Baccio Bandinelli (1487 or 1493–1559), was a Florentine sculptor and jealous rival of Michelangelo but eventually became one of his most servile imitators.

64   A room in a theatre for the accommodation of actors when off-stage.

65   This footnote first appeared in the fifth edition (1851) following Ruskin's defence of the Pre-Raphaelites (see introduction).

VOLUME II

1   From Tyrtaeus, a Spartan poet of the 7th century BC who composed martial songs.

2   Eccles. iii.11.

3   Ruskin's choice of the term 'theoretic' is evidence of his debt to Aristotle who argues in the *Nicomachean Ethics* that the object of human life is happiness and that perfect happiness is a kind of contemplation ('theoria'). See especially book 10 of the *Ethics*.

4   In a footnote to the 'Re-arranged Edition' of 1883 (the sixth) Ruskin described this paragraph as 'the radical theorem, not only of this book, but of all my writings on art'.

5   Luke viii.15.

6   Ruskin inserted the word 'quite' in the 1883 edition, explaining in a note that the sentence needed it and that he meant it. But, he went on, 'I must beg the reader to observe that I don't, even now, think myself *quite* right in all matters, even of taste.'

7   The previous chapter, entitled 'Of false opinions concerning beauty', has been cut. In it Ruskin attempts to dispose of 'four of the more current opinions respecting Beauty' (IV.66): that the beautiful is the true; that the beautiful is the useful; that beauty depends on custom; and finally that it is dependent on the association of ideas – i.e. that 'the agreeableness in objects which we call Beauty, is the result of the Association with them of agreeable or interesting ideas' (IV.70). Ruskin regards the last as

the 'most weighty theory' but insists that 'no two consecutive sentences were ever written in defence of it, without involving either a contradiction or a confusion of terms' (ibid.). His argument at this point is weak and reflects his desire to elaborate an aesthetic system which is untainted by contingent, subjective influences. Nevertheless, Ruskin himself acknowledges the importance of the association of ideas later in the same chapter and expresses doubt about whether 'the minor degrees and shades of this great influence have been sufficiently appreciated' (IV.72). He admits that 'the eye cannot rest on a material form, in a moment of depression or exultation, without communicating to that form a spirit and a life — a life which will make it afterwards in some degree loved or feared, — a charm or a painfulness for which we shall be unable to account even to ourselves, which will not indeed be perceptible, except by its delicate influence on our judgement in cases of complicated beauty' (ibid.). Ruskin finally reaches the important conclusion that since nobody can distinguish 'the unconscious underworking of indefinite association peculiar to him individually, from those great laws in which he is comprehended with all his race', it is impossible to draw 'absolute and incontrovertible conclusions on subjects of theoretic preference' (IV.74). See also page 348ff.

8 Wordsworth, *Intimations of Immortality*, stanza v, ll. 66–77.
9 'Laurati' is Vasari's name for Pietro Lorenzetti. 'Benozzo' is Benozzo Gozzoli.
10 According to C & W, the *Madonna del Cardellino* is in the Uffizi, while the other two are in the Pitti Palace.
11 *Ecclesiastical Polity*, Book I, para.xi.
12 Both works by Fra Angelico.
13 A purpose not fulfilled.
14 *Of the Sublime and Beautiful*, Part III, Sec.iii.
15 Ibid. Part III, Sec.ii.
16 A camelopard is a giraffe; a turnspit is a kind of dog (which turns a spit).
17 A small force of Spartans held the pass of Thermopylae for three days against a huge invading Persian army in 480 BC (Herodotus, *Histories*, vii. 207–28). See also page 497.
18 Exod.xiv.13.
19 The *Theseus* is a figure from the East Pediment of the Parthenon (part of the Elgin marbles, in the British Museum). The *Dawn* and *Twilight* are works by Michelangelo from the tomb of Lorenzo de' Medici, in the Medici Chapel, Rome.
20 Louis François Roubiliac (died 1762) was one of the foremost

sculptors in eighteenth-century England, though he was born in France. There are several tombs by him in Westminster Abbey (e.g. the Duke of Argyll, 1748). Antonio Canova (1757–1822), a Venetian, was the foremost exponent of neo-classical sculpture.

21 Jacopo della Quercia (1374/5–1438) was from Siena. The tomb of Ilaria di Caretto is the earliest work attributed to him (c.1406).

22 I John i.5.

23 Rev.xxii.1; xxi.18–21.

24 Chapters x and xi have been omitted.

25 See p. 198.

26 The passage referred to has been deleted. It begins: 'In the range of inorganic nature, I doubt if any object can be found more beautiful than a fresh, deep snow drift, seen under warm light.' (III.445–6)

27 See p. 221.

28 George Herbert: 'Providence' from *The Temple*, ll.133–4.

29 Rev.vii.2.

30 Sic. The *Oxford English Dictionary* gives no appropriate definition. Perhaps it was a misprint for 'lenten', but on the other hand lentils do soak up water thirstily!

31 2 Sam.xvi.13.

32 Commenting on this passage in 1883, Ruskin wrote: 'It is extraordinary that the real motives of the book have never been asserted till now, and even here, thus hastily. I had no memory, myself, when I began the revision of the text, that it was anywise so pregnant with the design of subsequent works.'

33 2 Kgs.iv.38–40.

34 Fra Angelico.

35 In Bologna.

36 Guido Reni (1575–1642), a Bolognese painter who enjoyed great popularity in the seventeenth and eighteenth centuries.

37 Exod.xvii.13.

38 See letter 10 of *Letters on the Aesthetic Education of Man*.

39 Gen.xxiv.63.

40 An allusion to Wordsworth's *Intimations of Immortality*, stanza x, l.179.

41 Rev.xxii.3,4.

42 *Elements of the Philosophy of the Human Mind*, Part I, Chap.vii, Sec.I.

43 The quotations are all from Milton: (i) *Paradise Lost*, ii.706; (ii) ibid.vi.193; (iii) *Lycidas*, 25; and (iv) *Il Penseroso*, 65.

44 *Coriolanus*, II.i.166–70.

45 See note 53 below on Ruskin's changing view of 'fancy'.

46 See p. 206.

47 According to C & W, drops of molten glass, consolidated by falling into water; in shape resembling tadpoles. The thick end may be hammered safely; but if the smallest portion of the thin end is broken off, the whole flies into fine dust. These toys, if not invented by Prince Rupert, were introduced by him into England.

48 See *The Prioresses Tale*:

> '. . .whan that I had songe,
> Me thoughte, she leyde a greyn up-on my tonge.
> Wherefor I singe, and singe I moot certeyn
> In honour of that blisful mayden free,
> Til fro my tonge of-taken is the greyn.'

49 *Paradise Lost* i.222.

50 *Purgatorio* xxvi.4. In Cary's translation:

> 'The sun
> Now all the western clime irradiate changed
> From azure tinct to white; and, as I passed,
> My passing shadow made the umber'd flame
> Burn ruddier.'

51 The pholas is a kind of boring bivalve mollusc (the piddock). One species bores into gneiss, a very hard rock.

52 An allusion to Coleridge's *Rime of the Ancient Mariner*, ll.113, 114.

53 A lengthy passage has been omitted at this point in which Ruskin attempts to distinguish 'fancy' from 'imagination'. 'Fancy', he claims, 'is able to give a portrait of the outside, clear, brilliant, and full of detail.' 'The imagination', on the other hand, 'sees the heart and inner nature, and makes them felt, but is often obscure, mysterious, and interrupted, in its giving of outer detail.' (IV.253) Ruskin later (1883) downgraded the distinction, saying that he was 'entirely indifferent which word I use' (IV.220).

54 The passage referred to has been deleted.

55 According to C & W, Lecture iii, *Life and Writings*, ii.176.

56 Hylas was a young man beloved of Hercules who was carried off by nymphs when drawing water from a fountain.

57 John ix.7–11. Christ restores the sight of the man born blind by rubbing mud on his eyes and telling him: 'Go wash in the pool of Siloam. . .'

58 According to C & W, the 'Torre del Fame' was at Pisa and was destroyed in 1655. Count Ugolino and his children were starved to death in it (Dante's *Inferno*, Canto 33). Capraja and Gorgona are two barren islands off the coast of Tuscany.

59 *Paradise Lost* ii.666.

60   *Paradise Lost* iv.977–90.

61   On 'fancy' see note 53 above.

62   See p. 226ff.

63   The etching is signed and dated 1650. Impressions are in the British Museum.

64   In the Sistine Chapel.

65   The cartoon in the Victoria and Albert Museum, London.

66   The majority of the frescoes in the Campo Santo were destroyed in the Second World War.

67   The passage referred to has been omitted.

68   Better known as the Last Supper.

69   Now known as the Palazzo Medici-Riccardi, in Florence.

70   The Arena Chapel in Padua contains Giotto's famous fresco cycle. C & W said (in 1903) that the Perugino fresco in the Albizzi Palace was 'not now known to be accessible'. Ruskin saw it in 1845 and described it as 'a most heavenly work'. The subject is the Entombment of Christ.

71   *Paradise Lost* i.600.

72   Fra Bartolommeo's *St Stephen* is probably that in the Duomo at Lucca. Raphael's *St Catherine* is the one in the National Gallery, London.

73   Ruskin had in mind a Fra Angelico in the Uffizi about which he wrote to his father in June 1845: '. . . I spent an hour and a half before a Fra Angelico, and hadn't enough of it neither. I learnt how *ladies* dance from Simone Memmi [in the Campo Santo at Pisa]; and I saw *angels* dancing to-day, and so I know how *they* do it. I wish you could see one of Angelico's, either dancing or singing. One that I saw today had just taken the trumpet from his lips, and—with his hand lifted—listens to the blast of it passing away into heaven. And then to see another bending down to clash the cymbals, and yet looking up at the same instant all full of love. And their wings are of ruby colour and pure gold, and covered with stars, and each has a tongue of fire on his forehead, waving as he moves.'

VOLUME III

1   See p.8.

2   See Vol. I, note 5, above.

3   From Byron's *Prisoner of Chillon*, stanza vi. Ruskin, as usual, quotes from memory. The second line should begin 'Its massy. . .' and the third line, 'Thus much the fathom-line. . .'

4   *Iliad* vi.390–470.

5   Now known as Carlo Maratta (1625–1713). One of the earliest neo-classical painters.

6   Fra Angelico.

7   Charles Robert Leslie (1794–1859), Professor of Painting at the Royal Academy and author of the life of Constable (see Vol.I, note 19 above).

8   Thomas Webster (1800–86), painter of rustic and genre scenes.

9   Phil.iv.8.

10   This anecdote is recounted in Vasari's *Lives*.

11   See p. 8.

12   Luke ii.7.

13   A term which, according to C & W, was very common in eighteenth-century art criticism, and meant the maintenance of the proper relations between nearer and more distant objects.

14   In the Louvre.

15   A reference to the Nazarene school, founded by Overbeck and Pforr in the early years of the nineteenth century.

16   See p. 245.

17   In the Scuola di San Rocco, Venice.

18   Rev. i.19.

19   *Inferno* xii. 77–80.

20   *Iliad* ix.209. The earlier reference has been deleted.

21   See note 103 below.

22   *Fairie Queene*, Book i, Canto iv, ll.30–1. Ruskin has left out five lines between '. . . about his jaw' and 'All in a kirtle. . .'

23   'if ever a mule becomes king' [of the Medes]. Herodotus, *Histories* I.55.2. The first words of the Delphic oracle's reply to Croesus when he asked whether his reign would be a long one. The oracle went on to warn him that in this event he would do well to take flight. He was eventually defeated and taken prisoner by Cyrus, king of the Medes, who, like a mule, was of mixed parentage.

24   Not visible in the plate. According to C & W, Ruskin marked in his copy for revision that this statement was wrong of the griffin at Verona; but he also referred to instances at Ferrara, both with and without wheels.

25   Ezek. i.19,20.

26   See Vol.I, note 2.

27   Titian's *Entombment* and Veronese's *Marriage at Cana* are both in the Louvre. Tintoretto's *Adoration* is in the Scuola di San Rocco, Venice.

28   See pp. 14, 34ff.

29   *The Church Porch*, stanza 54.

30   See p. 256.

31 An allusion to *Twelfth Night* II.iii.

32 An allusion to 1 Cor.i.28 and Rev.i.19.

33 Acts xvii.11 and 18.

34 According to C & W, from *Astraea*, a poem delivered before the Phi Beta Kappa Society of Yale College, by Oliver Wendell Holmes (1850).

35 Originally from Chap.xxvi of *Alton Locke* by Charles Kingsley (1850).

36 *Inferno* iii.12.

37 *Christabel*, Part i, ll.49, 50.

38 *Odyssey* xi.57, 58.

39 *Hamlet*, I.v.162. 'ground' should read 'earth'.

40 Jude 13.

41 *Pastorals*: Summer, or Alexis. Four lines are omitted after the second in the quotation.

42 From the lines beginning ' 'Tis said, That some have died for love', composed in 1800. Another quotation from memory, with various minor inaccuracies.

43 *Endymion*, Book ii.349–50.

44 *Iliad*, xxi.211–360.

45 Gen. xxxii.1; xxii.11; Josh. v.13; Judg. xiii.19.

46 *Iliad* v.846 ff.; the following reference is *Iliad* i.43 ff.

47 *Iliad* xxi.489 ff.

48 *Iliad* iii.365.

49 *Illiad* iv.141–7.

50 *Odyssey* v.55–75.

51 e.g. *Iliad* ii.88.

52 *Odyssey* ix.132–41.

53 *Odyssey* xiii.242–7.

54 *Paradise Lost* ii.620.

55 *Inferno* xi.16 ff. and xviii.4 ff.

56 *Purgatorio* x.24 ('three times the length of the human body'); and xii.100–5.

57 The references are to *Paradiso* xviii.70–96 (letters and words); 97–114 (eagle); xiv.100 ff. (cross); xxviii.22 ff. (circles like rainbows); xx. 31–6 (eye of a bird); xxx.117 (white rose).

58 *Inferno* i.77.

59 *Inferno* i.1–7. The following reference is to *Inferno* xiii. The 'one exception' is the wood in the terrestrial paradise, *Purgatorio* xxviii, referred to in the next paragraph.

60 *Purgatorio* xxvii.131–2. Ruskin mistranslates the second line, '*Fuor se' dell' erte vie, fuor se' dell' arte*', taking '*arte*' to mean 'art'

when it actually means 'narrow': 'Thou art beyond the steep and the narrow ways.'

61 The reference is to *Oedipus at Colonus*, the tragedy by Sophocles, l.668 ff. (An earlier reference to this play has been deleted.)

62 *Purgatorio* xxviii, opening lines.

63 *Purgatorio* xxviii.40 ff.

64 *Purgatorio* xxviii.68 and 80,81.

65 Countess Matilda of Tuscany (1046–1115), known as La Gran Contessa, famous for her loyal support of Pope Gregory VII in his power struggle with Emperor Henry IV. It was to her castle at Canossa that Henry came barefoot in the snow to pay penance to the Pope in 1077.

66 *Purgatorio* xxvii.97–110. Cary's translation.

67 *Paradiso* xxxi.93.

68 *Purgatorio* xxxi.118–23.

69 *Purgatorio* xxvii.108.

70 *Purgatorio* xxviii.41.

71 *Purgatorio* xxxi.92.

72 Ruskin attempted to dispose of the apparent contradiction between this passage and pp.379–80 (which was pointed out to him by a correspondent), arguing that the earlier passage is 'speaking of the *habitual* mood of casual everyday contemplation, which was light with the mediaeval and deep with the Greek.' The present passage, by contrast, deals with 'the sealing difference in the hard work and thought of the two' (See V.431–2).

73 See also pp.455ff and 601ff.

74 See p.376.

75 *Inferno* iv.118: '*sopra 'l verde smalto*'.

76 Ibid. ix.53.

77 *Purgatorio* vii.73–6.

78 *Purgatorio* viii.28.

79 See p.375.

80 *Inferno* iv.118.

81 Mark vi.39.

82 e.g. Sonnet xxxiii where 'glorious morning' kisses 'with golden face the meadows green'.

83 *Iliad* ii.467, 468.

84 *Odyssey* v.398, 463.

85 *Purgatorio* i.105.

86 Isa. xl.6: 'all flesh is grass'.

87 The Biblical references are: Gen. i.11; Matt. vi.28; Isa. xlii.3; Matt. xii.20; Ezek. xl.3.

88 The preceding chapter, 'Of Mediæval Landscape: – secondly,

the Rocks', has been omitted in its entirety. In it, Ruskin discusses Dante's descriptions of rocks, mountains and skies. He notices that Dante's rocks are always described as being a 'colourless grey' (V.302) and that his mountains are nothing but 'broken stones or crags' while 'all their broad contours and undulations seem to have escaped his eye' (V.307). As far as the sky is concerned, Dante's only pleasure, according to Ruskin, depends on its 'white clearness' (V.310). He never takes any notice of clouds, for which, Ruskin claims, he has an 'immitigable dislike' (V.312). Ruskin also illustrates the inaccuracy of the rock drawing of the mediaeval and Renaissance Italian artists, from Giotto to Ghirlandaio.

89   *The Clouds*, 316–8, 380, 320.
90   Allusion to Wordsworth, *Miscellaneous Sonnets*, Part ii, no.36, l.13: 'The river glideth at his own sweet will'.
91   Eph. ii.12.
92   Wordsworth, *Miscellaneous Sonnets*, Part ii, no. xxxiii, ll.9–10.
93   Sir Arthur Helps (1813–75), a popular Victorian writer and eminent civil servant, author of *Friends in Council*, dialogues on ethical and aesthetic questions.
94   *Marmion*, Introduction to Canto ii.
95   *In Memoriam*, xi and xv.
96   ibid. xv.
97   *Ode to Melancholy*.
98   *Tintern Abbey*, ll.76–7 and 81–2.
99   See pp.348–9.
100 John Howard (1726–90), prison and public health reformer.
101 Wordsworth, *Poems of Imagination* no.v, 'Yew Trees', ll.13–31.
102 *The Excursion*, Book I, ll.211–3.
103 The White Lady is a spirit with whom the hero of *The Monastery* enters into an alliance. At their first meeting she describes herself as 'Something betwixt heaven and hell, / Something that neither stood nor fell, / Something that through thy wit or will, / May work thee good; may work thee ill.'
104 Mark iv.19.
105 See p.397.
106 Job xxxviii.1.
107 See p.520ff.
108 Job xli.18, 22.
109 Matt. vi.28.
110 See p.409.

VOLUME IV

1   The passage referred to has been deleted.
2   In *The Seven Lamps of Architecture*, Chap. vi, para. 12.
3   Stanfield's *Coast Scenery*, a series of views in the British Channel (1836). Turner's *Windmill and Lock* was no. 27 in the *Liber Studiorum*. See fig.67.
4   See p.304.
5   Num. xi.26, 27.
6   See p.248.
7   See pp.266–7.
8   See pp.61 and 201.
9   See p.299.
10 The intervening chapters have been omitted. They provide, firstly, a highly wrought, symbolic account of what, in Ruskin's words, 'the proper effect of the natural beauty of different objects *ought* to be on the human mind' and, secondly, a remarkably detailed account of the physical structure and form of the different varieties of mountain scenery, with particular reference to the Alps. Needless to say, Ruskin seeks to demonstrate that Turner alone among artists has accurately depicted the true appearances of Alpine scenery. Ruskin himself acknowledged in a letter to Charles Eliot Norton of 1879 that the geological sections of *Modern Painters* were 'wholly irrelevant to the matters in hand' – see Letter 328, *The Correspondence of John Ruskin and Charles Eliot Norton*, Eds. Bradley and Ousby, Cambridge 1987.
11 Isa. iii.24.
12 Luke x.31.
13 Gen. iii.8 (Vulgate).
14 Jer. iii.6.
15 Mic. vi.2.
16 Pss. lxxii.3.
17 The rich King of Phaeacia who entertained Odysseus.
18 According to C & W, a quotation from *The Fulfilling of the Scripture*, a book by Robert Fleming the elder (1630–94).
19 See pp.461–2.
20 Ruskin delivered a series of lectures on art and architecture in Edinburgh in 1851 at the end of the fateful Highland holiday in the company of Millais. See introduction.
21 The Bible quotations in this paragraph are: Gen. viii.4, xix.17 and 19, xxii.4; and Pss. cxxi.1.
22 Deut. xxxii.49.

23 Eph. iv.13; Heb. iv.15.
24 Matt. xvii.1.
25 This is a paraphrase. Luke ix.29–30 reads: 'And as he prayed, the fashion of his countenance was altered, and his raiment was white and glistering. And, behold, there talked with him two men, which were Moses and Elias.'
26 Matt. xvii.5.

VOLUME V

1 Parts VI and VII, entitled respectively 'Of Leaf Beauty' and 'Of Cloud Beauty' have been omitted in their entirety. They occupy approximately the first half of Vol. V.
2 A paraphrase of Col. i.16, 17.
3 It has been suggested by Elizabeth Helsinger in her *Ruskin and the Art of the Beholder* (1983) that Ruskin's fascination with historical philology, which emerges particularly clearly in the last volume of *Modern Painters*, was a consequence of his contacts with F.J. Furnivall and his reading of R.C. Trench's *Study of Words* (1851). Both Furnivall and Trench were closely involved in the creation of the *Oxford English Dictionary*, which was first conceived in the late 1850s. Ruskin's approach to etymology is, however, distinctly idiosyncratic and creative.
4 From the Te Deum; Ruskin has translated 'Sabaoth' into 'hosts'.
5 Ruskin commented in *Unto This Last*, Essay III, 'Qui judicatis terram', that his principles of Political Economy 'were all summed' in these two sentences.
6 A reference to the term Aristophanes used in describing the school of Socrates: *The Clouds* 94.
7 The epitaph written by Simonides on the Spartans who fell at Thermopylae (Herodotus, *Histories* vii.228.2). See also Vol. II, note 17.
8 Plato, *Phaedo* 60e. Throughout his life Socrates had had a recurrent dream which gave him this command. Before his execution, he decided to clear his conscience by obeying it and therefore wrote some poetry.
9 See p.249ff.
10 'another precept of this knowledge is...that [men]...should make a show of perpetual felicity in all that they undertake; which cannot but mightily increase reputation' (*Advancement of Learning*, Book II, xxiii.34, Oxford, 1869 edition).
11 *The Seven Lamps of Architecture* (1849).

12 Benjamin Robert Haydon (1786–1846) and James Barry (1741–1806) were both painters of ambitious, large-scale, historical works in the grand manner.

13 Book I, Chap. iii ('Les Imperceptibles Constructeurs du Globe').

14 'the modern pathetic school' refers to the Pre-Raphaelites.

15 Needle-like.

16 During the winter of 1857/58, Ruskin devoted himself to the cataloguing and conservation of the drawings contained in the Turner bequest.

17 See p.249.

18 Now in the Tate Gallery, London.

19 See p.248/9.

20 Gen. i.26 (the Vulgate).

21 1 John iv.16.

22 See Deut. xxxii.4.

23 See Isa. lv.8.

24 1 Cor. xiii.12.

25 For Rio, see introduction p.xxvii. Lord Lindsay (Alexander William Crawford, 1812–80), author of *Sketches of the History of Christian Art* (1847) which Ruskin reviewed.

26 Pss. xxiv.4.

27 See *Odyssey* x.495.

28 Pseudo-Anacreon 4(3), ed. Rose—a conflation of two lines:—
4 and 10.

29 Luke vi.44.

30 Tintoretto's *Paradise* is in the Great Council Chamber of the Ducal Palace, Venice. Titian's *Assumption* is in the church of the Frari, Venice. For his *St Peter Martyr*, see Vol. I, note 11 above. His *Presentation* is in the Accademia, Venice. For Veronese's *Marriage at Cana*, see Vol. III, note 27 above.

31 Rom. v.3, 5.

32 See note 30 above.

33 This reference has been deleted.

34 1 Cor. xv.54.

35 A sulphurous volcanic vent near Naples.

36 The tradition that Salvator Rosa spent his youth amongst bandits has now been shown to be a myth.

37 The reference is to the *Temptation of St Anthony* (see fig.54). According to C & W, the quotation that follows is from an inscription which appears in an etching by Salvator Rosa entitled *The Genius of Salvator Rosa*.

38 Pss. xc.10.

39 Eccles. ix.10: 'Whatsoever thy hand findeth to do, do it with thy might; for there is no work, nor device, nor knowledge, nor wisdom, in the grave, whither thou goest.'

40 See p.598.

41 The term 'classicus' usually referred to the highest class of citizens in Roman society.

42 The Library Edition at this point prints '*fio*', as does the 1888 edition. But this is clearly a mistake. The point about '*fides*' being distantly related to '*credo*' is well taken; it is not 'faith' in the modern sense, but 'confidence' or 'reliance'. (I am grateful to Dr Roland Mayer for this observation.)

43 Better known as the *Last Supper*.

44 See p.537ff.

45 See note 30 above.

46 The *Supper at Emmaus* is one of the three large Veroneses which Ruskin studied in Turin in 1858.

47 It is curious that Ruskin makes no reference to Stubbs.

48 The 'Adoration of the Shepherds' was one of Jacopo Bassano's most frequent subjects. A well-known example is in the Royal Collection at Hampton Court.

49 The previous chapter ('Of Vulgarity') has been omitted. In it, Ruskin concludes that vulgarity 'consists in a deadness of the heart and body' and 'shows itself primarily in dulnes of heart. . . [and] in inability to conceive noble character or emotion' (VII.359).

50 Presumably Francesco Albani (1578–1660), a Bolognese painter and contemporary of Guido Reni.

51 Sic. But it is surely a misprint for 'wit'.

52 St Arnulph, Bishop of Metz (according to C & W).

53 Turner's childhood home has long since been demolished.

54 Dante's *Paradiso* xxv.5: 'The beautiful sheepfold where I slept as a lamb' – i.e. Florence.

55 See *The Garden of the Hesperides* (plate 19).

56 John Narraway. He was an old friend of Turner's father. There is a story of Turner staying with the Narraways in 1800, on which occasion he is supposed to have borrowed a pony which he failed to return.

57 Apart from the *Téméraire*, the pictures referred to are: *The Battle of Trafalgar, as seen from the mizzen starboard shrouds of the Victory* – commonly called *The Death of Nelson* – in the Tate Gallery, London; *The Battle of Trafalgar*, painted for George IV and presented by him to Greenwich Hospital and now in the National Maritime Museum, Greenwich.

58 This seems to have been in 1785 or 1786: it is not clear whether

the fit of illness referred to was Turner's or that which led to the death of his sister in March 1786.

59 Sandycombe Lodge. He moved there in 1813 from his house in Upper Mall, Hammersmith. Originally he called it Solus Lodge.

60 Turner made several drawings of the refectory at Kirkstall Abbey in or around 1798. One of them is in Sir John Soane's Museum, London. There is also a plate in the *Liber Studiorum*.

61 The title which Turner gave to the manuscript poem from which he drew the mottoes for many of his paintings. It seems only to have existed in fragmentary form.

62 In a footnote Ruskin identified the two works referred to here as *The Tenth plague of Egypt* and *Rispah watching the Bodies of her sons*. Both are in the Tate Gallery, London. There are also plates in the *Liber Studiorum*. See fig.64.

63 Joel iii.13.

64 For these works see XIII.89–181 and 227–316. The passage cited here is on p.251.

65 *Paradise Lost*, Book V, ll.185–8. The painting is in the Tate Gallery, London.

66 In the Indianapolis Museum of Art, Indiana.

67 For the *Tenth plague* see note 62 above. *The Battle of the Nile* is apparently lost. *Narcissus and Echo* is at Petworth, Sussex. It was first exhibited in 1804, not 1805.

68 *Theogony* 211–25.

69 'short-withering': literally 'black' or 'dark', or, figuratively, 'malignant'.

70 See Euripides, *Hercules* 394. Their names are given by Apollodorus, in *The Library*, II.v.11. Modern texts alter 'Hestia' to 'Hesperia'.

71 The passage referred to has been omitted from this edition. (See VII.182.)

72 Hesiod, *Theogony* 333–6.

73 Ibid. 233–6.

74 Ibid. 375, 378.

75 Euripides, *Hercules* 398.

76 Pss. cxxiv.13,14,15. In fact, the Septuagint speaks of the 'heads' of the dragon. The following reference to Etham is Exod. xiii.20: 'And they took their journey from Succoth, and encamped in Etham, in the edge of the wilderness.'

77 Hesiod, *Theogony* 334, 335.

78 Euripides, *Hercules* 394–400.

79 Apollodorus, *The Library* II.v.11.

80 Hesiod, *Theogony*, 281, 287, 295.

81 'another garden': an allusion to Matt. xxvi.49; xxvii.3.
82 *Inferno* xvi.133, 134; and xvii.1–3.
83 Job xli.29, 30 (Ruskin has reversed the order).
84 *Inferno* xvii.7–27.
85 Ibid. 100–5.
86 Ibid. 133.
87 Hesiod, *Theogony* 287 ff.
88 *Inferno* vi, last line: '*Quivi trovammo Pluto il gran nemico* ' – 'Here we found Pluto, the great enemy.' Ruskin gave the title '*Quivi Trovammo*' to his engraving of Turner's dragon (fig.65).
89 *Paradise Lost* i.679.
90 Job xl.18 and xli. 18.
91 Apollodorus, *The Library* II.v.10.
92 C & W thought that Coleridge was a slip of the pen for Bacon, who offers this interpretation in *The Advancement of Learning* (i. viii. 7: Oxford, 1869 edition).
93 *Iliad* xi.10.
94 Ibid. iv. 442, 443.
95 *Aeneid* vi.280–1.
96 Hesiod, *Theogony* 230.
97 *Iliad* xix.91.
98 *Fairie Queene*, Book IV, Canto i, ll.28–30.
99 *Hippolytus* 741–51.
100 *Aeneid* iv. 484–92.
101 In fact the Garden of Proserpina, as the quotation itself reveals. *Fairie Queene*, Book II, Canto vii, 52–5.
102 Acts xvii.23.
103 The title of a painting by Turner in the National Gallery, London (see Vol. I, note 29 above).
104 Hesiod, *Theogony* 294.
105 The passage referred to has been deleted. In it Ruskin asks 'What value ought this attribute of clouds to possess in the human mind? Ought we to admire their colours or despise them?' (VII.161).
106 e.g. Lev.xiv.4.
107 Ladon was the name of the dragon who guarded the apples of the Hesperides. (Apollonius of Rhodes, *Argonautica* IV.1396).
108 Matt.v.5.
109 *Caligula's Palace and Bridge* is in the Tate Gallery, London.
110 For Dante's '*bello ovile*' see note 54 above. Casella was a Florentine musician and a friend of Dante. He appears in *Purgatorio* ii, where he sings one of Dante's own love songs to refresh the poet's soul.
111 See p.431ff.

112   All of these drawings were reproduced in the *Liber Studiorum*.

113   *War. The Exile and the rock limpet.* Exhibited in 1842. In the Tate Gallery, London.

114   Matt. vii. 1 and Ezek. xlv. 9.

115   Prov. iii. 3.

116   He never did.

117   See p.405.

118   The story about Milton appears in Carlyle's *Past and Present*, Book I, Chap. iii. The Dürer anecdote comes from Dürer's diary of his journey to the Netherlands, according to C & W.

119   See Michelet's *L'Insecte*, Book II, Chap. i.

120   According to C & W, Ruskin wrote here in the margin of his copy 'General Havelock', presumably a reference to Major General Sir Henry Havelock (1795–1857), the hero of the first relief of Lucknow (1857).

121   The Houses of Parliament.

122   Holman Hunt was very hard up in the 1850s and but for a loan from Millais might have emigrated to Canada or Australia. *The Finding of the Saviour in the Temple* was exhibited in 1860 – the year Ruskin finished *Modern Painters*. See plate 24.

123   From James Russell Lowell's poem *Columbus*. Lowell's works were introduced to Ruskin by Charles Eliot Norton, an American scholar whom he first met in 1855 and who was to become a lifelong friend.

124   Matt.ix. 28.

125   2 Kgs.ix. 31.

126   See p.538.

127   John iii. 16; viii. 12.

128   Tennyson, *The Princess* iv.

129   Matt. xi. 14.

130   Hesperus, the Evening Star; Heosphorus, the Morning Star.

131   Matt. xii. 50: 'For whosoever shall do the will of my Father which is in heaven, the same is my brother, and sister, and mother.'

INDEX

Italicised numerals indicate illustration